UNDER THE SUN

UNDER THE SUN

◄○►

The Letters of Bruce Chatwin

SELECTED AND EDITED

BY

Elizabeth Chatwin

AND

Nicholas Shakespeare

VIKING

VIKING
Published by the Penguin Group
Penguin Group (USA) Inc., 375 Hudson Street,
New York, New York 10014, U.S.A.
Penguin Group (Canada), 90 Eglinton Avenue East, Suite 700,
Toronto, Ontario, Canada M4P2Y3
(a division of Pearson Penguin Canada Inc.)
Penguin Books Ltd, 80 Strand, London WC2R 0RL, England
Penguin Ireland, 25 St. Stephen's Green, Dublin 2, Ireland
(a division of Penguin Books Ltd)
Penguin Books Australia Ltd, 250 Camberwell Road, Camberwell,
Victoria 3124, Australia
(a division of Pearson Australia Group Pty Ltd)
Penguin Books India Pvt Ltd, 11 Community Centre, Panchsheel Park,
New Delhi – 110 017, India
Penguin Group (NZ), 67 Apollo Drive, Rosedale, North Shore 0632,
New Zealand (a division of Pearson New Zealand Ltd)
Penguin Books (South Africa) (Pty) Ltd, 24 Sturdee Avenue,
Rosebank, Johannesburg 2196, South Africa

Penguin Books Ltd, Registered Offices:
80 Strand, London WC2R 0RL, England

First American edition
Published in 2011 by Viking Penguin,
a member of Penguin Group (USA) Inc.

1   2   3   4   5   6   7   8   9   10

Letters by Bruce Chatwin copyright © The Estate of Bruce Chatwin, 2010.
Preface and annotations by Elizabeth Chatwin copyright © Elizabeth Chatwin, 2010.
Introduction and notes copyright © Nicholas Shakespeare, 2010.
Compilation copyright © Nicholas Shakespeare and Elizabeth Chatwin, 2010
All rights reserved.

Extract from *The Unquiet Grave* by Cyril Connolly. Copyright Cyril Connolly, 1945.
Reprinted by permission of Rogers, Coleridge & White Ltd.

Extract from *Ups and Downs* by Frances Partridge. Copyright © Frances Partridge, 2001.
Reprinted by permission of the Partridge Estate c/o Rogers, Coleridge & White Ltd.

Additional acknowledgments for permission to reprint copyrighted works appear on pages 527–528.

LIBRARY OF CONGRESS CATALOGING IN PUBLICATION DATA

Chatwin, Bruce, 1940–1989.
[Correspondence. Selections]
Under the sun : the letters of Bruce Chatwin / selected and edited by
Elizabeth Chatwin and Nicholas Shakespeare.
p. cm.
Includes index.
First published in Great Britain in 2010 by Jonathan Cape.
ISBN 978-0-670-02246-5
1. Chatwin, Bruce, 1940–1989—Correspondence.   2. Authors, English—20th century—
Correspondence.   I. Chatwin, Elizabeth.   II. Shakespeare, Nicholas, 1957–   III. Title.
PR6053.H395Z48 2011
823'.914—dc22
[B]
2010033591

Printed in the United States of America

CONTENTS

PREFACE

——◆◇▶——

I first met Bruce in late 1961 at Sotheby's, where I came to work for a couple of years. I was the first American that the auction house had employed in London and was, of course, a curiosity. Not long afterwards, Bruce was sent on his first trip to New York, to look at collections of paintings for possible sale. He was enchanted by everything, especially the glamorous old wealthy Wasp milieu which made a fuss of him. After that trip – from which he returned wearing a large checked woollen jacket and hat to match, the sort worn by country people at work – I became more interesting.

During the next few years we spent weekends in the Black Mountains, walked the Malvern Hills with his father, and one summer we almost rendezvoused in Libya. We were married in 1965.

His letters and postcards from that time have disappeared. I managed to keep most of the subsequent ones. I am thrilled that a collection of his correspondence is to be published. Letters are the most vivid writing of all. His mother kept his weekly notes written from prep school and these are already full of different interests and enthusiasms. It is fascinating to see the child develop into an art historian at Sotheby's. He was always good at stories, which became his eventual career.

Bruce was Sotheby's expert for the Impressionist and Modern Art (excluding British) and the Antiquities Departments. The latter meant artefacts from India, the Ancient Near East and Europe and Amerindia, the Pacific and Africa – the World – and involved endless research at the British Museum and Musée de L'Homme in Paris. He became more and more disturbed by archaeological objects brought in to sell – some of which were stolen from unrecorded sites — and fakes. He began to regret that Sotheby's had cajoled him into not going to Oxford when a place came up. They persuaded him that he would do very well without a degree.

By 1966 he was looking at universities with the idea of reading archaeology . . . Only Edinburgh and Cambridge offered a degree course for undergraduates, so to Edinburgh he went. It would mean a dramatic fall in income but we reckoned we could manage.

Edinburgh in those days was very grim in the winter. The Royal Mile on which we had rented a flat in a newly built block had 23 pubs and none with chairs to sit on. To get green vegetables and salad, I had to go to the New Town (across the bridge in the eighteenth-century part) where there was a proper greengrocer. The huge North British Hotel did not know what a salad was. The best things were the fish and the outside oyster bar. You took your white wine and they provided brown bread and butter with the oysters. Freezing but fun.

Bruce worked terribly hard and well into the night. He was very competitive and at 26 was a mature student up against teenagers just out of school. He studied Sanskrit as well as archaeology and came out top of his class, to his delight. Then, after two and a half years of a four-year course, he quit. He did not even tell me he was going to. He became disillusioned after going on digs in the summer and realising he didn't like disturbing the dead.

By this time he had become fascinated by nomads and he began to write about them. Thanks to a fee to go and look at a collection in Egypt he had enough money to travel a bit. In 1969 he and Peter Levi went to Afghanistan on a grant Peter had from Oxford. This was Bruce's third visit. I joined them after two months and was utterly beguiled by the country. Nine years later, the Russians upset the balance forever.

He worked on the nomad book for several years, but it was and remains unpublishable. Then he was persuaded to go and work for the *Sunday Times* magazine, quite a distinguished publication in those days. He made many lifelong friends there.

Bruce began as the art expert to replace David Sylvester who was leaving. He ended up doing articles on Algeria, Mrs Gandhi, André

Malraux as well as on art. He met Eileen Gray, an Irish designer of furniture and interiors who was an important influence in the use of new materials such as Perspex in combination with traditional ones. She had lived in Paris since 1904. Gray encouraged him to go to Patagonia for her, as she had always wanted to go but was now too old.

So again he made a dramatic move in his life, without telling anyone till he was nearly on his way. He wrote a letter to the *Sunday Times* on a little piece of yellow foolscap now lost or stolen. He usually telephoned me from some tiny bar on the road as he was moving south. He was full of praise for Moet & Chandon Argentine bubbly. To find champagne in an unlikely place was a great lift to his morale. He loved it.

He nearly always travelled alone: two people have a defence, but a single person is approachable. He could never have managed Patagonia with me tagging along, or *The Viceroy of Ouidah* or most of his books.

He slightly altered the people he met along the way – the brothers in *On the Black Hill* were not twins; a nurse in *In Patagonia* was a devotee of Agatha Christie, not Osip Mandelstam. It enraged the people thus altered, as Nicholas Shakespeare and I found when retracing his steps in 1992 in Patagonia – all part of his storytelling. *The Songlines* has completely invented characters.

People used to ask me how I felt about his endless absences from home. Sometimes it was annoying that I had to cope alone, but I knew he was working; he had to be free. At the very beginning of our marriage he said he hoped I didn't mind, but he had to go off by himself – *The Cat that Walks by Himself*, a lovely picture by Kipling is on my kitchen dresser.

Bruce always kept in touch by letter or telephone from the ends of the earth and I simply wasn't curious about what he was doing. He would entertain me with stories on his return.

In the early 1970s I was given my first Black Welsh Mountain ewes, and from then on my calendar was set to a sheep timetable. I still have their descendants and am just as fond of them.

Bruce attracted all sorts of people throughout his careers. He had a talent for making friends wherever he was: on buses, trains, ships. Somehow he discovered a stranger's abiding interest within minutes, and they chattered away like old friends. It always amazed me. They thought it was friends for life. Exchanging addresses meant letters coming to him from all sorts of unlikely places. A Nigerian had a plan to start a shop and asked for a huge list of things like socks and shirts and pants and cotton thread to stock it with. More lists would arrive. I'm afraid we ignored them.

Once Bruce began to write books he became addicted to it and woke up in the morning thinking of the work. When we travelled together on the Continent he would become very restless if he had not been able to write for more than a couple of days. He would rearrange the room we were staying in so he could sit and work. I was sent out to sightsee for myself.

It is wonderful how many people kept his letters, even before he became a well-known writer. He never kept anything, including the first editions of his books.

I simply don't know what he would have thought of computers and of using them to write books on. He might have felt it was more fun than anything to talk to any person anywhere in the world, or he might have hated it. When we were trekking in the Everest National Park in 1983 we were approached by a lone American who tried to attach himself to our camp (repulsed by evasion eventually). He said that within a few years Bruce would be using a word processor to write with. He got a mocking reply from us, and indeed Bruce never even looked at a computer as far as I know. But he observed that most books published after the advent of word processors were much bigger. Nothing wrong with them, but too long, as it was so easy to correct and adapt with the machine.

His system was to write by hand on yellow (American) legal foolscap and correct and delete and discard sheet after sheet. When he was fairly happy, he typed it out with large margins and then corrected and changed it some more. Then maybe another handwritten copy and definitely more typewritten ones. He threw away mountains of paper, so there are no working manuscripts to be seen.

He never showed his work to anyone till he was satisfied with it, but he read it aloud to me. Everything had to sound right and flow easily.

The letters are the only unreworked writing of his. He felt that writing was a labour. A computer made it too easy.

And now that communication has become so fast and easy with mobile phones and e-mail, no one writes letters any more. No notes from the little darlings at prep school to treasure, maybe no love letters and no travellers' accounts. Does anyone print the communications they get for keepsakes?

So Bruce's letters, starting from a very young age and continuing through life, are a last example of a traditional form of communication which may now disappear.

ELIZABETH CHATWIN

INTRODUCTION

I am most certainly in the mood for writing letters

A year before his death in January 1989 Bruce Chatwin opened a letter from his London publisher Tom Maschler and read the following:

'I've said it before, and I'll say it again, there is simply no writer in England for whose work I have a greater passion than yours. This statement is made with all my heart.'

Twenty-one years on, Maschler finds no reason to alter his opinion. 'Of what I call "my lot" – Ian McEwan, Martin Amis, Julian Barnes, Salman Rushdie – Bruce was the one I was most anxious to know where he was going to go. I think had he lived he would have been ahead of all of them,' he told me.

Chatwin's compelling narrative voice was cut off just as he found it. In his last months, wrapped in a shawl beside the stove at Homer End near Oxford, he lamented to Elizabeth: 'There are so many things I want to do.' A work on healing to be called *The Sons of Thunder*; a triptych of stories after Flaubert's *Trois Contes*, 'one set in Ireland in the days of Irish kings'; an Asian novel about the Austro-American botanist Joseph Rock who lived in China; another novel, based in South Africa, which would explore the gossip and jealousies of a Karoo dorp. And, of course, his Russian epic *Lydia Livingstone*, a love story first and foremost which was to weave in three cities – Paris, Moscow, New York – and attempt to fiction-alise his wife's Jamesian family. 'Bruce had just begun,' says his friend Salman Rushdie. 'We didn't have his developed books, the books that might have come out of falling in love with his wife. We saw only the first act.'

One of the titles he liked, though he did not yet have a book for it, was *Under the Sun*.

It was a foreigner who asked the question: 'Why should the disappearance of Bruce Chatwin make such a difference?' Writing in June 1989 in the *Times Literary Supplement*, Hans Magnus Enzensberger answered his own question in this way: 'it is surely as a storyteller that Chatwin will be remembered, and missed – a storyteller going far beyond the conventional limits of fiction, and assimilating in his tales elements of reportage, autobiography, ethnology, the Continental tradition of the essay, and gossip.' For Enzensberger, with whom Chatwin had plotted a future walk along the Berlin Wall and down the East German border, it was not enough to say that he died young or was full of promise. 'Chatwin never delivered the goods that critics or publishers or the reading public expected. Not fearing to disappoint, he surprised us at every turn of the page.' Enzensberger concluded: 'Underneath the brilliance of the text, there is a haunting presence, something sparse and solitary and moving, as in Turgenev. When we return to Bruce Chatwin we find much in him that has been left unsaid.'

While we shall never know the surprise of his unwritten works, Chatwin has left behind a body of writing that is striking for its freshness; an authentic conduit which allows us to return to him and even to be rewarded in the manner Enzensberger hints at: namely the letters and postcards that he wrote from his first week at boarding-school, two weeks shy of his eighth birthday, until shortly before his death at the age of 48.

* * *

Assigned in Nazi-occupied Paris to censoring civilian mail coming from Germany, Ernst Jünger, the subject of one of Chatwin's best essays, confided to his diary: 'There's nothing people won't set down in letters.'

Whether typed on Sotheby's notepaper, or written with a Mont Blanc pen on sheets of blue stationery from a shop in Mount Street (with a proper die for his address), or scribbled on the backs of postcards with a blunt hotel pencil, Chatwin's correspondence reveals much more about himself than he was prepared to expose in his books.

Alone in his letters did he make known that he had been present on a February day near Johannesburg when a cracked fragment of antelope bone was prised from the floor of the Swartkrans cave, soapy-feeling and speckled with dark patches as if burned: evidence, it turned out, of man's 'earliest use of fire'. For all his brilliance, Chatwin could be disarmingly modest, hiding his light under the same bushel as his well-concealed darknesses. The Bruce Chatwin who appears in *The Songlines*, *In Patagonia* and *What Am I Doing Here* is his own best, most achieved character: observant, intelligent, sharp-witted, hetero-sexual, generous, intrepid. This persona was an essential part of the appeal of his writing. 'In his books you were addressed not merely by a distinctive voice,' observed Michael Ignatieff, 'but by the fabulous character he had fashioned for himself.' The Bruce Chatwin of the letters is less certain of who he is, more vulnerable but more human. Delicate about his health and finances; uneasy about his sexual orientation and his relationship with England; above all, restless almost to the point of neurosis.

In his passport, Chatwin put 'farmer' as his profession, but his life was spent on the hoof, a sizeable proportion of it in the study of nomads. An internal memo circulated at Cape in October 1982 gives a flavour of his travels, their tern-like spread. 'Publicity have no idea when Bruce Chatwin will be in Australia – neither does his agent! As far as we know he is still in Siberia/Russia.' He copied into one of his signature Moleskine notebooks this telling line from Montaigne: 'I ordinarily reply to those who ask me the reason for my travels, that I know well what I am fleeing from, but not what I am looking for.' About the motivations for Chatwin's restlessness, I have not yet found a more convincing explanation than this, by the Vietnamese writer Nguyen Qui Duc. 'Nomads in the old days travelled around looking for food, for shelter, for water; modern day nomads, we travel around looking for ourselves.'

Written with the verve and sharpness of expression that first marked him out as an author, Chatwin's correspondence gives a vivid synopsis of his interests and concerns over forty years. To read his letters and postcards is to be with him on the road: in the Sudan, Afghanistan, Niger, Benin, Mauretania, Tierra del Fuego, Brazil, Nepal, India, Alice Springs,

London, New York, Edinburgh, Wotton-Under-Edge, Ipsden – in pursuit of the restless chimera that was Bruce Chatwin, that 'haunting' and elusive presence who is at once 'sparse and solitary and moving'.

* * *

A life revealed through letters is not nowadays so linear as a biography. It zig-zags through time and space rather in the manner of Chatwin's accounts of his journeys to Patagonia and Australia; it is messy, repetitive, congested, of the moment. Nor, frustratingly, can you rely on it to deliver letters when you want – from periods, and about incidents and people, just when their insight might prove most welcome. But it has this virtue: it is a life told at the time in the subject's own voice and words. It is the closest we have to his conversation.

The multifaceted narrator of Chatwin's books is a person who says remarkably little. He is virtually a mime artist, a character of laconic observations and lapidary asides that camouflage what he is thinking – 'stepping back to hide himself,' as his friend Gregor Von Rezzori saw it, 'in the cultivated impersonality of a newspaper article'. This impression is misleading. In his letters, as in life, Chatwin was no less voluble than was Marcel Marceau when not being silent on stage.

'I don't believe in coming clean,' Chatwin famously told Paul Theroux. In his letters, he cannot avoid it. They are the raw matter of his thoughts, a way of trying them out on the page, the first version. They chart his struggle with who he was and what he wanted to be; art expert, husband, archaeologist, writer – first as an academic theorist, then as an unrepentant storyteller. They are as much a communication with whoever he is writing to as a continuing natter with himself.

Chatwin's Gloucestershire neighbour, Jim Lees-Milne, recorded in his diary the local Duke of Beaufort's opinion that 'posterity should never judge people by their correspondence, as what they wrote one day was often the opposite of what they thought the next.' The shifting stream of Chatwin's mental processes is part of what injects his letters with their vitality. It is not uncommon for him to change his mind from one letter to the next, even between the paragraphs of a single letter. He changes his mind about his house, Australia, Africans, about whether to join his wife in India. 'He's thinking on paper and clarifying his mind, like a conversation,' Elizabeth says. Especially volatile are his travel plans, more uncertain than the on-again-off-again sale of his Maori bedpost that once belonged to Sarah Bernhardt; or the saga of the long-awaited cheque from James Ivory to cover the cost of a week's car hire in France. No sooner does he arrive anywhere than he is shouldering his rucksack, plotting to leave. 'Everything is always perfect to begin with, but he gets fed up with a place very quickly and in no time at all he's picking holes.'

Then, sent as often as not from the next place – a postcard.

For Paul Theroux, with whom he once gave a talk at the Royal Geographical Society, Chatwin's postcards have the effect of miniature billboards, being 'the perfect medium for many boasters, combining vividness, cheapness and an economy of effort'; they allow him to stay in touch without the depth and commitment of letters. But another American writer, David Mason, is less sure that these postcards betray the vice of the self-advertiser. Mason met Chatwin just once, at a bus stop in Greece: 'His terse correspondence with acquaintances like me was surely the product of a gregarious sensibility. Some writers become self-advertisers out of a grating neediness. What I sensed from Bruce was more akin to uncontainable enthusiasm.'

This enthusiasm is certainly what appealed to Chatwin's editor, Susannah Clapp, for whom the idiom of the postcard chimed with his dash and mystery and elipses as a writer. He liked short sentences, short paragraphs; the condensed description of the Sotheby's cataloguer and postcard sender. 'Pungent, visually arresting and on the wing,' Clapp writes, 'for Bruce Chatwin postcards were the perfect means of communication' – and allowed him to startle with a bolt from the blue. Arguably his most famous sentence (though the hardcopy has not been traced) was the telegram (it may have been a letter) that he is reputed to have sent to his editor at the *Sunday Times* magazine, saying GONE TO PATAGONIA FOR FOUR MONTHS (it may have been six). A postcard to his Italian publisher (also missing) contained, apparently, the warning line: 'Australia is Hell.'

A phrase that does reoccur is 'I think of you often.' One of many to receive it was the Queensland poet Pam Bell, with whom Chatwin stayed on the last leg of his second and final journey to Australia. 'There was warmth in his postcards,' she said. 'You felt he really wanted to bring you up to date. People very often say they thought of you and it's just a skim, but with Bruce, you did feel that for some minutes he cared about you.' He posted a card to the classical historian Robin Lane Fox, whose ancestor General Augustus Pitt Pivers had amassed a collection of price-less Benin Bronzes seized by a British raiding party in 1897. 'Bruce wrote that if I didn't get in touch he would launch a punitive expedition and come and take my willow-pattern cups away.'

* * *

Chatwin is not everyone's cup of tea. Under-appreciated for most of his writing life – more or less until the publication of *The Songlines* (1987) – his reputation after he died ballooned very briefly into a cult-like phenomenon, only to undergo a deflation. The nation's favourite author, Alan Bennett, was turned into a 'mean-minded' reader by Chatwin's introduction to Robert Byron's *The Road to Oxiana*. 'One afternoon,' Chatwin writes, 'I took *The Road to Oxiana* into the mosque [of Shei Luft'ullah in Isfahan] and sat, cross-legged, marvelling both at the tilework and Byron's description of it.'

'It's the "cross-legged" I dislike,' Bennett wrote, 'partly because five minutes of it and I'd be crippled. But why tell us?' Bennett recoiled from what he perceived as Chatwin's 'snobbishness' towards travellers who had come after Byron, 'the droves of young people who took to the road in the sixties and seventies'. Nor was Bennett engaged by a description of how Wali Jahn helped Chatwin to safety when he got blood-poisoning, which struck him as 'sheer Buchan' in 'the permitted degree of male camaraderie, men caring and crying for each other, both nobly'.

Barry Humphries was typical of several former friends who pretended they were no longer beguiled, writing in the *Spectator* in May 2006: 'Starbucks, incidentally, is on my list of the grossly overrated, along with Bruce Chatwin, Cézanne's *Bathers*, French onion soup, Bob Dylan, Niagara Falls, *Citizen Kane*, the Caribbean, the novels of Patrick O'Brian, Pilates, lobster, *The Lord of the Rings*, and most sculpture.' And yet to a generation which has grown up grazing on the Internet, it can seem as though Chatwin, far from being overrated, has slipped back into the obscurity in which he laboured while he wrote and published his first three books. Interviewed in Australia twelve years after his death, I was asked by a puzzled young journalist: 'Who was Bruce Chatwin?'

My answer, roughly, was that Chatwin was a precursor of the Internet: a connective super-highway without boundaries, with instant access to different cultures. He was a storyteller of bracing prose, at once glass-clear and dense, who offered a brand new way of representing travelling; further, he held out in his six books the possibility of something wonderful and unifying, inundating us with information but also the promise that we will one day get to the root of it. And I quoted his friend Robyn Davidson: 'He posed questions that we all want answered and perhaps gave the illusion they were answerable.'

If his questions have not gone away, nor have queries over Chatwin's reputation. The interrogation mark omitted deliberately from the title of his last book continues to hover over the character of its author, who, on scant evidence, has been accused of making things up, of not telling the truth. He may be guilty of other sins — for example, not telling Anatoly Sawenko that he was modelling the principal character in *The Songlines* on him, or failing to send him a copy of the published book. And yet Chatwin was not a 'whopper merchant'. In following his trail, I found errors, but strikingly few examples of mere invention, fewer than in the case of one or two of his disciples; or, say, Norman Lewis, who, imperishable travel-writer though he is, enjoys a reputation as a 'truth-speaker' that would have amused him enormously, and probably did.

'I absolutely deny to the end of my days that Bruce was a fraud, a poseur and a sham,' says Robin Lane Fox. 'I don't think he was any of these things. He had sharp beams of knowledge and a range of fragmented, intimately observed allusions that he could piece together in the most extraordinary original whole, beyond the frontiers of normal publication. There was no object I could allude to that he didn't know — a Spartan bronze, the Vix Crater in Burgundy, a silver plate on a Greek Bactrian elephant and a drawing of a similar object known in the Channel

Islands in the nineteenth-century and since lost. He would have a wild card on the uses of it, and off we'd be on a vast horizon expanding all the way from Russia to Siberia – a phenomenal imaginative display, entirely spontaneous, but based on genuine knowledge. It wasn't fraudulent balls. He *understood*. I learned so much from Bruce. Boy, he knew.'

For Elisabeth Sifton, Chatwin's American editor: 'Bruce was an artist not a liar.' Paradoxically, he did not have a fictional gift. He had the imagination to tell stories, to connect them, to enlarge, colour and improve them, but not to invent. Whether this reflects the terror of the autodidact, Chatwin more than most writers felt compelled to meet the people he wrote about, go to the places, read the books – where possible in the original language. 'His art of arranging, composing and enspiriting the material was, though, more like a novelist's than a journalist's,' says Sifton.

Perhaps the way to understand his stories is to treat them as Graham Speake advises us to view the stories of monks on Mount Athos, the place which in important respects marked the end of Chatwin's quest – i.e. as 'embroideries of a fundamental truth'. At his worst, he can irritate like any writer can; he can be cold, peremptory, relentlessly exotic. At his best, though, he is less economical with the truth than spendthrift. He tells not a half-truth but a truth and a half.

Nowhere does Chatwin arouse more suspicion than in the manner he is perceived to have dealt with his final illness: he died of Aids, but denied in public that he had it. His denial bred a sense that if he lied about his life, he must have lied about his work. Some readers have taken this as a cue to pass judgement on his books – or else not to bother with them. It deserves repeating that Chatwin's medical reports confirm that he said nothing he was not given leave to believe by his doctors at the Churchill Hospital in Oxford. At the time he fell ill – the mid-1980s – all sufferers of Aids had HIV, but it was not known for certain whether every person infected with HIV automatically contracted Aids. The disease, which had appeared in New York in 1981, was relatively new to England and still 'mysterious and shameful' in the words of the gay writer Edmund White, one of a number of men who had sex with Chatwin.

Whatever Chatwin's private fears during this period of profound public anxiety, he clung to the shred of hope offered by the presence of a then-rare fungus that he might not, after all, necessarily develop Aids (the fungus is now known to be an Aids-defining illness). It is unfair to judge him for any pronouncements that he made once his brain had been poisoned. By the time his HIV had developed into full-blown Aids, he was much like his description of Rimbaud, who died in a Marseilles hospital in 1891, 'mumbling in his delirium a stream of poetic images which his sister Isabelle, though she had paper and pencil to hand, did not think to write down'.

Typical of Chatwin's Protean nature was that after he died friends should disagree about him almost to the extent of his readers and critics. In Australia, Murray Bail, one of his closest correspondents, reacted to news of his death with a single paragraph, a notebook entry Chatwinesque in its deadpan concision. '18.1.89 All head and bulging blue eyes. No sense of humour, yet could recognise and tell well a story – always based on a person, an experience, usually slightly extreme. Travelled – geographically, intellectually, aesthetically and, apparently, sexually. These strange confused feelings when a friend, or even an acquaintance, dies at a faraway distance.'

If Bail recollected Chatwin's lack of humour as a chief characteristic, for Patrick Leigh Fermor, writing from Greece, his child-like humour was the quality he cherished: 'though very mature in experience, discernment and learning and enormously travelled and worldly wise, he had the utterly convincing aura of an infant prodigy shot up like a beanstalk into a sort of open-air Radiguet. Everything – the striking looks, the fluency and verve of his talk, the extraordinary adventures, the urgency, the enjoyment and humour, the nearly fiendish laughter that ended some of his sentences – increased the impression of youth and made his vast conversational range seem more surprising still.' What Leigh Fermor missed most about his 'amazingly gifted and suddenly absent companion' was 'the energy, the originality and the laughter'.

To Salman Rushdie, Chatwin was one of the two funniest people he had known. 'He was so colossally funny, you'd be on the floor with pain.'

Trying to corner Chatwin's elusive quality, the novelist Shirley

Hazzard cast him as an illuminator, shedding light rather in the way of a lightning-struck bush dragged back to the Swartkrans cave. She wrote to me when I was struggling to bring shape to his life: 'What is difficult to convey is how much he gave, above all by the enchantment of his presence and his crystal renderings of what had seemed ordinary things.'

Not one of those Chatwin worked with at Sotheby's predicted that he would throw up a lucrative partnership to become a student archae-ologist, still less a writer. 'No one would have thought this belated youth capable of writing anything more than his own name,' believed Von Rezzori in *Anecdotage*. If the character Chatwin presented in the flesh was an ever-altering scrum – 'I think I hardly knew him, there were so many of him,' says his sister-in-law – so also his books, each of them set in a different continent, resisted categorisation. Few understood his enterprise and significance better than a German author whose only experience of meeting him was on the page. W. G. Sebald was foremost of those writers set free by Chatwin. In the last essay that Sebald published before his own untimely death, he touched on Chatwin's achievement in trampling down the fence-posts imposed by publishers, booksellers and critics. Taught by his example not to be tamed by conventional bound-aries, Sebald went on to suggest that Chatwin's invigorating legacy lay in pointing a way forward as well as back:

'Just as Chatwin himself ultimately remains an enigma, one never knows how to classify his books. All that is obvious is that their struc-ture and intentions place them in no known genre. Inspired by a kind of avidity for the undiscovered, they move along a line where the points of demarcation are those strange manifestations and objects of which one cannot say whether they are real, or whether they are among the phantasms generated in our minds from time immemorial. Anthropo-logical and mythological studies in the tradition of Lévy-Strauss's *Tristes Tropiques*, adventure stories looking back to our early childhood reading, collections of facts, dream books, regional novels, examples of lush exoticism, puritanical penance, sweeping baroque vision, self-denial and personal confession – they are all these things together. It probably does them most justice to see their promiscuity, which breaks the mould of the modernist concept, as a late flowering of those traveller's tales, going back to Marco Polo, where reality is constantly entering the realm of the metaphysical and miraculous, and the way through the world is taken from the first with an eye fixed on the writer's own end.'

* * *

The process of hunting down Chatwin's correspondence began in 1991, when I was commissioned to write his authorised biography. I spent seven years working on his life as a matter of choice and made liberal use of letters gathered in the course of interviewing people in 27 countries. Almost everyone – there was one exception – gave me permission to make full transcriptions. Some of his correspondents I talked to for long periods; others, I never bumped into. A notice placed in the *Times Literary Supplement*, following the biography's publication in 1999, attracted five replies, plus copies of Chatwin's letters to Michael Davie, David Mason, Charles Way and J. Howard Woolmer. This book represents about 90 per cent of material collected over nearly two decades. Our hope is that it might result in the discovery of more. A day after the manuscript was delivered to the publisher, a cache of four letters and a postcard written to Susan Sontag was traced to an archive in Los Angeles; we have been able to include these.

Chatwin's principal correspondents were his parents Charles and Margharita, who in the early 1960s moved from Brown's Green Farm outside Birmingham, to Stratford-upon-Avon, where they remained for the rest of their lives; Elizabeth Chanler, to whom Chatwin was married for 23 years, despite a brief separation in the early 1980s; her mother Gertrude Chanler, who lived in Geneseo, New York State; Cary Welch, an American collector who was married to Elizabeth's cousin Edith; Ivry Freyberg, the sister of Raulin Guild, his best friend at Marlborough; John Kasmin, a London art dealer with whom he travelled to Africa, Kathmandu and Haiti; Tom Maschler, his publisher at Jonathan Cape; Diana Melly, his hostess in Wales; Francis Wyndham, the writer, who worked with him at the *Sunday Times* magazine and was the first to be allowed to see his finished manuscripts; the Australian writers Murray Bail, Ninette Dutton and Shirley Hazzard; James Ivory, the American film director, who stayed with him in France in the summer of 1971; Sunil Sethi, an Indian journalist whom he met in 1978 while on the trail of Mrs Gandhi.

The business of love affairs is not prominent. Chatwin is often at his most intimate with those encountered fleetingly in faraway places. 'You do not find pining lovers among the Gipsies,' he wrote in a notebook. 'Romantic love is played down as to be almost non-existent.' Any letters he may have written to Donald Richards or Jasper Conran have not come to light, if, indeed they ever existed ('He never wrote to me,' says Conran); those to Andrew Batey were destroyed in a flood in the Napa Valley.

Missing as well are letters to Penelope Betjeman, Werner Herzog, David Nash, Robin Lane Fox, Gita Mehta, Redmond O'Hanlon, David Sulzberger; and from the archives of Sotheby's and the *Sunday Times* magazine during the years of Chatwin's employment there.

Incorporated in the footnotes are Elizabeth Chatwin's comments on the text. These are intended to have the effect of an ongoing conversation. The poet Matthew Prior put it well in 'A Better Answer to Chloe Jealous':

> *No matter what beauties I saw in my way;*
> *They were but my visits; but thou art my home.*

In order to include as many letters as possible and to avoid repetition, we have pruned, sometimes heavily; all cuts are marked by ellipses. On the occasions when Chatwin wrote the same version of events to several people, we have chosen the fullest or most interesting. At other times – notably in descriptions of Penelope Betjeman's death, the house that Chatwin rented in India while finishing *The Songlines*, and his illness – we have included different versions in order to show that these are not duplications so much as demonstrations of the way his elaborating mind worked. In one case a single word was deleted to avoid causing distress to someone still alive. Casting Chatwin in a good or bad light has not swayed us. We have attempted to follow the advice of Isaiah Berlin, who wrote in a letter: 'we have all far more to gain than to lose by the publication of even indiscreet documents, which always emerge one day and then do more harm than if they were published openly, candidly and quickly.' Our choice has been determined by whether the material is interesting or illuminating. Obvious errors have been corrected; punctuation, addresses and spelling regularised – although we have retained his school misspellings. Dating the letters, even when they bear a date, has not always been easy. Chatwin was uncertain even of his wife's birthday; several letters are marked not only with the wrong month, but the wrong year.

If Bruce Chatwin were to have written an autobiography to what extent would it be this? Had he yet been alive, how much of this volume would he have left out, or rewritten? These questions have been everpresent during our preparation of *Under the Sun*. The answers lie, inevitably, in the same realm as his unwritten books. But a fascinating version of his life is here, from the first Sunday at Old Hall School in Shropshire when he sat down after Chapel to write to his parents.

NICHOLAS SHAKESPEARE

CHAPTER ONE

SCHOOLDAYS: 1948–58

Bruce Chatwin was conceived in a hotel south of Aberystwyth and born on 13 May 1940 in the Shearwood Road Nursing Home in Sheffield. His father Charles Chatwin was a Birmingham lawyer; he was away at sea in the Navy when Bruce was born. His mother, Margharita Turnell, the daughter of a clerk for a Sheffield knife-manufacturer, brought him up in the homes of great-uncles, great-aunts and grandparents. He had a younger brother Hugh, born on 1 July 1944.

For Chatwin's first six years, mother and son were everything to each other as they fled from the noise of war. The carpet-bombing of Coventry in November 1940, in one night flattening the city centre, frightened Margharita into giving up – without telling her husband – the small house which Charles had rented for them in Barnt Green; Birmingham's Austin Motor works, making Hawker Hurricanes, lay over the railway line on the direct flight path of Luftwaffe navigators. Her memory of the awesome orange glow in the night sky continued to haunt Margharita long after she bolted north. She had panic attacks. She would talk to herself and shout out, hunting for her absent husband, 'Charles! Charles!' 'What is it, mummy?' 'Oh, nothing, darling. Nothing. It's all right.' As they shuttled on the train between a dozen dwelling-places, including poky lodgings in Baslow and Filey, Chatwin's duty was to be the brave little boy looking after his distressed mother: aunts and uncles told him so.

When Charles returned from the war, the family moved first back to Birmingham, taking a lease on a house in Stirling Road which had been used by the army as a brothel; then, in April 1947, to Brown's Green Farm twelve miles south of Birmingham, a 'fairly derelict' smallholding with eleven acres, for rent at £98 per annum. A lawyer during the week, at weekends Charles invented himself as a food-producer, keeping an eventual tally of pigs, geese, ducks and 200 chickens. 'We were brought up as country children, tied to the rhythm of the seasons,' says Hugh.

At the end of April 1948 Chatwin went away to Old Hall School in Shropshire. His first surviving letter was written after attending one of three Sunday services in Chapel. He was seven years old and would spend the next decade at boarding school.

Old Hall School, a fifteenth-century manor house set in 25 acres, was a preparatory school for 108 sons of the factory-owning and professional and commercial classes of the Midlands, and the personal fiefdom of Paul Denman Fee-Smith, a stocky and energetic bachelor who advertised it as 'The Best Preparatory School in England.' Fee-Smith was a man of rigorous Anglo-Catholic beliefs whose conduct of three Chapel services on Sunday was in full priestly regalia of cassock, surplice and cope. Stories of the Prodigal Son, Daniel and the Lion and the Conversion of Saul were favourite readings. To the boys, he was known as 'Boss'. Boss's penchant for vestments and his encyclopaedic knowledge of the Bible were to leave an indelible mark upon Chatwin.

At Old Hall School Chatwin wore a maroon and grey cap and blazer. He played games on Monday, Tuesday and Friday afternoons, and distinguished himself in boxing and acting. He was still known at this stage as Charles Bruce Chatwin; although through making a certain amount of noise he earned the nickname 'Chatty'.

Boss noted Chatwin's restlessness in his first report: 'He is rather a careless worker & his attention soon wanders. He is still very young & hardly out of the egocentric stage; his behaviour is childish & very noisy at times!' To Hugh, his elder brother's behaviour was easily explained. 'From my perspective, Bruce was escaping from the trauma of war by playing out parts of his own *devising, by telling stories good enough to deserve being the centre of attention.'*

Spelling was never Chatwin's strong point. Like most pupils, he filled his weekly letters home using formulas; beginning each, as taught, with 'I hope you are all well,' reaching the bottom of the page with resumés of films, orders for books, for balsa wood models of houses and farms, or reports on his flu – his health was frail even at this stage; and ending with a separate line for each word.

Dressing up, acting, religion – already he displayed what W. G. Sebald would call 'the art of transformation that comes naturally to him, a sense of being always on stage, an instinct for the gesture that would make an effect on the audience, for the bizarre and the scandalous, the terrible and the wonderful, all these were undoubtedly prerequisites of Chatwin's ability to write'.

To Charles and Margharita Chatwin

The Old Hall School | Wellington | Shropshire | 2 May [1948]

Dear Mummy and Daddy,

It is a lovely school. We had a lovely film called The Ghost Train. It was all about a train the came into the station every year at midnight and if any one looked at it they wold die. I am in the second form.

With love from

Bruce

The Old Hall School | Wellington | Shropshire | 31 October [1948]

Dear Mummy and daddy,

I got on very well with the aroplane kit, but it flew into a fir tree and got torn. It was going very well until it did that. We played Packwood Haugh yesterday, and it was a draw. I was eighth in form this week. Latin is getting on very well. I have got a plus for history. In Maths

I am tenth. Aunt Gracie[1] sent me a postcard of London Towr bridge. Thank you very much for sending my stamps and my cigerett cards. Boxing is getting very well. I have got to have some extra boxing. Please could I have some more stamped onvelopes because I am writing so many letters. And will you send me *Swallows and Amazons*.

    With love from Bruce

The Old Hall School | Wellington | Shropshire | 29 February [1949]

Dear Mummy and Daddy,

    Please could you get me a Romany Book, called *Out with Romany by Medow and Stream*[2] Because I want it for a friend of mines birthday. Yesturday we had a lantern lecture on a man's uncle who went to Africa to exploring and he took a lot of photographs on big game, and natives.[3] In my book *Wild Life* there are two photographs. One of some Rock Rabbits, and another of a jackel. It was very nice. I hope you are well. Please will you send me a book called *The Open Road*.[4] Tell Hugh it wont be long till I come home. Please will you save these stamps till I come home. When you see Aunt Gracie next tell her I send my love.

    'Love you pieces'
    Bruce

The Old Hall School | Wellington | Shropshire | 13 March, Sunday [1949]

Dear Mummy and daddy,

    I hope you are all well. I wrote to Uncle Humphry and Auntie Peggey

1. The younger and more extrovert of his father's two spinster aunts.
2. *Out with Romany By Meadow and Stream*, Bramwell Evens (1942).
3. John Kearton, nephew of explorer Cherry Kearton, gave a talk on the African veldt, illustrated with photographs of man-eating lions and rhino.
4. *The Open Road: A Little Book for Wayfarers*, anthology, ed. E. V. Lucas (1899). 'A garland of good and enkindling poetry and prose fitted to urge folk into the open air, and once there, to keep them glad they came.' With a green buckram binding 'and a flight of gilded swallows on the cover', it was Chatwin's most cherished travel book, along with Osip Mandelstam's *Journey to Armenia* (1933) and Robert Byron's *The Road to Oxiana* (1937).

yesterday.[1] I like the sound of Brig[2] very much. Tell Hugh it won't be long till I come home. Thank you for the addresses. Yesturday, IVa gave a Variety Show. There was a quiz. Someone had to go up on the stage and they were asked two questions. I went up and I was asked, what was the oldest structure in England, and, what was the wing-span of a helicopter, and then I had to be dressed up as a baby. Purce was nanney. I had to have a dummy and a rattle. I was in pram. On Thursday it was Mr Fee Smith's birthday. We had a Tresure Hunt and afterwards in the evening we some films. There were two cartoons, one was called Andy Panda in Nuttywood Cavern and the other one was called The Pecquiler Penguins.

Love you pieces

Bruce XXXX

Another one was 'For those in Peril'.[3]

The Old Hall School | Wellington | Shropshire | 4 May 1949

Dear Mummy,

This is only a short letter to ask you if you could get me some rubber bands.

Love you peices

Bruce

1. Humphrey Chatwin worked for the Gold Coast Railway. On 8 December 1949 he was murdered by his cook-boy in Takoradi.
2. Hugh Chatwin: 'Brig was a Staffordshire Bull Terrier pup whose pleasure was to play boisterously with all our farmyard creatures. Alas, undeterred by useless scolding, he went the way of all hounds that worried neighbouring farmers' sheep.'
3. 1944 film based on a story by fighter-pilot Richard Hillary about Air-Sea rescue launches that patrolled the Channel picking up downed airmen.

The Old Hall School | Wellington | Shropshire | 6 November [1949]

Dear Mummy and Daddy,

I hope you are all well. Yesturday the fireworks were absoutly wizard. There were 130 rockets, 14 cathrine weels, 4 christal fountains and a lot more. Have you heard, about the Poenix firework company. Sombody put gun-powder in some false fireworks, and there was a terrific explosion at Okengates, and all the panes of the windows in the district came out, and a girl of 17 was wounded. We had a lot, so we tied them up in a parcel and threw them in the boating pond. Half term reports are coming next time. On Wednesday, we had a match against Abberly Hall. We won 2–1. We had a Remberance Service to day in chapel.

Bruce

Whether Chatwin was always so buoyant at Old Hall School as his letters home suggest is thrown into doubt by a short story he wrote towards the end of his life which paints a less than 'wizard' picture of Bonfire Night and of school life in general.

On a wall in Chapel, a brass plaque commemorated a boy who had died at Old Hall School on 9 September 1923, aged ten. Hugh says: 'In my time, no matron ever refuted the oft-repeated boys' tale that Tommy Woodhouse died of constipation – the result of a silly, rule-breaking dare.' This became the genesis for Chatwin's virtually last finished piece of creative writing. 'The Seventh Day' features a nervous, skinny, religious boy – clearly based on Chatwin – eight years old, with thick fair hair, who hates going back to boarding school, so much so that he makes himself sick. He is teased by other boys about his constipation ('He wished they'd stop laughing whenever he had hard times on the pot. The lavatories had no doors.'). He is teased about his father's car ('It was not a car but a grey Ford van. It had windows cut in the back and Spitfire seats to sit on. Sometimes the van smelled of pigswill.'). He is teased for his perceived self-sufficiency. 'He hated school because no one would leave him alone. Because he was so skinny he hated being tickled by the headmaster. He hated the boy who stole his marbles and he hated the boy who pinned him on his bed and rubbed his chest with his hairbrush. At night, after lights out, the others whispered their plans for the future. They would have wives and children. He hid under the bed sheet and saw himself as the last man left on earth after the Bomb went off. He saw himself in white cloth walking over a charred landscape . . .'

The boy also hates Guy Fawkes Night. 'The Guys had pumpkins cut into faces. One Guy was Mr Attlee with a scarecrow hat and a witch's broom. Mr Attlee had Hitler's moustache. He hated the masters for working up the boys. He went off into the dark and cried for Mrs Attlee.'

This last experience probably followed the defeat of Clement Attlee's Labour Government by Winston Churchill's Conservatives in October 1951. To it, Chatwin attributed the fact that 'never, even in my capitalist phase, was I able to vote Conservative'.

Hugh says: 'There were two sides to Bruce's early life. There was his ability to relate to adults and their world, and to reflect back the joy they expressed in their hope for his generation of War Babies; and then there was the private business of being a small boy who had not been brought up with other children, who found himself confined in a very strict, highly disciplined, seminary-like institution. Old Hall could be a frightening place.'

The Old Hall School | Wellington | Shropshire | [1949]

Dear Mummy and Daddy,

I hope you are all well. The Rocket-a-Copter is going most beauti-fully. It goes about 100 feet high. It got caught in a mulberry tree. One of the boys climbed up and got it down. All the wings have broken but I have mended it again. I am making another model village for Hugh . . . At the end of term I am doing a play called Fat King Melon[1]. I am going to be a Highwayman,

   Bruce

1. Chatwin's first proper stage role, in A. P. Herbert's *Fat King Melon and Princess Caraway*, performed in December 1949. The reviewer called him 'a good-looking chap'.

The Old Hall School | Wellington | Shropshire | 29 January [1950]

Dear Mummy & Daddy,

I am in bed with flu. My temperature has been 103 but is now normal. I have nearly finished The Georgian Mansion. It is a bit dull but very nice. We had a film Arthur Askey in 'I Thank Thee'. It was extremely funny. I have been doing a terrific wooden jig-saw puzzle of the 'Queen Mary.' It has 400 pieces. I am sorry my writing is not very good.

  With
  Love
  From
  Bruce

The Old Hall School | Wellington | Shropshire | 4 February [1950]

Dear Mummy and daddy,

I hope you are both well . . . I have completely recovered from my flu. Thank you very much for sending me the *Meccano Magizine* and the *Chilrens Newspaper*. Please don't send me any comics when I am ill they bore me. A boy's magazine such as *Boy's Own* would be much more appreciated.

  Your affectionate son,
  Bruce

The Old Hall School | Wellington | Shropshire [autumn 1950]

Dear Mummy & Daddy,

Boss hopes to put on a *Midsummer Night's Dream* at the end of term and he has asked me to play the part of Billy Bottom. We had a Will Hay film on Tuesday called 'Boys will be boys.' We have not played soccer yet because of the rain. Please could you send me a tube of balsa cement, two + ⅛th of an inch square strips of balsa wood. And a piece of balsa wood 3″ x ½″ x 2′ because we are making a model of Mevagissy Harbour.[1]

Love

Bruce

The Old Hall School│Wellington│Shropshire│3 October 1950

Dear Mummy & daddy,

I hope you are all well . . . We have had snow here. It is thawing but it is extremely hot . . . I came 10th in maths exam with 38 marks. I came 4th in Scripture with 52 marks. In History I came 3rd with 54 marks. The play is getting on all right now. We are going to watch a *Midsummer Dream* which is on television today. Mr Fee Smith has hired a large 15″ screen set. We had a nice service in chapel to-day as it is Advent Sunday. My model speedboat is completed, so please could you send some blue and silver dope and two paint brushes. You will get it at the Model Aerodrome. On Monday I had the wacking[2], for refusing to give a chit in which was not true. I was beating the master (Mr Poole) in an argument. He knew he was losing so he said 'Well, it's too late now I have reported you to Mr Fee Smith, and he told me to write you out a chit, he told me.'

with love

from

Bruce

1. E.C.: 'He had great skill with his hands. He could paint and sew and mend things, stick handles back on, so that you could never see the join.'
2. H.C.: 'Form masters had different means of achieving discipline. Mr Peregrine (Latin) kept a slipper handy; Mr Pye (Maths) preferred to beat with the flat side of a set of wooden board compasses. For more serious misdemeanours, a "chit" would lead to an evening interview with the headmaster. Usually, Boss followed his reprimands with two to four neatly laid cuts of his four-foot bamboo cane. The bruised backsides were there for other boys to comment upon at bath-time. This was Bruce's only whacking – compared with my four. He did not complain.'

The Old Hall School | Wellington | Shropshire | 10 December 1950

Dear Mummy & Daddy,

I have just discovered that my bird-books are worth £10 for the set, and will soon be very valuable.[1] I have decided that I would prefer a lightweight sports bycicle than an ordinary bycicle with a 3 speed gear. The trunks have come up and the play is going on quite well now. Boss has put a lot of his imagination in it. I think that if acted propaly it will be very nice.[2] I came second in the term order. I didn't want to be first because it is to much of a fag. Thank you very much for sending me the Globe-Theatre Micro-model. I have made a lot of Christmas decorations for the holidays. Our dormitory is festooned with them.

The Old Hall School | Wellington | Shropshire | 4 March [1951]

Dear Mummy and daddy,

I hope you are all well. I have got a lovely little smoothing plane, it is only 3 ins long, and the blade is ⅞ of an inch thick. Please could you send me an Anorma Post Office. Please get the money out off my savings. Mr Whitton gave a lecture on archaeolagy, it was very interesting. Conjouring has taken itself in the school and I am very interested in it. I am making some tricks myself. I have made some more things for you and Hugh.

        With love from Bruce

The Old Hall School | Wellington | Shropshire | 18 March [1951]

Dear Mummy & Daddy,
        I hope you are all well . . . We had the Gym Competition on Tuesday.

1. H.C.: 'After we moved to Brown's Green Farm, Bruce quickly became proficient in recognising all the woodland birds to be seen there; an aptitude rewarded by great-uncle Philip passing on his four volumes of Thorburn's *British Birds*. This gift, with gold-edged coloured plates, was the first antique thing for him to own.'
2. Performed on 14 December 1950. 'Perhaps pride of place should go to Bottom the Weaver. A very young member of the cast this one, who had a lot to do and did it with great gusto. Ass's head or no ass's head, you did well, "sweet bully Bottom" . . .'

I boxed in the ring on Monday against a tough.[1] I won 5–3. I am in the final for the Junior Cup. I have got a very good chance.

With love from Bruce

The Old Hall School | Wellington | Shropshire | 15 July [1951]

Dear Mummy and Daddy,

I hope you are all well. There was a match yesturday against Yarlet Hall. It was a draw. We were 125 for two. They were 4 for nine. It will soon be the end of term . . . How are the little black pigs[2] getting on? I was awfully embarrassed yesturday, some weomen, and one man, sat on our bench, while we were watching the match. I had to entertain them.

With love from
Bruce

The Old Hall School | Wellington | Shropshire | 30 September [1951]

Dear Mummy and daddy,

I hope you are all well. I am afraid that I have not got much to say as I only came on Thursday. Have you enjoyed your holiday at Marlborough. Please will you plant the bulbs I bought. The romundculus are those tentacle looking things and the iascas the little bulbs. Are the gold fish all right? The new matron staff is most peculiar, especially Miss Griffiths who we have nicknamed 'The Grifon'. She is most peculier and waddles about like a duck.

With love
From
Bruce

1. Philip Howard. The ordeal took place in Hall. Boss wrote that Chatwin proved 'a hard, relentless hitter and gives the impression of immense solidity'.
2. Charles kept 37 pigs at Brown's Green Farm, driving the pigswill from Birmingham in the same all-purpose grey Ford van that shuttled Chatwin's trunk back and forth to Old Hall.

The Old Hall School | Wellington | Shropshire | 7 October [1951]

Dear Mummy and Daddy,

On Friday night the fireworks were very nice. There were very big cathrine weels. I had a lovely firwork to hold called a flying star. On Tuesday we had a lovely film called the Overlanders. It was about driving cattale over Australia. They went from the Northern Territory to Queenslands. They came to a deep river were there were two big crocodiles. When the cart was going over one of the crocidiles woke up and splashed into the water. It came up to the cart when one of the men took a shot at it and killed it and then they got to a city they took the catle through. Then one of the men fell of his horse and broke his arm and some catle trod on him and he broke his leg, so they took him to hospidle for three days and for six days they went with out water. They found some water at a windmill pump but the horses only had a little drink when it stoped. They rested them and there was a fire. The cattle rushed untll they smelt water, the men rushed to see what it was but it was a bog. They tried to get them back but the horses got poisoned and they ran very fast, but they fell over, and they died. They went back to the cart. One day when they were lying on a rock some wild horses came and they made a wire fence and they traped them and they broke them in so they had some more horses. They went up a mountain when they were nerby at the top a tree blocked up the way and a man climbed up but he was to late. Two of the cattle fell of. Then the man when he got to the top fastened the rope to the horse and pulled the tree out but the horse very nerly sliped but he cut the rope and they got down

With love from Bruce

To Hugh Chatwin

The Old Hall School | Wellington | Shropshire | 21 October [1951]

Dear Hugh,

I have got a Dinky Toy for you I will give it to you on visiting day
From Bruce

To Charles and Margharita Chatwin
The Old Hall School | Wellington | Shropshire | 17 February [1952]

Dear Mummy and Daddy,

I hope you are both well . . . I am going in for a competition in which you can choose your own prizes. We had a jolly good film last night called 'Riders in the Forest' it was about a New Forest Pony. I am most certainly in the mood for writing letters. I am shooting up the form. I came 5th in Maths this fortnight.

With love from Bruce

To Margharita Chatwin
The Old Hall School | Wellington | Shropshire | [May 1952]

Dear Mummy

Hugh is settling down well. Unfortunately he is in form I and has been placed miles too low. He has begun music and he wants his old music book. He has lost his mack and does not care the slightest bit. I have swaped a lot of stamps.[1] As soon as he got there he made friends with Cant. I have had a food rash but it is nearly gone.

Bruce

To Charles and Margharita Chatwin
The Old Hall School | Wellington | Shropshire | 25 May [1952]

Dear Mummy and daddy,

I hope you are both well, Hugh has had a spell of being good. He has had no blacks for a fortnight now. If he gets on well I have promised him a clockwork submarine, which dives and surfaces again . . .[2] Unfortunately Hugh dislikes Cant and Reynolds and has taken to a boy called Taylor III

1. H.C.: 'As a stamp collector, he went on to specialise in unused "British Colonials".'
2. H.C.: 'Months before, I had accompanied Bruce to Birmingham's Model Aerodrome shop where he bought this birthday gift. Formally presented on the day, the toy became mine to enjoy – albeit one of several "elder brotherly" things that remained in his custody, lest I should break or lose it.'

who has invited him to stay with him, and his cousin, Williams, who lives
2 miles away from Taylor III, has invited me to go to stay with him.

   With

   Love

   From

   Bruce

*In the summer of 1953 Chatwin passed his Common Entrance
Exam and was accepted by Marlborough College in Wiltshire. On
22 July Fee-Smith wrote to his parents: 'Thank you so much for
the cheque for Bruce's contribution towards a garden seat, his
name and date of leaving will be inscribed on it. I shall miss him
next term – such a nice boy & such good company.'*

*   *   *

*In September 1953, after a sailing holiday on the river Hamble,
Chatwin's parents drove him in their old black Rover to begin at
Marlborough, a public school founded in 1843 for educating the
sons of poor clergy. He spent his first year in Priory, a pleasant
out-of-college junior house situated in the middle of town, with two
acres of grounds sloping down to the River Kennet. Chatwin had
left Old Hall School already stage-struck, having picked up, in
Hugh's words, 'a respect – and fancy for – the vestments and rituals
of authority'. Marlborough, with 800 boys, was more like a university. Life was not so organised. You had to be your own Boss. Hugh
followed his brother to Marlborough four years later: 'Old Hall was
an enclosed, monastic environment, caged by absolutes. Marlborough offered freedom from all that. The symbol and physical reality
of freedom were bicycles. At Priory, so long as we promised to stay
in pairs (in case of trouble), from the age of thirteen we could ride
out of Marlborough in any direction to celebrate whatever Wiltshire's
Great Outdoors had to offer. Additionally, we were expected to join
three to five of the College's 50 boy-self-managing Societies, but it
was entirely down to our own taste and aptitude what we might
choose to do with our spare time, inside or outside the gates.'*

To Charles and Margharita Chatwin
Priory House | Marlborough College | Wiltshire | Sunday [September 1953]

Dear Mummy and Daddy,

I am thoroughly enjoying myself here and I am settling down well. The Shell form that I am in is Shell A. There are six Shell forms. Shell A is the first. I have made several friends already. I get on very well with Edwards. I have made friends also with a boy called Ghalib,[1] whose father is a Turk. The food in Priory is excellent and I have had no need to delve into my tuck-box yet. Don't bother to send on the cycle-clips as we have to cycle in shorts. I don't know what the Master's name is yet and he is always called the Master.[2] Yesterday he had a talk with all the new boys and he is very nice. My bicycle has proved invaluable as we have to clear out of the house for one hour every day and we have 3 half holidays a week. Please will you send me some books because for an hour in the evening we have to read. I have seen all the other ex Old Hall boys . . . Massey[3] is a house captain and is in charge of my dormitory. Any band instrument can be taken. I can have free coaching for the first term and if the music master thinks I am good enough he will ask for it to be continued. Most boys here play the trombone. But I don't think I will have enough time.[4]

With Love

Bruce

Little correspondence survives from Chatwin's time at Marlborough. He was under no pressure to write letters – family visiting arrangements were made from a coin telephone in B2 House, the spartan, less expensive in-house to where he moved in 1954. As well, a close friend of Margharita's, Barbara Farrington, provided 'open house' to the Chatwin family at Minal Woodlands House, two miles east of Marlborough. Hugh says, 'Margharita was free to come down and join in the social life of Marlborough masters and their wives.'

* * *

1. Raymond Ghalib (*b.*1939).
2. Tommy Garnett (1915–2006) had been appointed Master of Marlborough in 1952.
3. Christopher Massey (*b.*1939).
4. E.C.: 'Bruce never learned to play an instrument.'

At the end of his first year at Marlborough, the Bratt family in Sweden contacted Charles through a friend. Would Chatwin like to stay the summer at their lake-side home south of Stockholm and teach English to their son, Thomas, who was the same age? Margharita saw him off at Tilbury on the SS Patricia. Aside from family sailing holidays in France, it was Chatwin's first experience of abroad.

Lundby Gard | Sweden | [July 1954]

Friday

Dear Mummy and daddy,

I arrived safely yesterday and had a wonderful crossing . . . It was rather unfortunate that the passengers in my cabin were a young man who was hoping to become a monk and said his prayers aloud all night in Latin and another who I think was a Polish Jew who snored all night. So what with snoring and Latin I did not get much sleep. But I was sitting at table with some very nice people. They were Swedes living in Finland and both of them had a most marvellous sense of humour. They have a boat in Finland and had just been to Lymington to see Laurent Giles[1] about designing another. He and I talked boats solidly all afternoon.

When the boat docked everything went smoothly until I came to the customs. The officer thought that I was French, why I don't know and then proceeded to take out everything from my case, searched all the pockets in my suits and then stalked off. After I had got all my things together again I only just caught the train. But when I was sitting down I discovered the reason for the customs officer. A boy came in and produced from various places 1000 cigarettes! The train went very fast and by lunch we came to Katrineholm. I got out and there was only the station-master there. But after waiting about ten minutes came Mr Bratt. I had expected Thomas to be fair-haired etc but he has jet black hair and dark skin which makes him look like an Italian. We packed into their huge Cadillac and soon came to Lundby Gard which is just about a village not a farm. There is Mr Bratt's brother in one

---

1. A renowned English designer of cruising yachts.

house,[1] in another his father, and another his uncle Percy![2] The lake is only the odd 30 miles long and joins up with several others; opposite the farm is an island on which is a castle and that is nearly five miles long and two and a half wide. There is not a shop for miles and everything has to be ordered, so my £10 may come back unmolested, especially as I earned 10 kroner this morning. They have a motor boat, rowing boat, sailing dinghy, an ordinary canoe, a Canadian birch bark and a very narrow canoe in which I went in several times trying to balance it.[3] We are going to Stockholm next week. I hope Hugh has got his post card. I tried to get you a picture of the Smorgasbord, the Swedish national dish which is a kind of hors d'oeuvre only on a far bigger scale. Hope you got the cable. Bruce

Postcard, b & w photograph of Lake Yngaren | Sweden | 20 August, 1954

This is part of their lake. All the land you can see the other side is an island. Their house is between the island and the mainland. We are going on a boat trip to another lake; all the lakes are just about joined up with each other. We spent 3 days in Stockholm and saw it thoroughly. It's a pity I didn't bring my camera because it is so beautiful country. We went down a very deep iron mine the other day;[4] it was very interesting. I will telephone you as soon as I get to London and let you know what train I am going on. Bruce

1. The pine houses were painted blood red with iron oxide from the copper mine. One day, Chatwin would paint his house near Oxford with the same Swedish oxide. E.C.: 'He was always in love with Sweden. It's where his colour sense gelled. The moment you go to Stockholm, there are his colours. Grey green, grey blue and contrasted with amazing ochres.'
2. Percevald Bratt – 'A delightful old gentleman always dressed in a white smock and sun hat . . . he lived in a log cabin lit by crystal chandeliers,' *Anatomy of Restlessness*. Peter Bratt (Thomas's brother): 'Shortly before his death, Bruce came to Stockholm because he wanted to revisit us. He mostly talked about the conversations he had had with my great-uncle [Percevald], who was erudite and knew classic literature very well, and Bruce said this was what incited him to start writing.'
3. E.C.: 'Sailing wasn't his great passion, as it was with Charles and Hugh.'
4. Grängesberg.

In the summer of 1957, after passing his driving test, Chatwin
borrowed Charles's van and drove to the south of France, returning
with a cane-seated high chair. It made a pair with his first major
furniture acquisition, a grey Louis XVI chair costing £2.10s. Both
requiring restoration, he bought a set of wood chisels and, in the
next stage after model-making, stripped them down in the box
room at Brown's Green Farm. In recognition of this passion, his
parents gave him a book on French furniture.

To Charles and Margharita Chatwin
B2 | Marlborough College | Wiltshire | [autumn 1957]

Dear Mummy and Daddy,

Thank you very much indeed for that wonderful surprise. It really is a
wonderful book, and on really looking at it closely it seems even better.
Like many French books it is eminently sensible in that it does not deal
exclusively with those fabulous rarities that are locked behind glass cases in
museums, and on that account are apt to be dull. But most of the things are
all first rate examples that one would be likely to come across. It is not a
book for the super expert, because volumes could be written on each of the
subjects but it gives a very clear picture of what was going on, and of course
those wonderful pictures help immensely, because it would be nonsense to
suggest that the best way of learning about such things is to see them personally or failing that to look at them by photographs. I have been reassured
on several points. Firstly that it is justifiable to refurnish French furniture
completely, and secondly that the two chairs are definitely genuine . . . The
second chair really is a rarity, it appears; square-backed Louis XVI *bergère*
chairs with that standard of carving and those spiral legs are very very
highly sought after, and even in that book there are few that have its elegance.
Also the book does not appear to worry too much about *ébénistes* stamps,
though of course, they add to the value to a large extent.[1]

1. In *The Songlines*, Chatwin meets a young *ébéniste* (cabinet-maker) on the road from
Atar. 'Although he had no passport, he had in his bag a book on French eighteenth-
century furniture.'

What is the name of the painter of your picture of 'The America' at the office? for I think you will be interested to learn that during April a picture, painted contemporary with the first America Cup, by a hitherto obscure painter named Carmichael,[1] showing the America,[2] was sold to an American bidder, I think at Christie's, for somewhat over £2,000 owning to the exceptional interest show over here by the new challenge.

The book has made my birthday. Thank you very much.

Love B

PS Buns lovely! Best for a long time. Aunt Cicely and Uncle Philip[3] sent 10/- for a Wallace Collection catalogue. Hugh gave me a blue and white striped mug to replace one that I broke.

Love B

For his 1957 Easter holiday, Chatwin travelled to Italy with another Marlburian, Richard Sturt.

To Charles and Margharita Chatwin
Rome | Italy | 2 April 1957

We had a fairly uneventful journey; wonderful scenery from the train. The sun was blazing as we crossed the Alps, but a confectioner from Scarborough, and a German girl in the same carriage insisted on having the windows firmly shut. We got here rather tired, took a taxi driven by a very smooth gent and before we knew what had happened he charged us £1. We argued and argued, and when he began to get nasty we gave him half, but it only should have cost about 2/6. The pensione was very grand, and now we have got a nice, much cheaper place. We went on a tour of Rome today with Father O'Flaherty[4], Richard's friend, and

1. John Wilson Carmichael (1800–68).
2. The original schooner.
3. Philip Boughton Chatwin (1873–1964), architect and amateur archaeologist dedicated to the restoration of old buildings. E.C.: 'I met him once, a beautiful old man, very civilised, tall, thin, with white hair.'
4. Hugh O'Flaherty (1898–1963), Irish Catholic priest and notary of the Vatican who saved up to 4,000 Allied soldiers and Jews during the Second World War.

tomorrow morning, together with several hundred other people, we are going to an audience with the Pope himself. Frankly, except for the Coliseum, the arch of Constantine, and Trajan's column, the Roman remains are rather dull to compare with the fantastic Medici palaces and the like. But it really is an incredibly modern city moving at a colossal speed. We have been made honorary members of an English club where we had tea with five very jolly Irish fathers. Love B

'Always a good listener, Margharita was seldom stuck for words, except on one notable occasion,' says Hugh. 'This was on Bruce's return from Rome in 1957. He regaled us in the Brown's Green kitchen with features of that city, ancient and modern, of its Seven Hills, of the fountains, of his lodgings beside the Spanish Steps, of the contents of its museums, of the Cardinal through whom his visit and audience with the Pope was pre-arranged – of the glamour of Rome's streets, of fashion amongst its women. "Golly!" was Margharita's interjection, as Bruce paused for breath before continuing his report. Thenceforward, it became our mother's party piece to trade on her astonishment of her and Charles's friends, giggling all the while, at the conditions in which her elder son was growing up, gallivanting about the Continent, whilst she was still plucking fowl and scrubbing eggs for sale at Henley-in-Arden's packing station.'

*   *   *

As at Old Hall School, Chatwin concentrated his best efforts on acting. He was Secretary of the Shakespeare Society and played the Mayor in Gogol's The Government Inspector, *Mrs Candour in Sheridan's* The School for Scandal *and James Winter JP in L. du Garde's* The White Sheep of the Family. *His interpretation of Winter, 'an expert burglar', revealed to the critic of the* Wiltshire Gazette & Herald *'considerable acting ability; his speech and movement were well-defined and throughout the whole performance he* seemed perfectly at ease'. Less impressive was his performance in class. In 1955, following a blow on the head while playing rugby, Chatwin had to miss the Michaelmas term. He struggled to catch up. 'He still finds his term away rather a handicap,' wrote his favourite form master, Hugh Weldon, the following summer. His report for Michaelmas 1957 was typical: 'Thoroughness and consistent concentration do not come easily to him. Too often in school and, it seems, in preparation, he is led astray and his mind goes off at a tangent, usually interesting but usually irrelevant.' Towards the end of his time at Marlborough, Jack Halliday, Chatwin's housemaster at B2, put pressure on him to think about a career. 'The undoubted success he had on the stage in Memorial Hall shows that he is extremely capable at organising other people, while the undoubtedly unsatisfactory reports in this folder show that he is not very capable at organising himself. In the holidays Bruce simply must get to grips with himself and, with his father's aid, must evolve a plan for his future.' Halliday proposed the Law and Trinity Hall, Cambridge, but Chatwin was quite sure that he did not want to follow in his father's footsteps. In his third year, he planned to try for a place to read Classics at Merton College, Oxford – the college of his grandfather and also of Robert Byron, an Old Marlburian writer whose work Chatwin already revered. But then National Service ended, the university had to find space for an extra generation of students and Chatwin might have to delay coming up for two years. Instead, he proposed a stage career following his successful production of Tons of Money. Charles, however, was adamant that neither of his sons should go directly from the sheltered life of boarding school to student digs in London, and declined Chatwin's ambitions for RADA, countering with a suggestion that he might consider the family profession of architecture. Chatwin was not prepared to study the science of building. His next idea was a job in Africa, following the example of his best friend at Marlborough, Raulin Guild, who had gone to work in Northern Rhodesia, but Margharita objected: Africa was where Uncle Humphrey had met his sad end. Then she read an article in Vogue

about a firm of fine art auctioneers.'What about Sotheby's for Bruce?'
So Charles contacted an old school friend Guy Bartleet, a chartered
surveyor who had sold at Sotheby's a Monet of 'a train going over
a bridge', to effect an introduction to Peter Wilson, the Chairman
of Sotheby's.

To Peter Wilson

Brown's Green Farm | Hockley Heath | Birmingham | 15 April 1958

Dear Sir,

Mr Bartleet has been good enough to give me the enclosed letter of
introduction to you.

I am very anxious to learn the best way of making a career in Fine
Art. If you would find time to see me before I go back to school on May
1st, I should be most grateful, and would hold myself ready to come at
any time at short notice,

Yours Faithfully,

C. B. Chatwin

A date was fixed for 3.30 Tuesday 29 April. The meeting went suffi-
ciently well for Charles to give notice to Marlborough that Bruce
would not be returning.'I shall miss that cheerful and accomplished
boy,' wrote the registrar Reginald Jennings by return, on May 2. On
7 May Wilson wrote to Charles:'I very much enjoyed meeting your
son and shall look forward to seeing him again during the summer.'

To Peter Wilson

B2 | Marlborough College | Wiltshire | 13 June 1958

Dear Sir,

When I came to see you in April, you said that I should write to you
again in June, by which time you would probably know if there was a
place for me at Sotheby's.

If there does happen to be a job available, I am very keen to take it. If you would like to see me again, I could easily arrange to come up to London at any time except from the 7th July for about a fortnight, when I am taking my exams.

Yours Faithfully,

C. B. Chatwin

Eventually, Wilson saw Chatwin in September and offered him a job as numbering porter in the Works of Art Department for £6 a week.

CHAPTER TWO

SOTHEBY'S: 1959–66

Chatwin was lucky to join Sotheby's at a time when Peter Wilson was expanding the auction house from four departments to fifteen. He rode the crest of this expansion. 'There is no doubt in my mind that Sotheby's was the main stimulus of Bruce's life,' says David Nash, an Old Marlburian who worked alongside Chatwin in the Impressionist and Modern Art Department, and travelled with him to Afghanistan. He learned from Wilson, and from the Antiquities Department adviser John Hewett, how to look at and handle a work of art, describe it concisely and to judge its market value. Sponsored by Sotheby's, he visited countries where these objects had originated and, 'slavishly' aping Robert Byron's itinerary, tracked his footsteps through Greece and Afghanistan.

Hugh remembers how, at Brown's Green Farm, Chatwin's family marvelled at his work-life pattern: 'his freedom to fly to Athens, thence to visit the sights, and the sites of digs, and his cosmopolitan friends at their island homes – journeying as if a university professor on long vacation and not an auction house trainee aged 20!'

Sotheby's enabled Chatwin to meet a network of aesthetically minded, rich enquiring dealers and collectors like Robert Erskine, Christopher Gibbs, John Kasmin, Teddy Millington-Drake, Edward Lucie-Smith, George Ortiz, Simon Sainsbury and Cary Welch.

It also introduced him to his wife.

* * *

For his first two months in London, Chatwin lodged with his uncle John Turnell, at 111 Cleveland Road in Ealing. He next moved to digs in St John's Wood, before signing a lease in August 1959 on a mews flat behind St George's Hospital. To share the rent, he took in Anthony Spink who worked at the family firm of coin dealers. The only friend Spink recalls Chatwin inviting home was Ivry Guild.'She was here a lot.'

Ivry (b.1937) had met Chatwin on a bright sunny morning in his last term at Marlborough. On Sunday 20 July 1958 the Oscar-winning film-maker Emeric Pressburger had driven her down from London in his greeny-yellow Bentley. Ivry, dressed like a 1920s flapper, sat in the front seat wearing a green suede hat. 'We alighted in the centre of Marlborough College courtyard and caused a sensation,' she recalls. 'Emeric brought a huge chocolate cake specifically ordered from Madame Prunier in St James's for Raulin, and some smoked sturgeon from The Czarda in Dean Street, along with horseradish cream that we all ate for lunch.' Ivry's brother Raulin was Head Boy and Captain of Games, and a close friend of Chatwin. 'Raulin took us in the afternoon to Bruce's study because he wanted me to see what fascinating furniture and objects Bruce had collected from local shops.'

Ivry became for Chatwin the epitome of London glamour; he was to keep in touch with her for the rest of his life and inscribed her copy of On the Black Hill *to 'my abiding friend'.*

To Ivry Guild
Beirut | Lebanon | 21 March 1959

This place is blissful – rather like the south of France. I am sitting on my balcony overlooking deep blue sea & snow-capped peaks. Wish you were here. I hope you are well & behaving yourself. I should be back in two or three weeks. I look forward to seeing you then. XXX Bruce

To Charles and Margharita Chatwin
Postcard, The Gulf of Porto Conte | Sardinia | 24 July 1959

Had an amusing time in Paris & Rome, and met people. Arrived Alghero in blazing heat. Went coral fishing with a crew of Neapolitans for a whole day yesterday. Bicycled to rock cut necropolis this morning. Food good but wild boar out of season. Arrived Sassani this evening by diesel. Met in Alghero squadron yachts from Majorca. No wind far out to sea but always breeze on coast in August. Invited aqualunging by German couple at Golfo di Aranci.

To Charles and Margharita Chatwin
Postcard, Figorolo Island | Golfo Aranci | Sardinia | 29 July 1959

As I rather hinted in the last card, Sardinia, though fascinating is quite impossible in this heat without a car.[1] And rather than go to the south, which is the wrong direction, at a cost of over £12 in travelling expenses,[2] I have decided to go from here to the mainland. Stay for a few days in Tarquinia and explore the Etruscan painted tombs and really leave Sardinia for another time. 10 minutes swimming in this sun produce one 'inglese arrosto',[3] as my friends call me. They are going back today. My nose bled solidly for no apparent reason the day before yesterday for 1½ hrs. B

In May 1960 Chatwin invited his mother to the Balmain sale at Sotheby's.

---

1. E.C.: 'For him to complain about the heat means it's desperately hot. Most of the time he didn't notice.'
2. A huge cost, when you could take only £50 out of the country.
3. Roasted Englishman.

To Margharita Chatwin
18 Grosvenor Crescent Mews|Belgravia|[May 1960]

Mummy Dear,

Am not lunching so can you have it with me. Spring cleaners are here all day today and are doing stairs to-morrow. Phone me as soon as you get in.

XX B

Within a short space, Chatwin held the reins in both Antiquities and Impressionists and Modern Art, or 'Imps'. In the summer of 1960 he was also involved in the sale of a small panel painting by Fra Angelico, one of two owned by Edward Peregrine, who had taught him Latin at Old Hall School. The painting of St Benedict, 15⅜ inches by 5⅜, was part of the collection of Peregrine's grandfather, physician to the Duke of Wellington; the other panel portrait was of St Anthony Abbot. Chatwin was given the sale to handle because he had known Peregrine and proved 'a very useful friend at court'. Archives, incredibly, are non-existent for this period, and Chatwin's correspondence affords a rare glimpse of Sotheby's behind the scenes. Employees of the auction house were not supposed to do private deals with Sotheby's clients, and what is going on remains elusive, but the tone suggests a Byzantine intrigue.

To Edward Peregrine
Sotheby's & Co.|34 & 35 New Bond Street| [May 1960]

Dear E.F.P.,

It was very nice to see you too the other day, even though the occasion was not as happy as could be.[1]

1. John Peregrine: 'This refers to my mother arguing what they were going to do with both pictures and feeling Sotheby's were out to swindle her.'

I am sorry that this should have cropped up. However the decision has now been made, and the one panel is being shown to prospective buyers, and Mrs G[1] is confirmed more than ever that the decision is the right one. So I think that the best thing to do is just for all of us to relax until we come to the question of a reserve price just before the sale.

Hoping for the best, Bruce

To Edward Peregrine
18 Grosvenor Crescent Mews | Belgravia | 9 May 1960

APOLOGIES FOR DELAY IN WRITING SALE DATE 22 JUNE WILL WRITE SOON WITH MORE DETAILS BRUCE

To Edward Peregrine
Sotheby's & Co. | 34 & 35 New Bond Street | 10 May 1960

Dear E.F.P.,

I must apologise for the frightful delay in replying to your letter but I have been away and the sale date has only just been fixed.

Mrs Gronau is at the moment on the Continent and does not return until Monday 16th May and there are one or two points that have arisen which she would like to discuss with you personally. I had a word with her on the telephone this morning and she wonders if you, Mrs Peregrine or both of you, could possibly manage to come up to lunch on Monday 16th May and talk them over directly with her. Could you give us a ring or drop a line to let us know?

Looking forward to seeing you.

Yours ever, Bruce

---

1. Carmen Gronau was organising the sale. Some friction may have been caused by the amount of restoration required. The restorer Herbert Lank had sent a bill of £231. 10. 9d. On 22 July 1960 Gronau wrote to E.F.P.: 'As you know it was a terrible business getting the blue over-paint away from the gold which had to be done immensely carefully by hand and penknife and could not be done by solvent.'

To Edward Peregrine

Sotheby's & Co. | 34 & 35 New Bond Street | 16 June [1960]

Dear E.F.P.,

Many thanks for your letter. With regard to the question of the reserve price, I wonder if you would fill in the slip that was enclosed with the catalogue for £6,000, at the same time making the provision that we can increase it at our discretion nearer the sale.

The old gentleman is at the moment sitting on an easel on a table in the entrance gallery and is attracting a lot of attention.

Looking forward to seeing you on the morning of the 22nd.

Yours, Bruce

At the auction on 22 June, the panel sold to an American dealer for £9,500.

To Edward Peregrine

18 Grosvenor Crescent Mews | Belgravia | 30 June [1960]

Dear E.F.P.,

In the present state of the market the price of £9,500 was a very good one and is by most people considered to have been the highest relative price in the sale. I think that the way to approach them is to inform them that having sold the other successfully at auction you are now rather reluctantly prepared to sell the other quickly privately. You must emphasise the fact that they are absolutely unseen and that the restoration was carried out by Mr Lank entirely on your instructions. Sotheby's name must on no account be used in connection with St Anthony Abbot and it must appear that the decision to sell only one stems entirely from you.

I do not think it would be wise to withdraw the picture from Sotheby's until you find out whether they are still prepared to buy, as you would burn your boats here and all the contacts that this place affords.

With regards to the question of price my own feelings are that you should start off at £8,000 and be prepared to come down reluctantly to £6,500 if need be, but one simply doesn't want the thing stranded on one's hands with nobody interested.

However, I think it would be unwise to hurry the matter and please would you not do anything without my being in the picture as it would not make things easy for me here.

Enclosed is a photograph for you to have, but it is essential not to show it to <u>anyone</u> yet.

Looking forward to having your comments.

Regards to Mrs P.,

Yours,

Bruce

To Edward Peregrine
Sotheby's | 34 & 35 New Bond Street | 19 July [1960]

Dear E.F.P.,

Very many thanks for your letter. I think that the way is all clear for you to write to Rawlinson[1] and find out if their American client is still interested.

Enclosed is a full and I think complete cataloguing description of St Anthony Abbot which will I hope lend weight to its authenticity.

Should he be no longer interested, do please let me know quickly, because I think that I may be able to arrange something else. If Rawlinson does fail you though, I think we should urge Mrs Gronau into activity first. If they are interested may I please somehow see you with the picture before showing it to them?

I am going to Greece for a month on September 7th which should be marvellous.

Regards to you both, Bruce

1. Rawlinson & Hunter, accountants representing an American client interested in the second panel of St Anthony Abbot.

*In September 1960, following Robert Byron's traces, he travelled
through the Greek islands on his way to Crete. His enthusiasm for
Byron was a constant that remained undimmed. Ten years later
he talked about the writer to Robin Lane Fox. 'No way did he model
himself on Byron, who he described as childish and irresponsible;
what he admired was Byron's ability for brilliant descriptions of
objects before him, combined with a slight transporting sense of
another world.'*

To Charles and Margharita Chatwin
Postcard, Cape Sounion | Temple of Poseidon | Greece |
15 September 1960

It rained today for the first time this summer. Spent weekend on island
of Aegina where I met O Marlburian. Food very good. Xenias Melathron
v. expensive and not as good as Tambi, at a third [of the] price. I had
no cheque book so please will you pay for table-cloth and I'll pay you
back, B

To Charles and Margharita Chatwin
Postcard, windmills at Rhodes | [September 1960]

So that's what you took a pot at![1] you naughty fellow! Yacht trip to
temple at Lindos with Lord Merthyr (R.C.C.)[2] and British Ambassador
+ Jill Kannreuther. B

1. Charles Chatwin had served in the Mediterranean on the light cruiser *Euryalus*. 'Bruce
was very cross because we bombarded the grain stores on Rhodes. "You bombarded
beautiful windmills." It was a show of force.'
2. Royal Cruising Club to which Charles belonged.

To Charles and Margharita Chatwin
Postcard, Dionysus mosaic | Delos Island | Mykonos | Greece |
19 September [1960]

Do come here, but for God's sake <u>not</u> in the boat[1]. Blows force 8 at least
all the time from the North. Last night from Rhodes, asleep on deck
when wave came right over me taking with it my hat and a little bag that
I bought. <u>Full</u>. Am going back to terra firma and shall go to Crete by
AIR. B

*Margharita wrote to Hugh at Marlborough about Chatwin's post-
card from Mykonos. Hugh says: 'I appreciated it as part of Bruce's
studied sense of filial duty to educate his parents in all matters
Hellenic. Three years before, he had expounded to me, sotto voce,
that Charles and Margharita had served more than their fair time
as Birmingham worthy-plus-squaw – should widen their horizons,
should see Rome, should experience the Lascaux wall paintings,
the flamingos of the Camargue and the Glories that were Greece.
Bruce's encouragement worked real wonders upon Charles. That
winter, he announced to his disbelieving law partners (and to me)
that, although only in his early fifties, he needed to earn less money
instead of more, precisely so that he and Margharita could set
forth on travels of their own. The outcome was that both parents
followed in his footsteps and they became happier with themselves
and each other for so doing.'*

*   *   *

*In Crete, Chatwin stayed with Allen Bole, 'a rather hopeless but
highly entertaining American' who lived in a house in Chania
near the harbour. Bole, a musician, had been Wanda Landowska's
assistant on the harpsichord and was now trying to write. Chatwin*

1. At Easter 1960, Charles had launched the *Rakia*, a 26-foot family cruising boat, to
be shared with his partners at Wragge & Co. Hugh Chatwin: 'Father had me ask Bruce's
classics master at Marlborough the ancient Greek word for rags. Hugh Weldon gave
us: ro, alpha, kai, iota, alpha – hence the name *RAKIA*.'

used to say of him:'He doesn't realise that the Mediterranean is very tough. People come here and think dolce far niente *– it's nice to do nothing – and it ruins them.'*

Chatwin several times returned to Crete before his marriage, to walk but also to seek out rare plants. 'I once spent the whole month of April combing the White Mountains in search of the rare Fritillaria sphaciotica, *and my search was a total failure.' He was possibly influenced by Robert Byron who, when visiting Mount Athos, had dug up for his mother, who had implored him to bring her 'something living from the Mountain,' a species of crocus. ('Grasping pseudo-trowels of living marble we gouged a dozen sepulchred bulbs into a biscuit tin.') In a draft for a botanical essay on the flowers of Greece, Chatwin wrote of these pleasures: 'If you will take a light-hearted walk through the hills of Attica in spring time, or wander through the upland pastures of Crete, your bag full of late oranges and hard goat cheese, resting in the odd shepherd's hut and drinking his staccha, the rich soured ewe's milk of spring, and possibly clamber up to the snow line of Ida for the sheets of the blue* Chionodoxa nana *and the tricoloured Cretan crocus,* C. sieberi, *there are rewards that no life in sombre cities can dispel.'*

To Ivry Freyberg[1]
18 Grosvenor Crescent Mews SW1 | 10 October 1960

My dear Ivry,

Have just got Avril's[2] mother's invitation for the 24th with a note from A saying that you're having a dinner party. Should love to come. Feeling much better[3] and am back at work. Sorry short note. Love B

1. Ivry had married Paul Freyberg, second Baron Freyberg, in July 1960.
2. Avril Curzon had lived with Ivry at 34 Boscobel Place.
3. I.F.: 'He was going to paint my bedroom and then had a cold.'

To Charles and Margharita Chatwin
Postcard, Matisse window | Chapelle du Rosaire | Vence | France |
25 May 1961

Went today to see this.[1] Marvellous weather. Have done absolutely nothing except get really quite a good colour. Love B

On 17 December 1961 he flew to Cairo to buy antiquities with the dealer and collector Robert Erskine.

To Charles and Margharita Chatwin
Cairo | Egypt | Christmas 1961

Arrived safely but 1 day late owing to fog. Weather marvellous. Writing from the Step Pyramid.

On 27 December he travelled to Wadi Halfa, his first trip to the Sudan.

To Charles and Margharita Chatwin
Postcard, The Khonsu Temple | Karnak | Egypt | 30 December 1961

Having a wonderful time. Back from the Sudan to see Abu Simbel. Return to Cairo and back Mon. XXX B

To Charles and Margharita Chatwin
Postcard, Panarea, Isole Eolie | Messina | Italy | [summer 1962]

Had a cable from Hugh yesterday. He appears to be in Athens by now. I may meet him in Sicily next week.[2] This island is absolute paradise.

1. E.C.: 'He later took me. It was like stepping into a rainbow.'
2. They met by accident in the Via Veneto in Rome in August, Chatwin on his way back from Greece; Hugh from Africa, on the last leg of a 10,000-mile hitchhike from Cape Town.

It's very easy to take a little house here in the summer for almost nothing, and money is virtually still unheard of. B

To Charles and Margharita Chatwin
Postcard of Brooklyn Bridge | New York | 3 January 1963

An average of –
4 parties a day,
4 times the work.
4 hours sleep
4 times as expensive
– and I'm fine. B

Eager to go further in tracing Robert Byron's footsteps, in the summer of 1963 Chatwin travelled with Robert Erskine to Afghanistan, the first of three visits.

To Margharita Chatwin
Herat | Afghanistan | 10 September [1963]

Darling Mum,
Afghanistan at last! It took three days to penetrate this far from Meshed which is only 250 miles away over the Persian border. Robert had a fetish that the bus service was totally useless. We were told that oil tankers crossed to Kandahar daily and duly made arrangements to accompany a Mr Huchang Fesolahi at 7am the next morning. We were half an hour late. Mr Fesolahi was nearly a whole day late. We drove with him for a hundred miles in acute discomfort and apprehension; it makes one nervous when the thousand gallon tank is behind one's head and in spite of a large DO NOT SMOKE sign Mr Fesolahi has smoked at least 5 packets of nasty cigarettes. He then let go of the wheel and shrieked with alarm. The receipt for his load had apparently blown out of the window. He expressed his intention of returning to Meshed at once. He didn't though and drove to a road hut built of mud and straw.

He entered and slept; the inhabitants drove us out. We attempted sleep in the cab which was worse than useless. At dawn I caught Mr Fesolahi escaping. He meant to leave us in charge of the tanker until his return two days hence. A gale was blowing, billowing sand in our faces and blotting out parts of the road. We did not mean to stop. We found two friendly Afghans in a lorry with scenes painted from Shakespeare's Avon, the monarch of the Glen and other pictures taken from Mehem-Sahibs Christmas cards of 45 years ago.

Arrived after two hours with them at a tea-house at Turbat-Jam where there is a 15th century shrine. I ran to it and back in 12 minutes, and when I returned the Afghans and Robert and a host of others were sitting round in front of the lorry smoking marijuana through a hookah. In pieces together with the hookah was the dynamo. The result – need for a new one. It was 7 o'clock. We waited till late afternoon sipping tea and very irritable. A posse of Land Rovers driven by dashing Afghans then gave us a lift. By 10.30 we were over the border. Wild eyed frontier guards were armed with bayonets. Customs officers at this post have great difficulty at night. They have one hurricane lamp. It was blowing another gale as we stopped at the only rest house, a mud affair built below the ground. The gale howled; the proprietor, wall-eyed, continually blew his nose on the end of his turban. A mess of chicken appeared which I was unable to face. The others all did, I sipped tea. Herat at last at 3 in the morning. The Park Hotel was built by Amanullah in the days of his 'folie de grandeur'. Furnished extravagantly in the manner of the Paris World's Fair of 1925, it has the appearance of an expensive hotel in Juan-Les-Pins. The garden is attractive; it is well-painted, deckchairs and cheerful awnings are on the terrace, within a gracious loggia, tables and chairs ranged all around; but this is Herat and not the South of France. Demand for lunch produced a triumphant smile. Yes, sir, no meat, no rice, no butter, no Pepsi-Cola, no Coca-Cola, no drink, no fruit. Bread and tea only. 'Eggs? Maybe yes! Tomorrow!' Flanking the portrait of the King however are a pair of dusty vitrines of misplaced flashiness. If they were in our imaginary Juan-les-Pins hotel they would contain beachwear, ties, scent of works of art. Here no! There are two tins of corned beef, rusty and probably useless, 1 tin of nescafé, opened dampened and caked, a tin of tuna fish, some old lard and a carton of Californian honey. The corned beef costs about £1. Robert is famished and so we settle for the tuna, only a little less expensive.

To the bazaar in a curricle, jingling with bells and hung with red pom-poms. You sit back to back, the form of these vehicles hasn't changed since Alexander used one to cross from here into India.

The bazaar is quite incredible. All women are in yashmaks. The men storm about with artificial ferocity, flashing dark and disdainful glances. In fact their eyes are made up, but then the outward appearance is all important. Turbans are often yards of ice-pink silk and reach gigantic proportions. Behind a street of little booths we found a vast caravanserai, an enclosure with two layers of arches, built at the time when Herat was one of the greatest trading posts in Asia. Camel trains are still to be seen all over Afghanistan but they have deserted this one. It has become a cloth market; from every arch row upon row of colourful clothes are suspended and are blown about in the breeze. What is extraordinary in this last outpost of untrammelled orient is that all are Western. A genius has bought up a gigantic horde of American ladies dresses and has sold them here. A student of modern fashion could find no better museum of modern dress. From Maine to Texas, from Chicago to Hollywood the wardrobes of thousands of American ladies over forty years are hanging into the breeze. Gowns that could have been worn by Mary Pickford, shiny black velvet with no back, or by Clara Bow, red lace and bead fringes, Jean Harlow, flamingo pink crepe off the shoulder with sequin butterflies on the hips, Shirley Temple, bows and pink lace, the folk weave skirts they square-danced in, the crinolines they waltzed in, fiery sheaths they tangoed in, utility frocks they won the War in, the New Look, the A line, the H line, the X line, all are there, just waiting for some Afghan lady to descend from her mud-built mountain village and choose the dress of her dreams all to be closely concealed under her yashmak.

I am sure she will get far more pleasure from it than its original owner.

Tomorrow we will ride out to Gazar Gah, the 14th century tomb of a saint called Ansari; he was a prodigious old bore who had visions while sucking his mother's milk and who went through life moralising until he was over 90.

We will start for Kabul on Thursday.

XXX Bruce

PS I forgot to tell you that the total cooking arrangements for a first-class hotel with 20 bedrooms consist of one noxious primus!

To Margharita Chatwin
Postcard, ancient mountain fortress near
Bamyan | Afghanistan | [September 1963]

Off to Peshawar in the Embassy truck tomorrow, so that we can eat curry to burn out Robert's cold and see Taxila, a Buddhist site on the Indus. X B

Chatwin's lease on Grosvenor Crescent Mews was due to run out in September. While away in Afghanistan he had sub-let the flat to a Frenchman called Pascal on the understanding that he would collect his belongings upon his return. However, when Chatwin got back he found that Pascal had changed the locks; further, Pascal claimed the flat's contents as his. Someone suggested that for £20 Chatwin could hire 'two goons' to knock down the door, but his father's name was on the lease and he did not have the stomach for this. It would involve more than a year of legal action to retrieve his belongings, Pascal settling out of court on the eve of the trial. Even so, Chatwin lost several favourite possessions, including his christening mug and a watercolour of a Roman mosaic pavement in Gloucester that he had wanted to donate to the British Museum. Increasingly, from this time on, he supplemented his meagre income from Sotheby's through private deals and running errands. He later wrote: 'It was still possible in the early 60s to buy Greek antiquities without causing legal harm.'

To Edward Peregrine
New address: 119a Mount Street | London | 27 December 1963

Dear E.F.P.,

I was just about to write to you. I had news from America just the other day to say that the picture safely arrived there. The cleaning took ages, and I saw it before it was sent over. The man did a most wonderful job and there is no cause for worry about it at all. Eugene Thaw[1] asked me to tell you that he wants just a little more time as nobody does anything around Christmas in America and it naturally slowed things up, the death of Kennedy. He will certainly be getting in touch with you direct in the middle of January. He is a charming person and I have 100% faith in him and his judgment.

Merry Christmas (belated) to you, Molly and the family.

Bruce

To Charles and Margharita Chatwin
Postcard, ivory ointment box in Brooklyn Museum | New York |
May 22 [1964]

Total chaos here as usual and horrible humidity. Hope to be back Tuesday after reopening of Museum of Modern Art here, love B

In 1964 Sotheby's purchase of the New York auction house of Parke Bernet required Chatwin to make frequent trips to America. But after six years, a loathing had started to set in. He confided his frustrations to Cary Welch, an American curator and collector of Indian miniatures and nomadic art. Described by Chatwin as a 'hypnotic character', Welch (1928–2008) was married to Elizabeth's cousin Edith; he had been introduced to Chatwin in Paris by Welch's old Harvard room-mate, the collector George Ortiz Patino. 'We became instant friends,' said Welch. 'In life, one does run into

---

1. New York dealer and collector. On 15 April 1964 Chatwin sent Peregrine a cheque for £6,000. It can be assumed that he took a commission.

people who are the perfect ping-pong opponent. In some ways I became the mentor/father figure.'

To Cary Welch
119a Mount Street | London | 27 July 1964

Dear Cary,

We are now the proud possessors of Parke-Bernet which I personally think is a highly dubious venture but do on no account want to be quoted as such. Am given over to much private melancholy on the subject as well as to my own future. The great golden handshake seems to have turned out to be of baser metal.[1] It's like a game of snakes and ladders and as far as Sotheby's are concerned I have slid down the snake to square one. This means that to go up the ladders again it will be a question of threats, imbecilic charm, insinuous manoeuvring and a better spy-ring. One day I shall kick the whole thing in the pants and retire to Crete. Sorry to be so devious – the details I'll fill in when I see you.

I have bought nothing and am not interested in doing so.

I am going again to Afghanistan with a friend.[2] We are going to walk this time in the Eastern part of Kafiristan. I am saying hell to works of art and have been given equipment and supplies from Kew on condition that I collect plants for them.[3] The area has never been botanised before at all. It is one of the last botanical unknowns in the world. This is my ambition – BOTANIST written in my passport. The sale of works of art is the most unloveable profession in the world.

1. This is the first suggestion that Peter Wilson had lured Chatwin with the temptation of becoming a Sotheby's director, only to renege on the offer.
2. David Nash, or 'Nashpiece'. Chatwin had known him at Marlborough. Before joining Sotheby's he worked as a gravedigger in a Wimbledon cemetery and as an electrical engineer at the Horton lunatic asylum.
3. Rear-Admiral Paul Furse (1904–78), botanist and plant collector, had been forced to abandon a mission from Kew Gardens to bring back a sample of cow parsley growing only on the northern slopes of the Hindu Kush. Chatwin decided to complete Furse's quest.

Am just a touch cross over the painting by Daulat,[1] but don't let on to Howard.[2] I think it is a very good thing and that you should have it. Please bear in mind that whatever I may say about not wanting works of art I do want to buy sometime soon a really good Mughal painting. Perhaps we could go into a huddle and find something in the Spencer-Churchill sale. This last has really thrown Mr T.[3] He even flew back from Greece to see the poor old thing almost breathing his last, and is now astonished to find that the lot are going to be sold. I do envy you your boat and wish I were on it.

All the best to the Knellingtons[4] and their mother,

Bruce

To Charles and Margharita Chatwin
Postcard, Zamzama or Kim's Gun, Lahore | Pakistan | [August 1964]

This is the gun that Kim used to sit under. We are doing a tour of N Pakistan because my arm went septic (as usual)[5] and we had to return after having got a third of the way. We are spending a week in Chitral then return via Beirut.

XX Bruce

1. Indian miniaturist, (1600–27). C.W.: 'On the afternoon I first met Bruce I took him to Charles Ratton, a great dealer, and the flat from which he sold. At about 3.30, I found a magnificent signed Mughal painting of the Infant Prince Shashuja by Abul Hassan. Bruce then came back ten days later, bought the Daulat and sent it to Howard Hodgkin, who sent me a photo. One year later, I bought it off Howard. Bruce was cross that Howard had made money by selling it to me.'
2. Howard Hodgkin (b.1932), British artist.
3. George Ortiz Patino (b.1927), millionaire collector known by Chatwin as 'Mighty Mouse' and grandson of Bolivian tin magnate Simon Patino, who since 1949 had used his fortune to build a collection of art from the ancient world; also known as Tizberg. C.W.: 'We always had nicknames: Bruce was known as Marcel Bruce, or Preuz; Elizabeth and Bruce as "the Chattys".'
4. Welch's children – Nellington. Thomas, Adrian, Sam, Lucia – were known by the collective noun Knellingtons; Ortiz's children as the Tizbergs.
5. Hunting for a specimen of cow parsley among small bushes of holly oak, Chatwin fell and scraped the skin off his arm. D.N. diary: 'Awoke next morning, B feverish and his arm v swollen & septic. Decide reluctantly to return to avoid gangrene.'

To Stephen Tennant
119a Mount Street | London | 20 October [1964]

Dear Stephen Tennant,[1]

I do so much look forward to the 2nd of November. We did decide to come by car after all as the drive is so pleasant in the autumn.

I'm longing to see the cottage[2] and do fervently hope that no one else takes it in the meantime. I'm sure from what you say that it's absolutely charming.

Delighted that you enjoyed the Gauguin[3]. The two figures have an immutability and ineloquence that recalls Piero.

Till the 2nd,

As ever,

Bruce Chatwin

Aside from his arm, Chatwin was having trouble with his eyes. Sotheby's acquisition of Parke-Bernet had demanded a succession of transatlantic flights which exhausted him. Plus he was responsible for two important sales. On 16 and 17 November 1964 Sotheby's auctioned the Ernest Brummer collection of Egyptian and Near Eastern Antiquities, which Chatwin had catalogued with Elizabeth Chanler, Peter Wilson's American assistant. He had also helped catalogue 540 works for the Impressionist sale four days later, including Cézanne's Grandes Baigneuses, *acquired by the National Gallery for a record sum of £500,000. By his own account,*

---

1. British aesthete and eccentric (1906–87) who spent much of his latter years in bed in Wilsford Manor, designing jackets for a novel set in Marseilles that he never wrote: *Lascar, A Story of the Maritime Boulevard, A Story You Must Forget.*
2. Probably the cottage on the Wilsford estate later rented to V. S. Naipaul.
3. Tahitian Woman and Boy, 1899. A photograph of Chatwin holding up this painting appeared in the *Daily Mail* on 24 November 1964 under the headline: 'Lot 32, star of the biggest sale of Impressionists and drawings ever held.' The article went on: 'It was Chatwin who arranged the Gauguin sale. Sotheby's had a telephone call from Mrs Austin Mardon, American-born widow of a tobacco company director. She has nine children, lives in Ardross Castle, Ross-shire. She said she had a painting to sell. Chatwin went to Scotland, was staggered to see the Gauguin in a bedroom. Its whereabouts had been unknown for 40 years. Mrs Mardon bought it in 1923 for £1,200.'

he went blind after these sales. On 31 December 1964 he visited
the eye specialist Patrick Trevor-Roper and told him:'When I look
upward I feel brown clouds.'The symptoms seem to have been a
flare-up of his 1955 complaint. Trevor-Roper advised him to give
up concentrated work and get away from the office for a few
months.

'"You've been looking too closely at works of art. I suggest long
horizons. Where do you want to go?"

'"Africa," I said.'

To Stephen Tennant
119a Mount Street | London | Sun [January 1965]

Dear Stephen,

New York turned me inside out and has left me in a highly nervous
state also without the power to focus my right eye. Exciting yes but it
would kill me to live there.

Have you been getting *Art News*? I have sent you 1 year's subscrip-
tion as a Christmas present so if you didn't get it I shall raise a storm.

I saw none of my friends in New York, but spent many tedious
evenings with the so-called 'Great Collectors'; they reduce one to a state
of physical and visual indigestion.

May I come again at the end of Jan? I have to go to hospital for my
eye soon, but after then.

As ever Bruce

To Cary Welch
119a Mount Street | London | [January 1965]

Dear Cary,

A quick note. Am rather depressed because the focussing in my right
eye has packed-up. Apparently the result of over-doing it in America.

You don't have any worries about the tax people looking into the accounts of Parke-Bernet unless you have a Federal Tax investigation against you in which case P-B are obliged to open their books to them. Many thanks for everything.

Am not intending to return until I can SEE.

British Paintings Dept suggest reserves

Sutherland[1] – £125

Palmers – £150 each

Please let me know.

If you think too little, I think I can sell the geometric Palmer for that at least to Derek Hill[2] who wants it but is neurotic about bidding in sales.

Say boo to the Knellingtons,

as ever, B

On 5 February 1965 Chatwin set off for the Sudan where he was the guest of a former girlfriend; Gloria Taylor had married Tahir El-Fadil el Mahdi, the Cambridge-educated grandson of Siddig el Mahdi, who had won Sudan's independence from Britain. After a week in Khartoum, Chatwin met Abdul Mohnim, a geologist who was leaving on an expedition to the Red Sea Hills to look for kaolin deposits. 'I asked if I could come along and he said I could.' Here, on a short camel trek in the Eastern Sudan, Chatwin experienced his first taste of nomadic life.

To Charles and Margharita Chatwin
Postcard, camel riders at El Obeid | Sudan | 13 March 1965

Many thanks for your cable. That makes life a lot easier. 3 more books I've remembered. Palmer's *Myceneans and Minoans*. Weigall's *Travels in The Upper Egyptian Desert, The Red Sea Hills of Egypt*. Do you have

1. C.W.: 'I had a small Graham Sutherland which Bruce talked me into selling and a Samuel Palmer sketchbook page.'
2. Derek Hill (1916–2000), landscape and portrait artist who had been at Marlborough and known Robert Byron; Bruce and Elizabeth often stayed with him at St Columb's, Letterkenny in County Donegal.

the christening mug? If not the swine [Pascal] has that too. Have got a cold – now better. <u>Bruce</u>

After six weeks recuperating in the Sudan, Chatwin returned to London by way of Greece.

To Charles and Margharita Chatwin
Postcard, fish plate in Museum of Corinth | Athens | Greece |
[27 March 1965]

Arrived here . . . 3 days ago because it was hotting up too much. I must say I had a marvellous time there. Will be in Crete as from tomorrow. It's bitterly cold in Athens but the sun shines and the flowers are out. The eyes vary from day to day, and are obviously still far from right, although they got much better at one stage. Let me know how things are. XXX Bruce

To Derek Hill
Chania | Crete | 10 April 1965

I have been trampling over the White Mountains hunting for a fritillary for Paul Furse. No luck so far. Eye better. See you soon. Bruce

In London, Rear-Admiral Furse had told Chatwin about an exceedingly rare flower, the Paeonia clusii, *endemic to Crete. One 'wild April day' Chatwin decided to dig up a seedling for Furse. He borrowed Allen Bole's Volkswagen and drove to a gorge above the village of Lakkoi in Western Crete. Ignoring Pliny's advice to dig at night, he found his* Paeonia clusii. *Curious things then happened. 'The seedling was minute, but the fleshy root vast. Growing as it was among boulders, the business became a major excavation, and when the precious root had been secured I was ashamed at the devastation I had caused. As I entered the village, with one peony and a few tulips in a basket, a stout Lakkiot was haranguing the crowd, but I was aware that I was the centre of attention. Shortly after, two police officers stopped me and there began a very curious cross-questioning. Barely understanding the questions my answers were unsatisfactory, and they began to scrutinise each tulip and the peony. I was at great pains to point out that neither were opium poppies and the interview dissolved into laughter. The explanation came a year later. There were two versions and both originated in the stout Lakkiot, the first that I had been walking down the mountainside with an antique vase filled with gold coins, the second that I had been sent to recover a hoard of gold sovereigns buried by the Germans before they evacuated the island.'*

On his return, Chatwin gave the peony – at that time the only one in England – to Furse. When Furse died, it went to John Hewett's wife Diana, a keen gardener, and then to Chatwin's old girlfriend Gloria Taylor.

To Charles and Margharita Chatwin
Chania | Crete | [10 April 1965]

What about the PASCAL affair[1] and am I expected back in April, if so when? Can I know soon? Try to postpone till mid-May. I shall return by sea and land as the aeroplane, for CERTAIN, does me no good. Eye took 10 days to recover after KHARTOUM-ATHENS. Much better now, in fact am very fit. Walked Knossos to Phaestos along the ancient Minoan Road. Would mummy like to meet me in Paris for a couple or 3 days on my way back at MY expense?

 Love B

To Ivry Freyberg
Chania | Crete | [20 April 1965]

Your letter went half way round the world before I got it. I lost the focussing however in one eye, but it has at last recovered. I'll come back

---

1. The case was at last coming to court.

in May. Crete is wonderful, but is in the throes of a great spring, hail, thunder and earthquakes.

Will ring you on return, Love Bruce

To Charles and Margharita Chatwin
Postcard, hall of the double axes, Knossos | Crete | [21 April 1965]

Suggest we leave the Paris excursion to the autumn when I go on business. It sounds a bit complicated now. Shall be there probably for 1 or 2 days in May, but don't want to be tied down as the Pascal case is not fixed. Quite right about the mug. Am going to Rhodes for 5 days over Easter. Back to climb Mount Ida with the Sinclair Hoods[1] on the 3rd–4th and then start for home. Will return before the 12th. XX Bruce

Chatwin had made an important decision in the Sudanese desert. Encouraged by Cary Welch, instead of going to Rhodes for Easter he invited Elizabeth Chanler to Paris. There, in the Cabinet de Medailles in the Louvre, he proposed. The engagement was still a secret when he met her parents a fortnight later in Ireland.

To Gertrude Chanler
119a Mount Street | London | [25 May 1965]

Dear Mrs Chanler,

I did enjoy my weekend in Dublin[2] enormously. Thank you very

---

1. Chatwin called more than once on the archaeologist Sinclair Hood who was excavating at Knossos. Together with Hood's wife Rachel, they went to look for the endemic Cretan tulip on the Nida Plain on Mount Ida. 'We did find one example, growing up through a terribly prickly thorn bush!' This may have been the specimen he brought back for Admiral Furse.

2. E.C.: 'It was the first time my parents ever met Bruce, and then I announced I was engaged and they hadn't paid much attention. "That's nice," but they couldn't remember him.' On 26 June, Gertrude Chanler wrote to Margharita: 'At the time we did not realise that all this was so serious . . .'

much. Liz obviously had a good ten days. She came back looking wonderfully well. She certainly needed it. Sotheby's is frantic at the moment and having taken things at my own pace for the past few months I find the changeover alarming. We were all turned upside down by the Telstar broadcast[1] the other night. Contrary to everyone's gloomy predictions it was a riotous success.

Liz[2] and I went to the Chelsea Flower Show yesterday morning for the preview. The flowers are so overbred and look more and more like plastic with each year that passes. There are one or two places from Scotland and Ireland who stick to straight-forward plant species and they are always infinitely preferable. I do hope to see you both again before long, and again many thanks.

Yours ever, Bruce Chatwin

To Ivry Freyberg
119a Mount Street | London | 8 June 1965

My Dear Ivry,

Bless you for your cable! The deed is done, and in about three months I'll no longer be a free man. Secrecy is rather necessary for a bit, partly because we both find the word fiancé(e) difficult to pronounce with the right expression.[3] May we come down and see you sometime during the summer?

A beaming face waved and shouted from a taxi this afternoon. It was Raulin,[4] looking marvellously well I must say.

Love to you both, Bruce

1. The first transatlantic sale using the Early Bird satellite, featuring paintings by Winston Churchill. E.C. to G.C.: 'The Early Bird sale went like a bomb. Churchill made unheard-of figure – £14,000.'
2. E.C.: 'He'd overheard my parents calling me Lib and misheard it as Liz.'
3. E.C.: 'We kept the engagement secret because we didn't want people at Sotheby's to rag us.'
4. Ivry's brother, Alexander Raulin Chevalier Guild (1940–66) had come back from Northern Rhodesia and was working for the Conservative Party in Woodbridge.

To Gertrude Chanler
119a Mount Street | London | June 22 1965

Elizabeth calls you M & B[1]. I think this is irreverent, but I haven't an idea what to call you. I've discussed it for an hour, but she's offered no constructive suggestion. I'm amazed by the elaborate detail of her letter – Not a word to tell you how happy we both are, and how much we look forward to the end of August (? or September) and seeing you again. Please don't worry too much about the Chatwin contingent. We will fit in entirely with your plans. I simply can't make it vis-à-vis Sotheby's before the 21st, and I'm sure it would be a horrible rush for you too. So any day from the 21st on will be perfectly all right.

Also I don't really see why it has to be on a weekend. Surely during August people are fairly relaxed in their offices? I have a very few friends in New York who will be able to come, and also Cary and Edith Welch from Boston. I imagine we will be twelve at the most. I'm not intending very light grey[2], and my mother is not in a flap; that crisis seems to be solved already.

I do hope you will not worry about my not being a Catholic.[3] I have always been brought up according to the Church of England, as were both my parents. A few relations of my grandfather's generation were Catholic converts. I am absolutely willing, not to say anxious, that any of my children shall be brought up as Catholics, and I intend to talk to a great friend of mine Peter Levi[4] who is a Jesuit. I know you'll agree that it would be a great mistake to take steps in this direction just at this moment. All I can say is that at the time I left school I was influenced strongly by Catholicism and have an entirely open mind about the future.

I've got a small flat in Mount Street just opposite the Connaught Hotel. We have decided we would prefer to live there for the time being

---

1. Mummy and Bobby.
2. E.C.: 'This is exactly what he did wear, a pale grey suit.'
3. The Chanlers were Catholic. G.C. had written to E.C.: 'One thing you must do is see what can be done about Bruce getting the required religious instructions . . . This is very important.'
4. Peter Levi (1931–2000), Jesuit priest, author and poet. Through Levi, Chatwin found a Jesuit priest, Father Murray, to give Pre-Cana instructions.

rather than face a major upheaval just now. It's a bit like a couple of staterooms on a liner, but its advantages are its economy, cupboard space, living-in housekeeper in the basement, and the fact that it is 2 minutes flat from Sotheby's.

My father and I have entered our little boat into the Round-the Island race on Saturday,[1] and Lib[2] will be on the finishing line to greet us (if we make it!) Looking forward to August <u>immensely</u>. If I can help with anything at all do let me know,

Love Bruce

To Stephen Tennant
Postcard, Historiska Museum, Stockholm | Sweden | 29 June 1965

Would love to come down after July 10 and will drop a line to see which day's covenient.

Bruce

On 12 July 1965, after Elizabeth had flown to New York, a notice appeared in The Times *announcing the engagement 'between Charles Bruce elder son of Mr and Mrs C. L. Chatwin of 16 College Street, Stratford on Avon and Elizabeth Margaret Therese, eldest daughter of Rear Admiral and Mrs Hubert Chanler of Washington DC and Geneseo, New York. The marriage will take place in America in August.'*

To Ivry Freyberg
119a Mount Street | London | Saturday [July 1965]

My dear Ivry,

So very many thanks for your letters. Sorry that everything was still in its early stages when I first wrote. I do hope you didn't see that terrible

1. At Cowes.
2. E.C.: 'Now he's got it.'

little piece in the *Evening Standard* entitled 'Love among the Pictures'. Elizabeth's already gone to America and I leave on the *Queen Elizabeth* in ten days – a good 5 days rest. We are getting married in their family chapel on their estate which is at the back of beyond in New York State near the Canadian border. We're going to give a party when we get back in the autumn. I need your advice. Where is a good room for 350 people to dance in?[1] I've no idea about these things. We both send our love and long to see you. Bruce and Elizabeth

To Elizabeth Chanler
119a Mount Street | London | Wednesday [15 July 1965]

My Dearest Liz,

Please write to P. Wilson. Katherine[2] says there is a slight huff[3] about you leaving at all. Typical of course, and don't give it a thought. But write your charmingest letter to say how sorry you were that when you came to say goodbye he wasn't there, and that you're horribly sorry not to have given more notice.

The Greek head[4] arrived, and is quite incredible. I think I see how to work it all out. But we won't be able to have much else for years. Do you mind if I divest us of the green head, because I shall probably have to? Why don't you say for wedding presents credit at John Hewett,[5]

1. E.C.: 'We never gave this party.'
2. Katherine Maclean, personal assistant to Peter Wilson or 'P.C.W.'
3. There was also slight amazement. E.C. wrote to G.C.: 'We told Katherine and P.C.W. last Friday & then ran. They were really flabbergasted.' Another person to register surprise was the American writer Leo Lerman, who had been asked by Wilson to write a history of Sotheby's. On 13 July 1965 Lerman wrote in his diary: 'Elizabeth is marrying Bruce. We couldn't be more astonished at this Sotheby's romance.'
4. Female, 3rd c BC. E.C.: 'People said, "What do you want for a wedding present?" and we said "You can give a contribution to the Greek Head." It was one of the things Bruce had to sell when he needed money.'
5. Close friend of Wilson and Bond Street dealer (1919–94) with a special love for tribal and ethnographic art, who virtually ran the Antiquities Department; also known as 'K.J.H.'.

173 New Bond St W1? Father Murray[1] is a real treasure and we're going to have the sessions alternately in the flat and Farm St.

May be in America sooner than you think. Having eluded the 10 journalists on Monday morning I find a P.P.[2] directive saying that my presence is required for certain antiquities in N.Y. in August anyway. Nothing happens here so I might just as well come over. What about that?

    All is love,

    B

To Elizabeth Chanler
119a Mount Street | London | [22 July 1965]

My Dear Liz,

After our telephone conversation I had a sleepless night. The real reason for my insomnia was caused by the recollection of a conversation we had before you left, a conversation of which I only just realise the horrendous implications. You said that you were going to learn how to work a deep freeze!![3]

Now all week I have been instructed about the evils of paganism and heresy. I have learned the implications of life everlasting, the light of Heaven, the darkness of Hell, and the mist of Purgatory. But I now find myself faced with the greatest HERESY known to man, the DEEP FREEZE.

Imagine if you were put in a deep freeze. Your outward form might remain, but where would your soul be? Flitting about the Fields of Asphodels or knocking at the Golden gate. But vegetables have no souls; they die. It is a major article of my faith never to eat dead vegetables.

1. John Courtney Murray (1904–67) SJ, American theologian.
2. Peregrine Pollen, head of Sotheby's New York office.
3. E.C.: 'He didn't understand about deep freeze. He thought it was unhealthy, a new-fangled thing that made food taste awful. Even his parents thought this. I used to give them half a lamb and they ate it up as fast as they could, as if it was going to go bad in a freezer. Of course, he came round to it completely.'

A doctor friend of mine nearly dropped down dead in Harley Street as a result of eating dead vegetables. It is a complaint known as scarlatina. So give up all this nonsense of a deep freeze, do not deprive me of the pleasure of eating fresh food in its due season and learn to make a proper apple pie and the best chowder.

xxxx B

To Elizabeth Chanler
119a Mount Street | London | [July 1965]

Dearest E,

I'm in a vile mood today. I went to Hugh and Connie's[1] party last night, drank champagne and feel lousy and lonely. Connie is really quite a dish, isn't she?

Katherine had obviously what was a catty letter from Leo,[2] and is purring. P.C.W. has gone to Lady Sarah Russell. George O[rtiz] sends his love . . . Took Gouri[3] out to dinner at the Narain.[4] This gave me fearful attack of wind which was embarrassing at the tailor's. Your trust money came in and was about £1200 for which congratulations.

Had the nicest letter from Cary [Welch] which got me through yesterday. He suggests that we all drive together to Maine, and why ever not. We'll have our hire-car man disguised as an azalea at the bottom of your drive, change in the rhododenrons, give the car over to him and jump into the Welch station waggon. When I am cooped up in that

1. Hugh Hildesley, who worked in Sotheby's Pictures Department, and his Amercian wife Connie; he later became Rector of the Church of Heavenly Rest in New York.
2. Leo Lerman (1914–94), American writer, had been engaged by his friend P.C.W. to write a history of the auctioneering firm, to be called *The Seismograph of Taste: Sotheby's 1744–1964*. 'He felt hampered at the start by the lack of business archives at Sotheby's. The auction house also did not intend that Leo write honestly about auctioneering practices, which involved a great deal of obituary watching and sharp dealing.' *The Grand Surprise – The Journals of Leo Lerman*, ed. Stephen Pascal (Knopf, 2007). E.C.: 'I had to read the obituaries in New York when I first worked for Sotheby's and find out if the deceased had had a collection and then Sotheby's would write an oily letter.'
3. Gouri Dixit, E.C.'s Bombay flatmate who worked for Air India.
4. Indian restaurant.

miserable boat you will simply have to telephone once a day, otherwise I shall arrive a jabbering wreck. We shall have to look on our telephone calls as capital investment.[1] I should never have let you go. Letters are all very well, but by the time they reach they are old hat. Can you imagine what it must have been like in the 18th Century, with the husband disappearing for years to India, and with a postal service of three months? I now have all the right papers signed by Church, notaries and State. I assume that it is all right to bring them over with me? My uncle Anthony just came in with an unbelievably hideous and special metronomic (?) clock which was exhibited in the Great Exhibition. There is also a postcard signed Alfred (Friendly);[2] it shows a long Italian tunnel with apparently no ending. How right he is? I can't lay my hands on it just now, but will send it on.

The sight of you at the docks will be worth all this trial.

Love, love love, Bruce

Have a marvellous Hawaiian feather necklet for you.

To Elizabeth Chanler
119a Mount Street | London | 30 July 1965

My Liz,

Would we like as a wedding present, a yacht trip around the coast of Crete next summer with a character called Allen Bole, who is a rather hopeless but highly entertaining American living in Chania. I think so, don't you? Also the nicest letter from Henry Mac.[3] We are invited to Glenveagh for the stalking in Oct. Or would you prefer Sir James

1. E.C.: 'In those days you had to book through the operator, you couldn't just dial. It was terribly expensive, we never did it. He sent me telegrams from the *Queen Elizabeth*. EACH TURN OF THE SCREW BRINGS ME NEARER TO YOU.'
2. Alfred Friendly (1911–83) philanthropist, journalist, and a friend of Elizabeth's from Harvard.
3. Henry McIlhenny (1910–86) Philadelphia collector, philanthropist and bon vivant whose grandfather invented the gas meter. Chatwin had stayed with him in Donegal at Glenveagh Castle. 'He has 8 gardeners, 8 indoor servants, 20,000 acres and 28 miles of fencing to maintain . . .' James Lees-Milne's diary, 4 August 1971.

Dundas's[1] fishing lodge opposite Mull which is ours whenever we like in the autumn. Cheque from New Zealand cousins.[2] Am much cheered this morning by your telephone call, the host and the weather. No houses on the market. Chairs, blinds, etc all arriving soon, must shampoo carpet.

A million hugs!

B

On 21 August Bruce and Elizabeth were married at a Nuptial Mass in the Chanler family chapel at Sweet Briar Farm, Geneseo. David Nash was best man. Elizabeth's aunt Maria gave her this advice for their wedding night: 'Don't forget to cut your toenails.'

The Chatwins honeymooned off the Maine coast in a 42-foot yawl chartered by Elizabeth's father, who had not consulted either of them but had heard that Chatwin liked sailing. They were joined by Cary and Edith Welch on another yawl, spending much of the week fog-bound in the lobster harbour of Cape Split.

To Derek Hill
119a Mount Street | London | 15 October 1965

We long to tell you about it – every succulent detail – the admiral's jig – the Holy Water flicked in my eyes – my drunken sister-in-law doing karate on the lawn – the stove[3] that exploded during the wedding feast and covered the house in black smoke – those brothers-in-law who put fire-crackers in the car – the honeymoon (dreadful word) in Maine, stuck in the fog in a small yacht . . . And we think you have something to tell US of balls (?) in Donegal. Longing to have the picture[4] but we have no house to hang it in. What are we to do? Love B

1. Sir James Durham Dundas, 6th Baronet (1905–67).
2. Philippa Chatwin, daughter of Charles's late brother Humphrey.
3. E.C.: 'A great big cast-iron range that was not used in summer; it was lit without opening the flue and smoked like mad.'
4. A panel of Tory Island off the Irish West Coast where Hill used to paint.

To Cary Welch

119a Mount Street | London | [1965]

What I have omitted to tell you is the PARTY[1] for Teddy Millington-Drake.[2] Having been squared and explained to about it in Geneseo, the Admiral becomes terrified of missing something, and the day before down they come to New York, specially (ostensibly to see us off). Teddy sends round a huge quantity of flowers and that is considered very strange. Twenty or thirty people expected. The admiral puts out twenty-five glasses of all kinds. Twenty-eight people come all of whom I know except for two of Teddy's friends and a host of Elizabeth's. The Admiral glowers as Michele Morgan's daughter arrives in a glittering pants suit. He then takes up a position at the front door, and glowers to each and every person who comes through the front door, leaving me to do the drinks, and saying to each in turn 'I am Admiral Chanler; I don't know who you are; but then I don't know anyone here and this is my house.' By this time he had had far too much to drink having started at four, and started to make such observations as 'There are many people here who, under normal circumstances, I would regard as of questionable honesty,' singling out in particular a friend of mine called Tristram Powell, ex-Eton, son of the novelist Anthony Powell, as a 'very suspicious man with a beaky nose'. My mother-in-law's curiosity was aroused into grilling me over dinner about the marital status of everyone present. 'Are they married or living together?' 'He's not married, is he?' 'No, I thought not' and so on, and I would love to have invented so bizarre a sex life for each of the characters in turn that they would have a whole-dark-Geneseo-winter-full of conversation and speculation. THEY NEED IT. The Admiral also claimed that no less than seventy people arrived.

1. E.C.: 'We were staying in my mother's flat in New York and decided to give a party. My father came and got drunk. I found the whole thing mortifying: he said to one lady in trousers, "Do you always go out in the evening dressed like that?"'
2. Edgar Louis Vanderstegen ('Teddy') Millington-Drake (1932–94), painter and son of Sir Eugen Millington-Drake, British Minister in Montevideo at the time of the scuttling of the German cruiser *Admiral Graf Spee* in 1939. Chatwin stayed with him at his houses in Greece and Italy, and towards the end of his life said that Teddy was one of two men he had loved. E.C.: 'Raulin Guild was probably the other.'

The Chatwins returned to London in October and immediately started house-hunting.

To Gertrude Chanler
119a Mount Street | London | [23 October 1965]

Dear Mrs C.,

I'm sitting propped up in the flat because yesterday we went to stay with a friend called John Hewett[1] whose prize ram escaped. I needless to say came off worst and cut my leg right open on a barbed wire fence. The ram of course was unperturbed, was at length recaptured, only to escape again, this time for good. It later that day walked into the local garage.

No luck with houses so far. The market is apparently depressed at the moment and we may have to wait till spring because that's the time people put them on the market. Patience is the great thing. Just when you give up, the right thing comes along.[2] I've been going to board meetings for the first time[3] and more often than not they're long and tedious, but sometimes they are very funny especially when all my own contemporaries stand on their dignity and get all pompous and silly. There was a marvellous piece of nonsense the other night when they held that big sale in New York. There was a black-tie audience in London and an additional auctioneer to relay bids from London through an amplified two-way telephone connection. Unfortunately something went wrong and the New York audience heard Cockney swearing, and the London audience heard a few new bits of New York slang. All that could be heard were the operators rather than the auctioneers.

1. Hewett owned a farm in Kent.
2. Not until February 1966, after several false starts, would the Chatwins find Holwell Farm, a pink seventeenth-century house set in 47 acres near Wotton-under-Edge in Gloucestershire. Gertrude advanced £17,000 as a wedding present for them to buy it.
3. In the summer Wilson had at last appointed Chatwin a director, not with a vote as he had expected, but one of nine new subsidiary directors without voting rights. A new tax law meant that the partnership would not come into effect until the following April, by which time Chatwin had made the decision to leave Sotheby's.

Did Lib tell you we're probably going to Russia for eight days in December? John Hewett and I have always wanted to see the archaeological stuff in the Hermitage and so we've cooked up an expedition. Then we are going to Donegal to Derek [Hill]'s for Christmas, and I think that the chances are that we'll be able to come back to America in the Spring because there's a sale I shall have to catalogue which is scheduled for June. All rather in the air at the moment though.

So it won't be too long before we'll all be back. Lib says to tell you that a friend of ours called Allen Bole may look you up.

With love,
Bruce

To Elizabeth Chatwin
119a Mount Street | London | [November 1965]

I now feel at liberty to forget your birthday present
    xxxx B
PS do you normally keep your stockings in the 'frig?'[1]

In January, after their visit to Russia, Chatwin took Elizabeth as his secretary to Paris to catalogue the Helena Rubinstein collection. This would be his last major sale for Sotheby's.

To Gertrude Chanler
Hotel de L'Université | Paris | France | 7 January 1966

I have you horribly on my conscience because I didn't yet write to thank you for my Christmas present. I tried to send something but it was of a highly perishable nature and I hated the idea of it mouldering at Rochester

---

1. E.C.: 'There was a time when we all kept our stockings in the fridge. Word got about that if nylon was left out it would ladder quicker, so you put it in the fridge and it supposedly lasted longer.'

airport. The odds are even that we'll both be able to come over for about a fortnight in February, but I'm not yet counting on it. Helena Rubinstein[1] wore a lot of people out during her long life, and she retains that capacity in the grave. We work from 9.00 till 8 in the evening and we still get nowhere. Then we go back to this peculiar hotel which has now become less than a joke (bathwater from midnight to 5am). Paris is wonderful for holidays but horrible to work in. I'm going to insist that E. gets paid a fortune.[2] We are sitting in an Italian restaurant and the woman next to me is a blonde with a khaki face. E. and I are speculating how it got that way because she is not a negress. E. has eaten an enormous pizza, half a chicken, and is now proposing to embark on an elaborate sweet. Nobody would say she doesn't eat! But what really irks me is that she doesn't appear to get any fatter while I blow out like a balloon [Elizabeth: that's because he eats candy all day long . . . It's not my fault that this letter's all full of spots either. David [Nash] and Judy[3] are here and we think the affair is all washed up but we're not sure]. Bruce again: We rather hope so secretly because it would be very limiting for David. E and I put different interpretations on the whole business [E: the whole thing started at Uncle's[4] party for us!]

On 4 March 1966 Chatwin bought three paintings of nineteenth-century Indian fruits at £25 a piece.

To Sven Gahlin[5]

Wasn't it lucky that E found some little cheques in her handbag? Otherwise!

Bruce

---

1. Helena Rubinstein (1870–1965) founder of Helena Rubinstein cosmetics.
2. E.C.: 'They didn't give me anything except my board and a little suede evening bag.'
3. Judith Small, American dealer. E.C.: 'They did marry and had a daughter, but divorced.'
4. Porter Chandler had given a party in New York.
5. London dealer in Indian art.

Since his return from the Sudan, Chatwin had been unable to focus on Sotheby's. He told Robin Lane Fox how he explained the matter to Peter Wilson: 'I don't want to go on perched on the podium having sham orgasms as I knock down another lot.' His disillusion over his degraded partnership added to his growing frustration with antiquities. Elizabeth communicated his malaise to Leo Lerman. On 13 July 1965 Lerman wrote in his diary: 'Elizabeth Chanler says she was looking at some antique jewellery in the showroom. And one of the porters said she shouldn't touch this Egyptian jewellery, because some fifteen or twenty years ago a man brought in a mummy in a case. Then he didn't call for it for about five years. It was put on a top shelf. Finally he wanted it. When the porter tried to get it down, it broke open, and a mess of "black" matter fell on the porter, who became sick immediately, went home, and died that evening. Ever since, porters believe that "antiquities" are cursed.'

Only part of Chatwin's dislike was aimed at grave-robbers. Closer to home, he found himself becoming tangled in a scheme to disperse the Pitt-Rivers collection. This unique collection of ethnographic art (including 240 works from Benin retrieved as bounty by British troops during an expedition in 1897) was stored at the Farnham Museum in Dorset. Still mired in secrecy, the deal which saw their dispersal involved the tight circle of gentlemanly rogues who were Chatwin's immediate bosses. On 27 August 1988, six months before he died, Chatwin focussed his rage against John Hewett, John and Puntzel Hunt in Ireland, and the Sotheby's chairman, Peter Wilson: Chatwin claimed that he left Sotheby's because he was being forced to sell the Pitt-Rivers collection 'fraudulently' to American and other collectors.

In June 1966 Chatwin shocked colleagues at Sotheby's by announcing his resignation to read archaeology at Edinburgh. The idea had been simmering ever since he had decided not to go up to Oxford. It had presented itself again in December 1965 on a visit to the Hermitage when he stood before the embalmed body of a Pasyryk chieftain who had been brought back to Leningrad in 1933 by the archaeologist Rudenko. On his return to London, Chatwin had borrowed Rudenko's report from Robert Erskine, once an archaeologist at Cambridge, and began to look into archaeology degrees.

Archaeology had interested Chatwin since his schooldays when his great-uncle Philip Chatwin, a force behind the Birmingham Archaeological Society, had taken Chatwin on his excavations at Weoley Castle. From Sotheby's, Chatwin would visit Hugh at Marlborough, especially to revisit West Kennet Long Barrow, Silbury Hill and the Avebury stone circle. 'It was in his bones,' says Hugh.'He was looking for absolutes, for why we are as we are, and shifting from Anglo-Catholic certainties to pagan rites.'

Cary Welch tried to discourage him – 'I know, from experience, that you are too alive for the academic world' – but agreed to write to Stuart Piggott, Professor of Prehistoric Archaeology at Edinburgh. Their meeting at the end of May decided Chatwin. Thereafter, Welch backed him. 'Your decision to study archaeology is very exciting . . . it may be that you MUST prove yourself to yourself in the THING area. Inasmuch as its rewards can be predicted, it is a wise, safe choice. Stuart P[iggott] could not be a better sort, to my mind, and I think you are to be warmly congratulated.'

*   *   *

On 24 June 1966 Elizabeth wrote to her mother: 'Bruce has finally decided to leave Sotheby's. He is going to go to Edinburgh University to get a degree in archaeology and this will take about 4 years. Sotheby's is having fits of course and are trying everything they know to make him stay another year, but it just won't work. He's been accepted at Edinburgh and is quite determined to go now, especially as we have geared ourselves up to it . . . He said he is going to write to you himself about it all, but I thought I'd just tell you in case you found out some other way. Anyway it's nothing to get alarmed about so don't worry. He's been thinking

about this for ages, but couldn't find out how to start, and where
to go and it's taken quite a while to get it all organised, especially
finding the people to talk to, as most of them were out in the desert
digging or something. The mechanics of his leaving Sotheby's
have not been worked out yet as he only told them a week ago, but
I expect they will make the arrangements for him to sell his shares
back etc.'

To Gertrude Chanler
119a Mount Street | London | 24 June 1966

Please don't have a fit. We'll survive, and before you know it Lib will
be turned into a SCHOLAR![1] I'll write soon: I'm sorry it's all so
precipitate but its no use chewing it over and over once one's decided
to take the plunge.

    With love, Bruce

To Gertrude Chanler
119a Mount Street | London | 6 July 1966

Dear Gertrude,

    I am sorry that we took you by surprise the other day with my
decision to give up Sotheby's and read archaeology. The fact is that
I have been chewing this idea over for at least four years. When I
took up the partnership in April I had got no further and was content
to let the thing drift. The main difficulty was that in this country you
cannot read prehistoric archaeology as such, but have to take a first
degree in classics or some such subject, and then go on for another
three years with a doctorate in archaeology; the other alternative is a
rather ineffectual diploma which takes two years and is not much good

---

1. E.C.: 'I was enrolled at Edinburgh in a Russian course and language lab.'

nowadays vis-à-vis a job at the end of it. During the last week in May I met Professor Stuart Piggott[1] who has the chair in Edinburgh; he has recently reorganised the department and has a four-year honours degree; he has hardly any students to start with and will be able to take the whole thing tutorially, and he is also one of the finest archaeologists in the world. I took a very rapid decision, and it is arranged that I start in October. Over the last fortnight I have been talking to the people at Sotheby's and although they at first wanted me to stay on for another year, they now understand that it would bring no advantage either way. By putting it off another year would be of no particular advantage financially this end either. The cost of living in London looks after all my salary and more each year but there is a definite possibility that I can get what is called a mature studentship[2] which is enough to live on each year. We shall be able to spend more time at the house[3] because the terms are only seven and a half weeks.

Until last year when my salary went up I was only paid a pittance, and have always had to earn my living in a number of different ways. In fact my income since becoming a partner has gone down because I did not have a free hand.[4]

My view is that the subject is so vast and complex that there is no time to be lost, and I believe that Peter Wilson at least sees this point of view, because he is gifted with a great deal of imagination and spirit. I am afraid that the art world, at least the world of art dealing, is coming to a grinding halt. It is no longer the reasonably civilised occupation it was five years ago. At any rate, it was making me extremely miserable and I feel that what I am doing is the right decision. Elizabeth does, and

1. Stuart Piggott (1910–96) held the Abercromby Chair of Archaeology at the University of Edinburgh. Chatwin had known of Piggott at Marlborough for his excavations of West Kennet Long Barrow. At the time of their meeting he had just published *Ancient Europe*, which included an illustration of Welch's Siberian plaque. On 15 July, after inviting Chatwin to lunch, Piggott wrote in his diary: 'Bruce C. very good value and should be a pleasure to teach.'
2. E.C.: 'He did, but it was only £275. We spent £8 a week on food.'
3. They had taken possession of Holwell on 9 May.
4. He was not allowed to have dealings once he became a partner.

it was to a certain extent her firm mindedness that encouraged me to see the last few weeks through.

I shall surrender my shares in September when I leave. I am working until October 1st; we intend to take the car to France during the second half of August returning in the first week in September. The house is coming on fine, but slowly and I'm afraid we shall not be in before Christmas at the earliest.[1] Could you let me know into which account you would like the share money returned?[2] It is just possible that David Nash, to whom they are being allotted, will want to make the payment directly in America, but this is an accounting problem, and there is no immediate hurry.

With love to you all, Bruce

Sorry

To Derek Hill
Postcard, skull of Cro-Magnon man, Les
Eyzies | Paris | France | [August 1966]

Overleaf is one of Elizabeth's <u>many</u> relations whose loss was a terrible blow to us. We hate to think of you going the same way but just wait till you come and stay with us. Love B and E

Michael Cannon had shared a room with Chatwin at Marlborough. This postcard was photocopied by Chatwin's secretary, Sarah Inglis-Jones. 'He gave it to me in Modern Paintings and said "Post this", as he was rushing off somewhere. He was always, always rushing somewhere in a drama, rushing from behind his desk. So I photocopied it thinking he might be well-known one day.'

1. The Chatwins would not, in fact, move in until the following July.
2. Gertrude had loaned half of the £6,500 that Chatwin needed to buy his shares.

To Michael Cannon

Sotheby's | 34 & 35 New Bond Street | London | [September 1966]

You may not have heard that I have LEFT Sotheby's to read a degree in archaeology at Edinburgh. Change is the only thing worth living for. Never sit your life out at a desk. Ulcers and heart condition follow.

CHAPTER THREE

EDINBURGH: 1966–8

Sotheby's kept Chatwin to the bitter end, not releasing him till 5 p.m. on the day before Edinburgh University required him to register. That night he took the sleeper to Edinburgh. No digs existed for married students. While he hunted for an unfurnished flat, he lodged for £10 a week at the Avondale B & B on the main road south out of the city.

He had arrived in high spirits. He was part Scottish and coming back to his roots, the land of his forebears, the Bruces; and of his maternal grandmother, the gypsy-like Gaggie from Aberdeen. He was enrolled to study the discipline of his great-uncle Philip; the profession claimed by Robert Byron when he had sought admission to Mount Athos.

Archaeology was a four-year course. It was arduous work. Chatwin attended from ten to fifteen lectures a week, which went on till seven in the evening; and was expected to write a weekly essay. Prescribed texts for the autumn term covered eighteen subjects, from the barbarian kingdoms of Western Europe to the uncertain frontiers of the Mongol horsemen. He also chose to learn Sanskrit.

But, as at Sotheby's, disillusionment set in.

He was away from the bright lights; no wine or food in shops; he had to work hard; and as an older student he did not fit in. Here was someone who had been twice to Afghanistan, to the Sudan, to Istanbul; others, fresh from school, found him shy or stand-offish.

Nor was archaeology the discipline he thought it was. 'Totally

bewildering to me,' he wrote in notes for his first lecture, on 8
October 1966, featuring a cairn at High Gillespie. 'Two middle
chambers only really indicated by depressions in the earth.' Four
days later, he scrawled 'Terrifying' – underlining the word three
times. He was repeating himself, his repellence with 'things'. As
his friend Robert Erskine put it: 'He went into archaeology
thinking he'd be the next Howard Carter, walking into a room of
Egyptian antiquities – and not spending his time with his bottom
in the air, in the mud, groping around a megalithic site.'

He would last two and a half of the four years; he described
his period here as his 'saison en enfer'.

To Ivry Freyberg
Department of Archaeology│19 George Square│Edinburgh│
24 October 1966

My dear Ivry,

I have just had the immeasurably sad news that Raulin is dead.[1] You
must try to forget these past few years with their sense of impending
tragedy. Instead you must try and imagine that some invisible power has
carried him off as he was – open, fair, free-minded and ruthlessly honest.
He was one of the very few really remarkable people I have known and
for that I shall always be grateful.

with love Bruce

While Chatwin studied, Elizabeth rented Lower Lodge at Ozleworth
Park in order to oversee the renovations at Holwell Farm. She
wrote to her mother: 'Bruce sends his love. I don't think you'll ever
make a correspondent out of him . . . he hardly even writes to me
when I'm not here, and then only scribbles giving orders etc.'

1. I.F: 'Raulin shot himself in a totally uncharacteristic moment of aberration rather
than allow himself to be sent back to a nursing home near Woodbridge. I don't think
anything has hit me as badly as that hit me. He was like Bruce, a man of magic.'

To Elizabeth Chatwin
Avondale|Edinburgh|30 October 1966

Sat

Dear E.

Tried to ring you but this is cheaper.

1. Will you come straight here next Fri as I won't be able to meet the plane?

Will try and get hold of James Dundas.

2. Daddy should deal with the Burnley[1].

3. Can you bring typewriter if it's not too much trouble.

4. I'll pay Feaver but only when Sotheby's pay me my pension etc.

5. Dagger[2] must wait till I've had a proper search. Am telling F.N.[3] to keep Lloyd Williams[4] informed.

6. Suggest 6x6 square tiles, not the octagonal ones as they'll look a bit corny[5].

Am seeing Eddie's[6] friend Peter Davis[7] today after beagling (!) with Bill Spink[8]. We're now in a tiny room which is sad.

XXX

B

p.s £6-10-0 is a sleeper to Edinburgh

---

1. Burnley Building Society, for the £4,000 mortgage on Holwell Farm – to rewire, reroof, put down floors and replace the beams.
2. Mogul, jade-handled. E.C.: 'He wanted to sell it.'
3. Felicity Nicolson, who had taken over from Chatwin as head of Antiquities. E.C. to her mother, 13 December 1965: 'She is a very small person, with a gloomy sort of face, but is really terribly nice and rather funny, as well as very clever.'
4. Chief accountant, later chief executive of Sotheby's, who was one of those furious over Chatwin's resignation.
5. For the kitchen.
6. Hon. Edward ('Eddie') Gathorne-Hardy (1901–78), botanist; known by Francis Partridge as 'wicked old Eddie'. Chatwin had met him with Allen Bole in Crete.
7. Peter Davis (1918–92), botanist, expert on the flora of the Middle East and author of the multi-volume *Flora of Turkey*.
8. Brother of Chatwin's former lodger Anthony Spink; he lived at 11 George Square.

To Stephen Tennant
Avondale | Edinburgh | [October 1966]

There is a great friend of mine here called Peter Davis. He is one of the leading botanists of the day and is embarked on a complete Flora of Turkey, in 14 volumes! He is also one of your fervent admirers. He bought a picture in your London exhibition and is desperately keen to have another or more. Do you think he could buy one? I seem to remember that there are two in Sotheby's, and maybe he'd like one of those. But then I couldn't know how much to ask. Do let me know if you can spare one, one with Lascars? He really is terribly keen and asks constantly.

Yours ever, Bruce Chatwin

PS The weather is unbelievably horrible here, but at least one breathes fresh air which is a change after London.

On 1 November, Chatwin took a three-year lease on an apartment in the Royal Mile.

To Derek Hill
Avondale | Edinburgh | 8 November 1966

We have a flat . . . but I do not think we'll be in it by November 20th. Address is c/o Dept of Archaeology, 19 George Sq, Edinburgh, but no phone. We had the Chanlers here. Great dramas over regular feeding[1] times. Considerably recovered after that horrible auctioneer had nearly drunk the last drop, but will I pass the exams? B

To Elizabeth Chatwin
Flat 6 | 234 Canongate | Edinburgh | 30 November 1966

Tuesday

Term will soon be over and I'm in a state about exams. At least they can only chuck me out at the end of the year. Had a very funny lunch on

1. Elizabeth's parents came and stayed in the North British Hotel. 'My father had late onset diabetes which meant he had to eat at regular hours.'

Sunday with the Talbot-Rices[1] who you'll love. She is a big Russian version of Penelope Betjeman[2], and he beams. They live at Fossebridge and so we are going over to see them soon. Otherwise nothing but the orange linoleum. I think I've changed my mind again about the floor and want plain pine again. I want to experiment with dirt and caustic on a piece. When I come back through London I'll make some enquiries. I thought I might stay with old Simon Snell[3] for two nights. I also want to see about getting some crushed terracotta for painting the house. I think the Rokeby[4] colour needs toning down a bit for Glos. Would the Victorian curtains[5] be nice in the back bedroom? The only place for them. Had just remembered how nice the Persian textile will look in dining room. Redman[6] sounds a real menace. Terrible dramas about getting a painting by Stephen Tennant for Peter Davis. S[tephen] T[ennant] writes illuminated letters to the Department and tells me he has dedicated a poem to me called the 'Supreme Vision'.[7]

1. Tamara Talbot Rice (1904–93), Leo Tolstoy's god-daughter and author of *The Scythians*. 'It was first through me that Bruce came to be interested in nomads.' She had fled St Petersburg in 1918, pulled, so she claimed, behind reindeer under white skins in the snow. In 1927 she married David Talbot Rice (1903–72), art historian and Watson Gordon Chair of Fine Art at Edinburgh University. His friendship at Eton with Robert Byron, pointing Byron in the direction of Byzantine art, drew Chatwin as part of his second-year course to study Fine Art under him. Byron described him as a sedate heron 'sober always, even in insobriety'.

2. Hon. Penelope Chetwode (1910–86), daughter of Field Marshal Lord Chetwode, m. 1933 John Betjeman; traveller in and writer on India. E.C. to her mother, 5 April, 1966: 'She is sort of nuts but lots of fun and crazy about horses. She practically always rides everywhere even to dinner and takes the dog along. The whole performance is a scream. She has straight grey hair with bangs and is very round with an extraordinary voice & is also crazy about Indian architecture.'

3. Simon Sainsbury (1930–2006), collector and philanthropist. Chatwin had had a brief romance with him in the early 1960s.

4. Intense ochre red.

5. Bought in Edinburgh.

6. A neighbouring National Trust farm tenant had applied for permission to build a house on a corner of the Chatwins' field. E.C.: 'I had cards printed up and got friends to sign them whenever his application went in.'

7. On 6 November 1966 Tennant addressed a letter to Chatwin in pink and green inks: 'My dear Bruce, Your enchanting letter gives me joy. Please give my greeting to Peter Davis. Could I go on taking *Art News* Bruce? I do so love it. I'm dedicating a poem to you in my new volume. It's called the Supreme Vision.'

One can only pray to God it will never be published. He also says that he has been asked to go to the University of Wisconsin to give a seminar on Willa Cather.[1] If he does it would be one of the spectacles of the century, and we ought to go and write a book about it. Peter Davis is giving a dinner party for the Southern blonde and her husband on the Thursday. Sotheby's kept my pension and contra-ed it which I thought was rather forward of them without asking. One can't complain really and I shall take even longer to pay the rest off. Very patronising letter from Llewellyn. 'With each day that passes, the fatter their arses.'

xxxx B

In November an illuminated letter had arrived from Tennant at the Archaeology Department to say that he was writing a play set in Aix les Bains, Madame is Resting, *which he hoped to sell as a brisk farce. 'Edinburgh must be very handsome in sombre autumn. You do sound studious: what period are you studying? Boadicea? Camelot? Constantine? Bion?'*

To Stephen Tennant
Flat 6 | 234 Canongate | Edinburgh | 24 November 1966

Dear Stephen,

I have never been so overworked in my life. Even duchesses take up less time than history essays. It really is a most extraordinary sensation going back to school. I have learnt never to offend the second-year students, who are immensely full of their own self-importance. One second-yearer leaned across my shoulder and asked me why I was reading a particularly devious book, and then said that first-year students were not able to understand its mysteries. A rigid stratification divides the years and the twain shall never meet let alone for a conversation. There are some anti-conventional characters as well. There's a wonderful

1. Nebraska novelist (1873–1947), known for her depictions of prairie life.

young man with carrot-coloured plaits who wears a red plastic coat and no shoes even though there's ice on the pavement. I have only once been out of Edinburgh and that was to stay in Traquair; the hills above Glen were covered in snow even in October. May I come shortly after Christmas or else immediately before on about the 20th. I have to take exams here which I feel sure I shall fail, and will be in need of cheerfulness.

As ever, Bruce

To Elizabeth Chatwin
Flat 6 | 234 Canongate | Edinburgh | 27 November 1966

I still think that the 9in tiles would be nice in the dining room and don't think they would be too noisy. We could put an easy chair up by the fireplace with a rug in front to give it a bit of warmth. They might look very well laid diagonally but I'm not sure about that. I think you can get Dutch Delft copies with the little figures in the middle; they might be better than nothing. Also make sure they sink a space for a door mat (big) inside the back door.

XXX B

On 20 December 1966 Stuart Piggott invited Chatwin to dinner ('smoked salmon & venison, ananas au cognac'), afterwards writing in his diary: 'I became bored as he stayed until 1.30 a.m. oh my God. I suppose he was enjoying himself but oh when will the young realise that three hours is the ideal time to come and stay for a meal?' On 6 February 1967 Chatwin invited himself to dinner again, 'revealing all in the same breath and too obviously that Elizabeth had gone back to their Gloucestershire house, and sounding rather gay and relieved about it'. Piggott speculated whether Chatwin 'has homo. tendencies. No change to be had from me!'

To Derek Hill

Flat 6 | 234 Canongate | Edinburgh | Saturday [February 1967]

Dear D.,

My parents have lent us their car and we got out of this place, thank God, for the first time. In Perth we found a huge Wemyss *jardinière*[1] which I thought was horrid, but could scarcely be considered an expert judge. Enclosed is the shop's card. Run by a <u>very</u> swishy number who couldn't decide whether he was going to talk Highland or Hairdresser. I thought it was fiendishly expensive, but considering the prices here for really bad and beaten up bowls I suppose you would be getting value for money. Green bands above and below, green handles and cabbage roses on the body. Am very keen about this Hermes glass[2], which I have tried to monopolise, but E. thinks she would like to wear. I have just bought her a lacquered Javanese coolie hat. When are you coming to see us in Glos? We can put you up as yet in a state of intense discomfort, but the food is delicious, or perhaps you'd prefer the rival attractions of our nearest neighbour, Alvilde L.-M.[3] I say you were right about Peter Saunders[4]. After greasing about for months sending messages about how keen he was to meet us, when I said that I was an undergraduate he looked slightly nonplussed, spluttered something about Sotheby's and after the truth had dawned, ignored us. Poor thing to have wasted a whole money-making evening; he was quite crestfallen; I feel he may have wanted a free evaluation. He seems to have a beastly collection of modern pictures. Did you see his house tarted up by David Hicks[5] in that decorating book? It is quite the funniest book to appear last year.

1. E.C.: 'Derek was always telling us, "Keep an eye out for Wemyss." His house in Donegal was full of Wemyss ware, even with large pigs sitting up like a dog.'
2. Hermes magnifying glass in the shape of an eye. E. C.: 'Bruce is lying: he thought it a ridiculous present.'
3. Alvilde Lees-Milne (1909–94), gardening expert m. 1951 James Lees-Milne (1908–97), architectural historian and diarist; they lived at Alderley Grange near Ozleworth.
4. E.C.: 'Jewish son of famous equestrienne who escaped from Germany, married a Minnesota mining heiress and bought a beautiful Palladian house near Malmesbury, Easton Grey.'
5. English interior designer (1929–98), author of *On Living – with Taste* (1968).

We are going down to Glos in Mid-March and don't have to be back again till the end of April. I HAVE to go and excavate in Bangor, on some beastly Neolithic site being developed for industry just opposite the front gates of Vaynol.[1] As it is very easy to get on the ferry to N. Ireland from there I thought we might come over to Ireland for a week. Are you going to be there in early April? We can't make it definite because it rather depends on the state of the house. Do let me know?

What are you doing in the summer? I intend to go to Afghanistan and Persia and possibly N. India and Nepal for four months with E. joining me for some of the time only because she is going home for her brother's wedding. I really feel I am justified in opting out. It's bad enough raising the wind for one air fare let alone two. Spent the whole of December having my teeth seen to in Birmingham; owing to incompetent dentistry of the most expensive Harley St kind, they were on the point of falling out, but were rescued just in time. I went to Sotheby's for two hours and felt that feeling of helpless rage coming over me again. I am afraid it is terribly boring here; I expected it, and have to convince myself that it's good for me. But the intense relief of not having to turn up each morning to that lugubrious firm is a compensation. And I dare say that a really massive trip will put me right. I haven't had a proper holiday for two years. You are lucky to be going to Greece at this time of year. I once went on the Acropolis in February and there was nobody else except a party of Russian sailors. Edinburgh station is draped in Hammers and Sickles for Mr Kosygin,[2] and there is a ramshackle bunch of demonstrators demanding freedom for the Ukraine.

Love, Bruce

To Derek Hill

Holwell Farm | Wotton-Under-Edge | Glos | 29 March 1967

V. sorry cannot make it. At the moment, I have a streaming cold. That's what comes of excavating in the snow.

---

1. Vaynol Park, estate belonging to Sir Michael Duff.
2. Alexey Kosygin (1904–80), Soviet Premier 1964–80.

To Derek Hill
Flat 6│234 Canongate│Edinburgh│8 May 1967

I have a Wemyss pot and cover with strawberries for you. No one could accuse me of divided loyalties. Bruce

In June 1967, after sitting his first-year exams, Chatwin left Edinburgh for the summer and moved in to Holwell Farm. The renovations had taken more than a year.

To Gertrude Chanler
Holwell Farm│Wotton-Under-Edge│Glos│5 July 1967

Dear Gertrude,

We are covered in paint. Things are suddenly beginning to happen, like the electricity is going to be switched on and the central heating given its trial run. Needless to say when we are really settled down to a job of work there is always a country drama. I have spent half the morning chasing somebody else's cows out. The kitchen is all but ready and we aim to move into it, one bedroom and the little study at the end of the house very soon. It will be a great relief to get out of the lodge and begin to lead a civilised life again.

The examinations went off all right, and in fact I was top of the year and a prizewinner,[1] something that never happened to me at school, and despite my gloomy predictions to the contrary; it was all very encouraging. Stuart [Piggott] is not excavating this year and I am off in ten days to Czechoslovakia, Rumania and Bulgaria to see some museums and excavations. He has given me a whole battery of introductions. This year is International Tourist year and it does seem rather amazing that one does not require visas for an Iron Curtain Country except Russia. An old school friend[2] is in the embassy in Sofia which will make life more comfortable and interesting there. I am then going to Turkey for

1. Wardrop Prize 'for the best first year's work'.
2. Andrew Bache had been at Old Hall.

about three weeks with Andrew Batey[1] and hope that Lib will come out and join us on the way back. I have just finished an article I am writing for a book on the flowers of Greece, not really my subject and I am afraid it's been more hard work than it's worth. I dread that it is inaccurate and that learned botanists will tear it to shreds.

I have been howling with laughter at all the hoo-haa in the press about the art forgeries. This is in fact only the tip of the iceberg and more will come. But I do take a certain pleasure in the fact that I threw Mr Legros[2] physically out of Sotheby's by the neck some four years ago.

Last weekend we went to Penelope Betjeman's. He is about to be made Poet Laureate[3] and wasn't there, and she is so exhausting that we came back here to collapse. This weekend we hope to have a real work corvée, and Felicity [Nicolson] is expected too. The cat has had kittens and this time they are doing fine even though she is a hopeless mother. Poor David Nash has mumps terribly badly in New York and has temperatures up to 105. They are now recovering in Brittany and I am going to wait for them to arrive here before setting off. I hope that Cary [Welch] will come over this autumn. We have just had a totally incoherent letter from him. They are building a house in Greece with Billy Wood's brother Clem and one day it'll be lovely for us to use it as well. Then he has schemes for other hide-outs in Mexico: and the Burning Ghats in Benares!

We must go back to the scraping. I'll send John and Sheila[4] a cable from darkest Moravia, but this time the cables office must send them on.

Lots of love B

No sooner had he moved into Holwell Farm than Chatwin set off for his summer's excavation at Zàvist, south of Prague. He took with him for the first and last parts of the journey a 23-year-old American architecture student, Andrew Batey. This was 'the

1. American architect (*b.*1944).
2. Fernand Legros (1931–83) art dealer and former ballet dancer who sold forgeries of Elmyr de Hory. Legros and de Hory had recently been charged with fraud and jailed.
3. John Betjeman was not made Poet Laureate till 1972.
4. Elizabeth's brother John was getting married to Sheila Welch.

steamer-chair character' whom he had met on board the Queen
Elizabeth *when sailing to get married. Batey, then studying history
at Occidental College in Los Angeles, was sailing home. 'We had
adjacent deck chairs on the stormy, freezing crossing. One moved
over and it turned out to be Bruce.' So began a fifteen-year friendship. Chatwin, says Elizabeth, was 'very, very keen' on the willowy
Batey, who in 1966 matriculated at St Catherine's College, Oxford.
Batey visited the Chatwins at Ozleworth and pestered Chatwin to
go travelling. In July 1967 they took the Orient Express to Venice,
stopping off at the Villa Malcontenta to meet Dorothea Landsberg.
Batey continued by train through Bulgaria to Turkey; Chatwin to
digs in Czechoslovakia, Hungary and Rumania. They planned to
reunite in Istanbul.*

*This letter would, twenty years later, inspire the opening of
Chatwin's novel* Utz *about a collector of Meissen porcelain in Cold
War Prague.*

To Elizabeth Chatwin

Hotel Kaiserhof | Frankenberggasse | Vienna | Austria | [July 1967]

Dear E,

I am very late in my time-table because I should be through Hungary
by now. I arrived here today from Bratislava and spent the afternoon in
the Volkerkunde museum as everything else was shut. There are three
feather Aztec objects here, which I knew vaguely about but was totally
unprepared for. One is Montezuma's fan (from the collections of H.
Cortez and Charles V – no less), a circular arrangement of brilliant
feathers with an acid green butterfly in the middle. Then there is his
green feather headdress with blue and red stripes and little gold plaques
and another circular fan with a coyote in violet and orange in a raspberry fan. These three objects make the Bliss collection[1] et al sink into
nothingness, and there is heaven knows what besides.

1. Bliss Collection of pre-Colombian art at Dumbarton Oaks.

We failed to get into the Stocklet Collection[1] because the objects and the furniture were all put away for the summer, but Mme S[tocklet] was very accommodating and asked me to come again in the autumn. She even remembered my visit of 1960! Then we went to Aix and looked at Charlemagne and the Schatzkammer where there are some objects that nearly made me die, especially the engraving on the back of the cross of Lothar and Richard of Cornwall's sceptre. We separated at Cologne after looking over that monstrous cathedral and I went to an exhibition of 'Rome on the Rhine' which was only fairly instructive and visually barren. I then went on to Bonn, to Habelt[2] the bookseller where I found a copy of Dörpfeld's[3] *Troy* and the v. rare Berlin Troy catalogue both of which I bought. The Bonn Landesmuseum has the gold Fritzdorf Cup which is paralleled by the Wessex Culture Rillaton Cup[4] and one from Mycenae. There was also a smashing Hunnish cauldron which I had not known about. On to Nuremberg where I had the row with the hotel[5] and would never have set foot in Germany again were it not for the great kindness on the part of the manageress of the next hotel who was so appalled that she treated me to breakfast. In the Dom is the fantastic, hideous but rather wonderful 'sacrament haus' of Adam Kraft[6] who portrayed himself with his mason's mallet supporting the monstrous load. The museum is quite wonderful with Durers and manuscripts of Otto III's scriptorium at Endernach. I made the happy discovery that the chalcedony salt [cellar] I bought from David Lethan[7] is Augsburg c.1600, and that means it's really worth something.

Prague is one of the most curious places in the world. The whole place is utterly bourgeois and always obviously was. Communism sits on it in a most uneasy way, and I would have said cannot last long. It is virtually impossible to meet a single communist. Even in the trains and

1. Palais Stocklet, Brussels.
2. Rudolf Habelt, bookseller.
3. Wilhelm Dörpfeld (1853–1940) German archaeologist.
4. The Fritzdorfer gold cup is the oldest gold cup in Germany. The Rillaton gold cup was excavated from Bodmin Moor in Cornwall in 1837. Lost soon after, it turned up years later in George V's dressing room as a receptacle for his collar studs.
5. E.C.: 'They'd been incredibly nasty because he was English.'
6. Adam Kraft (1455–1509) German sculptor.
7. Edinburgh dealer.

buses they joke about it. Some of the younger generation might be communist but would not dream of owning up to the fact. It must be one of the few places in the world where one can hear the American position in Vietnam actually defended. They loathe the Russians and Chinese with an emotional fervour. A great many speak English, and I had a long lecture from a man on the excavation who could only be described as a peasant on the merits of Eton and how England was an education to the world. The world is full of surprises.

I rather fell on my feet and met a charming couple called Plesl.[1] He directs the excavations of a Celtic oppidum called Zàvist, nr. Prague and I was given the professional suite at the camp which meant that I didn't have to live in town. We went on a tour in their car of S. Bohemia to see another friend digging another Celtic oppidum called Trisov. Nearby is a Schwartzenburg castle called Chesky Krumlov[2] with a theatre with the Commedia dell' Arte figures in a sub Tiepolo manner. We drank pre-war Burgundy in a wine-cellar. Also on the Zavist excavation was an Italian called Maurizio,[3] who is my new friend. There is every reason why I should dislike Maurizio but somehow I do not. He is over six and a half feet tall and indecently fat. Despite the solid nature of Bohemian food he needs to be refilled every half hour. In July he was awarded a doctorate at Rome University and is vaguely connected with Tucci[4] and his nefarious crew. His thesis, calculated to make me hate him, was on the close of the Indus Valley Civilisation and the coming of the Aryans. He got it all wrong, and used a number of inapplicable analogies about the movement of the Maya from Guatemala to Yucatan. Maurizio is never at a loss for some apparently brilliant remark about some obscure facet of Central European archaeology, but I fear that his knowledge is about as superficial as mine. He tells me he was once employed in smuggling microfilms from East to West Berlin. He is a man of many parts, an archaeologist of sorts, a smuggler, an International Socialist and also a self-styled great lover. Maurizio cannot talk about the stratigraphy of the Lower Quetta valley

1. Emilia and Evzen Plesl took him along in their Skoda from Prague.
2. E.C: 'In 1987 we went back to see it.'
3. Maurizio Tosi (*b.* 1944), Italian archaeologist.
4. Giuseppe Tucci (1894–1984), Italian scholar in Tibetan and Buddhist studies.

without finding two bulges which remind him of firm breasts. He bent double, which for him is no mean feat, to kiss the hand of a ferocious Slav lady archaeologist. She was somewhat affronted, but in general it must be said he enjoys considerable success. He is engaged to a girl in Andover, the Wessex bird as he calls her. This is not to say that Maurizio doesn't have birds in any European town one cares to mention. The current object of his affections is Eva. 'Eva, the first woman, she gave herself utterly to me.' Eva is an enthusiastic wide-hipped blonde with sparkling blue spectacles and buck teeth, who lives up the hill from Zàvist with her refined but calculating mother, and I fear that Maurizio did not bargain for her as well. Mother and daughter work as a team, and they are determined to catch Herr Doktor Maurizio. Both have visions of a splendid Roman future, and Maurizio has built up such a baroque image of grandeur that it will be hard for him to dispel their illusions. He has already invited them to Rome. 'Supposing they really come,' he moans. 'How would I explain it to my family – and the Roman bird?' In the mean time Maurizio is eating them out of house and home – vast quantities of duck and dumplings, chocolate cake, red currant tarts and apricots. He sits on the sofa, and while mama presses her attentions and Eva ladles yet another spoonful of cherry jam down that ever open mouth, he contemplates himself in the mirror occasionally inclining his head to admire that strange Roman profile. I cannot imagine how he will extract himself from the situation, especially as mama has specially rented a riverside cottage for the two lovers this weekend. Despite a lingering feeling that he may have made Eva pregnant, Maurizio faces the prospect of the final parting next week with equanimity. 'It is very simple,' he says. 'I shall burst into tears, and when I cry who can be angry?' I cannot imagine it will be so simple and Evsen Plesh is full of gloomy prognostications of the scene that will follow.

In the meantime on Tuesday another bird turned up, the Moravian bird as opposed to the Bohemian bird, a passing affair from last year's conference when she had made terrible confusion of lantern slides while fondling Maurizio in the dark. News of her arrival in Prague from Moravia caused Maurizio to break off abruptly a deep conversation he was having about the affinities of the Beaker Culture in Bohemia, and to hurry to the Hotel Flora where apparently she was staying. I must say the Moravian bird was ravishing and did much better credit to Maurizio than Eva. She had a pointed turned up nose, dimpled chin and masses of hair piled up on her head and her sensuous little mouth flickered when she was silent. But there was a terrible snag. She had come to Prague to get married. The bridegroom was an ineffectual young German from Magdeburg with a fall-away chin and pointed shoes. She had known him for three years. 'And to think,' exclaimed the outraged Mauriuzio, 'that when she was making love to me on the Linear Pottery site at Bylany,[1] she knew him all the time. It confirms my opinion of the faithfulness of women. How could she give herself to the dirty German.' Anyway for the time being she apparently could and would and the reason for her contacting Maurizio was that he should be best man at the wedding. He at once changed tack and agreed with alacrity, and also insisted that I come too as a witness. The time of the wedding was eight-thirty in the morning on the next day at the church of St Ignatz. 'Don't you understand?' he said, 'she is only marrying him because she is pregnant. I shall play the part of the faithful and wronged friend and in two years I shall have her.' I think that Maurizio may have miscalculated again because the two seemed absolutely devoted and stood in the foyer of the hotel kissing and fondling each other to the fury of the headwaiter who finally told them to desist.

So the next morning at a quarter past eight found Maurizio and I in archaeological clothes but with carnations in our buttonholes on the steps of the baroque church of St Ignatz in Charles Square.[2] One old woman was desultorily cleaning the aisle and another prayed loudly and devotedly in the chapel of the Holy Sepulchre, a real rock cut tomb with a plastic Christ looming over the boulders which were rather unsuitably planted with gladioli and gloxinias. An untidy man appeared and was under the impression that I was the organist. When I protested, he shrugged and said he would play himself. This he did on two chords only and to this cacophony the bride arrived in a large Tatra saloon accompanied by her parents and the bridegrooms mother, a solid German hausfrau in a crinkled pale blue suit. The bride's mother was a

1. Danubian Neolithic settlement 40 miles east of Prague.
2. This wedding became the funeral scene in Chatwin's 1988 novel *Utz*.

good-looking woman evidently in a savage temper, and her father a mild mannered little Czech who squinted through his spectacles. Maurizio bent double and kissed the ladies hands to their evident surprise. The bride must have been wearing her grandmother's wedding dress, and the bridegroom's shoes were more pointed than ever. And so this comic little procession made its way up the aisle to the thump-thump of the organ, and came to rest inside the pink marble altar rails where the priest was waiting. St Ignatz is a vast building, about the same size as Bath Abbey with astonishing pink and white plaster decoration and angels and saints dripping from every cornice. The grey marble pillars rippled like the waters of an oil-covered sea, and the organist thump-thumped while the ceremony proceeded in an undertone. I winked at the mother who winked back and began to look more cheerful. And finally the organ stopped while the priest gave a short address. On either side of the altar-piece St Peter exhorted and St Paul comforted while St Ignatius was wafted up to heaven in a rosy sunset and above supercilious cherubs pouted on plaster clouds, and for a moment there was peace. Then the organ thumpthumped again, and never was an aisle so long. By nine-ten the seven of us were in the Hotel Miramar in a corner of the cocktail lounge drinking the happy couple's health with a savage Hungarian wine that tore to my liver. In the corner by the deserted bandstand was a stuffed bear which a cleaning woman dusted as she cleared up the squalid mess of the night before. And that was the most curious wedding I have ever been to.

Mon.

I must say I like Vienna more and more. The museum is fabulous and as luck would have it the collections are closed to the public. This means that they are available to be taken out of the cases by the likes of me. There is a charming assistant of Prof Kromer who spent a year at Edinburgh, poor thing but he survived well enough. Over lunch time I went to the Schatzkammer. The Imperial mantle of 1125!! with gold lions attacking camels on a scarlet ground is the most wonderful thing I ever saw. Compare the fact that King William of Sicily had the coronation robe inscribed with an Arabic legend with today's petty nationalism and realise how we have regressed. The sword of Charles the Bold has a narwhal tusk sheath and handle, and I must say I am more than resigned to the extravagance of a tusk since seeing the unicorn presented to the Emperor Rudolf one of the inalienable treasures of the Hapsburgs together with a sumptuous Byzantine agate bowl, once considered to be the Holy Grail.

Now what are you going to do? I go to Hungary on Wednesday and will be incommunicado till I reach Sofia on the 15th or so. You know the address c/o Bache, British Embassy. I feel that I may not go to Cyprus but instead go to Maurizio's professor's excavation at Bari which sounds v. interesting and you could come too, or do you want to go to the Turkish Aegean coast in September. I must say I would love to go to Samos from Turkey, then we might descend on Teddy [Millington-Drake] before making back. Or we could meet in Italy. The possibilities are endless. Why don't you suggest something? If you came to Turkey I wouldn't recommend the train all the way but a single air flight to Istanbul and no return. If you want to see Istanbul with me[1] you must let me know via Andrew or c/o Bache because we'll leave it out till later and go into Anatolia first.

I'm in a horrid hot little room and I miss you.

xxxxxx

B

P.S. Can you imagine it? The Schmallclothes[2] actually turfed Andrew off at Hyde Park Corner instead of taking him back? I'm afraid – to be written off!

B

To Ivry Freyberg

Postcard, Aachen Cathedral | Vienna | Austria | 1967

Rang you up when we were in the South once or twice with no luck. Am on an archaeological peregrination in E Europe while E. is in America. I have been excavating in Czechoslovakia in a Celtic fort which was fascinating despite my forebodings to the contrary. Am now being a

1. E.C.: 'I didn't see Istanbul till 1970.'
2. Judith Nash.

common or garden tourist for a few days before facing the rigours of Rumania for a fortnight. I do believe I shall go to see the Merry Widow. Love Bruce

To Cary Welch
Postcard, Volkerkunde Museum | Vienna | Austria [1967]

From the collection of H. Cortez. Not a bad provenance and I bet that if all the schlemiels in Madison Avenue saw it, they'd say it was a fake. I think your Sassanian dish[1] is a marvel, and that you're very wise, brilliant, etc and it's the best object you ever had etc. etc.

I have been grovelling about in the dust with a whole lot of enthusiastic Czechs, and will write at length when I have the time. Will be in Turkey on Aug 20 c/o British School of Archaeology in Ankara. Love B

To Charles and Margharita Chatwin
Postcard, El Greco's Ascension, Budapest Museum | Hungary |
15 August 1967

E Hungary

Am excavating for a few days at a Bronze Age site on the River Tisza, before going on to Rumania. In Transylvania there has just been found what may be the earliest evidence yet of writing yet known. I must say I shall not come here again without a car. The trains are packed and take for ever. Harsh white wine on an empty stomach for breakfast. Bruce

1. On 27 March 1967 Welch had written: 'Dear Prewz, About to buy a very early Sassanian dish, 8 in dia., very heavy, so alive and stunning in quality that it just has to be bought. The subject is a REAL DISH: a fertility goddess who makes me believe in them. She dances in her buff and blue with great bodily vitality. She waves a sash overhead, and is accompanied by two big birds (peacocks?). Her face is so alive and benelovent that it might be a portrait.'

To Elizabeth Chatwin
Béke Étterem | Hungary | [August 1967]

The dining room of the Béke Étterem is a long corridor with barely room for the three rows of tables. The modernistic lamps have quaint green glass shades half of which work. In between the Gentleman's which smells horribly and the Ladies which smells less is the orchestra, three violins, a double bass and a xylophone. Cream coloured walls have sprouted a curious fungus and in the far corner is a mutinous green tile stove. Each table has a single bedraggled carnation, and a sprig of asparagus fern that has seen many carnations. Also a blue metal hatstand behind each chair. A few foxed engravings are hung out of sight, level with the helmets. I have never known an orchestra with a greater capacity to shock. We have been running through Lehar waltzes, and whenever we hit a high note it is like crossing a hump back bridge, never fails to hit the wrong note. 'We are going to Maxim's' with a noise that sounds like a thousand Siamese cats in part song. The noise is quite deafening. Thieving Magpie, drab potbellied gentlemen with their shirt tails flapping. Sweaty fingers. Dark rings around their eyes. As I understand no word of the menu, and as I am constitutionally able to endure almost anything, although I did draw the line at the hen's head which peered out of the soup at me at luncheon, I have been experimenting with everything called Parizi. The influence of the French capital was never really strong in Eastern Europe and has still been further diluted in recent years. The object I am eating seems to be a hybrid Wiener Schnitzel and onion omelette, the one wrapped in the other deep fried in batter and served with a few rings of batter and chips. An original omelette surprise, like the orchestra!

To Gertrude Chanler
Ankara | Turkey | 4 September 1967

I've just been to see your friend Captain Trammel[1] who is badly laid up in hospital here, and I'll go again tomorrow. I've been having a

---

1. Bill Trammel, a naval friend of Admiral Chanler, as was the US Consul Betty Carp, who never left Turkey. E.C.: 'My father was here in the 1920s and tempted to stay.'

fascinating trip, in fact a lot of hard work, but I've learned an incredible amount. There's nothing like going to see the material first hand. I can never really grasp the implications from books. Over the past week I've been tramping about in the wilds of Anatolia. Andrew Batey was so beguiled by my Turkish friends in Istanbul that he stayed. Betty Carp[1] who we saw said 'I have known people go up to Anatolia and like it.' I do, but I'm now in the state of longing to go home.[2] Love, Bruce

To Gertrude Chanler
Holwell Farm | Wotton-under-Edge | Glos | 4 October 1967

How nice to get your letter! You beat me to it because I was on the point of writing to you to say that we had definitely decided to come over for Christmas. Your offer to pay the tickets comes as a marvellous surprise and we both look forward to it immensely. I think we must spend a few days here immediately after the term ends, and imagine that we'll fly on the 20th or perhaps the day before. We must book now. There will be a number of odds and ends to tie up here. One rather unfortunate thing is that our farmer John Jones may be going. He has been offered a sheep farm of 45,000 acres in Northern Scotland, and obviously we can't begrudge him that. In fact we have been actively helping him find the necessary finance. But that will mean we shall probably be having to find a replacement and that is difficult enough. They all seem to be so sharp and on the make here. I think that the best thing to do now that we have it properly fenced is to stick out for a high rent for a series of short lets. The trouble about letting for a long period is that one can create what is called an agricultural tenancy which means that one can never get the encumbent out, and we must avoid that. The next minor disaster occurred when the main water pipe burst,

1. Cary Welch, also sent by Chatwin to Carp, reported back that she had invited him to 'a six-Princer dinner'.
2. Notebook, 29 August 1967: 'I am not too thrilled with Turkey. Today it has occurred to me what is missing – a sense of the absurd. Stung by a wasp in the lorry.'

apparently owing to the action of static electricity on a galvanised pipe laid in wet clay. We were without water for four or five days and had to fetch it in milk churns. They then came to lay the new polythene pipe with a mechanical digger. When the man came to fill it in again, Lib was in Wotton doing the shopping and I had settled down to some Sanskrit. There was a yell from the front, because he had got trapped by the grab and was pinned against the cab. The plumber rescued him and announced that he had some ribs broken. I then called for the ambulance and not only did it arrive but three fire engines and half the county police force together with reporters for the local and Bristol papers. Of course in the meantime the driver had recovered and I felt I wanted to hide in view of what appeared to be a false alarm. Otherwise the whole place has taken a terrific turn for the better and is becoming simply beautiful inside. The kitchen is the most pleasant I have ever known and I think we will almost live in it. I am in the middle of painting the study which will be ready before we go. I once learned a very good technique for colouring walls. You paint them with flat white oil, and then put a very thin layer of coloured wax glaze. This gives the walls a slightly transparent look. We are doing the study in golden ochre which sounds horrible but I think you'll like it. The bathroom doors which I glazed green over grey blue are a great success. A painter friend of mine is seriously thinking of adopting the technique. The boiler at last works after its teething troubles and the whole place is remarkably warm and has dried out in a way I never thought it would.

Off again to Edinburgh in a few days. It is a far better course this year, and in point of fact one in which I have covered more of the ground than last year. I can't slack off though and be a flash in the pan. We are hoping that the Linlithgows may have a flat or cottage for us at Hopetown which is five miles from the city in wonderful country which leads down to the Forth. She is American and apparently gets very bored with the locals. So I would have thought there was a chance. In any case we must move from the smokey zone into the New Town if possible because one gets absolutely black where we are.

Captain Trammel was very nice to me in Ankara. He didn't look at all too good when I went the first time, but was up and cheerful the second time. I didn't ask Betty Carp what was the matter because it was obviously tactless to do so. It seems that he was waiting the results of tests which had been sent to Germany. I did gather though that it might have been quite serious. He was very interesting about Turkey and appears to know Istanbul backwards. Another person who knows Istanbul backwards by now is Andrew Batey. My Turkish friends almost ate him up entirely, and although he was supposed to come in to the wilds of Anatolia with me he never left the city for five weeks. I warned him in advance that it would happen if he weren't firm minded and it did.

The things that Elizabeth brought back are wonderful particularly the plain George II silver plate, which is in my opinion exactly how silver should look. I love its simplicity, and the tankard looks grand on it. I had one bit of luck in that I found an agate and silver gilt salt cellar in Edinburgh, and when I was in Vienna found almost the pair to it. Instead of being 17th century as I had thought it turns out to be Burgundian circa 1480, and the Vienna example comes from the Imperial treasury. When I have to learn German we'll go to Vienna rather than Germany. I had three most enjoyable days there, which was a great relief after Nuremburg where I had a fight with a hotel keeper.

Congratulations on your wedding anniversary and wish Bobby many happy returns of the day. Too late, I'm afraid, but as I once forgot my own birthday until it was a week too late, frankly it's not surprising. There'll be so many people to see again at Christmas and its very exciting. Cary [Welch] says he'll be in India but I am not sure I believe it yet. But as he was going through a craze for the Beatles, and since they are going too, I feel there may be more in it this time.[1] I would rather like to go to the Philadelphia University Museum for

---

1. Welch had pitched to his friend the director James Ivory a film on the Mughals featuring the Beatles. (Welch had heard 'Rain' and written to John Lennon saying it was the best Indian music since the time of Akbar). He wrote to Chatwin: 'Also on the path of the Mughals would be a gang of international art dealer-thieves . . . If the idea comes off, I see you in it too.' Ivory, apparently, was 'wild about the idea'.

two or three days, and we could stay with Billy and Mia Wood. Otherwise the slate is clean. We both look forward to it immensely. It seems ages since last October. So much water has flown under the bridges, but I've never felt a twinge of regret about Sotheby's, and every time I go back and see my poor ex-colleagues, I find they all want to do the same.

With much love, and please forgive the typing,

Bruce

Chatwin started his second year as the lone male on his course, which had slimmed from 41 students to seven. A favourite lecturer had also moved on.

To Elizabeth Chatwin

Flat 6 | 234 Canongate | Edinburgh | 24 October 1967

Horribly cold here, bring plenty of warm clothes. Edinburgh the same. Charles Thomas appointed professor at Leicester.[1] Am going to Stuart [Piggott] on Sunday. Otherwise nothing. Will you please bring Huxley's *Flora of Greece*[2] RHS pamphlet in the journals, also his flora of the Mediterranean in the attic and Piggott's *Penguin Approach to Archaeology* in the Lodge.

On 16 November 1967 Hugh had a car accident in Birmingham. 'I was travelling down Bradford Street in a red Austin 1100 when a lorry jumped the lights and I swerved to avoid it and a bus I had overtaken came in and spat me out under the lorry. I wasn't wearing a seat belt. They scraped me off the road and got me to hospital, I had 57 stitches in my head and was unconscious for two days.' During this time he dreamed about Bruce.

1. Charles Thomas (*b*.1928) had lectured in archaeology at Edinburgh since 1957. He first excited Chatwin in Darwin's visit to the Yaghans of Patagonia. Chatwin was now stuck with studying Roman Britain. E.C.: 'This was a blow. He wanted to do the Dark Ages.'
2. Anthony Huxley, *Flowers in Greece: an outline of the Flora* (1964).

To Hugh Chatwin
Flat 6 | 234 Canongate | Edinburgh | 1 December 1967

Dear H,

All this business about dreams. I never knew we were telepathic.[1] Believe it or not I had a dream about you to coincide with yours about me. It's this wild Celtic blood. Very sinister. I nearly came down today, but Father said you'd prefer it when you're a bit better. Congratulations on your exams.[2] I've got some at the end of next week. My whole life consists of struggling from one exam to the next. Felicity Nicolson is here for the week and she and E. have been charging down to Galloway and have come back with a couple of whopping Benin bronze heads.[3] Everyone writes to me to see if I can get them into Sotheby's. Any one would think it was the Christian Church in the 4th Century. I was always of the opinion that Sotheby's was some kind of religious cult. Now I know. How awful to have been an unbeliever. An unrepentant pagan. If you want some light if rather embarrassing entertainment get hold of a copy of a book by Connor and Pearson called *The Dorak Affair*, with a totally fictitious conversation with your brother not one word of which did he say.[4] The so-called treasure worth millions never existed so it is

1. H.C.: 'That telepathic thing, we both had with our mother. A year later, the girl I was in love with announced that she was going to marry one of my friends, and my mother shot up in bed. "Something's happened to Hugh, something's happened to Hugh."'
2. The finals of professional surveying exams. Hugh was a chartered auctioneer and estate agent for Grimley & Son in Birmingham.
3. E.C.: 'Sotheby's sent us there. The heads belonged to an old lady whose grandfather had brought them back from the Benin Punitive Expedition of 1897. She remembered them being put in the yard in Galloway and hosed down and blood coming off and the yard running red.'
4. *The Dorak Affair* (Michael Joseph, 1967) by Kenneth Pearson and Patricia Connor. The story of the Dorak hoard concerned the British archaeologist James Mellaart, and described the kind of hunt which, until now, had thrilled Chatwin. Mellaart had earned his reputation in Turkey where he had dug up the world's first mirrors, polished chunks of volcanic glass. In the summer of 1958, as Chatwin prepared to join Sotheby's, Mellaart claimed to have met a young woman called Anna Papastrati while travelling to Izmir by train. 'She was very attractive,' Mellaart said, 'in a tarty sort of way.' On her wrist was a solid gold, prehistoric bracelet. 'She said she'd got lots like it at home

naturally somewhat difficult to find out where it has disappeared to. It's like finding the Holy Grail. We have done rather well with our sales so far and haven't had to sell the silver, because we got £150 for a picture[5] I TOLD Elizabeth to buy for £35 in a Sotheby's sale a year ago. How's that for a good profit.

Get well soon.[6]

B

In the winter of 1967 Cary Welch recommended Chatwin to curate an exhibition at the Asia House Gallery in New York devoted to the Nomadic Art of the Asian Steppes to be called The Animal Style. *The exhibition was not to open until January 1970. Until that time Chatwin was expected to use his Sotheby's training to contact museums and collectors and to gather the best examples of nomadic art. This was where he now directed his energies.*

---

and asked if I would like to see them.' Mellaart went to her house in Izmir, 217 Kazim Dirik Street, where lapis, obsidian and fluted gold objects glinted in cotton wool in a chest of drawers. Mellaart understood them to be relics of the Yortan culture. He wanted to take photographs, but she would only allow him to draw them. In November 1959 his drawings were published across four pages of *The Ilustrated London News* under the headline: 'The Royal Treasure of Dorak – a first and exclusive report of a clandestine excavation which led to the most important discovery since the Royal Tombs of Ur'. His reputation declined soon afterwards. Attempts to track down the woman proved fruitless. Mellaart was either a dupe, or trying to dupe. Chatwin, touched for his expert opinion, knew about the site of Hacilar where Mellaart had excavated. Once, the authors of *The Dorak Affair* quoted him saying, 'a dealer came in with a box of stuff from Hacilar. You know, pots and the usual goddesses. He left them with us until the date of the auction. One day one of our men was shifting the stuff and he dropped it. Well, that's enough to make anyone go cold, but funnily enough it didn't turn out that way. We had a look at one of the broken goddesses and it had got pink dental plaster under the armpits . . .' The authors noted that the experience of working for Sotheby's had somehow 'soured' Chatwin.

5. A gloomy painting by John Atkinson Grimshaw (1836–93) of moonlit autumn leaves. E.C.: '£150 pounds would keep us going for months.'
6. H.C.: 'I took six months off and decided to go to London, to the chartered surveyors, Weatherall, Green and Smith, where I remained for 20 years.'

To Cary Welch

Flat 6 | 234 Canongate | Edinburgh | 13 January 1968

Dear C,

Since you seem prepared to spend vast sums on works of art, I enclose the following three photos (three life size) of an object I want to buy. It is Archaic Eskimo probably from North Alaska, exactly which of the eskimo cultures I wouldn't like to predict. It is in MAMMOTH ivory. I have had this checked by the Natural History Museum. It belongs to a jeweller in Glasgow. I believe he will ask a hefty price for it. He has always promised to sell it to me one day, and I would like not to refuse to pay it. It is of course an arrow-shaft straightener of a type well attested from the Madgalenian to the Eskimo of today. I personally hardly know of a more satisfying Eskimo object, it has gone the colour of rich mahogany tempered with a sort of cloudy effect on the surface. I have been thinking of Eskimo objects for the exhibition and this is what has brought the question again into the open. I don't think I will be able to afford to buy it at the moment, but would buy it for you if you were interested, providing I am able to buy it back after your death in the unlikely event that you should DIE before me. Or maybe you think it is boring.[1]

I am on the verge of buying however a really exquisite Parthian silver earring [of an elephant head], the head and ears unbelievably fine with the trunk curling round in a loop, in silver, very hard and fine, the ears like some kind of ruched curtain, as in Uncle Nasli's[2] dish. 1½ in diam, it seems raving but not considering my preoccupation with objects that fit into a matchbox.

Mercifully, the Edinburgh library has all the books I need for the Animal Style. It becomes more and more exciting as I spot, or think I do, wide ranging new possibilities. I have also found a fabulous 19th century travel book, with plates in the manner of Gustav Doré, called *Una Estate in Siberio*, fantastic engravings of shaman offerings and fetishes in dark mesolithic woods. They would do wonderfully as end covers, and could

1. C.W.: 'I did.'
2. Nasli Heeramaneck Collection, New York.

be elaborated ad nauseam by Mr MacCracken.[1] I spent the whole day with a friend from London on the prowl round the shops. The barrenness was numbing. I think I will buy a 19th century wax cast of the face of an Australian aboriginal reputedly from the collection of Charles Darwin or maybe a coco-de-mer. I did buy a Peruvian *maté* gourd 18th century, with silver mounts, the best I have ever seen, and that is not saying much.

Love, Bruce

To Cary Welch

Flat 6 | 234 Canongate | Edinburgh | 30 January 1968

Dear C.,

This letter is being written in high dudgeon, and is really to let off steam. The dahling[2] despite frequent warnings that they should be insured, and a strict injunction not to consign them to the tender hands of the GPO has lost her pearl necklace valued in 1936 for £7,000, or rather the postman 'lost' the registered package on his delivery round, thinking it must have slipped out of his postbag when the bus turned a sharp corner.

Consequently the whole of my life for the past three days has been full of the wails of the dahling, disgruntled telephone calls to America, who are needless to say not best pleased, expensive lawyers, devious jewellers, obdurate post-officials, lightfingered (in my opinion) postmen, hopeless policemen etc., just when I had hoped to do some work on the Exhibition.

The dahling is QUITE HOPELESS about her possessions. She is rapidly divesting herself of all her jewellery (and her and my clothing) on planes, trains and buses, when it could either be turned into CASH or mortgaged, or merely kept in a Bank. It is a stupid waste to LOSE it. It makes me a. socially conscious b. furious that I could have used the money much better. It now would appear that we can recover at least some of its value due to Gross Negligence on the part of the Post Office though that was not without an intense struggle.

1. James MacCracken, a young hippy painter from Detroit, whom Welch had discovered in Boston.
2. Elizabeth. Edith Welch was also called this.

I also wanted to go for the weekend to the Shetlands to the annual Viking Festival the 'Up-Helly-Aa' at which they burn a replica of a Viking ship and send it off to sea, although admittedly I was secretly glad that I didn't have to face the 80mph gale in which the boat got stuck . . .

I shall go to Glasgow next week to see about the Eskimo object. We have a new car, a Volkswagen to replace my beloved Citroen van[1] which the dahling always hated. I don't like the image of the former. Who is this Peter Avery?[2] The name rings a big bell. I have bought this Parthian silver earring, very cheaply. It has apparently been vetted as ancient by some lab, God knows where. It is very appealing, but I cannot help wondering if it is marvellous quality Art Nouveau, if so what a conception. The Professor[3] and I would love to have a look at a slide of the FIBULA with a promise not to publish etc. We are also very taken with the idea of the silk[4]. If it is silk then it is the first occurrence in West Asia, but very interestingly there is evidence of an incipient SILK ROUTE leading to Celtic Europe in the 6th Century BC, where it is found in the Heuneberg,[5] conveyed by our old friends the Scythians on their stocky ponies with their animal style trappings. Or is the fragment really too small to tell even under the most powerful microscope.

Elizabeth is going down to London to see about the BLOODY pearls, and so I shall have the weekend to do some work. Give my greetings to the infant MacCracken

Love

B

1. E.C.: 'He didn't have to drive from Edinburgh to Holwell in a 2CV which had no heater.'
2. Peter Avery (1923–2008) British historian of Persia.
3. Stuart Piggott.
4. A Phrygian cloak pin made of gold and electrum that Chatwin and Welch had seen at John Klejman's gallery in New York. C.W. to B.C, 11 January 1968: 'The climax came when [Mr Young of BMFA] took out some tweezers, reached into a little crevice, and plucked out something that he put on a slide. He then whisked the slide over to a powerful microscope and looked and looked and looked. I asked what was happening. "I think I've found a piece of ancient silk," he said. "Something left over from when it was last worn."'
5. Heuneburg-Museum at Hundersingen on the Danube.

PS I went to London the other day and saw the Knight[1] at a party, wife in Portugal, and he was off there the next day. I have never liked the Knight more and we had an endless conversation. We wished you had been there to see the English in Fancy Dress. All my old friends in multi-coloured silk finery and furs or transparent plastic. I had a fascinating conversation with a Qantas Air Steward who told me a long saga of the secrets of AIR LOVE. Elizabeth was rather offended not to be introduced[2] though it would have shut him up like a clam.

To Derek Hill

Flat 6 | 234 Canongate | Edinburgh | 8 February 1968

Dear D.,

How badly I want to see you! I wish we could come down but we simply cannot. I am up to my eyes in work and debt and cannot stir. Edinburgh is a penance for frittering away all those years of doing nothing. I am going to organise an exhibition for the Asia Society in New York. It is John D. Rockefeller's plaything of the moment, though the chances of his continued enchantment with Asia in general are, I imagine, dimming. The title is 'The Animal Style of Mounted Asian Nomads'. The J.D.R. fund for Asiatic research is packing me off first to Finland, Sweden, Germany and a string of eastern European countries in March, and in the summer to Russia and my goal of the moment, Mongolia, if the Mongols are receiving. My collaborator is the topical Emmy Bunker whose father-in-law is ambassador in Saigon. Consequently she prefers not to be seen in Soviet circles. It opens in the winter of 1970. I would so liked to have come on that Iranian conference, but the dates conflict with the term. Beware of a gentleman called Mr M who will be intimately entwined in the whole business. He has silvery hair and the manner of Vittorio de Sica.[3] He is married

1. Desmond Fitzgerald, 29th Knight of Glyn (*b*.1937), architectural historian, Christie's representative in Ireland.
2. E.C.: 'He was continually not introducing me to people. He kept them in separate compartments.'
3. Italian film director and actor (1901–74).

to a Persian lady who secured him three archaeological concessions '*une pour la recherché, deux pour la commerce*'. I was once at a curious lunch at the Cavalry Club at which Signor M tried to sell the ex-conservative M.P. for Plymouth, a Captain Plugge, a monstrous fake silver vase purporting to be 2nd Millennium BC. Also present were Dr Barnett of the B.M. and the Air attaché of the American Embassy, whose only counsel when asked a question was 'Bomb North Vietnam' and whose wife 'just adored antiques'. The Captain was attracted to Mr M's girlfriend, who was being let off for the day. Dr Barnett who was called upon to authenticate the vase sat in a cold sweat, and I laughed . . .

I suppose you'll never come here again now that poor Mrs Crabbie[1] has died . . . Our house is in the doldrums. It is finished structurally; the central heating keeps it warm and dry. There are some expensive pieces of furniture, but neither carpets, curtains nor paint. Nor have we the time to see to it. We make the best of Edinburgh, but it is very second best, and our immediate reaction on leaving here is to get abroad.

What are your plans for the summer? I secretly may go on to Japan on the Trans-Siberian railway, but cannot imagine how I would get back. I suddenly feel a great fascination for the far north but imagine it is only a phase; I don't think I shall ever be a serious archaeologist because my whole approach is wrong. I can only see it in terms of getting someone else to pay for my travels . . .

We stayed four days in the Chanler apartment in New York. It really is inconceivable to me that they should have <u>copied</u> curtain materials that should have been swept away in 1918. There are a number of other touches that you would appreciate such as my father-in-law's proud hanging of the pictures, where neither he nor anyone else can see them, particularly the Chardin[2] which is totally concealed from view.

Love, Bruce

1. Of the family who made Crabbie's Green Ginger Wine; Hill used to stay with her when in Edinbugh. E.C.: 'If I go to a pub and someone says "What do you want?" I'll have green ginger wine on the rocks.'
2. A tiny Chardin oil, *La Lavendeuse*; Bobby put it behind the door.

To Gertrude Chanler
Flat 6 | 234 Canongate | Edinburgh | 8 February 1968

Dear Gertrude,

What a week it's been! I must say that when the postman arrived on the doorstep and said they'd lost the package, bedlam broke loose. We were in awful suspense over the weekend, and it was only slightly relieving to hear from Cartiers that they were insured. The police pulled very grave faces and said they doubted it would ever be found again. They were the only people in the whole business who were enjoying themselves. I imagine that in Edinburgh they are constantly being sent off for worthless bits of rubbish, but valuable <u>purralls</u> really captured their imagination. Eliz[abeth] went to London because we decided to get Ian Murray[1] to handle the whole thing for us, and that evening there was a loud rat-tat-tat on the door, and the two most comic CID detectives standing outside. They looked at us as though they had stepped out of a very slow moving comedy thriller of the 'thirties, one six foot five at least and nearly as wide with a beetroot coloured face, the other less than five feet a sort of ashy colour. With the maximum of ceremony they pulled it out of an envelope, and asked me to identify it. I pulled out my glass in a very knowledgeable way and said 'Boucheron 1920' in a very knowing way. Then they told the story. The postman must have dropped it out of his bag onto the pavement at the top end of Princes Street. A shop assistant walking to work after 'a tiff with er boyfriend' and in a blind fury sees a little package and kicks at it, not once but for half a mile like a football. When she gets to the shop, she sees some cotton wool poking out from one end and inside 'a wee string o' beads' which she keeps at the bottom of her shop bag for a week. In the meantime she makes it up with her boyfriend (quite bright the boyfriend) who says <u>purralls</u>. She takes them to a jeweller for valuation so she can get the reward for finding them ha! ha! and the jeweller who was apparently not very bright but who had a visit from our friends the detectives the day before telephones the police. We are now trying to get the girl off because under Scotch Law she has to be charged for withholding them.

It sounds all very well after the event but I had a feeling that

1. Elizabeth's solicitor.

something might go wrong and said that the post wasn't the proper place for them. In any case I have now <u>made</u> E. get them insured.

We have sold the old van very well to a friend of mine[1] who set her heart on it and despite the fact that I have told her twice what it was worth. We have got a rather smart green Volkswagen instead which is what E always wanted. Last night we went to see Mrs Murray[2] who was very nice and asked to be reminded to you. She has a fine portrait of Mrs Wadsworth by Thomas Sully. She says that she can fix up some stalking for me next year on her old estate.

We did have a wonderful time at Christmas. I have never really enjoyed America more, because always in the past there was the gloomy shadow of Parke-Bernet looming up in the background. I will have to come over to talk about the exhibition and then of course we must come for the opening which will be Christmas the year after next and that time we won't be in a rush at all because the days of exams will be over. We have been having the vilest weather here and were knocked off our feet in the great gale the other day. It was dangerous to be out at all because the air was filled with flying rubbish. But so far we haven't had the fantastic snowfalls that they have been having in the south.

Lots of love, Bruce

PS Hugh much better

To Cary Welch

Flat 6 | 234 Canongate | Edinburgh | 8 February 1968

By Air Love

Dear C.,

I was not aware that E. had spoken to the unspeakable Roger.[3] For me

---

1. Ruth Tringham, lecturer in archaeology. R.T.: 'The bottom fell out of it after a year.'
2. Barbara Murray, cousin of Elizabeth's uncle Porter Chandler, lived outside Edinburgh.
3. Roger Wollcott-Behnke, journalist on *Daily Telegraph* magazine. E.C.: 'An American friend I'd known since I arrived in London. If you weren't careful, he'd come and lodge and never go. A perfect mimic and talented in lots of ways, he had *folie de grandeur* and died of liver cancer when he was in his early thirties.'

personally R. has the same effect as Edith's friends who I met on Crete, a reaction that is rarely less than physical. In my view it would be a bad idea, though I don't want it to get back to E. that I said so. Everything Roger touches has the kiss of agonising DEATH. It could be that he has turned the corner, but as I have been an appalled witness to such endeavours as a motor-racing magazine, a colour book about maharajas in decline, a collection of Holbeins belonging to an Irish peer, a collection of ikons belonging to an Austrian prince, plus God knows what in the way of trying to sell an Egyptian mummy to Kathmandu, the last I admit not without its funny side, I rather doubt his ability to handle anything, least of all Mr Mac C., who will undoubtedly have a ferocious chemical reaction too. Worse Roger has two hangers on called the Princess Toy and the Prince Chip, while he hangs on to a very pleasant lady called Mrs Brydon Brown[1] on the principle of little fish suck bigger fish. The combination would be fatal. No wonder E. didn't confess to her indiscretion.

Will you let me know if you have any spring plans in our direction because we wouldn't want to miss you. I shall leave here on about March 16th en route for Helsinki, probably to be birched in the sauna at the expense of Asia House. I've never been able to make up my mind if I like the idea or not. Wouldn't it be awful if one suddenly found one was a physical masochist as well as everything else? My friend Mr Batey wants to come and look at the architecture of Alvar Aalto but I'm not sure if it's a good idea as he's wildly unreliable and unpunctual, and as I have work to do, it would be a distraction. I have promised though to take him to the Stocklet House, which is a marvel. Last time I sat in a white leather sheepfold, drank wishy washy tea from rock crystal cups, and watched the Rembrandts and a Simone Martini wheeled by on a stainless steel trolley. When the lights in the theatre go up, they shine through Mexican alabaster masks on the Han tomb reliefs flanking the auditorium. Mr B[atey] is marrying his childhood sweetheart in California in late September, and his father in law to be seems to be that rich that he is doshing out air tickets to friends for the CEREMONY. He has also given him the fastest and most expensive Mercedes that money can buy in which I shall probably be killed if he

1. Louise Brydon Brown, American pharmaceutical heiress.

comes to the continent. I have already had the nastiest moment of my life in his £20 Austin Seven.

I have bought the largest coco-de-mer I have ever seen. Beautiful and obscene. We take it to bed.[1] Did I give you the message that Mr H[ewett] will NEVER sell the Migration style brooch away from you, and I am going to take a photo when I go down there. I am buying a bellows for my Asia House Tour.

Love B

PS Got your letter this morning and will reply soon, but I am plunged in the Neolithic of Bulgaria, who is a very demanding master.

To Emma Bunker
Postcard, greenstone sculpture of Neolithic elk, Alunda, Uppland.
Flat 6 | 234 Canongate | Edinburgh | [April 1968]

Will write again when my photos of the objects are printed. I couldn't make Budapest or Bucharest because the visa complications were vast. Ortiz collection has proved to be a great success and photos expected in 2 weeks. Would you ever go to Toronto where the Royal Ontario museum has Borowski's Ordos Coll. Bruce

In April 1968 Cary Welch wrote to say that he had seen another early Sassanian dish with a motif of Shapur I slaying lions with a bow. 'I think it is the best hunting piece I have seen.'

To Cary Welch
Holwell Farm | Wotton-under-Edge | Glos | [April 1968]

Your letter of this morning re the Sassanian dish. You may think I am mad, but I urgently counsel you not to buy it. I am certain from the photographs that it is a forgery – although a damn good one. If you'll forgive me saying so, I think you are judging it by the same standards

1. E.C.: 'Nonsense.'

you would apply to Indian painting from Rajasthan around 1800. I have always been of the opinion that the forgeries of Iranian objects rely on Indian inspirations, if not actual workmanship.

Anatomically I think that the foreleg of the deer is horrible, also the position of the lion's paws wholly out of keeping, also the rib cages of both animals are like car radiators. Furthermore the animal is a deer and should have <u>antlers</u>; instead it has antelope horns which should be curving backwards, except those of the saiga antelope (which this is not) which curve backwards before their tips begin to come forwards. No a thousand times NO. IT IS NOT GENUINE. It is less of a joke than the object from the Kimble Foundation in the Asia House Exhibition which is grotesque.

I simply cannot imagine how you could be bothered to fling away genuine objects for this. Sassanian silver dishes and Sassanian art in general may be clumsy and inaccurate at times, but never slick (and sleazy) like this.

It was for peddling this sort of object round America that Mr Safani[1] offered me 100,000 dollars a year.

Forgive the ranting.

Love B

On 19 April 1968 Chatwin had lunch with the journalist Kenneth Rose and two South American girls. Rose wrote in his diary: 'We have a jolly lunch, all shouting at once. Bruce tells us that his great-grandfather was a celebrated swindler, who cheated the then Duke of Marlborough out of many millions as his family solicitor. "He cheated old women out of their few pounds, too.". . . Bruce has tried to get his father to talk about the case, but cannot get a word out of him. He asks me to see.' On 30 April 1968 Rose wrote to Chatwin of his discovery that Robert Harding Milward had owed his creditors £108,595.15.11, for which he was sentenced to six years, dying in prison a few months after receiving his sentence.

1. Edward Safani (1912–98) Iranian dealer, established the Safani Gallery in New York in 1946.

To Kenneth Rose[1]

Flat 6 | 234 Canongate | Edinburgh | [April 1968]

A real operator — £108,595.15.11 is no mean sum. If only he hadn't been found out! One can hardly breath for fog and rain. A visit from you in May would be a blessing, but I may try to escape south to do my revision. Do let me know if you are going to be up here. Winston must have known R.H.M[ilward] for there to be a reference to him at all.[2] His hey-day with the Marlboroughs was a good twenty years before in the '70's and '80's. I'll try and whip up the Gounod, Wagner, Richter correspondence for you to see. Bruce

To Ivry Freyberg

Holwell Farm | Wotton-under-Edge | Glos | 10 June [1968]

Lovely party. I couldn't have enjoyed it more. Maddeningly I missed the train but there was a perfectly good one later at 11.30. I can't imagine why I was taking the 10.30. Come down, PLEASE, to Glos. It's quite beautiful at the moment. Can put you up in minimal comfort! but GOOD FOOD! Am in the middle of sitting exams. Lots of love, Bruce

In the summer of 1968 Stuart Piggott invited Chatwin to join him and Ruth Tringham on an official tour of archaeological museums in the Soviet Union. On Sunday 30 June 1968 Andrew Batey drove Chatwin and Piggott to Dover; from Ostend they took a train to Warsaw to meet Tringham – also George Ortiz, whom Chatwin had invited separately. Elizabeth was to join Chatwin for the second part of the journey, through Rumania and the Caucasus. On 3 July, Piggott wrote in his diary that foreign travel was an

1. Founder and writer of Albany column, *Sunday Telegraph* (1961–97) and royal biographer (*b.*1924); Chatwin had met Rose at Derek Hill's in Ireland.
2. Randolph Churchill in his biography of Winston Churchill made a brief reference to Milward's conviction for 'fraudulently converting to his own use moneys entrusted to him'.

escape-route clearly for Chatwin, 'who is running away from himself by travelling'.

To Elizabeth Chatwin
Hotel Orbis Bristol | Warsaw | Poland | [July 1968]

Dear E.,

Visit to Warsaw of high fantasy with ambassadorial dinner parties and visits to the Academy. Freedom of movement circumscribed owing to lack of transport. Also our official Soviet invitation came through some two days <u>after</u> the visit was supposed to begin. This may mean we have to scrap our whole programme for the Caucasus/Iran but God alone knows! Could you try and bring with you my compass which is somewhere in my room I think, and failing that can you buy a fairly good one? Can you also bring my copy of Parvan's *Dacia*,[1] a small green book in my shelves and a map of Rumania. I only hope you'll be able to come on the Transylvanian jaunt.[2] Also remember to put the <u>tent</u> in the car + a <u>small</u> billycan for gas in case you run out.

While enquiring about the Bulgar/Rumanian section in the car can you find out if one can cross the Danube by ferry going due north from Sofia, through Vraca and thus missing out Bucharest. I think the best thing is to miss out Hungary if this is going to be difficult by taking the Yugoslav autobahn from Belgrade to Lyubliana. On looking at Stuart's map I see that one cannot cross the Danube anywhere else but at Guirgui nr Bucharest.

Love, B

To Elizabeth Chatwin
Hotel Orbis Bristol | Warsaw | Poland | [July 1968]

Dear E,

We are faced with a totally Kafka-esque situation. We are now on two tours, one organised by ourselves going Leningrad – Moscow – Kiev

1. Vasile Parvan, *Dacia: An Outline of the Civilizations of the Carpatho-Danubian Countries* (1928).
2. E.C.: 'I didn't go. It was too complicated, obviously.'

and the Caucasus, the other at Ministerial and Ambassadorial level going to Leningrad – Moscow – Suzdal – Siberia and Moldavia with camping equipment and excavation tools provided. Flurries of cables have been exchanged between half the British embassies of E. Europe. Ambassadorial and ministerial receptions and dinner have been arranged. George [Ortiz][1] is arriving tonight and may well be collected from the airport in a Rolls-Royce. How can one explain his Bolivian nationality – as a fellow of Che Guevara? Ruth has apparently lost her passport and the British Council Representative is a collector of Bloomers in the [Eddie] Gaythorne-Hardy manner.

   Love B

PS Please try and bring 3 tubes of Dylon – quick wash – excellent! We may now go to Moldavia rather than the Caucasus after all. Will write c/o British School of Archaeology in Athens. Please contact for messages. B

Piggott's group broke up on 20 July, Chatwin heading off to Bucharest. In August he was in Kiev where he watched 'a squadron of Cossack cavalry exercising down a cobbled street: glossy black horses, scarlet capes, high hats worn at an angle; and the sour resentful faces of the crowd.' One month later, Russian tanks rolled into Prague. Chatwin by then had joined Elizabeth at the Welches' house in Spetsai. The invasion of Czechoslovakia and the événements in Paris that summer passed him by, his concentration focused on the Asia House exhibition. On 7 September Piggott wrote in his diary: 'Bruce rang up on Monday in London; caught night train; breakfasted with me; collected some books he wanted and returned to London by the 10 a.m. Very mad.' Days afterwards, he flew to New York for a meeting with his fellow curators, Emma Bunker and Ann Farkas.

1. S.P. diary: 'This morning Bruce's friend George Ortiz has joined us. I hope he will prove congenial – an odd young Bolivian millionaire.' Ortiz was travelling as 'Doctor Ortiz of the Basel Museum'.

To Elizabeth Chatwin
1030 Fifth Avenue | New York | [September 1968]

Dear E,

Flight at present is fixed for the morning of the 10th approx 8am. <u>But</u> I may have to go to dinner with the Rockinghorses[1] the night before and leave from NY rather than Boston. Possibility of massive research grant from Rockerfeller. Asia House Exhibition neither better nor worse than expected. Emmy [Bunker] is fine but listens to not one word. Ann Farkas severe academic, but not unsympathetic. New possibility of exhibition at Museum of Primitive Art to coincide with Asia House.

English invasion in force. Mr Fish,[2] Blades, Annacat,[3] all up Madison there are slow English drawls. Steph[4] <u>decorating Blades</u>. Desmond Guinness,[5] David Hicks – *Tous*. Many parties. Charities etc. Go to Philadelphia tomorrow. Atmosphere very nervous with possibility of vast negro vote for Wallace (!) to precipitate to struggle. Please go to Holland if you feel like it but let me know if you're going. Otherwise see you sometime on 10 Oct . . .

Dining with Cousin O'D[6] this evening at 7.0. Brendan & Ali[7] with the Irish Georgians on Tu.

Love B

Chatwin – 'a compass without a needle' as one friend called him at this time – now replaced Piggott with a new guru. Peter Levi, the Jesuit priest and poet whom he had known since Sotheby's, was teaching in Oxford. Elizabeth says, 'I'd go and wander round the Botanical Gardens with my cat while Bruce and Peter talked

1. John D. Rockefeller III (1906–78), patron of Asia House.
2. Michael Fish, British fashion designer responsible for the kipper tie.
3. The British boutique Annacat had opened on Madison Avenue.
4. John Stefanidis (*b*.1937), interior designer and partner of Teddy Millington-Drake.
5. Hon. Desmond Guinness (*b*.1931), founder of the Irish-Georgian society.
6. O'Donnell Iselin, Elizabeth's cousin.
7. Brendan Parsons, Lord Oxmanton (*b*.1936) m. 1966 Alison Cooke-Hurle; succeeded father 1979 as 7th Earl of Rosse.

in Campion Hall.' For Chatwin, the thin and handsome Levi was a figure of glamour. Levi said: 'He thought it a wonderful idea to have all these pads all over the place: a room at Campion Hall; a room in Athens; a room in Eastbourne, where my mother lived. He wanted from me a way of life that was largely in his imagination. He thought my life was some kind of solution: I travelled and I was a writer.' A main topic of discussion was the introductory essay on nomadic art that Chatwin was contributing to the catalogue for the Asia House exhibition. Levi said:'He was then in the process of transforming himself from an archaeologist into a writer and so far as any advice was called for, it was I who advised him to make the change. You write in order to change yourself in my view. He was trying to remake his life and become a writer.' Another topic was Afghanistan: Levi had been commissioned by Collins to write a travel book on the Greek influence in Afghanistan. He suggested that Chatwin come with him and take the photographs. 'You can look at nomads and I can look at Greeks.'

To Peter Levi

Holwell Farm | Wotton-under-Edge | Glos | 15 October 1968

Dear Peter,

Many thanks for the poems.[1] It would have been delightful to think that we might have met up on Saturday but I'm afraid that Edinburgh is calling.

My summer was disastrous too, or rather wasteful. I shall not repeat the experiment of travel in the Soviet Union until there is clear sign of a change. Every plan was frustrated, and I'm afraid that most traditional Russian hospitality is a deep-seated desire to see foreigners drunk. I did manage to see Professor Masson[2] under his own table, while reciting a

---

1. *Pancakes for the Queen of Babylon* (1968).
2. A.V. Masson, director of Institute of Archaeology at Leningrad.

Shakespeare sonnet for the benefit of his wife. It was not worth the supreme effort for I was crippled with a liver attack for days after.[1]

I am certainly going to Afghanistan next summer, if not before. I refuse to delay it one moment longer in the interests of spurious scholarship in Eastern Europe. I have been to Lahore, but not to Swat. I have every intention to go to Swat, Dir, Chitral (which I know), Hunza and Baltit. In the Lahore Museum there is a suit of leather armour which belonged to a stray Mongol dessicated in the desert of Sind. We could even try to go to Pir-Sar, which Aurel Stein identified with Alexander's Aornos.

Didn't you find America in a curious calm? A negro told me that the word was out 'Vote Wallace! He don't give you no shit.' Refugees of 1938 now talk openly of returning to Europe. People discuss when and how the country shall be split. In the Ukraine they talk darkly of big trouble in Lvov, and the Khirgiz virtually push the Muscovites off the pavement. Are the Super-powers superannuated?

I'll try and come and see you soon. Bruce

After attending Andrew Batey's marriage in Pasadena – 'Bruce gave me a Mogul dagger with a jade handle as a wedding present (for an exquisite death)' – Chatwin returned to Edinburgh on 10 October. He had moved out of the Canongate flat in the summer. On 22 October Stuart Piggott wrote in his diary: 'B now staying at the Abercromby Hotel up the road; madder I think. He and/or his marriage will crack up before long.'

In late November Elizabeth drove up to fetch him – they were flying to America for Thanksgiving. She found Chatwin fed up with having to study Roman Britain, and fed up as well with

1. S.P. diary 12 July 1968: 'At 4.00 we were suddenly switched into a room in the museum & plied with vodka and wine & salads. Very jolly if it hadn't been for the first of three parties that evening. On returning we went to more drinks with some Americans met in the Institute library & then to an awful interminable evening with Masson and a female cousin. More vodka more wine and fortunately a pilaff to sop up some of the alcohol. I survived miraculously as did B[ruce].' E.C.: 'When Bruce got back to his hotel room, George said: "I have to congratulate you," and was upset when Bruce then was sick over his dressing gown.'

Piggott, whose attitude towards him, says Elizabeth, had become bizarre to say the least, even frightening. An entry in Chatwin's notebook, one of several on this theme, attest to his mounting suspicion that 'most archaeologists interpret the things of the remote past in terms of their own projected suicide'. Elizabeth says, 'More than once Stuart suggested that the three of us go away and kill ourselves.'

The Chatwins spent Christmas in Geneseo, but Bruce did not reappear in Edinburgh. On 9 January Piggott wrote: 'Absolutely no news of Bruce Chatwin. He came to me in a great state last term saying he was £6,000 in debt owing to buying the Glos. house, wouldn't take money from Elizabeth's family & simply had to take a job – offered one at £1,000 a year, one day a week from Christie's. Shot off to London to investigate & hasn't been heard of since.'

◄◦►

CHAPTER FOUR

THE NOMADIC ALTERNATIVE:
1969–72

On their return from Christmas in America Elizabeth asked Bruce: 'Aren't you going back to Edinburgh?' 'No.' Fired by the example of Peter Levi, Chatwin had fastened on expanding his Asia House essay into a book: his proposed subject – 'nomads here, there, past and present.' He hoped that the book would shed light 'on what is, for me, the question of questions: the nature of human restlessness'. Almost thirty, Chatwin was mindful of the words of a Marlborough master: 'Every man who ever stretched himself has one book in him ... although it may be a better book if he delays delivering it to publishers until he has attained the age of sixty.' Through the poet Edward Lucie-Smith he met the literary agent Deborah Rogers in London and she agreed to act for him.

To Gertrude Chanler
Holwell Farm | Wotton-under-Edge | Glos | 20 January 1969

Dear Gertrude,

We had such a marvellous time and couldn't have enjoyed ourselves more. It was such a pity about the 'flu. There was a huge storm while we were away that knocked down our windbreak and demolished the local farmer's beech tree, but we remain unscathed. I am going up to town tomorrow in search of a publisher for a book based on the Asia Society Introduction.[1] So I hope that comes off. We are still living in American

---

1. *Animal Style (Art from East to West)*, Bruce Chatwin with Emma Bunker & Ann Farkas, New York: The Asia Society Inc. (1970).

time and it gets worse rather than better. By next week we shall be sleeping in the day and awake at night. Do let me know if you want me to try and find out anything about those secretarial schools in London for Felicity.[1]

Again, many thanks for a lovely Christmas and we hope to see you soon, love Bruce

To Cary Welch

Holwell Farm | Wotton-under-Edge | Glos | 1 February 1969

Dear Cary,

All well here. The winter is mild and delicious, and I am sure we shall have to expect snow in April. We have been planting more trees and the first snowdrops and crocuses have appeared. Charles Tomlinson[2] and I go for long walks and we are planning an anthology of shaman poetry.

Mariano[3] called today and wondered what effect his letter had had on you. I told him I didn't think much, because you couldn't understand it. It now seems that he may accompany Andrew [Batey] and I to Egypt in March and if so that will be a real *fête triangulaire* the outcome of which is hard to see.

Asia House sent today the very good photograph of the Mogul carpet fragment. Now could you set one of your students on to the matter and do my homework for me? What I want to know is this? What are the immediate origins for this particular design, the animal symplegma? Is there anything in it that we can specifically connect with Central Asia, such as the northern influences that come into Tabriz. I want just a few notes, scholarly and to the point, and then I shall swing it on my academic ladies whether they like it or no. My part of the exhibition does, I have to say, become more and more difficult as more and more European museums refuse to lend or offer to send casts or electrotypes. In my view there is NO substitute for the real thing that is worth bothering with, and one might

1. The eldest of Elizabeth's sisters.
2. Charles Tomlinson (*b*.1927), poet and translator, the Chatwins' closest neighbour; m. 1948 Brenda Raybould.
3. Mariano Rivera Velasquez, a Mexican friend of Batey's whom Chatwin had met in Paris at the house of Jimmy Douglas. He later killed himself.

just as well use photographs. The latest blow is the British Museum, all lovely and pliable on the phone to Gordon;[1] when it comes to the point of course, they have A. done nothing about it B. tell me IN CONFI-DENCE (mark you!) that they intend sending the Trustees a report coun-selling against their dispatch to America, and letting the Trustees then decide for themselves. Upon refusal the Trustees are to blame for helping to spoil an important exhibition, because of course the matter was entirely out of their hands, and what can one do with Trustees like that anyhow? The Peabody have kindly consented to one bear mask and a Hallstatt bull.

I am having a fine time dashing up to London seeing publishers from which I hope that something will emerge. At present I am focussing my attention and blandishments on Mr Maschler,[2] who was the publishing genius behind *The Naked Ape*, but am resisting a recent account of art auctioneering to be called *An Ascension Myth* in favour of a work on nomads here, there, past and present.

The cat[3] is sick and I have been buying a number of silly bits from Christopher,[4] who is lovelier than ever.

Love B

Tell the darling not to fret about her tea caddy as I shall buy her a lovely one in plastic.

To Tom Maschler

Holwell Farm | Wotton-under-Edge | Glos | 24 February 1969

Dear Tom,

You asked me to write you a letter about my proposed book on nomads. I cannot provide a history of nomads. It would take years to write. In any

---

1. Gordon Washburn, Director of Asia House.
2. Tom Maschler, head of Jonathan Cape, had published Desmond Morris's *The Naked Ape* in 1967. On 23 January 1969 Deborah Rogers had sent Maschler Chatwin's text for the Asia House Exhibition. 'Can he come and see you tomorrow? I am sure he is worth your spending half an hour with. I have a good feeling about him.'
3. Kittypuss, ginger female.
4. Christopher Gibbs (*b*.1938), antiques dealer and collector.

case I want the book to be general rather than specialist in tone. The question I will try to answer is 'Why do men wander rather than sit still?' I have proposed one title – *The Nomadic Alternative*. We obviously won't use it. It is too rational a title for a subject that appeals to irrational instincts. For the moment it has the advantage of implying that the nomad's life is not inferior to the city dweller's. I have to try and see the nomads as they see themselves, looking outwards at civilisation with envy or mistrust. By civilisation I mean 'life in cities', and by civilised those who live within the ambit of literate urban civilisation. All civilisations are based on regimentation and rational behaviour. Nomads are uncivilised and all the words traditionally used in connection with them are charged with civilised prejudices – vagrant, vagabond, shifty, barbarian, savage, etc. Wandering nomads are bound to be a disruptive influence but they have been blamed out of all proportion to the material damage they cause. This blame is rationalised and justified by false piety. The nomads are excluded; they are outcasts. Cain 'wandered over the surface of the earth.'

The first chapter might ask the question – 'Why wander?' It could start with the Greek legend of Io and her compulsive wandering, and be called *Io's Gadfly* (if that's not too trite). The word 'nomad' comes from words meaning 'to pasture' but it has come to apply to the earliest hunters as well. Hunters and herdsmen shift for economic reasons. Less obvious are the reasons for nomads' intransigence in face of settlement even when the economic inducements are overwhelmingly in its favour. But the mutual antagonism of citizen and nomad is only one half of the theme. The other is much nearer home – ESCAPISM (a good personal reason for writing the book). Why do I become restless after a month in a single place, unbearable after two? (I am, I admit, a bad case). Some travel for business. But there is no economic reason for me to go, and every reason to stay put. My motives, then, are materially irrational. What is this neurotic restlessness, the gadfly that tormented the Greeks? Wandering may settle some of my natural curiosity and my urge to explore, but then I am tugged back by a longing for home. I have a compulsion to wander and a compulsion to return – a homing instinct like a migrating bird. True nomads have no fixed home as such; they compensate for this by following unalterable paths of migration. If these are upset it is usually by interference from the civilised or semi-civilised half-nomads. The result is chaos. Nomads develop exaggerated fixations about their tribal territory. 'Land is the basis of our nation. We shall fight,' said a nomad chief of the 2nd century BC. He cheerfully gave away his best horse, all his treasure and his favourite wife, but fought to the death for a few miles of useless scrub. This obsession for tribal land lies behind the tragedy of the Near East. The High Seas do not evoke quite the same emotional response, and territorial waters lie close to land. Sailors' emotions are directed towards the feminised ship that carries them far and their home port.

Looking at some of today's studies of animal and human behaviour, one can detect two trends . . .

1. Wandering is a human characteristic genetically inherited from the vegetarian primates (No fleas).
2. All human beings have the emotional, if not an actual biological, need for a <u>base</u>, cave, den, tribal territory, possession or port. This is something we share with the carnivores. (Fleas).

Chapter II will deal with the omnivorous weapon-using ARCHAIC HUNTERS. They can be traced from the Lower Palaeolithic to the present day. They <u>follow</u> their food supply; they return home to <u>base</u>. They <u>take</u>, gratefully, what nature offers (Chapter title – PREDATORS?), but make no practical effort to propagate their food supply, except by ritually identifying themselves with animals or inanimate objects in the environment. Living for the moment they are distinguished from us by having a radically different concept of time and its significance, though differences of this kind are matters of degree rather than kind. Their lives are not one long struggle for food, as many imagine. Much of their time is passed in gross idleness, particularly the Australian Aborigines whose dialectic arguments know no bounds of complication. Though capable of bouts of intense concentration while actually getting their food supply, they do not take kindly to manual work. The leaders lead; they do not coerce. The whole point of receiving a gift is to give it away; a pair of trousers given to an Aboriginal will pass rapidly through twenty hands and end up decorating a tree. Vendetta is a private rather than a public affair. If they kill one another, it is usually for ritual reasons. Mass extermination is a speciality of the civilised. The 'neo-barbarism' of Hitler was Civilisation in its most vicious aspect.

Chapter III will be a discussion of Civilisation (as something to escape from). Chapter title – THE COMFORTS OF LITERACY. 'Put writing in your heart. Thus you may protect yourself from any kind of labour' – Egyptian scribe to his son *c.*2400 BC. The triumph of the white-collar worker was achieved over the backs of sweated labour. The Civilisation of the Old World crystallised in river valleys where the soil was fertile but the choice was 'Make dams or be swept out to sea.' Note the hero's medals offered posthumously by a grateful Mao to those 'human dams' drowned while blocking the Hwang-Ho in spate. Diffusionism is unfashionable but I believe (with Lewis Mumford among others) that civilisation as such was an accident that happened once and once only in the very peculiar conditions of Southern Iraq, and that the consequences of this 'accident' spread as far as the Andes before Columbus. This proposition is highly debatable. On it hinges the question 'Is civilisation something natural – a state to which many different cultures have irrevocably led?' Are those that did not failures – or are they alternatives to civilisation? Or is civilisation an anti-natural accident? If so, the evolutionary analogies, of Darwinism and the survival of the fittest, are misapplied drastically when used with reference to human cultures. In any case WRITING develops hand in hand with civilisation, standardisation and bureaucracy, and with them a stratified social and economic hierarchy, and the repression of one group by a ruling minority. The first written tablets record how much the slaves are bringing in. Literate civilisation freed some for the higher exercises of the mind, for the development of logical thought, mathematics, practical medicine based on scientific observation rather than faith healing etc. But in Mesopotamia the two highest gods were Anu (Order) and Enlil (Compulsion). Breasted writes of the 'dauntless courage of the architect of the Great Pyramid'. However, the 2½ million blocks were hauled up by fettered labour. Civilisation was lashed into place. We inherit the load.

Chapter IV HERDSMEN (or PASTORALISTS)

The herding of domesticated animals was one of the technical advances that led towards the formation of civilisation, but it was always combined with some sort of agriculture, and was, therefore, reasonably settled. True pastoral nomadism, with herds on the move all the time and no agriculture was not a stage towards civilisation. It developed as an <u>alternative</u> to it. It was directly in competition with it, especially in border regions. The art of riding provided the means of mobility; it was the 'tip-over' factor that enabled some groups to abandon agriculture and be permanently on the move. The pastoralists had much in common with the hunter – they believed in a mystical bond between animal and man. But from civilisation they learned the idea of the unity of the State, and from the techniques of herding and killing domesticated animals, they discovered those of human coercion and extermination.

This is a long chapter and perhaps best divided into two. I will then trace the origin of the great nomad cultures, the Scythians, the Huns, the Germanic 'waves', the Dorian Greeks, the Arabs, the Mongols and the Turks, the last (semi-)nomadic people to aspire to world conquest.

There will be an account of nomadic life; its harshness and intolerance, its illiteracy and obsession with genealogies; the comparative lack of slavery, though that did not prevent nomads from being the most successful slave traders; the renunciation of all but the most portable possessions in times of emergency; the failure to appreciate civilised standards of human life balanced by a natural adjustment towards death, which the super-civilised have lost; the communality of property and land within a tribe. 'All are God's guests. We share and share alike.' (Bedou chief); the position (remarkably emancipated, especially in Northern Asia); the sanctity of the craftsmen etc.

Chapter V will continue the story of the nomads in the face of a triumphant agricultural and then industrial civilisation. I may call it *Civilisation or Death!* the cry of the American frontiersmen. This will be a record of the hard line towards nomads; its rationalised hatred and self-assured moral superiority. Nomads are equated with animals, and treated as such. I will discuss the fate of the gypsies, the American Indians, the Lapps and Zulus, also nomads within highly civilised societies, tramps, hobos etc. I would give an account of the Beja in the Eastern Sudan, the Fuzzy-Wuzzies of Kipling. They have been able to resist all civilising influences since they were first mentioned in Egyptian annals some three thousand years ago only because they are prepared to tolerate the lowest level of personal comfort. They are sensationally idle and truculent as well. Most of the morning for the men is taken up by a fantastic mutual coiffure session (grooming urge?). There is also the depressing moral and physical effect of civilisation on the Arab. 'Law and order have settled in like a blight on Sinai and Palestine.' G. W. Murray, *The Sons of Ishmael*.

Chapter VI will be the reverse of Chapter V and will trace the longings of civilised men for a natural life identified with that of the nomads or other 'primitive' peoples. To be called *Nostalgia for Paradise*, the belief that all those who have successfully resisted or remained unaffected by civilisation have a secret to happiness that the civilised have lost. It is bound up with the idea of the 'Fall of Man', with Paradise myths, and Utopias, the Myth of the Noble Savage and primitivist writings from Hesiod on. Its most extreme form is Animalitarianism, the assumption that animals are endowed with superior moral qualities than human beings. 'I could turn and live with the animals . . .' Walt Whitman. Hence at a different level the popularity of such books as *Born Free*. Otherwise it may emphasise the essential unity of animal and man, an intellectual tendency far older than Aesop and still with us. We also have a lingering idea that eating animals is sinful, and it is interesting to find that some North Asian hunting tribes preserve legends of a Vegetarian Paradise, a folk memory of our vegetarian primate days.

Chapter VII. THE COMPENSATIONS OF FAITH

Nomads are hated – or adored. Why? It cannot be sheer chance that no great transcendental faith has ever been born of an Age of Reason. Civilisation is its own religion; religion and state are wedded; at the apex the god king of Egypt, the deified Roman emperor or the papal monarch. In its own day 'Pax Britannica' was a religion, and one 19th Century sceptic described religion as 'civilisation as inflicted on the lower races at the end of a Hotchkiss gun'. The great faiths renounce material wealth and the idea of progress in favour of spiritual values. Their ideologies hark back to the religious experiences of the early hunters and herdsmen – a complex of religious beliefs known as Shamanism. The Shaman is the original religious mystic, androgynous and ecstatic. The nearest the Chinese have to a transcendental faith – Taoism – is 'little more than systemised shamanism'; Judaeo-Christianity, Zoroastrianism, and the

Hindu-Buddhist traditions preserve their pastoral past (Feed my Sheep – The Lord is a Good Shepherd – The Flock of the Faithful – The Sacred Cow). Islam is the great nomadic religion. Even in the Middle Ages the ecstatic dualist cults of the Bogomils and Albigenses had their origins in Manichaeanism and the shamanic traditions of the western end of the steppe – and they paved the way for the Reformation. The religious leaders of the civilised give way to the shamanic type of religious hero, the self-destructive evangelist, the celibate, the wandering dervish or divine healer. Note the difference between the Shakers (ecstatics) who shook themselves out of existence and the Mormons (enthusiasts) who aspired to the Presidency. The nomad renounces; he reflects in his solitude; he abandons collective rituals, and cares little for the rational processes of learning or literacy. He is a man of faith.

The Jewish diaspora obviously violates every attempt to categorise it. I would think it worth a chapter to itself. Title –? THE WANDERING JEW – a daunting subject. There are two questions I would like to ask – was Jewish 'exclusivism' kept alive by the loss of the 'Promised Land', their tribal territory? And were their energies diverted as a result towards the nomad's other great stand-by – portable gold?

Incidentally, while we are about it we can lay for all time the Great Aryan Myth; it surfaced again the other day in a new disguise – the wishful thinking of a frustrated lady archaeologist. Northern nomads – The Blond Brutes – were not the active masculine principle that fertilised an effete south. The Amazons are not my idea of femininity; they could not aspire to womanhood till they had killed their man. Neither are the Maenads nor the Bacchae. They were all nomad ladies. There must be some other explanation.

Chapter VIII will continue some more general aspects of nomadic behaviour, and may be called the NOMADIC SENSIBILITY; their sense of values; the importance of music (the drum and guitar are pre-eminently nomadic instruments); the craving for brilliant colour and the reassuring brilliance of gold. Nomads wear the most elaborate jewellery; a Bedou woman will wear her whole fortune around her neck; the nomads' roads to ecstasy – Turkish Baths, saunas, Indian hemp and mushrooms. Nomadic art is intuitive and irrational rather than analytic and static. I could use some illustrations to make my point and this chapter will obviously be expanded as I go along.

Chapter IX to be called the NOMADIC ALTERNATIVE calls into question the whole basis of civilisation, and is concerned with the present and future as much as the past. There have been two main inducements to wander, ECONOMIC and NEUROTIC. For example the International Set are neurotics. They have reached satiation point at home; so they wander – from tax-haven to tax-haven with an occasional raid on the source of their wealth – their base. How often has one heard the lamentation of an American expatriate at the prospect of a visit to his trustees in Pittsburgh. The same thing happened in the Roman Empire in the 3rd Century AD and later. The rich abdicated the responsibilities of their wealth; the cities became unendurable and at the mercy of property speculators. Wealth was divorced from its source. A strong state took over and collapsed under the strain. The rich wore their wealth, and the governments passed endless laws against extravagance in dress. Compare the diamonds and gold boxes of today, and the aura attached to portable possessions. The mobile rich were impossible to tax, the advantages of no-fixed address were obvious. So the unpredictable demands of the tax-collectors were laid at the feet of those who could least afford to pay. Wandering passed from the neurotic to the economic stage.

True nomads watch the passing of civilisation with equanimity; so does China, the unique combination of civilisation and barbarism. There is a good Egyptian text to illustrate the patronising attitude of the super-civilised in his self-confident days. 'The miserable Asiatic . . . he does not live in one place but his feet wander . . . he is not conquered, neither does he conquer. He may plunder a lonely settlement but he will never take a populous city.' Civilisations destroy themselves; nomads have never (to my certain knowledge) destroyed one, though they are never far away at the kill, and may topple a disintegrating structure. The civilised alone have control of their identity, and I do not believe in any of the cyclical theories of decline, fall and rebirth.

Now for today. We may have enough food even, but we certainly do not have enough room. Marshall McLuhan asks us to accept that literacy, the lynch-pin of civilisation is OUT; that electric technology is by-passing the 'rational processes of learning' and that jobs and <u>specialists</u> are things of the past. 'The world has become a Global Village,' he says. Or is it Mobile Encampments? 'The expert is the man who <u>stays put</u>.' Literature, he says, will disappear and the social barriers are coming down; everyone is free for the higher exercises of the mind (or spirit?). One thing is certain – the Paterfamilias, that bastion of civilisation (not the matriarch) is right OUT.

McLuhan is correct in much of his analysis of the effects of the new media. He does not seem to appreciate their probable long-term consequences. They are likely to be rather less than comfortable. The old nostalgic dream of a free classless society may indeed now be possible. But there are too many of us and there would have to be a drastic drop in population. Much of the world's population is on the move as never before, tourists, businessmen, itinerant labour, drop-outs, political activists etc. Like the nomads who first sat on a horse, we have again the means for total mobility. As anyone who owns a house knows, it is often cheaper to move than to stay. But this new Internationalism has activated a new parochialism. Separatism is rampant. Minorities feel threatened; small exclusive groups splinter off. The £50 travel allowance was not imposed for purely academic reasons.

Are these two trends not representative of the two basic human characteristics I mentioned earlier?

Yours ever,

Bruce Chatwin

P.S. Sorry I have a fiendish typewriter. B.C.

On 26 February 1969 Deborah Rogers submitted Chatwin's letter to Maschler. 'The idea is emerging with greater clarity as he progresses, despite the intentional looseness and preambly-ness of the enclosed. The next stage is probably for him to tackle a full chapter.' Maschler replied to Chatwin on 3 March 1969: 'I read the synopsis you will be amused to know in my cottage in the Black Mountains, surrounded by deep snow for miles in all directions. The book is indeed beginning to take shape, and to look exciting. Deborah mentioned that before you move onto the next stage, that

is to say, you tackle a full chapter, you would like to see me again
. . . I have a hunch, as we say.' On 13 March 1969 Maschler wrote
again: 'I do just want to put into writing that I am convinced it
will be an important book. Important in the way The Naked Ape
was important . . . I very much look forward to the first chapters
of the book just as soon as you can manage them.'

To Tom Maschler
c/o David Nash | 42 Eaton Square | London | 12 May 1969

Dear Tom,

I was delighted to get your letter. I'm sorry I didn't answer before, but my wife thought it was a bill and kept it from me. I have just returned from Tunis where I bought some South Sea sculpture[1] and tried to see some Sahara nomads, who, poor things, hardly exist in that mean little country. Algeria must be a better bet for them. Next week I hope to go to Le Mans. I have a new friend, a self-employed motor bicycle ace, who follows a prescribed range from Grand Prix to Grand Prix, and shows all the characteristics of a true nomad.

I am delighted with Desmond Morris's comments.[2] He's very kind to bother. I too have come to the same conclusion. The word NOMAD must go. It is too vague unless used in its strictest sense, that is a

1. A South Seas Maori door, covered with faces, sold to George Ortiz.
2. Desmond Morris to T.M., 4 April 1969: 'I was interested to read Bruce Chatwin's Nomad summary. It is positively bursting with ideas and clearly has the makings of an exciting book. Just the kind of thing I like. I have only one criticism . . . a matter of definition. What exactly is a nomad? It gets a little confusing at times as I read his chapter summaries . . . It seems to me that there is a fundamental psychological difference between wandering away and then back to a fixed base, on the one hand, and wandering from place to place without a fixed base, on the other. As I said in *The Naked Ape*, the moment man became a hunter, he had to have somewhere to come back to after the hunt was over. So a fixed base became natural for the species and we lost our old ape-like nomadism. Maybe the answer is to get rid of the word nomad altogether and think in initially vaguer terms of "HUMAN WANDERLUST". Then he can relate man's urge to be mobile to its different causes and functions without implying that he is dealing with the same basic phenomenon in each case.'

'wandering herdsman', and too loaded with emotional prejudices. In my view hobos and other dropouts are not nomads at all. They are vagrants. Nomadic wandering is purposive, and is usually contained within a fixed home range or territory. Vagrancy is aimless. I would have thought that the Jet Set are vagrants along with the tramps. After all both are parasitic, and one could never describe them as socially secure in this age. Their 'fabulous fixed home bases' are little more than temporary encampments.

Taking him up on his first point, total nomadism, herdsmen permanently on the move, evolved as a technology, in direct competition to the city's control over surrounding agricultural lands. The first true nomads came later than the first urban populations. To talk of hunting nomads or nomadic apes, as everyone does, is stretching the point.

I am leaving England in mid June to follow the Silk Route with Peter Levi. It's also the hippie route to Nepal. I'll be away about three months. I have been reading heavily in the literature of animal behaviour for my first chapter. When it's ready do you think Desmond Morris would look over it?

As ever, Bruce

Is Deborah back?

To Tom Maschler

c/o David Nash | 42 Eaton Square | London | 15 May 1969

Dear Tom,

The first will be a Wandering Beast chapter, preceded by an introduction. This you will have by October as I don't think it will be watertight before I go, although most of the notes are ready. I estimate that the manuscript should be ready to hack together by this time next year, that is providing we don't decide to enlarge it with a section on the Lone American, who is beginning to be a much more significant figure than I had imagined.

Desmond Morris has a very good point about the contrast of nomad and civilisation. I am beginning to think that there are two interlocking sets of ideas here which I should separate. The second set I should write as a sort of anarchist tract to be called the BARBARIC ALTERNATIVE,

as ever, B

On 26 May 1969 Stuart Piggott received a letter from Chatwin 'admitting that the idea of his becoming an academic archaeologist was a mistake and formally withdrawing'. Meanwhile, Chatwin prepared for his Afghan journey with Peter Levi. 'It was evident archaeology was over for him,' says the Italian archaeologist Maurizio Tosi, whom Chatwin introduced to Levi at Campion Hall. 'His references to archaeology were mainly humorous ... He spent one full day with me at the Institute of Archaeology to photograph pot shards from Baluchistan which I had been studying. But it was very much like an elder brother helping the naïve dreams of his younger brother. His eyes were shining with excitement only when he spoke about the trip to Afghanistan which he and Peter were to undertake that summer.' Chatwin invited Elizabeth to join them in August.

To Peter Levi

c/o Robert Erskine | 2 Cambridge Place | London | [May 1969]

Dear Peter,

Help! The Afghan Embassy have issued me with a transit visa of one week only. They require now that you write a supporting letter saying that I am going with you. What a performance. I suppose they imagine that I was some sort of hippie, and there was a terrible scene in which the consul was determined not to lose face. Can you please write two letters, one to him, the other to me. He says it'll only take a day. It is the never never land of the nearly impossible!

As ever, B

PS We both need <u>3 month</u> visas and must say so.

To Elizabeth Chatwin
c/o British Embassy | Kabul | Afghanistan | 6 July 1969

Have just been up a mountain at 12,000 ft and we're both feeling rather whacked out from the heat. We're hiring a Land-Rover for a fortnight at vast expense but it does seem to be the best way of getting about. Very comfortably installed in the Embassy in a wholly unreal atmosphere of the latter day British Empire.

XXX B

To Elizabeth Chatwin
c/o British Embassy | Kabul | Afghanistan | 12 July 1969

We went to Isfahan by air at a vast extravagance. British School in Teheran was populated by the most awful Cambridge archaeologists you can imagine. Breathing tomb fungus. We barged in on the Bala Hissar, a military fort, and both got lashed at by a very irate infantryman with his belt. Very uncomfortable but in fact quite funny. Flowers are still marvellous. Ambassadress a botanist. Have arranged to stay with the second secretary.[1] Would you be prepared to come at a cable's notice. Get your jabs, visa etc NOW for Afghanistan. Prepare to leave early August.

To Kenneth Rose
c/o British Embassy | Kabul | Afghanistan | 12 July 1969

The embassy was built to the order of Curzon to dominate Kabul. Kabul grew the other way and it is now stranded like an English country house. There no flowers grow that one wouldn't find in the Home Counties. As I sit one can hear the noise of tennis balls and click of croquet mallets. We are off to Badakhstan in a day or so. By mistake we infringed the military area in the Bala Hissar and were belted by an outraged infantryman, inflamed by the heat of the day and our retreating hindquarters . . . Bruce

1. Christopher Rundell.

To Elizabeth Chatwin
c/o British Embassy | Kabul | Afghanistan | 21 July 1969

Dear E.

Have just returned from the mountains of Ghor, and have visited the minaret of Jam etc on horse 4 day trek. Cholera raging in Herat and there's no question of getting out of Afghanistan while it continues. Also (wait for it) I have seen and photographed The Mausoleum of Gohar Shad in the heart of a military area being the first (I believe) person to do so except for a Russian lady from Tashkent, and this is the monument that D[erek] has been longing to get at for years but was refused permission. I simply got myself up in a turban and fitted a jeep with Afghans, presented bottles of coca cola to the soldiers and drove by. Whoopee! I hope that I have been taking some rather sensational photos and so I am not too discouraged about finance. Guy H[1] should have paid you £312.10.0 already and they will owe me the same amount on Aug 25 as they are back-dating my retainer (which I have accepted and the hell with the rest of all those backbiters!). So what I suggest is this — that as it is really bloody hot here, and as Peter, I think, is quite ill — drinking bad water against my advice — and also as I am only going to pay rather a perfunctory visit to Pakistan — that we meet somewhere in Western rather than Central Asia on or around Aug 25th. This will have given me time to photograph the North — I have permissions to go right up to the Oxus and Badakshan — go to photograph Nuristan for a few days — pass on to Swat, Dir and Hunza then fly back from Lahore or Karachi. Now as always when I am festering away in exotic climates I have a longing for CIVILISATION with a capital C. and I suggest that the best thing may be for you to drive the car to Rome/or Athens if you can face it though I don't really see much point except that I may have rather a lot of books to carry home — having extricated the £812 from Guy Hannon on say

1. Guy Hannon, managing director of Christie's. Chatwin had agreed to work for Christie's on an annual retainer of £1,250. On 7 June, on his way to Kabul, he flew with Hannon to Cairo on an abortive mission to secure the sale of the contents of the Cairo Museum.

Aug 10 instead of the 24th. You would then fly either to Teheran (which I doubt the merit of) or to Cairo depending on whether they want me there) or to Cyprus (if I can get there from Cairo – which I must be able to do via Beirut) or possibly Ankara or Istanbul. I will certainly take you to Istanbul as I want to go and look at the Fatih Album properly. We will go to Patmos to stay with Teddy [Millington-Drake]. In short I think the best way of arranging all this may be as follows. You meet me in Cairo – car in Athens or alone. My baggage sent on ahead from Kabul – air freight – we then go by air to Cyprus – boat to Rhodes – Patmos – cross to Turkey (Smyrna) Istanbul – Athens and back. How's that?[1] Then on the return through Italy <u>Tuscany</u> etc and the <u>Dordogne</u> late Sept.

I have realised several things on this trip. You know – they are very good for me. They act as purgatives. a. I have decided to condemn Miss Smallclothes . . . and that lot to a bottomless perdition and not to speak to them again. b. I am pleased about it and have decided to act upon it. c. I am going to be a serious, and <u>systematic</u> writer d. I am fed to the back teeth by the happy hippie hashishish culture, (jail is the answer) and the artworld (<u>finally</u>) and the little Bo-Peeps Corps,[2] and it's just as well one isn't a member of the drop-out generation (just). e. I love you.

XXXX B

To Elizabeth Chatwin
Postcard of camels, Nekzad Market | Kabul | Afghanistan | 21 July 1969

This CANCELS letter if you get either in time. Finance isn't all that bad in view of Christie's extra £600. Please COME now. Take the car to ROME and fly via Teheran. On arrival contact Chris Rundle 2nd Sec at Embassy who will put you up if we are out of town, as we are leaving for 10 days to the NORTH. We will then all go to Nuristan before going to W. Pakistan. On return I want to have a few days in Teheran before

1. E.C.: 'I flew straight to Kabul. Can you imagine me driving all that way by myself?'
2. Peace Corps.

flying to CAIRO if Christie's want me to. If you come later than Aug 1st here there is really no point in spending all that money for 3 weeks. I fancy a drive through Italy and France as an antidote to all this. Guy Hannon will I am sure give you extra cash as my retainer which was backdated to March comes due on Aug 24. Please bring basic minimum in clothing as I am horribly overweight and am contemplating AIR-freighting my stuff to Rome or England from here. Please ensure that yr cholera is OK as there is a scare. 15 rolls Colour Ektachrome 35 shots to each. Ask Semple[1] to give you £100 if he wants me to buy cheap and v. good kelims, dhurries etc. More if he can spare it as there is plenty to be bought. I'll account to him. If you can't make it please cable and I suggest we meet up in Cairo Athens or Istanbul. Mrs Seiferbitch,[2] Madame Smallclothes, Master Rash and the ever-exploding S[3] can all boil in their own filth. xxxxxx B.

Pay for fare if poss. Also get £200 from Hannon. Finance not so desperate. £1250 from Xties. Good prospects for book etc

To Derek Hill
Patmos | Greece | 19 September 1969

Well, I have a couple of tiles from Masud's Palace (probably) at Ghazni. I jolly nearly got out a large piece of marble frieze, but honestly showed it to the Museum who promptly seized it. This shows honesty does not pay necessarily. I am longing to see you. I hope with successful photographs of the Mausoleum of Gohar Shad at Khosan – probably the most beautiful of all Timurid buildings. AND those of the Nouh Goumbed at Balkh which escaped the notice of the ever-unobservant French though they surveyed and excavated not half a mile away – a mosque of the 9th century with brick work as fine as Sultan Ismail at Bokhara and vine scroll stuccos finer and earlier than

1. John Semple, Arabist with antique shop in Lower Sloane Street.
2. Helene C. Seiferheld, New York dealer. She had rented Grosvenor Crescent Mews off Bruce.
3. Illegible.

Naylu. Have also located but not seen the Gate of the Arabs which has a brick mosque probably of the 10th/11th Cent at 11,000 ft in the Hindu Kush.

To Peter Levi
Holwell Farm | Wotton-under-Edge | Glos | [Winter 1969]

Dear Peter,

I have just found a piece of paper on which is scrawled in your handwriting 'The 9th Century Mosque at Balkh, the Lion Throne, 4 copies of the horse photo.' The horse photo I trust you now have. In enlargement you really do have a savage look . . .

I shall be going to America immediately after Christmas to devote myself to many forms of Oriental art and, worse, people devoted to Oriental Art. Thence I shall go to Morocco, I suppose to devote myself to Orientals, if such they can be called in the Far West.

Very interesting the use of the word 'nomad' as a term of abuse in the Sharon Tate murder case.[1] 'A band of hate oriented 20th century nomads' is as bad a condemnation as one can get. I have written two chapters of my book. Then I decided they were boring. So they will have to be rewritten. If only I didn't have an argument to follow. Arguments are fatal. One always forgets what they're about.

Love, Bruce

PS Try and come here before you go.

Late in 1969, at Howard Hodgkin's house near Bath, Chatwin met the American film director James Ivory. A friend of Cary Welch, who nicknamed him 'Jungle Jim', Ivory was preparing to make his fourth feature film, 'Bombay Talkie'.

---

1. American actress (1943–69) m. 1967 to film director Roman Polanski; she was murdered when eight months pregnant by followers of Charles Manson.

To James Ivory
9 Kynance Mews[1] | London | December 8 1969

Dear Jim,

I have just returned to a grey London from the country, where I have written a chapter of my book, and decided on the train that the whole thing must be rewritten. This evening I am spending with someone called Galt MacDermott who wrote the music of *Hair*. In a moment of enthusiasm, or rather infatuated by a member of the cast,[2] I wrote a scenario for a musical one bright spring day. It has been languishing around ever since, but now sparks from elsewhere, scriptwriters, lyric writers and musicians. What a performance! The Living Theatre. And furthermore lunch with Noel Coward on Friday. I'm a sucker for theatrical camp. Hence the Mongol outfit.

Alas I am gradually being railroaded into going to New York after Christmas, to the extent that I have just reserved the tickets. I have this wretched Asia House Exhibition, shared with two supermale ladies, who are sharpening their knives. Other forms of torture are being greased and oiled for the intrepid English amateur who has dared plant his unwary feet on the hallowed ground of American scholarship. I received the official invitation to meet myself in the presence of Mrs Rockefeller; this has its comic implications. Charmed to meet myself but nobody else. The opening of the show is for the 14th, and I will possibly linger on for some days after. I intend to go to Morocco, and then possibly to Mauretania, one of the great unknowns. I'd vastly prefer to come your way, and go to the south, but immediate financial prospects are not that favourable for the enterprise.

I went to the Kervorkian Sale of miniatures,[3] and fiddled around with low bids on some of the grander numbers. I came away with a

1. In April Chatwin had signed a short lease on 9 Kynance Mews.
2. Peter Straker, a 19-year-old Jamaican, played the part of Hud in *Hair*. Chatwin believed that he resembled the Pharaoh Akenaten. The outline for Chatwin's musical is lost, although Straker remembers its drift: the sun-worshipping and hermaphroditic Pharaoh uproots his court from Thebes to the desert, getting away from old conventions.
3. At Sotheby's on 1 December.

Jahanghir period picture of an Arctic Tern,[1] the bird that has the longest migration of any species. It is like the best of the animal painting of the period, but a bit rubbed. Beautiful clear line of the wing and tail feathers. Your Basawan[2] sounds wonderful. You can always find things wherever you go. Two days in the auction room brought back a flood of gruesome memories. The nervous anxiety of the bidder's face as he or she waits to see if she can afford to take some desirable thing home to play with. Like old men in nightclubs deciding whether they can really afford to pay that much for a whore. But things are so much better. You can sell them, touch 'em up at any time of the day, and they don't answer back. H[oward] H[odgkin] came to dinner the other night and told me that he and Kasmin[3] acquired some Devgarh pictures which sounds fine. I am perhaps going to try and buy one.

One day I want to make a really long and slow trip right across Asia, by the most obscure frontier posts and along the least frequented routes. I would write the whole thing into a semi-imaginary picaresque journey, which is a form that has always appealed to me. Have you ever read a weird book called *The Asiatics* by Frederick Prokosch,[4] a bit hammy in parts, but really quite interesting. It would be a way for me to incorporate all my fragmented diaries of episodes of my travels. I have always thought that an archaeological fraud film has possibilities. I was once very closely involved in one, which in reality was far more fantastic than anything one could ever write. It had everything from the Persian Royal Family, Armenian ladies in Beirut, American Museum directors, and a leprous-faced recluse living in the Place Vendome, writing and rewriting an imaginary biography of the young Michelangelo.

Till January 8th I'll be in the country. Holwell Farm.

Do write. I had a good time too.

Bruce

1. The Arctic Tern was one of few works of art he kept, along with the Peruvian feathered cape.
2. Mughal painter (1550–1610).
3. John Kasmin (*b*.1934), British art dealer.
4. *The Asiatics* (1935), picaresque novel featuring a nameless 22-year-old American who walked, hitchhiked and sometimes travelled in luxury from Beirut to Damascus and across India to China.

To Derek Hill
9 Kynance Mews | London | 8 January 1970

Off on Thursday morning with Penelope Betjeman to New York[1] ...
So the machinations of Sir Noel[2] worked – I'm really glad. Think of all
the theatrical knights one has never heard of – let alone seen. love, B

*In the spring of 1970 Chatwin submitted an untitled chapter of
his book to Tom Maschler. On 23 March an anonymous reader at
Cape reported back:*

*'Bruce Chatwyn [sic] is obviously a lively-minded and content-
ious young man, not afraid to take a swipe at all the ethnologists
within reach and some out of it ... His sample chapter is all over
the place but I am inclined to think that it would be better to give
him his head for the moment and let him do his own disciplining
as he goes along, which I have a hunch he will, cutting out the
wilder digressions and more outrageous statements, which only
damage the impression made by his more sensible ideas. He sets
out to explain the wandering urge in man, which is an interesting
basis for a book, and if he keeps his eye on the subject he may
produce a rather good book.'*

To James Ivory
Holwell Farm | Wotton-under-Edge | Glos | 9 April 1970

Found your letter on arrival back from Mauretania – probably the most
pleasant country on earth in which to travel. Had intended writing about
it for travel magazines etc but how could one write for the <u>public</u> about
a place where police are non-existent as well as passport controls? Nothing
but blue men walking through orange and purple landscapes and a few
left over Spanish who run their settlements as brothels for imported
Senegalese. Should be here in the summer unless I go to rent a little

1. For the opening of the Asia House Exhibition.
2. Noel Coward had been awarded a knighthood.

house in Patmos to write in June/July. Will inform. Flat let in London.[1]
Money exhausted by journey. Love B

To James Ivory
Holwell Farm | Wotton-under-Edge | Glos | 21 May 1970

Dear Jim,

Letters from you and Cary [Welch] today. A good post. Cary in fine form having, he says, bought a farm in New Hampshire, where the Welches can retire to and grow vegetables if the WORST COMES TO THE WORST as many people seem to be predicting in America right now: though in the unlikely event of that happening, I dare say there would be hordes of hungry barbarians in flashy clothes, probably on horseback,[2] who would dig into their radish patch with their swords (ammunition being no longer available). Small quick crops of quick growing things like cress would be all that would have time to grow before the hordes swept down again. The key to the whole thing surely is that book *The Making of the President*;[3] nothing is more violence inducing than a sense of individual powerlessness.

You must be bloody hot out there. You might let me know if you're going to be there next winter, because we have plans to come in October and remain till May. I want to go if possible to Sikkim in the spring and also to the far south in the winter. This is something that has been planned for four years, and as with all long term plans I shall only decide two weeks beforehand.

I spend the weeks in Oxford now, heavily disguised as a skiiing undergraduate, and, I confess, celebrating my thirtieth birthday with a skittish affair. Merton College, jasmine tea, shades of Max Beerbohm[4],

1. To Oliver Hoare, the carpet expert at Christie's, on the stipulation that Bruce and Elizabeth had squatting rights once a week.
2. E.C.: 'I had a horse at Holwell Farm and I was approached by someone saying "Because you have a horse, you'll be able to get around. Will you help?" There was a doom atmosphere, as if everything was going to collapse.'
3. *The Making of the President – 1960* by Theodore H. White, about the 1960 presidential race between Senator John F. Kennedy and Vice-President Richard M. Nixon.
4. Max Beerbohm (1872–1956), English caricaturist.

red lacquer, ecclesiastical drag, mystical excesses of the Early Church Fathers combined with the intellectual mentality of Ronald Firbank.[1] You get the picture? <u>Not serious</u>, very pretty.

I may go to Patmos in July and August, where I have undertaken to rent a house, providing a. I have finished my so-called research b. I have the funds. Do you know that island? The most beautiful in all the Aegean. Couldn't you come there?

Off to Ireland for a week or so then here.

Do write.

love B

To Derek Hill
Holwell Farm | Wotton-under-Edge | Glos | 8 June [1970]

In the course of a letter to Hill, Elizabeth wrote:'They are thinking of making a film of Lady Sale.[2] Don't you think Loelia[3] would be perfect as the star?' Chatwin then added this PS:

Do you know the story of her retreat from Kabul? Refusal to cut her personal staff below 46. Insistence on removing her grand piano down the gorge in midwinter, and solemn devotion to her needle-work throughout capture and possibe rape. L[oelia] wouldn't have to act.

Dog has torn up my last jersey, but it is all quiet without the parrot[4] for whose continued absence I pray. Love B

---

1. Ronald Firbank (1886–1926), English novelist.
2. Lady Florentia Sale, *Journal of the Disaster in Afghanistan, 1841–2.*
3. Loelia, Duchess of Westminster (1902–93).
4. E.C.: 'I had a parrot before I was married and gave it away and I moaned and groaned so Bruce got me an African grey. It hated men, and Bruce couldn't go anywhere near it – even if it saw Bruce through the window it would shriek. I gave it back to the vendor.'

To Elizabeth Chatwin
Chora | Patmos | Greece | [July 1970]

Monday

Dear E.,

Am very well installed after an uneventful journey with the Father[1] who sends you his love. We stayed two days in Athens with his friends, which was not entirely thrilling except for one hilarious interlude. *La Vache sacrée* of American anthropology, Margaret Mead[2] no less, at luncheon in a restaurant with her students – or rather her menagerie, one of each ethnic type from Eskimo to Javanese, obviously all hating each other and her in particular. She, garrulous and white fleshed, held forth on a number of very audible topics. When I heard her say 'Well, I think we've got a bunch of silly egalitarian ideas about the place,' I fixed her with my well known acid blue glare, and if it didn't shut her up entirely, at least it made her profoundly nervous.

Ginette Camu, Bill Bernhard and Thilo von Watzdorf's brother are here.[3] Otherwise the horde has not yet descended. The weather is perfect, and the *melteme* doesn't come for another fortnight. I am feeling human again. As one gets older, one realises that there are some places that suit one, and others that emphatically do not. One can only find out by experience. Paris and this place are two of them. I don't think we could afford to live in Paris, but I must say I wouldn't mind a try. Can you let me know how you get on with the unholy alliance of trustees? Please also can you contact David and Judy [Nash] at 42, Eaton Square, and retrieve from them the Inca as and when you take the feathers.[4] Please be doubly careful of the

1. Peter Levi.
2. Margaret Mead (1901–78) American anthropologist. Her daughter Catherine Bateson had been at Radcliffe with Elizabeth.
3. Friends of Teddy Millington-Drake. Ginette Camu, a famous Belgian beauty m. to Bernard Camu, banker and bon vivant; William L. Bernhard, who bought a ruin in Patmos; Stephan von Watzdorf, brother of Thilo who worked at Sotheby's.
4. A poncho with checker-board patterns, sold to finance Chatwin's journey to Patagonia. The feathers were a rectangular hanging of blue and yellow parrot feathers, possibly intended for an Inca temple, discovered in an earthenware drum near the River Ocana in Peru. Bruce and Elizabeth had bought the feathers in New York with their wedding money.

frame, and use blankets. Remember it is very heavy, heavier than you would think, and once the edges are bashed up it will be very difficult to repair.

When a book comes from Blackwells for me by Bruning, called *Biological Clocks*,[1] will you let me know at once. Then I will have you send it to someone coming out here like Ron[2] . . . Clem and Jessie[3] were well in Paris, and were driving to Greece today. Poor Iain Watson[4] had bronchial pneumonia which loused up their plans for Istanbul.

Incidentally, that gramophone record we heard at Derek [Hill]'s was *Autour du Celebre canon de Pachelbel*. I just found the note of it today. Why do you not order a copy from Discurio in Shepherd's Market?

The post takes for ages – about one week from London, and so we will have to cable if anything becomes urgent. Work begins in earnest in two days time. Meanwhile I have swum several miles, and will swim several more.

B

P.S. Will you buy 2 small Winsor-Newton Watercolour brushes for me. I only have the smallest and 2 large.

P.S. Can you try and do something for me? It is rather complicated. Either at the Bodleian or the British Museum they have services for photo-copying articles. I have decided that I must have that famous Lorenz article copied and then translated. The reference is . . . Konrad Lorenz, *Die Angeborengen Formen Moglisher Erfahrung in Zoologische Tierpsychologie*, V, 1943, pp. 235–409. (God help us for the number of pages) I shall need it directly I get back and will have to find someone to translate it. If the cost is desperate, obviously don't do it. The Bodleian card number is 20374 if they have any queries.

1. J. L. Bruning, *Biological Clocks in Seasonal Reproductive Cycles* (1968).
2. Ron Gurney, Quaker banker; Chatwin had met Penelope Betjeman at his house near Wantage.
3. Clem Wood married to Jessie, daughter of Louise de Vilmourin, shared a house with the Welches on Spetsai.
4. Iain Watson (*b*.1942) m. in 1967 Miranda Rothschild (*b*.1940). Miranda was, in her own description, 'a tragic young widow'. In 1964 her previous husband, an Algerian, had been assassinated as a gun-runner. 'I found him in a charnel pit.' Rescued by her mother, Barbara Ghika, who discovered her in a hut living off worms, she went to live in Athens with her two-year-old daughter, Da'ad Boumaza.

To Elizabeth Chatwin
Chora | Patmos | Greece | 1 August 1970

Dear E.,

. . . You may complain of my lefty views, but God I'm right. We have the daughters of the upper classes here in force and I have been listening to a baklava of snobbery and prejudice for the past week. Maxime McKendry[1] and John are here, which is quite fun, but they are rather brittle too. Shilly shallying conversation and no desire to go to the beach. I go down and talk to Irina[2] occasionally in her little house. Otherwise nothing. I would sell the car if you want to. I really don't care for it as you know, though as I definitely do not want one myself I leave it entirely to you.

Heaven knows what we can do about the money situation. If you like why don't you flog those chairs back again if you feel it would solve anything. Also if you feel like it, I have a mustard pot that could go.

I am not particularly keen on entering India with cash on the black in Kabul if I am only coming in with a rucksack. I simply can't think why you can't arrange your money problems in India in advance. I shall take about £150 of my own, but I am not keen on the idea of being searched. Please get in touch with Robert [Erskine] and ask him what he does over his picture buying. I cannot believe you would have to get the rates of the bank.

I sold the dagger[3] for about £120 which I have in cash. The bed shop was closed and so I shall probably arrange it[4] on my return through Paris. On the other hand I have become more and more anti-possession minded except perhaps for 2 little portable things, that I really may scotch it. You can also flog the Anglo-Indian chair of mine which I certainly

1. Maxime Birley (1922–2009), fashion model, food writer and mother of Louise ('Loulou') de la Falaise (b.1948), m. to John McKendry, curator of prints and photographs at the Metropolitan Museum of Art, who influenced Robert Mapplethorpe to take photography seriously.
2. Irina, elderly Greek woman who lived by herself.
3. A Mogul, jade-handled dagger.
4. A Napoleonic campaign bed, supposedly 'Marshal Ney's steel campaign bed with its original lime green hangings'.

don't want and never really liked, though I would like the money to go towards the thing I bought in Christies, which is <u>marvellous</u>.

. . . The other thing is that I think the best thing would be to get the flat off my hands, so when O.[1] arrives back if it's not before you come out, what do you think about setting that up too? Or perhaps you might find out from the Grosvenor estate what they have going in the way of one-roomers or two roomers.

The writing is not coming along too badly. I have done two chapters in the rough. I have a new method and am leaving whole sections very rough and charging on to finish and absorb all the material before cutting and polishing. As you know I make no promises as to when it will be finished but it should be by November. Where the hell's name am I going to stay in England? I really cannot see why I shouldn't have the use of the house and my study until I go, and I think you'd better warn Monica[2] accordingly, though Lord knows I don't find her exactly palatable company.

Margaret Mead plainly the Queen of Hags

Love B

To Elizabeth Chatwin
Chora | Patmos | Greece | 12 August 1970

Dear E.,

God how the time flies. Have written nearly 40,000 words and that isn't fast enough. I keep on getting terribly stuck for two or three days at a go, and then it starts to come right again. Am just rewriting the first three chapters again for the fourth time.

This letter is being posted in London by M. Van den Bosch, the Belgian Ambassador, who is leaving for London tonight. We have had some really sweltering windless days and Chora sizzled. Tremendous

1. Oliver Hoare (b.1945), with whom Chatwin shared 9 Kynance Mews. B.C. diary: 'V restless as myself, v likeable and attractive.' He later achieved celebrity as one of the Princess of Wales's lovers.
2. Monica, a dressmaker, who lived on the top floor at Holwell.

drama when Bessie Schwartzenberg's mother collapsed of a haemorrhage caused by heatstroke and died at once. Then Bernard Camu reported to have skin cancer in New York and they are all leaving at once. Magouche Phillips[1] is here and quite wonderful, a great relief after rather a procession of fine looking but dreary ladies. I couldn't have been more pleased when Maxime McKendry left. God what a bore. Forever reminiscing about amusing *boites* on the Left Bank in the old days when we were young and gay. Then followed by alcoholic soulful looks. If you see Ron [Gurney], can you put some coriander and cumin in a little package as I want to do the <u>fainting imam</u>.[2] Also you couldn't I suppose send me another little Schaffers[3] as mine disappeared from the room together with my penknife, but I don't think I can make a fuss about it. I shall go from here to Samos, then to Smyrna and Istanbul when you are about to appear, then come back here for a fortnight or so; after that I can use Peter [Levi]'s room in Athens until I am ready to go to London. Iain [Watson] and Miranda [Rothschild] hate Istanbul so that is that. God alone knows what they'll do about it all.

Magouche is very funny about her ex-husband and yesterday we went on very long walks. Letter from my Romanian admirer. I seem to think he was the station master of the logging railway, or he may have been an archaeologist or the beekeeper. I can't be sure but have sent him a postcard.

I really think the answer is NO to Straker. It[4] is quite unsuitable to be worn out in the open at all, and I won't have it rained on by all that filthy Edinburgh. Apologetic regrets. It would swamp him anyway.

Must get on with Martin Buber.[5]

xxxxxxxxxxxx B

1. Agnes Jean Magruder (*b*.1921), Boston-born daughter of American naval commodore, m. 1st Arshile Gorky 1941–48, Armenian artist who coined the nickname 'Mougouch', which meant 'my little powerful one' in Russian; 2nd John C. Phillips Jr in 1950; 3rd Xan Fielding in 1979.
2. Turkish dish with aubergine.
3. E.C.: 'He liked fountain pens. Like books, they had to be guarded.'
4. E.C.: 'A beautiful ikat chapan from Afghanistan, a man's silk coat put on over garments, as worn by Hamid Kharzai.'
5. Martin Buber (1878 –1965), Austrian-Israeli philosopher.

To Elizabeth Chatwin
Kardamyli | Messenia | Greece | [30 August 1970]

Dear E.

I am sitting on the terrace of Paddy and Joan Leigh Fermor's[1] house in the Mani. Quite heavenly here. The whole Taygetos range plunges straight down into the sea and eagles float in thermals above the house – a low arcaded affair of limestone beautifully marked with red karst. Olives and pencil thin cypress clothe the terrace between the mountains and the sea. From the house one can dip into the water. Magouche Phillips and I came here from Patmos having spent 2 days in Athens to get my teeth seen to[2]. We were both rather glad to go. Apart from the nannying that went on, Patmos is the most enervating place – bar Edinburgh – I have ever spent any time on. One was really ready for the Revelation.[3] Beautiful though it is – the wind howls – or it blisters in the sun, those pinnacles of jagged rock finally pierce through to the subconscious. Smart English girls of brittle conversation burst into tears after a week. No food or water, but above all that terrible feeling of not being able to get off which is psychologically devastating. If I hadn't had something to do I would have gone mad. As it is I <u>have</u> done – in the <u>rough,</u> five chapters each of about 12,000 words, despite constant interruptions. I am not exactly thrilled by all of it – and it can be polished and resorted later, but still it is something done instead of flailing about.

I am coming to the conclusion that there is no point at all in coming back to England in the autumn. Llama Ghika[4] has got to be in Athens all the time which bores her stiff and I can sit in a sort of penthouse they

1. (Sir) Patrick Leigh Fermor (*b.*1915); author, living in Greece; m. 1968 Hon. Joan Eyres-Monsell, photographer (1912–2003), whom he had met in wartime Cairo.
2. E.C.: 'He had an infection of the jaw. Eventually, I sent him to my London dentist, Russell King, who sorted him out.'
3. E.C.: 'Everything having been paradise on earth suddenly turned into the biggest bore. It happened everywhere, except the Black Hill.'
4. Barbara ('Llama') Hutchinson (1911–89) m. 1st 3rd Baron Rothschild, 2nd Rex Warner, 3rd Nico Hadjikyriakou-Ghika, painter and sculptor; mother of Miranda Rothschild.

have – or in Peter [Levi]'s room which is the nicest room in Athens facing Lycabettus, the Parthenon, Hymettus and the sea. Going back to England would only disrupt the book further and make me a month later in India by the time one had got there and I really do think it will/or can be ready in its first draft by <u>November</u> (early). I would then send a copy to London – and get them to annotate a version and have it sent to India somewhere. Anyway going back to England is bound to cost £200 at least by the time one has fiddled about. I suggest therefore we meet in Salonika – if you pass through Salonika on yr Istanbul voyage + 1 winter suit and some cold weather clothes for Turkey in winter. <u>Gloves</u>, my windjammer <u>rucksack</u> – the one I had for Mauretania and boots and new laces and socks. Also you'd better bring my camera en route. I don't know quite what to do about money, but I believe I do get £1,000 on delivery of the manuscript. The other thing that has struck me is that <u>I</u> might establish non-residence in England this year in case any decent money ever came from it. Apparently I can – for a time – become non-resident without you at all – and after next July 15 would anyway be entitled to 3 months in England. Anyhow we can discuss it. I do suggest that you pre-pay a cable to the Nash's in N.Y for permission to get out the Inca Poncho before you leave – and apprise Oliver [Hoare] and Ferdy Mayne[1] that I don't want the flat. We should rescue the <u>bed</u> and the <u>Navaho</u> carpet – and that spit roaster (but I'm not sure about the latter because it's on the H/P with the frig). Anyhow I'd be prepared to let the whole thing go and those beastly cushions if I did not have any expense of any kind to <u>pay</u>. If you can't arrange it I suppose H.P.C. [Hugh Chatwin] can be called in if necessary. If the Maori[2] sells, it sells. If it doesn't I'm not sorry because damn it it is still a very good

1. Ferdy Mayne (1916–98) owner of Kyance Mews studio leased by Chatwin; MI5 informant and German actor, famous for playing Count von Krolock in Roman Polanski's 1967 film *The Fearless Vampire Killers*.
2. A bargeboard from a Polynesian hut that had belonged to the actress Sarah Bernhardt, who used it as a bedhead. On 30 June 1968 E.C. wrote to her mother: 'Bruce has swapped the Greek head for a fantastic piece of Maori sculpture, for which he has already been offered more than twice what he paid. It belonged to Sarah Bernhardt: she brought it back in 1902 when she made a tour of New Zealand & she bought it from an already old collection then.'

work of art. Robin Symes[1] was in Patmos with a couple of King's Road shits. Don't wear well in the sun those antiques boys – they acquire a fake patina. I do want that Maori piece paid for and collected at Christie's – a great buy quite beautiful – also the Arctic Tern is at Pollack Blue Boar Yard[2] and should be ready mid Sept if you had time.

Very entertaining <u>here</u>. Much more my style than those brittle conversations about blokes and sofas.

write c/o Nikos Ghika, Kricozotov 3, Athens

xxxx B

PS Let me have yr dates + itinerary soonest. May want to meet you <u>Igoumenitza</u> if I go to see the <u>Vlachs</u>.[3]

To Derek Hill
Corfu | Greece | [September 1970]

Dear D

Patmos was buzzing with the helicopters of <u>your</u> friends. Visits from Jackie and Lee[4] disturbing the Revelation. Would to God that Greece was preserved as overleaf – as it is bad Beaulieu-sur-Mer in summer – with an overdose of hippies – decapitations under LSD on Spetsai – and new love from island to island for the rich. May go direct from here to India – await the yellow caravan of ladies in Salonika, Love B

In September 1970 Elizabeth set off for India in a converted yellow grocery delivery van, an eight-month expedition that would take in India, Afghanistan, Iran and Turkey. Her passengers were Elizabeth Cuthbert, a schoolteacher, and the artist John Nankivell ('a young male pencil artist of real talent', John Betjeman wrote to Stuart Piggott). The journey was made at the instigation of

1. London antiquities dealer, sentenced in January 2005 to two years in prison; he served seven months.
2. Framer.
3. Nomadic shepherds inhabiting the northern Greek mountains and central Balkans.
4. Jaqueline Kennedy Onassis and her younger sister Lee Radzwill. E.C.: 'Derek knew everybody.'

*Penelope Betjeman who wished to investigate pagoda temples in
the western Himalayas. Betjeman herself drove in a second Morris
van with another artist, Elizabeth Simson. Chatwin,
originally to be part of the group, reneged. He did, though, agree
to meet Elizabeth and Penelope in Istanbul and to show them the
city before the next stage of the journey, and to meet up with them
again in India once he had finished his book.*

To Charles and Margharita Chatwin
Postcard, ancient houses of Istanbul | Turkey | 28 September 1970

[Elizabeth's handwriting] B just getting his train ticket to Paris & should
be with you in a week. This is a marvellous place – we leave Wed for
Anatolia & beyond.

[Chatwin's handwriting] Overeating here – stuffed mussels with
hazelnut sauce. Starvation trip on train without sleeping car. Discipline
needed in Stratford, please work all day – exercise at weekends.

XX B

To Derek Hill
Postcard, compote service of gold encrusted with diamonds,
Topkapi Sarayi | Istanbul | Turkey | 28 September 1970

If only you had the money for this <u>and</u> Wemyss Ware. Much love Bruce
and Elizabeth

To Patrick Leigh-Fermor
Yenikoy 177 | Istanbul | Turkey | 1 October 1970

Dear Paddy,
        . . . Unfortunately, I have to return to England because our tenant[1]

1. Monica, the dressmaker, had married a policeman.

ratted two days before Elizabeth left with Penelope and the rest of the caravan for India. The house cannot be left untended, and I go on the Orient Express tomorrow. I'll look out the Comparative Dictionary of Indo-European languages for you in Blackwell's, and would like to give you some of it as a present anyway. Do let me know if you have already done anything about it.

I escorted the caravan of ladies and their one sensationally ineffective gentleman across the Bosphorus. I dread the result. The cars lost each other for five days in Yugoslavia and Bulgaria. One attempted rape on Penelope and her friend by a Turkish infantryman in a maize field near Edirne. Penelope selflessly offered herself instead of the girl. Offer finally accepted as rescue came. Not before the soldier himself had offered five Turkish lire, his week's pay, for the younger specimen. In Istanbul two exposures behind bushes, from sailors; but if the ladies will picnic in Gulahane park on a Sunday . . .

I have just returned from watching a party of fishermen hauling a drowned horse from under Galata Bridge, and am now going to the hammam.

As ever Bruce

To Elizabeth Chatwin
Holwell Farm | Wotton-under-Edge | Glos | 15 October 1970

Dear E.,

Have just had your letter from Malatya. That John [Nankivell] does sound unbearable and spoilt. I'm very sorry I simply can't send 100 dollars as the financial situation is as you said rather desperate. I have decided to go down to barricade myself into Holwell because it is terribly confined here. Linda,[1] I must say, keeps the place like a surgery except that the flies in the upper room are appalling and make it impossible. I

1. To cover running costs, the Chatwins had loaned Holwell Farm to Linda Wroth, a girlfriend of John Michell. Chatwin had walked with her in Wales; on 13 December 1969 he described Linda in his diary as having 'the wide staring intense eyes of the American intellectual initiate'.

shall occupy the bedroom. Stayed in London with the Knight and Olda[1] in their very agreeable new house in Fulham Road area.

Drama in excelsis about my teeth which were the cause of real anxiety. For a week they made tests on the tissue of the gum to make sure it wasn't <u>cancer</u>. The teeth may have to come out anyway and the gold filling removed. Incompetently done in the first place and rubbing for years caused it. I had visions of half my jaw coming off, and got rather alarmed. Mr King has been very good about it all, but I have to have about six sessions before they will be able to clear it up. The cost! I shall probably have to flog a few things to keep going, and might sell the Pomeranian suite. Sandy[2] thinks he's sold the Maori, but then he permanently seems to think he's sold it and no money is forthcoming. The Nashes are here. The Arctic Tern has arrived back and looks marvellous. *Vogue* delighted with the piece I dashed off in a morning and are paying £200 for it.

Now UTA[3] are prepared, I think, to fly me for free to Ceylon in January. What about that? I could I might add also go to Tahiti, Madagascar or the Cameroons. I would write a piece.

. . . Went riding with Rich Ron [Gurney] last weekend on the Berkshire downs which was quite beautiful.

Some of that later Seljuk architecture can be appalling. Never cared one bit for that elaborate portal at Sivas, but have never been to Divrigi or Malatya. I don't quite agree with you over Hittite art. I think that Yazilikiya is most remarkable. It's very tough and solid, and requires a bouleversement of all one's ideas as to what is beautiful. I like it all the same in the time of the Old and early New Kingdoms. You're not, I suppose, going to Nimrud Dagh.

I am just going to move my stuff to Holwell in the land rover and must dash this to the post or it won't get you in Teheran. Most mystifying. A huge consignment of gold and silver dishes arrived from some dealer in Teheran for me at London airport. I replied I knew nothing about it and had the whole lot sent back. It might have been some

1. Desmond Fitzgerald married Olda Willes in 1970.
2. Sandy Martin, dealer and one-time partner with John Hewett.
3. Union des Transports Aériens, French airline.

smuggling operation, and I simply don't want to be involved. It wasn't the textiles of last year.[1] That for one is certain.

Love and all.

xxx B

To Derek Hill
Holwell Farm | Wotton-under-Edge | Glos | [October 1970]

Some cutting away required, but not <u>malignant</u> cancer which is what the biopsies were about. If only we knew less about medicine and were able to trust to the mercy of God, we might live less long, but be saved innumerable alarms. See you soon, I hope. Much love, B

To Elizabeth Chatwin
Holwell Farm | Wotton-under-Edge | Glos | 22 October 1970

Dear E,

Vastly windy day and the leaves pouring off the trees, and the house buzzing with flies, and a new addition – bats, long eared bats that mysteriously secrete themselves into the bedroom and hover around at night after the flies. It's a curious sensation the noise of fluttering air, more mechanical than animal, and I could even hear the high-pitched screech.

My parents have been here this morning to try on the overcoat.[2] *Un vrai sac*, I am afraid. She must have thought I was a giant. I can see my father ending up in it.

Lunch the other day with Sally[3] and later a walk with her and Master, and needless to say I succumbed to his entreaties about cutting down the tree on the path. Lenny[4] is going to do it.

1. Silk from Afghanistan.
2. Margharita had made Chatwin a tweed overcoat. E.C.: 'She did eventually make him one that fitted.'
3. Sally Perry (1911–91), m. 1945 Gerald Grosvenor, 4th Duke of Westminster (1907–67); and companion of Henry Somerset, 10th Duke of Beaufort (1900–84), Master of Queen's Hounds; neighbour of Chatwins at Wickwar Manor.
4. Lenny Ballinger, the Chatwins' tenant farmer.

I have taken to staying in the Knight and Olda's basement in London which is very convenient and pleasant, but I don't know how long it'll last. Teddy [Millington-Drake] is here from Patmos and is going back to New York 'because I don't have anywhere else to go'. Poor thing. We may both come out to India, but as I have firmly maintained I make no promises as to the date. The book progresses. There is no doubt about it. But as I have cast the whole thing in a different literary form, and have abandoned the confining institution of the paragraph in favour of a more militant SLOGAN, the whole thing has had to be recast. Am having a great row with *Vogue* magazine as they intend to publish my article under the title 'IT'S A NOMAD, NOMAD, NOMAD WORLD.'[1] Either the title is changed or it's coming out. Thank you.

Have heard from Cary [Welch] who is busy as usual with the young folks. New Young Folks this time with art classes and Zen cookery lessons.

If you get a chance can you let me know what you have decided to do about the fencing which has to be done because the sheep have been in the garden. Who is supposed to be coming to do it? A ghastly new vicar,[2] a really priggish vandal has come and proposes a real clean up of Ozleworth, this involving the removal of the tombstones in the interest of Hygiene. Fury all round. It's the stupid fault of the Fergussons[3] for not attending to it properly.

Thank God my teeth really do seem to be better. A very nasty week that was, waiting to hear the results of the biopsy on a piece of my gum from the Cancer Clinic.

Vandalism is in the woods. That horror Mr Woodward is chopping near Newark Park now. Thank heaven for our little bit of scrub.

She is awfully curious that Linda. Secretive in a funny way. Frankly I thought she'd leave when I came. She said 'I suppose it's your house, isn't it?' but now she seems to have got used to the idea of my presence. She is silent, moves stealthily about the house, has the most terrible

1. 'It's a Nomad Nomad Nomad NOMAD world' appeared in *Vogue*, December 1970.
2. Mr Ball, known as Canon Ball.
3. William and Rosalie Fergusson, neighbours at Holwell.

friends, really terrible friends, professional snivellers – except John[1] who came one night. I receive nobody, except that I may be having Keith[2] plant some more trees. I am afraid I cannot find time to DO the garden, only to offer some useless advice. Lenny [Ballinger] is very helpful, and is chopping the apple tree up for firewood. I intend to plant some more of those willows in the willow patch.

If I'm through by Christmas I may go to Darling D[erek]. I don't know whether it's a good idea or not. We shall see. In India please look out for hand made paper, old looking but with all the bits in it. Also anything you can find in the way of original natural not aniline colourings paints etc. When I have finished the book I am going to have a really big painting and drawing session. I have got all worked up about the old passions Seghers,[3] Leonardo landscapes, Sung masters etc. There is a North West Coast stone whale in Sotheby's looking rather neglected, unillustrated, unloved by F[elicity] N[icolson], Sandy [Martin] etc, but really beautiful. May try and buy it. Am selling kufic lettering, maybe the Green Man[4] if I can get enough and some other footling thing. Nothing of yours – yet!

love, B

PS Have read another horrendous article about Heraclium[5] and have eradicated 2 by the peonies. Where are the others?

To Elizabeth Chatwin
Holwell Farm | Wotton-under-Edge | Glos | 28 October 1970

Dear E.,

If you are that desperate for money, we will send some, but the question remains how much do you need and where do you want it. Quite

1. John Michell (1933–2009), English author. *The View Over Atlantis* (1969) popularised ley-lines, 'referring to ancient stone circles, menhirs and graveyards which are laid out in lines across Britain,' as Chatwin wrote in *The Songlines*. Chatwin walked with him in Cornwall and Wales.
2. Keith Steadman, horticulturalist neighbour at Wickwar.
3. Hercules Seghers (1589–1638), Dutch painter. Cary Welch owned a Seghers oil painting of a skull.
4. Miniature drawing of a sikh grandee.
5. Giant hogweed. E.C.: 'Bruce thought you'd get poisoned if you stood next to it.'

frankly we have had so much expense here that I don't know whether I'm coming or going, with rates, oil and the mortgage payments who demand monthly payments at the rate of about £500 per year. We simply cannot go on asking my parents to fork up, as there will come a limit. I have been doing some more journalism which brings in a bit, and I think I have sold the Maori board but I am reserving all the money from it for an emergency.

My pectoral[1] has been the success of the year £50, sold the fish hook off which nearly paid for it; the pectoral itself comes from the famous Caroline Islands, and is worth about £400, at least John [Hewett] offered me three.

The flies are incredible here, and I have caught worms and a terrific resurgence of ringworm, which must be from the cats[2].

I am much less depressed about the book though, which does seem to be getting along far better if slowly. I have changed the literary form.

A red writing case came for you here this morning, will I pay for it £6 or so and what do you want done with it. Kept?

The posts must be very bad between here and Teheran if you didn't get my letter, but of course the first week after my arrival back in the country was so fraught with anxiety that I didn't get one off before.

Elizabeth Simson. If she drives you mad which she plainly does, imagine what she'd do to me. I might even become a homicidal maniac.

Did you meet up with Roger the Lodger?[3]

love, B

To Elizabeth Chatwin
Holwell Farm | Wotton-under-Edge | Glos | 6 November 1970

Dear E.,

It's all very well you complaining about no news, but I have no idea as to how fast you are travelling. You are a. miles behind schedule but

1. Maori shell.
2. E.C.: 'He really didn't know anything about animals.' Chatwin's notebook: 'Hell is a house – house dog is Cerberus.'
3. E.C.: 'I didn't.'

b. failed to get my letter in Teheran. Yet today we have one quick as lightning from Afghanistan. I don't know, so you'll now have to put up with a boring succession of correspondence in Delhi.

All is well enough; the house has been filled this weekend with Linda's friends including Japanese. The Hodgkins and Kasmin and Tomlinsons are coming tomorrow night. I have met some rather nice people called Roberts who are relations of yours in a way I cannot fathom. Iselins as usual, but they are as county English as you can imagine. The girl hunted with the Genesee Hunt but was not available for cross-questioning. I am going to exercise their hunters once or twice a week in Cirencester Park and have become quite horsey, stamping around the house in riding boots. Would you like to write to me to tell me what to do about the Forest and Orchard Nurseries, and whether they are to plant the beech hedge. If they come don't you think they might as well tidy up a bit. Fred[1] is far too busy with the transformations at the Bowlbys'[2] and you know my horror of turning the sod. Might plant a tree or two, but that's my limit. Miranda [Rothschild] after endless procrastination seems to have bought a very pretty 17th Century house in Cheyne Row (the p–a–and s of this type-writer are giving out causing me endless pain and fury). What am I to do?

. . . Teddy [Millington-Drake] and John [Stefanidis] came for lunch. I cooked deliciously but naturally neither were hungry. 'Fancy serving haricot beans with lamb. Fancy!'

When you are in Delhi will you please make detailed enquiries about the following. The North-West Frontier Province, Bhutan, Sikkim, Nepal, and Ladakh. I will quite definitely want to go into the high Himalaya in the spring, and that's that. I simply can't think of it at the moment to make plans, but I want any amount of gratuitous information. I want to write a very specific travel diary about it to publish, but I do not have to have a camera with me if that is the obstacle as I fear it may be with the frontier problem. Is there any literature available. Also can you find out for me the name of the man who arranges expeditions with sherpas in Nepal?

1. Fred Mewis, the Chatwins' gardener.
2. Anthony and Doe Bowlby lived at the Old Rectory in Ozleworth.

Imagine my horror when *Vogue* proofs came back with the title changed to ITS A NOMAD NOMAD NOMAD WORLD. Jesus what horrors editors. Am tackling the Jews in the book, god what a nasty lot! Everywhere the smell of singeing flesh. Do you mind if I sell the Green Man to buy an Eskimo seal coming up in Sotheby's. His eyes have been haunting me for the past two weeks as seals' eyes do. Bloody typewriter collapsing as I write. I hate typewriters.

Love B

Notice came that £200 or so was deposited by Mellon[1] to your Bank.

To Elizabeth Chatwin
Holwell Farm | Wotton-under-Edge | Glos | 15 November 1970

Dear E.,

I have your letters from Delhi today, which is also if I recall correctly your birthday[2] though I am not very good about remembering things like that. In any event the anniversary of your birth has been marked by a ceremonial planting – Holwell farm now has a *Salicetrium* and you can guess what that is till you return.[3] It has also been graced by a beech hedge, which I have had put inside the apple trees, and it looks and is far nicer than if it were outside the apple trees. The back has also been graced by a mixed planting of spurges, hostas, White Buddleia, pale pink clematis, Rosa brunonii and it will be absolutely charming.

There is a creature called David Hann who is supposed to be coming to work in the garden. I have sold a coin of Euthydemus to Hon R[obert Erskine] to pay for same. I think he may say that a very firm hand ought to be taken with the cross paths etc. in order to eradicate the weeds. In the yard is a ziggurat of reddish topsoil of the finest quality, because at 40/- per ton I said they might just as well bring five tons and three for the hedge.

You will have to admit that my instincts about P[enelope] were fully

1. Elizabeth's trust at the Mellon Bank in Pittsburgh.
2. 16 November.
3. Willow plantation.

justified. Eccentricity carried to that extent is egomania, and not particularly interesting. John B[etjeman] is having her letter describing the rape photostatted and circulated, so Jim L[ees]-M[ilne] told me.

Phone rings at 8am brightly yesterday. Sally [Westminster] inviting herself to lunch. And last night I was at Keith [Steadman]'s to meet the Garnetts[1] when Derek [Hill] rang saying he had something vital to talk to me about, the worst possible news, something really serious had happened. For some reason I could not sleep and when I did I dreamed horrible nightmares of Derek and the Andy Garnetts in a futuristic house. This morning too at 8-30 Derek in a funereal voice, spent five minutes telling me how serious and terrible the situation was without telling me what it was.

It seems that Faber's have turned his Morocco book down unless D[erek] manages to produce £8000 to cover the printing costs. Did I know a foundation who would put up the money. What I did not say was that D[erek]'s photos are so atrocious that it would be a miracle if any publisher looked at them with or without the £8000. Anyhow I suggested the Mellon Foundation, and much cheered he said he would write AT ONCE to Bunny Mellon, and of course etc. etc. she'd do everything to help being such a close friend. I am afraid that was the cruellest thing possible because poor Mrs Mellon if she has any sense will say no and there will be an embarrassing scene and a broken friendship (by whom?). The simple fact remains that it is unpublishable. Why are all one's friends lunatics?

Charles T[omlinson] came to dinner with the Hodgkins and Kasmin the other night, and the morning before Charles appeared with his latest monotypes, which I like in a way as they have a certain quality. Would I mind hanging them in the drawing room so that Kasmin etc might take a look, and possibly have an exhibition etc. etc? Really quite dotty because the Kasmin Gallery only goes in for Candy stripes twenty feet long, and not black blodges 2⅔ by 3¼ in.

I have sold the Maori so it seems. It has to be confirmed. I shall hang on to that money, but will probably buy an Eskimo seal with plaintive

1. Polly Devlin, journalist, married to Andy Garnett, entrepreneur, neighbours at Bradley Court near Alderley.

eyes that have been looking at me for three weeks. How I am bored with large things! Never liked them anyway. A phase – only a phase, but in fact my collecting if such it be is becoming less and less expensive as I can only bear a smooth pebble or a simple harpoon.

Writing not bad. Refuse to be hurried, and one IS in a much better frame of mind if one exercises one day in four. No doubt about it. You couldn't send me a cheque on your Geneseo account could you because I want to order one or two paperbacks from New Directions.[1] Or can I ask your mother for them?

The carpets finally arrived from Morocco with a consignment of C. Gibbs, but the one I bought was so hideous in the grisliness of England that I gave it promptly to the Knight and Olda who were Thrilled by it. This shows their terrible judgement and everyone is happy all round. I keep on paying little bills for you . . .

F[elicity] N[icolson] says she wouldn't have you interrupt your plans and drive specially to Bombay for her as she still won't decide what to do. Neither will I, though I will be able to give you some idea in a month. She thinks the best thing is for you to do what you like, and she will fit in or not as the case may be.

XXXXX B

Linda [Wroth] is the most interminable telephonist I have ever known up to three quarters of an hour to London.

To Gertrude Chanler

Holwell Farm | Wotton-under-Edge | Glos | 16 November 1970

Dear Gertrude,

As Elizabeth probably told you I had to come back because of a hideous episode with my teeth. A rotten dentist years ago made a complete muck of a filling and it went horribly bad underneath.

I am sitting here in the farm for a bit, writing each day. These things take far longer than one imagines and I procrastinate over every word.

---

1. Independent American publishing house, founded 1936.

Have celebrated E.'s birthday by a massive planting session. A pyramid of top soil arrived and we now have some proper borders in the back with tree paeonies and big species roses plus a very pretty plantation of willows. I want to try and pave the back this winter, but can't find the stone slabs at the moment.

One thing. We have bust the Cape Cod lighter burner,[1] and Elizabeth will be furious. This being an American ritual the English don't understand, how can I get some more? I think we'd better have two or three so that they'll last.

I keep hearing about the lady adventurers from time to time. Penelope [Betjeman] seems to be very demanding and I'm afraid that eccentricity has an uncommon tendency to develop into egomania. This is perfectly all right as long as you don't have to travel with it. I think I'd have gone absolutely crazy already.[2] Three days was enough in Istanbul. I will fly out in January. I can't see that going overland would solve anything, and the spring gets very hot by March

with love,

Bruce

To Elizabeth Chatwin
Holwell Farm | Wotton-under-Edge | Glos | 24 November 1970

Dear E.,

Many thanks for yr Kampur and Delhi letters which arrived together. Felicity [Nicolson] is writing to you about her visit – and is procrastinating. I simply cannot see any chance of coming out immediately after Christmas. End of Jan is the earliest possible. You must realise if I don't do this thing now it'll sit here for ever as I have a million other plans as well. I'm very sorry but there it is. I am going on and on until the first draft is available for Tom Maschler and have his opinion. Then I'll decide. I know the whole thing is very irritating for you especially with your

1. A stoneware firelighter soaked in kerosene.
2. 'I love her dearly but she is impossible to be with for longer than two hours at a stretch.' James Lees-Milne diary, 5 September 1972.

companions – and incidentally Penelope [Betjeman] is the last person I want to show me round Delhi and would put me off for ever. You still have never said when you want to be back here – and Linda [Wroth] would roughly like to know where she stands. She is v competent etc but somewhat gloomy to be with!

. . . As I've told you I have sold the Maori and am treating myself to the most astonishing object belonging to C. Gibbs my favourite of all his things – a <u>Shinto</u> Mitsutomoe (C17 at latest maybe C15) symbol in gilt bronze 3 ft across like a Brancusi only better – £250 for nothing![1] In part exchange am letting him have the little Moroccan table for which he'll give a good price. One bit of replaceable tat for something really stupendous. Otherwise nothing very much of note here except for the mildness of the weather and corresponding legions of flies. Have you met this rather famous man Ajit Mukherjee[2] in Delhi who runs the crafts museum and is a great one for folklore etc. I believe he is very very weird but interesting too. Why don't you buy a lot of the Penguin and other cheap Indian texts and really study while the others draw and mooch around. All books are terribly cheap.

The hedge as I told you arrived and is planted. I contemplate another tree order – one to plant the Amur oak whose bark provided the Imperial Yellow dye for the Chinese Emperors. Available at Hilliers . . . I thought I might take a day off and go over there myself and collect them personally which is a much better bet than all that delivery horror.

I'm rather alarmed that the Death Watch beetle in the beam above the bedroom seems to be active. I will try and get someone to look at it. No sign of Mr Elms.[3] Also Linda and I both have Holwell Farm stomach ache and we wonder if it could be anything to do with the well.[4]

Must begin again upstairs. Have just spent the morning shopping for the week in Wotton as I am alone till Friday

xxxx B

1. E.C.: 'I still have it.'
2. Ajit Mukherjee's *The Art of Tantra* (1970) generated an interest in Tantric Art.
3. Elms & Sons, the Chatwins' builders.
4. E.C.: 'The water was perfectly all right. The Etheridges, who owned the Lodge after us, had it tested.'

Chatwin had been writing The Nomadic Alternative *for almost a year and kept thinking that it was about to be done – in much the same way he continued to believe that he had sold Sarah Bernhardt's Maori bedstead. In this state of mind, he made plans to join Elizabeth at various dates over the winter and spring. But the end of the book was unreachable, 'a Sisyphean job' in Elizabeth's words. A month-long postal strike made communication difficult since the post office ran the telephone system as well.*

To Elizabeth Chatwin

Holwell Farm | Wotton-under-Edge | Glos | 1 December 1970

Dear E.,

Today I start on a new chapter. The last one on the Hunters now finished has gone on for nearly thirty thousand words and will probably have to be halved. I don't know what I can say about coming. I wish I did. I can't tell you how much I long to get away. But if I break the threads of concentration now, I'm honestly afraid that the whole thing will go down the drain. I sit here from 9 a.m. till 10 p.m. but of course the length of time offered does not necessarily make a complete working day. Some days it comes easily, others I battle with 500 words.

I think you can <u>calculate</u> on Feb 7th, let's say as a firm date, and if there is any likelihood of it happening any quicker I'll be the first to let you know. The main difficulty is that HAVING written this enormous bulk I may want to refine the whole thing down to my inimitable (!) style with the exception that this time I want it to glitter like a diamond. Maybe I'd better sit in the Red Fort and correct the proofs.

F[elicity] N[icolson] has been rather remiss. She has had your addresses for four weeks and told me yesterday she hadn't even written. The chances of her coming are I tell you REMOTE. Do not make any effort to go to Bombay to meet <u>her or</u> me. When I come I will find you wherever you happen to be.[1] I shall be virtually without luggage and such as I have will be left at Bombay or Delhi . . .

We are the proud proprietors of an Eskimo seal at nearly £100 per inch. It's tiny, but the most appetising Eskimo animal I have ever seen except for the archaic Point Hope walrus. It is so balanced that when I write at the typewriter on this table it bobs up and down exactly as a seal does, and looks at me with a pair of dark sympathetic melancholy eyes. It's even got a suggestion of whiskers from the crystalline centre of the nose and a wholly seal-like expression in the mouth. When you stroke it, it responds back. It is exactly a similar model that Brancusi took for his Lying Seal. There are one or two other little treasures such as the pipe and tobacco box of an 18th Cent Welsh shepherd of unbelievable elegance and simplicity.

Last weekend full of Gloucestershire dinners. Ninety laughs a minute. 'What do you do?' 'I'm writing a book. What do _you_ do?' 'DO? What d'ye mean DO? I hunt four times a week. How d'ye expect me to Do anything?'

Am going to some people called Clifford who live in Frampton Court, a great Vanbrugh pile. Conversation with Mrs Clifford is like talking to a portico. Long letter from Penelope [Bejteman] which I cannot read. Also from your mother in answer to one from me requesting a Cape Cod lighter burner as the one here seems to have finally collapsed. I am employing someone called David Hann who works for Keith to do some things in the garden. We only have occasional visits from Tigger[2] who has gone very wild. It's no use keeping him in as he just howls to be let out.

I have to take a little time off occasionally, and one day before Christmas I mean to go to the hawking centre in Newent. They train eagles like the Kirghiz – imagine!

love, B

---

1. E.C.: 'I went back to Bombay twice to meet Bruce because he said he was coming. I traipsed back, driving hundreds of miles, and he didn't come, ever.'
2. E.C.: 'A half-Siamese ginger cat completely focussed on me. When I left, he went mad and never recovered.'

To Elizabeth Chatwin
Holwell Farm | Wotton-under-Edge | Glos | 11 December 1970

Dear E.,

Have just had yours from Gwalior this morning and am going up to the dentist tonight. I wrote to you yesterday but haven't posted the letter because it was quite a stream of invective against that Linda. She really is quite awful. I can't stand her, and she's been making such a fearful scene because I'm here at all. When I suggested she GO and I STAY, there was no question of it. She was intending to STAY. Not that she's had to pay one penny so far. I footed all the bills. She even complains about not having enough money to eat, because she's not prepared to sell her shares, but is quite content when her boyfriends eat and drink all the drink on me. I'm hardly ever here at all. Sitting in the study. Have asked no one here for fear of disrupting her, and when Miranda and Fatby [Miranda's daughter, Da'ad Boumaza] came for a couple of nights she threw the most almighty scene and refused to speak. Very unpleasant.

Coupled with a fearful row with Sotheby's. Jessie Wood gave me a very nice gold box to put into Sotheby's with a res. of £800. I phoned up after the sale and was assured it had been sold for £800 on the reserve. Then no confirmation of sale. I ring up and they say that the last bid in the room was £760, and that it had never reached £800. They are all such liars because they've contradicted themselves several times over. There's some shenanigans about the whole thing, and I am insisting they cough up.

I just don't know what to do about the book. I am going to talk to Deborah [Rogers] today about it. It is very nearly finished but is in the most unholy mess. What do I do? Come to India and work in Bombay. The books etc will not be needed because it will all be in the files. Cable me if you feel like it from Hyderabad. F[elicity] N[icolson] now says flatly she's not coming. I may have found a lead into Sikkim and Bhutan and will let you know. I'll go to the Indian High Commission tomorrow.

Furthermore I have strained my back, and may even have slipped a disc GARDENING. Winter flowering cherry planted, now in bloom.

Very beautiful. Charles T[omlinson] has been coughing blood. Very worrying, now in bed. I hope he hasn't got T.B. Been looking awful recently.

Never want to write another thing again.

much love, B

PS Have talked to Deborah today. First draft v. nearly done. B

To Valerian Freyberg
Holwell Farm | Wotton-under-Edge | Glos | [December 1970]

The enclosed is an 18th century sherbet spoon[1] which should be used by my godson Valerian for his first ice-cream or water ice. I am very keen on my godson[2] and want to see him, often, when is his birthday?
PS Should be used but not if he's going to bite it to bits. I detected a certain firmness of attitude to crowds and the House of Lords. I had one winning smile and for that am grateful.

To Elizabeth Chatwin
Holwell Farm | Wotton-under-Edge | Glos | 2 January 1971

Dear E.

I have your letters today, as I've come down from London to the farm for a night to get some things. Iain and Miranda have let me stay in Llama [Ghika]'s house in Little Venice, which I share with Coote Lygon.[3] At the end of the month if I'm still here, I shall have the place

1. E.C.: 'The sherbet spoon was mine.'
2. Valerian (b.15 December 1970), 3rd Baron Freyberg; 'my godson and perennial favourite', Chatwin described him in an inscription to On the Black Hill.
3. Lady Dorothy ('Coote') Lygon (1912–2000); 4th d. of 7th Earl Beauchamp: 'I was working at Christie's in Old Masters, making a card index based on early picture sales. I was on the second floor at Blomfield Road, Bruce on the first. He had a beautiful brown silk robe which he said he had bought from nomads in Central Africa. I was very jealous of it. It had voluminous, big sleeves, so he'd put his hands up the opposite sleeve and keep himself warm.'

to myself. I am afraid I simply couldn't stand the atmosphere here one minute longer and one day filled up the car and fled. She infuriates me to the point of no return and has mercifully gone to Bath for the night which is why I have come today. However she does look after the house well despite everything. Though a sinister crack has appeared in the beam in the dining-room due to the jolting of her constant intercourse. SHARK'S CUNT Miranda and I have called her. She and Fattles [Miranda's daughter] came down for the night before Christmas, and Miranda did some wonderful cooking which she did not deign to touch. Though the lot which we had hoped to eat for lunch next day was spirited away in the night.

Then the drama of my back. GARDENING My Dear! Lugging soil for the new planting at the back of the house. A slipped disc, no more no less – and three weeks of agony. The third vertebra in my back, and it has caught the nerve which leads to one's crutch and balls and I felt someone had given me the most almighty boot where it hurts most. Two sessions with the back man at St Thomas's and he wasn't too optimistic, and then suddenly it's gone. Touch wood! I still have to be careful about getting in and out of bed and lifting things.

The next drama. Sandy Martin said he had sold the Maori the opening day of his exhibition. It got the red spot and was duly considered sold. I found out it was to G[eorge] O[rtiz] P[atino]. The payment to be made Jan 1st. Dec 30th phone call to Sandy. He wouldn't buy after all. Says he told Sandy he would buy on one condition that it was prior to 1800. Took the photos to an expert in New Zealand who said Very fine quality but 1810-1820. K. J[ohn] H[ewett] says this is nonsense. Now there's an almighty stink broken out, but Sandy who had written to my bank guaranteeing the money, then wrote off to cancel it before even telling me. They're all such liars. K.J.H. being very helpful about it. Overdraft now £1,250. Oh God!

I'm taking up to London the Persian silk textile[1] and will probably be able to get £500 for it. The Moroccan one is ready and looks marvel-

---

1. Pale blue silk in geometrical squares and triangles; it had belonged to the Director of the Victoria & Albert Museum.

lous and so it can hang in its place. I vastly prefer it anyway. That'll relieve the situation temporarily at least. Am rather loath to sell anything else just at this minute. The Mitsutomoe is a huge gilt roundel Japanese of uncertain date but probably Muromachi that is to say 15th–16th Century with three enormous blobs like ying and yang except the Japanese Shintoists with their flair for the ambiguous have gone in for HE SHE AND IT. Magnificent. It's like having your own Brancusi 2½ feet diam. Best thing I've ever had except for the Eskimo seal another Brancusi-ish object.

The lights have gone off. The third power cut in two days apparently. The deep freeze stuff is a wreckage according to the note left by Linda. They had a fourteen-hour cut. There is one candle in the Japanese lantern, and I am thankful I am going out to dinner with the Gascoynes,[1] and will refuse to be put off. Bamber and his wife have spent a winter in India and are writing a Mughal book – such a _novel_ idea. They're rather silly.

PLANS. In a way I'm rather sad you think you must be here in May – like May 1st? Especially as I have been laying a series of very well conceived ones to be invited by the King of Bhutan and you as well. All the papers have gone off last week. Oh dear! What to do about? As you know, to me this book is really important. It is, though I say it myself, coming on all right. There are parts I am pleased with and parts that are a mess. One cannot hurry something that can't be hurried. Am lurching through the last section quite rapidly now, next week will come to the Hero and the road of trials, followed by anarchists and modern revolutionaries, and then a concluding chapter where all the heavy guns are fired. Nerve required. I am quite unaware at the moment if I have gone off my head or whether the ideas are so novel, so outrageous, so shattering that no one will be able to put the book down. Or neither, just a silly mess? Iain Watson who is normally a stickler about such things is highly enthusiastic. I read him passages and he corrects it. Quite toughminded Iain when it comes to the point. We shall see. _The Book must_

---

1. Arthur Bamber Gascoigne (_b._1935), author and broadcaster; m. 1963 Christina Ditchburn. _The Great Moghuls_ is still in print.

be done. The back of it may get done by mid-Feb in a state visible to Tom Maschler i.e. in an intelligible first draft. I don't want to be disturbed till then particularly. That is if you are happy, and you sound infinitely more cheerful than previous letters which were giving me a slightly guilty complex. My father has made no holiday plans. He I think would come out and help you. I believe that if one asked he might very well like to come anyway, but I think one should provide some entertaining diversion in India or en route for him.

So I wouldn't worry if I were you. The thing with me is that if I break the continuity it always goes to pot. This has happened before, but as I hope to remain comfortably installed in Blomfield Road it should be OK. Incidentally it's the nicest place to live in London and really convenient because the Oxford motorway streams right by. There is none of that Cromwell Roadism, it's also very convenient for the West End and the City.

In spite of my screamings or I suppose because of them the *Vogue* article appeared with title. The typography made it look as though it had the title NOMADS, and the shrieks of acid laughter were not quite as loud as I feared. Lesson learned. Never write an article for the fashionable press after a hangover in two hours. It doesn't pay off in the end.

I am really quite worried about Charles [Tomlinson]. For three years he has worked on translations of the poetry of Ungaretti.[1] Oxford guaranteed to publish etc. Now he has found that some snake who he told about it, extracted from Ungaretti's publisher the rights to all translations in English, and Charles can't even publish at all. Coupled with that he is really ill. Now I think this is something we must look into. He has a permanent pain in his intestine on the right side accompanied by a constant urge to pee and couldn't eat anything for days. But before Christmas I had exactly the same. I couldn't sit at the typewriter because of the agony in my stomach, coupled with really terrible nervous depressions. C[harles] says it was so bad for him some years ago that he went to the Bristol Hospital with suspected kidney disease for check ups and they found

1. Giuseppe Ungaretti (1888–1970), Italian modernist poet.

NOTHING. I went up to the Doctor in London three times and he found nothing. I am having the water tested. I am quite decided it isn't my fertile imaginations. It is quite definitely something biological in the water, local virus etc. God knows! But we really must find out.

Great drama. A rogue sewage lorry dumped all its filthy effluent on the drive in that open patch. We i.e the police and I believe the Spyvees[1] put them up to it. If I wasn't in so financially tight straits I'd have sued both of them. The only thing I have made them do without going to court is to cover the whole thing with lime. Really filthy. I think it does give us a stronger hand with the Glos. C.C. over the private road, and when you come back you and C.L.C. [Charles Chatwin] should have another go at getting it closed.

Am taking a few days off actually to write an article on the horrors of Konrad Lorenz for the *New York Review*. I've really got him. 'The Jews, through inbreeding have formed a tumerous growth in a civilised nation.' 'Tolerance towards the inferior is a danger for the people.' I also have a new friend Lord Chalfont[2] who helps my schemes. Although this is the nadir of our fortunes, I am not sure that one or two little plans are not working out.

Lights have gone on again. Thank God! We've had the worst frosts ever. Today I looked in at Roger Warner[3] and bought a very nice old boomerang and three of those cloche tops with rather ropy bottoms which we could easily have fixed, or have new ones made. The border at the back of the house my dear is going to be a blaze in fact not a blaze at all because it's all white and soft blue and yellow and greyish green. I think you ought to have a plant licence, because if you come through Afghanistan in April you'll be able to get handy with your trowel. One thing very nice. Japanese winter flowering cherry, about twelve willows. *Magnolia Sieboldii* if it survives, a dream my dear a dream.

Robert Skelton[4] is going to get Penelope's camera equipment out

---

1. Neighbours on spur of the valley.
2. Alun Gwynne-Jones (*b*.1919), Minister in Foreign Office 1964–70; Baron Chalfont from 1964.
3. Dealer. E.C.: 'We lost the boomerang when we moved.'
4. Keeper of Indian and South-East Asian art at the Victoria & Albert Museum.

to her by Feb 11 if I can't come out. He has someone going, and they will be dropped off at the High Commission in Delhi. She can use my camera if she likes <u>on condition</u> she replaces anything lost, and repairs all defects.[1]

Your mother has been getting your letters because I have heard from her. I wrote asking her to send another Cape Cod lighter which Linda finally broke. Chatty letter in return to the effect that your father had sprained or broken something and she'd fallen from a horse. Thank God you did not buy the *Encylopaedia*.[2] Never heard such a ridiculous idea. In India of all places.

I hope you bought the Maharajah's Dumbbells.[3] They sound very nice. Kitty Puss is fatter than she was. She went through a bad patch, but is now better. Probably pining.

PLANS AGAIN. Will you cable me where you are on Jan 28th–Feb 7th and I will let you know mine. I think that's the best way of leaving things. If by then, the thing is looking like completion within a reasonable time I will come out maybe just on an ordinary return fare for a month or so if the return journey can be sorted out. I'd no idea you were going to be in Bombay as we were without news till yesterday when the letters from both Bombay and Hyderabad came together.

Lovely New Years party at Susanna's[4] then passed on to the Erskines – and horrors. I have never been in a room with so many people lacking one redeeming physical feature.

Have decided to do nothing about UTA and Ceylon. Too complicated. You don't any way know how lucky you are not to have to face the flight!

Cable if you'd like your reactions to Plans. Address c/o Ghika, 27 Blomfield Road, London W.9

Love as ever, BBB BBBBBBB B No pen.

1. E.C.: 'Penelope had lost her camera. The reason we went so slowly is because she would say, "I want the evening light" and spend two nights in every place.'
2. E.C.: 'An *Encyclopaedia Britannica* 1911 that I found in Hyderabad. It had quite a lot of holes from silverfish.'
3. Made of wood and bone and lacquer. E.C.: 'I bought them.'
4. Susanna Chancellor m. 1958 Nicholas Johnston (*b.*1929) architect.

P.S. Have just got here from the farm again, and after loading the car with books I think I've done my back in again. Agony. There's really going to be no point in sitting cooped up in a car if it goes on, and frankly I become more and more convinced I won't be able to make it. I did it shovelling earth into the border behind the back of the house. Sitting in a confined position makes it worse, and one has to have an upright chair with a pillow in the middle of the back.

Write soon. Must get on with the *New York Review* article. Real acid.

Love B

P.P.S Had a sudden panic this morning as I couldn't find this and wondered if I'd left it on the kitchen table for Linda to see.

B

To Elizabeth Chatwin

c/o Ghika|27 Blomfield Road|London|[but franked on envelope
Lisbon|Hotel Tivoli]|1 February 1971

Dear E,

What with the postal strike[1] and everything closed here, how are we going to be in touch. Suggest the best thing as per my cable is to cable c/o G. Ortiz office in Paris, or c/o Jessie Wood, 16 bis Rue L'Abbé de l'Epee, Paris VI.

Rather depressing here in London, and the book still grinds on with remorseless slowness. If I start at 9–30 in the morning and finish at four I am intellectually exhausted. In theory one ought to be able to go on all night, but it always turns out badly if I do.

Went down to the farm last weekend for Sunday night to get some books. Everything is OK but Linda [Wroth] continues to rule. I wanted to go down this weekend but she rang on Tuesday and said it was inconvenient. We shall have to cut the tree in the lane as the oil people simply will not deliver any more until it is out. He breaks the driving mirror each time. Please give instructions, as I said the hedge ought to be laid

---

1. On 20 January 1971, 200,000 British postal workers began a seven-week strike.

and everyone else says you have said no. What also shall we do about the garden? I can't dig any more even if I'm there. Shall I employ David Hann, Keith [Steadman]'s helper, to come and do some things or not. If so where's the money coming from?

My back's still there. Some days it's O.K. others not. Particularly bad with driving. Last night we had Stephanides and the Johnstons here for dinner, and Miranda [Rothschild] and I got frantic with boredom half way through. They arrived an hour late after the dinner was spoiled, and then batted on remorselessly about what Jeremy and Antonia, or Amabel and Clive were or were not doing with each other, stayed yacking till 1-30. God the English are a bore. I have never felt such a yearning to be something else.

Let us know through Jessie [Wood] what your plans are and what you want me to do.

Much love, XXX Bruce

P.S. Have absolutely no money since the Maori fiasco but just <u>manage</u> as long as there are no expenses.

To Elizabeth Chatwin
c/o 27 Blomfield Road|London|or as next week
c/o Wood 16 bis Rue L'Abbé de l'Epee Paris VI|[February 1971]

My dear E,

Have just heard via Patrick Kinross[1] that Jack Richards is bringing a lot of films to Penelope and so I'm scrawling a few lines to catch you because the whole country has seized up with the postal strike – and I haven't heard a word since about 5 weeks I thought it'd be a good opportunity. Apparently you can send cables via Western Union.

The book isn't bad but of course still not over. Oh God when will I get it done. I've worked and worked for example 8am to 12 midnight yesterday. I am beginning to think it's rather good in parts at any rate

---

1. Patrick Balfour, 3rd Baron Kinross (1904–76), author, broadcaster, specialist in the Ottoman Empire. 'The dearest old thing in the world,' according to James Lees-Milne.

but it is an endless drama of shuffling and reshuffling the component parts, turning passive verbs into active verbs etc. Miranda and Iain are going to Paris on Thursday and I am hitching a lift with them to give myself a break – collect the famous bed and get Iain [Watson] to bring it back in four days. Then I shall have the house to myself for about a couple of weeks and then Llama [Ghika] comes back. I would really then like to move back to the farm but because of the Linda situation I don't know what to do. Shall I kick her out before you come back or leave her? Can't stay under the same roof. Unbearably rude whenever I go. Apparently Sally [Westminster]'s broken something hunting[1] so I must ring up. Sold some absolute rubbish inc. that Punic head brought in Tunis £68 and some others. Then I found another Moroccan shroud like ours. Rather beautiful £10. Finances bad but not so bad.

Am writing the anti-Konrad Lorenz article with great excitement and this is going to be a bomb for NY *Review of Books* – already accepted.[2] I would love to go away and will probably come and fetch you part of the way out. I would like some sort of instructions! I think now March-April for the book ending. The garden's in chaos at the farm as there has never been so much as a trowel lifted except for my operations at the back of the house. But the vegetable patch – horrors!

Miranda [Rothschild] has found out she has no female hormones!! and is turning into a man – imagine! Chaos with endless visits to the endoliologists. I cannot now decide if she wants to be a woman so the position is very complicated. She is having a long confab with Patrick Kinross (who sends his love) on the subject. M[iranda] has struck up a friendship with Gloria,[3] Sedig and Da'ad are fast friends and make a great noise.

My parents are well and had a funny time in Majorca. H[ugh].

---

1. Her wrist.
2. Chatwin's article on Lorenz did not appear in the *New York Review of Books* until December 1979. He was to interview Lorenz in July 1974 for the *Sunday Times* magazine at his home in Altenberg outside Vienna.
3. Gloria El-Fadil el Mahdi, Chatwin's former girlfriend; her son Sedig (Chatwin's godson); and Da'ad Boumaza, Miranda's daughter.

P. C[hatwin] seems to be much better after his operation but my God what stitches all over his head.

Bhutan is now off because I cannot do it in time. Just for the hell of it I have the permission forms in for September. What to do? As I say, have no plans till the bloody work is finished. One's 30th year you know is make or break year. I'm rather superstitious about it. Must be over by May or something awful might happen. Having dinner with Magouche Phillips, very nice with paintings by Gorky.[1] First line of the book – the best travellers are illiterate. Last line quotation from Chinese. To allow the people to pass freely for that is the Way of Heaven.

Darling D[erek] here in London. We dined at the Johnstons on Wednesday and this weekend he has gone to Jim and Alvilde [Lees-Milne]. We shall have to have the hedge cut apparently. Also there is great trouble. The Middle East oil shortage means that oil is v scarce. We can't get it at Blomfield Road. Send cable c/o Wood. Jessie has sent her Max Ernst to Sotheby's and I get I/C.[2] Still hopping mad with them, but am cushioned from the horrors by v amiable Thilo Von Watzdorf who works for Shellers[3] and finds that my antipathy is mirrored in him.

Oliver Hoare and I went to a Japanese masseuse.

Everyone sends love.

XXX

Bruce

On 29 March 1971, in response to an SOS from Elizabeth, Chatwin flew to Teheran to drive her back. She brought with her a 19-year-old Pathan boy, Ghulam Akbar, whom they had met a year before in Multan. They dropped Akbar off in Greece to sort out his Italian visa.

1. Arshile Gorky (1904–48), Armenian-born painter and Magouche's first husband.
2. Introductory commission.
3. Michel Straus had worked at Sotheby's with Chatwin in the Impressionist Department.

To James Ivory
Postcard from Achilleon | Corfu | [May 1971]

. . . I had to go to Persia to bring back Elizabeth and her companions. Beautiful Persian spring followed by dismal Anatolian winter. Turkey does not unfreeze till May. A series of near calamities on the way – the loss of passports – then of Elizabeth's Pathan in Brindisi found later by a friend of mine on the streets of Paris[1]. We shall be here till August at least while I try to finish my book. Great sessions yet to come. One month away has quite broken my train of thought and after one day I am already shaking with the malaise of settlement. I do hope I haven't missed you

    love B

On Friday 14 May 1971 Prince William of Gloucester unveiled a sculpture in St Mary Church of Grace, Apsall, in memory of Raulin Guild who had died five years earlier.

To Ivry Freyberg
Holwell Farm | Wotton-under-Edge | Glos | 17 May 1971

My Dear Ivry,

    Of course it was all perfect. The weather, the service and the lunch. It was as though we were all celebrating the gift of life. I don't think anyone missed Raulin because he was quite emphatically <u>there</u> in everything we said and did.

    The sculpture is very beautiful. I think you did very well to commission it.

    Elizabeth sends her love and hopes to see you both soon.

    Much love

    Bruce

Three years after buying Sarah Bernhardt's Maori headboard, Chatwin sold it to Cary Welch for £3,000.

---

1. Miranda Rothschild. She and Akbar became lovers.

To Cary Welch
Holwell Farm | Wotton-under-Edge | Glos | 17 May 1971

Dear C.,

I am having T. Rogers, Mason's Yard, SWI send you Air Freight the Maori artwork. I've declared it for £1500 and insured it for £3000. Anyhow you get it through the customs as it's not dutiable; have dated it circa 1800. I'll let you have the details of its publication, a book by Portier and Someone else called *Decoration Oceanienne*[1] which I have never seen. There is no hurry about payment at all, so take your time within reason, but please pay Gertrude Chanler or someone else of her choice in America, and not here, if that's possible. The reason being she is helping me finance a flat in London and I will want the money to come from America anyway. With it I am sending the metal stand which hitches the thing up diagonally, two sort of hooks fitting through the open work. It will need a bit of experiment to see which hole fits, so don't try and strain it. It does look marvellous on this stand because the line now follows the line of the house roof. With the exception of the pieces in Wellington and Auckland I have still yet to see a better piece of house decoration, and I don't care what anyone says. The bits in the B[ritish] M[useum] and the Pitt-Rivers just simply lack the movement and that tornado quality. The reason for delay in writing is that I went to Persia to drive Elizabeth back, and had with one or two major tragedies a rather wonderful time. Saw the Q'ashgais on their spring migration which was thrilling, and for five days filled a British Embassy Land Rover full of sheep, tribesmen, women suckling babies etc.

All well here. The Chanlers went yesterday. The Madame of Glyn goes into hospital to produce, one hopes, the Knightlet. I had to assist Prince William of Gloucester unveil a memorial plaque to a mutual friend who died, and imagine the shock when we saw the memorial underneath the veil – a sculpture of a boy, naked and beckoning in a Michelangelesque way with the caption under '. . . of all sorts enchantingly beloved'. Not far from the truth and that was the trouble.

1. *Décoration océanienne*, André Portier and François Poncetton (1931).

Elizabeth's young Pakistani friend Akbar couldn't get into England and is now stuck in France, where he is adopted by the Rothschilds as their latest amusement and a lot of talk about the Lost Tribes of Israel. We are prevented from talking to him on the phone so jealously is he guarded. Very irresponsible performance on the part of everybody. O to finish the book. I wrote the last sentence before I went away. Since when some ideas have evaporated and new ones have taken their place. Two three perhaps four months of revision. But the general plan is an American autumn and a South American winter. Might we even all go to Maine or swan around the New Hampshire farm, which I am very keen to see. March is the very worst time to come to England with everyone at their level worst. Now the spring is here tempers are less frayed.

love B

PS have written to Jungle Jim [Ivory]. He will see you soon, come over for the festival of his filums in June??

To Cary Welch

Holwell Farm | Wotton-under-Edge | Glos | [June 1971]

Dear Cary,

I had just written you and yours came. So now I start again. Sarah Bernhardt has been sent via Rogers to Boston . . . As you know Sandy sold the thing to me three years ago, and he couldn't sell it since. On the other hand Maori art is very very unfashionable. There was in Christie's a marvellous <u>huge</u> canoe prow which was not as exciting as the Bernhardt and it only brought about £5,000. The argument obviously seems to centre on whether they are Pre- or just post-Cook, which is a magic word for the difference between metal or stone tools. Sandy emphatically believes it to be pre-Cook and bought it with the recommendation of Ken Webster, who as you may know was the great Maori expert in England and buyer for the New Zealand museums. He said it was pre-Cook. The centrepiece I know about and is apparently in a private collection in Paris. I have never been able to get to see the photograph of the three together and Miss Small Clothes never told me that she had a copy. She sold hers to Elliott[1] for 12,000 dollars. I do know that. I think – and this was K.J[ohn] H[ewett]'s objection – that the principal argument against them is the way in which they are broken, but when you get it on the stand I have had made you will see that it hardly matters.

Family Tree 2 pieces

Rasmussen Paris
|
Ralph Nash London   _
| |
Merton Simpson via Small Clothes   Sandy Martin
| |
John Elliott   BC

Christopher Gibbs and Kasmin are here for the weekend and there is a sudden call to walk to the Hodgkins for lunch four hours away. And this letter which might have gone on for some pages more is coming to an <u>abrupt</u> halt.

    love B

On 2 June 1971 Welch wrote to Chatwin: 'Maori piece arrived yesterday . . . I cannot understand why I am so fortunate as to have it. After all I did nothing to deserve it other than a. encourage you to buy it and b. tell you I'd buy it if you could not sell it at a profit. But why is the art market so stupid as not to realise that this piece & its marvellous companions are the only things of their marvellous sort outside of New Zealand. As such they are of the utmost importance – not to mention their beauty.'

---

1. John Elliott, New York dealer.

To Cary Welch
Holwell Farm | Wotton-under-Edge | Glos | 11 June 1971

Dear C.,

The weather is so infinitely frightful that I have just decided to go to the South of France with my typewriter and E is going to follow later.

As I told you the £3,000 for the Maori is going to be used on a flat in London for me. But I am also owed about £700 in August and at the moment am flat broke. Would it be asking too much for you to send me (or rather <u>Elizabeth</u> because she has an external account) £300 or $800 to keep me going through the summer?

Many thanks if you can.

love Bruce

In France Chatwin had rented a house in a village belonging to his Gloucestershire neighbour, Jeremy Fry.

To Elizabeth Chatwin
Le Grand Banc | Oppedette | Basse Alpes | France | 22 June [1971]

Dear E.,

Have just arrived and been out on a long walk for my first day. I had no idea about this stretch of country. It's quite beautiful and completely unspoiled. Not a tourist in sight, and any amount of crumbling farm houses to buy, my dear. High up, plenty of air and wind. One wouldn't need a garden for the wild flowers are a treat, all wild briars and honeysuckle, my dear. The restaurant, if one and a half tables qualifies as a restaurant, serves a perfectly decent meal for ten francs. The village is quintessenially FRY,[1] with any amount of ingenious gadgets which don't quite work. The famous phone has been *enlevé* as he didn't pay the bill.

Madame Luc at the café says she knows of someone who has a *hameau* (whatever that may mean under the circumstances) which may

1. Jeremy Fry (1924–2005), artist, inventor, philanthropist.

or may not be to let during August. If so, would you like to up-sticks and come here during August. If not, we must think again. One couldn't live here all the year round without going slightly potty, but I do think it would be well worth while looking for a rough house. It's far nicer than Natasha Spender's[1] and all that Basse Provence part, and it doesn't take any more than an hour to get here by car from Avignon and the Paris sleeper.

Love B

To James Ivory

Postcard Apt church | Le Grand Banc | Oppedette | France | 3 July 1971

Come, do come, but quickly. I have this place which is incidentally a whole village all to myself till 17th–18th July. After that I must <u>station</u> myself elsewhere. It is remote and beautiful, high on a mountain. The phone has been cut off. I have no car. Neighbours fetch me to dinner occasionally, or I walk to the shop ½ hr away. So if you come you <u>must</u> hire a car. Fly to Marseilles and come here. Then we're mobile and you won't be bored. If you have my telegram, we will have talked on phone. If not leave message with Telephone Publique at Oppedette. Have tried twice with no success.

Or a message with HIRAM WINTERBOTHAM RUSTREL 2

To James Ivory

Oppedette | France | 3 July 1971

DO COME BUT QUICK STOP HIRE CAR MARSEILLE STOP CABLE OPPEDETTE LOVE BRUCE

1. Natasha Litvin (*b.*1919), pianist, m. 1941 poet Stephen Spender; had a house at Les Baux. From Chatwin's notebook: 'A description of the Stephen Spenders. *Il y aura chez lui des personnes qui vous connaissez parait-il trés bien, la femme joue au piano et écrit un livre sur les sensations auditives. L'homme est peintre. J'ai oublié le nom . . .* J-Claude-Roché.'

To James Ivory

Le Grand Banc | Oppedette | Basse Alpes | France | 12 July 1971

Dear Jim,

Have just intercepted your letter. The postman calls every other day so I have it one day earlier. I <u>have</u> rented another house from the 18th c/o Jean-Claude Roché, Aubenas-les-Alpes, Haute Provence. Tel 1. Aubenas. He is a great expert on birdsong and periodically leaves for Patagonia or the Galapagos to record the dawn chorus. Very unusual for a Frenchman to have an enthusiasm. The father was a famous old art collector called Henri-Pierre Roché[1] who knew Picasso in the good old days of 1910 and wrote *Jules et Jim*. The snag to this one is that Mrs C[hatwin] wants to come to France. I have told her the 25th would be the right date. This could be delayed a bit but not much. Do please try and come after the 19th for a few days. You can always fly on to Tangier from Marseille. Perhaps I could go to Tangier too, but that might be a bad idea until I negotiate a cheque from Edith's for something I sold Cary (note the order of progression: the Dahlink is paying). And money matters take a horribly long time in France. Also I am very very anxious about getting this book done. I know myself too well. Once in Morocco the footsteps lead to another horizon. I am a bum and I do not believe in work of any kind.

But I do badly want to see you – for lots of reasons. Apart from the obvious one, I want to ask your advice. I have in the rough a story, which doesn't really work as a novel because I have tried it. It is also a true story about someone I met by chance. I have a *goût de monstres* but this was the best ever and I ended up feeling the deepest compassion for him. He was a real estate agent in slum property in down-town Miami; each year he spent his entire income on coming to London as Cinderella from the Ball. His letters to me are great pieces of Americana; unfortunately they are in Glos. To my knowledge – and you will probably be able to correct me – nobody has ever dealt <u>compassionately</u> with the idea of going to Miami to die. Also <u>visually</u> Miami is

---

1. Henri-Pierre Roché (1879–1959), Dadaist whose semi-autobiographical novel *Jules et Jim* was filmed in 1962 by François Truffaut.

surely the most extravagantly beautiful example of holiday camp horror in America. I called my story 'Rotting Fruit'.[1] Do you think there might be something in it for you?

When you get this can you cable me at Oppedette <u>and</u> at Aubenas when you will be at a particular number in London and I will call you? But if I have to make an expedition of six kilometres to the phone box it isn't worth the bother and find you not there. You should also allow that you'll be at least one hour in the same place, because the lines have a tendency to whistle for half an hour.

Love, B

To Elizabeth Chatwin

Le Grand Banc | Oppedette | Basse Alpes | France | Tuesday 15 July 1971

Dear E.,

So the cheque came OK thank God! I have endorsed it and it is for you to pay into your external account FOR ME, but you can use it if it gets you out of a fix. I would like you to have your bank send me £100 to a bank of their choice in Apt, Vaucluse, <u>by cable</u> and fairly quick. I have about £30 odd still left but don't want to get stuck at all, and to inform me at once WHAT BANK.

Now the house. A couple I met with Hiram Wintherbotham[2] are called the Rochés, father was a famous old art collector and author of *Jules et Jim*. Jean-Claude is the greatest expert in France certainly on birdsong and has a chateau rigged up as a recording studio.[3] He is renting

1. 'Rotting Fruit' exists in rough draft, but not the letters. Edward Lucie-Smith heard it several times over 'and laughed till I was nearly sick each time I heard it . . . There was going to be a mausoleum in which this rich American was going to be buried with his Mom, with a "bronze dog" reposing at their feet.'
2. Hiram Winterbotham (1908–90), Glos textile manufacturer, who changed his name to inherit the business of Hunt & Winterbotham in Old Bond Street; had moved to France, near Apt, with his ex-guardsman servant.
3. Roché recorded birdsong that he sold commercially on cassettes. Requiring someone to say the names in English, he asked Chatwin – whose voice enunciates the names of 406 separate species.

me his mother's house two rooms all mod con when I want it till the 18th or so of August and even then it's not the end of the world because there is apparently bound to be something else.

I suggest you come around the 23rd or so with a car <u>plus</u> another typewriter as I suspect there will be typing to do, and the two large Oxford dictionaries and some money – enough money – mine if not yours and also the *New Yorker* article about Chomsky[1] which I left behind. It's not coming along too badly at all. At least I know how to do it.

. . . Jungle Jim Ivory wrote saying he wants to come to France and I've asked him here only if he brings a car. You can if you want buy a car with that money of mine, but I don't particularly want to own it. Did anything happen with my flute delivery from Parke-Bernet? If so please bring it with you, WELL WRAPPED. Also I suspect that Rogers and Co will have sent me a bill for the shipping of the Maori. Should be about £30. Please pay it.

Still quite beautiful up here. Never gets too hot. No mistral but a breeze. Apparently its freezing in winter but always bright.

love, B

P.S. Did you know, my dear, that Chatwin means 'a spiralling ascent' in Old English?

To Elizabeth Chatwin

Le Grand Banc | Oppedette | Basse Alpes | France | Tuesday [July 1971]

Dear E.,

Further to the phone call of today. I have a card from Charlotte today saying that the Max Ernst fetched £6500 which by my calculation should bring in about £150 or a bit less, and then there is Porter Chandler's Picasso which I don't know the price of. Plus the cheque from Cary [Welch] which if you haven't received it by now you should be calling the alarm, by cabling me at Aubenas or phoning there. Will you then

---

1. Noam Chomsky (*b*.1928), American linguist and political activist.

please do the following for me – buy and bring with you if he's there the little Plains Indian female figurine from K J[ohn]H[ewett]. The price I believe he quoted at me was £220 or so. Don't pay more and if he asks you say he'd better speak to me about it.

I go with Hiram [Winterbotham] to Douglas Cooper's[1] for dinner on Thursday and hope on Friday morning that the money will have arrived at the Société Général in Apt, that is if your confounded bank don't muck the whole thing up as usual. Otherwise I want and need nothing but perhaps a few more clothes. Rather low on shirts. Plus the things mentioned in my last letter.

See you, love B

Very nice American couple here! Jane Kaplan or something like that. On permanent staff of *New Yorker*.

Ivory duly rented a car and stayed for a week at Oppedette. 'We had a very good time together, driving around, meeting Bruce's friends (people like Stephen Spender). We went to see a sort of gay encampment of rich Englishmen who had bought a whole village on a mountaintop, including the deconsecrated church. He took me to Ménerbes for the first time (most likely in the hope of spotting Dora Maar climbing up the hill) and we went to St Tropez. We slept on mattresses on the floor of the rather bleak little house he'd rented, which was baking hot. Everything was fine, but the thought of Elizabeth driving across France at that time to join him, as she said she would, and maybe walking in on us some morning made him nervous. Eventually, reluctantly, I had to leave to join some American friends in Morocco.'

---

1. Douglas Cooper (1911–84), heir to Australian sheep-dip fortune and Cubist art collector who lived at Château de Castille.

To James Ivory
c/o Jean-Claude Roché | Aubenas-les-Alpes | France | 2 August 1971

Dear Jim,

No alarm calls so we presume all is well. By the time this letter reaches London you will probably be in New York. I had a note from a friend asking me to meet him in Marseilles which arrived eight days after the sending, and two days after he'd gone. I look forward to your acerbic comments on the riff-raff life in Tangier. Did you meet someone called Yves Vidal, known commonly as Ma Vidal, who owns some castle that sounds tasteless and hideous and is or is not normally for sale at a million dollars. All *meubles en matïere plastique*.

We have had the Mistral for four solid days and I have had a solid stomach ache. The house has become like a gas oven. Really, he might have had more sense than to plonk it on a south facing hill with a nice stretch of gleaming gravel to reflect the heat into the house. I doubt that Mummy will leave her apartment in Neuilly often to fry in these rooms.

Despite the heat and stomach I have gone racing on with the book. Forty pages have been done since you left. I do hope it's not all nonsense. I have also finished Mr C[1] I must confess with rising exasperation over the chapters on the minorities. I am afraid that like so many intelligent people he has fallen victim to a complaint called Aryan Nonsense. The mysterious blond brutes have an uncanny way of unhinging people's common sense.

I will leave here on the 18th or so and then go for eight days to Porto Ercole to see some old friends,[2] then back to England with the manuscript I hope pretty well intact. Never never never will I write anything longer than a few pages. Never – at least for a very long time – will I try anything that demands RESEARCH. I think on that

1. Chatwin is probably referring here to Lorenz, not Chomsky. His long 1971 article 'Excavating Lorenz' was never published; although he reworked many of its ideas into his 1979 review of Lorenz's *The Year of the Greylag Goose* for the *New York Review of Books*.
2. Thilo von Watzdorf, whose mother owned L'Annunziata in Porto Ercole.

day we were all under a cloud. You were anxious. I was anxious and I hadn't thought what I was going to be. Quite an emotional crisis, but it passed. What's to be done? America not before the 15th Sept. but I have really no idea. All depends on Tom Maschler at Jonathan Cape. Anyhow I miss you.[1]

    love, B

One of several film ideas that Chatwin pitched to Ivory was an episode from his 1969 Afghanistan trip. On 25 June 1969 Chatwin had dined in Kabul with Peter Willey, a major in the Territorial Army and senior housemaster at Wellington College who was leading a team of former pupils to the northern province of Badakhshan to make a study for the Anti-Slavery Society. It reminded Chatwin of a mission to Kabul in 1841 by a Society for the Suppression of Vice among the Uzbeks. He wrote in his notebook: 'They are, if the whole story bears credence, investigating the bond relationship between the growers of opium and Indian hemp and those who control the market. This constitutes a master-slave relationship. [The Anti-Slavery Society] has therefore provided funds and button microphones, and miniature cameras. The expedition lives on corned beef.'

To James Ivory
c/o Jean-Claude Roché | Aubenas-les-Alpes | France | 12 August 1971

Dear J.

    O my! that housemaster. As I have written to the *Times* in high

---

1. Ivory wrote to Chatwin on 6 September 1971: 'A young man asked me more or less out of the blue what place I would choose to live in for a year (you couldn't leave) and comprising an acre. I said in the south of France, thinking of Aubenas and its environs . . . you can see from this reply how fondly I recall my week with you in that perfect countryside.'

dudgeon and irony – so high they won't publish it – no spectacle, not even the Angel Gabriel on a trip, was more bizarre than one puffy public school master followed by three of the most exquisitely dressed and pretty and flirtatious boys, one with boots and marginally more masculine than the other two with handbags, as they picked their way delicately from the Ministry of the Interior to the Ministry of the Exterior to the Ministry of Education to the Ministry of Culture and finally when the Afghan government had made it abundantly clear that they didn't want to be investigated, least of all by an ex-British army ex-major, the party dropped in on the PM to be shown the door, first of all quite politely and then really rather rudely. The major, believe it or not, is the self-appointed expert on the Old Man and the Mountain and the hashashins,[1] and his real motive in attempting to queue barge his way into the northern province of Badakhshan was to try and contact a group of Ismailis who live there. To do this he invented a great yarn to [the] head of the Anti-Slavery Society of London and presumably Ltd., because it must be a profit-making institution, about the slave markets of Afghanistan. As I first heard it, the original slaves to be investigated were Czech and Hungarian women, enslaved in Bulgaria, traded in Afghanistan with officers in the Chinese Army for Opium. As that tale wore rather thin and to justify Major Gordon[2] the expenses, not only for the air tickets, but also for the button-microphones and miniature cameras, and tins of corned beef and the packet soups he had so generously provided (one couldn't expect boys that delicate and attractive to eat the native food), they found the slaves in the bazaars of Kabul, because Kabul was where the Afghans said the expedition must remain and remain it did.

My Dear, it was funny, very funny. And that really is worth a filum. Or maybe we might incorporate it. My mind has been on my book. O God that book, now lurching into the final chapter and letting off heavy ordnance at random, thereby probably murdering it myself. E and I are

1. Peter Willey, *Castles of the Assassins* (1962).
2. Actually, Colonel Patrick Montgomery. The Anti-Slavery Society published Willey's report *Drugs and Slavery* in July 1971.

going to the observatory this afternoon so that I can get a little celestial guidance and this letter as you can see is being ripped off at an alarming rate.

She THE FINANCIAL MASTER-MIND whose mind works only in terms of the Mellon Bank in Pittsburgh says you owe HER not me, the sum of 128 dollars – what a hideous expense that tiddly little car was, and then apparently the ticket came to more than we had imagined, because when we went to settle in Manosque the man said he was some short. Can you possibly send it to E direct at Holwell Farm?

The house at Aubenas is now filled at nights with little black flies that you can neither see nor hear.

Will be in touch as soon as ever I can.

xx B

To Charles and Margharita Chatwin
c/o Jean-Claude Roché | Aubenas-les-Alpes | France | 23 August 1971

Have had 2 very entertaining days with the <u>Mayoress</u> if that's what she can be called – of <u>Marseilles</u>. Am going to Italy for 8 days then return. All but the last 10 pages are done. What a relief when it's over! Bruce

To James Ivory
Holwell Farm | Wotton-under-Edge | Glos | 15 September 1971

Dear Jim,

Sorry for this hasty note. Elizabeth is flying to Boston and then to Upper New York State to face her sister's[1] wedding, and she will post it. I am two-thirds of the way through typing the book out, but the last

---

1. Felicity Chanler was marrying Steve Young.

chapter will require some energetic doctoring before I can bestow it on the unsuspecting publisher. When and as it is ready, I shall come, but not before I am released by him. Once in the US I don't particularly want to go back to the UK but still plan the South American trip, all being well.

She'll phone you in NY, because the poor thing is penniless, more penniless than I, which is a happy state of affairs but not likely to last. This means she will HOUND you for the dollars, so that she can go on little shopping expeditions to Abercrombie and Fitch.

Once I'm through I'll apply my febrile mind to the idea of the film about THINGS. Incidentally I have a splendidly macabre story about a compulsive collector of Cherry Blossom Boot Polish tins, set in North London between the wars, and ending with the most enigmatic death. See you I hope in about 6 WEEKS. Oh dear! What a long time!

Love

B

To James Ivory
Holwell Farm | Wotton-under-Edge | Glos | [October 1971]

Dear Jim,

You're an angel to send the cheque. Lord knows why you should have had to pay for the bloody car anyway though we'd have been pretty stuck without it. Anyway it eases the financial situation here somewhat. I have hardly earned a penny for the past four years, though I manage to survive somehow – a mixture of meanness and cunning but nothing more. The bright star on the horizon financially is that I have a feather cape from Peru bought for 300 bucks in 1966 in NY. Yesterday the phone rang from a friend asking whether I would accept $22,000 for it. You bet I bloody well would.[1] The deal has yet to go through, but God . . . just one further proof of the lunacy of the times.

1. Chatwin never sold the cape.

I have found the letter[1] to my great joy. Quote . . .

'According to you I have no appreciation of art. Well, I guess under certain circumstances maybe I haven't. Now take your Egyptian stuff. I wouldn't give you thruppence for the lot. But I have stood before the Absinthe drinkers in the Jus de Pomme for hours on end. I surround myself with the most beautiful objects this horrible world has to offer – including people. I am undoubtedly one of the most beautifully dressed men in the world. Everything I put on my body is the very finest of its kind that can be bought in the world so I think I can appreciate fine art or at least some aspects of it. Here is a little something you might like to think over. I have known many people in my long long life from garbage collectors to kings . . . etc etc' page upon page of it. I can't tell why I find it so funny.

We have just had a lunch party for thirteen people including my parents, some cousins of E.'s and their cousins – some local unspeakables. So I am feeling rather washed out.[2] The manuscript is at the typists. Regrettably there will have to be some radical alterations because I have just read some latest books on my line, and they show where I am wrong. Whole tracts will have to be rewritten, though the main thesis doesn't change. I hope to give the thing in to the publisher in early Nov, and then come with Howard and Julia Hodgkin to Boston and then to NY mid or late in the month. I keep on saying this and then nothing happens. I'm appalled at how long everything takes to get done. Living in the country doesn't help because one has to go hurtling up to London or Oxford to check a reference. In the end they'll probably turn the bloody thing down. It'll be interesting however to see which way the escape route runs. It really is too funny. Two friends of mine, ex colleagues and partners at Sotheby's resigned from the board because they, as non-

1. From the Miami collector (see p. 193).
2. E.C.: 'He was a wonderful guest, but a terrible host. He forgot to pass the bread around, he got the people he wanted to sit next to him and never bothered with anyone else, he never helped – and then he'd disappear and someone would say "Where's Bruce?" and he'd gone to write.'

smokers, objected to Sotheby's allowing Wills', the tobacco firm to bring out a cigarette called <u>Sotheby</u>. I had a good laugh and said very loudly in the salesroom that another brand name for cigarettes is 'Passing Cloud'.

ACTION in film is to my mind the answer. I'm afraid film without fast action is for me nearly a non-film. To me it's the whole point of the medium. I am very keen to do something on the <u>pilgrimage</u> theme myself – the idea of <u>finding oneself</u> in movement. Any ideas?[1]

Must stop I fear.

love Bruce

On 2 November 1971 the Chatwins' neighbour James Lees-Milne dined at Holwell Farm. Afterwards, he wrote in his diary of Chatwin: 'What does this boy want? He is extremely restless. He hates living at Holwell, wants continuously to be on the move . . . He has finished his nomad book and I wonder how good it is. When the 'or' has worn off his 'jeunesse', how much substance will be left?'

To John Kasmin

Postcard, A Kirgis Woman in Pamir Making Curd | Holwell Farm | Wotton-under-Edge | Glos | 29 November 1971

'Owing to constant dirt his clothing swarms with parasites which he amuses himself by killing in a most unceremonious way. It is a common sight to see an official of high rank open his sheepskin or kaftan wide open to catch an offending insect and execute him on the spot between his front teeth'

1. J.L.: 'Perhaps I was too stupid to understand that Bruce was <u>serious</u> about his film ideas, while seeming to play them down or making a joke of them. It never occurred to me that he wasn't just being entertaining in his letters, in the same way that Cary [Welch] always was, with preposterous plots and characters. When I read all his letters together, I see – too late – that Bruce might have been in earnest. I must have seemed like a poor friend, letting him down all the time.'

Lt-Col Prejevalsky, *Mongolia*.

Love Bruce

Please may I BUY the Kotah drawing of an elephant all falling down? £80.

To Joan Leigh Fermor
Holwell Farm | Wotton-under-Edge | Glos | 30 November 1971

Dear Joan,

I agree with you. I think the collections of the Hermitage <u>are</u> worth the price (usually heavy) one has to pay to get to them. Being outside a tour is equally ghastly, because then you are not at the mercy of Russian hospitality. This entails drinking sessions till two in the morning which start up again at ten. Liver pains and Animal style are intertwined in my consciousness, though, to my credit I may boast, Professor Masson, the Head of the Leningrad Archaeological Academy, slumped <u>under</u> the table while I stood on it declaiming Shakespeare for the benefit of his sister.

I do hope to see you in England. When do you come? Paddy [Leigh Fermor] I know is going to D[erek] Hill for New Year and we are supposed to be in Ireland for Christmas. But I have the most itchy feet and want to go to <u>Niger</u> – more nomads, the Bororo Peuls, the most beautiful people in the world who wander alone in the savannah with long-horned white cattle and have some rather startling habits like a complete sex-reversal at certain seasons of the year. So I may be off.

I have finished my book, but am so heartily dissatisfied with it, I hope it won't be published. I was brow-beaten by the publishers, who didn't like the idea of *Nomads in Central Asia*, into something far too general. It's turned out to be the great unwriteable. But there's no point in letting it ruin one's life.

Would Paddy put me up for the Traveller's Club? As I'm never really going to live in London it might be a convenient place to stay for a night or two in the week. I resigned from mine[1] because it was full of backgammon playing freaks. Anyway, it's an idea.

Have made it up with Miranda [Rothschild]![2]

Love

Bruce

Late in 1971 Chatwin borrowed a 16mm camera from Robert Erskine, who, since their journey to Afghanistan, had become well-known on television presenting a series of on-location archaeological films, The Glory That Remains. *Inspired by his discussions with Ivory, Chatwin planned to make a documentary about the market in Bermou, Niger.*

To Cary Welch
Holwell Farm | Wotton-under-Edge | Glos | [Christmas, 1971]

Dear C.

Got your letter by sheer chance. I managed last week to wrangle a free ticket to the heart of blackest Africa, and should by now have been celebrating Christmas among the baobabs and bowerbirds. This was not to be. When I came to present my ticket, I found that it was stamped for January 1st and not before. So I am back at the farm rather disgruntled and listening to a Moroccan record of pipe music made by a new friend called Brion Gysin,[3] who in turn is a friend of the dreaded

---

1. St James's Club, 106 Piccadilly, also home of Dilettanti Society, with separate room devoted solely to backgammon. Chatwin never did join the Traveller's Club.

2. M.R.: 'Suddenly I get a letter from Bruce – blue paper, blue ink, Mont Blanc pen, very permeable: *My dear M, I want to see you more than anything else in the world. I want you to forgive me more than anything else in the world. Yours B.*' Blaming himself for bringing Akbar into her life – resulting in Miranda and Iain Watson divorcing, with Akbar's letters being read out in court – Chatwin went to see her in Paris. 'He gives me a Mesopotamian duck-weight made of haematite. He'd affected my life to a tremendous extent. He owed me one.'

3. Brion Gysin (1916–86), English painter, poet, and inventor of cut-up technique used by William Burroughs (1914–97), American novelist and prominent member of the Beat Generation.

Mr Burroughs. I am at my lowest ebb at the minute, but will probably recover once the voyage starts. I have been trying to decode from the German a paper entitled *Uber epilepti che Wanderzustande* or the wandering mania.

About the money for the Maori board. The trouble is that it is an essential ingredient towards buying this flat,[1] and I can't do without it. Otherwise all the complicated transactions I have with the bank to buy it will be fouled up unless I have it ready before completing the purchase. This does I fear mean NOW – BY RETURN! If you haven't already put it in the post can you send it direct to my bank Lloyds Bank Ltd 23 Corporation Street, Birmingham 2, attention Mr Williams, marked for my <u>Property Account</u>. I calculate the sum to be 1482 dollars at the current rate of exchange. If it is on the way, will you let E. know by cable so that she can open the letter and pass it on. Sorry about this but it is as you see rather vital. I have had to raise all the money myself without asking for a sou from the USA side, because the last time I talked about it with them, they promised and promised and when it came to the crunch refused to lift a finger. Since when prices have doubled. I have sold literally everything I possess – which has also been very disheartening (not yr wedding present!).

To Charles and Margharita Chatwin
Agades | Niger | 29 January 1972

Hope all went off OK with the flat, though I have to confess it all seems so remote to me here. I can't understand why one has to live anywhere special at all. I have been looking again at nomads. Amazing group of cattle breeders called the Bororo Peuls who have no possessions, no houses, no tents even but follow their magnificent lyre-horned cattle about the bush. May go on from here through Nigeria to Lagos – thence by air to Cameroun and back mid-March. Much love Bruce

1. Chatwin had found a flat off the King's Road, 8 Sloane Avenue Mansions.

To Elizabeth Chatwin
Hotel de Rivoli | Niamey | Niger | [February 1972]

Dear E,

Cabled you from Agades but didn't know if you ever had it. Asked you to ask Nigel Greenwood[1] not to sell the feathers. Don't know why I think it's the one thing we should keep. Have just come back from the Mts of Aïr – camel journey of 10 days. Feeling very Beau Geste[2] and have grown neat military moustache to match (am being horribly interrupted by a pair of delicious tarts in bonbons and bandanas armed with portraits of President Pompidou who left yesterday – my fault for sipping champagne on the sidewalk). Haven't heard from Kasmin if he wants to go to Cameroun or <u>not</u>. I am tempted having £280 left. Will go up to Tahoua tomorrow to take the film of the market at Bermou. Most aesthetic market I've ever seen. Tuareg Bouzous Peulhs and Hausas, camels cattle that might have come from Egyptian tomb paintings etc

Hoping you might have had the proofs of the *History Today* article[3] to send to the above address, but if you cannot get them here by <u>Feb 8</u> at the latest I think we better forget it till I get back.

Have one marvellous story to write up[4] – French colonial setting (for which reason a round of the bars and cabarets tonight).

May go from here to Nigeria – Jos Ife Benin Lagos then to Cameroun up to Fort Lamy. Don't yet know. It'd be hellish hot.

Love B

---

1. Nigel Greenwood (1941–2004), dealer.
2. Character in 1924 novel by P. C. Wren who leaves Britain to join the French Foreign Legion.
3. 'The Mechanics of Nomad Invasions,' *History Today*, 22 May 1972.
4. 'Milk' was published in the *London Magazine*, August 1977.

To Derek Hill
Le campement, Tahora | Niger | [February 1971]

Not a scrap of architecture except the famous mosque of Agades which is little more than a mud-pie. Everything here is made of mud or dom palm fibre. Still the French colonial/New-Independent-inspired-African-Republic manner is an endless source of fascination. Le Style Neo-Sodomite[1] – Anarcho-Egyptian – Annamite-Pagoda – Cap Ferrat Mauresque – Functional Mud Hut moderne. Quite homogenous . . . I don't think I shall travel any more. Have just had a very tiresome session with black drunk muslim racists and am in a highly chauvinistic frame of mind. Love Bruce

To Elizabeth Chatwin
Hotel de Rivoli | Niamey | Niger | 5 February 1972

My Dear E.,

Have just returned here after shooting the bloody film. God knows how it'll be. I <u>hated</u> doing it – a blank day in my life. Can't remember anything of it. All is a very spectacular market where the desert folks meet the settlers. Anyhow it's worth a try, but I simply won't lug around all that camera equipment in future without a car – and how I hate cars!

Two things are new. I have started writing a long story – may even be a short novel. You know how I have an incurable fascination for French hotel/bordel keepers of a certain age in an ex-colonial

---

1. Notebooks: 'Barmou, Niger. A Hausa boy, after listing the attractions of his village
– You have seen the "grand omosexuel?"
– No
– You want to?
– Absolutely not!
This person turns out to be a tough, moustachioed Frenchman from Lyon, ex-Foreign Legion, a borer of artesian wells, builder of police-posts and village schools, who travels around in a Land Rover with eight spindly black boys between the ages of sixteen and twenty.
These all take turns to sleep with him.
– And when I need a white one, he says, there's always the Peace Corps.'

situation. Well I've been in on a most amazing series of encounters with one in Tahoua. Even held the fort while she had a *crise cardiaque* after sleeping with a Togolese bandleader (*L'Equipe Za-Za Bam-Bam et Ses Suprèmes Togolaises*). Much better than writing a travel piece because one can lie.

Second my moustache. It's beginning to curl up at the edges in a raffish, almost Blimpish way. I have to confess it is highly chic and for the first time in my life I feel I have got away from that awful pretty boy look and can envisage the possibility of growing old – if not with dignity at least with a certain style.[1] At the moment one might well have had a career in the movies in the age of Ronald Colman.[2] It's sort of d'Artag-nanesque. The card was from Christopher [Gibbs] inviting me (in purplish prose) to stay in the pinnacled folly in the Ourika valley – I don't know if I shall. I have now £200 left and all my air tickets. May very easily decide point blank to go through Dahomey, thence by boat to Douala and up through Fort Lamy.

XXX Bruce PTO

PS. Enclosed please find the AIRWAY BILL for a sack which I have sent air freight today. It contains in my rucksack at the bottom – the <u>film</u> which you should give to <u>Robert</u> [Erskine] as soon as possible + a whole lot of Sudanese cottons for my flat + the camera tripod (also for R.E) + some books + a box containing a number of highly precious possessions, including a dried chameleon and the eardrum of a lion.[3] Guard this box very carefully for reasons which will be explained later. I thought it would be best if you cleared the package rather than R[obert] E[rskine]. You'll need the car. Package went off today 7 Feb to Paris.

XXX B

PPS leave for Dahomey tonight.

---

1. E.C.: 'I thought his moustache was fine, but everyone hated it.'
2. Ronald Colman (1891–1958) actor, known as 'the English Valentino'.
3. E.C.: 'I was telephoned by customs. "What do you think is in here? It says CLOTHES." I said my husband had left here in winter clothes and obviously didn't need them. They never opened it. They'd have had a fit if they'd seen the lion's eardrum.'

To Charles and Margharita Chatwin
Postcard of Chatwin with moustache | Ouidah | Dahomey | [February 1972]

This town, an old slaving port, is one of the most fascinating places I've ever been in. The architecture is Brazilian baroque and owes its character to the liberated slaves who returned to their African home – often exceedingly rich – and built up a sort of Creole aristocracy whose descendants still walk the streets. Latin-American Catholicism is all mixed up with Voodoo religion from both sides of the Atlantic. The upper crust of Ouidah are all direct descendants of a Portuguese who managed to extend the slave trade clandestinely forty years after it had in theory been abolished by the British. Fascinating material for a book.

To Elizabeth Chatwin
Hotel de Douala | Douala | Cameroun | 16 February 1972

This place is something between Lausanne and a Turkish bath. Perfectly ghastly. Am on the hunt for a sculpture in the bush – one of the Bamileke dance masks of which four examples are known. Kasmin to whom I talked on the phone is sending some money. One or two other things to buy and I hope to recover the expenses of the trip. If I get the mask I shall probably fly back with it in a week or two   xxx B

Dahomey was absolutely fascinating with voodoo dances etc.

To James Ivory
Holwell Farm | Wotton-under-Edge | Glos | [March 1972]

Dear Jim,

So I'm back, never thinking to be back, and all the time I was in Africa having the guilty feeling of not having written you. Not having your address there was nothing I could do about it.

I have a moustache. I am thinner. I am crazy about Africa and the Africans. There aren't enough of them here yet. The thing I most miss here is the <u>proximity</u> of people. There one is quite used to a big mama with the fat rolling on her slapping you in the face with her tit as she humps it out to feed her infant. Here they recoil at the least touch.

I am still writing the bloody book. I finished it once to my satisfaction, but not the publisher's, and now I firmly believe it to be a load of humourless, egotistic, sententious rubbish. And I've set it aside to write a little story about an old style-French whore who retreats into the desert to run a hotel, and then there's another one about a young Hong Kong salesman of cheap cotton, who catches syphilis in Free Town and cannot return to his wife and newborn son. I've got to pick up better Chinese patter before this one will come off.

I also made a short filum. Hated doing it I might say. People threw things at the camera when I pointed it at them. It's about the markets in Niger, where trade is a sort of language which prevents people from cutting each other's throats. I thought – and still do – that it's far too amateurish to be of any use, but Vaughan Films are prepared to hack it into something, and then hawk it about the television companies.

Cary and Edith [Welch] were here and I just caught them in Paris on my way back from Dahomey. Seemed in very good form. They were with that zombyish creature called David Becker. They also said you were coming to Europe, especially for the Cannes Festival. Will I see you?[1] May even go to the Grand Banc with my writing for a bit.

I do have a flat. A hideous one-room affair, shaped 'in the form of a pompadour wafer' to quote the estate agent. I bought it because the rents are so capricious. Its merit lies in its being on the 9th floor overlooking half London, and its position, just off the King's Road. Can't move in quite yet till the painters come. The address is L8 Sloane Avenue Mansions, London SW3. Am about to send a letter to an African boy, who has just written 'I am very happy I have saved the money to

1. Chatwin was Ivory's guest in Cannes on 8 May 1972 for the opening of *Savages*.

write to you', also hoping that I am well and strong enough to do my job.

That Andrew [Batey] story[1] is fascinating. Maybe we could do something. Sorry must catch the post. Otherwise this will be delayed three days or more.

Will write soon.

much love, Bruce

To Derek Hill
Holwell Farm | Wotton-under-Edge | Glos | 29 March 1972

Please can you ring up over the weekend to resolve our dilemma. Ivry Freyberg's Floral Luncheon – this is not my style at all <u>but</u> though I will not go if you do not go, I cannot not go if you do. Wind blowing everything flat here.

Love, B

To James Ivory
Holwell Farm | Wotton-under-Edge | Glos | 8 April 1972

Dear Jim,

I had your letter today. I have been mouldering as usual in the country. It all seems so prissy after Africa. I think really considering the life I lead, I should try to <u>live</u> three months of the year in NYC which nobody could ever describe as dull. England is now little England with a vengeance, the world of boutiques and bitchery and little else.

Savages sounds a bit like NYC. What may very well horrify your smart friends is this. Everybody is prepared to slum. Ultra Violet you

1. J.I. to B.C. 12 January 1972: 'I told a friend of mine . . . that story of your friend Andrew Batey, as best I could recall it, and he was fascinated and also thought it was potentially wonderful material for a film.'

could film upside down with dildo up her twat[1] surrounded by 10 year old lesbian nymphettes providing her <u>surroundings</u> were suitable and everyone could draw comforting moral conclusions. Once you transfer that sort of thing into a Waspish Upper New York State it becomes less funny because you have moved into a province where innuendo and suggestion are the rule. I look forward to seeing it.

I did see Mr Chaudhuri.[2] And I enjoyed it. But I do think he's an almost impossible subject because you can't make a conversation piece out of someone who hasn't the vaguest idea how to converse, only to lecture. And on our set with its rotten reception he was all but inaudible. My dear, you have got to tell the public everything. My publisher says my book is exactly the same. We have to make the conclusions the preface or nobody will read a line more.

I'm going to have a word with Jeremy [Fry] about Le Grand Banc, but he is in Bangladesh selling boats to Bengalis. The alternative is a folly, literally, in the Atlas mountains about twenty miles south of Marrakesh which Christopher Gibbs will lend me. Please signify interest, rather quick as I'll have made up my mind.

Meanwhile I have to stay in London a bit to supervise the doing up of my minuscule flat. It resembles the bridge of a second-class cruise ship of the 1930's. The building was a famous call-girl warren before and after the war, and the whores are still there, mainly Hungarian, who drop their handbags in the lift and ask you 'Zahling, plis . . .' to pick them up. I am on the 9th floor with a panoramic view over London, which at that height doesn't remind me of London, so that's all right.

The Batey story. I think it is good. And my feelings are now totally numb and dispassionate. Quite good to start off on the 'France' or some such liner with the seduction – for the hell of it – by a young ravishing

---

1. Ultra Violet (*b.*1935), convent-educated French actress, notorious for wearing torn vintage mauve dresses and colouring her hair with cranberry juice.
2. Ivory's 54-minute documentary, broadcast on the BBC on 1 April 1972, about Bengali writer Nirad Chaudhuri (1897–1999) who four years after independence dedicated his first book to the British. J.I. to B.C., 12 January 1972: 'He's quite incomprehensible, but that, I firmly believe, is half the film's charm.'

American of an older less ravishing Englishman (young don?) on his way to get married and the subsequent chaos[1].

Where are you going to be in the summer. I have a rather less than defined longing to go to the US.

much love, in haste

B

To Cary Welch

Holwell Farm | Wotton-under-Edge | Glos | 8 April 1972

Dear C

England is gradually closing in on me again, and the moments of euphoria become rarer and rarer as one gets paler and paler and fatter and fatter and the backbiting conversations grow bitchier and bitchier, and everyone thinks and talks of selling something to somebody else. Mrs Chatwin and Mrs Kasmin are thinking of going into partnership in their idea of gathering together the folk arts of the world in a single emporium for taste-ridden, guilt-laden semi-intellectuals to browse among the indigo stuffs of Africa, the gauze saris of Rajastan, the basketry of Indo-China. It'll be a fine business.[2]

I have been making art works. The first a green fetish container called the God Box,[3] then a night blue affair called the Skinner Box, and I am presently cutting out Mainland Chinese literature to make a vivid red collage called The Colour of Immortality.

I rather liked your friend David Becker. Everyone here who met him couldn't understand why you were going round with 'an impossible zombie'. He wasn't really a zombie at all. Very tortured about

---

1. A.B.: 'I just imagine a Merchant-Ivory re-make of *Death in Venice* – my Tadzio (they found the real one – he died in Warsaw in 1986) to Bruce's Aschenbach – in German with English Subtitles.'
2. E.C.: 'A lovely idea, but a complete fantasy.'
3. The glass-fronted God Box was the only one of the three that he kept. E.C.:'He never talked about it, never explained. It was completely personal. I honestly don't know what it meant. Magic, I suppose.'

something. That ashen quality. But he kept on making intelligent, if unsure remarks. This in contrast to oneself, who makes cocksure, but unintelligent remarks. My filum is not at all too bad. I was quite amazed, considering my extreme irritation at the whole process. They say they'll be able to cut it into a picture of about twenty-five minutes and sell it to European television.[1] Now I want to do another one.

My African artworks are so much appreciated that Mr [Sandy] Martin wants me to go back to Africa at once and buy the things I didn't buy. I am tempted, but feel it's tempting fate. Remember what nearly happened last time. Nemesis building up? Warning signals? Don't touch the ju-jus, massa. Dont want no buy carved stick, massa. Carved stick he have bad medicine, massa. And talking of bad medicine I appear to have a jigger in my foot. Elizabeth expressed the hope that I wouldn't have elephantiasis. Last week she thought I might have sleeping sickness. Incidentally we would not know of the existence, let alone the symptoms, of these dread complaints were it not for a Little Red Book put out by the Royal Geographical Society called the *Traveller's Guide to Health*.

It is written in the most beautiful military prose and concentrates on the prevention of disease rather than its cure, with such admonitions as 'The Tse-tse fly is the vector of Sleeping-Sickness, which usually proves fatal to the European. If the traveller must penetrate Tse-tse fly regions, he must be sure to clear the forest to within a quarter of a mile radius of his camp.'

Must now stop and pay bills,
much love Bruce

In the summer of 1972 Chatwin had a call from Francis Wyndham 'who master-minded the Sunday Times *colour supplement' – and was offered a position, which he accepted, as adviser on Art. 'The job, as I understood it, was to commission articles from people who knew about art. I was at my wit's end. All my schemes to work had*

1. The 25-minute documentary for Vaughan Films, with Erskine's voiceover, was lost while being hawked around European film companies.

come to nothing. My confidence was at zero. I was in debt.' The job
would start in November. On 25 July he abandoned London for
America, where Ivory had lent him a clapboard cabin in Oregon.
Here, goaded by the publication of Peter Levi's account of their
journey to Afghanistan, Chatwin determined to finish his nomad
book once and for all.

To Elizabeth Chatwin

P.O. Box 464 | Harriman Route | Klamath Falls | Oregon |
28 August 1972

Dear E.,

We've had a succession of brilliant days here, and I must say it's
quite pleasant. The house is a bit gloomy because it's under vast pine
trees and doesn't get much sun till about 11-30. But there's a dock you
can sit on which juts out into the water. And now everyone's going home
for labour day and the noise of the motor boats will happily cease for
weekends. There's a mountain called Mount Pitt at the end of the lake,
and endless trails through the forests. I wandered along the Brown Mountain trail STARK NAKED for fifteen miles without coming across a soul[1]
but deer and birds and that made me very happy.

The Book is coming on well. Not fast. But I have now found myself
with it and I know what I'm doing instead of flailing around in a disorganised way with marvellous material and no sense of direction. When
I went to Geneseo I bought a beige Volkswagen with a loan of 700 dollars
from your mother. I thought it better to buy a good one rather than some
rattle-trap that will collapse. Jim [Ivory] got your cheque before he left
NY but now we have a note saying it isn't payable in Continental USA.

---

1. Chatwin did once come across the caretaker at Lake of the Woods, Charlie Van,
who reported back to Ivory: 'I saw this guy back in the woods a ways, hiking. And
this son-of-a-bitch was stark naked, except for his big hiking boots, going along
like he was in a nudist colony and owned the place. I shouted Hey you! and he
turned around . . . And you won't believe this, but he'd tied some flowers round
his pecker.'

What can be done? I cannot imagine what happened . . . Can you correct the same? Because I find it rather embarrassing. Failing that can the Mellon send it direct?

God this country's so expensive. I don't know how anyone lives here at all. I'm down to 300 bucks and will have to borrow more from Jim to get back. So that's why I'm anxious about the other. He is leaving in a week and I will drive him down the Northern California coast route just to San Francisco for two days and then return here for the whole of the rest of the month. What do you intend to do? I will have to be back in England I suppose for the wretched *Sunday Times* by October 15th at the latest. The idea of a job horrifies me. I am more doubtful about the thing than ever before.

I think they'd like you to come over at Geneseo. It was very pleasant when I was there. I suppose before there have always been too many people swamping me whenever I've been. Lonely for them too now that everyone's gone.

Of course what I should really like to do would be to go and sit in a little house in Yucatan and watch sharks and fiddle about in the ruins of Tulum.

Much love Bruce.

To Charles and Margharita Chatwin
P.O. Box 464 | Harriman Route | Klamath Falls | Oregon |
30 August 1972

Hello!

I'm sorry I left in such a precipitous hurry, but there we are. I usually do and I did. I was getting totally exasperated a. by the weather which had given me the worst chest and lung combination I have ever had. London in July and one was literally coughing up grey slime. b. that film company was driving me nearly desperate. I always think I'm pretty disorganised but they are something else. I'd go in each day prepared to work on it and there'd be some hold up. I couldn't use the cutting room or my assistant was needed to play court on some movie mogul. It's a terrible business. At least if you write, you are your own master. The

only way to get my little film out of the way was to announce my departure. Then it happened. At least I hope it did, because there's not been
a single word. And I must finish the book before I begin with the *Sunday
Times*. Otherwise it'll never be done.

Of course I've completely unscrambled it. In fact I'm completely
rewriting it. It'll be about half as long and instead of six whopping chapters with an argument linking them all in a continuous flow (which not
even I could understand let alone the poor reader), we now have about
thirty chapters, each one I hope intelligible by itself.

Oregon is simply beautiful. The house I have borrowed is a little log
cabin on a lake called Lake of the Woods, surrounded by tall pines. There
is a canoe and I can paddle up a river to look at beavers making dams
and it's very warm for swimming. The nights are cold because we're
five thousand feet up. The nearest town is thirty-five miles away so I've
bought an old Volkswagen for the summer. I'm staying here till about
September 10th; then I'm going to take a short break and go up to Puget
Sound and Vancouver. It's only a day's drive from here to Seattle, your
old stamping ground[1], though I bet it's changed. I'd very much like to
see all that rain forest they've preserved as a national park on the Olympic
Peninsula. Elizabeth may come and join me but since she's been away
we haven't been in touch. It is an awful hassle to get out all this way,
and one really feels like completing the circuit having got thus far.

Nearby there's a Shakespeare Festival of all things, the oldest in
North America founded in the early twenties. The town Ashland is full
of banks and hamburger joints got up to look like Ann Hathaway's cottage.
Teenage girls float around with syllabub trays and if you want to eat
there's always an English tart. 'It's sort of like a pecan pie, but we call
it English tart . . .' The performance was horrendous. The women were
like the daughters of the American revolution at a bridge party and the
men all came from Texas and gassed about on phoney hobby horses
waving silk handkerchiefs at each other, shouting 'Hi . . . yeee . . .' I
have refused an invitation to go to the *Taming of the Shrew*.

1. In 1943, Lieutenant-Commander Charles Chatwin RNVR had crossed North America
by Canadian Pacific Railway to pick up a large new mine-sweeper at the naval base,
under Britain's 'Lend-Lease' arrangement with the USA.

I don't know how long it will take. I am simply going to sit here and finish it. I refuse to be budged. My book, whatever anyone may say, is far the most important thing I've ever attempted. This place is quite conducive to work. So there we are.

Much love, XXX

Bruce

To Elizabeth Chatwin
P.O. Box 464 | Harriman Route | Klamath Falls | Oregon |
14 September 1972

c/o Charles Van

Dear Hurrubureth,

Charles Van is the caretaker here and as all the post is directed through him it's best to put his name on letters because the main supplies of post have gone, the summer people having flown and I seem to be left entirely alone with the beavers.

So we went to San Francisco which is so unlike anything else in the US it doesn't really bear thinking about. It's utterly light-weight and sugary with no sense of purpose or depth. The people are overcome with an incurable frivolity whenever they set foot in it. This doesn't mean that one couldn't live here. In fact I think one could easily, preferably with something equally frivolous to do. I stayed with the Oppens[1] and they were lovely. They have no money. He is very Jewish of the muscular outdoors type and they sail all round Maine in an open 16ft dingy with a light plastic awning. Imagine. He considers every word meticulously and makes one feel slightly foolish. I think his poetry is some of the best in America. She is sort of homespun with one of those little girl-straight-from-the-ranch simplicity faces, even though she's nearing seventy. We went one night to the grand San Francisco poet Robert Duncan[2] who is famous with the young for his grandiloquent and skillful outbursts on the

1. George Oppen (1908–84), American Objectivist poet, married to Mary Colby.
2. Robert Duncan (1919–88), American San Francisco Renaissance poet.

Vietnam war. I on the other hand thought him one of the most unpleasant people I have ever met, with a waxen witch-like face, hair tied in a pigtail and a pair of ludicrous white sideburns. He gassed on and on in a flat monotone and it was impossible to decide if the tone was hysterical or dead pan. The house was a creepy-crawly nightmare, and betrayed *la moralité des choses*, all *art nouveau* of the worst kind. Bloodless fingers fingering the objects as he spoke, and I suspect that if he weren't fingering *art nouveau* objects he could just as easily be pressing buttons or ordering napalm, so sinister and obsessed with the demonic alternative he was.

There's a beautiful little town on the north coast of S.F. called Mendocino with marvellous clapboard buildings and water towers and sculpture of the latter-day Greek revival and if it gets too cold here I might try and find a room down there on the coast for a week. So beautiful there with sheer cliffs going down to the sea and wind-blown pines and sea-lions on the rocks, and redwood in the mountains behind. The northern section of the road is utterly deserted, then one meets the real estate signs, then the developments in varying degrees of artyness, then the funeral parlours. The one thing I feel about S.F. is that it doesn't reek of death, whereas almost everywhere else does. I intend to stay here or nearby until October 5th or so and should have a great hunk of this done by then. I am writing fast, then hitching the things up for the finer points of style later. I had terrible trouble with my back at one stage. It hurt all down my right side, not the left as was usual. It was sitting down to type that did it, plus the most horrible bed that meant one was floating in an oily sea. Plus I imagine the <u>diet</u>. So I went to health shop in S.F. and spent 50 bucks on emetic food. Needless to say I ran into the dreaded Linda who was buying her molasses and brown rice at the same time. Grown enormously fat she had, and she was with the Sufis.

Yes I should like to go to Africa this winter and preferably to Dahomey, and would certainly be prepared to go THERE with the Kasmins. We could take a car perfectly easily from Cadiz or Barcelona or wherever to Abijan in Ivory Coast. It gets there in three days and there's no earthly problem and it means one doesn't have to have something that crosses the Sahara. But to be comfortable one must go in January at the very latest. Otherwise the heat and the rain start to set in. Preferably of course before. Like November. God knows how to finance. Means I must work like a black. The more I cogitate it the more I dread the *Sunday Times* business as being something I don't want to do. I have sent a host of letters from here about this and that, none of which gets a reply. I'm exasperated without having begun. One's independence is so fragile a thing and I hardly think the money matters. Frankly, I prefer to flog the flat or long-let it rather than have to work in London. I find it fine for three weeks, but thereafter, WHAT IS THERE TO DO? I hate the theatre and the weather kills me. I seriously contemplate a cabana near Hiram [Wintherbotham]. What do you think? Or the Pyrenees. What do you think of the Kasmins',[1] a bit like Holwell for scenery?

Not one bit surprised by P[eter] Levi's expulsion from Greece[2] and frankly and being rather cruel I think he richly deserved it. Though naturally he wanted it to happen, being such a publicity seeker. He courted the police to make them think he was suspicious. I found it immensely irritating, though less so than the Afghan book[3] which drove me wild with rage and I think I'd better not read it or I shall become apopleptic. I hope HIS book won't mean <u>we</u> are expelled from Afghanistan. What he really seems to enjoy is implicating other people in his own mess. All that harum-scarum Scarlet Pimpernelery only implicates his other English friends like Paddy and Joan [Leigh Fermor] and he can waltz about calling them crypto-fascists when they disassociate themselves from him. That's about the level of his political carry-on. O what a subject for a novel. I really think I must write one. P.L. is really about on the level of Major Willey when it comes to that sort of thing. The thing that really infuriates me about the Afghan book is that all my remarks and observations are repeated verbatim as an integral part of his text. Much love B

Have found 18th Cent Hawaiian food bowl.

1. Kasmin had a house in the Dordogne.
2. P.L.: 'My name was on a list. I was at the British School of Archaeology in Athens and had been helping to get Greek citizens out who wanted to escape. I was arrested in Corfu and sent out.'
3. *The Light Garden of the Angel King: Journeys in Afghanistan* (1972).

To James Ivory
P.O. Box 464 | Harriman Route | Klamath Falls | Oregon |
14 September 1972

Forgotten what day of the week it is.

Dear Jim,

All well here. Fine but cold. This is the last letter. Hope it's not a declaration of total war from your sister. Cary [Welch] writes me that he hasn't yet gone to England and will do so before the end of the month and will then be in the flat. You'll have to arrange it between you who has it, and there's not room for two, UNLESS OF COURSE . . . But that is impossible.

Off to Ashland to shop.

love B

P.S. Elizabeth says it's YOUR BANK'S STUPID FAULT. There was No reason why that cheque wasn't payable in the US. They simply don't use their eyes. Anyhow the money's been cabled.

When Chatwin left Oregon in late September he carried with him a manuscript that he believed to be virtually finished. In Los Angeles he called on the writer Christopher Isherwood and poured out to him its essence. On 28 September 1972 Isherwood wrote in his diary: 'Yesterday, we had a visit from Bruce Chatwin, a blond, blue-eyed but somehow not really attractive friend of Peter Schlesinger. He is an anthropologist – and has spent time with native groups of hunters in the lands south of the Sahara; Mali, Niger and Chad. He maintains that hunting-groups aren't religious; religion only begins when people settle down and have individual possessions. (I didn't want to get into semantics so didn't challenge this, because it was obvious that Chatwin attached a different meaning to the word "religion".) But he was extremely interesting, describing how the boys between thirteen and sixteen wear a sort of drag and are regarded as girls. The whole hunting-group is perfectly adjusted to its environment; even the young children know what stars are rising and setting and when the migrations of birds take place and what habits the various animals have. As Chatwin put it, they differ from us in that they never try to interfere with Nature in any way. They also think that our preoccupation with possessions is crazy; according to their way of thinking, you share everything you have, so they "steal" from tourists, only it isn't really stealing because they don't want to keep what they take.'

On 30 September, Isherwood wrote again: 'I had some more talk with Chatwin yesterday morning on the phone – I think he has now left Los Angeles, on his way to see some of the pueblos of New Mexico. He repeated some of the things he told me when he came to the house – that he regards the hunting-groups as being fundamentally unaggressive; that "much of what passes for aggression is a response to confinement" and that where there is no confinement giving replaces aggression – when two groups are in the same territory they don't fight over it, they exchange gifts, one group leaving its gift at a certain place and the other accepting it only when the gift seems sufficient; if the gift is not accepted, the giver adds to it until the recipient thinks it adequate and takes it away, leaving another gift in its place. Chatwin is very scornful about Konrad Lorenz's On Aggression *and says that his philosophy is derived from the same sources as that of the Nazis.'*

On his return to England early in November, Chatwin delivered his manuscript to Deborah Rogers, who waded conscientiously through it: 'I remember the heart sinking.' She found the writing leaden, the content plodding. Unable to see a way to salvage the book, she nevertheless sent it to Tom Maschler who read 50 or 60 pages and stopped. 'They were terrible. They were completely sterile. They were a chore to read and I imagine a chore to write.' Maschler told Chatwin his verdict face to face, saying: 'Something's going wrong here and maybe you should not be doing this.' He says, 'I remember Bruce saying as he left: "I'll think about it." I hoped I'd put him off.'

To Derek Hill

L8 Sloane Avenue Mansions | London | 24 November 1972

Why don't you move into the farm pro temp. The whole upstairs can be made into studio etc. We can go away more often and it'll all be lovely.

CHAPTER FIVE

SUNDAY TIMES: 1972–4

Chatwin began work at the Sunday Times *on 1 November 1972. He found himself part of a tight-knit editorial team that considered no subject too ambitious or too trivial.'For a time it was the best photo-journalism magazine in Europe. I remember angry Frenchmen demanding their money back from the kiosk outside the Café Flore. That was the Sunday when, for "economic reasons", the magazine was not sent to France with the paper.'*

Although hired as arts consultant, Chatwin was given leave by the senior editor Francis Wyndham to spread his wings.'At our first meeting I made suggestions – and one was adopted. We chose a photographer.

'"Now," I said,"we shall have to find a writer."

'"Don't be silly," said Francis."You'll write it yourself."

'"I can't," I said."I can't write."

'"I've never heard such nonsense."

'The article was that on Madeleine Vionnet.

'The rest followed.'

After three years of tussling with his nomad book, the magazine offered Chatwin a deadline and an audience.'We soon forgot about the arts, and under Francis's guidance, I took on every kind of article.' As a journalist he would file from Paris (on the couturière Madeleine Vionnet, the artist Sonia Delaunay, the writer André Malraux); New York (on the Guggenheims); Moscow (on the collector George Costakis, the architect

Konstantin Melnikov, Nadezhda Mandelstam, widow of the poet Osip); Vienna (on the animal psychologist Konrad Lorenz, the 'Nazi-hunter' Simon Wiesenthal); Upper Swabia (on the aesthete Ernst Jünger); Marseilles and North Africa (on Algerian migrant workers); Peru (on Maria Reiche and the Nazca Lines); India (on Mrs Gandhi, Shamdev the Wolf Boy). 'He was better in short stretches,' says the historian Robin Lane Fox, who came to know him at this time.'He was an unsurpassed feature writer. He had an ability to evoke a place and build supportable castles in the air which were actually well founded.'

Few letters from this period have come to light.

Almost the first subject Chatwin suggested for a profile was the 93-year-old Irish architect, and designer of the chrome chair, Eileen Gray, who had lived in Paris since before the First World War. One winter Sunday afternoon at 3 p.m. he called on Gray in her apartment at 21 Rue Bonaparte.

To Eileen Gray

L8 Sloane Avenue | London | 21 December 1972

Dear Miss Gray

I cannot thank you enough for the most enjoyable Sunday afternoon I have spent in years.[1] This morning too I have looked at your cahiers with Alan Irvine[2] and I am completely bowled over by them.

I do hope you'll come over for the exhibition. It is going to be most

1. Chatwin never wrote the profile, but something else came of his interview. In Gray's salon hung a map of Patagonia, which she had painted in gouache. '"I've always wanted to go there," I said. "So have I," she added. "Go there for me."' From 'I Always Wanted to Go to Patagonia – The Making of a Writer,' *New York Times Book Review*, 2 August 1983.
2. Alan Irvine, curator of an exhibition of Gray's work, *Eileen Gray: Pioneer of Design*, staged at the Heinz Gallery of the RIBA, 8 January–23 March 1973.

exciting; but if not could I please come again sometime to the Rue Bonaparte.[1]

I am sorry this has taken so long. The first letter ended up in Spain by mistake!

yours sincerely, Bruce Chatwin

To Valerian Freyberg
Dordogne | France | 25 April 1973

Two godfathers staggering out of a marginally drunk lunch in a fairly obscure part of Perigord send their warmest greetings to their godson and hope he will not follow their example. Bruce David.[2]

To Stella Astor and Martin Wilkinson[3]
Postcard, Ambrosius Holbein, Portrait of a boy with blond hair, Basel, Kunstmuseum | Glos | 13 September 1973

How I envy your eyrie in the hills. Especially after returning to the dreaded London. I walked to Kington from you, then to Penelope Betjeman nr Hay where I had two exhilarating days riding the Black Mountains bareback on her Arab. West Glos seems very heavy and dreary after the fun and games on the border. Many thanks. Much love to you both.

1. When Gray died, Chatwin tried and failed to persuade the Victoria & Albert to buy her room intact. In March 2009 a 24-inch tall wooden and leather chair that she designed was sold at auction for £22 million.
2. David Rogers. Paul Getty and Ralph Dutton were Valerian's other godparents.
3. Stella Astor (b.1949) m. 1974 Martin Wilkinson. They lived at The Cwm in Shropshire.

To Elizabeth Chatwin
Telegram | October 1973

NO PHONE HOPELESS COME ALGIERS 9 OCT STOP BRING
DESERT SHOES ONE DRESS AND NOT LESS THAN
250 POUNDS WILL REPAY WILL GO CENTRAL SAHARA
BRUCE

To Ivry Freyberg
Holwell Farm | Wotton-under-Edge | Glos | 2 November 1973

Can I come and see my godson – and his parents(!) in the near future.
My life at present is the way I like it. Perpetuum mobile, so it'll have to
be a snatch visit. What about a mid-week commuter special overnight
stay?? Much love B

*In November 1973 Chatwin stayed with the Rezzoris at their
home near Florence. Rezzori (1914–98) was an Austrian-born
author, best known for* Memoirs of An Anti-Semite. *'It gave us
great pleasure to exchange useless curiosities,' he wrote of
Chatwin in* Anecdotage. *'He went into virtual raptures when I
told him that about the only thing I remembered from my studies
of mining geology were the names of the five sites where gold is
found in the former Dual Monarchy: Schemnitz Chemnitz
Nagybanya Ofenbanya Vöröspatàk (mineral resources of the
Danube region). He tried to learn these names by heart which
given the challenge they posed to his Anglo-Saxon speech
apparatus was no simple matter. This only doubled his enjoyment.' In the same vein, Chatwin left this entry in their visitors'
book.*

To Gregor and Beatrice Von Rezzori

Donnini | Florence | Italy | 31 November 1973 [sic]

Menu

Huile d'olive vierge gelée avec sauerkraut

Sardines mordecai (eat a live sardine)

Gravelax (prepare 2 sides of a salmon and press between 2 slabs of stone with salt and dill. Leave 2 weeks)

Stuffing for pintade or pheasant (must wrap bird in bacon)

Sorbet aux mangues avec Rhum blanc

Cheese: formaggio tartufato – gorgon Emile Zola

Wines: Papa Blumen 1970 Vinsanto – Eger Bull's Blood 56

Camel's milk. Infusion d'hibiscus.

PS As alternative Boile of duck (with vinegar) serve with a horse-radish ice-cream

In spite of commitments to the Sunday Times, *Chatwin had not abandoned his nomad book. His article on the blood-sweating horses of the Chinese Emperor Wu-Ti, and their possible descent from Alexander's battle-horse Bucephalus, drew a fan letter from Robin Lane Fox, a young classical historian then preparing his biography of Alexander the Great. Chatwin wrote a two-sided letter back. Their correspondence is lost, but Lane Fox retains a clear memory of the contents. 'Of course, Bruce wrote, many friends had told him that there was no future chasing horse bones through the steppes of Central Asia, but he gathered that I, too, had been in Afghanistan [in 1972], and he would like to meet and discuss the discovery of Alexander's route across the desert and what I thought of Ai Khanum, the Greek city many thought was founded by Alexander. We met in London and he gave me his essay on Animal Art. We struck up an immediate friendship. I thought: "Here is someone whose horizons stretch way beyond property prices in Bayswater; here is someone who can use allusions – Tacitus, Ibn Khaldun, Flecker, Louis Sheaffer's* The Golden Peaches of Samarkand; *here is someone who has devoted his life to objects* beyond "that last blue mountain barred with snow". My book came out in November 1973 and Bruce was back in touch with a letter saying how much he caught. "I know it mattered as I missed the buff-coloured uplands of the lower slopes of the Hindu Kush in your company, with the scent of bitter wormwood in the air and white wild roses ahead of us. I want to talk to you about the Dionysiac adventures of the Macedonians in Nuristan. I have photographs which I think will appeal to you." The photos were black and white, of boys with dark eyes, their hair entwined with long vine leaves and ivy, returning to their village in the evening. Bruce understood that Alexander's troops believed in that area they'd discovered the groves of Dionysus.'

In the same year, Lane Fox became a lecturer in Classical Literature and Languages at Oxford. When, the following November, Chatwin telephoned and asked him to come to Patagonia, he had to decline. 'I couldn't have wandered. I had a family to feed. I opted for a world of syllabus and system and approved footnoting and references, departmental collegiality, evidence and proof – and I funked it. Bruce makes me realise that there are more things in the universe than our systems and merit awards allow us to dream of.'

Reflecting on their conversations, Lane Fox says: 'Bruce wasn't really romantic. He was well-informed about apparently romantic and exotic things. He talked of Diogenes and Lorenz and the animal in us all. He told me that man was essentially restless and it was an illusion he could settle in one place. Once he invited me and my first wife Louisa to lunch in Wotton-under-Edge. He had hired two horses to ride to Westonbirt. He talked the whole journey about his nomadic project, the nomads' craving for the colour of mud on brown steppes light of tulips, and how the only way they could maintain it was in their textiles. There was incessant talk of the book he was writing about nomads. This is where conversation would come back to rest.'

To Elizabeth Chatwin

La Fonda|Plaza Santo Cristo|Marbella|Spain|9 April [1974]

Dear E.

I have got your first letter but not yet the second – and I may never get it now as I think the best thing will be if I go for a bit to the Atlas. I do love my walks so much and I get well unblocked on them, though today I have had a ? brilliant (tomorrow it will be poor) idea for one of my chapters. I am going to write my hunter's chapter in the manner of Turgenev's sketches. My first chapter is called *Diogenes and Alexandra* being the least and the most. I went from Ronda which was appallingly bleak at this time of year to Janetta's¹ House near the sea. Very well ordered days with Magouche and a beautiful garden etc. House was love-ly<u>ish</u>. Too much care attached to <u>maddening</u> details. Incidentally, I honestly believe that what Holwell needs is the whitewash pail inside. It really is terribly easy to slap a new coat on each year. It takes a morning. And a lot of sofas covered in cotton and a lot of cushions. I'd bring down that old reed mat from the bedroom again for the drawing room – and I'd whitewash inside the fireplace. If you get the chance in Bristol why not have the Mahdi's flag² and the Moroccan (it is 16th cent) textile put behind glass – they fit exactly.

To help the house problem etc. I'd like to give you that Ibibio head (black) which you can sell. I believe it should be worth about £500 but is perhaps best sold in France or Belgium. Ask F[elicity] N[icolson] what she thinks. Also I do think that Jap box is an awful extravaganza at the moment. Perhaps we could send it back? She'll yowl in agony but *tant pis*. You should also whitewash the wall by the kitchen at the back and have masses of potted plants like they have here all round.

1. Janetta Woolley (*b*.1922) m. to Dr Kenneth Sinclair-Loutit; Robert Kee 1948–50; Derek Jackson 1951–6; 1971 to Jaime Parladé, Marques de Apesteguia, Spanish archi-tect; lived at Tramores on the lower slopes of the Ronda mountains. She had worked for *Horizon*.
2. The banner carried in battle by Muhammad Ahmad (1844–85), Sudanese leader who in 1881 proclaimed himself the Mahdi, leading an uprising that culminated with the fall of Khartoum. Gloria Taylor had married his grandson, Tahir.

I saw the Connolly thing[1] in the *Sunday Times*. Boring. But also *tant pis*. In fact it was silly egocentric drivel, but that is what goes down, so one can't mind. I've really gone off him. Magouche couldn't read *The Rock Pool* either.

I will come back at the end of May for June–July hopefully and then I suggest we think of going somewhere adventurous together? <u>S America.</u> <u>S. Seas?</u> (except that I'm still keen on Francisco de Souza as an idea) What are the options on the house? A professor from Bristol here for the Academic Year? Possibly Steph[anidis] might want it. Could even be persuaded to put things in it? Staff it? Why not ask him. Also say that the year's tenure is coming to an end in June on the Feathers. What to do?

Rang R.S.T.[2] and will be dining with him in Tangier tomorrow night. Alistair Boyd[3] is an extremely nice intelligent Hispanic nut, married to a second wife, who was once married to Kingsley Amis and is hopelessly drunk all the time. They are further wedded to an enormous Palazzo called Palazzo Monchagon, Moorish – 16th Cent Spanish which will be their grave unless they rid themselves of it.

Do whatever you think with the flat. I never really want to set foot in it – or ever to live in London. But cannot be bothered. XX B

In the summer of 1974 Bruce and Elizabeth stayed in Norway at Fiva, a traditional white painted wooden house above the River Rauma.

1. Cyril Connolly (1903–74), English critic. Almost his last piece for the *Sunday Times* magazine was *Cooking for Love* on the Andalusian cookery of Janetta Parladé, 'a phenomenon of our time it would take too long to describe . . . the pleasantest and most stimulating companion that an artist could hope for, one who would drive you to Ankor at the drop of a map'.
2. Richard Timewell, head of Furniture at Sotheby's, had a house in Tangier.
3. Alasdair Boyd (*b.*1927) 7th Baron Kilmarnock, married to Hilary ('Hilly') Bardwell. Her first husband, the novelist Kingsley Amis (1922–95), came to live with them at the end of his life.

To Hugh Chatwin
Fiva | Aandalsnes | Norway | [Summer 1974]

Dear Hugh,

We are thinking of you here because we feel you would be better off than us. The River Rauma is apparently the best salmon fishing in Norway. Our hosts – the Bromley-Davenports[1] – own about five miles of it. Recently a salmon, more porpoise than a salmon, of about 60 lbs was hauled out of it.[2] All we do is watch the ten-pounders lift themselves like aeroplanes over the falls.

We are glad, too, to escape here from the angst-ridden place we left. Imagine if you can a nervous artistic German aristocrat,[3] married to but hating a Guinness, pretending in Norway to reincarnate her English suffragette aunt of 1905, wearing crinolines and parasols, even on the glaciers, and introducing a company of musically minded drunks, who played an awful wheezing bagpipe and were dreadful in their Irishness. It was, I tell you, frightful. It was enough to turn maddest of men into raving Whitelaws.[4]

It is a charming country, this, but ouch the expense.[5] Back soon,
Bruce

1. Sir Walter Bromley-Davenport (1903–89), Conservative MP, and his American wife Lenette.
2. The salmon was transported back to Fiva strapped to an oar.
3. Princess Marie-Gabrielle ('Mariga') von Urach (1932–89) m. 1954–83 to Desmond Guinness. E.C.: 'She'd inherited from her suffragette aunt these log cabins in the woods north of Oslo. We were there several days. We had to pay to go up in a helicopter onto the glacier – and there she was, walking around in a parasol and long dress.'
4. William Whitelaw (1918–99) Conservative Secretary of State for Employment who confronted the National Union of Mineworkers over pay demands.
5. E.C.: 'The expense was staggering. I even had milk out of a cow and had to pay for it.'

CHAPTER SIX

GONE TO PATAGONIA: 1974–6

On 1 October 1974 Elizabeth's father died. Bruce flew out for Bobby's funeral in Geneseo and stayed on in Gertrude's apartment on Fifth Avenue. He had $3,500 expenses from the Sunday Times *and was supposed to be writing a story on the Guggenheim family. But he felt at the end of his tether with the magazine – 'which we all felt was being wrecked from "above"'. On 2 November, 'on the spur of the moment', he made a break for it; he plotted to meet up with Elizabeth and Gertrude in Peru in early April.*

Magnus Linklater, the magazine's editor, has no recollection of the telegram that Chatwin claimed to have sent to the Sunday Times: *GONE TO PATAGONIA FOR FOUR MONTHS. The telegram most likely took the form of this letter to Francis Wyndham.*

To Francis Wyndham
Lima | Peru | 11 December 1974

Dear Francis,

I have done what I threatened. I suddenly got fed up with N.Y. and ran away to South America. I have been staying with a cousin in Lima for the past week and am going tonight to Buenos Aires. I intend to spend Christmas in the middle of Patagonia. I am doing a story there for myself, something I have always wanted to write up. I do not, for obvious reasons, want to be associated with the paper in Argentina, but if something crops up, I'll let you or Magnus [Linklater] know. I'm working on something that could be marvellous, but I'll have to do it in my own way.

The third part of the Guggenheim saga[1] is already complete in note form and will take only a day or two to write, but we will have to compress the rest together. Later on I'll be looking at the Guggenheim mines in Central Chile because my cousin's husband runs a mine near Chuquicamata.

Can you tell Magnus that Ahmet Ertegun[2] is definitely on, but I want to wait until the spring and go with him to Turkey (at his expense) and watch the king of rock music, who firmly intends to be President of Turkey, in action.

I'll give you an address in Buenos Aires through which I can be contacted, but I don't want to receive any official S.T. correspondence in the Argentine.

as ever, Bruce

In Lima Chatwin stayed with his cousin Monica Barnett.

Monica was the daughter of Charles Amherst Milward, a clergyman's son and 'spectacular adventurer' who ran away to sea and by 1897 had circumnavigated the world 49 times. In that year, however, his ship sank after hitting an uncharted rock at the entrance of the Straits of Magellan; he later bought an iron foundry in the Chilean port of Punta Arenas, the southernmost city in the world, where he worked both as British and German consul.

It was Milward who had sent back a salted scrap of giant sloth skin to his cousin, Chatwin's grandmother, in Birmingham.

Already when in New York, at the instigation of the literary agent Gillon Aitken, Chatwin had outlined Milward's story in a proposal for a book to be called O Patagonia. *'Among my first recollections in life is being held up to my grandmother's cabinet of curiosities and being allowed to handle a thick dry piece of animal skin with some reddish hair like coconut fibre. My grandmother*

1. 'The Guggenheim Saga,' *Sunday Times* magazine, 23 November 1975.
2. Ahmet Ertegun (1923–2006), New-York based Turkish founder of Atlantic Records.

*told me it was a "piece of brontosaurus" and I developed a fetishistic
obession for it ... the piece of brontosaurus began my continuing
interest in palaeontology and evolution.' The book Chatwin wanted
to write would be 'on Patagonia – and a lot more besides ... The
form of the book must be dictated by the journey itself. As it will
be – to say the least – unpredictable, there is no point in even trying
to guess what it will hold. I shall start the diary the moment I cross
the Rio Negro (I do not intend to fly unless it is absolutely vital;
descriptions of landscape from the air are the most boring descriptions of all). I may cast a backward look at the horrors of Buenos
Aires, but then I shall zig-zag down the country from the coast to
the mountains and so on.'*

But first he had to fly to Lima to find out more about Milward.

*Monica, a former journalist, had started to put together
Milward's sea stories with the idea of publication. She allowed
Chatwin to make rough notes, but insisted that he did not remove
the 258-page journal of her father's life from the house. Chatwin's
misunderstanding about what material he was permitted to use
would have repercussions.*

To Elizabeth Chatwin
Lima | Peru | 12 December 1974

Hello,

I like my cousins enormously. Monica Barnett is exactly like Aunt
Grace to look at. The diary of Charlie Milward is fantastic, even if it could
never be printed in its present form. The story of the wreck, of Louis de
Rougemont, of Indian massacres, of life at sea on the Cape Horners is
exactly like something out of Conrad. Am going to Buenos Aires tonight,
and will give an address of some of Monica's friends when I get there.

Lima is dreary because covered with a grey blanket of cloud. It is
not a good time to go into the sierra until late March at the earliest, as
the rains are just about to begin and the roads get washed away. But late
March early April is the absolute best, with spring flowers etc. The

Barnetts have offered to lend us their camper, which sleeps five in comfort and that would be wonderful if you think Gertrude could stand the jolts. It is 3000 km to Cuzco from here, and the most interesting places will all be on dirt roads. We can see nearer the time.

We went up to 12,000 feet the other day on the central highway and it had the same bracing effect as Afghanistan. But I do not think there is anything of the hilarity.

XXXXXX X

B

P.S. Do find out if your uncle Willie and/or your grandfather sank the 'Maine' as they are alleged to have done in Hugh Thomas' *Cuba*.[1]

To Elizabeth Chatwin

Hotel Lancaster | Buenos Aires | Argentina | [December 1974]

Dearest E,

Buenos Aires is utterly bizarre a combination of Paris and Madrid shorn of historical depth, with hallucinating avenidas flanked with lime trees, where not even the humblest housewife need forego the architectural aspirations of Marie Antoinette. I have been mixing with Anglo-Argentines who have lost command of English and all knowledge of home and with some of the crustier Argentines who speak it far better than I do. Wonderful houses like Meridian House[2] but still thriving with *boiseries*, Louis XV and *paté en croute*. There is always the vague feeling that the high-flown French or English conversation may be interrupted by guerrillas, but no-one seems unphased by it.

Please be on the look out for my best friend here – a young writer called Jorge Ramon-Torres Zavaleta,[3] who is absolutely enchanting and

1. At 9.40pm on 15 February 1898 the US battleship *Maine* blew up in Havana harbour with the loss of 2 officers and 258 men. Hugh Thomas writes in *Cuba* (1971): 'One story suggests that she was blown up by a mine planted by a US millionaire and eccentric, William Astor Chanler . . . already engaged in gun-running to Cuba.' Thomas blames the explosion on new gunpowder needed for heavier guns.
2. Washington home of Elizabeth's diplomat grandfather Irwin Laughlin.
3. Argentine short-story writer and essayist.

of a culture and sensitivity that has died out in Europe. He has written short stories that were plagiarised by Borges. He is travelling – for the first time – outside Argentina to the U.S. in Jan (?20th) for 3 weeks with one in N.Y and probably with 2 friends.[1] He probably can't take much cash out, even if he comes from the Martinez de Hoz family who are the biggest blood-stock breeders in the country. I said that if he was stuck he could probably stay in the apt, but he will in any case be writing to you.

Did I tell you in my last letter that we have the Barnetts' camper in Peru to go up to Lake Titicaca if Gertrude's back can stand it. Uncomfortable but probably not more so than the hotels and we would have much more fun. The size of a biggish caravan. They are going to England in Jan and will go to Stratford.

Not much fun in London with bombs in my lunchtime pub on the King's Road,[2] thank you.

Off tonight to Patagonia.

XXXX

Bruce

Address for urgent contact is Hotel Lancaster.

In the third week of January, marooned in the small village of Baja Caracolles, Chatwin wrote to his wife. He was stranded in the middle of nowhere, but he had arrived.

To Elizabeth Chatwin
Baja Caracolles | Prov. de Santa Cruz | Argentina | 21 January 1975

Dearest E

I have begun letters I don't know how many times and then abandoned them. Now I am stuck, for 3 days at least, because the justice of

1. EC: 'Jorge came on a freighter to New York with three friends, sons of *estancieros*, one of whom owned the site of the W. H. Hudson story *El Ombu*. He spent the entire day looking all over New York for *dulce de leche* for me.'
2. On Saturday 14 December 1974 the IRA threw a bomb through the window of the King's Arms.

the peace, to whom I confided some of my things, has run off with the key.

Writing this in the archetypal Patagonian scene, a *boliche* or roadman's hotel at a cross-roads of insignificant importance with roads leading all directions apparently to nowhere. A long mint green bar with blue green walls and a picture of a glacier, the view from the window a line of lombardy poplars tilted about 20 degrees from the wind and beyond the rolling grey pampas (the grass is bleached yellow but it has black roots, like a dyed blonde) with clouds rushing across it and a howling wind.

On no previous journey am I conscious of having done more. Patagonia is as I expected but more so, inspiring violent outbursts of love and hate. Physically it is magnificent, a series of graded steps or *barrancas* which are the cliff lines of prehistoric seas and unusually full of fossilised oyster shells 10″ diam. In the east you suddenly confront the great wall of the *cordillera* with bright turquoise lakes (some are milky white and others a pale jade green) with unbelievable colours to the rocks (in the pre-*cordillera*). Sometimes it seems that the Almighty has been playing at making Neapolitan ice-cream. Imagine climbing (as I did) a cliff face 2000 feet high alternatively striped vanilla, strawberry and pistachio in bands of 100 feet or more. Imagine an upland lake where the rock face on one side is bright purple, the other bright green, with cracked orange mud and a white rim. You have to be a geologist to appreciate it. Then I know of no place that you are more aware of prehistoric animals. They sometimes seem more alive than the living. Everybody talks of pleisiosaurus, or ichtyosaurus. I met an old gentleman who was born in Lithuania who found a dinosaur the other day and didn't think much of it. He thought much more of the fact he had a pilot's license, at the age of 85 being probably the oldest solo flyer in the world. When he was younger he tried to be a bird man.

I have been caught in the lost beast fervour and 2 days ago scaled an appalling cliff to the bed of an ancient lake . . . and there discovered to my inexpressible delight a collection of fragments of the carapace of the glyptodon. The glyptodon has if anything replaced the mylodon in my affections – there are about 6 whole ones in the Museum of La Plata – an enormous armadillo up to 9-10 feet long, each scale of its armour looking like a Japanese chrysanthemum. The entertaining fact about my discovery, and one that no archaeologist will believe, is that in the middle of one scatter of bones were 2 obsidian knives quite definitely man-made. Now Man is often thought to have done away with the Glyptodon, but there is no evidence of his having done so.

Not an Indian in sight. Sometimes you see a hawkish profile that seems to be a Tehuelche i.e. old Patagonian, but the colonisers did a very thorough job, and this gives the whole land its haunted quality.

Animal life is not extraordinary, except for the *guanaco* which I love. The young are called *chulengos* and have the finest fur, a sort of mangy brown and white. There is a very rare deer called a Huemeul and the Puma (which is commoner than you would think but difficult to see). Otherwise *pinchi* the small armadillo, hares everywhere, and a most beguiling skunk, very small, black with white stripes; far from spraying me one came and took a crust from my hand.

Birds are wonderful. Condors in the *cordillera*, a black and white vulture, a beautiful grey harrier (also amazingly tame), and the black-necked swan which has my prize for the best bird in the world. On the mud flats are flamingoes – these are a kind of orange colour – the Patagonian goose inappropriately called an *abutarda*, and every kind of duck.

You would think from the fact that the landscape is so uniform and the occupation (sheep-farming) also, that the people would be correspondingly dull. But I have sung 'Hark the Herald Angels Sing' in Welsh in a remote chapel on Christmas Day, have eaten lemon curd tartlets with an old Scot (who has never been to Scotland) but has made his own bagpipes and wears the kilt to dinner. I have stayed with a Swiss ex-diva who married a Swedish trucker who lives in the remotest of all Patagonian valleys, decorating her house with murals of the lake of Geneva. I have dined with a man who knew Butch Cassidy and other members of the Black Jack Gang, I have drunk to the memory of Ludwig of Bavaria with a German whose house and style of life belongs rather to the world of the Brothers Grimm. I have discussed the poetics of Mandelstam with a Ukrainian doctor missing both legs. I have seen Charlie Milward's *estancia* and lodged with the peons drinking *maté* till

3am. (*Maté* incidentally is a drink for which I also have a love/hate relationship). I have visited a poet-hermit who lived according to Thoreau and the Georgics. I have listened to the wild outpourings of the Patagonian archaeologist, who claims the existence of a. the Patagonian unicorn b. a protohominid in Tierra del Fuego (*Fuego pithicus patensis*) 80 cm high.

There is a fantastic amount of stuff for a book – from the Anarchist (Yes, Bakunin inspired) Rebellion of 1920, to the hunting of the Black Jack Gang, Cassidy etc. the temporary kingdom of Patagonia, the lost city of the Caesars, the travels of Musters, the hunting of Indians etc. Everything I need.

TIME is going rather quicker than I hoped. One is inclined to get stuck. I am aiming now to the Jamiesons at Puerto Deseado, then the Frazers (son of the man who raped Monica's mother) at St Julien, then Rio Gallegos which is apparently little England, then I may if poss, hire a car and do the touristy glacier of Lago Argentino, then back to Rio Gallegos and to the Bridges[1] in Tierra del F. Then to Punta Arenas where I have contacts and then hopefully up to Puerto Montt by boat; thence back into Argentina ending up in B.A. for a short spell. How long this will take I honestly don't know, but I do think that Peru in April rather than March – or at the earliest March 18–20. Maybe sooner.

Can you please check for me if either N.Y. Pub Lib or Harvard have copies of a journal (from about 1931–the '60's) called 'Argentina Austral'. It is going to be v. imp for me and I must not go from Argentina if I can't get hold of copies elsewhere.

Dying of tiredness. Have just walked 150 odd miles. Am another 150 from the nearest lettuce and at least 89 from the nearest canned vegetable. It will take many years to recover from roast lamb.

xxxxxx B

Will cable address Rio Gallegos.

---

1. Thomas Bridges's great-grandson, Tommy Goodall (*b*.1933), continues to manage Estancia Harberton with his wife, American biologist Rae Natalie Prosser.

To Tegai Roberts[1]
Punta Arenas|Chile|10 February 1975

I am sorry that I have to press on from Esquel south, but I expect to return in early March. In the meantime I must thank you and everyone for my welcome in Gaiman. Off to Tierra del Fuego in the afternoon. Bruce Chatwin.

To Elizabeth Chatwin
Hotel Cabo de Hornos|Punta Arenas|Chile|10 February 1975

Dear E.

I came here more or less because the aeroplane to Tierra del Fuego was so erratic that it proved impossible to get from Argentine Patagonia to Argentine Tierra del Fuego. Punta Arenas, the little I have seen of it, is a town utterly to my taste. Rather like Victoria, British Columbia in atmosphere, with a catholic rather than a protestant bias. The houses of the English, mansions in the style of Sunningdale lie up the hill, the palaces of the Braun-Menendez family, Jewish/Spanish millionaires with cypresses and monkey-puzzles that are lashed by a perpetual hurricane. These houses were imported piece by piece from France and still look as though they have been miraculously dislodged from the Bois de Boulogne. I dined with the Brauns last night among their palms, their Cordoba leather, their aseptic marble goddesses, their bronzes of fishermen, their Louis-the Hotel-Quinze suites, their painting (of two geese with disjointed necks) by Picasso's father, their marquetry floors their billiard table, the bird-like French patter of their black dressed ladies and the assumed upper-class accents of their men.

Captain Milward's house, which I mistook for the Anglican church, is a towered crenellated building with overtones of Edgbaston, Birmingham, now turned into a claustrophobic Chilean middle-class home. In the garden there was an octagonal summerhouse and crazy paving paths bordered with London Pride, with Sweet Williams and Canterbury Bells in the borders.

1. Roberts ran the museum in Gaiman in Welsh Patagonia.

I am going on to the island [Tierra del Fuego] this afternoon by the air taxi, a 10 minute hop and will be incommunicado till I get here again on March 1st or 2nd. What I have been able to do is to make plans.

The boat to Puerto Montt leaves here on 12th March and arrives after steaming up the Canales Fueginos on the 16th. I want 3-4 days in Chile, to go to Chiloe and the region around Valdivia and then will re-enter Argentina by Bariloche where I want 5 more days in the province of Neuquen, going thence by train to Viedma (Carmen Los Patagones) on the east coast 1 day, then Bahia Blanca 1 day; then to Buenos Aires for about a week where I must do quite a lot of homework in Amando Braun-Menendez's library. I had the idea of going by bus from B.A. to Juyuy the Northern Province then into Antofagasta, and thence by bus to Lima up the Pacific highway, air freighting my bags ahead. But this may not be possible. I suggest then that April 7th is our date in Lima, all being well, revolutions permitting etc. we should stay a month. How does this suit? If it is all right, cable here, and write to Monica Barnett (husband is John) because she is going to book us into a nice English pensione by the sea, which I can assure you is infinitely to be preferred to the Sheraton or any of the other big hotels with their glass panelled doors cracked with bullet holes. Ask too about the camper and get yourself an International Driving Licence. Just in case mine will not do. I had to have special permission in Argentina, but I imagine there will be no problem.

Met a woman in a remote estancia in the cordillera who worked for the Milwards. Said they were <u>dreadful</u>. He used to pray to God that she would not be deceitful and put her on a bread and water diet for a week for breaking a bottle of brandy. She was 14 at the time

xxxx B

P.S. Please tell Jorge Ramon [Zavaleta] that I might want him to put <u>me</u> up in B.A. for a bit – or arrange it – and also to receive a parcel if I air freight it from Bariloche to B.A.

Am also asking Francis Wyndham to contact you if there is anything vital re the Guggenheims.

My rucksack is taking [on] the most beautiful patina.

B

To John Kasmin
Cueva del Milodon | Ultima Esperanza | Chile | 10 February 1975

This is the cave where my great uncle Charlie Milward the Sailor dug up the remains of the Mylodon, or Giant Sloth, perfectly preserved in salt-petre. Have been sleeping everywhere from the open pampas, to peons huts in the rain forest, to (last night) a Jewish millionairess's residence (*c*.1900) that looked as if it had been translated bodily from the Bois de Boulogne to this, the most southerly city in the world. Much love to all XX B

To Elizabeth Chatwin
Punta Arenas | Chile | [1 March 1975]

Dear E,

Notepaper of the British Consulate cut off to avoid offending la Reina Isabel!

<u>Now</u> re Peru.

I may be able to get though quicker in BA than I had hoped. So what I suggest is the following. For you and Gertrude to fly to Lima on/or around the 1st April (no later) and stay in the pension on the beach that Monica knows, see Dum Tweedie[1] (whom I can personally be without) and the dreaded Mrs Porras,[2] visit the museums (which are wonderful) Gold Museum, National Museum, Herrera Museum, visit perhaps Pacha-camac great Inca site on the coast − in other words finish with Lima which I have done and I will turn up any time in that week not later than the 7th so that, in this way, we have wasted no time − because you, bless you, will have made all the superlatively organised arrangements that our expedition requires. I suggest we then go up the Andean highway onto the tableland and loop around Lake Titicaca via Cuzco, Macchu Picchu coming back through Arequipa.

---

1. A friend of Sally Westminster.
2. Chatwin was staying with Diana Porras when some men appeared on the skyline above and looked down, arms folded, motionless. 'Who are they?' Mrs Porras: 'Our future murderers.'

Important points to remember.

1. Try and get hold of some decent maps in the U.S. because you can bet we'll get none in Peru.
2. Bring pair of binoculars, for watching condors (A pair hovered above my head 15ft up in Tierra del Fuego. Incredible. Like a bombing raid.)
3. 1 pair of jeans <u>please</u> button-up 32 waist 34 leg. Mine were mangled without apology together with all my other clothes by a woman who did not know how to operate a washing machine. The hotel even tried to charge me for rags!
4. My canvas sided boots. Also really sensible light boot/shoes for you both. Wouldn't mind a good thick woollen sweater. Light warm/wind proof gear. Remember it is 14,000 ft.
5. Some form of camp cooking equipment.
6. A new battery for my exposure meter to fit the small Leica CL; it is like a small pill ½ in diam.
7. If the camper is not going to work out: this you will have to check on the phone with Monica. I suggest we have an emergency tent; because I gather it will be <u>much</u> more comfortable than the hotels. Gertrude should invest in a big double-size sleeping bag that zips down the side + air mattress.[1]
8. Read Prescott's *History of the Conquest of Peru* for a start. Also bring with you if you can some <u>sensible</u> but not sensational accounts of Peruvian Archaeology. See if you can find the dope on the Nazca Desert Drawings, because if all works out well we will go to interview Maria Reiche,[2] octogenarian Austrian? mystic-archaeologist-recluse for the *Sunday Times* and then charter a plane (at S.T. expense) and get them photographed from the air.

. . . Nowhere is smaller than Patagonia. Of course the good-looking American couple in the Hotel Cabo de Hornos lived near Barrytown,

1. E.C.: 'I brought all this stuff and never used it because the camper was equipped.'
2. Maria Reiche (1903–98), German-born archaeologist. 'The Riddle of the Pampa', *Sunday Times* magazine, 26 October 1975.

New York. Of course, he was painted as a boy by Robert Chanler.[1] I have been hurtling around Punta Arenas in search of the ghost of Charlie Milward. Fascinating place. For example parked on a beach with a rash of tin shacks almost on top of it is the *Kabenga*, the boat that took Stanley up the Congo. There is a concrete replica of the Parthenon which is the Gymnasium, there are little octagonal summer houses that could be Turkish. My menu of last night was as follows –

Loco de mer mayonnaise (Abalone)

Jambon Cru de la Terre de Feu

Pejerrey a la planche

Latuna nature (prickly pear)

Café

I am really looking forward to Peru and our circuit round the sites. How about your learning Quetchua (?sp) if you want to be really useful – or at least some Spanish.[2] Could probably do with some sunglasses if only for the wind.

Don't forget International Driving Licence

Bless you,

B

PS. Don't forget a big – and I mean big bag – or bags – of bran. Hopeless line. Apparently it's always the same

xxxx B

To Charles and Margharita Chatwin

Cueva del Milodon | Ultima Esperanza | Chile | 15 March 1975

The story of Charlie the Sailor is, as I originally guessed, absolutely fascinating. Monica has the manuscript, albeit unfinished, of his autobiography, which introduces me into a Conradian world of sailing ships. Then from this end I have unearthed an extraordinary mass of documents of his

---

1. Robert Winthrop Chanler (1872–1930), E.C.'s eccentric great-uncle, muralist and painter of screens, briefly married to Italian soprano Lina Cavalieri.
2. E.C.: 'In Peru I could tell he was speaking Argentine Spanish, full of expressions the Peruvians didn't understand.'

extraordinary activities in Chile. He was German vice-consul as well as English. No wonder Winston Churchill and Lord Fisher thought he was a German agent. Am returning up the Canales Fueginos and Magellanes to Puerto Montt, thence to Buenos Aires to work in the libraries for a week and will meet Elizabeth and Gertrude in Peru on the 5th April. Much love B

Early in April, Elizabeth and Gertrude met up with Chatwin in Monica Barnett's house in Lima. After visiting Arequipa and the Convent of Santa Catalina, they travelled by train to Cuzco in order to see Machu Picchu, and then flew back to Lima where they picked up the Barnetts' camper van, driving to Huaraz, Chavin and Nazca, before returning to New York.

Unwilling to work at Holwell, Chatwin rented a house on Fishers Island, a private island off the Connecticut coast, while Elizabeth returned to England to oversee renovations.

To Elizabeth Chatwin
1030 5th Avenue | New York | 7 June 1975

Dear E.

When you have Mr Elms fix the study at the end why don't we lay your sisal on the floor, BUT making first very sure that the floor is sealed with some insulating material to keep out the draughts and the cold from underneath. Also let us plan on having a Franklin or a Shaker stove. Ask him how complicated it would be to remove the fireplace entirely. I don't think very.

Went last night to the most ghastly, chicy, swanky occasion at George Plimpton's,[1] all the people I most hate, which left me in a vile depression. I think I might try my hand at a short story called THE GADARENE LEFT.

Longing for you to see my Norman tower on the beach.[2] It is slightly

1. George Plimpton (1927–2003) journalist and founder of *Paris Review*.
2. Stone Cottage was a conical gatehouse once owned by Margaret Stone, widow of Austin Tappan Wright, author of the Tolkien-like novel *Islandia* (1942).

like a set for a Hitchcock movie, with a castle beyond and flights of ferocious seagulls. I got slightly alarmed about the cost, and went to Nantucket to try my hand there for a house – and hated it. Full of maddening boutiques and middle class American children pretending to be hippies. Fishers Island on the other hand though it may be stuffy as all hell has a dreamlike vaguely surrealist atmosphere that is not at all disagreeable.

Adrian[1] is here and looks a bit better and less depressed. Perhaps he is getting the upper hand.

much love,

B

To Elizabeth Chatwin
Box 271 | Fishers Island | New York | [July 1975]

Dear E.,

Got your letter. R[obert] E[rskine] is here. We have had an enormous lunch of steamed clams and grilled shrimp, and will have lobsters for dinner. Whew? There is a grey fog. Did I not tell you this house is not near the beach but in the beach. To such an extent that I have seagulls nesting in the house. Moules, delicious moules, not fifty yards from where I type, that is at low tide.[2]

Among the books I shall need are: Marshall Sahlins. *Stone Age Economics*. Lovejoy and Boas, *Primitivism and other related Ideas in Antiquity*. And *Il Jimmy, the story of a Patagonian Outlaw*. The first I once lent to Charles [Tomlinson] who may still have it. Of course there is too much furniture in the end room [at Holwell]. It should have: a desk, a chair, an easy chair, the stand, the French chair *y nada mas*.

Was supposed to go to N.Y. next week, but am having cold feet about it, because I do not like going off the island.

I had wondered why the main house had an astonishingly beautiful appearance and was full of amazing things. Huge Hawaiian bowl to keep

1. Adrian Chanler, E.C.'s brother, with his then wife, Teri Blackmer. They divorced.
2. E.C.: 'There was constant fresh fish. Fishermen would give us sea-bass and bluefish. The water's so polluted now, you can't eat the fish.'

the magazines. French Empire painted screens of Incas. Hokusai wave in the bedroom, but have since learned that it was decorated in 1932 by the famous Lady Mendl.[1] Now being turned, rapidissimo, into the spirit of Bloomingdales, like everything else in the U.S.

XXXXXXXXXXXXXXXXXX B

P.S. Did you send the Ladies of Lima[2] to Monica. If so, good. If not, why not and how do we get it to her? One way is to get it to Christopher Barnett who would I suppose take it to Lima. I haven't heard from Monica.

In a lost letter to Robin Lane Fox, whom he had invited to go with him to Patagonia, Chatwin explained: 'I'm having to write my account and you will think it is a contrived attempt at noticing, and I step out every morning looking at the ordinary world as if through a kaleidoscope of fractured glass – that's what you will say, but I'm aware I'm doing it.' Lane Fox says: 'He later showed me a draft of In Patagonia. *I said: "It's too brightly lit, you've decided to go and notice everything." Chatwin replied: "But the point of it is precisely that." '*

To Charles and Margharita Chatwin
Fishers Island | New York | 25 August 1975

Dear C and M,

Well, I have done about half the book of Patagonia. There is a 3-inch pile of manuscript, much of which will have to be scrapped when I come to the revision. This island has been well worthwhile. We rented a tiny Norman style garage stuck right 'out in the middle of the sea. It belongs to a family of mattress makers who have the big house. Seagulls virtually live in the house. Fifty yards away is the hideous mansion of

1. Elsie de Wolfe, known as Lady Mendl (1865–1950), American interior decorator. E.C.: 'She had rag-rugs in Persian carpet patterns that were stunning and real French provincial furniture. I stole a rug and a lamp that they'd chucked out.'
2. Ethnographic picture.

Mr Henry Luce, the proprietor of *Time* Magazine, whose banal conversation makes one long for England.

I am just starting in on the part of the book which deals with the legendary Charlie Milward the Sailor. What a history! The life as a cadet up the mast of the Cape Horners. A shark-riding episode. Shanghaiing in San Francisco. Mad passengers etc. Monica has let me have a copy of his manuscript which describes the wreck on Cape Pillar at the entrance to the Straits of Magellan. The extraordinary thing about Milward is that he could never shake off Birmingham. The house in Punta Arena is pure Edgbaston arts and crafts. In his letter book there are a number of letters from L.B.C.[1] Evidently he was fond of his cousin Isobel. From time to time he sent odd curiosities of Patagonia, such as a bow and some arrow heads of the Ona Indians. And I imagine he sent the piece of Giant Sloth at the same time.

Many thanks for your letter, which was also a bulletin of the doings of the family. In doing this piece about Charlie Milward I have wondered about them from time to time. I must say I was amazed to hear that the Joneses[2] were still with us. That really takes me back. I'm told by people, here even, that John Chatwin[3] is considered quite a name among young modern architects in England.

We leave here next week and go to New York for a few days. I am going to the West to Utah to do an article for the *Sunday Times*. Absurd subject. Butch Cassidy, the most famous cowboy outlaw of the West, skipped the USA in 1902 and managed to shake off the men from the Pinkerton Detective Agency. He and his friend the Sundance Kid got a concession of land in Northern Patagonia at a place called Cholila, where they lived from 1903 to 1910. There are people who remember them quite well, and their log cabin survives with its wall-paper intact. Later they were supposed to have been killed in Bolivia but Cassidy's sister, now in her 90's in Utah says her brother spent the twenties as a country gentleman in Ireland and returned to Utah for burial. This is the case of the Hero that never dies.

1. Leslie Chatwin (1871–1933), Chatwin's grandfather.
2. Hubert Jones, cousin of Chatwin's Milward grandmother.
3. John Chatwin, Chatwin's first cousin.

I am in two minds about coming back before this is finished, but I think it will probably be better to come over in October, stay at least a couple of months and do my extra research in Oxford rather than Harvard. I talked to Cary [Welch] today and he's going to give me a room in their house. So I am going to have 2 weeks at least in Harvard!

I must say Gertrude was very remarkable in Peru. We had her climbing up mountains at 10,000 feet. Her friends say she has stretched upright since going away. She had never been on a camper before and although she got a bit tired, I think she enjoyed it. Peru was extremely beautiful, but it gives you the cold shudders. The Spanish colonial empire does have a very lowering effect. In Argentina, though, where everything was chaos, and one was supposed to be machine-gunned at every second if you believe the foreign press, it struck me as being about as peaceful as Stratford-on-Avon.

I'm sorry I'm so hopeless at writing. When you pore over the typewriter all day it's the last thing you want to do.

   X B

Chatwin stayed on in Fishers Island till after Labour Day in September, returning to England on the new Queen Elizabeth II. *He had a second-class ticket, but obtained permission from a steward to work in the first-class library, until he was discovered and ejected. 'He came home in a rage saying how horrible it was, all plastic furniture and terrible muzac.' He was still writing* In Patagonia.

That November, he rented a house in Bonnieux belonging to Anthony Carver, brother of the Field Marshal. Elizabeth says, 'I am sent on ahead AS USUAL to drive on my own, 500 miles, to the Vaucluse, to prepare it. The place was impractical, uninsulated and insanely badly arranged, the top two floors of a house built into a cliff. We had a catalytic gas heater which ate up all the oxygen, and were feeling cold and nauseous, until we realised that we had to have the window open all the time.' Visitors over the winter included Kasmin, some friends from Paris and Chatwin's parents.

To Charles Chatwin

Postcard, Bonnieux | 12 Rue Droite | Bonnieux | France |
2 December 1975

Our terrace marked with a pretty indistinct arrow. Weather fine, clear and quite cold. Mountain air etc. make one feel very well. I will be signing a cheque for £900 shortly. Could you please check with bank that this is O.K. in view of the £650 from *Sunday Times* due at the end of Dec. If not please transfer funds to cover. Many thanks. See you. B

To John Kasmin

12 Rue Droite | Bonnieux | France | 12 January 1976

Dear Kassl,

Seems ages since you left. Probably because I have the family here.[1] I haven't lived with them like this for twenty odd years and I feel I am back at school. Everyone holds opinions and airs them at great length while I am trying to write or think or even breathe.

Reached a crisis the other morning and so I packed a little section of my writing into the leather rucksack[2] and headed for the Luberon. By lunch next day I was at Le Beaumanière at Les Baux and sat down to a solitary and enormous lunch of *Paté des Anguilles aux pistaches*, *Noisettes de Chevreuil* etc. The maitre d'hotel was charmed by the leather rucksack and bore it in his arms to the cloakroom, showing it to the owner's wife who bought me a glass of champagne. I have conceived a plan of walking to all of the best restaurants in France from a distance of fifty miles.

We have admittedly had ten days of the clearest weather, some days so hot I had to sit in the shade rather than let my brain burn up in the sun. I have packed my family out house hunting, but can't decide if I

---

1. Charles and Margharita had come for Christmas. E.C.: 'Most of the time we went off on picnics and left Bruce behind for the day.'
2. A dark brown leather rucksack, copied from a canvas bag, without a frame but with special pockets, that Chatwin had made up by a saddler's in Cirencester. He left it to Werner Herzog.

like the region well enough. I do find that phoney Provencal atmosphere rather trying.

I had quite a funny letter today from the Rasputins[1] who enclosed the particulars of that *nouvelle cuisine* restaurant and spa at Eugénie les Bains. Somewhere obviously to be avoided at all costs. I don't see the point of taking a health cure at a place so pretentious that it would give you an apoplectic seizure after two hours.

I enclose a cheque payable to David[2] for £133. I hope this is enough. I also have your *Guide Gourmand de la France* which I conveniently and truthfully discovered half an hour after the Sulzberger contingent left. I have taken to reading it in conjunction with Pound's *Cantos* as bed-time reading. My parents will bring it back to you, unless I go up to Paris and give it to Sulz[berger] to bring over.

Let me know if you plan to go skiing with Grisha[3] and I might come over to Sestrìere and join you.

Love to Linda.[4] Keep your marriage guidance counsellor posted on that front.

Love, Bruce

To Derek Hill

12 Rue Droite | Bonnieux | France | 12 January [1976]

My dear D.,

We have let the house to Alistair Sutherland[5] and are squatting here for the winter in a rather Spartan dwelling. But the sun seems to shine

---

1. Michael and Sandy Marsh (*née* Alexandra Acevedo Kirkland) had driven from Paris with Chatwin's friend, David Sulzberger. The bearded Michael was third son of a Texas rancher with petrol and helium reserves, and brother of Stanley, who erected a fence from half-buried new Cadillacs. Sandy eventually jumped out of a window in New York.
2. David Sulzberger (*b*.1946), oriental dealer and former lover of Sandy Marsh; Chatwin used to write in his apartment at Quai Bourbon on Isle St Louis.
3. Gregor Von Rezzori.
4. Linda Adams, Kasmin's girlfriend. J.K.: 'I was divorcing my wife Jane and I used to pour my heart out to Bruce.'
5. Son of Countess of Sutherland and a former policeman in the Metropolitan Police.

with regularity, and I must say it's comforting to have to sit in the shade outside while writing.

I was in England for a month only in the autumn, and before that I was in Argentina, Chile and Peru, taking Gertrude round the Andes in my cousin's camper truck.

I am writing about my cousin Charlie Milward the Sailor, who ran away to sea; was shipwrecked near Cape Horn; introduced reindeer to South Georgia; found the Giant Sloth in a cave in Last Hope Sound, preserved in salt; was accused by Churchill of being a German spy in the First War. I am cobbling his diaries together with Patagonian Giants; an Anarchist revolution against British estancia owners; the albatross; E. Allan Poe; the Patagonian Welsh; Boers; Butch Cassidy and the inevitable Mr Darwin.

I am going to sit it out here until it's done. Once you break it, fatal. I like this country and we're thinking of buying a *cabanon* here, even if it is a bit like the geriatrics ward . . .

We hear you're writing your biography.[1] That'll give reviewers like Mr [Douglas] Cooper some fun. I always used to like him in a perverse way, but no more. Last November in New York I went to a dinner, and suddenly heard floating from the next table: 'My dear, I can't IMAGINE what Grace Dudley[2] thinks she's doing bringin' in that piece of trash.'

I do wish you'd come here on one of your lightning tours. You just might over the next three months.

Love from Elizabeth and from me,

Bruce

That summer, Chatwin visited Ronda in Spain where his friend Magouche Phillips (now living with Xan Fielding) had bought a house. 'It was raining,' Magouche remembers. 'I was looking out of the window. "Why, why, why do I have to put myself on this perch?" Suddenly I saw Bruce. He just appeared through the apple orchard, like an angel.'

1. Hill never completed his autobiography.
2. Grace Kolin (*b.*1923) m. 1961 William Ward, 3rd Earl Dudley.

At the suggestion of Magouche, Chatwin called on the British writer Gerald Brenan (1894–1987), best known for The Spanish Labyrinth, *who lived at Alhaurin-el-Grande – 'the Garden of Eden, though with Adam much older than he ought to be'. At first, the two men hit it off. Brenan wrote to Chatwin: 'I so much enjoyed your visit – it was a great stimulus though I felt terribly envious of your travels. Travel gives immediate pleasure, writing only satisfaction – or dissatisfaction. But it's the combination I should like to have had.' Chatwin, in turn, fell in love with a small house in Pitres: one of many that he would contemplate buying over the next two decades. In Kasmin's opinion: 'Bruce's biggest problem was where to be. He never knew where to be. It was always somewhere else.'*

To Gerald Brenan

In the Lot | as from Holwell Farm | 26 August [1976]

Dear Gerald and Lynda[1] and Lars,

This morning my voice returned. (You must forgive the whirlwind of conversation). All the same I wish I were back in the Alpujaras. I've always found this part of France suffocating and depressing, one's thought leaden, and head hanging dead weight like a pumpkin.

At Malaga airport there was no unbooked seat for days, so I went out for the day to Alhaurin-el-Grande, and in the evening Zalin[2] put me on the night train to Madrid. He is, as you say, tormented by Vietnam, and I think it will be years before the horror of it heals.

Next morning I rested in the Prado in the room of black Riberas,[3]

1. Lynda Price (*b*.1944), nicknamed 'Tiger' and a student from Chelsea Art School, had lived with Brenan since 1968. 'I loved him but I loved him as one loves an uncle.' Brenan never even once kissed her passionately. In 1978 she married the Swedish painter Lars Pranger.
2. Zalin Grant, neighbour of Brenan and author of *Survivors*, who spent 30 years trying to establish what had happened to the missing journalists Sean Flynn and Dana Stone. 'Of course the Vietnam War was always with us.'
3. José de Ribera (1591–1652), Spanish painter. E.C.: 'Bruce had decided Ribera was the greatest artist ever, the usual hysteria.'

the least frequented room in the museum, and after lunch took the milk train for Bordeaux. On crossing the frontier I asked some German boys to make sure I didn't miss the station and woke up with the light and the outskirts of Paris. The next day I spent getting back down here and the whole journey cost rather more than an airfare, but at least I didn't have to set foot on a plane.

I loved the house at Alhaurin-el-Grande, so cheerful and workman-like, but the Alpujaras are definitely for me. Elizabeth sounded delighted at the prospect of terraces, shivering water and Muslim architecture. Providing the price is within the margin we discussed, I think we'd better buy it. If we sold Gloucestershire and moved to Spain, we'd have to find something bigger but I'm sure we could sell it later, and if not, at that figure, it's not the end of the world.

To my immense relief Jonathan Cape have taken my book on Patagonia;[1] so I shall be taken up revising and rewriting for the next month or two. But if things came to a crisis, Elizabeth could perhaps find a cheap fare to Malaga and straighten things out. She is far more competent about property than I am. We have the money set aside in an American bank account, so we can by-pass the labyrinths of the British Treasury.

Do please, if it's not too inconvenient find out the price, but do not on any account, put yourselves to any further trouble. You must promise this. If it falls through or is unavailable, we shall come back in the late spring of next year and look for another.

I shall send you Sinyavsky, Isaac Babel and the Prose of Mandel-stam. Don't order them yourselves.[2] Thank you – all of you. Bruce

On 6 September 1976 Brenan wrote to inform Chatwin that he had visited Chatwin's 'dream house' in Pitres the day before, but the owner was not yet prepared to sell.

---

1. Maschler agreed to pay an advance of £600 under the terms drawn up eight years earlier for *The Nomadic Alternative*.
2. Brenan would leave to Chatwin all his Central Asian books bought during the First World War.

To Gerald Brenan
Holwell Farm | Wotton-under-Edge | Glos | 21 September 1976

Dear Gerald,

Though I'm sad the little dream house No 1 isn't for sale immediately, perhaps it's all for the best. Elizabeth and I will come out and prospect further sometime in the fairly near future. After all, one can't expect to find the ideal place in a single afternoon.[1]

I am sitting in London, working over some unresolved sections for my book, before embarking on a new project. Some years ago I went to a place called Ouidah on the slave coast of Dahomey and met members of a family called de Souza, now totally black. The original de Souza was a Portuguese peasant, who went to Bahia, became captain of the Portuguese fort on the slave coast and successively the leading slave-dealer, the Viceroy of the King, and one of the richest men in Africa. At one point he had 83 slave ships and 2 frigates built in the Philadelphia dockyard, but he could never leave his slave barracoon and his hundred odd black women in Ouidah. The family went mulatto and are now *feticheurs*. A de Souza is high priest of the Python Fetish, which Richard Burton saw on his Embassy to Dahomey in the 1860's. At that time it was in decline but, since independence, has taken a new lease of life. Tom Maschler of Cape's says I should go and try and chronicle the gradual blackening of the family. I'll probably leave for Dahomey in November and then go to Brazil for a month in March, returning through Spain.

I hope you've got the Sinyavsky, Babel and Mandelstam by now.

Love to Lynda, Bruce

---

1. E.C.: 'He would wear out people in certain places and then have to move on. Everything was absolute paradise etc for about a month and then things were not quite what he wanted them to be. I discovered after years of this nonsense that the sure-fire way of making Bruce not buy a house was for me to agree.'

———————————◁◇▷———————————

CHAPTER SEVEN

THE VICEROY OF OUIDAH: 1976–80

On 25 November 1976 James Lees-Milne wrote in his diary after visiting the London Library: 'Ran into Bruce Chatwin in St James Square, overjoyed that he had handed in his book on Patagonia.' Chatwin was now free to concentrate on the story of the Brazilian slave millionaire Dom Francisco Felix de Souza. Meanwhile, his cousin Monica continued to express concern about what exactly from her father's journal he planned to include.

To Monica Barnett

as from Holwell Farm | 8 December 1976

My dear Monica,

A few lines to keep you abreast of developments here. By the time, though, this reaches you I'll be in West Africa in a country called the Republic of Benin to do some research on a book about a slave trader.

Patagonia is finished and delivered, down to the last Spanish accent (which I hope are right). Reasons of space have obviously restricted the amount of C[harles]. A. M[ilward] material I could – and would like to have used, but this is all to the good. I have printed verbatim in the first person the story of the boys getting lost overboard (my literary friends say it's better than Conrad) and two others The Bushmen dancing and the Indians' Canoe, both v. short, about 2pp each. The others I have duly compressed, sometimes to a line or two and put into the Third Person.

The book ends with the following:

'This book would not have been written without Charley Milward's daughter Monica Barnett, of Lima, who allowed me access to her father's papers and sea-stories. This was particularly generous since she was writing her own biography in which the stories will appear in full.'

This leaves absolutely no room for question about matters of copyright.

In December 1976 Chatwin flew to West Africa with Kasmin to research his new book. Dahomey had changed name since his first visit in 1972 and was now the Marxist Republic of Benin. A curfew began at 11 p.m. and officials of President Kérékou were wary of foreigners unless they were North Korean.

To Elizabeth Chatwin
Abomey | Benin | 9 December 1976

K[asmin] & I have been walking round the north of the country making a preliminary tour. We have had an audience with the king – born in the year of Burton's visit in 1863.[1] The story is wonderful, already forming in my mind, but I've hardly touched on it yet. I think it will have to be written in the high style of *Salammbo*. If you liked & could afford it you can come out in Feb for 3 weeks – fare to Cotonou £320. I will have lodgings in Pto. Novo hopefully, but it is hot sticky and I'll be working.

1. Notebook: 'The king sat down on the green plastic seat of the throne. He was a very old king. A man called Burton came to see his father the year he was born. That made him a hundred and twelve. He had thick glasses and a big square jaw. One of the queens held a yellow parasol over his head. He knew all about Dom Francisco. "My grandfather's best friend," he said. "My grandfather called him Adjunakou, The Elephant. He was a big man, bigger than both of you together. My grandfather took him out of prison. He lifted him up a ladder and over the wall. My grandfather was even bigger than Dom Francisco."

'The queen was bored. She sat and mended the parasol which had a broken strut. She steadied the handle with her big toe. A man came in and kissed the concrete floor. The King went on with the story. At the end he held out his hand and we paid a thousand francs. He told another story and we paid a little less.

'He could go on all day. He liked telling stories. He liked getting paid for them. There was not much left for a king to do.'

To Francis Wyndham
Parakou | Benin | 29 December 1976

Teacher's at under £2 a bottle. La lutte continue. B

To Elizabeth Chatwin
c/o Sebastian de Souza | P.B.40 | Porto Novo | Rep du Benin |
14 January 1977

Maxine,[1]

Here am I sweltering in a room I've rented from an aged doctor in a street lined with Portuguese houses built by creole nabobs who returned from Bahia in the 1850's. It is infernally sticky and I have to confess the whole of this part of the trip is something of a trial – climatically. I went to see Lynda Price's brother[2] (that is, Gerald Brenan's girl friend) in Ibadan in Nigeria. That country has diabolical energy which one can't but admire, however impossible it may be to exist there. A room in Lagos costs about £40 a night at the cheapest reasonable standard. Dreadful English misunderstood nursery food dinner [3] at least £10 per head. Here is quite expensive if you go in for French food but otherwise not so.

Hope K[asmin] has rung you up with details of our run-around. Quite exhausting because one could never tell when he would begin one of his British sense-of-fair play outbursts. One or two near scrapes but he was an excellent fellow traveller and we both enjoyed our little tour. Saw the game park in the south. Beautiful but an irritating atmosphere in the hotel.

---

1. E.C.: 'He called me this ever since our honeymoon, when we all bought name tags in a petrol station on the way to Maine.' The labels stuck. Chatwin was Max; Elizabeth, Maxine; Cary, Earl; Edith, Darleene or The Dahling (as sometimes was Elizabeth).
2. Keith Nicholson Price. Brenan had sent Chatwin his address in Ibadan, writing on 8 December: 'Do go & see him.'
3. E.C.: 'There was a dish called "baked vegetables", covered with a thick white sauce and cooked in the oven.'

At Ibadan I met the famous Pierre Verger[1] Afro-Brazilian scholar of encyclopaedic knowledge but little practical use. Tight with information. A fantastical old queen, having a tiff with his Yoruba boyfriend.

I've been reading some Balzac and think the only way to treat de S[ouza] is to write a straight Balzacian account of the family beginning with a description of the place and then switching back to him and writing through to the present. Quite a mouthful.

Frankly I don't now see any point in your coming out because it isn't a joyride and the only way is to get it over as soon as I can.

I'm a bit alarmed about my affairs with Sotheby's, somewhat in desperation I borrowed £1500 on a whole lot of my little things – and frankly F[elicity] N[icolson] thought she promised one thing and then asked for more things later. I don't mind selling the haematite frog and the Eskimo man – if I have to – but the others I do rather mind about especially if there's going to be money coming in from the book. At any rate I couldn't let myself be put off doing this for the sake of a few things. But I leave it to you to do what you think. Perhaps we ought to protect them by saving them up. Feathers are now at K[asmin]'s.

But, O dear, what are we going to do about the farm? I really can't stick the Alistair[2] situation again, and as you know, find it very hard to work there. On the other hand, travelling about the world makes one less and less feel like quitting England – which I think will get better not worse. But I do think we have to be comfortable there.

Let me know how it was in N.Y. With the market crowing outside my window, I envy you . . . Rambling letter written in the light of a guttering lamp. Must plunge under the mosquito net.

XXXX B

P.S. Going with Sebastian de Souza[3] to a football match in Togo and

---

1. Pierre Verger, alias Fatumbi (1902–96), photographer, self-taught ethnographer and Yoruba priest, was an expert on the slave trade between West Africa and Brazil.
2. Sutherland had looked after Holwell when Elizabeth was in India. 'Bruce didn't get on with him at all.'
3. Chatwin's guide – 'a young, honey-coloured mulatto with a flat and friendly face, a curly moustache and a set of dazzling teeth' – was a direct descendant of de Souza.

will write from there again with more news. Please tell Charles Tomlinson that I had no success in getting anything on Blacks in the French Revolution. Perhaps he should look at the career of Toussaint L' Ouverture.

On the way to the football match Chatwin was caught up in a coup. Mercenaries had landed at Cotonou in a DC-7 and shot their way through the western suburbs with the intention of overthrowing President Kérékou's Marxist state.'By eleven the President reported a "glorious victory" for the Benin Armed Forces with news of the enemy fleeing towards the marshes "en catastrophe".' A "witch-hunt" for foreigners took place in which Chatwin and several hundred others were taken to Camp Ghézo and strip-searched. Three days later, he flew to the Côte D'Ivoire from where he rang Kasmin, who wrote down their conversation:
'Friday 21 January. Woken at 7.30 this morning by Bruce calling from Abidjan. He escaped from Cotonou yesterday and related his experiences during the mysterious coup of last Sunday. Was arrested, roughed up and locked up with hundreds of other Europeans and some blacks. Some shootings, much brutality and chaos. Was the coup genuine or a stage effect to strengthen Kérékou's position as saviour of the country and keep alive the notion of an imperialist enemy eager to attack the Marxist state. His story of hiding in a de Souza closet and then at the Gendarmerie a mercenary type being brought in with gun and dressed in camouflaged combat suit who transpired to be the Fr Ambassador found while out on a partridge shoot and the Amazon who kicked him for being slow at undressing on command. Poor B was worried whether he was wearing under-pants or not.'
From Abidjan, Chatwin flew to Monrovia to catch a KLM flight to Rio de Janeiro – 'penniless (for my travellers' cheques had gone), a bit bruised about the face, and with a very sore big toe which a lady corporal had stamped on'.

To John Kasmin

c/o Brit Vice-Consulate | Salvador da Bahia | Brazil | 7 March 1977

Dear K,

Necessity will damn well have to be the mother of invention. Everything's gone wrong! Where was it we were hexed? Somewhere I have it in my mind you said we'd been hexed. Well, not only the arrest, the visa withdrawn, the traveller's cheques stolen, the bronchitis (from the Beach Hotel of Cotonou), the bags sent to Cairo instead of Rio, the ten-day pointless wait, now Tom's proof of *Patagonia* has got lost in the post between Rio and Bahia just when I have to go off north.

I have to say Brazil is very fascinating. Not very taken with the big cities to which I have been chained, but last night for instance I went to a *candomblé* in a *teneiro* (fetish house) way up a mountain with the 'daughters of the god' trance dancing in colossal white lace crinolines and the boys – girlie boys – in silver and lace all shuddering as the God Shango[1] hit them through the shoulder blade and one boy twisting and whirling off the platform his silver thunderbolts glittering down the mountain and coming back up again and collapsing into the arms of the 'mother' – a middle aged white lady with spectacles, hair in a scarf and the air of a bank manager's secretary.

As and when I get the proof I am going north through the *sertão* – cactus scrub – to San Luis de Marañón, where Ghézo's mother Agontimé was sold into slavery and was got back by de Souza. In the meantime I'm kicking my heels in the country round Bahia, walking round crumbling plantation houses. The architecture is wonderful. 18th century Rococo with genuinely Chinese overtones brought direct from Macao whose towns look like the willow pattern. Bahia itself is rather a bore, one of those self-congratulatory places like San Francisco.

I may meet E. and her mother for a week in Spain or Portugal in April and then come back to England. I think I'll sit out the summer at the farm because this will need a lot of other men's books if it's to be

1. Xango, the Orixa god of fire.

anything – though I'm still taken with the story. Have traced Domingos José Martin's family and will in Bahia. An interesting figure is a man called Joaquim Pereira Marinho – Martin's and de Souza's banker – who made his first fortune in charque salt dried beef and was known as a *carne seco* who died in the 1880's in a colossal palace, a Viscount of the Empire. (The de Souza's are convinced they still have a fortune in Bahia).[1] Pereira Marinho in turn was a cousin of the biggest family in N.E. Brazil, the Garcia d'Avilas who – from 1550 on were the biggest cattle barons the world ever knew with ranches stretching 1000 miles. Their house is in ruins but still standing – a palace of granite blocks in a coco plantation. The only medieval castle in the Americas. In the *souẓala* or old slave quarter the blacks are all de Souzas!

But then everyone is a de Souza or has de Souza cousins in Brazil.

Much love. Be good. Hope your love life is working out. See you all summer.

B

To Elizabeth Chatwin

c/o British Vice-Consulate | Salvador da Bahia | Brazil | 9 March 1977

Dear E.

Oh, I hope this new arrangement works out. Probably because I have had to kick my heels round Bahia so long, I am heartily sick of it. Full of folklore, bad art, intellectuals in search of Atlantis and smart folks who go to candomblé in jangling earrings. I am staying with the missionaries of the British Church and when got down I retire into a damp retreat in the graveyard where I read while marble personifications of sleep mourn our English gentlemen victims of yellow fever.

I don't promise Portugal or Spain until a. the wretched proof comes b.

---

1. N.S.: 'The situation remained unchanged in 1995 when I accompanied the Bahia street musician Rasbutta da Silva to Benin to seek his African ancestors. At the Maison Familiale da Silva in Porto Novo, the clan, all descended from the Bahia slaver José-Rodrigues da Silva, imagined Rasbutta to be immoderately rich, like his namesake. They crowded around him, saying: "When are you going to take us to your big house in Brazil?"'

I don't find something wonderful in the province of Pianhy or Marañón. In any case I'll phone you again 1 week before you go i.e. round the 23rd. Incidentally, I do think you're going very early for Spain. You remember how perishing it was when we were in Madrid. Also the weather in April is liable to be tricky in Andalusia. Downpours for Holy Week in Seville. Never been so cold as in Ronda in April. You may be lucky, but I would have left it till 2nd half of the month and then go from Madrid to Aula, Salamanca, Trujillo and the Extremaduran towns (I imagine you are hiring a car) then to the south Cordoba, Seville, Granada. Don't miss Yuste, Charles V's retreat or the monasteries of Guadalupe with the Zurbarans – there's an equally good series in Cadiz. You shouldn't miss Salamanca either – cold or no cold. The best city in Spain. Old cathedral out of this world.

I can fly Varig very easily direct to Portugal and want just a snuff around Lisbon for a few days. Perhaps we could meet in the Hotel Seite Aix in Cintra – the most beautiful looking hotel in the world. One night wouldn't break the bank.

Next day.

All this is, as I said on the phone, rather dependant on future timing, posts etc. and whether any startling development occurs. In any case I'll phone you from wherever on the 26th/27th to find out how things are . . .

In haste. xxx x B

At last, in early March, Cape's proofs of In Patagonia *arrived from England.*

To Belinda Foster-Melliar

c/o British Vice-Consulate | Salvador da Bahia | Brazil | 9 March 1977

Dear Belinda Foster-Melliar,

Many thanks for your letter which got stuck in the post between Rio and Bahia – 2 weeks instead of two days and was unstuck for me by a gypsy cabocla or fortune teller who prophesied, after a certain amount of greasing, that it would arrive today – which it did.

Answer to your queries:

P41. He was white, sickly white. We might even put in 'unhealthy white body.' Persians pride themselves on their whiteness anyway. Aryan = Iran = fair . . .

P133 Don't like either. What about this? 'When he had to retire, he couldn't face the coop of England and had sought his own camp taking with him 2500 sheep and "my man Gomez."'

. . . P278 Don't know what 'at night' is doing here at all. Should read: 'He came back to breakfast . . .'

MacLennan. I simply can't do without a ref book in Glos. My impression is MacLennan. Is that a Scottish name at all? The name is taken from an Argentine book which may well have got it wrong . . .

I hope this is comprehensible and I do apologise for the delay.

Yrs ever, Bruce Chatwin

My love to Susannah.[1] Say I'm a bad correspondent.

PS Please confirm by cable that you have received this. Then my mind will be at rest.

PPS Don't really care too much for dedications.

To Francis Wyndham

c/o Price Waterhouse | 63 Praca Machada Assis | Recife | Brazil |
10 March 1977

Dear Francis,

Do you still have any clout on the magazine? Or is it not worth bothering with?

The matter is this: In 2 weeks I'll be in Recife where there is a most interesting man: Its bishop Dom Hélder Camara[2] who is a. perhaps the greatest expert in the world on the problems of the urban poor (The Brazilian N.E. being a testing ground like Bangladesh) b. an

1. Susannah Clapp, Chatwin's editor at Cape.
2. Hélder Camara (1909–99), Roman Catholic Archbishop of Recife, famous for saying: 'When I give food to the poor, they call me a saint. When I ask why the poor have no food, they call me a Communist.'

anti-Marxist of the Far Left c. with Sister Cecilia[1] of Calcutta the nearest thing to being a saint and who will probably be canonised at once when he dies.

He is, I have to add, much lionised by certain New York ladies, who gave me his stuff to read. Also Oriana Fallaci[2] has already interviewed him. But as far as I can judge, his position is one for which I have the greatest possible admiration. The Camaras were (and are) great sugar moghuls with old slave plantations in Pernambuco.

Let me know by cable what you think. If the magazine proves hopeless perhaps the paper might take something. I imagine, Recife being a colossal city, that I could get a reasonably decent colour photo of him. The money I can arrange through the above company, but we'll have to pay them back.

Otherwise Brazil is rather lowering. People in Rio cowed and lacking in personality.

As always, B

To Elizabeth Chatwin
Juazeiro | Rio Sao Francisco | Brazil | 11 March 1977

Dear E,

The last letter was posted in a rush. I am now on my long-delayed tour of the north-east. The arid cactus and thornbush country that stretches from Bahia to the Amazon. I am making for San Luis de Marañón which is almost up to Belem, and is where Queen Agontimé of Dahomey was sold into slavery and brought back by de Souza. I know exactly what to do with the book: write it in one long stretch without even the favour of chapters. Balzac's *Eugénie Grandet* gave me the idea. You begin in the present in the present tense and you flash back into the past and then write through to the present. I am beginning with the family celebrating their annual commemo-

1. Chatwin means Mother Teresa.
2. Oriana Fallaci (1929–2006), Italian journalist.

rative mass in the Church in Ouidah and retiring for the dinner in Simbodji which means the Big House or Casa Grande in Fon. None of the black de Souzas are aware of the big House in Brazil from which de Souza was expelled as a boy and which he reconstructed in Africa. The scene is then set for his life and what a life! Cattle drover turned man drover who ends up the prisoner of the King of D[ahomey] and dies of rage at being trapped when all he wants to do is get out of Africa and retire to Bahia. I hadn't quite realised we had got as far as March 11. However, I'll ring up as planned on the 26th probably from Recife. But I may want to try and get an interview with the Bishop Hélder Camara for the old *Times* (if they'll have it).[1] He is the greatest world expert on the problems of the urban poor and the nearest thing to being a saint. He and Sister Cecilia of Calcutta are in fact the 2 who are up for immediate canonisation.

Re Spain: I don't think I can make Rio before say April 8–10. Don't want to stay more than a day or so and there are flights every day to Lisbon and Madrid. The best thing might be for you to ring Margaret Mee[2] again and say where you are.

All this depends on what happens here.

Lots of love

B

PS Please have my typewriter repaired xxx B

This is the only letter that Chatwin wrote to his father independently of Margharita; an apology for having caused him great pain. Hugh says: 'I remember Charles speaking to Margharita and me in his drawing-room: "This all happened a very long time ago and it was quite wrong of Bruce to drag the matter up, upsetting our elderly relatives, again." '

1. The *Sunday Times* did not commission the article.
2. Margaret Mee (1908–88), English botanical artist living in Rio de Janeiro.

To Charles Chatwin

8 Gloucester Gate | London | 20 September 1977

Dear Charles,

Of course, the footnote about Robert Harding[1] can be cut out of the paperback.

I had attached a lot of importance to it at the time, but now see that it is rather superfluous. It's terribly difficult to get such things in perspective when you're close to them.

The trouble is that he, your grandfather, became one of my childhood obsessions, ever since I discovered that court suit (and dressed up in it), in the red spotted trunk at Brown's Green. I felt that his vertical rise and fall somehow offset Charley's horizontal wandering.

Anyway I <u>am</u> sorry.

as always,

B

After their times together in France and Oregon, Chatwin saw less of James Ivory. 'I went down one time to Holwell Farm,' Ivory remembers. 'Strolling about with him in a long upstairs hall with polished floorboards he privately told me that he had given up homosexuality – that he didn't have those feelings anymore.' However, at a wedding in Long Hanborough in June 1977 Chatwin met Donald Richards, a 27-year-old Australian stockbroker who had arrived with the artist Keith Milow. 'I

---

1. The footnote on page 148 of the first edition of *In Patagonia* read: 'My great-grandfather, Robert Harding Milward, did not go into the family's Worcestershire needle business, but went into the law. He was a wonderful-looking man, eaten up with snobbery and delusions of grandeur. He was the Duke of Marlborough's man of business and went to America to negotiate the Vanderbilt marriage settlement. (The Duke later sacked him for "grose incompitance".) He was a friend of Richter, the Wagnerian conductor; of Madame Patti, and of Charles Gounod, whose son, Jean, was briefly engaged to my great-aunt Dora. His financial manoeuvres were bound to land him in trouble. In 1902 he went bankrupt for £97,000 and the Lord Chief Justice gave him six years for embezzlement. In Ventnor Jail a tumour developed in his brain and he died.'

introduced brown-eyed Donald to blue-eyed Bruce and their eyes met,' says Milow. 'Something seemed to click which I was not prepared for.' Before, Chatwin had had passing affairs with men. 'This was the first time he'd committed his life to a man,' said Teddy Millington-Drake. 'Bruce was infatuated with him.' No correspondence survives of their relationship, which lasted five years, save for a postcard from Richards two months after their meeting: 'I long to see you, so I can relax, and tell you <u>everything</u>. Rest assured I do look forward to <u>that</u>. Meanwhile take care, and keep writing, with my love XXXX D.'

*   *   *

In October 1977 Chatwin drove with Elizabeth through Switzerland and Austria ('bought the inevitable loden coats and had two thrilling days in the Ost-Ture romping round in the snow')
to Siena, where he had rented from Millington-Drake the annexe at Poggio al Pozzo in order to begin writing The Viceroy of Ouidah. *'When he came to stay,' wrote Millington-Drake, 'he settled in and made his nest in whatever part of the house he had been assigned; then when it suited him, he would move on to another nest in someone else's house. He expected to be fed: "What's for lunch?" he would cry as he breezed in at half-past twelve. Occasionally he would contribute a couple of bottles of champagne or, as a great treat, some wild rice. Then there was the telephone bill. He telephoned continually to his agent, his friends, to a young man he'd fallen in love with in Brazil. At the end of the visit he would offer 10,000 lire (about £4), saying he hadn't used the 'phone much. But his friends didn't mind because we were so fond of him, though he was selfish and self-centred like most artists are.'*

To David King[1]
Poggio al Pozzo | Siena | Italy | [October 1977]

Dear King,

On leaving England we moved to Geneva and stayed with my friend George Ortiz. I played with his little girl Graziella aged 5 and now the only trace of her is a chloroform soaked rag left in a falsely registered car abandoned near the French border. The real nightmare of being rich is that even if you gave away every cent, no one would believe you and you'd then have <u>nothing</u> to protect yourself with. G[eorge] O[rtiz] is innocence at large and that this should happen to him monstrous.[2]

Otherwise we didn't have too bad a time in Austria and I am quite well installed here. In Florence yesterday we met the Director of the Karlsruhe Museum who said that anti-Hitler jokes during the war were exceedingly funny. An example: Hitler, as everyone knew, would sometimes grovel on the floor in a rage and bite the carpet. The story: Hitler goes to a big store in Berlin and buys a new carpet with a very thick pile. The salesgirl says: Mein Fuhrer, will you take it away or eat it now?

Drop me a line to say how it goes with T[om]M[aschler]

as always, Bruce

In Patagonia was published in England on 14 October 1977 with an initial print run of 4,000 copies. Paul Theroux was one of the first enthusiastic reviewers, writing in The Times. *'He has fulfilled the desire of all real travellers, of having found a place that is far and strange and seldom visited like the Land where the Jumblies live.'*

1. David King (*b*.1943), art editor of *Sunday Times* Magazine 1965–75.
2. Graziella Ortiz was kidnapped from the grounds of Chateau Elma near Lake Geneva. The trail led to an abandoned Alfa Romeo near the French border. She was released ten days later, slightly chubbier – 'obviously from being fed starches,' her father said – following the payment of a $2 million ransom.

To Francis Wyndham
Poggio al Pozzo | Siena | Italy | about the 20th Oct. [1977]

Dear Francis,

This is better than the Welsh mountains. Bare hills, bright light and most of the English gone back for the winter. I cycle to Siena for groceries and speak to shopkeepers in an incoherent mixture of Spanish, Portuguese and Latin; they smile breezily and ask if I want peanuts.

[John] Stefanidis is here and says the doctors have taken Violet[1] off some drug and that she's much better – and going out to lunch! I am so glad. It would be wonderful if she could go on as she was.

The two of them have gone for lunch at Lord Lambton's[2] new papal villa, bristling with statues. I have stayed behind to write the bit about the Dahomean coup, have written four bad pages and will reduce them to a single line. So it goes. I am also holding the fort for the arrival of guests: Mme Lillaz and Mme Picasso,[3] no less.

So far I have seen the reviews in *The Times* and *Observer*. Not at all bad. Gratifying, in fact. Neither quite got the hang of it – or what the brontosaurus stands for. Who is Nicholas Wollaston?[4]

I spent my solitary lunch thinking of the enormous amount I owe to you . . .

As always, Bruce

1. Wyndham's mother, author and socialite Violet Leverson m.1923 Guy Percy Wyndham (1865–1941). On 25 October, Wyndham replied: 'Yes, Violet is a million times better – it seemed like a miracle cure, though of course all it really consisted in was not taking what the doctor ordered.'
2. Antony Lambton, 6th Earl of Durham (1922–2006), Conservative MP, author and owner of Villa Cetinale, a 17th century villa in Tuscany.
3. Kitty Lillaz, Parisian beauty married to philanthropist George Lillaz, had driven to Tuscany from Grasse; Jacqueline Roque who had married Picasso in 1961 was to have come with her but suddenly was unwell.
4. Writer and traveller (1926–2007) who had reviewed *In Patagonia* in the *Observer*. 'Chatwin's telling is masterly, as tantalising as the synopsis of a newly discovered Conrad novel.' Wyndham wrote: 'Perhaps none of them quite get the hang of what you are doing, but they all seem to love the book and that will make lots of people read it, some of whom may get the hang!'

To Elizabeth Chatwin
Poggio al Pozzo | Siena | Italy | 24 October 1977

Dear E.,

I appear to have lost two library books belonging to the Museum of Mankind. They are Money Kyrle *The Meaning of Sacrifice* (green) and Donald Pierson *Negroes in Brazil* (beige). God knows what happened. As I remember it, I went through them in the Library itself, found only a few things of interest, and left them, without however getting back my borrowing slip. Could you a. check at the farm? (I know they are not at Carney).[1] b. check to make sure I didn't return them to the London Library by mistake?

The whole of last summer is like a bad dream to me.[2]

love,

B

P.S. Can you ask Pat Trevor-Roper to send 3 Betnesol N eye drops. Winter's supply. B

On 17 October Chatwin's father posted a batch of reviews. 'My reaction to them – worthy recognition of a lot of endeavour & hard work put in by you, and a full appreciation that the book is, to my mind, completely free of any padding . . . Thank you for your very understanding note before you left in reply to my letter.'

To Charles and Margharita Chatwin
Poggio al Pozzo | Siena | Italy | [October 1977]

Many thanks for the enclosures. Tom Maschler sent others with the news that we have an enthusiastic American publisher and several offers for foreign translations. Eh! Hiu! Bruce

1. Tom Maschler's cottage on the Welsh Borders; one of Chatwin's myriad writing places.
2. E.C.: 'It rained all summer.'

To John [Michell]
Poggio al Pozzo | Siena | Italy | 29 October 1977

Dear John,

Many thanks for your card.

The pianist! Ah! The pianist!

E. Hemingway, who knew a thing of two though it's fashionable to put him down, said if you take something OUT of a piece of writing it always shows. What I took OUT of that story was the head falling backwards at the end of the mazurka, automatically with no hint of it before, and lifting him off the piano stool into the bedroom.

But that is off the record and should be torn up.

Reviews rather good, the ones I've seen so far. All rather missing the point, but gratifying all the same. Nightmare interview with the *Guardian*. He had somewhere done his homework on my Sotheby period, which I was more than anxious to suppress. I suppose it can't be helped. But I will never give an interview again, nor will I interview anybody. (He says!).

Much love,

Bruce.

On 19 October Welch wrote praising In Patagonia. *'Perhaps I particularly like it because it has the qualities I find in Mughal pictures: extraordinary portraiture, very deep and psychological, superb technically, with all sorts of enrichments.'*

To Cary Welch
Poggio al Pozzo | Siena | Italy | 5 November 1977

Dear C.,

What a welcome letter! I hadn't thought of *In Patagonia* in terms of Mughal Art but the connection exists. *The Babur-Nama*[1] has influenced

---

1. *The Baburnama*, the memoirs of Zahir ud-Din Mohammad Babur (1483–1530), founder of the Mughal Empire, translated by Annette Beveridge.

me greatly in what I write. With the possible exception of Isaac Babel,[1] I know of no writer capable of such economic portraits of people. What I love is the clear, staccato line with a fantastical flourish at the end.

I must fish out my first piece of 'writing'. It was on the masterfully described descent of Omar Sheikh Mirza (is that what Babur's father was called?) from his pigeon loft.[2]

Such directness in Babur, Such awesome GAPS. I haven't got my Miss Beveridge here, otherwise there would be quotations. So there you are!

Is there anything else in Indian literature as good? I once bought Abu'l Faz'l[3] but sold it; it didn't have the same effect. Perhaps it's to do with their having being in Turki. I have often suspected the Turkish languages of having wonderful reserves of expression. It comes out in a lot of Russian literature.

So far the critics have been very complimentary, but the FORM of the book seems to have puzzled them (as I suspect it did the publisher). There's a lot of talk of 'unclassifiable prose', 'a mosaic', 'a tapestry', a 'jigsaw', a 'collage' etc. but no one has seen that it is a modern WONDER VOYAGE: the Piece of Brontosaurus is the essential ingredient of the quest. Patagonia, as the farthest place to which Man walked from his origins on foot, is a symbol as well as a country. I think the photographs were a mistake. If it gets reprinted I'm going to have them out.[4]

Tom Maschler writes today that we have at last found a 'really enthusiastic American publisher'[5] but doesn't say who. I suppose it's the agent's business to tell me.

The days pass with the landscape of Southern Tuscany spread out before me. In human terms it's all rather dreary. I don't speak Italian: for every one word I master in Italian, I feel I'm massacring twenty in Spanish.

Unfortunately the book I'm writing has to be a novel: the story is

1. Soviet short story writer (1884–1940).
2. Untraced. Babur's father was drunk or the steps to the pigeon loft were rickety.
3. Abu'l Faz'l (1551–1602), author of the *Akbarnama*, the official history of Akbar's reign.
4. *In Patagonia* did not have photographs in its American edition.
5. Jim Silberman of Summit Books at Simon & Schuster paid an advance of $5,000.

wonderful, but the facts are too few and contradictory to permit any other form. I had thought of giving it up when I was kicked out of Benin last winter. Then thought that was weak-kneed and so I go on. I am in no position to judge how it will turn out.

I haven't rung up the Tiz [George Ortiz] yet. When I did so there was a recorded announcement; so I imagined they didn't want callers. We were in the house a week before, and presumably being watched. It does seem uncanny that I said there were no kidnappings in Switzerland yet, and she gave me a look of despair and said YET.[1]

I can't think the H[oward]H[odgkin][2] situation is all that painful. The trouble is that it got out of hand. In the English 'art world' his became the most publicised private life of the century, and he didn't know how to handle it. When everyone else overdramatises your life, it inevitably becomes more dramatic.

What are your plans? I have said I will go to Afghanistan to watch horse-games on the Oxus Plain in March–April. Will you let me know if you are ever contemplating an Indian visit alone? I do want to go to India, but I want to find it for myself or be helped by really expert hands such as yours.

What's Jungle Jim's filum?

as always B

To Deborah Rogers
Draft letter, Poggio al Pozzo|Siena|Italy|1 December 1977

Dear Deborah,

I am delighted by the news. From all you tell me I would much prefer someone like Jim Silberman to handle it than be pressed through the

---

1. Welch had written to Chatwin: 'We telephoned G[eorge] O[rtiz] this morning. Graziella is back and not discussing her 10½ days of captivity . . . she is "resilient & strong" says G. and the captors did not treat her badly. But how utterly horrible!'
2. Howard Hodgkin, married father of two, had come out as gay and left his wife for a younger man. Welch had written to Chatwin: 'RS, in London, told me that life had been painful for H. on the personal front. Sad.'

mangle of Harper and Row et al. Especially with this peculiarly dotty book. The 5000 bucks sound fine to me: the dollar just would have to go down, now of all times. I don't think I shall come over. The cost by air is horrendous and I can't face the train or bus in this weather. The best thing is that Kasmin brings out the contract on December 23rd.

I would like to [write to] Silberman myself, because I have certain minor changes that could, if he thinks fit, be included in an American edition. The thing that most concerns me is the blurb: Don't repeat this to T[om] M[aschler] but I thought Cape's blurb a. rather over the top b. downright misleading.

There were certain things I flatly refused to say in the text for fear of sounding pretentious, but as none of the reviews picked up agreed that the book had, despite the collage effect, a pattern, a form even, but no one quite picked out what the form was, I wonder if it would help to do a bit of explaining.

Lots of other things have been said about Patagonia. I saw and did lots of other things in Patagonia, but cut them out for a specific [reason].

A. The book is the narrative of an actual journey and a symbolic one, admittedly using very concrete symbols.

B. Patagonia is the furthest point to which Man walked from his origins on foot: therefore it is a symbol of his restlessness. Maurice Richardson described it as a 'springboard to the Void'.

C. From the moment of its discovery, the southernmost tip had a tremendous effect on the literary imagination, especially writers obsessed with The Voyage in this world and the Voyage out of it. Hence in the text: the Baudelaire, Coleridge, Poe, Donne, Cendrars, even Shakespeare, are never chosen at random.

D. The form of *In Patagonia* described in the *Daily Telegraph* as wildly unorthodox is in fact as old as literature itself. It is supposed to fall into the category or be a spoof of Wonder Voyage: the narrator goes to a far country in search of a strange animal: on his way he lands in strange situations, people or other books tell him strange stories which add up to form a message. [Is not the Gilgamesh epic nor the Argonautics nor *Beowulf*.]

E. All the stories and characters were chosen because they illustrate some particular aspect of wandering and/or exile – all the reasons for emigration are there: political, criminal, pressure of family, the lure of the sea, or the passion, simply, to move. Cain, Abel, Moses, Aaron etc

I am of the view that the photographs even perhaps the map <u>don't</u> help.

I had in mind to write in another text beside the one of Blaise Cendrars which I love. Which should give the game away a bit more:

The most important from Chapter 1 *Moby Dick*.

'Then the wild and distant seas where he rolled his bulk; the unbelievable, nameless perils of the whale: these, with all the attending marvels of a thousand Patagonian sights and sounds, helped sway me to my wish.'

I did not put this in because George Gaylord Simpson, doyen of American palaeontologists, has used it already for his 1930's travel book *Attending Marvels*. And a very good book too!

In Lima Chatwin had learned from Monica that her mother Isabelle had been raped by her employer when hired as a governess to a Scots family in Patagonia. On 28 November 1977 Monica wrote to Chatwin expressing her 'pain and shocked horror – yes, horror' over a paragraph in In Patagonia *which dealt with this 'pitiful experience'. ('One night the whisky-soaked proprietor went for her and laid her down. She ran from the house, saddled a horse and rode through the snow to Punta Arenas.') She sent the letter via Chatwin's father, to whom she wrote the following day:'Bruce came to me knowing some of this story – I told him the truth and begged him – literally begged him, in your home that night, not to print anything of my Mother's story . . . But I am asking you now, if you can, because you are a lawyer, to urge Bruce to change the text of page 173.' On 3 December she also wrote to Cape: 'This paragraph is full of conjecture and half truths and quite clearly impugns the honour of both my parents.' Chatwin had given an impression of Isabelle – 'never Bella!' – as a 'rather cheap adventuress' preying on the soft heart of a lonely old man when, in fact, she was 'respected by all who knew her'. Another objection was to*

the footnote in Chapter 72 concerning the bankruptcy and impris-
onment of Chatwin's great-grandfather, Robert Harding Milward.
And there was a question of copyright. 'While I gave Mr Chatwin
access to my father's "Journal" and a letterbook covering the years
1912–16, I certainly did not give him my permission to photocopy
my father's Journal.' To Chatwin, she wrote: 'I understand now
why you insisted on staying on, shut up in your room upstairs
while we were in the process of moving house.' She accused him of
having 'lifted' sections 'word for word from my father's Journal –
'which is our one inheritance from him.'

To Monica Barnett

Holwell Farm | Wotton-under-Edge | Glos | 14 January 1978

Dear Monica,

I am most sorry not to have written before. The postal service has all but broken down in Italy. I did not receive your letter until after Christmas, acted on it, and returned to London to see what could and should be done.

In Patagonia will be published in the United States by Summit Books, who are a subsidiary of Simon and Schuster. The process had already gone farther than I knew, but, mercifully, the letter came just in time to halt the printing.

I deeply regret what has happened and take full blame for misinterpreting your wishes. I had understood that you wished to exclude all reference to the circumstances of your brother's birth.[1] I phrased the episode vaguely and this has led to the trouble.

1. Monica's brother was born, and lived, in England. In her letter to Charles Chatwin, Monica had written: 'As I'm sure you know, rape usually results in two victims, and did so in this case – and herein lay the tragedy ... The tragedy of my brother is never-ending for he found after many years that he was not even a British citizen – this after serving 8 years in H.M. Forces during and immediately after the war, and having obtained a job with Municipal Welfare services in the UK (he never returned to Chile after 1928).' About the identity of the rapist, she wrote to Chatwin on 25 March 1978: 'I do know the man's name, and believed he suffered a terrible retribution as I understand one, maybe two of his children went down in the "Aviles" on their way to the war.'

The picture I wanted to convey was of two people, of different ages and backgrounds, both stranded at the end of the world; both wronged by a society (which, for all I can learn of it, was considerably off-beam), both of whom found consolation in each other's company and fell in love. Otherwise, to me at least, their behaviour is inexplicable.

That your father should have looked after her is typical of him: his sympathy for the underdog was automatic; hypocrisy was an anathema to him. That your mother should have returned to a place that must have been hateful to her, that she should have supported him through his disaster, is surely proof of her rocklike character and her devotion. That the Milwards (please let us mention no names) misunderstood their relationship is history. That the 'true Britisher' element in Punta Arenas ostracised them is something I learned from two people, who recalled events before 1919 with astonishing precision (though I fear one of them hispanicised the name 'Belle').

But the idea that your mother, in her condition, would have had 'carnal relations' before her marriage is something that never entered my head. If there are innuendos to that effect, I most humbly apologise for them and promise they are not there intentionally. It is safe to say that no reviewer (and I think no reader unaware of the facts) has picked on the episode.

The image of my great grandfather loomed over my life almost as much as 'the piece of brontosaurus'. After my grandmother's death I found his court suit and sword in a tin trunk. But you are quite right about the footnote, though it does give a hint of the somewhat fantastical nature of C[harles] A. M[ilward]'s family in England. It does not now belong in the text, but it did have a place in the original draft.

I did not take the facts of Harding Milward's bankruptcy from family sources, but from a standard biography of Winston Churchill. Milward apparently looked after the finances of the young Winston. The naval historians whom I consulted also make it clear that the decision to ignore Consul Milward's report on the *Dresden* came from Churchill himself, then First Lord of the Admiralty. I voiced the possibility that the two were connected, but that paragraph sat like a lump in the text and I cut it out.

It is quite clear that the footnotes and the offending paragraph must come out of future editions. There is a paperback in the pipeline; possible foreign translations, and then a reprinting since the first edition was small.

The changes I have forwarded to the US publisher are as follows.

p.148 Cut footnote.

p.157 Cut 'The Milwards' and 'as Milward gossip maintained . . .'

p.173 Para 1 should now read:

Meanwhile the ex-consul's life had taken a new direction. He had met a young Scotswoman called Isabel, who had got stranded penniless in Punta Arenas, after working on an estancia in Santa Cruz. Charley looked after her and paid her fare back to England. He was lonely again once she had gone. They wrote to each other: one of his letters contained a proposal.

Belle came back and they started a family . . .

p. 174 Change Bella to Belle . . .

2nd para 'Belle kept the books: she would carry on for nearly forty years . . .'

The question of copyright. In your house I made rough notes from the letter-book and the stories. Only when you allowed me to take the manuscript to the photocopier, did I get copies of The Wreck, Smallbones, The Doctor and his Wife, The Albatrosses, The Emperor of Brazil, The Dancing Pygmies, Hobbs and the Onas, The Salesians and the Alakalufs.

The Albatross story is probably the 'best'. The Wreck was essential to my tale but I had to paraphrase it to bring it down to size. But by far my favourites are Smallbones and the Doctor's Wife, both of which I would love to have used but are long and plainly belong to your story rather than mine. Instead, apart from the marvellously funny paragraph on Dom Pedro, I stuck to three small stories which concern the fate of nomadic peoples, a vital sub-theme of my book.

In Patagonia went to press when I was in Brazil last spring. In Cape's view my letter confirming your ownership of the stories was sufficient as long as there was an acknowledgement. I, however, insisted on crediting you on the copyright page for those stories which were reprinted almost verbatim; though not for the ones which were, for better or worse, contracted, paraphrased or adapted.

I always wanted C.A.M. to [do] the talking. His tone is inimitable. Had I never seen the manuscript the result would have had the character of a reconstruction from secondary sources. For me it is clear when he does talk, he is talking out of your source-book.

To clarify the position we should retain the copyright on the title page and adapt the note as follows:

Captain Charles Amherst Milward.

I could not have written this book without the help of Charley Milward's daughter, Monica Barnett, of Lima. She allowed me access to her father's papers and the unpublished manuscript of his stories in her possession. This was particularly generous since she is writing her own biography[1] in which the stories will appear in full. My sections 73, 75 and 86 are printed with minor alterations. His other stories, from sections 72 to 85, have been adapted from the original.

Please can you confirm whether you agree? I hate to try and rush you after what has occurred, but additions and subtractions are complicated and costly at this stage. The book is being offset in America and not reprinted. The publication is announced for the spring and if it fails to meet the date, it will have to be delayed till Fall. I have asked them to hold back till I hear from you. As each day counts, would it be too much for you to send me a cable to Holwell Farm?[2]

Please forgive.

yours ever,

Bruce

To Valerian Freyberg
Inscription to *In Patagonia*, 16 February 1978

For Valerian, when he's a little older and feeling restless. Affectionately, Bruce

To Ivry Freyberg
Holwell Farm | Wotton-under-Edge | Glos | 22 March 1978

I'm crazy about my godson and want to see him more and more often.

1. Monica never completed her father's biography.
2. On 26 January 1978 she telephoned Elizabeth at Holwell Farm, dictating this message: THANK YOU LETTER JUST RECEIVED STOP AGREE CHANGES PAGE 173 AND APPRECIATE REVISION OF ACKNOWLEDGMENT NOTE CONGRATULATIONS BOOK'S SUCCESS MONICA.

'It is slightly like a set for a Hitchcock movie, with a castle beyond and flights of ferocious seagulls.' Engrossed in a book, Bruce Chatwin bicycles from the gate-house he rented on Fishers Island, Connecticut, where he began writing *In Patagonia* (Elizabeth Chatwin, 1975).

(*Above*) Chatwin in 1955 aged 15, with Hugh (far left), Margharita with sister Kay and her two sons, going to the wedding of Margharita's brother John Turnell; (*above right*) the Chatwin family in France; (*right*) Hugh Chatwin on his 21st birthday; (*below right*) Charles and Margharita in the 1980s; (*below*) Chatwin taking the helm at Cowes, May 1964 (James Crathorne)

'I don't want to go on perched on the podium having sham orgasms as I knock down another lot.' Chatwin surprised everyone at Sotheby's when, in 1966, he resigned as a director to go to Edinburgh University to study archaeology. He later wrote to James Ivory: 'Two days in the auction room brought back a flood of gruesome memories. The nervous anxiety of the bidder's face as he or she waits to see if she can afford to take some desirable thing home to play with. Like old men in nightclubs deciding whether they can really afford to pay that much for a whore. But things are so much better. You can sell them, touch em up at any time of the day, and they don't answer back.'

In 1963, Chatwin (*left*) travelled through Iran with Robert Erskine (*below left*) to Afghanistan. This was the first of three visits in the footsteps of Robert Byron whose own fascination with Persian art had been sparked by image and by the Radkam Mausoleum built in 1281 AD of Gumbad-i-Kabus, the great 11th-century tombtower in northern Iran (*below*).

In 1969, Chatwin (*above*) returned to Afghanistan with the poet Peter Levi, 'a great friend of mine who is a Jesuit'. One of several mentors whom Chatwin later outgrew, Levi played a role in encouraging him to become a writer.

Chatwin wrote to Elizabeth after Levi (*above and right*) published an account of their journey in *The Light Garden of the Angel King*: 'The thing that really infuriates me about the Afghan book is that all my remarks and observations are repeated verbatim as an integral part of his text.'

On 19 September 1969, Chatwin wrote to Derek Hill: 'I am longing to see you. I hope with successful photographs of *the* Mausoleum of Gohar Shad at Khosan (*above*) probably the most beautiful of all Timurid buildings. AND those of the Nouh Goumbed at Balkh (*below*) which escaped the notice of the ever-unobservant French though they surveyed and excavated not half a mile away – a mosque of the 9th century with brick work as fine as Sultan Ismail at Bokhara and vine scroll stuccos finer and *earlier* than Naylu.'

Elizabeth (*left*) in 'a lacquered Javanese coolie hat' and Chatwin (*below* and *below left*) while studying archaeology at Edinburgh — a period that he called his 'season in

Visitors to the Chatwins' Canongate flat included: Hugh (*below left*) and the art dealer John Kasmin (also seen posing in a bobble-hat); and the collector Cary Welch (imitating a vampire). Welch, whose wife Edith was a cousin of Elizabeth, said of Chatwin: 'In life, one does run into people who are the perfect ping-pong opponent. In some ways I became the mentor/father figure.'

In February 1966, after several false starts, the Chatwins found Holwell Farm, a pink seventeenth-century house set in 47 acres near Wotton-under-Edge in Gloucestershire. Elizabeth's mother, Gertrude Chanler (*left*) advanced £17,000 as a wedding present for them to buy it. Elizabeth swiftly grew accustomed to her husband's absences. 'Everything is always perfect to begin with, but he gets fed up with a place very quickly and in no time at all he's picking holes.' In 1978, Chatwin wrote to Nigel Acheson: 'Wherever I go, particularly in deserts, the image of that misty Gloucestershire valley passes before my eyes. But one should never go near it, except to recharge the IDEA of it once every two or three years.'

Chatwin with Ivry Freyberg ('my abiding friend') whose brother Raulin had been his best friend at Marlborough; at the christening of Chatwin's godson Valerian Freyberg in 1971. 'I am very keen on my godson and want to see him, often, when is his birthday?'

FOLLOWING PAGE
Patagonia, 1975. 'On no previous journey am I conscious of having done more. Patagonia is as I expected but more so, inspiring violent outbursts of love and hate.'

Chatwin the nomad; and one of his 'cubby-holes'. L6 Albany was a former maid's room that he borrowed off Christopher Gibbs. 'It is not a flat, in the English sense of the term, but a one-room *garçonnière* such as one might find in the *Cinquième*. My tastes are also rather Spartan. It has a kind of kitchen, a minuscule shower and basin, but the lavatory is out on the landing.'

Chatwin the photographer:
(*above left*) West Africa, (*above*)
China, (*left*) South America.

On the black hill: The Tower (*above*) in Powys 'is, I have to say, a lovely place to work, the only distraction being a view of a white farmhouse through a slit window.' The house was owned by Diana Melly (*right*, with her

Another regular visitor was Francis Wyndham (*above*, with Diana Melly), who was the first to be allowed to see Chatwin's finished manuscripts.

Le Thoronet, an unfinished Cistercian monastery near Draguignan. Chatwin urged friends like Murray Bail and Derek Hill to visit. 'Whoever was "the mastermind" at Le Thoronet has, in my view, to have seen the Seljuk madrassas in Anatolia on the way to the 2nd Crusade.' For Bail, the austerity and elegance summed up Chatwin's aesthetic: 'Everything has been removed. It was plain, immaterial and resonant because of the emptiness.'

In November 1985, the Chatwins visited Beisha in northern Yunnan.
'We met a village doctor and herbalist, a sort of Taoist sage who went gathering
herbs in the mountains, painted orchids and bamboos and wrote calligraphies
of the great Tang poems.' Doctor Ho invited them to a feast for his new-born
grandson. Elizabeth says: 'This is the place where Bruce ate a black "1,000 year
old egg". It was a ritual course, and none of us ate the eggs except Bruce.
He said, "We have to make an effort, we've got to be polite." He ate one
and was sick almost as soon as left the house.'

Dionysus and Christ Pantokrator: a photograph taken by Chatwin in 1969 of a Nuristan man in trailing vine leaves; and the iron cross below Stavronikita monastery on Mount Athos which convinced him 'There must be a God'. In his last months, Chatwin took instuction in becoming Orthodox.

I may be off to India in the week to interview the redoubtable Mrs G.[1] now making a comeback. Wonderful to see you all! Much love, Bruce

To Cary Welch
Holwell Farm | Wotton-under-Edge | Glos | 21 May 1978

Dear C.,

I got back from Injuh to find your very welcome cheque, all the more welcome in that I have bought a flat in Islington, tiny but remarkable flat sitting in a garden with wild ducks nesting all round.[2] You would never have guessed what I've been doing: interviewing, travelling with that nightmarish lady, Indira Gandhi, have covered virtually the whole of India, from Cape Cormorin to the Himalayas, on her whistle-stop tour.[3] She's far worse than you'd ever imagine. I was prepared to allow her at least a dimension of greatness, but all you find is a lying, scheming bitch. If she were really evil, that would be something. If she were really Indian, that also would be something. Eventually I decided she was the memsahib behind the silver teapot congratulating General Dyer[4] on his courageous action at Amritsar. One of her ex-Cabinet Ministers said to me: 'The atmosphere round Mrs G[andhi] is like that of Arsenic and Old Lace.'[5]

She charmed me at first, I have to admit. But I couldn't stomach the pettiness of the lies. Her enemy Charan Singh[6] summed her up when he said: 'Mrs Gandhi is incapable of telling the truth even by mistake.'

1. Indira Gandhi (1917–84), after her election defeat in 1977, in which she lost her seat, was campaigning to be re-elected, possibly as a prelude to running again for Prime Minister. The *Sunday Times* magazine had commissioned Chatwin to write a profile.
2. E.C.: 'The flat was near Canonbury Square. At the last minute, he pulled out. He suddenly realised that it was too far away and no one would come and see him.'
3. 'On the Road with Mrs Gandhi,' *Sunday Times* magazine, 30 July 1978.
4. Brigadier-General Reginald Dyer (1864–1927), British officer who gave orders in Amritsar on 13 April 1919 to open fire on unarmed civilians, resulting in more than 1,000 deaths.
5. *Arsenic and Old Lace*, 1944 film directed by Frank Capra based on Joseph Kesselring's play.
6. Charan Singh (1902–87), Prime Minister of India 1979–80.

I did have some extremely funny times. Not the least was our visit to the Durga Temple in Benares, where a monkey with mastitis tried to rip off her sari. When I told the Rajmata of Gwalior that she had dipped herself in the Ganges, she said: 'Sacrilege!'

Now Benares is a place I wouldn't mind holing up in. Where else do the Ancient World and Twentieth Century Decadence meet in such harmony? The only trouble was a temperature of 42 degrees centigrade, with the result that I came back feeling a bit dessicated.

Sorry for the quick note. We hope to be over shortly, love B

On Mr Dhavan's desk (her Assistant Private Secretary) I found a manual for ventriloquists called *Mimicry and Monoacting*.

To Monica Barnett

Draft letter, Holwell Farm | Wotton-under-Edge | Glos | 10 June 1978

Dear Monica,

Now it's my turn to apologise for the delay. Your letter reached here the morning I flew to India to interview Mrs Gandhi (and that's another story). The one to Deborah Rogers had got there three days earlier. I spent six weeks in India and since coming back have hardly had time to eat, let alone think.

In the meantime the advance copies of the New York edition of *Patagonia* have arrived here, not seen yet. I'll have the publishers send you and Lala[1] a copy each. If there's anyone else you can think of I'd be very happy to do the same . . .

Now, with regard to the stories, I accept your position and most sincerely apologise for the misunderstanding. If I am in the wrong, then I am deeply in the wrong. But I recall the matter differently: I was not at all certain, in Lima, whether you would allow me to photocopy the journal, and was therefore extremely pleased, when one day after lunch when Gertrude and Elizabeth were there, you gave me the manuscript

---

1. Lala Leach, Monica's sister.

and told me I could go to the photocopiers. I have a copy of a letter to you dated 4th of May 1975, which starts:

This letter confirms that I have photocopied biographical material relating to your father the late Charles Amherst Milward, and also a great part of his uncompleted book. I have also taken extensive notes. I understand that you have no objection to my using it in the book I shall be writing about Patagonia. I also understand that this permission is subject to the following condition: that you hold full copyright over the material in your possession and that when you come to write the full biography of your parents there shall be no prevention to stop you using the same stories that I will have used. The same will apply to any photographs that will belong to you.

On my return to England I shall ask my literary agent to confirm this arrangement so that it is watertight.

yours ever,
Bruce Chatwin

To Desmond Morris
c/o Deborah Rogers Ltd | 5–11 Mortimer Street | London | [June 1978]

Dear Professor Morris,

I did enjoy our conversation last week about my wolf child[1]. I enclose a fiendishly bad photocopy of the piece and hope you didn't mind my quoting you – or half-quoting you – in the final passage. If you feel that it's wrong, please don't hesitate to let me know through Deborah [Rogers].

I thought you might like a copy of the book I wrote for Tom [Maschler] last year. American edition, I'm afraid.

Yours sincerely, Bruce Chatwin

While following Mrs Gandhi on her election tour, Chatwin had met Sunil Sethi, 'the 23 yr old whizz-kid of Indian journalism', who was starting out on India Today. *Chatwin found him 'an exhilarating companion. He had been everywhere in India,*

1. 'The Quest for the Wolf Children' appeared in the *Sunday Times* magazine, 30 July 1978.

roughing it. He could take in Hindi and spit it out in English from the sides of his mouth.'

To Sunil Sethi

Holwell Farm | Wotton-under-Edge | Glos | 18 June 1978

Dearest Sunil,

Well, that was a cheering letter. I had been waiting for it with a certain tetchy anticipation. Admittedly, it came at the end of a more cheering week. Had it come the week before, I might very easily have taken the next plane to Delhi. I was laid out. Laid out with such a monumental depression that I couldn't drag myself out of bed in the morning for fear of what frightful things the day had in store. I <u>think</u> I gave you to understand I was going back in such haste to see someone.[1] This is not my usual practice: usually I delay departure for England (*Le Tombeau Vert*) until the last possible moment. However, when the someone met me at the airport, I knew that something was seriously wrong (frightening how people can change in a month), and for three weeks the wrongness built up in a crocodile of misery, while I battled at my typewriter with that beastly woman who had ruined my journey to India. Emotionally, I always seem to suffer from transcontinental dislocation. Anyway for the past month I've been cursing myself for leaving YOU and you'll have to put up with it.

So, on Monday, stuck in bed at 10am on a bright sunny morning, Tom Maschler my publisher rang to say that *In Patagonia* had won the Hawthornden Prize for imaginative literature (previous winners include Evelyn Waugh and Dom Moraes!). So I stopped mooning and pulled myself together. Not that I am normally a mooner, but I have discovered I am far less hard-boiled than I thought.

Of course, *In Patagonia* isn't meant to be a travel book, but only you and the T.L.S. reviewer had the wit to see that, while I have been so browbeaten by people saying it is a travel book that I half came to believe it – or believed that I had failed in my purpose – to write an

1. Donald Richards. Frances Partridge, diary 4 May 1974: 'Donald good-looking (and knows it) but charming . . . He is Australian and has worked among aboriginal children, is now trying to write a Ph.d on the Indian Raj, loves opera, is drawn to the idea of death, calls everyone by their Christian names at once, but in a way that doesn't offend.'

allegorical journey on the classic pattern (narrator goes in search of beast etc). Thank you for 'a matter of multiple passions resolving into a final simplicity.'

Then there were rows at the *Sunday Times*. I felt the only way to tackle the woman was to do it obliquely, elliptically. How can any European presume to pontificate about India? Vainly, I tried to describe what I saw and left the readers to make up their minds. The copy came back scrawled all over: WELL? IS SHE COMING BACK OR ISN'T SHE or WHAT IS THE POLITICAL SCENE? That kind of thing, with a request that I rewrite.

But why should I? Print or don't print, but don't bother me. That has been my attitude over the past week. Preferably, don't print, because anyway I don't like writing about people I don't like.

English newspapers are dreadful. Unreadable, so why should one presume to write for them? The besetting sin of all English writers is their fatal attraction for periodicals, their fascination for reviews, and their passion for bickering in print.

Resolution of the month: Never to write for newspapers.

Quotation of the Month (from Cyril Connolly's *The Unquiet Grave*):

'The more books we read, the sooner we perceive that the true function of the writer is to produce a masterpiece and that no other task is of any consequence. Obvious though this should be, how few writers will admit it or having made the admission, will be prepared to lay aside the piece of iridescent mediocrity on which they have embarked! Writers always hope that their new book is going to be their best, for they will not acknowledge that it is their present way of life which prevents them creating anything different.

'All excursions into journalism, broadcasting, propaganda and writing of films, however grandiose, are doomed to disappointment. To put of our best into these forms is another folly, since thereby we condemn good ideas as well as bad to oblivion. It is in the nature of such work not to last, so it should not be undertaken . . .'

But what about the rent and drink bills? When the bills of his *Horizon* mounted to intolerable proportions, he sold himself to the *Sunday Times* and died there.

I am not suggesting you walk out of *India Today*, but feel you have reached a point where journalism has taught you the necessary art of condensation and the technique of story-hunting, but as such has nothing to offer you. Nor am I suggesting you abandon your project on the dynasties of the demagogues (though that is grandiose and journalistic): but with your particular gifts, with your passion for India (though you needn't confine yourself to India); with your unbearable curiosity into the motivations of people; with your capacity to arrange characters on a written page; you should be able to produce at least one lasting masterpiece. Don't leave it too late. I've left it far too late.

India is the land of the short story. It will never have its *War and Peace*. Mr Scott's opus[1] is a tragic bore; Mrs Jabberwallah[2] can't write; R. K. Narayan[3] isn't good enough and Mr Naipaul[4] is a pontificator. Nor am I suggesting that you go out like the young Kipling with his notebook. But in a world where millions of hot-air-laden pages are printed annually, it becomes a duty to go, see and condense for future readers at some unseen date.

I like *Passage to India* but believe that E.M.F[orster] is a poor model, as Somerset Maugham is a lethal one. Forgive me for suggesting you go on a course of Chekhov, Isaac Babel, Maupassant, Flaubert (especially *Un Coeur Simple*) Ivan Bunin[5] (whom I'll get for you) Turgenev, and among the Americans early Sherwood Anderson, early Hemingway, and Carson McCullers especially *The Ballad of the Sad Café*.

I wouldn't take too much notice of this: it does reveal my inability to come to terms with English literature in general, excepting of course the Elizabethans and the outsiders. But we have nothing in the 19th or 20th Century to beat the narrative drive of someone like Poe.

My latest passion is Racine, though heaven knows where it's going to lead. But the past week has gone writing an introduction to another

---

1. Paul Scott (1920–78), British novelist best known for *The Raj Quartet*.
2. Ruth Prawer Jhabvala (*b*.1927), novelist and screenwriter who worked with James Ivory.
3. R. K. Narayan (1906–2001), Indian writer in English much praised by Graham Greene, who published him.
4. (Sir) V. S. Naipaul (*b*.1932), British writer of Indo-Trinidadian descent.
5. Ivan Bunin (1870–1953), Russian short story writer. One of Chatwin's unfinished projects was to write an introduction to *Dark Avenues* for Robinson Books.

passion, the prose of Osip Mandelstam,[1] the most important writer to be snuffed out by Stalin. Consider this, written at the time of the purge:

'The bourgeois is of course more innocent than the proletarian, closer to the uterine world, to the baby, the kitten, the angel, the cherubim. In Russia there are very few of these innocent bourgeois, and the scarcity had a bad effect on the digestion of authentic revolutionaries. The bourgeoisie in its innocent aspect must be preserved, entertained with amateur sports, lulled on the springs of Pullman cars, tucked into envelopes of snow-white railway sleep.'

Do try and come here – for or preferably not for *The Sunday Times*. If you can wangle a cheap ticket, I can fix you some money, not much, say £400, and you can pay me back some time in India.

But I, I warn you, have had quite enough of *Le Tombeau Vert* for the present. Nor can I face the idea of your country in the monsoon when I have work (sic) to do. I have chosen to go to the Spanish Pyrenees (Pray God, they are as I remember them) to hole up in some cheap hotel, with Racine, Flaubert and a manuscript. And probably to stare at blank sheets of paper!

I MAY not come back until the end of September, but you of course would be welcome wherever I am. A card (allow 10 days) or a cable to here will reach me, but I will try and furnish some kind of address.

with love – as always

Bruce

Please forgive this rather chaotic letter written in the small hours of the morning.

To Desmond Morris

as from: Holwell Farm | Wotton-under-Edge | Glos | 2 July 1978

Dear Desmond Morris,

I can't thank you enough for your help over the wolf child piece. Corrections noted and passed on to the *Sunday Times*.

1. Russian poet and essayist (1891–1938).

Though I say it myself, the photo of Shamdev the Wolf Boy in the arms of his rescuer is rather amazing. I think it will be out in about three weeks.

Best wishes, Bruce Chatwin

To John Kasmin
Barcelona | Spain | 10 July 1978

I ate the Hawthornden Prize at the restaurant of Michel Guérard.[1] Not what it's cracked up to be. <u>My</u> *cuisine minceur* seemed at least to <u>taste</u> more than his. Have been running the bulls in Pamplona. Now hopefully down to work. B

In the summer of 1978 Chatwin returned to Ronda, renting the former summerhouse of a convent.

To Sunil Sethi
Apartado 73 | Ronda | Malaga | Spain | July 26 1978

My dear S.,

I write also at once, but yours, alas, has had a hard time reaching me. Don't give a thought to your self-doubt: mine is in full flood. The last month has been a wearisome frittering away of time, unenjoyable, expensive, unproductive. I have at last found a place to hole up in, an exquisite neo-Classical pavilion restored by an Argentine architect who has run out of money. BUT I FRY. I feel hotter here than in Benares. Five hours of work and I'm exhausted. I will the words to come, but they won't; don't like what I've already done: feel like burning the manuscript.

No. I wasn't being dishonest about Someone [Donald Richards] . . . yet the fact is I have left England feeling exceptionally bruised, bruised

1. Les Prés D'Eugénie, Eugénie les Bains.

not the least by some of my closest friends, who use my obvious discom-
fiture to turn it into heartless gossip. There is something horribly claustrophobic about my country and yet, like you, I cannot get used to the
life of exile.

Yes. Cyril Connolly was a rotten novelist. He was also extremely
nasty to me. The dreaded Widow Orwell[1] first introduced me to him,
saying: 'You two must get to know each other. You're both so interested
in . . . er . . . the truth.' 'Oh?' said Connolly, 'and what particular aspect
of the truth are you interested in?' However, the *Unquiet Grave* is a book
I return to again and again, so brilliant yet so terribly indicative of the
pitfalls of English literary life.

Yes. Of course Mandelstam, in poetry, but more so in prose, is one
of my gods. I have just written an introduction – a memory of his widow[2]
– to his *Journey to Armenia*. I have had you sent a copy of the magazine
in which it has appeared, though I haven't seen it yet and dread the
mistakes. Don't be too put off by its ridiculous name – BANANAS. It
was started by a friend of mine[3] as a one-issue joke to put down a rival,
the *New Review*. The first issue was so successful, she got an Arts Council
grant and now she's stuck with the name.

No. I don't think I'll go to Australia in the winter. Someone is
Australian and the point is somehow missing. I am supposed to go to
New York in October, that is, if this piece of mediocrity is done with.
But after that, in theory at least, I'm free to float. I have a number of
short stories to finish: then I want to travel for a couple of years, trying
to put all my efforts into that form. I feel that Eastern (Post-Marxist)
Europe would provide wonderful material.

1. Sonia Brownell (1918–80) m. George Orwell 1949 and 1958–65 Michael Pitt-Rivers.
2. Chatwin had visited Nadezhda Mandelstam in Moscow, through the introduction of
Martha Gellhorn who advised him to take her 'champagne, cheap thrillers and
marmalade'. A dishcloth printed with a map of Queensland hung from a hook on the
door. She asked him to straighten a picture, explaining: 'I threw a book and hit it by
mistake. A disgusting book by an Australian woman. Don't you want to know what
the book was? *The Female Eunuch*.' Chatwin's introduction to Clarence Brown's translation of *Journey to Armenia* (1933) was first published in *Bananas, Russian Issue* (1978),
and later by the Redstone Press (1989).
3. Emma Tennant (*b*.1937), British novelist.

Yes. Of course I'll go on a journey with you. Where? India? Further West or Further East? With nothing but ourselves? No impediments? No 'other men's books'? Only notebooks.

The Wolf Boy article comes out next week in the *Sunday Times Magazine*. Of course they were much more pleased with that one than Mrs G[andhi]. My slight rows over Mrs G (which I don't want talked about) were concerned with the fact that I wrote down only what I saw, not what other people say. They seemed to want a lot of opinion, of hot air, of pontificating. All I wanted to do was to get down some of the woman's banality. When I read it to people, it was complete news to them. Most Westerners picture her as a cunning, devious schemer only (which of course she is) without getting a glimmer of her fatuous side. Anyway, unless it comes out soon, events will have superceded it. What's happening? I do hope the prosecutions aren't a panic move only. It'd be dreadful to have her back.

No. My smile would not be cryptic or dismissing, but open, cheerful and rather hopeful. I do wish you were here – or I there?

Let me know your plans. The trouble with London, for me, is that I have absolutely nowhere to stay.

XXXXXX B

PS If you know of anyone going to Kerala, can they bring some of the plain cotton lunghis – with coloured stripes.

To Sunil Sethi
Apartado 73 | Ronda | Malaga | Spain | [July 1978]

Dear S.,

The last letter was scribbled off in indecent haste: I doubt this one will be much better. The technical problems of letter writing here are as follows: I get up at sunrise at eight; over coffee I sit out on a semicircular terrace, contemplate the mountains opposite, and the hideous glazed pottery busts of a nymph and the Infant Bacchus on the arched portico: then settle down to work. Four and a half hours brings me to 12.30 and letter writing time if I am to catch the post which closes at 2. I leave the house at 1, bounce down the mountain in my little Fiat and zig-zag up the other side of Ronda, which perches on the top of a sheer cliff and looks like an iced cake. I unlock the aluminium PO Box, usually empty and hurtle to the market, which also closes at 2. Twice I have had a fight with the local condessa (a Southern Rhodesian called Faffie) as to who shall have the last lettuce. Then to a bar in a side street which has magnificent *tapas* (hors d'oeuvres) which I make into lunch. The other day I had a raw clam and was violently sick in the middle of the night. The proprietor is a fantastical, red haired queen, with draperies of white flesh hanging from his upper arms. I have seen him smile once, when the bar was full of soldiers.

Then usually I go for a swim at the pool of a friend called Magouche Phillips. She is an old friend, magnificent, stylish, the daughter of a US Admiral: her name was once Agnes MacGruder, that is, until she worked for Edgar Snow's 'Support Mao' campaign in New York in the 'forties, met the painter Arshile Gorky and married him. She still lives off the contents of the studio, is haunted by Gorky's suicide and quarrels frantically with all but one of her four daughters. One of these is married to the son of Stephen Spender, lives in Tuscany and is the most dangerous gossip I know (though I love her). Matthew Spender, a painter, has the mentality of an over-opinionated curate. A second daughter is married to a Chinese nature-freak in New York: a third (not by Gorky) to a really tiresome 'hope' of British philosophy: the fourth is an angel who will be here next month.

So the afternoon is usually spent bellyaching about Magouche's children. Then I look in on two peasants who keep the house, Curro and Incarna, who keep me in onions, raspberries, cucumbers. They live in a spotless white house shaded by walnut trees in the bottom of the valley. Then I try to work for another three hours, but can rarely get much done other than prepare notes for the next day.

After that cook dinner. Last night disgusting experiment with spices bought in Morocco. Then read Flaubert, Racine or Turgenev if I'm up to it: Maupassant or Babel if my eyes start to flutter.

Will you please cable me if any of your European plans are crystallising? Sorry to be insistent, but one or two people may be imploding on me and you are emphatically first on the list. As I have said, all you have to do to get here is to go to my travel agent, John Ferer, 54 Shepherd Market, London W1 and they will get you the ticket for Malaga, but you must say if you want to go back from there by plane or train, which takes some time, but is not a hardship, via Madrid and Paris. You must also think, enquire whether you need visas for Spain etc. I imagine you do: some Moroccans were kicked off the boat at Tangier for not having them.

Also you must tell me if you want me to write one of those shameful TO WHOM IT MAY CONCERN letters to cope with the UK customs. HH of Jodpur[1] had a terrible time getting through immigration: a lot of sneering 'Oh! Yes's?' when he tried to give them the Eton and King's number. Going with anyone through the British customs makes me writhe with shame.

What I mean by a Kerala lunghi (I think I mean a Calicut lunghi) is a piece of plain white thin cotton about five feet by four with plain coloured bands two inches deep or less, preferably green, running along the upper and lower edges and set in from the sides. Also a pair of those Gujarati sandals, English size 9½-10, but don't bother with anything else. My shirt, made up from the Benares tussore, should be ready by the time I reach London.

And now it's one already and I must think of going. Today I am salesman for Curro's raspberries to the ex-patriate colony. I seem to be able to get him twice what the wholesaler gives him: the English ladies will settle down this evening to making raspberry jam.

Have procrastinated about what to say next for five minutes and I must go.

all love, B

1. His Highness Maharaja Sri Gaj Singhji of Marwar-Jodhpur (*b.*1948), or 'Bapji', was at Eton and Christ Church.

To Keith Milow

Apartado 73 | Ronda | Malaga | Spain | [summer 1978]

My dear K.,[1]

Your letter came on a morning when I was quite unable to work: the Levante is blowing hot, white wind from the Sahara and my head is spinning. Added to the horrors of a meal in Ronda last night which gave me a liver attack.

Otherwise all is well: the Flaubertian conte is progressing *pero muy lentamente*. I might just manage to finish its hundred or so pages by the end of the year. What I had estimated at three months will be at least six, but that's the usual story. Yet imagine the *Chartreuse de Parme*[2] being written in eleven weeks and packed off to the publisher without need of corrections!

On the subject of Flaubert, read *Un Coeur Simple*, in French, or at least with a French text in hand. Best thing written in the 19th century – and ours?

Don't quite know what to do when the lease of this house runs out in late October. Whether to gruel on, or seek a change of scene. I had hoped to be in NY by November 1st. Hope dashed.

I too am impatient to see the crosses: there is no doubt in my mind you are the best artist of your generation in England: that those concrete crosses had the look of real grandeur (in the best sense); and that if (and I hope you'll forgive this) you keep away from all the slick and sleazy techniques of the photographer's studio, you have the makings of a great artist. So there! Don't flap too much about the critics either – and never try to please them – and don't even complain about them (it isn't worth it). The function of an artist is to work for a) himself b) to leave something memorable for the future, to shore up the ruins. Fuck the rest of them! However, I confess to a sneaking pleasure by a card I got yesterday from Jan Morris[3]

1. British artist (*b*.1945), specialising in crosses, who had introduced Chatwin to Donald Richards.
2. Novel written by Stendhal in 52 days (from 4 November to 26 December 1839).
3. Jan Morris (*b*.1926), British writer known as James Morris prior to sex change in 1973.

saying that my description of the Welsh in Patagonia 'actually moved him/her to tears'.

I also confess to wearing a blue shirt belonging to you: you'll get it back one day.

Give my love to Kynaston[1] and say I'll hope to see him soon. Anyone else there as well.

all love, Bruce

To Ivry Freyberg
Apartado 73 | Ronda | Malaga | Spain | 26 July 1978

Many thanks for enthusiastic note. Came at a good moment when I was in an impasse with the new book. Oh! what a mess! Have rented exquisite neo-classical pavilion on beautiful hillside, elegantissimo, but this week have been frying. Wish you could come here. Masses of room. Much love to all especially the godson, B

To Alison Oxmanton
Apartado 73 | Ronda | Malaga | Spain | 26 July 1978

My dear Ali,

I hope this catches you at Birr: E. said you'd be there the whole of August. I am sitting out the summer writing about your old stamping ground, Dahomey,[2] on a beautiful Andalucian hillside. The house – pavilion, I should say – that I have rented belongs to an Argentine friend of your friend Christopher Balfour, whose name figures prominently in the visitor's book. I do wish you'd come and put in a few days here on your way back to Algiers. It really isn't too far round – and none at all if you go by land and across the Straits.

1. Kynaston McShine, curator at Museum of Modern Art in New York.
2. Alison's husband Brendan had worked for the United Nations in Dahomey in the late 1960s; it was partly at his urging that Chatwin had made his first visit there in 1972. The Oxmantons were now based in Algiers.

I'm going to try and come and visit you during the winter, for a protracted stay, if you don't mind (you don't have to put me up). I have always been fascinated by the country of Camus, and some years ago I did a story for the *Sunday Times* about an Algerian who murdered a bus conductor in Marseilles.[1] At the time it put me in quite good odour with the regime, despite the bad things I said about it, for my full outrage was directed at the French and in particular the City and Mayor of Marseilles. Algiers is one of the oddest places I've ever been, but full of literary possibilities, and the fact that you are now there makes it all the more inviting.

Perhaps we could take a trip to the South?

All my best to Brendan and the Rosses, and do let me know if you're passing. Planes can be met from Malaga.

Much love, Bruce

To Derek Hill
Apartado 73 | Ronda | Malaga | Spain | 1 August 1978

On the strength of a rather meagre Argentine royalty I've rented a Neo-Classical pavilion of great elegance on the hillside opposite Ronda. Slogging away slowly at a book. E has gone to Geneseo to try and restrain Gertrude from building a large sub-Lutyens mansion which would be another Sweet Briar Farm but much more expensive. Do come here. Much love, Bruce

To Francis Wyndham
Apartado 73 | Ronda | Malaga | Spain | 1 August 1978

Dear Francis,

After a nightmarish week in the Pyrenees, humid valleys screaming with French children, I spent all the money I've got renting a Neo-Classical 'pavillion' on a high, dry hillside.

---

1. 'Fatal Journey to Marseilles – North Africans in France,' *Sunday Times* magazine, 6 January 1974.

Mr da Silva is once again progressing – or at least moving forward – though it's hard to predict what the end result will be. Looking back on the past few, extremely frustrating months – I can see they weren't quite so weird after all. I do have slightly clearer ideas about how it should be.

I'm completely out of touch here: no phone, no newspapers: BUT somebody told me last night that the *Sunday Times* is in full crisis. I can't say I'm too surprised – or for that matter sorry. But do let me know what's happening. Also when and if Mrs Gandhi is coming out.

I am going to stick it out here until October at least: by which time I'll either be finished or in need of a change. After that, who knows/Australia?

Peter Eyre[1] and I had a lovely evening in Paris seeing a bad production of *Phèdre* in the open air. In a Hotel in the Marais. A lunch with Sonia Orwell. My God, she's brittle. I hope I didn't offend when I suggested that English lawyers always take you for a ride.

As always, Bruce

Of course, if there were any logic in the world, you, James and Chloe[2] would take advantage of cheap flights to Malaga and come here for a holiday. There are three deluxe bedrooms. B

To Margharita Chatwin
Apartado 73 | Ronda | Malaga | Spain | 17 August 1978

Dear M.,

Often I can't think what I'm doing in this overelaborate house: it has fountains, potted palms, arcades, some hideous statuary, a wonderful view and every comfort but electricity. The last wouldn't matter if the days weren't so hot and lethargic. I feel quite lively at night. I've tried

1. American actor and director (*b.*1942).
2. James Fox, journalist on *Sunday Times* magazine (*b.*1945), m. Chloe Peploe.

working to the light of a butagas lamp, but the thing overheats so much you're back where you started, feeling lethargic again.

Nevertheless, I believe the book <u>may</u> be finished one day. This, I might say, I have [not] believed before: so that is already an advance. The technical problems have been for me so colossal: how to string so many disparate facts and ideas into the life of one man, <u>and</u> carry the reader sailing from page to page. It will also be extremely small. I doubt if it'll print up to much more than a hundred pages. But then I've never liked long books myself, so I don't see why I should try and write them myself. Unless you're Tolstoy, most of the 'great books' of the world should have been cut in half.

The American reviews of *In Patagonia* are coming through and, so far, are much the same as the English. Who knows? I might even make some money. In the Pop Magazine 'Rolling Stone' there is a cartoon of the author wandering about Patagonia with a cup of tea in his hand and a bowler hat.

After bellyaching about the Mrs Gandhi article, the editor of the *Sunday Times* magazine now says he likes it enormously. So where are you? It'll be out on August 30th or thereabouts, cut to ribbons I have no doubt, and I bet there's a printer's strike as well. The whole thing seems to be on its last legs. Do you wonder in an organisation where Old Etonians have to trim their accents to Yorkshire when they go <u>upstairs</u> to the Editor, to cockney when they go <u>downstairs</u> to the printing rooms?

Magouche Phillips and Xan Fielding[1] are here, about six miles away. I go and swim in the pool. There are a couple called Zulueta, he the son of the Foreign Minister in the Republic and a great expert on the anopheles mosquito: she English, rather a bluestocking but most agreeable. Otherwise society in Ronda revolves around the penniless Lord Kilmarnock and his wife the ex-Mrs Kingsley Amis; two Americans who are the Spirit of Lake Tahoe: another called Mr Finkel . . . with

---

1. Xan Fielding (1918–91), British S.O.E. agent and author, was writing a book on the wind, *Aeolus Displayed* (1991). He and Magouche would marry in 1979.

many extra syllables . . . stein: a German called Siegfried: a memsahib lady called Grace: a Chilean sculptor and the local Condessa who is a Southern Rhodesian called Faffie.

God knows what will result from Elizabeth's American trip: the Chanlers all seem at sixes and sevens and plainly need something to DO.

Fares to Malaga aren't expensive and it costs nothing to live here. Would you think of coming out in September?

much love, B

Following the coup in Benin, Chatwin had found himself on the same flight to South America as Nigel Acheson, a teacher at the Cultura Inglesa in Rio de Janeiro. Over the next two months, Acheson had become Chatwin's host and guide in Brazil.

To Nigel Acheson

Apartado 73 | Ronda | Malaga | Spain | 25 August 1978

My dear N.,

Nice talking to you. I thought Much Birch[1] might have its effect and have thought of the good lady mixing her China and Indian and shaking her head sadly over her son.

I'm not entirely sure I approve of feeding Joao[2] with Black Magic, unless he was going to the gym as he promised. To my eternal regret there has been a six month silence now. My replies in Portuguese were quite inadequate, both in literary and emotional content, to this kind of thing:

'*Tenho pensado muito em voce de dia de noite a toda hora nao me esquece* I do my love my beautiful, *tenho vontade de te abracer te beijar sentir o seu corpe que tanto bem me faz. Quando esta frio eu penso em sair de casa a sua procure para me esquentar aquecer meu corpo com o seu*

---

1. Acheson's family home on the Welsh Marches.
2. Joao was barman at the Othon Palace Hotel on Copacabana.

calor, mas logo me lembre que e impossivel te encontrar pois voce esta tao longe de mim.[1]

– which for rhythm and poetic expression could almost come out of the Song of Songs.

Ah! the geographical impossibility of passion!

Plans: I'd adore you to come here, and if in September you wanted to go to Lisbon, I have some research (minor odds and ends, like what would a Lt. Colonel in the Portuguese Army be wearing in the tropics in 1875?) – and of course YOU, if you wouldn't mind, would be an enormous help.

I would even pay the ticket as a research fee, so that honour would be satisfied all round. Let me know if you can make it and I'll send you a cheque.

The only minor complication is the possibility of the arrival of a friend from India: the 23 yr old whizz-kid of Indian journalism, whom I want to take around a bit. The three of us in my tiny car might make rather an ill-assorted group. The chances are, however, that he won't scrape up the money for the fare. Getting to Europe for an Indian is tantamount to disposing of a real fortune.

How is your Television project coming along?[2] Watch out for those people! They are professional time-wasters and you must get them to pay researchers' fees. Incidentally, I think you're quite barmey to have anything to do with films or articles. Your Iquique material and the family connections are the stuff of a marvellous novel. And you should sit down, hack it into a rough form and then go out again to fill out the details.

Cable me and I'll ring you. But do state a time because I have to book the call.

As always, B

1. 'I have been thinking of you a lot, day and night, all the time – don't forget me I do my love my beautiful, I really want to hug you, kiss you, feel your body that makes me feel so good. When it's cold I think about going out to look for you so that you can warm me, warm my body with your heat, but suddenly I remember that it's impossible to meet you because you are such a long way from me.'

2. Acheson's family had worked in Iqique during Chile's nitrate boom, before the discovery of artificial fertiliser in the late 1920s. The story of their overnight decline and humiliating suburban decay – 'still wearing tattered Worth dresses' – captivated Chatwin.

To Francis Wyndham
Apartado 73 | Ronda | Malaga | Spain | 2 September 1978

The sizzling heat seems to be over and Mr da Silva advances '*pero lenta-mente*'. Might get finished one day. Ow! the strains of composition and of keeping up the momentum. How to eliminate the longueurs without eliminating the sense. Will never tackle a historical subject again. Saw Julian Jebb[1] last week.

Much love Bruce

To Charles and Margharita Chatwin
Apartado 73 | Ronda | Malaga | Spain | 2 September 1978

Yes. A bitch to write – about a bitch. I went very sympathetic to anyone who attempted to govern the ungovernable, but in the end couldn't dredge up one particle of sympathy for the woman. A pity: I don't like writing about people I dislike. Even in the villains you can usually find something – but Mrs G[andhi] is the essence of bathos. XXX B
Atalante[2] my FAVOURITE movie

To Elizabeth Chatwin
Apartado 73 | Ronda | Malaga | Spain | 6 September 1978

Dear E.,

We were cut off in the middle of the call: no warning of course.

The letter from Whinney Murray,[3] dated 1970, makes no sense to

1. BBC television producer (1934–84).
2. *L'Atalante* (1934), French film directed by Jean Vigo about a honeymoon barge trip between Le Havre and Paris. Chatwin's parents were shareholders of an Atalanta class low-keeled boat, ideal for exploring estuaries and canals. H.C.: 'Margharita had fallen in love with the simple life of French couples operating the sand barges of the Seine. If born again into another existence, she said, this was to be her preferred occupation.' The Royal Crusing Club, of which Charles was a member, enjoyed mooring rights on the Isle de la Cité.
3. Chatwin's accountants, now Ernst & Whinney.

me at all. I propose to ignore it: if they come back yawling for money, I shall say that I had NO income for that year, and what was more, the accountant's bill but swallowed up the free-of-tax grant on which I was supposed to live.

I was 14 weeks at Teddy's: at £25 per week that makes £350 in rent: I don't think I paid quite that but with telephone calls etc.[1] we'll put in for that amount. Enclosed is a cheque for £400 to tide you over the next week or two: I suppose I can afford it: I've now completely lost count of what I have and what I owe. We'll just have to hope and pray that money does come from Messrs. Summit Books. The reviews (I have a huge batch of them) are simply extraordinary. *New York Times'* 'Most praised book of the Season' etc. A cartoon in the *Rolling Stone* which you will doubtless be getting of the author in bowler hat and cup of tea and Patagonian peak. 'Home of the unicorn' *N.Y. Times* – a Pepe Gonzalez figure with bagpipes. 'Youthful Briton finds adventure in Harsh Land' *Youngstown Ohio Vindicator*. The one that did go really to my heart was a Robert Taylor (*Boston Globe*): 'It celebrates the recovery of something inspiring memory, as if Proust could in fact taste his Madeleine' – ENFIN somebody's got the point: I wrote off at once and told him so.

Well, I hope Ali [Oxmanton] does come. I shall probably have Sunil [Sethi] here IF he can wheedle a ticket out of *India Today*; the whole thing sounds rather problematical, and I have sent off a cable for all of 1500 pesetas missing off one's letter of the address. Will have to send another in the morning.

At some stage this month I shall be going to Lisbon for a week, to try and inject some life into the Bahia section without actually going back.

I have to say I wish I'd never started this bloody book, but it does crawl ahead *pero muy lentamente*.

I simply can't begin to advise you about the farm from here, because

1. On 27 January 1978 Tom Maschler had asked Chatwin for £100 for bills that had accumulated at Carney. 'Sorry it's so much but as you will see most of it is your telephone conversations!'

a. I have no idea whether you have had any conversation at all with your bone-headed family financial experts on the pros and cons b. whether or what you will have to pay in capital gains tax on the land i.e. in what proportion to the house etc. It seems raving to go into the blue (for you, not necessarily me) and hand out money to the bloodhounds of H.M.G. Financially, that is, if you want to stay in England, it would be better to have more land and less house, rather than vice versa, or I should say better land.

My urgent requirement is a small base which I do not <u>have</u> to get into hock with mortgages: I do not want to have to make bread and butter doing journalism, because ultimately it corrodes.

Have had to send the dog down to Curro. Nightmare of howling in the night. And as I predicted, the worst has happened, the rug and the dining table cover, crawling with ticks. Felt an itching in the groin the other day, lo! a pinkish grey balloon. The *gatito* has needless to say become extremely *domesticado* and constantly gets under my feet.

Absolutely no news from Ronda. Am going to the coast for the weekend; a mixture of Bill Davis,[1] Gerald [Brenan] and Janetta [Parladé]. Magouche off to the funeral of her friend Missie[2] at Cadaques.

I may very easily come back to Inglaterra, or at least to Paris in mid Oct. But all depends on the next three weeks, as to how the final haul, 40 pages shapes up. It's going to be a very small book.

love B

PS Sunil's just been to the Pondicherry ashram and concludes that the profundities of Sri Aurobindo[3] are totally meaningless.

1. Social-climbing New Yorker and ex-drinking partner of Ernest Hemingway.
2. Princess Marie ('Missie') Vassiltchikov (1917–78), author of *Berlin Diaries 1940–45*.
3. Indian philosopher (1872–1950) who founded an ashram in his name.

To John Kasmin

Apartado 73 | Ronda | Malaga | Spain | 7 September 1978

Dear K,

Red letter day today: yours and the first batch of American reviews of *In Patagonia* to burn your eyes out. Not that there won't be a stinker somewhere in the pipeline. One, by the staff writer on the *Boston Globe*, really got the hang of what it was about and put it down better than I could. It's the review that pleased me most. But I <u>must</u> stop reading them. Paralysing!

I know Worth Maltravers[1] from my childhood and associate that part of the coast with unalloyed happiness. Felt a trickle of envy when I compared your cottage with the Green Hole of Glos, but this soon dissipated in a burst of joy for you. I was more than sceptical about that place in the la-di-da country round Banbury.

From here there is no news. I am well, calm, a bit lonely and writing. The house lies on a beautiful clean dry hillside in ilexes and olives over-looking the Serrania de Ronda, but for all its palm court and hygienic glazed statuary it was little better than an electric oven in August. Better now and cooler breezes blowing. The book is shaping up *pero muy lentamente*. Enormous technical problems yet to be overcome. Going to be very strange. I had bargained for big dramatic set-pieces but these are all reduced to a few lines.

A peasant couple called Curro and Incarna look after me and we are now all three glued to each other with dog-like devotion. He was being cheated on his raspberry crop by the wholesaler, and I found out he should be getting double the price. There's a Chilean sculptor across the valley, a mad German below and Magouche and Xan Fielding about eight miles away. A friend from India is coming in a couple of weeks, also Alison Oxmanton on her way back to Algeria. I don't know if E. will show up again. She has been in the US where her family are in the middle of one of their nightmarish brouhahas. Should the mother leave her huge

---

1. Kasmin had bought a mason's cottage in a gulley surrounded by footpaths on the Dorset coast.

unsaleable house and build, for half a million dollars, another large unsaleable house on the adjoining site? Not a subject that arouses sympathy in me.[1]

. . . I left England in a particularly bruised condition. I long to live there, but in a situation that doesn't get on top of me. You are right: the answer is to live alone. I was reflecting the other day that the people I really miss out here are, for some reason, my parents and you. I can't tell you how pleased I was to get your letter.

They say the weather's wonderful through October. The best time for walking if you could squeeze a week in. There are endless off season cheap flights to Malaga, two hours by car.

I'll be here till the end of Oct, then see how far I've got on, and maybe hoof it to New York for a spell.

What's the name of your pal in Barcelona? I'll be coming back through there to look up some Latin-American types.

See you soon, love, B

To Nigel Acheson
Apartado 73 | Ronda | Malaga | Spain | Monday 11 [September 1978]

Dear N.

Ay! I bleed for you. I had it very badly about twelve years ago: got it from a needle giving me an anti-histamine shot for a mosquito bite in Sicily: had it obviously much worse than you, for I would never have been able to compose such a letter. In convalescence I made a thorough study of Nerval and Baudelaire (two very suitable poets for the hepatitic) and conceived vague ideas of a literary future. In fact it changed my life: I suddenly had a horror of the so-called ART WORLD, and though I went on to be a Director of Sotheby's everything about the firm filled me with claustrophobia and disgust.

You have to rest: and let me tell you CHEW two cloves of garlic

1. Gertrude did decide to sell the main house in Geneseo and build another one.

before you eat anything else in the morning. The best thing for purifying the blood – and for keeping 'loved ones' away.

I agree: wherever I go, particularly in deserts, the image of that misty Gloucestershire valley passes before my eyes. But one should never go near it, except to recharge the IDEA of it once every two or three years.

My plans are uncertain after mid-Oct: depends on how I progress over the next month. I don't think I'll be in this house as it's far too expensive for one to rattle around in, and will be impossible to heat.

I'll write with news. This is a quick one to catch the post.

As always, B

To Christopher MacLehose[1]
Apartado 73 | Ronda | Malaga | Spain | 11 September 1978

Dear Christopher MacLehose,

I'd very much like to see the Peter Matthiessen book.[2] He's a writer I follow with great interest, though I couldn't take (despite some beautiful lines) the Zen-influenced novel of the turtle fishers. I'll be at this address till the middle of next month.

I take it you are publishing the book: do you want me to ask John Gross[3] if I can review it?

Yours ever, Bruce Chatwin

1. Editor-in-chief, Collins Harvill.
2. *The Snow Leopard* by Peter Matthiessen, American writer (*b.*1927); his previous book had been the novel *Far Tortuga* (1975) about nine men schooner-fishing for green turtles in the Caribbean.
3. Editor, 1974–81, *Times Literary Supplement*.

To Elizabeth Chatwin

Apartado 73 | Ronda | Malaga | Spain | 12 September 1978

Dear E.,

I've got masses of yellow pads. Bones[1] brought me 20 hundred pages from New York in June. My size for the button-front jeans is 32 waist 33 leg. Sunil [Sethi] is on around the middle of the month: he hasn't yet found out if he's getting a lift on a jumbo of Air India going for an overhaul in Toulouse, but if not *India Today* are giving him his ticket. Ay! the floods. Haven't heard a word since then.

Progress *pero muy lentamente*. Have just been for the weekend to Janetta [Parladé]'s and had my lounge on the beach and swim. Feeling very relaxed and well. For some weeks I had terrible stomach upsets, which I have put down to coffee made in the machine. Anyway they've gone, but they were worrying as I was sick three times in the middle of the night.

Magouche's Susannah is here: I brought them up from Malaga and we called in on Gerald [Brenan].[2] The bore is Xan: apparently when I came up with some more 'Wind' information, he took offence and thought I was trying to patronise him. Also resents my friendship with Magouche. I've tried my best to like him, gave Maro[3] endless lectures about how stupid she was being but I've come to the conclusion she was right. He's a silly, jealous A1 shit. He picks rows with M[agouche] the whole time and reduces her to a bag of nerves. She's deeply in love with him (she's crippled with the pinched sciatic nerve) and will to my mind not go without him. However. Sad about Hiram.[4] You're right: in places like

---

1. David Sulzberger; nicknamed Smallbones after a 'young scamp' in Milward's journal ('about 12 years of age, about 4 feet nothing,' who 'was exceptionally clever and could pick up anything almost at once . . . but he was a perfect little devil to handle, and he would do anything to humbug anyone in authority over him'). D.S: 'Bruce was very envious of, and kept using, my American legal pads, longer than A4, which I bought from the Coop in Harvard Square, Massachusetts.'

2. After his initial enthusiasm, Brenan had tired of his verbal ping-pong with Chatwin. 'He is a man enclosed like an insect in a tight coating of chitin – totally insensitive, needs to talk all the time,' Brenan wrote to V. S. Pritchett on 24 October 1978. 'I can't say I really like him – an egotistical little boy – yet his energy was impressive.'

3. Maro Gorky (*b*.1943) artist m. 1962 Matthew Spender (*b*.1945), writer and sculptor.

4. Hiram Winterbotham had had a stroke and was in a wheelchair.

Provence, unless you have something specific to do, you just disintegrate. Same goes for here. Alistair Boyd has taken on a completely new lease of life since he got into the House of Lords.

I bet they've chopped up the Mrs Gandhi piece: the sub-editor *manque le moindre étincelle d'intelligence et du goût et d'humeur*. I really am NOT going to write for them again.

Can you check with my bank and D[eborah] Rogers what has and hasn't been paid in. The statement runs up to August 7th with a credit for £1000. There should have been paid in the French advance, the Spanish advance, and £1000 or thereabouts from the *Sunday Times*. If all three have been paid in, then I'm far worse off than I thought, and will be running with an overdraft of around £1000. Never ends, does it.[1]

Reviews from U.S. to burn the eyes out. Doesn't mean to say they won't come up with a stinker, but mentioned in the same breath as *Gulliver's Travels*, *Out of Africa*, *Eothen*, *Monasteries of the Levant*, Kipling's *Letters of Travel* etc. People lose all sense of proportion.

Kasmin's cottage sounds a marvel. Why don't you go and sniff round the land agents of that part of the Dorset coast. Just get in the car one day and go.

Must go.

love B

To Elizabeth Chatwin
Apartado 73 | Ronda | Malaga | Spain | 16 September 1978

Dear E.,

Not much here either. Xannikins has gone off to climb in the Pyrenees and so everyone is much more relaxed. He is an area of LOW PRESSURE. Susannah[2] and I climbed the plateau of Torecilla by full moon.

---

1. E.C.: 'He would pay all these bills and say "I've no money left," and I would feel desperate about it. I had my tiny quarterly allowance of £250 from Mellon, a trust set up by my mother in 1958, and it was already spoken for.'
2. Magouche's daughter.

I for one am not too sad about the big dhurry not selling. I feel that at some point it can be used.

I've enough yellow pads to be going on with and don't really want foolscap size, as it will bulge out of my loose-leaf folders.

The *gatito* has discovered all four palm pots for use as its W.C. The place is beginning to stink of cat shit and buzzing with bluebottles. But the headboard of the bed has become the nest of a most elusive mouse. So there you are! Trapped as usual.

Gave the Magouche *ménage* a most fruity meal: an anchoiade of figs, anchovies and garlic (delicious); salad of leeks in uncooked tomato sauce with basil, oil and lemon juice (also delicious) and a monumental Moroccan tajine of chicken and quinces and almonds and dates and roasted sesame seeds. Also raspberries. That fearsome mother of Magouche expected next week. Sunil [Sethi] having frightful time extracting himself from the floods. Expect [him] to be here next week.

Love

Bruce

When at last Sunil Sethi arrived in Ronda he found Chatwin in a state of extreme anxiety over his book. 'He thought this was the end. He kept describing a scene – day after day – when de Souza and Ghézo make a blood pact. He couldn't get it right. He'd crumple the paper with his hand and get very angry, saying "Am I a one-track pony?"'

Chatwin returned to London at the end of October with de Souza's story still unresolved. Less than a fortnight later, he found a 'cubby-hole' in Albany, a former maid's room which he sublet from Christopher Gibbs. No sooner had he arranged for an architect to convert it than on 9 December he flew to New York, to spend the winter there with Donald Richards. Among those he mingled with were Robert Mapplethorpe, Lisa Lyon, Edmund White, John Richardson and Jacqueline Onassis, the latter introduced to him by Cary Welch. Of this period, Robin Lane Fox remembers: 'I'd heard he'd become the plaything of every grand American woman in sight.'

To Elizabeth Chatwin
66 East 79th Street | New York | 11 February 1979

Dear Maxine,

. . . Life in New York highly social. Dinner parties every night. Escorting Mrs Onassis[1] to the opera next Thursday. Met her again with the John Russells,[2] and my God she's fly. Far more subtle than any American woman I've ever met. A man called Charles Rosen,[3] who has a reputation for being THE CLEVEREST MAN IN AMERICA, was pontificating about the poet Aretino, and since nobody reacted or contradicted him, turned his discourse into a lecture. He was halfway through when she turned on him with her puppy-like eyes, smiled and said: 'Yes, of course, you can see it all in the Titian portrait.'

Also hilarious dinner with the Erteguns, Iris Love[4], the Turkish Foreign Minister and the representative in America of Mr Greater Turkey himself: am lunching with him at the U.N. tomorrow. His conversations start: 'Look at my skull and you will see that, really, I am a Hittite.'

Have written my piece for *Geo Magazine* and got paid three thousand for it. Have been interviewed for *New York Times*. 'Mr Chatwin looks like a schoolboy and his eyes light up with a schoolboy's enthusiasm etc . . .' despite the fact that both [legs] looked like lumps of raw meat after being cut open by Dr Espy.[5]

Kasmin marvellously well behaved in Haiti[6] – as he had to be because

---

1. Jacqueline Bouvier (1929–94); m. 1st 1953 John F. Kennedy, President of United States, 1961–3; 2nd 1968 Aristotle Onassis (1906–75). Notebooks: 'She came in: in black gold pyjama pants, looking wonderful. The whisper is conspiratorial, not affected. The whisper of a naughty child egging you on to do something mildly wicked. To behave badly without being rude.'
2. John Russell (1919–2008), art critic of the *New York Times*.
3. Charles Rosen (*b*.1927), pianist, music theorist and critic.
4. New York socialite.
5. In November, he had had varicose veins removed from his legs at St Mary's Paddington.
6. In January Chatwin had travelled to Haiti with Kasmin.

the silly ass went out into a carnival crowd – despite my warning – with a wallet containing 800 bucks in cash and travellers' cheques, and we were knocked over by four transvestites wearing Fidel Castro masks and relieved of it. I paid thereafter. Mad about Haiti.

Apparently this week my photo is published large on the cover of the *Barrytown Explorer*. Unbelievable letters about *In Patagonia* from Chanler Chapman.[1] 'A whiff of aconite, the deadliest of poisons, a tale more heartless than King Lear etc.'

But the BIG NEWS is this. We rang up Mr Shawn's[2] secretary on the *New Yorker* to see if he would like to see Mr Chatwin. She replied: 'But surely it is Mr Chatwin who would like to see Mr Shawn?' However, when Mr Chatwin was finally, after a positively Byzantine series of manoeuvres, ushered into Mr Shawn's pure, intellectually Bauhaus office he rose and said it was nice to meet a *New Yorker* writer who had never written for the *New Yorker*. The upshot was a commission to do my Chekhovian trip through eastern Europe directly I finish Mr da S[ouza] plus as many thousand dollars as I need.

Jane Kramer[3] and her husband were in a fearful motor smash between Ronda and Malaga when we were there. Crapanzano nearly died of an embolism at Malaga airport waiting to go to Switzerland. And that dreadful

---

1. Chanler Chapman, E.C.'s father's first cousin. On 3 January 1979 he wrote to Elizabeth's mother from his hospital bed in Rhinebeck: 'This morning at 4 a.m. I finished *In Patagonia*. It's a savage sour book with a vengeance built on a wilderness of horror, terrible climate. The pages are loaded with hatred. I stuck with it because of the well-balanced pen of Bruce Chatwin. He practically never gives way to journalism. When he does allow 3 or 4 words of wonderfully keen observation to take fire and make a whole page fly, he does it with the unconcern of a man lifting a piece of bread to his lips. There is a compulsion that comes from the bowels of death. Darned tiresome but somehow Chatwin makes it significant. I'm proud of Elizabeth for marrying Bruce. Give her my love.'
2. William Shawn, editor of *New Yorker* 1952–87, did not after all take a single one of Chatwin's offerings. On June 24 1980 he rejected *The Viceroy of Ouidah* – 'We did not think it quite worked out as fiction we could publish'; in 1982 Shawn also turned down *On The Black Hill* as 'too episodic', none of the episodes seeming to amount to short stories.
3. Jane Kramer, European correspondent for *New Yorker* and partner of Vincent Crapanzano, professor of anthropology at New York City University.

man whom we met at the Zuluetas was instrumental in having their daughter abandoned, aged seven in a rough tourist hotel downtown, where she almost got lost.

But the Albany[1] is ready to begin work and as the workmen are on hand I suppose I must go back. Kassl has found me a flat in Covent Garden for two months while the work goes on (at £75 a week) but that is the price. I am really rather undecided. I have to say that I would like to spend about five months of the year in New York rather than London, and or even Paris. The trouble is laying out all that rent. I imagine the best would be to buy a cooperative, but the small places are v. difficult to find.

Love

B

To Clarence Brown[2]
Postcard, Christo's Wrapped Walk Ways 1977–8, Loose Park, Kansas City, Missouri (15,000 square yards of silk over 4.5 km of walkways)|L6 Albany|London| 21 March 1979

Why you should get this of all postcards is beyond me: it's the only one that happens to be lying around. Best, Bruce Chatwin

1. The arrangement barely endured two years. On 15 December 1980 Chatwin received a letter from Lt.-Col. Chetwynd-Talbot, secretary of Albany, in reply to his request for a more permanent apartment. 'Some of what you say . . . is quite honestly, best forgotten. In telling me that Christopher Gibbs has lent you his top room for two years, you convict him of a breach of his lease with Peterhouse . . . On page 2 you urge me to connive in others breaking their leases! In any case, the top rooms, all part of their sets below, belong to different Proprietors and are not the property of the Trustees. So that, I fear, is that!'
2. Professor Emeritus of Comparative Literature at Princeton and biographer and translator of Osip Mandelstam.

To Charles Chatwin

Postcard, Jean Baptiste Chardin's Pipes and Drinking
Vessels | Vaucluse | France | 4 April 1979

I inspected Bonnieux — and concluded it was in far too tricky condition to buy; could be an endless structural headache not what we want. The Paris one was — on reflection — just that much too small: a rare *pied à terre* and nothing more.

Chardin evidently loved <u>his</u> drinking cup:[1] it crops up again and again in the paintings. Bruce

In April, Chatwin received a letter from Osip Mandelstam's translator, Clarence Brown, who asked 'with a certain trepidation' whether Chatwin was aware 'that the spirit of OM seems to peep out from behind this or that phrase or stroke of portraiture or landscape.' Brown also suggested that In Patagonia *was not second but third in a fascinating succession – 'for Mandelstam's title alone makes it clear that he was very mindful of Pushkin's* Journey to Erzerum.'

To Clarence Brown

as from Poggio al Pozzo | Siena | Italy | 14 April 1979

Dear Clarence Brown,

Coming from you — of all people — that was indeed a gratifying letter. I owe you an enormous debt.

A friend gave me a copy of your translation of *The Noise of Time* when it first appeared. It set me off to 'discover' [Isaac] Babel and the others. Soon afterwards I started to write.

Of course *Journey to Armenia* was the biggest single ingredient — more so even than met the eye. Perhaps too much so — 'skull-white

---

1. E.C.: 'I had given Bruce a silver drinking cup for Christmas. When in Peru with my mother, he was bowled over when she pulled out one from a fitted leather case.'

cabbages etc' (O that mad Veraschagin in the Tretyakov!) But one bit of plagiarism was quite unintentional (though indicative of the degree to which I had steeped myself in the *Journey*) Not until after I had passed the final proofs did I realise I had lifted 'the accordion of his forehead' straight. I rang up the copy editor in a panic. She said it was too late and, besides, all writers were cribbers.

You must by now be viewing the O[sip] M[andelstam] translation industry with a rather jaundiced eye. But for what it's worth – and at the risk of being a bore – I'd like to put it on record that you are surely the finest translator out of Russian alive; that you have a most finely tuned ear for the cadence of a sentence; that your literal translations of M[andelstam]'s poems are far better than the work of the versifiers, and, lastly that you are TOO MODEST.

In an ideal world you would be appointed *generalissimo* in charge of vetting all translations from the Russian; one only has to think of the horrors of the so-called Oxford Chekhov.

To my shame I don't read Russian and one day will have to go to the Berlitz. I know vaguely of Pushkin's *Erzerum* and, obviously, want to know more. No translation, I suppose?

Do give my very best to Richard McKane[1] and to Ted Weiss[2] if you see him. Also could you drop me a quick card at this address, saying whether you will be around Princeton on May 23rd?

I am working here, but vaguely tempted to come and get my prize.[3] If you were about, it would be an added inducement.[4]

as ever, Bruce Chatwin

1. Australian-born poet (*b*.1947).
2. Theodore Weiss (1916–2003), American poet and literary critic.
3. The 1979 E. M. Forster Award, a $20,000 grant to fund a period of travel in the United States.
4. Notebook, May 1979: 'Princeton. Visit to Clarence Brown: liked him but not a success. Waste of time for him I fear. Lack of communication. Both exceptionally nervous . . . I signed his copy of *In Pat*. But forgot to ask him to sign *Journey to A*. Was he offended? Came out of lunch with a decided spell of jitters . . . Not at all good at talking about my work with other writers.'

To Valerian Freyberg

Poggio al Pozzo | Siena | Italy | [Easter Sunday 1979]

Dear Valerian,

Your mother tells me you like shells. I used to have a collection of shells. During the war when I was three my father brought me a huge conch from Panama. He said you could hear the wind and the waves of the Caribbean Sea if you put your ear up close. I decided that my shell was a woman and we called her MONA, though I don't know why.

You can't hear the Indian Ocean in this shell, but I think the design is very beautiful and I chose it for you. The white things look like mountains, don't they?

When I come back to England in June, I'll come and take you out from school. I think we must find you a book on shells. If you promise to collect them and look after them, it would be lovely for me, because when I go round the world, I can find more shells and send them to you.

With love from your affectionate godfather

Bruce

To Peter Adam[1]

Poggio al Pozzo | Siena | Italy | Easter Sunday | 3 May 1979

Quick card to say hello. Stuck on Tuscan hillside trying to plough my way through to finish 30 pages of manuscript but must have finished 150 of them.[2]

---

1. Documentary-maker, author and longstanding friend of Eileen Gray whose biography he would write (1988). Chatwin had a brief involvement with Adam at this time.
2. Chatwin delivered the manuscript to Tom Maschler in the summer. On 14 November Maschler paid an advance of £2,500.

To John Fleming and Hugh Honour[1]
L.6 Albany|Piccadilly|London|11 May 1979

Dear John and Hugh,

Back in London with a belated thanks for – as usual – a lovely time with you both. By <u>far</u> the best house I know in Italy! I'll be back in the solitude of Chianti in about three weeks.

In the meantime, C. Gibbs still has the Duchesse de Berry's Granet,[2] measurements on the back. It has a whopping Chatsworth frame made up from bits of late 17th century English moulding which I think makes it look marvellous. He wants about £5–6,000 for it, but is absolutely open to the idea of a swap. Apparently the National Gallery of Wales are nibbling at it, but I wonder whether they have the <u>nous</u>

much love, Bruce

One of several Anglo-Argentines who objected to the depiction of British estancia owners in In Patagonia *was Millicent Jane Saunders. She took particular exception to Chatwin's 'false description' of her late husband, 'a highly respected Patagonian'. On p.195 Chatwin had interviewed an elderly Chilean: 'He had worked twenty years on the estancia and now he was going to die. He remembered Mr Sandars, the manager, who died and was buried at sea. He did not like Mr Sandars. He was a hard man, a despotic man ...'*

To Millicent Jane Saunders
L6 Albany|Piccadilly|London|27 September 1979

Dear Mrs Saunders,

... I deeply regret that you should have been upset by Chapter 94 of my book *In Patagonia*. I think, however, you will appreciate the

---

1. British art historians and life partners who lived in the Villa Marchiò above Lucca. They had first met Chatwin in Venice.
2. A huge interior of a Capucine convent in Rome, by the French painter François Marius Granet (1775–1849). H.H.: 'It was too big to fit into our little house.'

circumstances under which it was written. I was simply recording the words of a dying Chilean peon. He said that the manager of his estancia had been a Mr Sandars (my spelling), who had been buried at sea, who was an '*hombre duro e despotico*' (his words), though he remembered him in a favourable light compared to what came after under the Allende regime and later. Having lived, as I did, in peons' quarters all over Patagonia, it was the most common thing in the world to hear men grousing about their employers in that kind of language, usually as we sat around the *maté* kettle.

My business was to record what people said. I did not, I can assure you, intend to pass any judgement on a man about whom I knew nothing, and whose name, apparently, I did not know how to spell.

Yours sincerely,
Bruce Chatwin

To Peter Adam
L6 Albany | Piccadilly | London | 15 February 1980

Have gone to New York for 10 days but will phone on return. xxx Bruce

Chatwin was in New York to work with Jim Silberman, his American editor, on The Viceroy of Ouidah, *as his book was to be called. Previous titles he had considered were:* Dom Francisco, The Elephant, The Brazilian, Skin for Skin, The Merchant of Ouidah. *He had rewritten and typed out half a dozen drafts, changing Francisco de Souza's name to Francisco da Silva. What had commenced as the history of a Brazilian slave-trader was now a novel. An introductory paragraph composed for Silberman, and later deleted, shows that Chatwin had found it impossible to transform de Souza's life into a biography: '. . . when I tried to fit these pieces into a narrative, each fact seemed to contradict each other fact. The story gave out at the critical points and, with a mixture of relief and despair, I decided to write a work of the imagination. I changed the names of the*

principal characters, having a prejudice against making histor-
ical figures say things they did not say, or do things they did
not do. And having changed the names, I was then free to borrow,
to combine, to juggle with dates, to invent new characters and
new situations – to such an extent that even I can hardly disen-
tangle the real from the invented.'

To Jim Silberman
[19 February 1980][1]

Jim,

I haven't looked it over.

Parts I–II and III are I think as the Cape editor and I think they should be with <u>most</u> (!) of your suggestions incorporated.

Parts IV & V are my final retype but not yet edited by Cape's.

There are 2 small parts which I want to rewrite anyway. Please anyway be FIERCE over these final sections because they have had far less going over than the first 3.

The book is <u>not</u> a novel but a TALE (?)

?A Tale of Two Continents?

See you Tuesday,

Bruce

To Francis Steegmuller[2]
L6 Albany (top) | Piccadilly | London | 21 March 1980

Dear Francis,

You can certainly <u>borrow</u>, not rent the above, but I feel I must warn you of the drawbacks. It is <u>not</u> a flat, in the English sense of the

---

1. On 15 February Silberman had agreed an advance of $15,000.
2. American Flaubert scholar (1904–94) m. 1963 Shirley Hazzard (*b.*1931), Sydney-born novelist.

term, but a one-room *garçonnière* such as one might find in the *Cinquième*. My tastes are also rather Spartan. It has a kind of kitchen, a minuscule shower and basin, but the lavatory is out on the landing. It has a painted *Directoire* bed, 3ft 6in wide – and definitely for Francis: sharing with anyone not recommended. It has a smaller, also *Directoire*, steel lit-de-camp, which can be made into a bed, though it serves as a sofa. In this Shirley would have to sleep. I have, on occasions, and found it small but possible.

Otherwise, there are a Jacob chair, a *Régence* chair, a table, a telephone, the King of Hawaii's bedsheet with a design of fishes (framed), a Sienese cross, and a Mughal miniature.

You will feel very cramped. I discourage visitors, but if you're prepared to put up with it, it can be yours from the 5th to the 11th.

I cannot rent it to you, because I pay no rent myself, and only have it on a friendly basis. You would have to pay my cleaning lady, Mrs Robinson, who comes on Mondays and Thursdays. You would also obviously monitor all phone calls and pay those. If you then wanted to give me a present – a bottle or two of champagne never refused – that would be up to you . . .

If I am up that week, I can easily find a billet and it will only be for a night. I have started writing about my Welsh peasants, if that's the right word for them, and don't need interruptions.

As always,

love to Shirley, Bruce

On 3 April 1980 The New York Review of Books *published a letter from Dieter Zimmer in response to Chatwin's review, on 6 December 1979, of Konrad Lorenz's* The Year of the Greylag Goose. *'Mr Chatwin's central statement seems to be this: "His [Lorenz's] message is that all human behavior is biologically determined." Now no matter how long I look at this sentence, I am not sure I understand what it is meant to say. I am perfectly sure, however, that if it is meant to say what it seems to say it is altogether wrong. I suspect that there is some fundamental misunderstanding here which blurred Mr Chatwin's*

picture of Lorenz.' Chatwin was given a right of reply in the
same issue.

To the *New York Review of Books*

I do not agree. *The Year of the Greylag Goose* is not a 'friendly and harm-
less picture volume', but a sugar-coated pill. The exquisite photographs
merely served Lorenz with a vehicle to air, yet again, a philosophical
credo that may have changed in tone, but never in substance, since his
successful application for membership of the Nazi Party (No. 6,170,554)
eight weeks after the Anschluss on May 1, 1938. For this detail, as well
as an assessment of Lorenz's contribution to racial biology, readers are
referred to the brilliant series of papers by Professor Theo Kalikow of
Southeastern Massachusetts University (the latest being: *Konrad Lorenz's
Ethological Theory: Explanation and Ideology, 1938–1943* in *Naturwissenschaft
und Techniken Dritten Reich*, edited by Mehrtens and Richter, Suhrkamp,
1980.)

One should never minimise Lorenz's capacity to charm the public –
or influence events. It remains for future historians of ideas to document
the impact of *On Aggression* on our own times. For just as, in 1942, the
biologists confirmed Hitler in his belief that the Final Solution to the
Jewish Problem concurred with his Duty to the Creator, so in the 1960s
the notion of 'ritualised', limited combats seems to have lulled certain
strategists (and apologists) of the Vietnam war into a belief that they
were answering the Call of Nature.

To Sunil Sethi
L.6 Albany | Piccadilly | London | 29 April 1980

Dearest S.,

I have always wanted to have a letter from Macao: so the crumbling
green portals of the Hotel Belavista were, to some extent, worth the sixth
month wait.

I wouldn't go anywhere near New York at the minute: the whole of the US has gone collectively barking as the Ayatollah himself. I was there three weeks ago to do some pre-publicity on *The Viceroy of Ouidah* (as the new book is called), and even intelligent friends, who last year were cosmopolitan liberals were shouting 'Bomb Qom': it's one of those slogans, like 'I like Ike'[1] which conceal a complete vacuity of purpose, yet nevertheless have the power to sway the millions. The shops in 42nd street were all selling the rifleman's targets, presumably put out by some Gun Owner's Association, with the Ayatollah's photo superimposed, his nostrils being the bull's eye.

I have a sneaking regard for him, as did Wilfred Thesiger,[2] who when interviewed recently said: 'You can't blame him for not wanting his country littered up with plastic.' One simply does believe in God's angels when the helicopters came out of the sky.

I long, like you, to go to China, but have never been able to cope with the idea of constant supervision and red tape. Eve Arnold[3] went for four months last year, even to Sinkiang and Lhasa, but although her photos were conventionally beautiful, nothing about the trip actually inspired me to follow in her footsteps.

If you stay in Hong Kong for any length of time I may visit you. It seems possible that *In Patagonia* will be translated into Japanese, and I've said I'll accept a trip instead of an advance. I have a passion to see the North of Hokkaido, the Inland Sea and the Seamier side of Downtown Tokyo. I know a very entertaining cuss called Donald Ritchie,[4] who is the world's expert on the Japanese film and he had always made it sound astonishing.

No. Paul Theroux's[5] *The Old Patagonian Express* (such a cheat the

1. Slogan in 1950s for Dwight D. Eisenhower, President of the United States 1953–61.
2. Wilfred Thesiger (1910–2003), British explorer and travel writer. He met Chatwin once at the Hampshire home of Adrian House. 'He turned up and talked all through lunch and dinner and he sat outside my bedroom door and kept me awake talking and I rather wished he'd gone to bed.'
3. Eve Arnold (*b.*1912), American photographer; she took the photos for Chatwin's articles on Mrs Gandhi and André Malraux.
4. Donald Richie (*b.*1924), American-born director and writer on Japanese cinema.
5. Paul Theroux (*b.*1941), American travel-writer and novelist.

title!) although it's a success commercially is not good. He happens to be a friend of mine, though, and if I can't quite stomach what he does, he is one of the more lively spirits around London. In November we gave a combined talk to the Royal Geographical Society, which completely bewildered types like Lord Hunt,[1] as we took the audience breathlessly through a literary excursion to the Antipodes.

I, I might say, have started a new book – on a pair of Welsh hill farmers, identical twins who have slept in their mother's bed for the past forty-three years. Marvellous subject, but do I have the <u>poetic</u> talent for it?

To go back to the previous paragraph – Paul and I appeared on a TV programme[2] together with Jan Morris, in her/his twinset and pearls. Going back to London in the taxi she/he said: 'I was so interested by what you said about the dangers of travel. You see, having travelled all over the world, both as a male and as a female, I can safely say it's far safer to travel as a female.'

Elizabeth was in India for a couple of months this winter, while I was on my mountain top. She even had tea with your father. I fear that our relations are going from bad to worse. The trouble with living separate lives, as we have done for so long, is that you end up with totally different conceptions of life – to the extent that when you do try and make arrangements together, they end in disaster.

Last weekend I tried to show willing and put on my best tweed suit for the Badminton Horse Trials: the result was terrible. We have since had an exchange of letters that hint of separation/divorce.[3]

A dreadful worry: what to do?

1. John Hunt (1910–98), leader of the 1953 expedition to Mount Everest and president of Royal Geographical Society.
2. *The Late Show*, BBC2, 8 March 1979.
3. E.C.: 'I was furious with him, totally fed up and exasperated that he took me for granted. He brought down David Nash, but had never communicated to me (a) he was coming (b) he was bringing David, (c) never mind finding out any arrangements I'd made. I wrote to him and said "You'd better not come here till I tell you. I don't want you around, please."

Must go now. I have to lunch with my US publisher[1] who is the key to my present existence. Long for the news from Delhi. A friend, the Bombay popper, Asha Puthli Darling,[2] whom I saw in NY, had a very strange tale about Dumpy.[3]

as always, my love to you.

B

PS Do you ever read Flannery O'Connor?[4] You should.

1. Elisabeth Sifton, editor-in-chief of Viking Penguin.
2. Asha Puthli, lively pop and blues singer from Bombay who appeared naked in the Merchant-Ivory film *Savages*.
3. Akbar ('Dumpy') Ahmed, politician and school friend of Indira Gandhi's younger son Sanjay.
4. Catholic and reclusive short story writer (1925–64) from the American South who died of lupus.

CHAPTER EIGHT

ON THE BLACK HILL: 1980–83

*Three months after Elizabeth ejected Chatwin from Holwell Farm,
they met for lunch in London. On 22 July 1980 Chatwin wrote in
his notebook: 'On train to Newport. Ah! The joy of not going places
by car. The relief to find that you are in possession of yourself . . .
Lunch with Elizabeth. Poignant. Sad. We discussed our lives in
the past tense.' Their separation had become a fait accompli
without any discussion, but as a Catholic she refused to divorce
him. They had met to discuss the sale of Holwell Farm, their home
since 1966 and now too large for Elizabeth to manage on her own:
'I knew I couldn't end my days there. I couldn't bear the lack of
sun.' She was, she wrote to her mother, 'frantically looking' for a
house with light and enough land on which to graze her sheep.
'Bruce is v. busy writing and says he has so many projects for the
next 10 years that he can't really think about it so I must just go
ahead and find what suits me.' She did not speak directly about
her troubled marriage to Gertrude. Nor did Chatwin tell his parents.*

*Throughout 1980, as his relationship with Elizabeth continued
to disintegrate, Chatwin assembled material for a new book,
returning to the area he loved best: the Welsh border country which
he had discovered on school and family holidays. 'The Welsh border
I regard as one of the emotional centres of my life . . . It's what
Proust calls the soil on which I still may build.' He billeted himself
in several houses: Carney Farm, Tom Maschler's cottage not far
from Llanthony Priory, where Chatwin as a schoolboy had come
on a bicycling weekend from Marlborough; The Cwm in Shropshire,*

belonging to Martin and Stella Wilkinson; New House, Penelope
Betjeman's home in Cusop above Hay-on-Wye; and The Tower in
Scethrog belonging to Diana and George Melly.

To Ivry Freyberg
The Tower | Scethrog | Brecon | Powys | 9 July 1980

Lovely the 16th!¹ So happens have to be in town for that day only – but
anyway I'd leave my Welsh mountain for you XXX Bruce

In October Chatwin was staying in Greece with the Leigh Fermors,
waiting for a bus, when he fell into conversation with an aspiring
American writer who had lived in Alaska. David Mason had arrived
in Kardamyli two months before with his wife. His meeting with
Chatwin was to be their only one, but typical of several short,
single, intense encounters. Mason wrote: 'Though our acquaintance
was based upon little more than three hours of conversation and
a sporadic correspondence over several years, I can say that he
had a powerful influence upon my own life.'

To David Mason
L.6 Albany | London | 30 October 1980

Nice talking to you at the bus stop. Sorry it couldn't go on longer. Best
of luck with your novel. I'm just off to N.Y. to see about mine. Regards,
Bruce Chatwin   Copy of *In Patagonia* in post.

The Viceroy of Ouidah was published on 23 October 1980. Maschler
sent a telegram to Chatwin at the Albany. NO LIVING WRITERS
WORK MEANS MORE TO ME THAN YOURS STOP EVERY

---

1. I.F.: 'We gave a huge dinner party for 110 people. Bruce and Diana Cooper were
photographed together in *Vogue*.'

*GOOD WISH ON PUBLICATION DAY TOM. The novel had many
good reviews, but overall the reception was one of rather qualified
rapture, a feeling that Chatwin's fascination with the grotesque
had run away with him. Robin Lane Fox wrote 'a not very easy
review' for the* Financial Times. *'I got back a rather noble letter
from Bruce; he was sorry I hadn't liked the book, but he didn't feel
I'd understood it, or that it had the "brightly-lit superficiality"
that my review suggested. In his mind had been Flaubert's travels
in North Africa and the model of* Trois Contes.'

*The disappointing response – hardback sales were 4,938, fewer
than for his first book – accounted for the direction Chatwin now
took: to retreat into the Hardy-like solidity of a story about 'a
pair of Welsh hill farmers, identical twins who have slept in their
mother's bed for the past 43 years'.*

To Francis and Shirley Steegmuller
The Cwm | Ludlow | Shropshire | 15 December 1980

A thousand thanks for everything during that whirlwind visit. I am writing
this on a tempestuous night in Wales. The rain beats on the Gothic panes
of my little stable-study window. Miserable heat from a single bar
electric heater. Wish I was back in New York. Much love Bruce

To Derek Hill
Amsterdam | 1 January 1981

For months on end, I've been in a rather strange frame of mind, writing,
in a remote corner of the Welsh Border, about people who never go
out. All the hogwash of travel, of nomadism, etc, seems to have burned
itself out. I now find it harder and harder to move one inch. E. on the
other hand is now the footloose lady traveller – off with the Duchess
[of Westminster] on a tour of maharajahs. Will we meet soon? I do come
to London every now and then

To Susannah Clapp
L.6 Albany|London [8 January 1981]

Phew! Yes, we seem to have <u>just</u> almost got away with it. Am up to the armpits in the mud of the welsh Borders, but one day, perhaps, that too will pass.

    XXX Bruce

The following note accompanied the gift of a purple lacquer tile to Bill Katz, a New York designer and architect who had invited Chatwin to stay at St Maarten in the house of the artist Jasper Johns.

To William Katz
New York | 6 February 1981

This is Eileen Gray's only attempt – in all probability the world's only attempt – to make purple lacquer. Bruce Chatwin

To David Mason
[New York but as from] L.6 Albany|London|16 February 1981

Many thanks for your card – which was lost and is found. I hope all goes well with Alaska. I, on the other hand, am off to the Caribbean to work on Wales. Such are the habits of writers. As ever Bruce C.

On 24 February Chatwin visited Yaddo, a writer's colony near New York that provided its residents with 'room, board and studio space, and almost unlimited time in which to do concentrated work'. Previous residents numbered Flannery O'Connor, Patricia Highsmith and Robert Frost. Sponsored by Barbara Epstein, founder and editor of the New York Review of Books, *Chatwin applied for a six-week Fellowship during April and May to finish the last third of his Welsh novel. Spaces were tight, but Yaddo's Director Curtis Harnack recommended him to the*

Admissions Committee: 'I believe he would fit the "outright" invitation category – a writer whose work and worth is generally known, therefore usual procedures suspended.' Harnack wrote to Chatwin on 4 March: 'The Admissions Committee in Literature reviews hundreds of applications each year, and I am happy to report that your name was very high on the list. It is the hope of everyone that this time free of distractions will enable you to finish your book.'

To Curtis Harnack
c/o Jasper Johns | Terres Basses | St Maarten | French West Indies | 20 March, 1981

Dear Curtis Harnack,

Very many thanks for your letter – and if I haven't replied before, this is because the post from this island to the U.S. takes a couple of weeks and it seemed better to wait until someone was returning to New York.

I am very happy that you can have me at Yaddo during April and May: concentrated work is, at the moment, the order of the day.

I shall leave here around the 27th and fly back to New York, but it is just possible that my wife may fly out from England & spend a few days with me there. If so, I may not get to you till April the 14th or thereabouts; but in any event I'll let you know by phone immediately the plans crystallise.

I very much look forward to coming.

With all good wishes,

Bruce Chatwin

In the event, Elizabeth did not join him in New York and Chatwin arrived at Yaddo late in March.

To An Unknown Photographer
c/o Yaddo | Saratoga Springs | New York | 28 March 1981

Dear Everett,[1]

Yes, I was in New York around the 20th, feeling pretty low, one way and another, and also quite embarrassed about not calling you. I kept putting it off, and then the morning came to clear out, and it was then too late – which I regret. I like you a lot. I think you're a fine photographer. You have a fine eye, and compassion for your subjects. I was moved by your picture of the funeral, and wanted a copy of it. I did not want it because I am a collector of photographs. I have no photographs and I think the whole photography collecting business is a bit of a bore. Nor did I want it because it was taken by you, especially. I wanted it because it was what it was.

But . . . I asked you if you would have another copy made and find out from those in the know what would be a reasonable price to pay. Instead of which, you sent the only existing print, inscribed to me, and then, after you knew I had it and was pleased by it, priced it at five hundred bucks on the grounds it was 'unique'.

So it may be. But . . . there is uniqueness and uniqueness and there is also such a thing as a studio copy. Now my photography-buff friends tell me that almost every Steichen[2] print that gets sold in an auction is a copy. So I don't quite get the hang of the value of its uniqueness in cash terms.

I hate chisellers and I hate chiselling over the price of something one wants – and, as I usually want nothing, this doesn't present too much of a problem. But disregarding the fact that I am as usual, flat broke, five hundred bucks is far more than I would pay – or that it would be reasonable to pay, given the choice. Besides, if the print were that valuable in terms of your career why let it out of your ken,

---

1. It has not been possible to trace the identity of this photographer or his photograph. E.C.: 'The only photographs I know that Bruce bought were a little sepia print of wheat and a print by Edward Sheriff Curtis [1868–1952] of Kwakiutle dancers in Alaska.'
2. Edward Steichen (1879–1973), American photographer.

when you know as I know, that a copy would have been quite as acceptable?

I think the only thing for me to do is for me to get it back to you. This may take until the end of the month, because I am holed up in this soi-disant monastery for soi-disant writers, and because I will have to get someone to fish it out of my apartment in London and then get someone else to bring it over here.

A pity to get snarled up like this.

As ever   Bruce

To Diana Melly
c/o Yaddo | Saratoga Springs | New York | [April 1981]

My dearest Di,

Well, I must say the Caribbean is a perfectly acceptable tonic in the dead of winter. I had such a foul chest, such foul green phlegm in London that I really thought my last days had come. The house in St Maarten, of course, was designed for 'visual' people, that is to say, there was not a single spot to read a book, let alone write one, without breaking your back or lying on the baked earth with the ants. All the same, I didn't perform too badly there and was able to get one or two ideas into focus.

But now . . . now I am immured in this 'monastery' for artists, for composers, for writers. People predicted instant insanity, or important production. Neither, of course, is true: but the pile of pages does mount up. It's extremely strange to conjure up a vision of Radnor or Brecon, hemmed in, as I am between a racecourse and a kind of suburban pine forest. I suppose, anyway, that all fiction has to be illusion, and my cardboard surroundings make my subject seem realler than ever. The same goes for the inmates. They're a well-meaning lot – writing plays on the Russian Revolution; poetry about Little Italy; novels on Outer Space or Mississippi – but the dinner conversation is so unreal – or have I yet to learn the language? – that the characters of the day's fiction seem far more palpable by contrast.

All this may be wishful thinking.

I had hoped to go on long bicycle rides in the surrounding countryside. I even bought a bike for the purpose, but, after hubris, a most frightful fall!

Zapping through the State Park, and musing on the banality of America as a country where every kid who reaches the Sixth Grade thinks he must be the President or shoot one, a Chevy swoops up close behind: I wobble, hit a pothole, fly head first over the handlebars and bust my arm. Agony – total agony at first – but, by some great mercy, the bone-setter peered at the X-rays and said it didn't warrant a cast. Uncomfortable now, but at least I can continue to type.

Now what to do? What I would like to do, of course, is come to The Tower? But I really think I must go on here until – if that is feasible – I finish a draft.

All that, too, may be wishful thinking.

I'd love a card if you can face it: for I shall be here at least another month.

All my love to you,

XXX Bruce

To Charles and Margharita Chatwin
Yaddo | Saratoga Springs | New York | 13 April 1981

All well except for broken arm – not in any way serious – or even seriously incapacitating in that I can still type. A place of zero distractions, but a fairly breezy climate and outlook quite suitable for work, XXX B

To Martin and Stella Wilkinson
c/o Chanler | 66 East 79 | New York | 27 April 1981

Dearest Martin and Stella,

Silence profonde! – and for which a million apologies. No excuses are better, in this case, for lame ones. I went first to New York for a week of the usual round of varied pleasures – all ultimately the same. Then to an island called St Maarten, the wreck of somewhere really rather beautiful, wrecked in the sense that it was absolutely overrun by Yanks. However, the compensations were a quiet house and in the afternoons, WIND-SURFING. I have to say that I really do want to be seventeen all over again, and become a professional windsurfer. I am not bad. I stay up in Force 3–4 winds. I can bounce the board a bit over the wave-crests, but I shall never be good. Also went to Martinique, which is delicious, a kind of tropical Provence of the mid-20's – delicious food and the tourists penned in to a few Americanised playpens in one remote corner of the island. More wind-surfing. Then, I began to make a discovery. It was far easier to conjure up Jean the Barn and the rest of them when separated by five thousand miles of sea. Why, I can't say? I think it's because the story stands a chance of being a circular whole, when you can't get at any more material. If I am thinking, what colour are those clouds, or what are the twins up to, the story rapidly gets out of shape, becomes instead of circular – pear-shaped. So, I got a fellow-ship at a sort of 'monastery' for writers called Yaddo, and here I am, writing this now (the above address is E.'s mother in NY). Yaddo is a mansion, positively Arthurian in style, situated on the edge of the famous race-course at Saratoga Springs. Here congregate various types (for free) to cultivate their artistic sensibilities in conditions of unusual, rather melancholic calm. There are composers, there are poets, there are novel-ists, most of the Space-fantasy kind, and there are visual artists, rich young Jewish divorcees with sparklets on their cheeks, creating feminine sexual fantasies in sand and acrylic. What do I do, they say? Mixed media! I fit rather uneasily in this community, largely because I am outnumbered seven to one, female to male. They all adore Shakespeare and they adore my beautiful English voice and they adore it when I do Hamlet or Prospero, in the evenings, in an overstuffed medieval saloon. Or rather I did it once, weakly, and they've now decided this is going to be a regular entertainment. BUT, instead of having about 120 pages of the book, and because this place is entirely like sitting on the Moon, I now have some 300 pages, and there are moments when I do believe I am heading for the final canter. In fact, that is an illusion – the final canter of the first draft is more correct: this is a book where there will be endless bits of shading and colouring. But at least I do hope, someday not too far off, to have a framework on which to build. Every day, three times a week, I wish I were there, at The Cwm, not here.

Also I broke my arm. I bought a bike to zap around the surrounding countryside, and on my first day was thinking some rather anti-American thoughts when I daydreamed myself into a pothole and – wham! – over the handlebars. It does, mercifully, appear to be mending. After this place, I think I may go to the West on an early summer walk in some mountains, and then back home in mid June.

E. seems to think she wants to buy a 'thirties house[1] somewhere near Henley-on-Thames. Sounds as though one needs it like a hole in the head but there's no accounting for taste. As for me, I've got the itchy feet again, so I suppose it doesn't really matter.

I obviously missed Chiquita[2] in NY in February, but hope she had a good time and give her my love.

Forgive this rather demented letter, written very late at night, the trucks on the thoroughway howling past beyond the screen of *cupressus macrocarpa*.

all love to you, Bruce

Chatwin's brush with a pothole was not his only unfortunate encounter at Yaddo. On 1 May one of the staff reported: '3.00pm. Bruce Chatwin would like his bedroom sprayed. He has a rash he believes to be caused from bed bugs. He brought in something to show me that looks like a flea. Says a Doctor in NYC diagnosed him as having scabies. Should we give him a spray can – or will someone take care of the fumigating?? . . . or what?'

1. Homer End, Ipsden. Built as a school in the 1930s by the artist Eric Kennington, who had illustrated *Seven Pillars of Wisdom* for T. E. Lawrence. In the autumn of 1974 the author and disgraced politician Jeffrey Archer (*b*.1940) wrote his first book there, *Not a Penny More, Not a Penny Less*, also published by Tom Maschler. E.C.: 'Bruce did like the house when he saw it. It was light and not very big.'
2. Stella's mother, Ana Inez Carcano, m. 1944–72 Hon. John Jacob Astor.

To Paul Theroux

c/o Yaddo|Saratoga Springs|New York|4 May 1981

Your name, bandied about the breakfast table at this colony of insecure and initiated writers and artists, prompts me to send a card to say hello. V strange. A lot of lady artists – vaginal iconography in sand and acrylic. That kind of thing.

As always Bruce

To David Mason

c/o Yaddo|Saratoga Springs|New York|[May 1981]

Here we are sprung to the opposite ends of the earth. I hope to go to the Aleuthians/or Alaska in June[1] Bruce

To Diana Melly

c/o Yaddo|Saratoga Springs|New York|10 May 1981

Dearest Di,

What a lovely letter – a kind of letter prose poem! Ever since it arrived this morning, I keep wondering how I can use it. The idea of you and Francis [Wyndham] locked in a bucolic existence has a potent effect on the imagination. So different with the signals I have been getting out of England. I won't bore you with them. The gist of it being this: we were supposed to sell Holwell Farm so that Elizabeth could have a small house in the country; that I could have a shoe-box in London or wherever; and that she would have some capital to live on. Instead of which, she found the house of her dreams (sic) between Henley-on-Thames and Oxford (ie millionaire commuter country) for the same amount of money as Holwell. I said on the 'phone she should have it if that's what she really wanted – and then, faced with a bill from the Inland Revenue for five years back taxes, I simply couldn't face it and said NO.

1. He never travelled to either place.

What's the point in having a £160,000 house[1] if you can't buy a bottle of plonk? Anyway – as far as I can judge over the phone – terrible sulks and recriminations. I do think the £50 limit on possessions is the answer for the '80s.

Meanwhile, Yaddo has changed. Gone the April crowd. Gone the Maine-backwoodsman educationist and his 20-year old lithographer girlfriend: gone the vampire-painter ('vaginal iconography in sand and acrylic'). Gone the prose-poet (60 pages of a woman masturbating with a banana); gone too one very bright girl from the bayou of Louisiana. The newcomers are brighter, older, and more argumentative – and include a heroically proportioned N.Y. campaigner for women artists' rights; a bearded novelist from Oregon; a real charmer called Elizabeth Spencer – Mississippi novelist and friend of Eudora Welty.[2] But I am beginning to wonder if one isn't getting a bit exhausted in talk. What I want to do is to get a very rough 1st draft and then come and stay with you. Quite sizable it is – about 300 pp already and at least 100 to go.

The grave we must go and see is that of Dafyd Ap Gwilym 14th century poet at Strata Florida.[3] My version of the Welsh in the post to you.

XXXX B

While in America Chatwin met up again with Andrew Batey and his wife Hope in Yountville, California. They made a trip to Mexico, 'a carefully planned tour,' according to Batey, of the best houses and gardens of the Mexican architect Luis Barrágan (1902– 88).'Bruce regarded Luis as the greatest modern architect. He saw a picture of one of his buildings in English Vogue, *April 1966, and showed it to me as an example of what I should be doing. So*

1. E.C. had sold Holwell Farm for £170,000 and bought Homer End for £150,000. 'I gave Bruce $50,000 from the sale to buy the flat in Eaton Place. He thought that that should be his share.'
2. American novelist and short-story writer (1909–2001).
3. The ruins of a Cistercian monastery in North Wales founded in 1164.

I worked for him – no pay, for a year. Since Luis was quite ill, the visit had to be choreographed.' They started in Guadalajara, Barrágan's birthplace; saw his gardens on Lake Chapala, and stayed at his house in Mexico City. Batey returned to California and never saw Chatwin again.'My ex-wife died on the same day as Bruce and I flew to London for the Valentine's Day memorial service, and slipped out inconspicuously. I now know he had the greatest influence on my life – and countless others.'

To Ivry Freyberg
Change of address card: 'As from 10th September 1981,
Mr & Mrs C. B. Chatwin will be at Homer End.'

17 August 1981

Did my godson get a kite from me sent from San Francisco? B

To Francis Wyndham
The Scethrog Experiment | Brecon | Powys | Thursday [September 1981]

My dear Francis,

How funny you should have picked up on Michel Tournier![1] One day, I've promised myself to have a big go at Michel Tournier. He's obviously one of the most interesting writers in Europe – to me, at least, in that his themes (quite unintentionally on my part) seem to correspond to my own. For all that, whenever I try and tackle one of his books – the last was a version of Robinson Crusoe – either my French isn't up to it, or I start feeling there's something unbearably portentous about the writing; that he's an 'important' literary personage, and is concerned to let you know it.

But my involvement with *Gemini*, published in France as *Météores*, is rather droll. A French friend, married to an identical twin, told me to

1. French novelist (*b.*1924) who retold the Robinson Crusoe story in his first book *Friday and Robinson* (1967). *Les Météores* (*Gemini*) was published in 1975.

read it – which I did, or got half-way through. Then when I went on to read the psychoanalytic literature on twins, the only book that really impressed was by a Professor Zazzo, written, I think in the 'Forties.[1] Last January, I went to lunch with the translator of *The Viceroy* in Paris, and there, on his desk, was *Météores*. 'Funny,' I said, 'I'm writing a book about twins.' 'Funny,' he said, 'my wife is a psychiatrist who works with the leading expert on twins, one Professor Zazzo.' We rang for an appointment. The professor was in his eighties. Utterly charming! I apologised for disturbing him. My questions were those of a novelist. I wanted to make sure my story held together. 'But, Monsieur,' he replied. 'I have 1200 case histories on twins, and if I had your talents, I would be Balzac.' He then put me right on a number of points, and mentioned Tournier. It seemed that Tournier had also been obsessed by his book and had checked his plot with Zazzo, as I did mine.

This morning it was blowing a gale, pouring with rain and the sun was shining strongly as well . . . The sheep were the same golden colour as the dying grass. A rainbow stretched from one corner to the other, and under it, a flock of rooks was blown this way and that, like black diamonds, glittering.

Much love

Bruce

PS Diana's claim that I have colonised the whole house is quite without foundation. She is the puppet mistress who moves me around. We are expecting guests in quantity. One guest room reeks of elderberry wine – a smell resembling a dead mouse – the other of an unmentionable garden product hanging up to dry.[2]

---

1. Rene Zazzo, *Les Jumeaux, le Couple et la Personne* (1960).
2. Ten cannabis plants, nearly six feet high, were eventually discovered by the Welsh police. Chatwin smoked pot on occasion, if someone else produced it. From his short-lived diary, 12 December 1969: 'Hashish before going to bed. Light-headed.' In *Take a Girl Like Me* Diana Melly writes: 'Bruce stayed with me on and off for five years and never even made a cup of tea, although he did occasionally boil up some rather disgusting-smelling Mexican leaves [actually, Argentine *maté*] into a brew which he said gave him energy – not something I thought he lacked, rather he fizzed with it.' E.C.: 'He'd suddenly come down from the top floor and say, "Where's the coffee?" or "What's for lunch?" He wanted to be waited on all the time.'

To David King

The Tower | Scethrog | Brecon. | Powys | 9 September 1981

Seeing that we're both in the <u>collecting</u> game I would like – though you must <u>NOT</u> feel obliged to comply – to collect (and pay for!) one of your first editions (the 2nd won't be quite as valuable in years to come) i.e. the Black Lamp[1] which I admire immensely and want. As always BC

To Charles and Margharita Chatwin

The Tower | Scethrog | Brecon | Powys | 22 September 1981

The big novel (440 pp so far) creaks on towards the end: but there will be endless rewriting to do. Spent a week repapering[2] Homer End – which, I have to say, is extremely glamorous – if something of a threat to my writing. XXX B

To Francis Wyndham

c/o Von Rezzori | Donnini | Florence | Italy | 6 November 1981

Dear Francis,

All well here. The sun shines in Tuscany, and, so far, until I hit the snags, it isn't taking as long as I thought. I've revised 200 pages and type up a hundred. But there are still hundreds and hundreds of minor points. In London, however, there appears to be a fantastic brouhaha about my wanting to go to Viking. I hadn't realised that in all Simon and Schuster contracts there's a little clause slipped in about the right to see the next book; and they refuse to waive the right etc, etc. It's all very tedious,

1. A lamp designed by King, six feet high, one foot square, with a 25 watt lightbulb sunk into the top shedding a faint glow. Chatwin wanted to paint it dull grey; King refused.
2. E.C.: 'He spent two days. We moved in, slept on the floor and mattresses with the movers from Holwell Farm. Bruce tore the dark brown ribbed *moiré* wallpaper off the little sitting room to make one room habitable. He relined and painted it pale buttercup. Next day, he pulled off the black and white paisley wallpaper and sea-grass in the big room. Then he went away. He didn't carry any objects in, not a thing.'

because this is the moment when I need Elisabeth Sifton's[1] help, not later when the book is ready for press. Anyway, I refuse to be bullied by big companies; and I'm even gearing myself to present them with a book of my collected journalism, which, if they had the least grain of sense they would turn down, and that would be that.

Last night, Grisha Rezzori was visited by a Rumanian compatriot, who appeared, from what he said, to be at the top of the Writer's Union. We had half-expected Marxist platitudes: instead, during supper, he let out, 'Hitler had a very good reputation in my country' – which shows you just how careful you have to be in gauging the mood in Eastern Europe.

all love, B

To Charles and Margharita Chatwin

c/o Von Rezzori|Donnini|Florence|Italy|7 November [1981]

Hello!

I did my usual bolting act and went to Tuscany to the tower where I work extremely well, in order to retype the manuscript. Almost 500 pages! What a weight!

Unfortunately, there is a considerable amount of urgency. I shall have to deliver the whole thing at the latest by January 1st if it is to be published in the autumn. Coupled with which, I seem to have stirred up a fantastic brouhaha. Last summer, in America, I met a woman called Elisabeth Sifton, who is well known to be the best editor in America. She had said to a friend that the one young English writer she wanted to publish was me. When we met, it was, on my part, a love-match (literary variety), because we found that all of our tastes etc. were held in common. She read nearly all of the new manuscript and offered about £30,000 but apparently I now, because of an option clause that got left

---

1. Chatwin had lunch with Sifton in London on 20 October and agreed to leave Jim Silberman and go with her to Viking in America. On 26 October she offered an advance of $50,000 for *On the Black Hill*. In the UK, Cape paid an advance of £7,500.

in the last contract WHICH I GAVE SPECIAL ORDERS TO BE TAKEN OUT, can't leave the other publisher. You can imagine the fuss. I'm better off in Tuscany.

But I have found a flat. I spent a totally dispiriting week looking around Camden Hill and Notting Hill, and seeing one gloomier flat than the next. Then I realised, battling through the traffic to the West End that the one thing I need London for is to be in walking distance of the London Library. I said to myself, 'If I can't have Albany, then what I want is a one-room attic in Eaton Place'; and there, in the *Sunday Times* next day, it was! It's actually quite a large room, at least twice the size of the whole of Albany, but so hideously cut up, messed up, and hideously decorated that no one apparently wanted it. Price came down from £35,000 to £31,000. Grosvenor Estate lease of 53 years or so. The total outgoings are about £1,000 but that included a caretaker and constant hot water and heating, so I'm not unduly worried. It'll need quite a bit spending on it because there's no point in doing this kind of thing in dribs and drabs. I've left the matter in the hands of Gerald.[1] The banks are giving a bridging loan, and then we'll see how much of the American money to put in, and how much one should mortgage. Apparently, I should have some mortgage in view of the possibility of my income next year being somewhat over £40,000. When I'm finished it'll be very nice, though. Three big windows facing due south over the rooftops.

It represents the limit of my attachment to London, and I pray the whole thing doesn't fall through. Much prefer one nice room to a lot of dreary ones.

If you like phoning, evenings are the best around 8 your time.
much love, XX B

In February, 'in a mood of extreme recklessness', Chatwin signed 'an enormous cheque' to his architect, John Pawson, telling him 'just to get on with the flat'. He then flew with Donald Richards to Kenya, spending ten days on the Island of Lamu.

1. Gerald Hingley of Wragge's, Chatwin's lawyer in Birmingham.

To Charles and Margharita Chatwin
Lamu Island | Kenya | 7 February 1982

Dear Charles and Margharita,

I've had a week now of mindless hot windy days on this Muslim island on the North Kenya Coast. I managed to borrow a 17th century merchant's house, built of coral blocks and stuccoed inside with traditional Arab decoration. From the roof you see palm thatched roofs, the minaret of the mosque, a sea of bougainvillea and, beyond, the channel of bright blue water up and down which dhows speed past at all hours of the day.

One of the fishermen took me snorkelling on a coral reef about 9 miles down the coast, and I must say that the pictures you see of such things bear no relation to the staggering beauty both of the fish and the corals.

Before leaving I managed to get a commission from the *New York Review* to write a long article on the discoveries of Richard Leakey[1] on Lake Rudolf – L Turkana as it's now called. A few years ago he excavated the skull of a hominid – a near-man – dating from 1½ million years together with his stone tools, and evidence of his camp-site.

Leakey is a Kenyan MP, and even in the half talk we had – in between his visit to the Prime Minister and his work as head of the National Museum – I felt that we saw eye to eye on an astonishing number of points. The fact that he picked up on so many of the same references as I did with the nomad book encourages me to take it up again. The upshot of the visit anyhow is that he is going to take me up to Lake Turkana, probably next week.

Otherwise I've been windsurfing: the trouble with it here is that either the wind blows 5 knots or 20 – and I need 10. I always seem to get catapulted forward and end up in the sea about 15 feet ahead of the board – but one day I'm going to overtake Hugh in his ocean racer.

On my second day in Nairobi I went for a walk in the Ngong Hills, near where Karen Blixen[2] had a coffee plantation but had to beat a retreat from a herd of buffalo.

1. Kenyan paleoanthropologist (*b*.1944).
2. Danish author, also known as Isak Dinesen (1885–1962); her books include *Out of Africa*.

After a tremendous brouhaha – 6ft long telegrams flying across the Atlantic etc – the deal with Viking Press has gone through. Enormous relief all round! But what a fuss! However, I stick to my guns. The move was not taken light heartedly. It was taken because I felt that I needed advice, and that one should try and get the best advice. There's no real point in having a publisher with whom you cannot discuss a project beforehand.

Returning March 1st. Lord knows where I'll be staying. The architect says he'll have Eaton Place finished – but I don't believe that! Much love B

To Elizabeth Chatwin
Lamu Island | Kenya | February 1982

A few days of wind-surfing on Lamu Is before Richard Leakey flies me up to Lake Turkana. Howling gale most of the day: so I'm quite bruised from falling off. Snorkelling in the coral reefs unbelievably beautiful. Viking Press deal has gone through – apparently – at last
XXX B

To Deborah Rogers
In Kenya | Mid February [1982]

Dear Deborah,
    . . . Re *On The Black Hill*: we've got a fairly tricky timing problem, I'm afraid. I get back on March 1st, possibly a day later, but anyhow not later than March 3rd. Can we start at once? I have given a copy to my friend Joan Saunders,[1] who as you may know is a literary researcher, very

---

1. Joan Saunders of Writers' and Speakers' Research, a literary researcher whom he shared with Patrick Leigh Fermor. In January 1981 she had sent Chatwin a list of Air Crashes and Women Fliers.

accomplished in spotting inaccuracies etc. I then must go to New York around the middle of the month to consult with the new American publisher, Elisabeth Sifton of Viking, before returning to send off the final copy.

I haven't got one word of it with me here: but my own thoughts are that the Peace celebrations chapter (195–220) may need some revisions; also I am not at all happy about the character of Philippa (towards the end) and feel she should come out. She is modelled, quite accurately, on Penelope Betjeman, and I think the whole episode jars.

The other thing we have to watch out for are the phrases 'one fine morning . . . On a Thursday in June . . . etc' They are essential to get the sequence of events moving through time, but I feel they are repetitive and stereo-typed, and we must think of ways of turning them, dispensing with them etc . . .

As always, Bruce

To Susan Sontag[1]
Flat 7 | 77 Eaton Place | London | 3 April 1982

My dear Susan,

London's a fine place to be this week – the spectacle of the entire Houses of Parliament clamouring to send an ARMADA – no less a word – of 40 ships to relieve the Falkland Islands. Makes me wonder if one's gone mad. Presumably by the time they get there, the islanders will have been spirited off to the mainland anyway.

I loved our dinner of entrails[2] and hope for a repeat. Our friend Calasso[3] sends greetings: I am machinating to try and get his Satta *Day*

---

1. American author and political activist (1933–2004).
2. In Chinatown. S.S.: 'Bruce was the only person I knew whom I could invite to a hakka – fried intestines and toe-nails.'
3. Robert Calasso (*b*.1941), Italian author and Chatwin's publisher at Adelphi.

of Judgement[1] published. George Steiner[2] pronounces it one of the truly great works of the century etc.

Do let me know if and when you're coming to France or Italy. Also, I am seriously interested in the idea of Berlin: it might be ideal for the next project I have in mind.

As always, Bruce

To Susan Sontag
Flat 7 | 77 Eaton Place | London | [13 May 1982]

13 May – and to think that I am 42 today.

Dear Susan,

The New York dinner season may be winding down: here, in London, we have the HUNT SUPPER. The English, having found in a seedy bunch of pseudo-fascist generals THEIR IDEAL ENEMY, having tasted that enemy's blood, are now baying for more. Under the rhetoric, under the phoney talk of 'making the world safe for democracy', you can hear the yelp of the hounds. I suspect, however (just wait till the Montonero-style guerrilla squads get going – ? in London) that all is going to end very badly.

I did my little bit of sounding off on the Australian radio, an article here etc. Then, *In Patagonia* appeared in Italy and the critics found – as I had forgotten – that, in the last line but one, a Falkland Island boy says "Bout time the Argentines took us over, we're so bloody inbred.' This was interpreted as a case of history imitating art – and you can imagine the absurdity of the rest – interviews on TV etc – a whole ten minutes on the evening news – and a piece of footage which showed, not the sophisticated crust of BA but some Amazonian Indians thatching their huts with palm fronds.

The novel about the incestuous brothers is in the press. And <u>when</u>

---

1. *The Day of Judgement*, posthumous novel by Salvatore Satta (1902–75) set in nineteenth-century Sardinia; it was published in English in 1987.
2. Cambridge-based critic and philosopher (*b*.1929).

I get the proofs, I'll leave by the first boat or plane – passing of course through Paris if you're there – on my way to . . . ? Well, Outer Mongolia is a possibility.

Calasso sends greetings. We both agreed on the grotesque character of the reaction to your very simple – and – if you'll forgive my saying so – very evident statement,[1]

As always, Bruce

To Graham C. Greene[2]
Flat 7 | 77 Eaton Place | London | June 8 1982

Dear Graham,

I want to make it clear at the outset that ON THE BLACK HILL is not a *roman à clef*, not some kind of faction, but a work of the imagination that has its own structure and operates accordingly. True, it is set in the Black Mountains or, preferably, the Radnor Hills. The town of Rhulen could be either Hay-on-Wye, or Kington, or Knighton, or Clun. There is indeed a Black Hill on the eastern scarp of the Black Mountains, but there is another one, overshadowing the house, in Shropshire, where I began the first draft of the book.

I have used the Border Country (which I have known since the age of six); the eternal feud between the two farms; and the motif of twins (for whom there is no possibility of an advance) as vehicles for a sustained meditation on the concept of Cyclical, as opposed to Linear, Time. But I have done an immense amount of research, in life and from old newspapers, to root the story in actuality.

There are four houses in the book – The Vision, The Rock, Lurkenhope Castle, and The Tump. If there are any prototypes for these, none have any connection with the other, in real life.

1. In a speech at the New York Town Hall on 6 February 1982 to protest against the suppression of Solidarity in Poland, Sontag had said 'Communism is . . . Fascism with a human face' – drawing boos and shouts from the audience, and accusations that she had betrayed her radical ideas.
2. Chairman of Jonathan Cape.

1. The Vision. Read Chapter 1, 32, and p203 Chap 44.

About five years ago, my friend Penelope Betjeman (wife of the Laureate) took me to her neighbours, George and Jonathan Howells, two bachelor brothers now (1982) in their late sixties[1], who live on the eastern side of the Black Mountains in their farm called New House. The story she told of them (and which captured my imagination) was that sometime before the War their mother, seeing them to show no signs of interest in the opposite sex, had sent them to the fair at Hay-on-Wye to meet some young ladies. They came back with crestfallen faces, never having seen girls in short skirts before. This put them off forever.

Their farmhouse kitchen does in some way resemble that of The Vision (Chap 1); but then it is hardly different from any border farmhouse from before the War. The Howells brothers are not twins. They were not involved in the First War. Their mother was an ordinary Welsh farmer's daughter from Radnorshire. Both their parents survived till well after the Second World War. They have not lived in the house all their lives. They have one (I think maybe two) sisters. Also a younger brother, who, in turn has a son called Vivian, a dashing dark-haired boy, who stands to inherit their 300 acres, but has not to my knowledge yet done so. He, Vivian, had a rather beautiful blonde girlfriend, of whom the brothers disapproved; but they have since split up. He did not marry. He didn't take his uncles in an aeroplane p 236. He had no hippie friends. What he did do was wear sunglasses and fail to attend the agricultural training college.

I felt the Howells' situation was so tangential to the story of Lewis and Benjamin in the book that one needn't worry about it. That is until Penelope gave the manuscript of my book WITHOUT MY PERMISSION to a Mrs Mary Morgan (nee Penoyre, and thus one of the local gentry, and a bluestocking to boot!). She managed to get almost everything wrong; and though she professed to have loved the book, have wept real tears etc was full of fatuous suggestions as to how, in her view, it could be improved, and was determined to identify every character in the novel with someone she knew. She seems to have identified her own

---

1. 'The young men', Betjeman called them.

family with the Bickertons (false!); Amos Jones with a local farmer and a great friend of mine (completely false) etc. BUT she also got hold of Vivian Howells and told him that he was 'in my book'. I suspect she even let him read passages from it.

THE ROCK Read pp. 49 ff. pp. 128–131, pp. 154–55, pp. 169–71, pp. 195–200, pp. 210–212, p. 222, pp. 223–7; whole of chapter 47.

This is much more closer rooted in reality than The Vision, which is I repeat a creation.

The model for the Rock is a smallholding called Coed Major, high up on the hillside, the property of a family called Philips. Joe Philips, better known as Joe the Barn, was a great local character who died last year after spending twelve months in hospital after a stroke. Before the War, the Barn (as Coed Major was called) was famous for being a place where local farmers could dump their illegitimates. It was a place of wild female energies. The exact relationships of the inhabitants of the Barn are too complicated to explain in this letter; but the reader should bear in mind that Meg the Rock is the only character in this book who bears any real relationship to a living person. But also he should note the characters of Sarah and Lizzie.

The other chapter that should be read in connection with the Rock is the account of the murder in Chapter 34

LURKENHOPE CASTLE is a complete fiction. If the Bickerton family had any resemblance to anyone, it is to some Lincolnshire cousins of mine;[1] but the connection is far too remote for anyone to worry.

THE TUMP inhabited by Rosie Tilman. p.184

There is an old woman, in her advanced eighties, bearing no relation to any of the above, who lives alone in a cottage on the side of Hay Bluff. She is called Miss Tyler the Tack, and was once seduced by a young

---

1. Bickerton was the eldest son of the disgraced solicitor, Robert Harding Milward; he was in the Broken Hill gold rush, badly gassed in the First World War and ended his days living 'rather rakishly' in Broadway.

gentleman in a big house, and retreated to a place of total isolation where she has lived for more than fifty years. Otherwise I know nothing more of her.

Perhaps we should change the name to something less resembling Tyler?

Sorry about all this,

as always

Bruce

To Robyn Ravlich[1]

Flat 7 | 77 Eaton Place | London | 25 June 1982

Dear Robyn,

Now that many hundred Argentine boys have been slaughtered so that, for a brief period of weeks, not months, the trains in this country would run on time etc; and now that I have finished the unusually protracted birth pains of a book, I am turning towards both the idea and actuality of Australia with something like the fervour of a first love affair. It now appears that I shall be coming earlier than I thought, say, by the 1st of September, and I intend to be as footloose as possible for a bit.

But, of course, I'll be in touch with you at once in Sydney.

My best to you and Stan.

as ever

Bruce

To Susan Sontag

Flat 7 | 77 Eaton Place | London | 30 June 1982

My dear Susan,

So the trains ran on time in this tinpot country for precisely five weeks while, in the blighted Southern Hemisphere, the boys were killed.

1. ABC radio producer from Sydney; she had visited Chatwin in Albany in January 1980.

Now London is paralysed with rail strikes, which is proof that things are back to normal.

I will, for certain, be in NY around the last week in August, and long for a repeat in Chinatown.[1]

As always, Bruce

To Elizabeth Chatwin
Flat 7|77 Eaton Place|London|30 June 1982

My dear E,

I've spent the past week frantically trying to sort out my finances and have decided to transfer the accountant from Ernst & Whinney to a Mr Shah, 23 Harcourt St W.1. who is Deborah Roger's accountant and specialises in the chaotic affairs of writers. My position which seems to me frantic doesn't seem to phase anyone in the least; and perhaps in the autumn depending on the sale of *On the Black Hill* I'll be able to help with Homer End. I have so much to do, what with articles etc. and I'm off to Teddy M[illington]-D[rake]'s for 3 weeks.

Love

B

Leo [Lerman] and Grey [Foy, Lerman's partner] send their love: they were at an overstuffed soiree at Lord Weidenfeld's[2] last night.

---

1. Sontag replied on 11 July 1982: 'I loved the stamp on your last letter [commemorating Admiral Fisher, the First Sea Lord, and his 1906 creation HMS *Dreadnought*]. The vivid, curiously Negroid head of Lord Fishersomething (part of the name inked out by the postmark); his pale Dreadnought riding in the background; and a miniature grey silhouette of the Queen as Girl, hanging in the upper left. Worthy of Donald Evans, which shows once again that you know . . . I'm off for ten days – all quite unexpected – to Kiev. My only justification is that I've never been to the Soviet Onion and I want to smell it, and it's <u>only</u> ten days. I look forward to your visit toward the end of August with impatience.'
2. George Weidenfeld, British publisher (*b*.1919).

To Elizabeth Chatwin
Interior of Eski Cami 'Old Mosque' | Beyoglu | Turkey
[August 1982]

Amazing to think that this exists in what is really the heart of middle Europe. And did you when you were here see the hospital of Gullion Beyazit where they cured the mentally ill with music 3 times a week. You stay in a caravanserai by Sinan[1] with weeping willows, a chameau and fowls in the yard that wake you up by coming into the room. Still in a mess, creatively. May embark right away on my so-called Russian novel.[2] Back around the 15th August.

To Ivry Freyberg
Flat 7 | 77 Eaton Place | London | 13 August 1982

Oh! How sad to have missed the party. I've been rotting in a Greek Island for 6 weeks. Long to see you all. Bruce

To Susan Sontag
Flat 7 | 77 Eaton Place | London | 16 August 1982

Dear Susan,

And how was Kiev? Whiffs of that peculiar Soviet disinfectant, unrefined gasoline? And the sight of a Cossack cavalry brigade along a cobbled street. I was last there at the time of the invasion of Prague — and, from that vantage point at least, it seemed quite evident that the event was staged to impress the Ukrainians not the Czechs that they'd better try no more nonsense.

In recent weeks I've been strolling along the Turkish-Bulgarian border and seem to have contracted some dread stomach disorder. This means

1. Mimar Sinan(1489-1588), Ottoman architect of Suleiman Mosque in Istanbul.
2. The first mention of a novel which Chatwin did not begin until 1988, of which but a fragment exists.

that NY is postponed until mid-September – when I do hope to find you there!

As ever Bruce

To David Mason

Postcard, Nicholas Roerich painting, 'Overseas Guests', depicting
Vikings staring over the rail of their bright ship at the Russian
landscape | Flat 7 | 77 Eaton Place | London | November 1982

Rochester is a far cry from Kardamyli: it so happens that both loom large in my life: my in-laws (alas, now separated) live in the Genesee valley. Above address is reasonably permanent. Have just been following the route of the Vikings down the Volga.[1] Hence the card. As ever Bruce

Penelope Betjeman had introduced Chatwin to the central characters in On the Black Hill *and was one of the first to read the finished novel. On 10 June 1982 she wrote to Chatwin: 'When St Thomas Aquinas was dying he had a VISION and when he came to he made the following statement (with which you are no doubt familiar!). "All that I have written is like STRAW compared with the things I have now seen." All that you have written previously: your two books etc. are like STRAW compared to* On the Black Hill. *I have been walking all day in a DAZE after finishing it. I think it will prove to be the greatest regional novel of the century, as good as anything Hardy wrote.'*

The novel's publication in the autumn was accompanied by a television programme on ITV's The South Bank Show. *In November 1982 it won the Whitbread Prize in the first novel category, the judges appearing to overlook* The Viceroy of Ouidah *as a work of fiction.*

1. For the *Observer* magazine, 'Great Rivers of the World: The Volga', June 1984.

CHAPTER NINE

———— ◄◦► ————

THE SONGLINES: 1983–5

Still fragile after an operation in St Thomas's Hospital, possibly for haemorrhoids or else connected with his 'dread stomach disorder', Chatwin chose to recuperate as far as possible from England. On 19 December 1982 he gathered up the card index of The Nomadic Alternative *– 'a mishmash of nearly indecipherable jottings, "thoughts", quotations, brief encounters, travel notes, notes for stories' – and flew to Sydney. '. . . I planned to hole up somewhere in the desert, away from libraries and other men's work, and take a fresh look at what they contained.' Elizabeth expressed her relief to Gertrude: 'I'm glad he's finally gone as he's had a fixation about it for years. He'll either love it or hate it, but he might find it a vehicle for the nomads or it'll finish him off.'*

To Francis Wyndham
c/o Ben Gannon | 11 Gaerlich Avenue | Bondi | Sydney | Australia |
11 January 1983

Dearest F.,

It was such a treat to get your cable. Good for Sir Victor![1] The whole US publication seems to be going off rather well. An over the top review on the front page of the NY *Times* Book Supplement by Robert Towers, rather missing, however, the point. An equally over-the-top effort by

---

1. V.S. Pritchett reviewed *On the Black Hill* in the *New York Review of Books*, 20 January 1983.

John Leonard in the Daily *Times* – though I strongly resent classifying *The Viceroy of Ouidah* as 'homoerotic and sadomasochistic'. In fact the *Time* review was, from my point of view, the best of all – in that he got the message of the 'still centre'. However, I cannot possibly complain: the reviewers over there are simply far more attentive readers. *On the B.H.* is also, I may say, no. 4 of the *Sydney Morning Herald*'s hardback best-seller list . . .

I have to say I'm enjoying it here. Glorious summer days. A wonderful doctor seems to have completely restored me to health. In a week or so, I'm thinking of taking off into drought-stricken New South Wales. The dust is the worst in living memory.

Penelope and Ricky[1] send their love.

All mine to you and to James [Fox] etc.

Bruce

To Charles and Margharita Chatwin
c/o Penelope Tree | 19a Eastbourne Rd |
Darling Point | Sydney | Australia | 12 January 1983

Dear Charles and Margharita,

Well, I must say I'm feeling extremely revived. I seem to have recovered totally in the sun and wide open spaces. Physically, Australia is definitely for me: the land is so beautiful, and you get none of that terrible usurped quality I always feel about America. But so far, I've really done nothing, except recuperate, read books, windsurf and go to aerobics class in the gym with Penelope Tree. She, as you may know, was once the most photographed model in the world: but has now decided that she can't bear either England or the US and has settled here.

On the Black Hill is going great guns in the US. The idea of a 'still centre' is apparently something of real attraction to the American reading public; and they've already reprinted, and are thinking of a third. I'm

---

1. Penelope Tree (*b*.1950), Anglo-American model photographed by Richard Avedon, Cecil Beaton and David Bailey. She had lived in Sydney since 1974 m. to Ricky Fataar, South African musician who briefly played for the Beach Boys.

left with a tremendous problem as to what to do next, and have temporarily exhausted myself doing articles I didn't want to write. The instant I arrived here I was pursued like by the Furies, by a string of telegrams; 'will I write just 2000 words, on this, that or the other?' It can really give you such a profound distaste for writing that you long to take up landscape gardening or whatever.

Next week, however, I am clearing out of town with my rucksack, and will be more or less incommunicado for a month. I want to go to some of the Aboriginal reservations in the heart of the country; and if possible to Broome, the pearling town in the far North West. I am hoping that the concept of the new book will begin to germinate, however blank I feel about it at present. With so many 'cooked-up' books knocking around, I don't really believe in writing unless one has to.

I'm gearing up to the point when I tackle ringing up all six of the J. J. James's[1] in the phone book.

Much love

B

To Elizabeth Chatwin

c/o Penelope Tree | 19a Eastbourne Rd |
Darling Point | Sydney | Australia | 12 January 1983

Dear E,

This, I must say, is the country to settle in. You've no idea how beautiful the land is, and the climate, just on the fringe of the arid and wet zones. Rolling farm land, forests, vines, and none of that terrible property-mad usurpation you find in the U.S. The Hunter valley is like Provence or Tuscany but Anglo-Saxon. Wine and food delicious. And the trees! The Australian section of the Sydney Botanical garden is incredible, not just for the gums and banksias but hundreds and hundreds of other species. Also all the great flowering trees of temperate China seem to grow here as well. Of course, on one level, it's a complete

1. Childhood friends who had emigrated to Australia.

Cloud-Cuckoo-Land, really very far away from the rest of the world; and it's going through a recession; but if anywhere has an underlying optimism this is it. I think really a combination of things like the Malvinas (as I now persist in calling them) and Paul Bailey's snarky review[1] have made me feel so irreversibly un-English that I really had better start doing something about it.

On the Black Hill is apparently going great guns in the U.S. The reviews such as I've seen are not simply favourable; they understand what's going on. Robert Towers on the <u>front</u> page of the *New York Times* Supplement completely got the hang, but the one that pleased me most was the man in *Time*, and the concept of the 'still centre'. Anyway, all this makes very little impact on my tremendous difficulty dreaming up what to do next. I have an idea – yes. A relatively outlandish one, that will take me to Broome in the Far North West, or rather to a place called Beagle Bay. I have a card index of the old nomad book to plunder – but God knows what'll happen.

In the meantime, we surf, sunbathe, windsurf, and go to an aerobics class in the gym. Am vastly recovered but after such an infection am bound to feel a bit crotchety for a while.

xxx B

Penelope will take messages or Benny Gannon's[2] secretary at 02-357-XXXX

To Deborah Rogers
c/o Ben Gannon | 11 Gaerloch Avenue | Bondi | Sydney | Australia |
23 January 1983

Dear Deborah,

The sky is so blue, the sea is so blue, and the surfers so unbeliev-ably elegant that the room in which I have been trying to write has not

1. Bailey in the London *Evening Standard* had called *On the Black Hill* 'a curiously coarse-grained book . . . The writing is rife with cliché . . . At its worst it suggests Mary Webb on a very off day.'
2. Australian television producer with whom Chatwin stayed on Bondi Beach.

seen much actual writing . . . for the next month or so I shall be in the Outback and really quite unavailable. I think I'm on the trail of something.

The 'something' had been gestating in his system a long while, and stemmed from a conversation Bruce had had, back in 1970, with the Australian archaeologist John Mulvaney at the Pitt-Rivers Museum in Oxford. Chatwin – then curating his exhibition of nomadic art – had sought out Mulvaney in the hope he might be able to shed light on the nature of human restlessness. In particular, 'I wanted to know about the "walkabout", but you can hardly find it in the literature.' Mulvaney, apparently – he has no recollection of the meeting – had pointed Chatwin in the direction of the anthropologist Theodor Strehlow, who had lived and worked with Aboriginals in Central Australia. 'He is the man who really knows. You ought to come and see him.'

Strehlow had died in 1978, but his widow Kath lived in Adelaide. On 28 January Chatwin turned up at her house wishing to purchase a copy of Strehlow's Songs of Central Australia, *a difficult book, long-ignored and virtually impossible to get hold of.*

'When Bruce introduced himself on the phone, my words to him were: "Let me say hello to the first man in the world who's read it."'

Kath sold him an unbound proof. 'I put a map in the back so he could see where the songlines were.' She also produced her husband's daybooks and diaries for him to read. The next couple of hours defined Chatwin's next three years. 'I sat down, only for a morning,' he said, 'and I suddenly realised everything that I rather hoped these songlines would be, just were.*'*

Revitalised, Chatwin flew to Alice Springs to study Strehlow's book in situ and test his theory. 'I wanted to find how it worked.*'*

To Elisabeth Sifton
Alice Springs | Australia | 7 February 1983

My dear Elisabeth,

I wonder if you could ask Altie[1] to help. Iris Harvey who runs a magnificent bookshop in Alice Springs has been trying without success to buy copies of a book republished by the Johnson reprint Co. but cannot get a reply to her letters. The book is by the late Prof T. G. H. Strehlow,[2] *Aranda Traditions* and is an essential work for the study of Australian anthropology – indeed perhaps the reason for my being here in Australia. Mrs Harvey believes that Johnson have a remnant stock of about 500; and if so she'd like to buy up as many as possible. Could Altie, therefore, find out a. the address and phone no. of Johnson b. the name of the person in charge to whom Mrs Harvey could communicate. I believe that the reprint houses who xerox the original edition have a system of being able to reorder copies of course at extra cost. I don't know if that is still done.

Much love

B

To Elizabeth Chatwin
Haasts Bluff Aboriginal Reservation | Alice Springs | Australia |
7 February 1983

The Aboriginals though infinitely fascinating are also infinitely sad: so sad, in fact, that I am rapidly coming to the conclusion that to write a

1. Altie Karper, Sifton's assistant at Viking.
2. Theodor George Henry ('Ted') Strehlow (1908–78), anthropologist who grew up speaking Aranda on the Lutheran Mission at Hermannsburg, where his father was pastor, and made it his life's work to record 'in notebooks, on tape and on film the songs and ceremonies of the passing order'. The Aboriginals considered Strehlow to be a member of their people and, controversially, entrusted him with the responsibility of safeguarding their sacred objects and ceremonies. In May 1978 he caused outrage when he sold photographs of secret ceremonies to *Stern* magazine which were syndicated to the Australian weekly *People*. He suffered a cardiac arrest four months later. Chatwin wrote in *The Songlines*: 'Strehlow died at his desk in 1978, a broken man.'

book about them would be impossible. And as for the arid outback, it would be another *In Patagonia* minus the poetic dimension. Should be back mid to late March. XXX B

To David Thomas[1]
Alice Springs | Australia | 20 February 1983

At first I was dumbstruck with horror. Alice is a hornet's nest – of drunks, Pommie-bashers, earnest Lutheran missionaries, and apocalyptically-minded do-gooders. Gradually, however, I'm learning to live with it. A day or two in town . . . five or more out bush. The complexity of the Aboriginal Dreaming Tracks (bad expression) is so staggeringly complex, and on such a colossal scale, intellectually, that they make the Pyramids seem like sand castles. But how to write about them – without spending 20 years here?

Always
Bruce

To Diana Melly
c/o Ben Gannon | 11 Gaerloch Avenue | Bondi | Sydney | Australia | 1 March [1983]

Dearest Di,

Last night I got back to Sydney and we sat up watching Bob Hawke become the new Prime Minister. Secretly, although one can't say so, I think they'll regret it: not because he's LEFT or Republican etc but because he has the meanest mouth imaginable and terribly shifty eyes. However . . .

I have been on a marathon, extremely expensive zig-zag across the

1. Thomas had researched ITV's *The South Bank Show* on Chatwin, aired on 7 November 1982.

continent from Adelaide, rip through Alice Springs, over to Broome and the Kimberleys, down to Perth and back: Georgie[1] will probably have told you how I tracked him down to a sort of rustic amphitheatre in the forest.

You fry in the Centre of Australia: but I can't complain. I never once FELL for the country, except perhaps in the most abstract way with the landscape. The Aboriginal situation is too disheartening, the whites so disjointed, or plainly disagreeable, but I did, often enough, light on a situation that grabbed my attention. Also, I do have what I was looking for: the 'Australia' peg on which to hang my 'nomadic' material. The title is to be 'A Monk by the Sea' – where, indeed, I found him: a Cistercian ascetic[2] who had lived in London, entered this most severe monastic order, worked on an Aboriginal mission, and then had returned to a hermitage of corrugated sheet (the cross was made by a pair of crossed oars, washed up by a cyclone) on the most abstract beach in N. Australia. He also happened to be obsessed by the story of the Israelites wandering in the desert, by Sufism, Taoism etc. Anyway, I have begun to sketch . . .

I intend to do a trilogy of 3 tiny novels which can all be bound together. 1. The Monk (affairs of the spirit) 2. A new story I've been told of a black woman and a Scandinavian diplomat 3. The old tale of the man with porcelains in Prague.

We shall see . . .

The news of Donald [Richards] is that he's landed himself – after weeks of angst – with a wonderful job – as Deputy Director of the 'Future' Brisbane Festival. It was absolutely impossible to have him moping around, penniless and frustrated, and he's already become a creature transformed. As far as readjusting to Australia, it couldn't be better. He seemed excessively nervous here in Sydney, and has now

1. George Melly was appearing at the Perth Jazz Festival with John Chilton's Feet-warmers.
2. Father Dan O'Donovan. 'Yes, I remember well the day Bruce turned up at my paper-bark humpie, just south of Cape Leveque lighthouse . . . Regarding the pages which pertain to me [in *The Songlines*], apart from a couple of details accurately conveyed, the whole statement is purest fantasy.'

returned to his own.[1] So, as usual, I seem to have been sprung back to my usual condition . . . THE ROAD . . .

As for the US reception of *On the B.H.* Well! Review after review with endless comparisons . . . How they love comparisons! Hardy, Spencer, D.H. Lawrence, Vermeer. The review I most liked was in the *Houston Globe*: 'If you really want to sit by the fireside, going grey with a cameo tied round your neck, listening to a two-piece orchestra banging out the same old tune, good for you. As for me, I'm off to find my own excitement in the West Loop . . .' After a 10 minute read with Penelope Tree the whole lot enjoyed the hospitality of her garbage can . . .

I do hope Candy's[2] all right. How terribly worrying for you. I have to say that although she's very sweet, touching etc I could also BRAIN that Sophia[3]. Though I never met Marco I remember the whole thing starting. I took her to dinner one winter night in Siena, and she told me all about him. I remember having forebodings at the time – because, though they can't help it, those upper-class girls can be terribly and wantonly destructive. The Jasper Guinness[4] set in Tuscany has really a lot to answer for.

Plans? I can't begin to say. I want to go and hide and write. But can't decide whether to stay here or come back in April. Am feeling very pushed and pulled.

I really do have a mountain of mail – so here's all my dearest love. B

---

1. Richards ended up working at the Powerhouse Museum in Sydney.
2. Diana's daughter. Her Italian boyfriend, Marco Bellucci, a friend of Teddy Millington-Drake, had died in a car accident in Radda in Chianti. Chatwin wrote to her, the only person to do so. 'My dear Candy, A short and terribly inadequate note to say I am thinking of you in your sorrow. With all my love, Bruce.'
3. Lady Sophia Vane Tempest Stewart (*b*.1959), Marco's previous girlfriend.
4. Hon. Jasper Guinness (*b*.1954) lived near Siena.

To Paul Theroux

Postcard of 'The Breakaway' by Tom Roberts
(Australian artist, 1856–1931) | Sydney | Australia | 7 March 1983

All going well down-under – with a new Republican Prime Minister poised to cut the umbilical cord from the Mutterland. Have become interested in a very extreme situation – of Spanish monks in an Aboriginal Mission and am about to start sketching an outline. Anyway, the crisis of the 'shall-never-write-another-line' sort is now over. As always Bruce

In mid-March Chatwin flew to Jakarta to meet Jasper Conran, the young couturier to whom he had been introduced the previous summer at a restaurant in Greece. Twenty years younger than Chatwin, Jasper was more intellectually matched to him than was Donald Richards, whose relationship with Chatwin had petered out over the New Year. 'I was in love,' says Jasper. 'It was very much my first love. There was nobody like him. He was gorgeous and he knew it. To be clever, witty and bright is a devastating combination.' In Indonesia, the two of them swam out over the reefs, looked for Indian textiles and, in Java, visited the ninth-century Buddhist temple of Borobudur, parking outside a bat cave. On 6 April Chatwin returned to Sydney running a high fever.

To Deborah Rogers

c/o Ben Gannon | Sydney | Australia | 18 April 1983

Dearest Deborah,

I shall be back soon . . . Australia, I'm afraid, has been a bit of a flop. I feel a bit the same way as Lawrence in *Kangaroo*.[1] Flat, dried out,

1. 1923 novel by D. H. Lawrence (1885–1930) about his short residence in Western Australia and New South Wales, and reflecting his sense of persecution at the hand of the English.

alienated. None of the rich vein of fantasy you can tap by simply landing in S. America.

Oh Well! I have at least got one thing of inordinate fascination which can be worked into an essay. Then I'm rearing to go into more fiction. Sorry for this negative note: perhaps conditioned by the hideous food poisoning I got in Java last week.

To Lydia Livingstone[1]
Flat 7 | 77 Eaton Place | London | 4 June 1983

Darling Lydia,

Over a rather gloomy pre-election lunch (all the vegetables, in the middle of summer, were canned!) both Mr [James] Fox and I agreed that the best thing in Australia is Lydia Livingstone. His drama continues slowly: but I'm sure that, in his slow and thoughtful way, he's going to find a solution. Anyway, this is just to say how infuriating it is to think you're so far away BUT I am coming back. I had Mr H[2] on the phone for half an hour this morning from Melbourne. The money is there; the Aboriginal half of the cast is being 'rounded up' – or is that expression too strong? – and shooting is supposed to start on August 15th. I'll fly probably direct to Melbourne around the 5th. What I long for is that you should come to Coober Pedy in some nebulous but alluring capacity. You with your finely-tuned sense of the ridiculous would, I think, also enjoy it.

I'm sorry this is the shortest possible communication. I have myself ONE day to grapple with a mountain of turgid mail. I bought 40 air-letter forms and am now down to five. So I know you'll understand –

1. Sydney film producer; Chatwin was so taken with her name that he planned to call his projected 'Russian novel' *Lydia Livingstone*.
2. Werner Herzog (*b*.1942), German film director, was filming *Where the Green Ants Dream* in Coober Pedy, based on the Aboriginal Land Rights Movement and their lawsuit against a mining company. Chatwin had met Herzog in Melbourne on 8 March 1983, and talked for 48 hours non-stop, it seemed to Herzog. W.H.: 'It was a delirium, a torrent of storytelling. It went on and on, interrupted by only a few hours of sleep.'

this is not the best moment for enlightened correspondence. I feel quite awful about B[en] G[annon]. Two American cheques I gave him bounced because of the immense complications of my American account. Anyway it should be sorted out by now.

All my love to you.

XXXXX Bruce

On their visit to Ayer's Rock a year later, Chatwin would tell Salman Rushdie: 'I've been very unhappy lately and for a long time I couldn't work out why, and then I suddenly realised it was because I missed my wife. I sent her a telegram to meet me in Kathmandu and she sent a telegram back to say she would.' The way Chatwin and Elizabeth got back together did not in fact begin with a judicious exchange of telegrams but with a telephone call from Sydney. When Esquire *magazine offered Chatwin a commission 'to go anywhere I want', he telephoned Elizabeth at Homer End and asked her to suggest a place. 'He said he'd like to go to the South Sea Islands or to Nepal. So I said Nepal. I'd never been there.' He paid for his airfare to Kathmandu by reading* In Patagonia *in six instalments for ABC radio. In the middle of April the Australian novelist Murray Bail drove Chatwin to the Blue Mountains outside Sydney. 'I stepped back for him to admire the view, as you do up there. He looked at it for a second and then turned to me: "What's the date today? Next week I'll be at the base camp of Everest."' One year younger than Chatwin, the dry-witted and well-read Bail – he had worked on the* Times Literary Supplement *– was to become one of his most regular correspondents.*

To Murray Bail

Flat 7 | 77 Eaton Place | London | 4 June 1983

Dear Murray,

This is a very short communication. Before settling down to write, or at least to set down on paper, some of my Australian thoughts, I've set myself one day to grapple with a mountain of mail. I bought from the Sloane Square Post office 40 air-mail letters at 9am and at 7pm I am down to three. That says nothing about the English side.

I loved our drive in the country.[1] It should be the first of many more. I have in mind to rent a house in the Vaucluse for next winter, and if I do I'm going to try and tempt you over to Cézanne and Van Gogh country.

England, as usual, is in a soupy pre-Fascist condition. The weather has been vile. But I have been hardened and burnished by a month of trekking around the base of Mount Everest, so I'm up to it, for a bit.

Also I seem to be coming back to Australia in August, for five weeks, in connection with Werner Herzog's film,[2] and this will give me the opportunity to make another foray into the centre, at a less blistering time of year. Why don't you come?

In haste, and best to Margaret[3]

as always

Bruce

To Lisa Van Gruisen[4]

Flat 7 | 77 Eaton Place | London | 13 June 1983

Sunday

My darling Lisa,

It's hard to write this letter because I have deep physical ache to be back in Nepal. Gradually, over the past couple of weeks, I already

---

1. M.B. to B.C. 26 June 1983: 'I mentioned to S. Hazzard and Steegmuller we'd penetrated the Blue Mountains, but that our view of "Govett's Leap" was spoiled by a girl squeezing the pimples on the back of her fiancé's neck nearby, perhaps you noticed?'
2. E.C.: 'He didn't go back then. Werner offered him a bit part, but he decided that he didn't want to be in the film.'
3. Margaret Wordsworth (b.1944); m. 1965–91 Murray Bail.
4. Lisa van Gruisen (b.1951), m. 1986 Tenzin Cheogyal; marketing director Tiger Mountain Group Nepal 1974–97. She had organised the Chatwins' trek.

feel my knuckles whitening with impotent rage, and my guts twisting into knots. I had to write 75 letters. I had to cope with VAT. I watched the appalling spectacle of the election.[1] I was subjected to bullying demands to do this and that. *Esquire Magazine* wanted me to rewrite the piece in terms of a Yeti-hunt[2] – which as one damn well knows it wasn't. Altogether I feel shredded and sliced. Now to cap everything, I've lost somewhere between my flat and E's house my principal Australian notebook, without which I am truly sunk SUNK . . . SUNK . . . SUNK . . .

I am sorry to gripe on: but you do see the contrast with one's unalloyed happiness in Nepal, where I never for a second felt mildly annoyed. I'll write again soon, hopefully in a better frame of mind. If you want the flat for a week or so, let me know and I'll see if it works out. In the meantime there's a vague warning: it is JUST conceivable that my American bank which of course is completely computerised and therefore not amenable to the human will, will bounce the cheque. I have, in fact, in the account about 20,000 dollars, but I've been juggling the accounts round, and it may be that, despite instructions to honour all cheques, they will reject one on my old cheque book – without of course having provided me with a new one. If so, tell them not to be alarmed, because I'll fix it at once.

All my love to you. I AM sorry for this negative note . . . XXXX
B

1. On 9 June 1983 the Conservative Party under Margaret Thatcher won the most decisive election victory since that of Labour in 1945. Chatwin had been equally appalled when Harold Wilson's Labour Party hung on to power in October 1974. He had watched the result on Robin Lane Fox's television in London. R.L.F: 'I said, "This is so awful, I might emigrate." Chatwin said: "I can't think why anyone would want to live here in the first place."'
2. E.C.: 'We were near Gokyo-Ri, at 13,000 feet. We'd been in our tent and Bruce said, "Come over here. Look, what do you think of this?" There were tracks. I said, "Nah, can't be." I was hugely sceptical. Immediately, I thought: Someone with a broomstick and shoe can make those. But they weren't bootprints and they ended where the snow had melted off the bare rocks. There was no explanation.'

To Jorge Torres Zavaleta
Flat 7 | 77 Eaton Place | London | 16 June 1983

My dear Jorge,

It was lovely to get your letter, six months late, from John Sandoe.[1] And thank you for that excessively kind review. I have always been a bit mystified about the Book [*In Patagonia*]'s reception in Argentina, particularly since the Spanish translation, published by Sudamericana seems to have sunk without trace.

However, I do know the book is at least known. For example last week I heard that it was thought to be of consequence by Vargas Llosa,[2] to such an extent that there's a possibility I shall go on some TV chatshow[3] with him and, of all people, Borges,[4] who, to my astonishment, is apparently coming here for three days in the autumn. Could that be true?

The War horrified me rigid. Disregarding the very obvious Argentine right to the islands, and the obvious threat that the 'pirates' nest poses to Argentine security and ideals, it showed that the British are still the militaristic nation they always were; that they were itching to go to war with someone, no matter where; and that when the opportunity was offered, they went for it, blindly, without even contemplating the rights or wrongs. The *Belgrano* episode[5] has to be one of the most cowardly acts of the century, or else a fatuous bungle, but in neither

---

1. Independent bookshop set up by John Sandoe in Chelsea in 1957.
2. Mario Vargas Llosa (*b*.1936), Peruvian novelist.
3. *Frank Delaney*, BBC2, broadcast on 24 October 1983.
4. Jorge Luis Borges (1899–1986), Argentine short-story writer and essayist. 'What is wonderful about his writing is the compression of his thought,' Chatwin said on the programme. 'They say Borges lives in a world of imagination and dreams, but he's central to life.' His influence is evident in Chatwin's 1979 story 'The Estate of Maximilian Tod'.
5. The *General Belgrano* was an Argentine Navy cruiser sunk by HMS *Conqueror* on 2 May during the Falklands War with the loss of 323 lives. In notes for an unpublished essay on this episode, Chatwin wrote: 'I cling to the archaic idea that unjustifiable killing in peace or war eventually rebounds on the killer. The dead do haunt the living. There is such a thing as blood guilt.'

case forgiveable. I agree with you: Mrs T.[1] and Galtieri[2] are the mirror image of one another; and had the gamble not come off, as it might very easily not have, she would be where Galtieri is today . . .

I'm prostrated by paperwork. I had to buy 60 air-letter forms on my return, and wrote them all. Yours is the second batch. I've had a minor literary success, well and good, but what must it be like to have a major success? I'd like to think that there was still a place for me, an Englishman, in Patagonia. I'll try and get your story from Maxi and look forward to reading it. Chiquita [Astor] told me it was marvellous when I last saw her in December.

My contribution to the war was to find myself inveighing against it on Italian TV, where I suggested that no encouragement should be given to either belligerent by the Common Market Community. Next day Italy refused to renew economic sanctions – for which of course I was roundly castigated by the British Embassy. Someone even suggested I should be put in the Tower of London.

So there we are. I'd love to see you soon . . .

as always, Bruce

To Nicholas Shakespeare[3]
Flat 7 | 77 Eaton Place | London | [August 1983]

Can you, please, somehow, by the 28th Sept get me a copy of the Vargas Llosa *War at the End of the World* – in Spanish or whatever. This is about the war of Canudos about which I can wax eloquent – having been there. Etc. B.C.

---

1. Margaret Thatcher (*b*.1925), British Prime Minister 1979–90.
2. General Leopoldo Galtieri (1926–2003), President of Argentina 1981–2.
3. Nicholas Shakespeare (*b*.1957), author and broadcaster, had invited Chatwin to appear on BBC2's *Frank Delaney* with Borges and Vargas Llosa.

To Murray Bail

Flat 7|77 Eaton Place|London|3 August 1983

Dear Murray,

Alas! I'm not coming. These past three months have been little short of a nightmare. I feel I've been got at in all directions, to do things I didn't want to do etc. So in the end my only recourse was to cancel everything, and try and get down to some work. The only thing I have done is to accept an invitation to come to the Adelaide Festival in March: and that makes me feel somewhat less bad. Then, hopefully, I shall have quite a lot on paper, which will make sense of my return trip.

The weather in England has been tropical; my flat unbearable: so I've been holing up in a mediaeval tower in Wales.

Incidentally, is the pulped book on songlines, to which you referred, Mountford's *Nomads of the Desert* (or whatever the title)?[1] If so, I know it – but if not I'd be glad to have the reference. Oddly enough, it was the Germans who first cottoned onto the idea of the songlines: one of my favourite anthropologists is a Father Worms.

I've sent for *Correction* from New York. All of Bernhard[2] – or nearly all – is translated into French: though of course not into English. According to an article in the T.L.S. by George Steiner, fifty copies of the American edition of C. sold. So till March then, or maybe a bit before, and a thousand regrets it can't be sooner, unless of course you care to take a foray in this direction.

Love to Margaret, as always Bruce

---

1. Charles P. Mountford, *Nomads of the Australian Desert* (1976). Bail had written to Bruce: 'The entire edition was pulped after Aborigines complained that it revealed secrets of dreamtime etc.'
2. Thomas Bernhard (1931–89), Austrian playwright and novelist.

To Kath Strehlow[1]
Flat 7 | 77 Eaton Place | London | 24 August 1983

My dear Kathie,

We seem to have missed each other by several continents. I am, however, coming back to Adelaide, having been invited to come by the Festival in March. I want, too, to spend some more time in the Centre when it gets colder in April and May. I am writing away like a loonie. I have absorbed vast quantities of literature on Aboriginals; and my admiration for T.S. grows and grows. Sometimes, when reading *Songs of Central Australia*, I feel I'm reading Heidegger or Wittgenstein.

The real scandal, frankly, is that *Aranda Traditions* is out of print. It is a 20th century lynch-pin: you only have to look at the work of Levi-Strauss to realise this. I'm sure that something must be possible.

Incidentally, there's a man here, at Durham University, called Bob Layton[2], who was something to do with the Ayer's Rock case. I don't know what his role was, or really what his line is, but his enthusiasm for T.S. matches my own.

Let's keep in touch,
as always,
Bruce

I came back to a legal can of worms!

To David Mason
Flat 7 | 77 Eaton Place | London | 30 August 1983

Send a PC with your phone no. It's <u>conceivable</u> that I may come and spend Christmas with my wife's family in Geneseo NY (not 30 miles from you). If so, I would need some LOCAL moral support. As always Bruce.

1. Kathleen Stuart m.1972 Theodor Strehlow.
2. Robert Layton, Professor of Anthropology.

Their month in the Himalayas marked the beginning of Chatwin's rapprochement with Elizabeth. They had come back from Nepal together and there was no further talk of separation. Chatwin used Homer End as a base and treated it as home. 'He'd open up his boxes and play with his things, or sit outside under the cherry tree and write, which he was never able to do at Holwell. And it was very close to London. He'd take his little 2CV with a surfboard on top to the local reservoir at Eynsham, to Spain, to Greece, everywhere. It practically never came off. He loved it because it wasn't flying, but as close as you could get.'

To Elizabeth Chatwin
Chora | Patmos | Greece | 28 September 1983

Dearest E,

Most successful time in Patmos – in that, at last! I've found the right formula for the book: It's to be called, simply, OF THE NOMADS – *A discourse.* And it takes the form of about six excursions into the outback with a semi-imaginary character called Sergei during which the narrator and He have long conversations. Sergei is incredibly well-informed, sympathetic but extremely wary of generalisations – and is always ready to put the spoke into an argument. The narrator is a relentless talker/arguer. I've done two chapters and it really seems to work in that it gives me the necessary flexibility. Needless to say the models for such an enterprise are Plato's *Symposium* and the *Apology.* But so what? I've never seen anything like it in modern literature, a complete hybrid between fiction and philosophy: so here goes.

Patmos beautiful as ever but we now have Clarissa Avon[1] who, to my mind, casts rather a pall over the atmosphere: so I'm off for a couple of days to the dreaded Beatrice [von Rezzori] where Kässl [Kasmin] is celebrating his birthday:[2] then back to the horrors of

1. Clarissa Eden, Countess of Avon (*b.*1920), widow of Sir Anthony Eden, Prime Minister from 1955–57.
2. The Rezzoris had a house on Rhodes.

London, to Stockholm, back to London for the Borges, and then to the Tower. The cottage[1] went for £17,000: so I chickened out. It was quite wonderful in its way: but the responsibility and hassle of leaving it empty were just too much: and I would, definitely, prefer a bolt-hole in the Mediterranean, wouldn't you. I got so carried away by the book that the search, this time, was impossible: but I think one day next year, we should go on a tour of the islands and pick which one; then rent a place to make sure, and while renting, if possible, buy.

I should with luck be able to come to America around Christmas. I'm certainly not taking on anything, though, that's going to disrupt the flow. If only I can get this one off my mind, it will be an enormous relief and I might start living a relatively normal life thereafter.

I must say I'm itching to be back in Nepal.

I'll have to go down to Homer if only to get my loden coat: apparently it's freezing in Stockholm. *On the B.H.* has apparently come out in Germany to one or two rave reviews.

Much love to Lisa [van Gruisen]. I hope all your charges behaved themselves.[2]

xxxxB

To Kath Strehlow
Flat 7 | 77 Eaton Place | London | 9 October 1983

Dear Kathie

As I think I've told you, I shall – God willing! – be holding forth at the Adelaide Festival in March. Can we postpone the discussion of the foreword or whatever till then?[3]

I am absolutely delighted to think that you would have me as a fellow of the Strehlow Foundation – and, of course, accept.

1. A cottage near Hay-on-Wye.
2. E.C: 'A group I took to the Himalayas, a 22-day tour that started in Pakistan.'
3. To Strehlow's *Songs of Central Australia*. He never wrote it.

Forgive this scribbled note. I've just been in Sweden and Finland for a fortnight and am trying to catch up with a mountain of mail. I'll write when I have more news.

As always Bruce

To Murray Bail
The Tower | Scethrog | Brecon | Powys | 20 October 1983

My dear Murray,

All well here, but I've been sauntering here and there on entertaining, but fairly fruitless jaunts. First to Greece, where I actually made a proper start on the new work. Then to Sweden and Finland, where my books came out. The Finnish title of *On the Black Hill*, by the time it had been changed and translated, was *Erottamattomat* – which of course was the title I'd been looking for all the time! Then to cap everything, I went on a TV chat show in London with Borges and Mario Vargas Llosa. Llosa and I share some of the same ground, in that we have both written about a Brazilian village called Uaua:[1] we were even there in the same month. I thought it'd be rather a good thing to chat about the dreariness of Uaua: but he thought otherwise, and the moment the cameras were turned on him, he turned from being lively and entertaining into the WRITER-AS-PUBLIC-FIGURE! Of course, we both dutifully held our tongues when the Magus of B.A. appeared, and any attempt to have a chat there-after was drowned in a flow of beautiful 17th Century English and beautiful Castilian verse.[2]

Blast the Madison Avenue Bookshop! I still haven't had *Correction* yet, despite a reminder. Not a hope of getting it in this country. I suppose I better read it in the Edition Gallimard. George S[teiner] is inclined to exaggerate, you know – though don't for God's sake say I said so. I stayed with him the other day in Cambridge, on my way down from Scotland.

1. *The War of the End of the World* (1981).
2. On the show, in the moment before Borges came on, Chatwin enthused: 'He's a genius. You can't go anywhere without packing a Borges. It's like taking your tooth-brush' – to which Borges, overhearing this on the monitor, muttered: 'How unhygienic.'

He thought I had been with Updike et al. at the Edinburgh festival, but I said (revealing my fantastic error before I actually said it): 'No I've been doing something much more atavistic. Shooting stags!' – which, I'm afraid, was true.[1] It had the most terrible effect; and I'm sure that no matter what I say and do, he'll look on me, in his heart of hearts, as a murderer. Be that as it may, I've shot stags since I was a boy. And though I say it, I'm a good clean shot – when it comes to stags, and nothing else.

I secretly dread the Adelaide Festival. They wrote to me the other day, and said that 'since I fit into no known category' they are going to programme 'An Hour with Bruce Chatwin.' Lord save us! What shall I say?

I'm writing this in the half dark, in the mediaeval tower I've borrowed in the middle of the River Usk. Henry Vaughan[2] used to live in the ruined cottage in the field a hundred yards away. The typewriter is atrocious: so I can't go over any of the mistakes. My progress, if such it can be called, is equally atrocious. Dismal. The novel, if such it be, consists of the narrator (myself) and a Russian immigrant to Melbourne (based loosely on someone I met) having a long drawn-out conversation in the shade of a mulga tree. I think perhaps I should come and sit under a mulga tree in the hope that progress might speed up. Or would it? Australia, I find, even on the most superficial level, is extremely difficult to describe. More soon. Love to Margaret. Should be there by mid Feb.

To Elizabeth Chatwin
The Tower | Scethrog | Brecon | Powys | 20 October 1983

Dear E.,

So here I am alone in the Tower, which is, I have to say, a lovely place to work, the only distraction being a view of a white farmhouse

1. Not quite. Chatwin was staying with David Heathcoat-Amory at Glenfernate. At the critical moment, with the stag in range, he refused to take the rifle and pushed it away. 'No, I'd like you to shoot it.'
2. Henry Vaughan (1621–95), Metaphysical poet.

through a slit window. The new book at least exists as an entity and that, I suppose, is the main thing. The Swedish and Finnish (!) journey went off very well. I was definitely upstaged by the Golding Nobel Prize[1] which was announced at the same time: but I was so pleased to be there that nothing got me down. The title of *On the Black Hill* in Finnish is *Erottamattomat*, which I think should be the title all round. It's published there in a wildly distinguished list called the yellow Library – Faulkner, Hemingway, Joyce, Bellow – that kind of list: so I felt immensely flattered.

On the strength of this, and of the movie-rights being sold (not for much admittedly!) I bought myself in Stockholm an <u>incredibly</u> beautiful c. 1760 Swedish crystal chandelier[2] which comes out of a manor in Southern Sweden for which it was made. God knows what to do with it, because I'm not sure it'll look quite right in the flat: but my fantasies about Sweden are somehow connected with a lit chandelier and a cray-fish party on a half-dark summer night. I propose to do something to pay for half of it. It's not over big either.

Otherwise, nothing, except that I am inundated to write forewords for this and that. One could easily develop into an exclusive foreword-merchant: for a photograph book on Machu Picchu; for Clemente's[3] paintings of S. India; for the Sierra Club Calendar; and latest for Jackie O[nassis]'s book on Indian costume. By the last, I have to say, I was tempted in that it involved a trip to India in January. (Apparently the idea was not only hers but Mapu[4] somebody's who runs the Ahmedabad Museum). However, since Cary W[elch] was in on the act (it being in connection with the Met. Costume Institute etc.), I told Jackie I'd phone him for saying yes or no. C.W. was relentlessly hostile to the idea: you could literally feel him squirming on the other end of the line. So I chucked, and anyway the timing of it was horrendous, and might have

1. The English novelist William Golding (1911–93) had won the 1983 Nobel Prize.
2. Notebook: 'The old Swedish gentleman who told me "The Swedes are the only people who understand about chandeliers. The way ice hangs from a tree."' E.C.: 'Ever since Bruce stayed with the Bratts as a schoolboy he had been longing for a Swedish chandelier.'
3. Francesco Clemente (b.1952), Italian artist.
4. Maharaja of Kapurthala at the Calico Museum of Textiles.

put this book back six months. I must say she was extremely nice about it when I called. Your car is not ready yet, another three weeks or so; because it needs a new part. I'm not going to London if I can help it, and so don't need a car. I intend to go slogging on till December 15th and then I'll take a break. My working year was so mucked up, I think it's the only thing to do.

John B[etjeman] had a heart attack and very nearly died[1]. It was national news for a week, and now he's better.

XXXX B

To Ivry Freyberg
The Tower | Scethrog | Brecon | Powys | 3 November 1983

So glad it wasn't too embarrassing. I had no idea what I was doing in the programme at all. xxx B

To Elisabeth Sifton
Postcard of 'Mexikanische Miniatur-Maske aus der olmekischen Zeit' from the Schatzkammer der Residenz, München.
as from Flat 7 | 77 Eaton Place | London | 6 December 1983

How's this for a really hideous-and-marvellous object! The hands are gold, green enamelled. The 'work' goes laboriously on – and is <u>very</u> strange but now manageable. I can begin to see the end: but not before I've gone to S. Africa <u>AND</u> back to Australia Feb/March. I miss you. I almost came to N.Y. the other day, but funked it.

Much love,

Bruce

---

1. Betjeman died the following year.

To Murray Bail

Flat 7|77 Eaton Place|London|[December 1983]

March'll be upon us before one can shout. I am coming to Australia from – of all places – South Africa, where I have to go to meet a man[1]. It depends on what happens there and whether I make a trip with him into the Kalahari – as to whether I come to Sydney after March 7 or before. I'll call you, I think, sometime in January: then we can make a tentative plan.

As always, Bruce

To Shirley Hazzard

as from; 77 Eaton Place: but written nr Siena|[January 1984]

My dear Shirley,

... It's late at night; there's a peppering of snow on the ground, and the central heating's been turned off. I may easily be driven under the eiderdown before too long.

The piece of work which I gaily hoped to complete in a matter of months is proving far more intractable than my worst fears. Last January, in the Outback, I met an incredibly moving character whose job was to map the sacred sites of the Aborigines, especially those which might lie in the way of the new Alice-to-Darwin railway. He was the son of Russian immigrants; and when a policeman discovered his origins, he said, of us both, 'What did I tell you? A Pom and a Com.' Anyway, I went with this Anatoly on a surveying expedition, together with a group of Aboriginals, and on three successive nights, we sat up by the camp-fire discussing everything that came into our heads. Anatoly, I might say, had Cossack blood, and so was in a position to discuss my major obsession: the nomads.

I have, left over from my foray into the academic world in the late

1. Dr Charles Kimberlin ('Bob') Brain (*b*.1931), South African palaeontologist, director of the Transvaal Museum and author of *The Hunters or the Hunted?* described by Chatwin as 'the most compelling detective story I have ever read'.

Sixties, the draft of a projected book on nomadism.[1] I had written an essay which discussed whether the nomads were necessarily the destroyers of Civilisation, or whether they were the necessary impulse behind the First Civilisations; whether, in fact, the nomads gave to all Civilisations their restless and expansive character. It is not an angle that many historians have dared to tackle: I, of course, am completely incompetent to do so. Yet the subject is so compelling, I cannot leave it alone. For once you enter the world of nomadism, you have to tackle Renan's dictum, 'Le désert est monothéiste' – and from there the search for nomads becomes the search for God.

All last summer, I experimented, wrote, tore up, wriggled this way and that. Then on Patmos, I had the brainwave – revelation if such it was – that the way to do it was to hold an imaginary dialogue with Anatoly (who would, of course, become a fictional character!). Now you see what I've landed myself in for. I've done eighty passable pages; but as for the rest, a long, long tunnel ahead.

To give the whole thing greater veracity, I decided to go back to the Centre, and reconstruct our journey amid those scenes of hopeless desolation. Yet I have found, as I write, that there is something immensely moving about the dried-up continent, a place which has far from yielded its secrets and may yet surprise us. Anyway, when I got the invitation to go to the Adelaide Festival, I was mighty pleased.

As for the year of disgrazia '84 that, too, may surprise us – in that it does seem to have made people aware of the hollowness of the doom-mongers. For my own part, I am going to try, this year, to do my meagre share to add a small voice of dissent.

Fifteen years ago, with Vietnam in swing, I became aware of how the politicians were using some so-called 'facts' of our evolutionary past to justify their own squalor. Among these 'facts' was the idea that the human species had begun its career in cannibalism and bloodlust. The evidence for this was supposed to come from the Cave of Peking Man (since destroyed) and some caves in the Transvaal, which their

---

1. E.C.: 'Margharita had pulled the manuscript out of a wastepaper bin. "I'm sure he didn't mean to throw this away."'

excavator, an Australian called Raymond Dart[1], interpreted as the Original Human Bloodbath. Recently, a man called Brain, now Director of the Transvaal Museum, has reinterpreted the evidence, and has found that all the damage to the bones was the work of one particular (now extinct) carnivore, known to science as Dinofelis. There is, he suggests, the possibility that this creature was a professional Man-eater: in other words, by becoming human, we had to live and defend ourselves from this beast. The fact that we did so successfully is perhaps a measure of the Original Threat to our existence. Since then, it seems to me at least, the story of humanity has been the invention of monsters that do not exist. I put this rather schematically, because – please remember – it is very late at night. Anyway. I am sufficiently fascinated to fly to South Africa next week to try and make sense of the evidence for myself. Hopefully, I may be able to incorporate it into the final, imaginary discussion with Anatoly, under a gum tree.

Incidentally, our discussions took place at Neutral Station, N.T. I'm not sure that I can't play with 'Neutral Station' as a title . . .

If you need a billet in London, you're welcome to the above, providing no one's there. I suggest you call Jasper Conran at work 01-437-xxxx. He could arrange for you to have a key.

I'm thinking of quitting London for a bit, and of finding some kind of billet in Tuscany. One can work so much better there.

Much love, Bruce

'Australia is Hell' Chatwin wrote in a lost postcard to his Italian publisher Roberto Calasso. In another lost postcard from Australia, to Paul Theroux, he wrote:'You must come here. The men are awful, like bits of cardboard, but the women are splendid.' One woman he had met on his visit to Alice Springs in February 1983 was Petronella Vaarzon-Morel, an anthropologist of Dutch descent who

1. Australian anthropologist (1893–1988) known for his 1924 discovery of the first fossil of *Australopithecus africanus*, 'flesh-eating, shell-cracking and bone-breaking, cave-dwelling apes.' Notebooks: 'At his 90th birthday party I watched him swinging about a hematite dumb-bell with which he hoped to keep himself in shape.'

had worked on Walbiri land claims. They had a genuine rapport; on Chatwin's part, amounting almost to an infatuation. 'He made it clear he found me attractive,' she says. He would rework Vaarzon-Morel into the idealised characters of Marian and Wendy in The Songlines. *'The moment I set eyes on Wendy I could hear myself saying, "Not another one!" Not another of these astonishing women. She was tall, calm, serious yet amused, with golden hair done up in braids.'*

To Petronella Vaarzon-Morel
Donnini | Florence | Italy | 8 January 1984

My dear Pet,

I am terribly sorry for sloping off without warning and not coming back – as I fully intended. The truth was I got hideously ill in Java, with amoebas and all that – so ill, in fact, that for a moment they thought I had cholera. And though I did go back to Sydney for a week or two, I was in a considerably <u>lowered</u> condition.

But I'm coming back. By a stroke of luck the Adelaide Festival offered to pay the fare out: so on March 7 or thereabouts I'll have to sing for my supper, and then I'll be sure to come again to Alice.

I'm writing something very odd – which although set under a gum tree somewhere in the MacDonnells has nothing much to do with Central Australia. No, that is wrong, it has everything and nothing to do with Central Australia and I need desperately to know certain things.

What do you think the chances of being able to arrange a trip up to Kintore?[1] I missed the chance of going out of sheer stupidity and regret it. I'll probably be coming to Alice with a friend, Salman Rushdie,[2] who wants to go on a short jaunt before going back to England.

1. Aboriginal community 530km west of Alice Springs, renamed Cullen in *The Songlines*. Between 18–30 March 1984 Chatwin stayed in a caravan there at the invitation of the storekeeper, Rob Novak, whom he met at the Adelaide Festival.
2. British-Indian novelist and essayist (*b*.1947).

As for me, I want to stay in Australia for months and months. I imagine I will stay at the dreaded Melanka Lodge[1] . . . I do hope you're THERE! <u>Never</u> have I caught a bus in such a DIZZYING way.[2]

Give love to Toly,[3]

Bruce

To Tom Maschler

Kardamyli | Messenia | Greece | 29 January 1984

Dear Tom,

A quick note to tell you that I've gone to ground in Greece for the winter. I had thought of going to your old stamping-ground, Chania. But the only flat available was the top of the Stavroudakis/Haldeman[4] set-up, and I thought it really too sinister and depressing in its implications – to say nothing of the street noise below – and instead have found an ideal spot on the Mani, a few hundred yards from Paddy and Joan Leigh-Fermor.

I won't say anything about the work in hand, except that I work at it at least six hours a day and am pressing forwards rather than procrastinating – at least, I hope so!

The grape-vine tells me you're in fine fettle.

1. A back-packer's hostel in Alice Springs.
2. P.V-M.: 'I remember him embracing me, jumping on to the bus to Broome . . . There was a certain sense in which he was intoxicated by the place, the things he had found out, and I was part of it.'
3. Anatoly Sawenko (*b.*1950), Australian-born son of Ukrainian immigrants, then a consultant to the Aboriginal land rights body of the Central Land Council; Chatwin based Arkady, the central character in *The Songlines*, on him.
4. In 1963 Maschler had published *The Sun's Attendant*, a first novel by Charles Haldeman, an American whom he had met in Chania. T.M.: 'We ended up buying jointly, with a friend of Charles' called Stavroudakis, a flat in a tall Venetian building overlooking the water on No 1 Angel Street. One year in the early 1970s Charles was away in Athens, and his boyfriend, a beautiful Cretan boy, took it upon himself to take an axe and chop through the head of Allen Bole, a homosexual would-be American writer and friend of Chatwin's who lived in an apartment across the way. I never went back to the flat after.'

To Lydia Livingstone
Flat 7|77 Eaton Place|London|[January 1984]

Thinking of you often if not always. And now, next week, I take the first leg of my return journey towards you – if somewhat obliquely – just to Johannesburg and the Kalahari desert – then on March 2 to Sydney xxxx Bruce

On 1 February 1984 Chatwin stayed with Bob Brain in Pretoria. 'B. quiet, meditative, self-effacing with impeccable manners,' Chatwin wrote in his notebook. The next morning he accompanied him to the cave at Swartkrans in the Sterkfontein valley near Johannesburg. Brain's classic text on early human behaviour was based on his excavations here.

What happened on that day, 2 February, would reverberate in Chatwin's mind for the remainder of his life. 'Around 3.30 Bob came back from the dig with a piece of bone which he said was "highly suggestive". Antelope long bone: which layered beige white on the exterior and black on the inside, broken in 2. With it were some flecked fragments – speckled with manganese staining. He had, he said, so often searched for use of fire. It had been found by George [Moenda, Brain's foreman] lying alongside an arrangement of 3 stones 6–7" across and was slightly cracked. The question is whether this could conceivably be the hearth ... He had tried so often, had so many false alarms, that one must always expect the worst. At the same time he was visibly excited.'

To Bob Brain
Le Thalonet|Johannesburg|South Africa|[February 1984]

Dear Bob,

I found the following in the *Muquaddimah* of Ib'n Khaldun (the Father of modern history) ca. 1400 AD. 'The animal desire of attacking others and destroying them or being their master confronts man with the need to defend himself against wild animals which would destroy him if he lived alone. Man can protect himself only through organised communal defence. Instead of physical power, of which he possesses less than many other animals, he has to utilise the power in which he excels, namely the power of thought and practical reason. These faculties help him to become dexterous in the shaping of tools and to organise communities for producing them.'

If I remember the passage correctly (for all I have found is an extract) it goes on something like that 'in conditions of surplus, when the needs both of the individual and of the community have been surpassed, the war of all against all breaks out with the weapons devised to protect man from the beasts.'[1]

I had a wonderful day at Swartkrans: and, as luck would have it, I met Alun Hughes[2] at the tea-party who took me today to Sterkfontein. Yes, indeed! Quite another style! But most instructive. I'll hope to see you, if I may, around the 24th of the month. In any case I'd like very much to come again to Pretoria to see the museum at great length. I'd be most grateful, too, to have a copy of the photo of the juvenile skull and leopard canines . . .

I stupidly left a pair of shoes in the house. But please don't worry as they were extremely uncomfortable. I could perhaps get them on my return.

My very best wishes and thanks to your wife. As always, Bruce.

To Francis Wyndham
Holiday Inn | Botswana | 15 February 1984

This trip has proved really abortive – except for the S. African archaeologist/zoologist who should be given a Nobel Prize on the spot. Otherwise, in Botswana – heat, dust, spiders – and NO Bushmen.

Much love, Bruce

1. Chatwin had remembered it well. Ibn Khaldun's actual words: 'in moments of surplus, when the needs of the individual are surpassed, the war of all against all breaks out with equipment designed to defend himself against wild beasts.'
2. Alun Hughes supervised excavations at the nearby limestone caves of Sterkfontein where, in 1976, he found the cranium of Homo habilis, c 1.5 million years old.

Staying beside the Zambezi river with Kasmin, who had joined him in Botswana, Chatwin continued to dwell on the conversations he had had with Brain. About Birmingham, where Chatwin had grown up and from where Brain's father, finding England restrictive, had departed for the Cape. About Brain's son Ted, who died at 14 months when he choked on a piece of apple, teaching Brain – painfully – to live his life as though each day might be his last. Moved to review his own life, Chatwin wrote in his notebook: 'And in the morning while the car was in dock we sat on a fallen tree with a mat of weeds, looking out across the Zambezi which appeared to be being blown back upstream. The District Commissioner's House/mine recruiting camp with its mosquito screens and terraced gardens gone to seed. To think that I, in my schoolboy dreams, pictured such a place as the place in which I would spend my life, in khaki shorts, with Shakespeare and Shelley, dreaming of a leafy Warwickshire which no longer existed. I would go out in a hat . . . Had a dream of my parents, Margharita in her blue dress with the orange and green cummerbund, and Charles in tails, dancing in the moonlight. I felt that, in their way, they're the most romantic couple on the earth.'

To Gertrude Chanler

South Africa | as from: 30 Victoria Street | Pott's
Point | Sydney | Australia | 2 March 1984

My Dear Gertrude,

For the first day in a month of feverish coming and going I've got the time to sit down and write a letter or two. I was a little bit apprehensive about going to South Africa in the first place: but I must say things there are not at all what gets reported in the international press: some better, some worse, but never <u>bland</u>. As Lib may have told you, I came to talk to a man who wrote a book about the Earliest Man, and I've had perhaps the most stimulating discussions in my life. Prof. Brain has, for the past 20 years, been excavating a cave near Johannesburg in which you find at the lower level (Date: around 2 million years) a situation in which the ancestors of Man were literally dragged there and eaten by an extinct giant cat called Dinofelis. Then in the upper level, Man (the First) suddenly takes control and the Beast is banished.

The only way to inhabit a cave, which is also inhabited by predators, is to deter them with fire. And though archaeologists have been hunting for fire in Prehistoric Africa for thirty years now, the earliest hearth they could find was only 70,000 years old. On the one day I visited Brain's cave, at Swartkrans, I remembered how nice it would be to discover the human use of fire in the cave. Half an hour later, we excavated a bit of blackened bone. Brain, who is a most undemonstrative man, said: 'That bone is remarkably suggestive!' – which indeed it was. It turns out I was present at the uncovering of a human hearth, probably dated around 1,200,000 years old. The earliest by 700,000 years.

I'm off to Australia in the morning, where I have to give a talk at the Adelaide Festival next week (on what Lord knows!) and then I'm off into the Outback again for four weeks or so. My new book is a very slow operation, but if it comes off I think it could be very unusual.

I gather from Lib that we're coming over in the summer, and look forward immensely: but I certainly didn't want to wait to thank you for those two magnificent French goblets, in which we drank your health!

I hope to have something substantial to show to my publishers by then. There have been fearful upheavals at Viking Press, though I hope they all simmer down.

All my love to you, Bruce

Another Australian woman whom Chatwin admired was Ninette Dutton (1923–2007), an enameller and short-story writer, and one of the organisers of the Adelaide Festival. He had met her in Adelaide the previous January, after which he wrote in his notebook: 'Dined last night with Geoffrey Dutton and his wife Nina – a glamorous late middle aged couple – she particularly stylish in the manner of the 40's reminded me a little of Magouche. Grey hair and dangly earrings. Used to own a big station – Anlaby – which seems to have gone the way of all great landowners. He described by Bob

Hughes as "mildly rebellious scion of old grazing stock" . . . We discussed the whole Falklands affair with sorrow and disgust. A lot of booze. Gave me names of a variety of things and people to see in the North.' One year on, with her husband having walked out on her, Ninette was planning a thousand-mile drive to Queensland for a book on the wildflowers of Australia. She offered to take Chatwin along, so that he could see something of the back country, once he had finished his Aboriginal research at Kintore in late March. Elizabeth says: 'She became a muse to Bruce.'

Also at the Adelaide Festival, Chatwin met Anne-Marie Mykyta, whose 16-year old daughter Juliet was one of eight women murdered by two serial killers, James Miller and Christopher Worrell in what became known as the Truro murders. On 21 January 1977 Juliet was waiting at a bus stop when Worrell offered her a lift home. Instead, he drove her to Port Wakefield where he tied her up and strangled her. Mykyta had told the story in It's a Long Way to Truro *(1981). Chatwin was introduced to her because he wanted to speak to Ukrainians in Australia. 'My husband's family is Ukrainian so I invited Bruce to our house to meet my husband and his brother and his wife. The evening turned out very differently.' A television programme,* 60 Minutes, *had recently interviewed Miller and Mykyta concerning a book that Miller had written while in prison. 'During the evening a number of people rang begging/ ordering me to stop Miller's book from being published. I had already taken legal advice and knew there was nothing I could do, but in the end when Betty Ann Kelvin (whose son was murdered) started screaming at me, I started screaming back. My husband took the phone from me, I walked out of the room and Bruce followed me.*

'"You promised me a copy of your book," he said.

'I signed a copy of It's a Long Way to Truro *(which is about the impact on us of Juliet's death) and he signed a copy of* On the Black Hill.

'Over the few days left we spent time together every day, just very quietly, and planned to meet when he got back from Central Australia. We liked each other very much.'

To Anne-Marie Mykyta
Alice Springs | Australia | 14 March 1984

My dear Anne-Marie,

A quick note from the middle of nowhere to thank you for your beautifully conceived and, in the end, heartening book. Your courage is unsurpassed. Salman and I are having an enjoyable time in the Centre, but, needless to say, wherever I go in the desert, I always nearly get washed away. Love Bruce

After the Adelaide Festival Chatwin and Rushdie flew to Alice Springs where Chatwin introduced Rushdie to the characters who would reappear, without much disguise, in The Songlines; *he also introduced Rushdie (by telephone) to Robyn Davidson, author of* Tracks, *an introduction that was to have far-reaching consequences. They hired a four-wheel-drive Toyota and drove to Ayer's Rock. Rushdie went on to Sydney to meet Davidson; Chatwin to the Aboriginal settlement at Kintore. At the end of March, he joined Ninette Dutton for a five-day drive from Adelaide to Boona where they stayed with the poet Pam Bell, who became yet one more in the line of Australian women who admired Chatwin as much as he them. Bell listened to Chatwin talk about his experience with the Aborigines. 'He was desperately trying to go to the centre. It was the most important thing for him and he realised half way through he wasn't going to be able to do it, he was excluded. You have to* earn *mystery. It's only lovers who get there.'*

To Shirley Hazzard
Postcard, The New Moree Hotel | Newell Highway | Moree | Australia |
5 April 1984

I hope your aesthetic sensibilities will be OUTRAGED by this card – but this is, after all, the heart of New South Wales . . . [Ninette Dutton's handwriting] We are thinking and talking of you very much as we career across vast areas of this country while I search for the smallest of wild flowers. We hope to reach Cape York and see some Aboriginal painting. Much love, Nin, Bruce

To Shirley Hazzard
Flat 7|77 Eaton Place|London|[May 1984]

My dear Shirley,

Just back from Sydney to find your wonderful letter of January. I discovered the use of sleeping pills for a long distance flight, and considering the fact that I failed to notice Singapore or Kuala Lumpur or Abu Dhabi, they must have worked. I am only feeling <u>slightly</u> hazy the day after. I enjoyed Oz far more this time than the last. The Adelaide Festival was a little like going to a clinic for a week, in that there were always young, encouraging, nurse-like figures at one's elbow, with gentle words to say it was time to do this or that. I had never been to such an occasion; hope never to go again; but found that to have done it once was all right. I still maintain what I thought last year: that it is the interior of Australia which determines what goes on around the periphery. At a dinner in Sydney, a very intelligent man picked a quarrel with me; said he never met Aborigines; implied that Aborigines were irrelevant to the Australian situation. I then found voice and said that the Aborigines, or their destruction, were as important as the Penal Colony in the Australian consciousness. The enormous riches of Australia are generated by the heartland; and by the same token that your Sydney intellectual has never met an Aborigine, he has never seen the iron-ore trains approaching Port Headland – without which, of course, the cities of the fringe would not, in their prosperity, exist. But as a place, it is immensely intractable to the pen. How few writers really get the texture of, say, a small town in the Outback! Randolph Stow,[1] for Western Australia, is the exception. Why also am I moved, almost to tears, by the women, and indifferent to the men? Except, I may add, by the drunk truckie at a pub famous for its red-neck attitudes, who, when taunted for having abused his Aboriginal

1. Julian Randolph Stow (*b*.1935), Australian anthropologist, librettist and novelist.

wife, tried to explain to his tormentors the immense elaboration of Aboriginal society and when completely lost for words, shouted, 'I tell you, it's so com . . . fuckin' . . . plex!'

There is one astonishing film on the Bakhtiari nomads called <u>Grass</u>, made by Americans in the Thirties. I'm not sure it's the one your friends saw. I suspect not. The word 'rhythm' is the key to all: one has to remember that the cantillation of rabbis; the to-ing and fro-ing of the Passover and, for that matter, all the prostrations of the Islamic Hadj – are the ritualised versions of an original nomadic journey.[1]

I found South Africa of enormous interest. What on earth is to be made of a country in which one can be jailed for marrying a Vietnamese wife, yet be an honoured member of Afrikanderdom if married to a Japanese? The amazing aspect of S.A. is that Apartheid can no longer be seen as anything but a joke, a sick, black joke. Often, in Australia, one heard of South Africans who could no longer support the brutality etc, and had come to a better place. Yet my friends, mostly Jews, I might say, who have to put up with the indignities and yet fight inch by inch to make the system yield, were contemptuous of the runaways. There's nothing bland about South Africa: and if, by some miracle, the country is saved from the bloodbath so many people have predicted, then its salvation will have been hammered out all the way. The scientists I talked to in Pretoria, for example, seemed to be some of the sanest, most creative people I've ever met: there is, one felt, a certain advantage in being so isolated, for then one can take it for granted. 'Bob' Brain, the man I went to see, is I feel sure a genius fit to rank with the giants of the 19th century. He and his assistant have been completely rethinking the theory of evolution, in particular the mysterious transition from ape to man. I'm a bit too gaga to explain this all in a letter: it'll have to wait till I see you.

Murray B[ail] took me out to see Maisie Drysdale[2] on Tuesday and we had a marathon discussion in the car. I relish his company. I've no idea what I'll be doing, but I have to go away and write all summer. I intend to start on the 1st of May in a friend's house in France, and just go on and on . . .

1. William Dalrymple has in fact traced the origin of these prostrations to an Eastern Christian practice in the early Byzantine period.
2. Lady Maisie Drysdale, widow of Australian artist Sir Russell Drysdale.

If, ever, I manage to get the work in hand done, I intend to go and learn Russian in Paris with Les Pères Jésuites de Maudon. Russia exerts for me the most enormous fascination; and if one doesn't get to grips with it now, one never will.

I am sorry for this incoherent note and send you and Francis all my love,

Bruce

Nin Dutton and I sent you a post card from a small town in NSW. She is recovering from the dreadful shock of Geoff's disappearance,[1] and is putting the pieces together in an incredibly courageous way.

To Anne-Marie Mykyta
as from Flat 7|77 Eaton Place|London|1 May 1984

My dear Anne-Marie,

I am so sorry we never made it on my return to Adelaide. Things were a really terrible and hectic rush. I literally spent hours, rather than days, in the city. And now I'm infinitely far away in a more or less empty French farmhouse, trying to summon up my Australian experience and put it onto paper in some manageable form. We'll meet again before long, of that I'm sure. Do let me know if you're heading this way.

Much love, Bruce

To Kath Strehlow
as from: Flat 7|77 Eaton Place|London|4 May 1984

My dear Kath,

On getting back I found in my post the magnificent golden scroll. I hope you didn't think I'd omitted to thank you: it simply hadn't come before I left England. I adored seeing you AS USUAL; and you must promise me to signal PROPERLY THIS TIME when you're next heading

1. Geoffrey Dutton (1922–98) Australian author and historian, had recently left Ninette, his long-standing wife, for one of his students, Robin Lucas, whom he married in April 1985.

this way. The chances I have to tell you of getting me at the above number are remote. I can't do a thing of work in London (Depressing place!) and at the moment I'm holed up in a farmhouse in France trying to summon up Australia. The best contact is my agent in London: Deborah Rogers, who usually knows where I am, roughly!

In the hectic rush of leaving Australia, I didn't get the chance to go to Canberra and talk to Mollison,[1] which would be the best way of sussing out the ground. I certainly will write to [him] if you like: but I'd need to know <u>what</u> to write. He is a rather mercurial, but likeable character, and from what I gather he's been under fire lately. He staked a huge part of his reputation and the gallery's money on modern American painting; and it turns out the Australian public couldn't care less about American painting, even though Americans come on special pilgrimages to see the Canberra collection. As Geoff Bagshaw[2] rightly said: the place for the Strehlow Collection IS the National Gallery; but as I don't have to tell you, there are complications!

Look after yourself; and there is, as a postscript, one thing I beg of you (though it's absolutely none of my business!). Technicolour film has a tendency to fade unless stored in the right temperature. I do think you should consult an expert on the matter. I took some footage in the Sahara – beautiful footage – and the whole thing is now a shadow of its former self, because I was unaware of this fact.

Much love,
Bruce

To Elizabeth Chatwin
France | 25 May 1984

Not doing so badly in complete seclusion: Paris – a nightmare. Have put off Spain till after the summer if at all. Should – or rather will be – back 3/4 weeks for further research etc. XXX B

1. James Mollison (*b.*1931), director of the National Gallery of Australia 1977–90.
2. Australian anthropologist whom Chatwin had met at the Aboriginal community of Haasts Bluff.

To Penelope Tree
Apartado 73 | Ronda | Spain | 2 July 1984

Something always prevents me from having MY way and settling on a Greek island. For silly reasons am here in Spain. So you got the Renata A.[1] You wanted it, and got it. I couldn't read it, I have to say and frankly I'm glad you couldn't. I too adore her — what little I've seen of 'her': but it does make me realise that NY is a very small pond. A disaster with the Australian book — in that another, by accident, had cannibalised it — temporarily. Think of you always XXX Bruce

To David King
Ubeda | Andalucia | Spain | 2 July 1984

A crowd of small boys have clustered round my windsurfer — on the roof-rack. Recklessly — and with an American Ex card I bought a most elegant and speedy model. When I tried it out, of course, I fell off again and again. I have a ridiculous new book in hand — which has grown ORGANICALLY out of an article. As always B

To Lydia Livingstone
Apartado 73 | Ronda | Malaga | Spain | 23 July 1984

Am stiff and back-biting after 3 months of writing rubbish. But I did buy a windsurfer. Thinking of you often and long to be back. Much love B

To Murray Bail
Flat 7 | 77 Eaton Place | London | 31 July 1984

Dear Murray,
    I am reunited with my post after 5 months: so you can imagine the state I'm in. Fine. You can use the flat from August 23rd for two weeks.

1. *Pitch Dark* by Renata Adler (b.1939), American novelist.

I'll be around but can spend my odd nights in London with friends: but nearly all the time, flat out writing (I hope) about an hour away in the country. All going very badly! I hate all this business of writers doing places – or doing them in – and wouldn't dream of doing the same for Australia. Hence my problems, but I won't bore you with them.

The Cézanne watercolours are at St George's Gallery.[1] Call me the moment your plans firm up, so I can get you the keys etc.

In haste, Bruce

To Elisabeth Sifton
Flat 7 | 77 Eaton Place | London | [August 1984]

Dearest Elisabeth,

Enclosed 55 pages of this 'experiment'. There are many more, but in a chaotic condition, since this is like the jig-saw puzzle you despair of finishing.

The '<u>middle</u>' of the book, if it has one, is a revelation that, in the case of Swartkrans, the killer of the hominids was not any old <u>beast</u>: but a <u>specialist</u> predator who it appears preferred <u>our</u> kind to the exclusion of almost all other flesh. The coda examines the implication of the fact that at the particular moment in palaeontological history, when our intelligence suddenly appears with a Bang, there was a Beast with whom we were locked in a 1:1 relationship. All very speculative, I admit, but nonetheless arresting!

Love,

Bruce

P.S. I am now intent on getting the thing onto paper first – and then checking and 'Englishing' it backwards. Call you next week.

---

1. In St James's, where Chatwin and Bail bought their art books. M.B.: 'Bruce often attacked the British for not seeing the importance of Cézanne. In the 1920s it was almost impossible to see a Cézanne in London; you had to go to Paris.'

On 28 August Sifton telegrammed Deborah Rogers: 'Bruce's manuscript is tremendously exciting and I am very eager 1. to see the whole thing 2. to see it published.'

To Ninette Dutton
Flat 7 | 77 Eaton Place | London | 1 November 1984

My dearest Nin,

Sorry if our correspondence has gone a bit astray. I've been in the thick of it, beavering away on the book: by the end of the day it's as much as I can do to sign a cheque, let alone write. And what a monstrosity it is! About monsters, no less! But touch wood, over the last few days I reached a watershed, and can, I believe, see light at the end of the tunnel. The real cause of my distraction was the annual visit to London by my American publisher, Elisabeth Sifton, who has almost become my alter ego when it comes to books. She was wonderful: not only did she take the point, entirely: she also provided the wherewithal to continue – which considering the extremely cranky viewpoint was, to say the least, encouraging.

Alas, I can't see my way to coming out again this winter (ours). Who knows, another month of this dripping cold climate and I may change my mind utterly. It is after all possible these days to hop on a plane. But on balance I think I'd better try and slog it out. The only date I have in mind is Midsummer's Day in Finland at something called the Lahti Festival. By that time all being well, I'll have cleared the decks for my so-called 'Russian' project[1] – though, I have to say, I'm having second thoughts about beginning that at once. Wouldn't it be better, I ask myself, taking a real *wanderjahre*, my head empty of grandiose (and? unattainable projects), just to roam around and write short stories. Anyway to Finland I shall go, but what I wondered is whether that coincided with – or around – your plans for Moscow.

Many thanks for the clipping. I never read S[alman] R[ushdie]'s

---

1. The projected novel *Lydia Livingstone*, with a heroine partly based on Ninette Dutton.

Tatler article[1] because I had a feeling it might make me mad – and wouldn't it just? Silly arse! It's one thing to go knocking Australia if you're paid to do it by an American publisher – as I believe Shiva Naipaul[2] is doing – quite another when you're invited by the city, given that degree of attention, even adulation – and then what? He got it all from a rather painted-up, ogle-eyed and not-to-my-mind-so beautiful literature-groupie who went the rounds, it seems, of every writer at the festival before latching onto him. How silly can you be? The Mayor, in my view, was dead right. But then I do believe he's gone a bit barmy recently. He left his wife for my friend the 'camel lady' Robyn Davidson[3] – all my fault – or so I was told! – but now he's back again in London, full of the 'weirdness' of Australia. Frankly, I find the 'weirdness' of Mrs Thatcher's Britain quite enough to contend with without adding to the list. And it is strange to find myself, as a Pom, becoming more and more patriotic and defensive about Australia – thank God I wasn't so thunderstruck on my first visit – but now I see the whole thing in better perspective, I'm secretly tempted to up-sticks and move there.

I feel for you desperately about Geoff [Dutton] – but from what Tisi[4] said, I too did think it sounded – for all those reasons we discussed – as though he was going to stay. The awful thing was that I lost his letter (together with a whole lot of others!) – and although I tried to answer his questions about Afghanistan, I'm afraid it must have sounded a little limp-wristed. I haven't heard from him since.

My friend Murray Bail was here – a really good egg! We had the liveliest time together. It's funny to see how well his 'art-historical'

1. Rushdie had written an article for *Tatler* about the Adelaide Festival which included the passage: 'Later in the evening, a beautiful woman starts telling me about the weirdo murders. "Adelaide's famous for them," she says, excitedly. "Gay pair slay young girls. Parents axe children and inter them under lawn. Stuff like that. You know." Rushdie wrote in a postscript, 'some of the citizens of Adelaide were upset by its reference to "weirdo murders," even though I'd been told about such crimes by more than one resident of the city.'
2. Shiva Naipaul (1945–85), author and younger brother of V. S. Naipaul.
3. Robyn Davidson (*b*.1950), Australian travel-writer.
4. Teresa Rose ('Tisi') Dutton (*b*.1961), singer, d. of Ninette and Geoff.

biography of Fairweather[1] comes off in relation to David Malouf's novel[2] of the same theme.

We'll write again before the month's out. Otherwise slog. But I <u>did</u> have a <u>week</u>'s break to go to a writer's conference in Barcelona and find myself in the same platform as my No 1 hero: Andrei Sinyavsky[3]. Not very approachable, I'm afraid, for though he spoke perfectly good French – and rattled along when his wife was not looking – she caught us and said bleakly through the interpreter in Russian: '<u>We</u> have spoken enough French for today.'

Much love Bruce

PS Came back 10 days after writing this to find that the people in the house had <u>not</u> posted it. In the meantime I did read S[alman] R[ushdie]'s notorious *Tatler* article. The man is off his head! How dare he when I introduced him to Mrs Mykyta, make flip comments on that murder(s)!

Elizabeth got back this afternoon from Delhi of all places and is a bit shattered xx B

To Murray Bail

Flat 7 | 77 Eaton Place | London | [November 1984]

My dear Murray,

I've been wondering how you've got on since the Sudanese abortion.[4] I keep on kicking myself for not being <u>firmer</u> at that dinner: but

1. *Ian Fairweather* (1981).

2. *Harland's Half Acre* (1984).

3. Russian writer (1925–97), who published his novels in the West under the pseudonym Abram Tertz. Chatwin particularly admired *A Voice from The Chorus* (1973), a collection of his thoughts from the gulag where he was imprisoned from 1965–71. Chatwin had met him in Barcelona on 26 September 1984. Notebooks: 'Sinyavsky in a blue jacket with strange long brown shoes. The face of an agreeable peasant. Warm handshake. White beard, gold-rimmed spectacles.'

4. M.B.: 'I was in London and trying to get into Sudan. At this small dinner with Bruce – at Michael and Anne Davie's, whom he hadn't met – there was discussion on how best to go about it. When we left, Bruce tore into the British, the Davies – for their mundane, philistine, drab way of living and seeing the world. I went into the Embassy the next day. I was "interviewed" by a very tall man with tribal marks cut across both cheeks, and in the middle of the conversation a papier maché portrait of his country's leader fell off the wall behind him. I didn't get a visa. Harare was where I went instead.'

the *Morning Herald*'s letter looked so imposing, so irrefutable. Anyhow, I hope that Harare was at least something. I also felt we should have made some grand expedition in England. But you know how it is. I am usually so desperate to get the hell out of here that any moment for work is precious. The book grinds on slowly. I thought I was on top of it – that is until I began to re-read some, at which point I realised 'This will never do'. The American publisher liked what I had done – or so she said – but, out of sheer terror, I'm going to refuse the advance offered for fear of being stuck.

Salman, as you know, is back. What a drama! I'm a little bit cross with him for sounding off against the Adelaide Festival . . . Adelaide as an ideal location for a murder movie etc. A friend from Sydney also sent me Shiva Naipaul's embittered rant from one of your magazines.[1] All seems to me to be so pointless. I suspect that there's quite a market in the US for writers who will tell the Americans that Australia is not quite so great after all. Anyway, I, as a Pom, have moved into a high Pro-Australia-patriotic phase, and won't hear one word against it.

The other night, with the wind howling round this promenade-deck-of-the-Queen-Mary house of ours, I read *Ian Fairweather* from cover to cover. Absolutely A1. I haven't read so enjoyable an 'Art Book' (which it isn't) ever. What I never took in was how the later 'Chinese' pictures were all 'remembrances of Cathay.' What a figure![2] And what a destiny! In your hands he's totally alive – whereas the artist in *Harland's Half Acre* just isn't convincing. Why don't you turn your hand to Cézanne? Jon Rewald[3] is, of course, the expert; but he's a basically unimaginative man, and I reckon you could arrive at the 'texture' of Cézanne better than anyone. Anyway, it's only an idea.

Elizabeth has been in India for a couple of months. She got away

1. 'Why Australia?' had appeared in the *Sydney Morning Herald*.
2. At Pam Bell's house in Boona, Chatwin had seen a grey Fairweather guache, *Painting 1959*, that, in Bail's words, 'knocked his socks off'.
3. John Rewald (1912–94), German-born American art historian and author of *Paul Cézanne* (1948) who created a foundation to turn Cézanne's studio in Aix-en-Provence into a museum.

from Delhi the night before the assassination,[1] and managed to miss the real rumpus: all the same, she's pretty whacked.

All my love to Margaret and yourself,

Bruce

To Lydia Livingstone
Flat 7|77 Eaton Place|London|8 November 1984

Lovely to get your letter as always. Here the same old grind. Mirella Ricciardi[2] sent me to see 'Green Ants Dreaming' in a totally empty movie house in Chelsea. Really, my new friend W[erner Herzog] was really off his head. The script, when I saw it, was a warning. Anyhow, well out of that one. Much love to all. Ranald[3] here delighting us all.

To Anne-Marie Mykyta
Flat 7|77 Eaton Place|London|12 November 1984

Something terrible happened. Your letter – which I had in a mountain of mail – got lost between here and the country:[4] together with a stack of others. Inexplicable! The winter draws in here. The proverbial English gloom – and I am trying to write of the blinding light of Central Australia,

1. Indira Gandhi, Prime Minister of India, was assassinated in New Delhi by two of her Sikh bodyguards on 31 October 1984 on her way to be interviewed by Peter Ustinov for a documentary on Irish television.
2. Mirella Ricciardi (b.1933), photographer.
3. Ranald Allen, who had met Chatwin in Australia. In the 1970s Allen lived and worked as an Art and Craft adviser with Aborigines. Herzog had briefly approached him to advise on *Where the Green Ants Dream*. Some time later Allen talked to Wandjuk Marika who had appeared in the film along with his brother Roy, both Senior Law Men from Yirrkalla in North East Arnhem Land. 'Wandjuk told me how close he and Roy went to spearing Werner on the set when he got a bulldozer driver to keep driving at them during a protest scene and almost ran them over. They reckoned he was a crazy man.'
4. E.C.: 'The letter was probably blown out of the car or slipped behind the seat. He was very untidy at loading things. You should have seen his baggage. He had no system at all. It was all jumbled together.'

for which already I ache. I'm fed up with being a soi-disant 'writer'. It's my experience that the moment one starts being a writer, everything dries up. I think of you often. Much love Bruce

To Anne-Marie Mykyta
as from Flat 7|77 Eaton Place|London|26 November 1984

My dear Anne-Marie,

This is my last evening in England since I'm going to go doggo in the Aegean all winter: and am flying to Crete in the morning. I just thought I'd nip into the flat and there was your card.

I didn't mention the Salman R[ushdie] business because a. I knew you'd have been hurt: the question was how hurt b. I've had a terrific falling out with him over it. Really, it was too thoughtlessly cruel. And to what end? There he'd been feted, applauded – which apparently he needs – and then that! I'd rather if this was between us; but I do think he can be excused only on the grounds that he was going a bit off his rocker at the time. He wrote one wonderful book. For once the judges of a big literary prize were right at the right moment, but the whole business seems to have unhinged him a bit. The fatal thing is to turn oneself into a '<u>writer</u>'.

I could, I'm sure, get the *Tatler* to print what you have to say: but, in this tricksy city, people's memories are so very short, and it would, I feel, only titillate a morbid interest which would have nothing to do with Adelaide as such/or the Festival: but now S[alman] R[ushdie] has shot his mouth off again.

I can't quite remember whether you met him with me in all that hubbub; but he certainly knew of you through me and all that guff about the party was just a lot of blarney.

I'm riveted by the affair of Kath Strehlow and the Aboriginal collection.[1] What a mayhem it all is? Pint-sized egos being inflated all round.

---

1. Ted Strehlow had willed 1,200 sacred artefacts to his second wife Kath for safe-keeping, until their baby son Carl came of age. These *tjuringas* were the subject of a ferocious debate. On 29 May 1992 government agents raided her house in Adelaide and seized books, papers and objects. K.S.: 'One of the things bugging them was my friendship with the English writer Bruce Chatwin.'

She was here for a bit on her way to Canada: I must say I'm sympathetic to the fact that they – whoever they are – were definitely trying, for the most venal and short-sighted reasons, to dismember Ted Strehlow's life work: And he – make no mistake – was a real homespun <u>genius</u>: examples of which, as we know, are in short supply. His *Songs of Central Australia* – wildly eccentric as it is – is not simply some kind of ethnographical tract: but perhaps the only book in the world – the only real attempt since the *Poetics* of Aristotle to define what song (and with song all language) is. He arrives at his conclusion in a crabby way. He must also have been impossible. But nonetheless VERY great, and far too important, obviously, to be seized upon by a bunch of ambitious bureaucrats.

If the matter hots up, I may, indeed have to hot foot it back. In the meantime I'll plod on.

As always with love,

Bruce

<u>PS</u> Do let me know if there's anything you want me to do vis-à-vis para 2.

Excuse the yellow pad: it's all I have.

To John Kasmin
as from: Flat 7|77 Eaton Place|London|[November 1984]

Dearest Kaz, I have, <u>temporarily</u>, unfrozen myself vis-à-vis the book: it's rather like sailing round a headland in flat calm, every little puff helps. Well, I've had the teeniest puff and have gone to Crete for a couple of weeks to see how I like it there and whether or not I want to spend the winter there. See you around Christmas. XX B

To Murray Bail
Flat 7|77 Eaton Place|London|[December 1984]

Dear Murray

A quick note <u>in extremis</u>, ie from London. I had two glorious weeks in Crete, and then the Peloponnese where I have rented a flat for the winter.[1] Then the return, where as usual everything has piled up. Will I go and see a film about Freud's last patient? Will I write a foreword? Will I pay my tax (but what with?) Will I . . . will I . . . <u>NO</u>!

I don't know what to do. My impulse is to sell up and go away somewhere rather primitive – or at least isolated from the literary 'buzz' that nags at me with the insistence of a pneumatic drill in a neighbouring street. The answer is this: that no amount of comfort, padding recognition etc, is, in any way, a compensation for having one's head and time free. And London is such an abominable trap!

I had your letters simultaneously: the first with *The Plains*[2] seems to have been opened, and tampered with, presumably in case it contained a bomb. It actually seems to have arrived here <u>after</u> the second.

I'm going to sit down for a few days and read that, and the new Sinyavsky *Bonne Nuit!* (as yet in French) and a book on Rimbaud in Ethiopia and Ovid's *Metamorphoses*.

Aren't Victoria Falls a surprise? Nowhere else in the world, perhaps, can we look down on the sublime. There is, strangely enough, a rather wonderful 19th century painting of it in the Royal Geographic Soc[iety] by an artist whose name I forget.

I dread to do your bidding with the *Sunday Times* and *Observer* vis-à-vis Fairweather. I don't know them at all on S.T. . . . and it's all a mafia of sneer and pretentiousness with art critics reviewing etc. If you ever read the reviews that Marina Vaizey[3] puts out, you'd be amazed. She went to Paris the other day (imagine!) and panned an exhibition of Douanier Rousseau;[4] said the colour was crude. Tut! Tut!

On the other hand, I could I think somehow fix something better for the *T.L.S.*

1. Chatwin had based himself in the Hotel Theano, a five-minute walk from the Leigh Fermors.
2. By Gerald Murnane (*b.*1939), Australian writer. *The Plains* (1982) was a short Borgesian novel about a young film-maker who travels to an imaginary country within Australia where he fails to make a film.
3. Marina Vaizey, *Sunday Times* art critic.
4. Henri Rousseau (1844–1910), French primitive painter and customs officer, known as 'Le Douanier'.

Sorry for the disjointed and probably illegible page. But I feel I must reply at once to say how much I value your comments about not making the book so 'easy'[1] . . . I know exactly what you mean and have, any way, embarked on a different track.

Much love to Margaret as from E

Bruce

Will write from the Mani. I was swimming there last week. Here I am completely gummed up with green phlegm. Dining with Salman tonight.

B

To Ninette Dutton

c/o Leigh Fermor | Kardamyli | Messinia | Greece | [January 1985]

Forgive the silence: I've been estranged from my post for over a month, and will be for another. I have a flat overlooking olives, cypresses and the sea. The iris and anemones (of Adonis) are out. Some days, like yesterday, are balmy and beautiful, but in the night we had a non-stop gale from Kamchatka that broke the shutters. The book edges along. I keep wishing I was in Australia – and now consider myself badly bitten. Much love B

To Diana Melly

c/o Leigh Fermor | Kardamyli | Messinia | Greece | 30 January 1985

Dearest D,

Well, I've been here a month now, in the most beautiful place you can imagine. A view of olives and cypresses, a little island and the sea.

---

1. On 24 August Bail had visited Homer End where Chatwin had read to him the Swartkrans section, after which Bail wrote in his diary: 'Felt it was written too smoothly, lightly'.

Some days are clear and blue and the sun so hot it could be June. Occasionally, it blows from Siberia and the sea below my window is a churning mass. The place I'm staying in is ideal for writing: in fact, it would do for anyone doing a stint of work between October and May when the tourists come and make a bit of noise.

My mother's been in the flat next door. My poor father didn't get to sail the Atlantic[1]. Once they got to the Cape Verde Islands they ran into a strong trade wind, and apparently the boat became unmanageable, slewing this way and that, and burying her bow into the waves: so they decided it would be unsafe to go on, and gave up. We got some news of this, but in a garbled form, and there were one or two days of mild anxiety.

Up behind Kardamyli, there is a first line of hills with little villages dotted about, and then a line of snowy mountains. I usually break off at 2 and go walking with Paddy. Yesterday, he had a hilarious letter from Daphne Fielding about the 'Duke diggers'[2] at Badminton. Both she and Diana thought the two boys who did it were 'very romantic' and had 'wonderful cheekbones'. I can't think that Sally would have seen the comic side.

I have to come back to London for about a week, as from the 6th Feb, partly to sort out one or two odds and ends, to see JC[3] but otherwise to lie rather low. Please do be in London then.

Forgive the scrappy note,

Much love Bruce

---

1. Charles was supposed to be sailing across the Atlantic in a concrete boat. His childhood dream was to sail his own yacht on a trade wind passage, to arrive in time for Christmas at Nelson's Dockyard, English Harbour, Antigua – all in accordance with Royal Cruising Club tradition.
2. Two anti-hunt saboteurs had attempted to dig up the late Duke of Beaufort's grave in Badminton churchyard.
3. Jasper Conran (*b.*1959), English fashion designer with whom Chatwin had been involved since 1982.

To Murray Bail

as from Homer End | Ipsden | Oxford | 11 February 1985

Dear Murray,

Pam B[ell] sent me a copy of your essay on [John] Passmore:[1] very, very good. Imagine a single one of the art-blatherers in this country matching a single one of your lines. I now want to know what a Passmore really is like: and, stuck as I am, in the Southern Peloponnese, I won't find out for a bit.

The above is a white lie: I've been in Greece now for 7 weeks and have come back for 3 days ONLY! to cope with the mail, pay bills etc. Then I'm off back again. I have a room with a view of olives, cypresses, a bay. I work till 3; then walk in the hills; then read; then sleep. Not bad. Costs next to nothing. I go on with the book, and have reached such a stage, I simply daren't look back.

I'm home at the moment, after finding in Barcelona a wonderful Romanesque (Catalan) panel. 13th century – tempera: of King David and a stork – all reds, black and white – with incredibly lively, rather coarse drawing. Such a thing is apparently RARISSIMO – but I think it was just too lively for most people. E sends her fondest love, and so do I to you and Margaret. Bruce

PS I hear that S[alman] R[ushdie] and the camel lady are back again.[2]

To Pam Bell

c/o Leigh Fermor | Kardamyli | Messinia | Greece | 22 February 1985

This is more like it: at least I've been writing instead of procrastinating all the time. I now find city life rather hell except for the odd weekly

---

1. Australian artist (1904–84). Bail had contributed an essay for a retrospective at the New South Wales Art Gallery. He replied to Chatwin on 18 February 1985: 'I saw John Passmore as a peculiarly Anglo/Australian product, a slightly primitive man who raised himself with his kind of isolation.'
2. M.B. replied: 'Yes, SR is back on the camel lady. Personally, I don't think it's going to last . . . SR sent me a note a few weeks ago with a letter enclosed for P. White. He'd just reread *Voss* and this was "his first and only fan letter".'

visit. How was your trip to London? I have bought a wonderful painting! A 13th century Romanesque panel – from Catalonia – of King David and a Pelican. Many thanks for M[urray] B[ail]'s piece. A1 as usual. Much love, Bruce

To Valerian Freyberg
c/o Leigh Fermor | Kardamyli | Messinia | Greece | 22 February 1985

Your dreadful godfather has gone into hiding in Greece for months and months in the hope that he will be able to finish his 4th book. Each time round it gets harder and harder. But I will be around in England in the summer! I think of you often – and wonder how you're getting on. Much love Bruce

To Murray Bail
c/o Leigh Fermor | Kardamyli | Messinia | Greece | 1 March 1985
Dear Murray,

Got your letter yesterday. I don't get many here, because I've put a block on being available from London, and that includes the post. Without wanting to sound unpatriotic . . . I now find that a week in my own country is as much as I can stomach. It used to be two months, but now, like the dwindling pound, it gets whittled down and down and down . . . I went for 8 days, to sort out various affairs, in February, and by the 8th was nearly bonkers. E. too, is beginning to feel the same way. I think the way of solving the matter is to let things slide; not to take any bold, self-conscious decision to leave, but, in practice, to do just that. I shall stay here in Greece until the early summer; then, as I have to be in Helsinki, on midsummer's day, I thought I'd have a stint in the north. Then I've promised to go and do a 'small' job in Hong Kong. Then to America for six weeks to 'teach' – God save me! in October.[1] Then basta! BUT, the way my mind's working is to join E. in India on or around November

1. At Vassar College in New York State.

1st and stay, if necessary, for months and months. It's not that I want to write a book about India – though I am sure it still is the land of the short story. I simply want to float there for a while, from the plains to the hills. I want to see Orissa or Bengal in full monsoon: that kind of thing . . . It would be terrific if you were there too. In fact, I cannot imagine anything in the world I'd like more.

I may, in the course of these violent wanderings, have to show up in Oz, in order to check things out for the book. A very peculiar work, let me tell you. Far too diffuse and repetitive at present. How I long for the light exhilarating days on constructing *Patagonia*. This is altogether too weighty and serious and needs, I fear, a good shot of . . . well, I dread the word 'local colour' to bring it to life.

Vis-à-vis the Cézanne problem.[1] He is, surely, like all the truly greats, a somewhat hit-and-miss performer. And one never knows on what scale he's going to hit the bull's eye. If your pal[2] will look through the Christie's catalogues of Impressionist sales for the late '60's – say 68–70, but I may be wrong about that, he will find an oil sketch of Mont St Victoire – with literally about ten brushstrokes on a plain white primed ground. I honestly believe it is one of the most breathtakingly beautiful paintings I have ever set eyes on. It went for about 20,000 pounds – far less even then than a sketchy drawing of the same subject – and was bought by Beyeler of Basel, who sold it to a Swiss collector. It might just be worth following up. It is, admittedly, Mt. St Victoire reduced to almost Malevich-like abstraction: but that, if I were buying a Cézanne for a national Gallery is the kind of thing I'd aim for, rather than complete, early, or untypical 'Tentation' etc. Your pal obviously seems to know the market pretty well: and I am hopelessly out of date. Like some old dowager of the Belle Epoque, '*Je garde mes souvenirs . . .*'

1. M.B.: 'Bruce and I often talked about Cézanne, arguing for our favourite ones. Towards the end, in the wheelchair, he phoned me to say he had bought a Cézanne painting, unfinished, just a few brush strokes, of the mountain. As good as a fully finished work, "better than a Constable cloud study."'
2. James Mollison, director of National Gallery of Australia, was then looking to acquire a Cézanne. M.B. was a member of the Council. 'By the time they got one they could only afford a strange early painting of a bloke in bed with a woman.'

The most beautiful Cézanne in the world is to my mind Henry McIllhenny's *Portrait of Madame Cézanne*, a tiny picture by comparison with others, but . . . He is a nice, tough, open-minded man, who likes Australia a lot, and has of course recently sold the wonderful, but very conventional still-life to pay for his yacht. I wonder whether it would be worth putting some kind of proposal to him: that eventually etc, in return for keeping it now, and in return for X dollars now and Y later, he might even like the idea of it ending up in Canberra. Instead, that is, of Philadelphia, which is of course bursting with Cézannes.

Poor Madame de Chaisemartin[1]. In my day she was quite a character: a defending barrister, who specialised in the cases of poor Algerian immigrants on murder charges. I thought she was terrific. It was I . . . *Je garde mes souvenirs* . . . who set in motion the deal whereby the *Grandes Baigneuses*, then hanging in the maid's corridor, was bought by the National Gallery.

What am I reading here? I have the Sinyavsky, in French, but cannot finish it. Abram Terz to the fore, and less of Sinyavsky. Brilliant flashes, but on the whole, unacceptable lumps of fantasy. Don't know anything about *The Case of Mr Crump*.[2] *The Plains* I like a lot. Strangely Germanic in tone; but then I have thought that the Germanic suits Australia very well. I'd love to see what else he does. That's a real voice for you. Otherwise, three novels of [Italo] Svevo[3] who I'd never read before; *The Idiot*, which I last read in the Sahara; Michel Tournier, who is obviously inventive but I now think is far too kitsch; *Dialogues* of Plato, to see how you express ideas in dialogue (The answer is, 'I don't') plus the usual array of technical and scientific stuff. I have a new friend in Michael Ignatieff,[4] a Canadian-Russian,

1. Louise de Chaisemartin had offered to sell the painting, owned by her mother Madame Lecomte, at auction free of charge. It was sold to the National Gallery for 6 million francs, but there is no mention in the Gallery's archives of her association with Chatwin.
2. *The Case of Mr Crump* (1926), by Ludwig Lewisohn (1882–1955) Berlin-born American author. 'The opposite story to a feminist tirade-novel. A real horror story.' M.B. to B.C. 18 February 1985.
3. Italian novelist (1861–1928).
4. Canadian historian, author and politician (*b*.1947) who lived in Britain 1978–2000. He interviewed Chatwin for *Granta 21*, Spring 1987.

whose grandfather was Education Minister in the Duma. You might like to look at his essays published by Chatto, *The Needs of Strangers*. Otherwise, I am completely out of it . . . They were trying to get me to write something on the sinking of the *Belgrano*. I had a go, but was so disgusted by what I'd written – bellelettristic outpouring on events I knew <u>nothing</u> about, that I gave up – to everyone's annoyance. I wouldn't mind a glance at the S[hirley] H[azzard] Lecture;[1] I agree with you, the days of the *pontificateur* are over.

It's getting dark and a bit cold on my terrace; the bats are out, the sea is calm and grey, and there is a lurid orange line along the horizon.

As always, B

PS Let me know about India

Whew! The S[alman] R[ushdie][2] drama. Give them my love if you see them. I may have put my foot in it: because when he was in London, with his wife, I gave my congratulations etc when, in fact, he was leaving for Australia then and there.

To Diana Melly
c/o Leigh Fermor | Kardamyli | Messinia | Greece | [March 1985]

Dearest Diana,

Lovely to get your card. I couldn't think who would be writing from the Lygon Arms. Shades of my great-aunts[3] who would go to paint watercolours in the Cotswolds!

---

1. M.B. to B.C. 18 February 1985: 'Shirley H. has given the Boyer Lectures (Reith) on the ABC. Telling us where we've gone wrong. I didn't hear them, will read them instead. Good people here have called them sanctimonious. Woe is me! I fear they might be right.'
2. Rushdie had left his first wife for Robyn Davidson. E.C.: 'It was a very public, violent love affair, throwing each other out in the street and shouting, and then a reconciliation here at Homer End.'
3. Jane and Grace, his father's spinster aunts. Jane had lived as a young woman on Capri and was still painting at 84, not very good watercolours of turbaned Indians, churches, sailing boats and almost naked men with exiguous turquoise slips.

The weather here is alternatively lovely and tempestuous. But my room is always warm and, in a way, I rather welcome a storm. From the window I can watch the cypresses lashing about and the frothing waves a hundred yards away. After a storm though, I begin to get a bit chesty: but then everyone else does, so I'm not alone. I now realise the full enormity of this book, which seems to stretch before me like an endless tunnel. The only thing to do is press on regardless without looking back even, and then – only then – see if one can sort out the mess. It may take years.

I'm glad I came here. The winter in England is going to do me in, and I simply cannot summon up the concentration for a big work. They were after me the other day to write a piece for *Granta* on the *Belgrano*. I spent four days or so, fretting, getting unbelievably angry, and writing such drivel that, in the end, I had to give up. I cannot write about what I cannot know. The only letters I seem to get are from Australians: they're wonderful correspondents, as indeed they have to be. My great friend Nin Dutton is coming over in the summer, and I hope to spend some time with her in Prague. Otherwise, the only date is Midsummer's Night in Finland, where I have to make some kind of speech. The trouble is that this place fills up around the middle of May: so I will have to find somewhere else. Maybe Patmos even?

I know it's bad of me, but I'm not really inclined to leave Greece. I wish you'd come here in late April . . . Let me know because I'll have to make sure there's space. I'm sure there is.

Love to everyone. XXXB

PS I'm writing to Tom Maschler to see if he'll send me a copy/proof of Francis [Wyndham]'s book.[1]

On 4 February Tom Maschler had written asking to know when Chatwin might complete his manuscript. 'I assume it is the book we talked about! i.e. in shorthand AFRICA.'

1. *Mrs Henderson and Other Stories* (1985).

To Tom Maschler

c/o Leigh Fermor | Kardarmyli | Messinia | Greece | 1 March 1985

My dear Tom,

Lovely to hear from you. I'm stuck in here for at least another three or four months. In fact, the only date I have at present is in Finland, on Midsummer's Night, where I have to make some kind of speech. Otherwise, I don't intend to do another thing but write this long (How I dread the word 'long'!) book. Should we say it's longer than anything I've attempted before. It is, I suppose, a novel: though of a very strange kind; but as I have the most unbelievable difficulty slotting all the bits in, I'd really rather not talk about it. One thing I'm sure of, is that it won't be ready for publication this autumn. The fatal trap, I've discovered, is to think one is a 'writer' and to go in for all the paraphernalia that surrounds writerdom. So for what it's worth, I'm keeping things a bit close to my chest.

I'd love to see a proof of Francis [Wyndham]'s stories (or novel) depending on which way one looks at it. If you have one handy, you couldn't put it in the post. He's terrifically bucked by the care and trouble you've taken, and I know that all his friends must be very grateful to you.

Directly I have something to show – which will be when I dare go over what exists and do a re-write – I'll of course send it on to you.

as always Bruce

To Ninette Dutton

c/o Leigh Fermor | Kardamyli | Messinia | Greece | 1 March 1985

Dearest Nin,

Well, I was a saying to myself 'why don't I go trotting off to the post office and see if there's a letter from Nin,' and Joan Leigh Fermor knocks on the door and says, 'I've been to get your post' and there was a letter from Nin. Well, this is good news, about the trip.

I'd dearly love to go to Prague with you, but May 31st is a wee bit early. I'm not that keen to leave Greece so soon. On the other hand it could be that I won't be able to bear Greece another moment (unlikely!). The only fixed date I have for the whole of the summer is Midsummer's Night, in the arctic circle (or near it), in Finland – which does mean that I will be drifting round London and/or Paris in the 10 days or so before. I may not go to London – or for that matter to England – for the whole of next year. I have a US advance and fee from teaching at a US university in the Fall, and may very easily take what they call a tax-year. I can't promise it, quite, but can you signal if you want to borrow the London flat? There is somebody in it, on the understanding that he'll get out if I need it. But before even moving in that direction, the question is whether you want it. London is a nightmare of expense in June; and I wouldn't dream of staying in a hotel.

But if I didn't see you in England, we could have a fine time in Paris. This book is real Slow-Boat-department (how wonderful that yours is done!) but I do have a sense of it now and it does move in a more or less orderly progression. I was torn, terribly, by my decision not to come back to Oz this winter. But I think it was wise.

Foreign perspectives are often the best. I have a lovely room here: a view of olives and cypresses and the sea. Most days are clear and lovely, but tonight we have a Siberian tempest, and I have to run the gauntlet of 300 yards of muddy path in drenching rain, to go and cook Circassian chicken for Philip Sherrard,[1] expert on Greek poetry, with a wife who drones on about the Golden Section in Greek Art.

Next day. As I wrote the sentence above there was a knock on the door and it was Philip Sherrard who had lost the stupid wife in the storm and was afraid she was at the bottom of a ravine. We had to go out with torches, but she had taken refuge in a chapel and was subdued for most of the evening. He, on the other hand, was not: he banged on and on about what was in my book? What was my definition of a nomad? And so on. It then turned out he was a creationist, who seriously (I think) believed in 4004BC as the date of all things. At that point I clammed

---

1. Philip Sherrard (1922–95), British translator of modern Greek literature and 'astute observer of Athonite affairs' who converted to Orthodoxy.

up: 'There is one thing with which one simply cannot cope,' Konrad Lorenz once said to me, 'and that is plain stupidity.'

They went this morning and I have spent the day at my typewriter in the company of my Cistercian monk (or his fictional equivalent) on the beach north of Broome.

I may come to live in Greece: or at least have a hideout here. It's wonderfully anonymous in the winter, especially, and in the winter the cheapest bucket-shop fares to Australia are via Olympic Airways from Athens.

All my love to you and Tisi (it took ages for my postcard to get there!).

xx Bruce

On 21 March 1985 Patrick Leigh Fermor wrote to Deborah, Duchess of Devonshire: 'We've got a fellow-writer called Bruce Chatwin staying, very nice, tremendous know-all, reminds me of a couplet by O'Goldsmith.

And still they gazed and still the wonder grew
That one small head could carry all he knew.

'He's a great pal of Jackie Onassis.'

Deborah Devonshire replied on 4 April: 'Bruce Chatwin! OH how unfair you knowing him. He wrote a book (if it's the fellow I think it is) which I so adored I've never really felt like another.

'How ghoul if he's a know-all, but I wd like just to see & smell him to see for myself. Or is it like meeting royal people & actors, better not?'

(They did meet, eventually, at a Thai restaurant in Fulham.)

To Murray Bail

Hotel Theano | Kardamyli | Messinia | Greece | [April 1985]

Dear Murray,

This'll have to be a quick one since Paddy and Joan [Leigh Fermor] and I are going on an expedition to Arcadia and I want to catch the post.

Many thanks for the Shiva N[aipaul] piece[1] which I read without agreeing with it. The white Land Council heavies are, as you said, ludicrous in their pretensions and self-deceit: I ran up against the biggest operator in the business who had got an Aboriginal Council to buy him a plane. Of course S[hiva] N[aipaul] should never have been banned: but reading his piece you end up thinking he actually wanted to be banned in order to air his particular prejudice. The Land Rights Movement is not all bad; not all doomed; things do go better when they get back to the outstations. Instead of adopting a high-and-mighty tone about the historical process etc he should have discovered what incredibly artful dodgers they are. Aboriginal Australia was — and still is — one of the world's most astonishing phenomena — the anthropologists and linguists are still only scratching the surface.

Enough of that! My news — and this is <u>DEAD</u> secret for you alone! — is that I have been offered a trusteeship of the London Nat Gall — following in your footsteps![2] In fact, honoured though I may be etc, I think I shall turn it down. The idea of being present for at least 8 meetings a year in London fills me with terrible despair. My only reason for embarking on such a thing would be literary . . . !

I know, from reproductions, that *Afternoon in Naples* [by Cézanne]! Idiots! Why didn't they buy a sketch?

I'm leaving here in the weekend and going to a friend's house in Spetsai[3]. Then quite an adventure to stay with the Abbot of Chilandari monastery on Mount Athos for 2 weeks. Derek Hill is taking me — and has been every year for the past 15. Athos is obviously another atavistic wonder — then E. and I may drive to Finland via Hungary, Poland etc.[4]

---

1. 'Flight into Blackness,' *The Age*, Melbourne. The Northern Land Council had banned Naipaul from the territories under its control, following his remark 'that the Aborigines could not be considered to have created a culture as sophisticated — say — as the Chinese or Greeks or Indians or Egyptians had done.'
2. Bail was a trustee of the National Gallery in Canberra.
3. The Welches shared a house on Spetsai with Clem and Jessie Wood.
4. E.C.: 'We never did.'

All this depends on the progress of work between now and June. I now have a huge pile of paper – which has to all get under control.

Letters from now on best to Homer End, Ipsden, Oxford.

Funny I was thinking of Nov 7 for Delhi.

Much love to Margaret and yourself. B

To Pam Bell
Spetsai | Greece | 12 May 1985

All well. Adored your letter as always, but am so inundated and fatigued by words that I can't face anything grander than a p.c. – even to those I love the best. Greece in springtime is glorious but vaguely lethargic. Tomorrow I shall be halfway to 90![1] An 'Australian' book inches forward – para by para.

Much love B

A week after his 45th birthday Chatwin set out to fulfil a boyhood ambition: to visit Mount Athos. In 1980 he had wanted to come with James Lees-Milne ('No, Bruce, I said, you can't') who had known intimately Chatwin's boyhood hero, Robert Byron. Along with The Road to Oxiana, The Station *was one of Chatwin's 'sacred' texts: Byron's account of his 1926 sojourn on this 30-mile-long Greek peninsula – the spiritual centre of Orthodox Christianity – in the company of David Talbot Rice, Chatwin's art tutor at Edinburgh. Next, Chatwin turned to Derek Hill who had visited Athos 15 times. On 21 May they arrived at the small port of Ouranoupolis from where ferries depart for the two-and-a-half-hour journey to Daphni, below Mount Athos.*

---

1. Chatwin was born on the evening of 13 May 1940.

To Pam Bell
Mount Athos | Greece | May 1985

Strange to relate, the evening after I had posted the previous p/c, I found myself in the frontier village of Athos, Ouranoupolis, having dinner with an Austrian lady who lives there: the companion of an aged Mrs Loch[1] (born NanKivell). <u>Her</u> name Hanchin – something like that![2] She began to describe what she thought one of the most beautiful places in the world – the lake, the mountains – and do you know where it was . . . where she had stayed with Eileen Bell[3] etc. XXX B

To Francis and Shirley Steegmuller
Postcard, Stavronikita Monastery | On Athos, but as from
77 Eaton Place | 5 June 1985

I think of you often. Am having a fearful battle with my 'Australian' book. Really very difficult – and the end by no means in sight. I daren't go back, either, in case I am tempted to tear the whole thing up. Any chance of seeing you in London or Paris/Aug/Sept. Then I am supposed to teach at Vassar but will probably chicken out.

To Susan Sontag
Postcard, fresco of Last Supper at Stavronikita Monastery |
Mount Athos | Greece | 5 June 1985

Sorry to have missed you in London: but as you see, I've been out of the world a bit. Not too seriously! I'll be coming to NY in the Fall. As always, Bruce

1. Joice NanKivell Loch (1887–1982), Australian journalist (and Australia's most decorated woman) who worked with refugees and lived with her husband, Scots novelist Sydney Loch, in a Byzantine tower on a beach overlooking the Athos peninsula.
2. Martha Handschin was actually Swiss; she assisted Loch in dyeing woollen rugs, extracting colours from onion skins and almond leaves, and selling them to raise money for earthquake victims.
3. In April 1984 Chatwin had stayed with Pam and her mother Eileen at 'Aroo', outside Boonah south of Brisbane.

To Charles and Margharita Chatwin

Chilandari | Mount Athos | Greece | 6 June 1985

Among the stranger coincidences is the fact that the vintner, a wonderful Medieval character, Father Damian used to work at Brinton's:[1] a young novice – also of Serbian origin – was born in Barnt Green[2] and was apprenticed at Milwards in Redditch:[3] an experience that gave him his monastic vocation. XX Bruce

One entry in Chatwin's notebooks read: 'The search for nomads is a quest for God.' Staying on Mount Athos at the Serbian monastery of Chilandari – where his former professor David Talbot Rice had felt at his happiest – Chatwin woke up at 5.30 every morning and attended services. One afternoon, he walked to the monastery of Stavronikita once painted by Edward Lear. 'The most beautiful sight of all was an iron cross on a rock by the sea.' Whether moved by the rich liturgical worship or the tradition of mystical prayer or the unbroken continuity with the past, he then wrote: 'There must be a God.' The significance of his experience was later recorded by James Lees-Milne in his diary on 14 February 1990. 'Derek Hill . . . talked of his visit to Mount Athos with Bruce Chatwin, who was so moved by the experience that he could not write about it.' Elizabeth says, 'When he came back, he said to me: "I had no idea it could be like that." It wasn't like his other voyages of discovery. It was completely internal.' The inner change wrought on the white ledge below Stavronikita, the impact of that simple rusted metal cross, would result, three years later, in a firm desire to be received into the Orthodox Church.

1. A carpet factory in Kidderminster.
2. The village south of Birmingham where Charles and Margharita lived after their marriage.
3. In 1703 the Milward family started a needle and fish-hook factory at Washford Mills in Redditch.

To Murray Bail
Homer End|Ipsden|Oxford|9 July 1985

Greece in summer very bad for work. A mistake! The sun and wind destroy the brain cells at an incredible rate. Nonetheless, we do, I take it, still have our date in India. As always B

To Deborah Rogers
Homer End|Ipsden|Oxford|27 July 1985

Just got back. Catarrh started in the Pas-de-Calais.

To Derek Hill
Back at Homer End, but wishing I was still at Chilandari|29 July 1985

Gruelling drive across tourist-torn Europe; soggy fish and chips on the boat; catarrh on the by-pass – the usual tale of English woes! Much love, B

To Gertrude Chanler
Homer End|Ipsden|Oxford|6 August 1985

I thought of you constantly on Mount Athos – not that you're ever likely to get there! – but because I had in my ruck-sack the little telescopic Tiffany beaker; and whenever, wandering along paths that can hardly have changed since Byzantine times, I would come to a spring (at which there was usually a cross, a shrine and a bench for weary travellers), I would take it out for a drink. Everyone predicted that Derek [Hill] and I would quarrel: there were even bets on it between Barbara Ghika and Elizabeth Glenconner:[1] we were happy to report that not a cross word

1. Elizabeth Powell, mother of Emma Tennant; m. 1935 Christopher Grey Tennant, 2nd Baron Glenconner.

passed between either of our lips. The book is taking for ever, and I am cancelling everything to press ahead. By November, however, I'll be in need of a break. Much love, Bruce

To Charles Way[1]
Homer End | Ipsden | Oxford | [early August 1985]

Dear Charles Way,

I've been away solidly for five months and have only just caught up with your letter. If you would really want to, I can't see any objection to putting my two old twins on the stage. We'd have to talk about it. There is the possibility about a Channel 4 film.[2] Options have been bought; scripts have been written etc. But I'm afraid I can't take too much interest in it because, on the whole, I loathe films – and particularly films doctored for a so-called television audience. I can't for the life of me see how you'd do it: but that, of course, is your business. I very much like the sound of the Spanish Civil War play[3] – a subject which interests me passionately. Anyway, the point of this scrappy note is to say that we should meet sometime soon, that is, if you're still interested. I'll be coming down to Brecon sometime and will give you a call.

As ever, Bruce Chatwin

To Patrick and Joan Leigh Fermor
Homer End | Ipsden | Oxford | [August 1985]

Dearest Paddy and Joan,

At least I thought that going to England in August might lessen the shock, climatically. But no! Nothing but rain. Freezing cold. I went

1. Charles Way (b.1955). Playwright, who wished to adapt *On the Black Hill* for the stage.
2. Directed by Andrew Grieve, who wrote the screenplay; released in 1988.
3. Way was writing *Bread and Roses* for Gwent Theatre, about Welsh miners who walked to Spain to fight in the Civil War.

wind-surfing on a scummy little reservoir near Oxford, and my hands were white and numb after ten minutes. But what I miss most are the mountains! The country round here is tolerably attractive, immaculately kept: but then you keep running up against the cooling towers of the Didcot power-station; the antennae of Greenham Common; the nuclear installations at Harwell – all of which give me the feelings of claustrophobia.

The usual run of crises with the book, which, I suppose, does plod on slowly. Compression is what's needed. And when talking of compression, how's this for the thud of nomad horsemen into one line (I mentioned it on one of our walks). Juvaini[1] in his *History of the World Conqueror* reports this unconscious hexameter from the mouth of a refugee from Bokhara after the sack of Genghis:

'Amdand u khandand u sokhtund u kushtand u burdan u raftand'

> They came, they sapped, they burned, they slew,
> They trussed up their loot and were gone

Juvaini, quoted by Yule in his edition of Marco Polo, p233, says that the essence of all his book is contained in this one line.

I'm writing to Rudi Fischer.[2] I sent a letter apologising for my inability to show up, and got a splendid two pages in reply. Your ears would burn at all the things he says about you. If I could get clear of all the mess, I'd go on a visit, just for the sake of it.

Otherwise not much news. I seem to see Barbara and Niko [Ghika] constantly: I've gone up to London twice only, and each time to dinner with them. Miranda [Rothschild] very calm, composed, and almost regal in appearance.

Much love and from E.

Bruce

---

1. Tarikh-i Jahangushay-i Juvaini, Persian historian (*d.*1283). *The History of the World Conqueror* describes the conquest of Persia by the Mongols.
2. Rudi Fischer, an editor on *Hungarian Quarterly* and friend of Leigh Fermor.

To Ninette Dutton
Homer End | Ipsden | Oxford | 14 September 1985

Dearest Nin.

Lord how time flies. To think it was a month and a half since you were here. I've been in London three times only: the days go by; work, sleep, work, sleep – and the rain pours down outside. Yes, it was awful: I had to leave my race across Europe too late, and didn't get anything like enough time with you. Besides I was, as always, a little thrown by my first days in England after six months.

God knows when the book'll be finished: but the little bits I've shown around – to agents etc – have all been received quite well. E. and I are off to China: to Yunnan, which is completely new ground for me – around the beginning of November.

The *New York Times* are stumping up the fare: then we're going to rent a house for three months in Kathmandu, where we have a great friend[1] who has, it seems, endless Sherpa guides for treks into the mountains. I might just – towards the end of February – have got sufficiently far that I dare get on the plane for Oz.

Salman and Robyn came for the weekend and it was all rather jolly. It was the most sunny day and was something of an experiment in that we had no less than 8 soi-disant writers: a lot of egos sounding off, but we were able to open the windows so all the talk blew out over the sheep . . .

Much love, B

Love to Tisi

To Paul Theroux
Homer End | Ipsden | Oxford | 16 September 1985

Dear Paul,

Patagonia Revisited[2] isn't at all bad looking, is it? It'd be lovely to see you. I go to China in Nov. Bruce.

1. Lisa Van Gruisen.
2. *Patagonia Revisited*, based on the 'combined talk' given by Chatwin and Paul Theroux at the Royal Geographical Society in November 1979, had been published by Michael Russell.

To Charles Way
Homer End | Ipsden | Oxford | 16 September 1985

I should, in early Oct, be staying at the Tower for 2 weeks. Working – but there would be time off to talk.[1]

To Elizabeth Chatwin
Homer End | Ipsden | Oxford | [September 1985]

<u>E</u>. Oh God! – as Joan [Leigh Fermor] would say.

1. Jacob R[othschild] has twisted my arm to attend a meeting – attend only! – on Friday lunch.[2]

1a. where this puts the weekend, can't say.

2. I shall have to go to Oxford, tomorrow, have lunch . . . sign books, go to the Bodleian – then London.

3. The fireplace man is coming at 9.30 tom.

4. The glass man has been.

5. *The Times* rang up to try and get me to review. NO!

6. Possible to put creases in grey suit?

7. It's too much!

To Ninette Dutton
Birr Castle | Co. Offaly | Ireland | as from Homer End |
1 October 1985

E. has gone off to India for her tour. Tremendous drama at the airport as she lost her passport and couldn't fly with the tour![3] I have sloped off to Ireland on a 'memory tour' of old friends – Birr, now inhabited by my

---

1. Way met Chatwin in the Hen and Chicks pub in Abergavenny.
2. Hon. N. C. J. Rothschild (*b*.1936), succeeded father as 4th Baron Rothschild (1990), had become Chairman of the Trustees of the National Gallery.
3. E.C.: 'The passport had slipped under the seat of his 2CV and Bruce never looked properly. I had to take a later flight.'

friend Brendan Rosse,[1] has the most magical arboretum: 4 generations of plant-hunter earls. The leaves are just beginning to turn, and it is quite magical.

Could you drop on a postcard a piece of seemingly useless information. I need to know what in the way of <u>fanged</u> beasts a boy of 3 in 1954 would have seen in the Adelaide zoo. Would there have been a leopard? Or a tiger? Or lion? A dingo is a bit mild for my purpose. If not I shall have to make do with a fictitious Irish wolfhound or Alsatian in a neighbour's house.

Ah well, I'll be in touch with plans as I know them.

Much love, dearest.

Bruce

PS There is a totally weird Australian here, a Mr Bartlett from Perth. Knows Geoff [Dutton], slightly. Literary ambitions to write Australian short stories or an updated Suetonius, in the most haunted medieval town in Ireland.

PPS re the above. If there were such a <u>beast</u> i.e leopard I'd like a word about its history, name etc. How much was the age? Feeding time?

To Ninette Dutton
Homer End | Ipsden | Oxford | [October 1985]

Dearest Nin,

Many many thanks for your note on the feeding of the lions. Exactly what I need: if only for one line of the book.

The blow, of course, is Piers Hill.[2] What horrible decision to have to make – especially in view of the garden. My parents faced <u>exactly</u> the same thing over our house in Warwickshire – just that much too big. Running into just that more than they could cope with – and I

1. Formerly Lord Oxmanton; succeeded father as 7th Earl of Rosse in 1979 when he inherited Birr Castle, County Offaly.
2. Dutton's husband having married again, she was contemplating selling her home in the hills near Williamstown and moving to Adelaide.

must say that by taking the decision to move to a small house when they did i.e. in their late 50's and by their acquiring their shack in the south of France, they seem to live a happy, varied and very independent life.

But I'm sure you must have somewhere in the country. I know it sounds bananas to suggest it. But what if you not exactly demolished but let go half the house? Bankers and the rest always speak of ruining your investment without realising it is you who have to live there. The site at Piers Hill is so perfect, it makes me wish there was no house there at all, but a tiny log cabin. Of course you might find just such another site and build one.

I feel so hopeless so many thousands of miles away: but I wouldn't be rushed. My friends in Ireland, the Rosses, who have inherited a vast castle and garden with very little money are amazed by the way in which things are working back in their favour. Life in cities has become so drab and meaningless that there is, in Ireland, at least, a flocking back to land by people who want nothing more than the roof over their heads and food in return for really substantial doses of work in the open air.

We leave for Hong Kong on the 7th Nov. I'll keep you posted with the Nepal address as from Dec 1.

Much love B

To Ninette Dutton
Homer End | Ipsden | Oxford | [November 1985]

Gearing up for our long promised month in China – we leave on the 7th for Hong Kong. Then (???). I've rented an Englishman's bungalow in the Valley of Kathmandu. Dec-Mar. Be lovely if you could come.[1] Much love B

---

1. Dutton was not the only prospective guest. Chatwin had also invited his parents to Nepal for Christmas, plus Kasmin.

To Charles Way
Homer End | Ipsden | Oxford | [November 1985]

Dear Charlie,

Here is the book I promised to try and find.[1] My method, very often, was to check out the 'truth' of one of these photos – which would then unloose a flow of reminiscences . . . Best of luck, as always, Bruce

To Ninette Dutton
Homer End | Ipsden | Oxford | 5 November 1985

Dearest Nin,

A quick line on the eve of departure. Yes, we, apparently, do have the house all through Jan – and would adore you to come. But I do want to know what I'm inviting you to, before inviting you – if you get my clumsy meaning. What it boils down to is this. E leaves me in Hong Kong on Dec 3rd and I follow 10 days later. She is going to inspect the house – then we'll call you. Does that sound hideously complicated?

No. You mustn't move to town.

Much love, Bruce

---

1. *Welsh Rural Life in Photographs*, by Elfyn Scourfield (Stuart Williams, Barry, 1979). C.W.: 'He told me that rather than say to someone "What do you remember?" he'd show them a photograph of a particular landscape. One picture of Hay Harvest 1930, with a little girl and two boys in caps, looks uncannily like Louis and Benjamin.'

CHAPTER TEN

CHINA AND INDIA: 1985–6

On 7 November 1985 Chatwin flew with Elizabeth on the first leg of their journey to Kathmandu, where they had taken a three-month lease on an unfurnished house. They stopped off in Hong Kong to make an excursion into China, the New York Times *magazine having commissioned a profile of Joseph Rock, the Austro-American botanist who lived from 1922–49 in the Lijiang Valley. By late November, they were back in Hong Kong. They went to the races – where Chatwin placed a bet and won: he spent his winnings on some rare tea and a trip to the Taipei Museum in Taiwan. Then, while Chatwin lingered in Hong Kong and visited the bird market, Elizabeth flew on ahead to prepare the house in Kathmandu. On his arrival, he found her sick with bronchitis and the original house let to someone else.*

To Ninette Dutton

c/o Lisa van Gruisen | Tiger Tops | Kathmandu | Nepal |
Christmas Day 1985

Dearest Nin,

Well, I finally got here from China and Hong Kong. We had an unbelievably fascinating time in northern Yunnan, on the borders of Burma and Tibet. I have put off going to China for so long, for fear that the China of my imagination, a kind of ideal China composed of such congenial spirits as Li Po[1] and Tu Fu did not exist. But they are still there! We met a village doctor and herbalist,[2] a sort of Taoist sage who went gathering herbs in the mountains, painted orchids and bamboos and wrote calligraphies of the great Tang poems.

Hong Kong's a bit of a nightmare, but not without a certain fascination. On the Kowloon side is the area known as Mong Kok the most densely populated square mile in the world, but it really is astonishing how people <u>can</u>, if pressed, live in such numbers without friction.

To my bitter disappointment, our house in Kathmandu valley fell through at the last moment. The owner, a British ex-army type let it over our heads for six months instead of our three. Typical! I knew the house, knew it was somewhere I'd work well in, and it was quite a blow. Instead, for the time being we are in a minuscule cottage, built for one of the Ranas as a student right in the middle of town. Dust everywhere! And quite a lot of noise! Plus the fact that Kathmandu is the world's Number One capital of respiratory diseases (that I didn't know). Elizabeth promptly got bronchitis, and has half given it to me. This country is so wonderful the moment you get out of the city that I can't regret coming here. But I think we're a bit unsettled and quite honestly I think the only thing is to put on earplugs and knuckle down to the book for the whole of January and then think again.

I keep worrying about Piers Hill. Do let me know if you think there's anything I can do to help.

Had a card from Robyn [Davidson] and Salman, who are using Homer End as a weekend retreat. Bitter complaints from them about the London fog.

All my love to you, Bruce

PS Tomorrow night, for dinner, we are meeting a Mr Chang, the

---

1. Li Po, or Li Bai (701–762), along with Tu Fu (712–770), the most prominent poets of the Tang Dynasty.
2. Doctor Ho in the village of Baisha, where Joseph Rock had lived, was holding a feast for his new-born grandson. E.C.: 'This is the place where Bruce ate a black "1,000 year old egg". It was a ritual course, and none of us ate the eggs except Bruce. He said, "We have to make an effort, we've got to be polite." He ate one and was sick almost as soon as he left the house.'

Number One official in charge of foreign travel in Tibet. Now that really would be something, if we can swing a trip on him. All the places I dreamed of going to: Kashgar, Urumchi, The Takla-Maklan, Lhasa – are suddenly OPEN.

Over Christmas, the Chatwins were joined in Kathmandu by Kasmin – Ninette Dutton and Chatwin's parents having cried off. But Elizabeth's bronchitis had worsened. 'The city was cold and damp and polluted, I couldn't breathe, couldn't lie down to sleep.' Early in the New Year, Kasmin suggested that they leave. The three of them flew to Benares and drove to Delhi where Chatwin had arranged to meet Murray and Margaret Bail. Dropping Kasmin at the Oberoi Hotel, the Chatwins accompanied the Bails to Jodhpur. There, after inspecting several houses, Chatwin found the ideal place in which to complete The Songlines, *a red sandstone fort 20 miles from Jodhpur.*

To Francis Wyndham
Benares | India | [January 1986]

Have fled from disease-ridden Kathmandu: the world's No 1 capital for complaints of the upper respiratory tract – and am now on the loose in India. I have, even with near pneumonia and the constant upheavals, done some writing.

Love as always, BC

To John Pawson[1]
c/o Manvendra Singh | The Fort | Rohet | Jodhpur | India |
23 January 1986

Dear John,

At last I have an address that may last a month or two. Our rented house in the Kathmandu Valley turned out to be a catastrophe . . .

1. John Pawson (*b.*1949), architect and designer, whom Chatwin had hired to redo up his flat in Eaton Place. Pawson had been using the flat as an office. Chatwin wrote in

Can you let me know if the flat is now empty? And if not when it will be? Next, can you work out what's owing? As it's been such a long time, frankly I don't want to spend all of it on repairs. Some can go to pay off the mortgage.

Can you arrange the shower to be tiled first, and put completely in working order? The same tiles as you have in Drayton Gardens. I think it's very important that the whole thing is leak-proof. The next step, I think, should be to prepare the surfaces for painting, filling in old plaster etc. But I feel we should wait till I get back for its final colour. I don't think I want it dead white. Or if I did want it white, then I feel the colour of the floor should be changed, bleached or something.

I'll take a decision as to what to do with the place when I get back. Frankly, it must either be arranged so it is lettable: company lets etc., in which case I must remove all my things and have it anonymous. But the business of letting anyone into so small a space, if the things are there, is really not possible. Or at least, it causes more angst than it's worth. Everyone, in some way or other, is territorial, and there's no point in having a place that isn't one's own.

I have, here, a suite of cool blue rooms in a Rajput Fort. Turtle-doves cooing, peacocks honking, and little children with bells on their clothes playing hide-and-seek in the garden below. I battle on with the arid landscapes of Central Australia.

Do send other news. The baby? The projects in N.Y.? I've been completely out of touch now, without so much as a letter, only some asinine telexes from *Vanity Fair*, for three months.

as always,

Bruce

---

a monograph on him: 'About five years ago, without the least forewarning of what to expect, I was taken to a flat in an ornate, but slightly down-at-heel Victorian terrace, and shown into a room in which, so it seemed to me, the notes were perfect. The flat was the first work of John Pawson, yet the product of fifteen years' hard thinking as to how such a room could be. Here, at last, I felt was someone who understood that a room – any room anywhere – should be a space in which to dream. I found myself walking around it watching its planes and shadows in a state of trance.' Chatwin would be Pawson's first private client.

To John Kasmin

c/o Manvendra Singh | The Fort | Rohet | Jodhpur | India |

27 January 1986

Dear Kassl,

I must say communication in this country is really very dicey. We had calls from you, and then cancelled, and then when we did finally make it to the receptionist in the [Hotel] Oberoi [in Delhi] we were told you'd just gone. The first stab at this mythical beast 'the place to write in' was a dud. Babji Jodhpur said he had a cottage with a swimming pool in a mango orchard halfway to Udaipur, in a place called Ranakpur, where there is an astonishing Jain temple. The whole thing sounded wonderful, but wasn't; in that a bus load of tourists were liable to swoop on the place for lunch, and besides it was all a bit cramped and there was no place to spread.[1] We did, however, at H.H.'s birthday celebrations, meet an extremely pukkah gentleman, ex-zamindar type who said he had a fort in the country. Absolutely secluded, on a lake, with an ageing mother in the zennana, a kitchen full of cooks with traditions going back to the 17th century – and I might say, fabulous miniatures (though if you breathe one word to the other H.H. [Howard Hodgkin], I'll brain you!). On the lake, spoonbills, cormorants, pochards, storks, three species of kingfisher. Slight ruckus from the peacocks in the early morning. Anglo-Indian furniture of the mid-19th century. A cool blue study overlooking the garden. A saloon with ancestral portraits. Bedroom giving out onto the terrace. Unbelievably beautiful girls who come with hot water, with real coffee, with papayas, with a mango milk-shake. In short, I'm really feeling quite contented. The cold and cough has been hard to shake off. A dry cough always is. But thanks to an ayurvedic cough preparation, it really does seem to be on the wane. Today was Republic Day, with Mrs Chatwin on hand to present the prize to the volleyball team, and sweeties to 500 schoolchildren . . . she's gone today via Jaipur and Agra [to Delhi] leaving me to sahib-ish splendour. Over the past week I have at last been cutting some fresh furrows with the book, and

1. E.C.: 'There was also a big grey langur monkey which took against Bruce. He was in this fig tree and he threw fruit and shat on Bruce, who was outraged.'

I don't think I have quite the same sinking feeling that all the rest of it was in chaos. Murray [Bail] was, in fact, a great help with Australianisms.[1] I'll have to watch the whole thing like a hawk. What one can't help feeling is the degree to which English has been Americanised, compared to Australia. I've always thought that Australian writing, on a page, looks a little archaic: now I'm beginning to realise why. They went off to Udaipur, and we came here.

Lots of love to B[eatrice] and G[regori Von Rezzori] – and I hope all goes well with the party. And to you, always B

PS I wonder what you'd think of Gadda[2], *That Awful Mess on the Via Merulana*. My pal Calasso says Gadda is wonderful. Murray lent it to me. I love it.

To Charles and Margharita Chatwin
c/o Manvendra Singh | The Fort | Rohet | Jodhpur | India |
1 February 1986

Dear Charles and Margharita,

Well, all we can say is some little fly must have buzzed in your ear a warning, 'Don't go to Kathmandu!' I don't know if you've heard what happened. The house we were promised: an Englishman's house with servants and sofas, in the country etc fell through and E. was then offered a *cottage orné*, in a garden admittedly right in the heart of the city, not far from the Royal palace. She had to furnish it etc, which all cost money; and when I arrived from Hong Kong, I had, I have to say, misgivings. Almost immediately the offer came up of a trek in the mountains to prospect a new route for Shirley Williams,[3] so I went off walking for six

1. Chatwin and Bail sat at card tables under the trees and Chatwin would read aloud dialogue for correction. M.B.: 'He'd call out, "Does this sound right to you?" and I'd say, "No, no, no, not crude enough."'
2. Carlo Emilio Gadda (1893–1973), Italian author of *That Awful Mess on the Via Merulana*. M.B.: 'It's about a detective who becomes the victim. I was amazed he liked it. Most of his other favourite texts are very traditional and lean.'
3. Shirley Williams, Baroness Williams of Crosby (*b.*1930), British politician and academic.

days, came back feeling wonderful, only to find a message at the airport that E. had bronchitis, which for her, is very unusual. Within a couple of days, I then had a lung collapse on the scale of my Christmas performance last year.[1] The house, it turned out, was sitting in a pool of pollution, plus the fact that over the wall was the city shit-house, plus the fact that they burned the shit and other refuse at night so that the fumes would settle in our throats. All I can say is that it brought back a kind of bronchial misery I associate with Stirling Road winter '47.[2]

Kasmin, who misbehaved dreadfully, then came up trumps and suggested flight, at once, to India: not next week, now. The first flight we could get on was to Benares, and to Benares we went. I've become completely neurotic about overweight, seeing that I'm forty kilos over, in books: but we sailed through that, arrived; went to watch the Burning Ghat (which is not at all sinister, but calming. You literally stand within, say 15 feet, of half a dozen burning corpses: and after you get used to the smell – though I with my cold, could hardly smell a thing – it all seems perfectly natural and harmonious). We then drove to Delhi along the Grand Trunk Road (all planes and trains booked) in a taxi. I hoped to show Kas the <u>Martinière</u> which is an enormous 'French' 18th century chateau, now a boy's school, but since the fog was such that we couldn't see the bonnet of the car, there seemed little point.[3] On to Delhi where we stayed with my pal, Sunil Sethi, a journalist whom I first met while 'doing Mrs G[andhi]', now the editor of a new newspaper *The Indian Mail*. He has a new and beautiful wife: all very *soignée*. Then our Australian friends, Murray and Margaret Bail, he a novelist, she seems to run the welfare department of Sydney, and we went off to Jodhpur,

1. E.C.: 'He gets worse and worse in the recounting of it. But all of this is ME, not him. We had to move because I was ill. I had to go to the American Clinic where the doctor said: "I've seen five people like you this morning. This is the capital city for respiratory diseases." Bruce never went to any doctor. He was fine.'
2. The former brothel in Birmingham where the Chatwins lived after the War. The rooms lacked central heating and Chatwin caught bronchitis, for two winters coughing up green phlegm.
3. E.C.: 'I suddenly realised the driver couldn't read signs and I had to sit in the front seat and read them. I told Kasmin he couldn't smoke more than one cigarette every fifteen minutes.'

where they had already arranged to go and I know the maharajah. The palace in Jodhpur is the last great ruler's palace to be built anywhere: at least as large as Buckingham Palace and completed, finally, in 1949. My friend H.H. (or Babji), a totally wonderful character, replied to my note at once, saying he was overcome with his 40th birthday celebrations. Would we come for a drink now? This minute? Which we did: to find him also entertaining a real lunatic, the Belgian ambassador to Iran. The question then was how to get rid of the Belgian, and keep us back for dinner – which I might say then developed into a farce, with the ambassador hoping he'd been invited, we knowing he hadn't but too polite to say so, etc. It passed off. I said I was looking for somewhere to write, and Babji immediately proposed a cottage in a mango orchard laid out by his grandparents at a place called Ranakpur, about 75 miles away (we went there, later, with the Bails; but it wasn't really very satisfactory. Every day, tourists staying in one of Babji's hotels would descend for lunch, and there was nowhere really for me to spread my books). The next night, however, was the birthday; the maharanee choked solid with diamonds and emeralds;[1] all the courtiers in whirligig Rajasthani turbans and real white jodhpurs; the musicians playing ghazals; polo playing colonels; the British Ambassador – Wade-Gery,[2] distinguished for a change! And then we met a real charmer! Manvendra Singh.

He comes from a line of Rajput zamindars,[3] which is to say, a little bit more than squire: courtier and landowner to be more exact. I did my usual babble about finding a place to write in, and he said, 'I think I have the place'. He had, too. Although he lives four days a week in town, he has his family fort, a building going back to the 16th century, around a courtyard with neem trees and a lawn, its outer walls lapped by a lake with little islands, temples on them etc. The rooms we occupy are a self-contained flat, bluewashed, with 19th century Anglo-Indian furniture, photos of maharajahs, and a never ending procession of birds. The country is flattish, and almost semi-desert; and since there was no monsoon last

1. E.C.: 'Babji even had diamond eyelashes. He joked to Bruce: "Shall I wear my eyelashes?" I had to borrow Margaret Bail's pearls.'
2. Sir Robert Wade-Gery (b.1929), High Commissioner.
3. Actually *thakurs*.

year, the situation is quite grim. But the lake, which is filled from a canal, is one of the only tanks in the region, and the stopping off place for all the migrants on their way to or from Siberia. Almost within arms reach are ducks, spoonbills, egrets, storks, cranes, herons, bee-eaters, a dazzling kingfisher which sits in the nearest tree. Each morning brings something new. Tea arrives with the sun. Siesta. Buckets of hot water. Breakfast. Morning coffee (real). Lunch. Siesta. Walk. More work. Then in the evening you hear the muezzin being called from the Mosque, and incredible bangings and trumpetings from the Krishna Temple, then silence.

I have the most charming study to work in, and work I do. I have learned long ago not to make any prognostications about when this book will be finished. All I will say is that I've enlarged it considerably since I've been here. There's a tricky passage to come, and after that . . . Well, who knows?

But I'm afraid this gypsyish life cannot go on. I shall have, whether I like it or not, to get a proper bolt-hole to work in. Otherwise I find I can fritter away six months at a time without achieving anything, and that only makes me very bad-tempered. In a way, I like being in Italy, but the climate's quite tough in winter, and the villages (because I'm sure it must be in a village) are usually quite depressing. Our old stamping ground in the Basses-Alpes is not half bad. Uzès is another possibility. What it'll mean, I'm afraid, is that the London flat will have to go. I'm after 3 rooms: one to sleep and work in; one to live in, and a spare room. It'll have to have a terrace, somewhere to sit out at least; and walks in neighbourhood. Greece, I think, is too remote; especially when one sees the problems Paddy and Joan [Leigh Fermor] have to face.[1] I know nothing about it: but I'm told the mountain villages of Majorca are still extremely attractive. It's no use thinking I could have something like *Les Chênes Lièges*:[2] because I do need at least the minimum of a working library, and that will take up space. The point is that it must be available for me to descend on, as and whenever, I̲, not anyone else, wants. It must not be let out – as I've had to do

1. The Leigh Fermors were being encroached on at Kardamyli. 'We have spent the winter together at Kardamyli – now being very much wrecked by Teutonic Hordes,' Chatwin wrote in a postcard to David Mason, the American whom he had met at the busstop there. 'A hard-rock disco in Kalamitsi Bay!'
2. The Chatwins' permanent caravan in Gassin, near St Tropez.

with the flat, because it's my experience now that the moment you let anyone in to your surroundings, they are suddenly no longer yours.[1] Anyway, the conclusion of this little moan is that, as and when the book is delivered to the publishers, I am taking off some months a. to try and teach myself some Russian b. to find the bolt-hole and set it up properly.

I'm sending a post-card to College Street, in case by any chance, you've left by the time this arrives. Our contacts are c/o the above: and there is an emergency phone no. 21161 Jodhpur for messages. Manvendra Singh speaks perfect English, as does his wife, who is usually there. There are times, though, when only the servants are in the house. A cable, in a garbled form, gets through, because we've tried it . . . I don't intend to budge until I see my way through towards the downhill slopes. If it gets too hot here, I'll take, as they always did, to the hills . . .

The peacocks are honking and the cymbals sounding in the Krishna Temple . . .

Much love XXXX

B

PS E. tried calling you from Delhi but was told the number was unavailable.

To Deborah Rogers
c/o Manvendra Singh | The Fort | Rohet | Jodhpur | India |
1 February 1986

Dearest Deb,

Who was it made the witticism 'Any letter answers itself after six weeks'? . . . I'm completely out of touch, which is, as you know, the way I like to be.

I wouldn't mind going to Prague for my next effort (something quite small).

---

1. Chatwin had the memory of Pascal in Grosvenor Crescent Mews; also, of lending his flat in Royal Avenue to some Haitians. E.C.: 'They literally stripped it, every sheet, every pillow case; they stole pictures that were mine, including one of India by Thomas Daniell; they stole everything.' His fears were well founded – everything disappeared also from Eaton Place when he lent it to some people.

To Murray and Margaret Bail
c/o Manvendra Singh | The Fort | Rohet | Jodhpur | India |
9 February 1986

Dearest Murray and Margaret,

Well, I have to say the Fort is a real piece of luck. We couldn't be happier here. There is just enough going on, either in the court-yard or by the lake, to arouse one's interest, and not too much to distract me. I have had the devil of a time, though, shaking off that cold – but it does now appear to be on the wane. E. is off to Bombay to see her friends for a week: but I refuse to budge. It is ironic that this book of mine, which is a passionate defence of wandering, as opposed to sedentary habits, should involve its author in a more or less limpet-like existence. The squirrels have got so tame that they crawl up on our chairs.

I feel so juvenile compared to these Indians. Manvendra Singh is one year older than me, almost to the day, yet he represents the male world of my father: in his absolute fairness and tireless, unostentatious work for others. It would also be ironic if India were the last refuge of 'the gentleman'.

I have to say I did enjoy the Gadda. I'm not sure if it'll reach you with or without this letter. E. is posting a lot of things back to England by sea-mail, and she's going to see, whether it's not too exorbitant, whether she'll send it by air.

I don't know what it was about *The Awful Mess* . . . that made me like it so: even the sawn off ending I felt was right. If it had been written by, say, Nabokov, I wouldn't have endured the literary facetiousness for two seconds. But this one I felt comes off.

As for my own 'Awful Mess' I've now got to the critical stage in which there is a sudden shift from Australia, in order to answer Pascal's assertion about the man sitting quietly in a room.[1] If it comes off, then I'm on the downward stretch. If not, then there's a real crisis.

And as for plans, my aim is to get the whole book checked and edited,

1. Blaise Pascal (1623–62), French philosopher: 'I had imagined that all man's unhap-piness stemmed from a single cause, his inability to remain quietly in a room.'

and then make a flying visit to Oz to check the language. It is strange how elusive 'it' is as a written language, and how very different, in the subtlest ways, it is from English spoken in England.

I must stop, I'm afraid, because we have to go to the post-master for a tea-party: a 20-year old bachelor desperately in search of a fair foreign wife who is perpetually badgering us to swap our clothes for his, our watch for his, our pen, our radio . . . etc then she's off to spend the night in town before taking the plane tomorrow morning.

I wasn't really on best form on our little jaunt a. because of my cold b. the uncertainty of what I was doing. E. and I have the idea of moving here for 3 months every year. She sends all her love, and mine.

Bruce

To Diana Melly
c/o Manvendra Singh | Rohet House | Jodhpur | India |
February 15 [1986]

Dearest Diana,

. . . I have been working like an express-train: I wouldn't say it is over yet: but what I have done is to compress all my material out of the files, notebooks, card-indexes (where it has been accumulating for 20 years) and have got it – nearly all – in the folder. Almost all the 'Australian' part of the book is done: so it remains – and this is the hardest part – to weave in the outside stuff. More and more, I've been making the discovery that I can only concentrate if completely taken out of my surroundings. But this wandering uncertainty can't go on: it wastes so much time for one thing: so when I come back, I'm to sell the flat and look for a bolt-hole, somewhere in the Mediterranean, to work in: a place where I can lock the door and go in at any time of year. Easier said than done! I have a feeling that the fatal thing is to go for somewhere 'unspoiled' – as if one isn't a spoiler oneself – because it takes so much money and emotional effort keeping it unspoiled. I wonder whether those mountain villages in Majorca might not be bad . . . Not that I've ever been there! but I might go and have a look.

I've never felt more out of touch: not the least because Elizabeth insisted on having 3 months' worth of our post sent air mail to Nepal – despite the fact I told her not to – including cheques from American publishers, magazines and God know what else, and the whole lot's gone missing: apparently all foreign businesses there send all their mail by courier. So that may be that! A letter from my mother got through with a very good review of Emma [Tennant]'s book,[1] plus a profile [in the *Times*] by Nick Shakespeare: otherwise zero. I am reading, properly for the first time, Proust.[2] Just shows you where things have got to! E. goes visiting the village ladies, learns Hindi from the Brahmin school-teacher, and I've not seen her happier or more cheerful in 20 years (the time we've been married!) I think even she is coming round to the fact that those houses, and that particular way of life, are as bad for her as for me.

A post card takes about 5 days to reach here – and a trickle has already started. E has gone to Bombay to see friends for a week. Tomorrow begins the big push forward (with the book) – I hope! – so the evening I've taken off to write letters.

Love to Francis, George, Tom and Candy –
and, of course you xxx B

To John Kasmin
c/o Manvendra Singh | Rohet House | Jodhpur | India | 17 February 1986

Dear KAZ,

(Kaz – Turkic verbal root meaning 'to nomadise' or 'travel': hence – Kazakh Cossack etc).

But what terrible news of G.[3] I'll write to them next, but Lord knows it's difficult enough when you can't assess the situation. My own view

1. *The Memoirs of Robina by Herself; being the Memoirs of a Debutante at the Court of Queen Elizabeth* II (1986).
2. E.C.: 'I had brought out Proust to read.'
3. Gregor von Rezzori had suffered a stroke at Donnini.

– and you should pass it on if – and only if – you think it would be helpful, is that they should give up going to New York. Whenever I've seen Grisha in America, he always looks fraught, fractious and ill. The whole business of getting into a plane, followed by that particular city, can, if you have a heart condition and a tendency to cancer, only be BAD. I was horrified by that whole ridiculous business of trooping round Middle America in search of Nabokov.[1] He should be in his study in Tuscany doing his own work: not playing to the American gallery, because ultimately his reputation in America is less important than anywhere. When the winter at Donnini gets too bad, then they should move into a hotel. There must be perfectly adequate doctors in Italy; or if not in Switzerland, to which he can go by car – but to be at the mercy of American medicine, however good it may <u>seem</u> to be, is a terrifying prospect.

Enough of that! I adore it here. Lunch yesterday, for example, consisted of a light little bustard curry, a puree of peas, another of aubergine and coriander, yoghurt, and a kind of wholemeal bread the size of a potato and baked in ashes. A sadhu with a knotted beard down to his kneecaps has occupied the shrine a stone's throw from my balcony; and after a few puffs of his *ganja* I found myself reciting, in Sanskrit,[2] some stanzas of the Bhagavad Gita.[3] I work away for eight hours at a stretch, go for cycle rides in the cool of the evening, and come back to Proust.

I envy you your talent for rug-dealing:[4] there's something in me that stops me doing likewise. I cannot explain what it is. But you will, I am sure, make far more money than you imagine with *Kaputt*.[5] I will, if you want, write a foreword.

But this peripatetic existence of mine must stop. I must have *mon bureau, mes fauteuils, mon jardin (pas des bêtes!)* (as Flaubert writes in a

1. An essay for *Vanity Fair*, 'A Stranger in Lolitaland'.
2. E.C.: 'He'd learned Sanskrit for two years at Edinburgh, so it's not a boast.'
3. Sacred scripture of Hinduism, composed between 5th and 2nd century BC.
4. While in Katmandhu, Kasmin had bought a number of tantric concentration rugs with tiger patterns.
5. Novel by Italian diplomat Curzio Malaparte (1898–1955). Kasmin was contemplating starting a press to make reprints of forgotten books.

letter) – somewhere in a relatively good climate, which means the Mediterranean, and I must have it soon. God knows how I'll raise the cash, if it means the sale of my London flat + my art then *tant pis pour eux*! I have fallen, happily, on my feet here: but to be in the situation of Kathmandu just isn't on. I only like doing <u>my</u> work: not reviews, not articles, not commissions – and however eccentric or unsaleable it may get, I intend to go my own way. The latest development to 'Australia' in which I take a world tour – and more! – is quite something! I've even squeezed in Luderitz![1] XXX B

PS Maybe Uzès, too! Or Catalonia?

To Roberto Calasso

c/o Manvendra Singh | Rohet House | Jodhpur | India | 18 February 1986

My Dear Roberto,

Forgive the almost interminable silence. Things, as usual, got on top of me in England: and, as usual, I fled. First to China – where, in the remoter parts of, say, Yunnan, the world of Taoist gentleman-scholars, plant-hunters, poets, calligraphers – still very much exists.

I've had a terrible time with the 'Australian' book: have torn up 3 successive drafts: only to find, borrowing a leaf from *La Rovina di Kasch*[2] that the only way is the 'cut-up' method. Not that I can see the end – yet. But at least I <u>think</u> I know what I'm doing. You're the first person I want to show it to – as and if and when it's ready – even perhaps before. My friend Grisha von R[ezzori] has been horribly ill, heart-attacks and I don't know what, and I must come and see them. Possibly on the way back from here – end April, beginning May, but I'm not sure yet of the dates. Will you be there?

As always, Bruce

---

1. Nondescript mining town on the Namibian coast which Chatwin and Kasmin had visited in February 1984 after the *Observer* commissioned Chatwin to write 'My Kind of Town'.
2. Calasso's *The Ruin of Kasch* (1983), dedicated to the French statesman Talleyrand, examined the rise of the modern state.

To Elisabeth Sifton

c/o Manvendra Singh | Rohet House | Jodhpur | India | 18 February 1986

Dearest Elisabeth,

Ay! Ay! News of Grisha – bad! I had a post card from our pal, Kasmin, who was with us in Nepal for Christmas and then flew straight to the bedside. Can't we/you/all persuade him <u>not</u> to go racketing around America. There must be proper doctors in Italy and there certainly are in Switzerland (to which he can go by car). He should stay in his study, in Donnini – or if Donnini gets too cold in winter, now that Southern Europe has its annual Scandinavian freeze, in a hotel. All that *Vanity-Vogue* life is <u>not</u> good for anyone's health, mental or physical.

News is that I've been beavering away for 2 months in a Rajput fort: overlooking a lake, flashing kingfishers, peacocks on roof, cool rooms with photos of maharajahs etc.. No comment on the book – except that, once again, it's unrecognisable. A third method now being tried – with, I think, greater success. We'll see.

I <u>may</u> appear in the U.S. for my favourite sister-in-law's[1] wedding mid-May. But not to N.Y. except for a second to see <u>you</u> only – if you're there. Can't tell yet, because I don't fancy leaving here without something to show for it. I've decided to <u>leave</u> England. As Richard Burton said: 'The only country in which I do not feel at home.' E. is beginning to feel the same way: so we're going to look for a bolt hole: Has to be in Southern Europe. But nothing elaborate – like Donnini.

Don't bother to reply to this unless something crops up . . .

Much love,

Bruce

To John Pawson

c/o Manvendra Singh | Rohet House | Jodhpur | India | [February 1986]

Monday 10am. 1 week after receiving yours.

Dear John,

What a nice, expansive letter! The first I have had in 3 months because

---

1. Alida Chanler m. Dan Dierker on 10 May 1986.

Elizabeth, against my advice, insisted on having our mail sent AIR to Nepal, – and it has, all of it, failed to arrive: cheques for thousands of $, invitations, etc. – all, temporarily at least, gone.

First things first. The flat. I know you and I will not agree on the question of dead white. I suppose it's because I've lived at various times in the incomparably beautiful whitewashed houses of Greece and Andalucia that dead white walls, in England, always used to be just that: dead – because of the English light. I agree that the existing colour was too creamy: what I'd like is something the colour of milk (if there is such a thing) – and anyway it doesn't matter too much. I'm sure you're right: that the shower, all the minor repairs, and the painting should be done together – but what about hocking the books off the shelves – and the enormous labour of getting them back again? Elizabeth returns to England on March 15; and if the operations were to coincide with her arrival, she would make arrangements to have the books sent down to Homer End. If, on the other hand, the paint job could be done around then, I'd be a lot happier.

My only complaint vis-à-vis last time was that the venetian blinds were not sanded down, which made them a kind of dirt trap.

We've decided to hang onto the flat indefinitely, because at that price, a roof over one's head in London is going to be quite irreplaceable. I'm just not interested in letting it again. But the news also is that somehow, we as a family (my parents are going to chip in) are going to try and find (build?) a bolt-hole for me to work in – somewhere in the Mediterranean – for the winters and probably most of the year. I get such terrible colds and bronchitis in the winter; and if they start in November, they go on till May. And the longer I go on, the less I want to be for ever searching for a suitable place to write. It happens, for this winter, we've found one: but that was a lucky fluke. It is funny, too, that you should mention Majorca. I've never been – and, although I love Catalonia, I wouldn't want to live there. But I'm told that if you clear off the coast (into the mountains), there are many parts of Majorca which are like the South of France was in the Thirties. I had in mind, the moment this book was in shape, to go and investigate the possibility of land on which to build. I need a courtyard, a flat roof with walls with a room open to the sky, 2 bedrooms (1 a library-cum-bedroom) and a living-room-cum kitchen with an open fire. All simplicity itself like that Portuguese architecture from the Alentejo. So you can think about it.

There is no more wilderness in the Med: so one just has to make a compromise. Any house built there <u>must</u> turn in on itself.

You said 'at last a building in the round'. Do you mind my saying that you haven't – or strike me as not having – done enough to apply your unbelievable gifts for coping with interior space to the articulation of facades of buildings. I cannot quite imagine how a building by you would be.

You also list a catalogue of complaints about your partners: but I'm afraid you'll have to face the fact, with your sense of style and fastidiousness, that you'll have to be a one-man band. In order to do what you have to do, you have to be the tyrant who directs, not the partner who cajoles – and, in fact, many people would prefer working for you as an assistant rather than having a slice of the cake.

The only way to run a business these days is to keep a very tight ship – and not to sacrifice control. When scribbling off that article, I couldn't help having misgivings about POSA:[1] it struck me as a silly name, but that's beside the point: the work on the flat was yours. Others may contribute very valuable bits here and there, but they are not stylists – or if they are, not in the same sense as you. They are, however, bound to be fractious if they are all supposed to be on one level.

I hate submarines – I've been down in one once – from Plymouth. Hate the claustrophobia: the same as the clum-pf of an aircraft door closing.

We had a wild dust storm this morning, but that has now cleared and the birds are chirruping again. I <u>want</u> to go on a tour of Rajput and Mughal architecture. The place we're in is fairly marvellous, but it is ironic that my book which is a passionate defence of movement should involve its author in <u>years</u> of limpet like existence.

as always, Bruce

1. The firm started by Pawson and three young designers: Crispin Osborne, Claudio Silvestrin and John Andrews. Chatwin's monograph on Pawson appeared in *John Pawson* (Spain: Gustavo Gili, 1992).

PS I suppose, thinking about it, the choice of Venturi[1] was almost a foregone conclusion. As I said, they were after something 'Neo-classical' and, I'm afraid, hell bent on an American – who are supposed to know so much more about Museums than Europeans – though with the exception of the Gardner Museum in Boston, I don't think I've ever been in an American Museum whose pictures didn't cry to be released from it.

I've written a <u>very</u> irreverent piece on the Norman Foster Hong Kong and Shanghai Bank.[2] As you may know it went over budget four times over – and is, I think, <u>absurd:</u> a maintenance nightmare, not a vision of the future at all, but a backward, thoroughly retro-grade glance back to Soviet Constructivism plus a sort of nostalgia for the glorious days of the Royal Navy. I managed to find the 'feng-shui' man: that is to say, the traditional Chinese geomancer whose advice the Bank took – and ignored – before commissioning the architect – and you should hear some of the things he said about the cross-braces!

To Sunil Sethi

c/o Manvendra Singh|Rohet House|Jodhpur|India|5 March [1986]

Dearest Sunil,

We're coming to Delhi by train from Jodhpur, arriving on the morning of the 12th. E. leaves for London the night of the 13th, and I thought I'd see her off. Is that OK vis-à-vis the room for a few nights? If not we can easily stay – and after a most abstemious two months in whatever hotel. But unless I hear to the contrary, may we assume it is on? Could you, if not too terrible a bore, do something for me. Inquire

1. Robert Venturi (*b*.1925), American architect whose Philadelphia company had won a closed competition to build the Sainsbury Wing of the National Gallery in London. The Prince of Wales had compared the previous design, by Richard Rogers, to 'a monstrous carbuncle on the face of an elegant and much-loved friend'.
2. 'The Chinese Geomancer', published in *Hong Kong – An Illustrated Guide* (Odyssey); reprinted in *What Am I Doing Here*.

how – and the quickest way possible – for me to extend my Indian visa? It runs out on April 6th and I will want to stay at least another month – preferably without having to nip up to Nepal and back. I rather dread the bureaucracy of the immigration dept, so maybe there's a travel agent who can expedite it.

Anyhow, I've decided to come back here after Delhi, immediately after getting the visa, for another spell of work: at least until the end of the month. I have a vague sense that, in that time, I can get the whole thing between covers – which would mean I was free to pack up my notes and books etc., and be free to toy about with the manuscript. I can't see any point in moving from here – even in the heat (there are some cool, almost subterranean rooms) – and one is so well looked after, and above all, CALM. A new place might disrupt things. After that, I thought I'd take to the hills for a bit, and then maybe fly direct to America, to my favourite sister-in-law's wedding in mid May. Who can tell?

I wanted to write to you anyway to say how much I approve of the *Indian Mail*. No waffle! Clear, sensible English – such has not been seen in an English newspaper for the past 20 years – and none of the carping tone. You were absolutely right to leave *India Today*: re-reading it critically over three issues, I find the tone there both gloomy and trite: an unpleasant combination. It's about time people realised just how wonderful India is – not in the exotic sense – but day to day realities. Watching Manvendra here coping with the drought is the kind of thing that Mr Naipaul[1] would never 'see'.

We are still without post from Europe, but tant pis.

Much love, B

---

1. S.S.: 'V. S. Naipaul was an object of derision for Bruce: he irritated him, was part of the carping tone.' Chatwin's notebook, 23 May 1979: 'Read V. S. Naipaul's *A Bend in the River*. Old gloomy-jaws again. The inevitable result of not having a glimmer of humour is to portray all Africans, except possibly the slave class, as monkeys. Simplistic message: back to the primeval forest for Africans.'

To Patrick and Joan Leigh Fermor
c/o Sunil Sethi | G9 South Extension | New Delhi | India | [March 1986]

Dearest Paddy and Joan,

. . . We've managed to install ourselves in the wing of a Rajput Fort about 30 miles from Jodhpur, belonging to one of the old zamindar families: the grandfather, who is still omnipresent in the memory of the retainers, was Colonel of the Jodhpur Lancers and one of the best polo players in the world. The suite of rooms we occupy is where he'd entertain his English friends. The walls are blue; there are punkah hooks, old dhurry carpets, chintz curtains, prints of the Quorn or Pytchley, others of Norwegian fjords and wolves: 18th century miniatures of the family, enthroned or on shikar [hunting] and replaced, gradually, by the same subjects taken by the Rajputana Photo studio. My study leads out onto a terrace along the battlements, about the size of Montaigne's, from which there is a view of the lake, a Shiva temple on an island, the family memorials (in Mughal style) onshore and a rest house for visiting sadhus. There was an old rogue who arrived a few days ago, in saffron, with a hennaed beard[1] down to his ankles: a scion apparently of a great Rajput house who had quarrelled irrevocably with his wife and taken to the road. After a puff or two of his *ganja* I found myself reciting in Sanskrit the opening stanzas of the Bhagavad Gita.

The food is delicious and brought by delicious girls on solid mahogany trays. Last week, for example, we had for lunch a light Little Bustard curry, a purée of peas, another of aubergines and coriander, and bread rolls, the size of potatoes, baked in ashes. The lake is seething with duck – shovellers, scaup, pintail, pochard – awaiting the call to fly back to Siberia. Herds of black buck come down to drink with the camels. There are spoonbills, storks, cranes and ibis; and yet I long for walks in the Mani.

The temptation to take a siesta instead of a walk is irresistible. I've never been so immobile in my life. The afternoon sun is very strong;

1. EC: 'He used to wash himself in the lake and had built a house that became a shrine where he grew hemp plants as tall as the ceiling.'

and the plain beyond, having missed last season's monsoon, is an ashen wilderness with willy-willies blowing across it.

The book is by no means done; I've decided the only thing to do is to let it run its own course and shove everything in. I've been casting back over my old notebooks, and have managed to find a place for things like this:

Djang, Cameroon
There are two hotels in Djang: the Hotel Windsor and, on the opposite side of the street, the Hotel Anti-Windsor

Or:
Goree, Senegal
On the terrace of the restaurant a fat French bourgeois couple are guzzling their fruits-de-mer. Their dachshund, leashed to the woman's chair, keeps jumping up in the hope of being fed.
 — *Taisez-vous, Romeo! C'est l'entracte*

Don't bother to reply to this except, perhaps, a post-card to say when the book[1] is coming out; and whether, if I broke my journey in late April or May, you'd be there. Elizabeth has to go to her sister's wedding in the middle of May; and if I had something to show the other Elisabeth [Sifton] I should be tempted to go too. But that's all too early to decide. I might even stay here, and take to the hills. I'll be going to Delhi to prolong my visa and pick up mail around March 15th.

Much love, as always
Bruce (and Elizabeth!)

---

1. *Between the Woods and the Water*, the second volume of Leigh Fermor's travels. The first, *A Time of Gifts* (1977), had come out the same time as *In Patagonia*. E.C.: 'Paddy said to me: "It's very good, but he ought to let himself rip." Bruce said to me, almost simultaneously, of Paddy's book: "Its very good, but it's too baroque and overflowing; he should tone it down."'

To Ninette Dutton

c/o Sunil Sethi | G9 South Extentsion | New Delhi | India | 5 March 1986

Dearest Nin,

I <u>am</u> sorry for the prolonged silence. At the beginning of the winter (northern hemisphere) things got terribly out of hand. As I think I jotted on a card, we had this house all fixed up in the countryside outside Kathmandu, with wonderful views of the mountains etc. But then the Englishman to whom it belonged (Perfide Albion!) welshed out on the deal and we were left with a kind of *cottage orné* in the heart of the city: pretty enough superficially, but terribly damp and with the most fragrant smells of the city sewer. Nepal really is one of the great unhealthies. Much more so than India, and both E and I were really quite ill, before deciding to flee to India. Nothing makes me in a worse temper than having set aside X number of months in which to work, then to find one is junketing round from hotel to hotel, looking for a place to settle. We did, however, meet up with Murray and Margaret Bail in Delhi. They had been in Simla for Christmas – against our advice! – in a freezing hotel three feet deep in snow. Anyway, we all went to Jodhpur whose Maharajah is an old friend of mine: we share a part of some really riotous times at the Cannes Film Festival of 1969.[1] Although he has no political power he has now become a most magnificent ruler and also owns the biggest palace in India. At his 40th birthday party, we were introduced to all his courtiers, mostly polo playing types; *thakurs* that is landed gentry. Among them a total charmer (not a polo player) called Manvendra Singh, whose grandfather was Colonel of the Jodhpur Lancers and fought in Flanders etc.

I did my usual spiel about being desperate for somewhere to write, and he said 'Why not write in my fort?' We've been here now for 2 months: a 17th century Rajput fort, on a lake, with a Shiva temple on an island, every kind of birds: ducks, flamingoes, spoonbills, pelicans. A burble of life going on in the courtyard below: the buffalo to be milked, the laughter of children, the howling of peacocks – at seven as alarm call! I never left. I hardly even went to Jodhpur, only 20 miles away

1. *Savages*, the Merchant-Ivory film, was shown in May 1972.

except to get typing paper. I won't say I've finished the book: that would be going too far – but I do have the sense of an ending. The book is not just an 'Australian' enterprise, but sets down a lot of crackpot ideas that have been going round my head for twenty years. So this is not three years work but 20. We shall see. The terrifying moment will come when I dare to re-read what I've done.

We are, in fact, leaving tomorrow. Elizabeth has to get back to her lambing. The past week has really been too hot. It would be fine if I didn't have something critical to do. But it's too hot to take exercise, and the mind starts to go soggy too. So I'm taking her to Delhi and then going for the rest of the month and most of April to a guest-house[1] we've heard of not far from Simla. Spring in the hills should be lovely, I hope! My aim is to get a rough first draft, and then take it to America. In the editing stages, I think I will have to come to Oz: when going through some of it with Murray, I realised just how easy it is for a Pom to slip up on the tiniest mistakes.

I'll get the post from my pal Sunil in Delhi. It'd be lovely to get a scrap of news. Goodness I hope every thing's gone OK vis-à-vis Piers Hill.[2]

All my love to you, dearest. E sends hers.

Bruce

PS We <u>have</u> to leave! They're all hotting up for the Holi festival. This means grinding accordion music all night!

To Charles Way
c/o Sunil Sethi | G9 South Extension | New Delhi | India |
9 March 1986

Dear Charlie,

I had – feeling rather guilty – at one moment thought of getting on a plane and coming back again. But one of my (? unconscious) calculations

1. The Retreat at Bhimtal, near Nainital.
2. Dutton did not move from Piers Hill until the late 1990s.

was that the first productions of *On the B.H.* were by no means going to be the last. I had an immediate sense, on meeting you and the <u>Made in Wales</u> people, of the rightness of the enterprise: and obviously I was right![1] Many congratulations! I long to hear, and see more. But don't bother to reply to this, unless there's something urgent. I shall be here: the above is a better contact for mail – until April 25th, when I'm coming back.

I had no idea, when I set out to do the current book, what an enormous enterprise I'd let myself in for. I, who liked to think of myself as a kind of miniaturist, am now faced with hundreds and hundreds of chaotic pages. But I think that's the way it has to be. Every book – though of course not a play – seems to have its length predicated by the opening paragraphs, and one simply has to go on to the bitter end and then take stock of the matter. I do like being out of touch, though. Yours was the first – and welcome! – letter I've had in a month or so. I suspect the local P.O. of monkeying with the mail, but we have vaguely kept in touch with the weather in Britain etc . . .

As always, and again a thousand congratulations and thanks, Bruce

To Murray Bail

c/o Sunil Sethi | G9 South Extension | New Delhi | India | 11 March 1986

Dear Murray,

Hello there! The Fort at Rohet has proved a resounding success. The rooms were cool. I shed my cold. The desk was at the right height. Coffee – real – came at the right moment. There were bicycles to take some exercise. The timeless scenes of Indian life went on from day to day. The arrival of a new species of Siberian duck on the lake and, one morning, flamingoes were about as much as we got in the way of excitement. We went to Jaipur in the car for two days: Jodhpur twice, for the afternoon. Otherwise, a hard slog. I won't say I'm finished: but the experiment I was dreading so much,

---

1. *On the Black Hill* opened on 4 February 1986 at the Sherman Theatre in Cardiff. 'It is something quite special, a work of intensity, compassion, humour and tragedy,' David Adams wrote in the *Guardian*.

and have been putting off for months, is done – and there's now a lot of book. I'm only capable of functioning away from all the hullaballoo – although I sometimes find myself envying your very calm house in the middle of all that hullaballoo. Considering I now hardly ever set foot in a bookstore, or read literary journals, it's quite amazing how you and I pick up on the same things. I thought *Kolyma Tales*[1] very wonderful; what I would love to try and get down someday is the rightmindedness of Russians in extreme adversity. Also Ray Carver[2] has been a favourite of mine since the first collection came out and a girl who, herself, came from Washington State advised me to get them. He really does make most other American writers look like so much junk. He's the only one who knows that there is such a thing as prose rhythm, and he has to be the most sensitive observer of the American scene. He's apparently spawned a troop of imitators, none of them any good. I'm told he's at work on a big novel, and it'll be interesting to see.

[Mario Vargas] Llosa's quite something, if you get a chance to meet him. Robbe-Grillet[3] is something I've never taken in.

I'm off this evening to the hills: a guesthouse with separate chalets in a nature reserve at Bhimtal, owned and run by ancient refugee Czechs.[4] E returns to England and her lambs. We shall see.

Forgive this chaotic note. Hot evening outside. Whirling with mosquitoes. Rohet, alas, has been unbearable for the past week with temperatures in the hundreds.

1. *The Kolyma Tales* (1980), by Varlam Shalamov (1907–82) short stories about a labour camp in the Soviet Union.
2. Raymond Carver (1938–88); his first collection was *Will You Please Be Quiet, Please?* (1976). After finishing it, the American writer David Plante wrote to Chatwin: 'As I read them I thought of you – in the same way, I'm pleased to know, you thought of me as you read them. Do you think we are having a kind of literary love affair – filled of course with jealousies and competitiveness but admiration and devotion? That would be nice. So often, reading a book, I wonder; what would Bruce think of this? And if I decide, well, really, Bruce wouldn't think much of it, I don't think much of it.'
3. Alain Robbe-Grillet (1922–2008) French filmmaker and writer, associated with the Nouveau Roman.
4. Fred Smetacek and his son Peter. E.C.: 'Smetacek was a Czech national who had lobbed a knife at Hitler and escaped, went to India, which he liked, and was interned by the British for the duration of the war. He met a moghul princess through an ad in the marriage columns and they married. They swapped nationalities so he could buy the resort.'

Write to England sometime but don't bother here unless urgent. We are still without our backlog of three months post, and chasing letters round India is not a pastime for me.

Love from E. Love to Margaret and from me to you both.

Bruce

Magnus Bartlett (b.1943) had been the photographer on Bruce and Elizabeth's trip to Yunnan. Based in Hong Kong, he was the publisher of a series of guides to or around China, including Tibet *by Elizabeth Booz. He had persuaded Chatwin to contribute a short piece to a forthcoming illustrated guide to Hong Kong, 'on a Feng Shui man "doing" the just-finished Norman Foster HSBC building'.*

To Magnus Bartlett

c/o Sunil Sethi | G9 South Extension | New Delhi | India | 12 March 1986

New Delhi but as from: Homer End, Ipsden, Oxford

Dear Mag,

. . . I have, in the past, had requests for just one <u>page</u> of manuscript from well-wishers in the United States. At Rohet, where we were staying, I was often appalled by the way in which our servant would empty the contents of my waste paper basket from the rampart, littering a patch of ground in front of the lake with a kind of *papierarie*.

This is not a complaint – and not to be broadcast around – but I don't think you have any idea of my intense loathing of magazines and magazine editors: there <u>are</u>, of course, individual exceptions, but each case must be judged on its merits. I would like to think that I never have to work for one again.

I want you to get Ducas[1] to get my piece <u>back</u> from the *Connoisseur*

---

1. Robert Ducas, Bartlett's New York-based agent, had submitted 'The Chinese Geomancer' – which Chatwin had written for Bartlett – to the *Connoisseur* magazine in London.

– though they must pay me (to England) the kill fee. And I want the original copy, too. I'm not interested in publishing it, and certainly don't want him touting it round the New York magazines, thank you. If anyone's going to do that, I will or my agent will – but I don't want to get any crossed wires . . .

Otherwise, nothing dims the memory of Yunnan – and nothing would have been better than my 2 months in Rajasthan – in that I've got a terrific lot done. I'm now going to the hills till the end of April – hoping, at last, to break the back of it. All contact had better be through E. in Oxfordshire. She leaves first week in May for the US.

All the best to you and Paddy, Johnson and Prof Tea.[1] The Tibet guide is first rate. I've read Elizabeth Booz's introduction – a masterpiece of tact and common sense. Pictures A1 etc. E. would like to know more of what's involved vis-à-vis the Silk Road project.[2]

B

To Magnus Bartlett
c/o Sunil Sethi|G9 South Extension|New Delhi|India|
[March 1986]

Dear Magnus,

Postscript to last screed. I'm told by people here who've worked for them, that the editorial staff of the *Connoisseur* (the word is enough to make one squirm) are deeply bonkers: and that to do anything for them, even at a long distance, is to drive oneself into the looneybin with them. So please get the text back!

B

1. Paddy Booz, son of Elizabeth Booz; Johnson Chang, Chatwin's translator in Yunnan; Professor Tea, the title bestowed on Michael Ng of Wing Kee Tea Merchants, a real connoisseur of Chinese tea whom Chatwin had met in Hong Kong, 'who only specialises in the finest possible Oolong special leaf', as he wrote to Derek Hill, enclosing a gift of a tiny amount of high altitude white tea.
2. Bartlett had discussed with Elizabeth the possibility of her doing a guide to Gujarat.

To John Kasmin

The Retreat | Bhimtal | Nainital | India | March 1986

Have moved up into the hills. Old English tea plantation now run as a hotel guest house by Czech adventurer type, ex inhabitant of Punta Arenas in Chile, refugee from Germany in the 30's for having thrown a knife at Hitler. B

To Elizabeth Chatwin

c/o Smetacek | The Retreat | Bhimtal | Nainital | India | 27 March 1986

Dearest E,

Quick note because some U.S. Embassy people are going down to Delhi and will post it, a saving of five days or so. Yes. It's very nice here: not too cold. I have a house to myself, with a verandah and Banks's rose clambering over it, a view of wheatfields etc. On the mountain above lives a charming sadhu, the father of the Forest, whose business it is to protect the trees. Old Smetacek has gone to Germany for four months. Sounds an incredible character. Hounded from Germany for throwing a knife at Hitler;[1] Chilean citizen (resident of Punta Arenas, where else?). Ended up in Calcutta during the war, and married a Muslim girl through correspondence column in the newspaper. I think I'll stay on as long as possible. There's no point in lumping oneself to Manali, or even Nepal, when the Kumaon is obviously very fascinating. Badrinath is a two-day bus ride: besides this is Jim Corbett[2] country – and as I'm writing about man-eaters I appear to have landed in the right spot. Below the sadhu's cave there is a leopard lair, but the animal is supposed to be very friendly. The Smetacek dogs though, if you take them on a walk, are inclined at certain places to get jittery.[3]

xxx B

1. In another version, Fred Smetacek was involved in a plot, discovered by the Gestapo, to dynamite a railway tunnel in the Sudetenland.
2. Jim Corbett (1875–1955), Indian-born British hunter and author of *The Man Eaters of Kumaon* (1944).
3. E.C.: 'A leopard's favourite thing is dog. People lost their pets very, very quickly.'

To Elizabeth Chatwin

c/o Smetacek | The Retreat | Bhimtal | Nainital | India | 10 April 1986

Dear E.,

Well, it's still very nice here but the heat increases each day with hot dusty winds coming from the plain. I've done some very good work. The cut-up method does actually solve the problem. I've just been writing the tramp and the Arctic tern. I'm not going to <u>finish</u> needless to say, but I've done all the back-writing i.e. there are now few gaps in the narrative.

I'm not quite sure what to do. I'd like to go on a trek before returning and in a week or so I'll be in the mood to pack the book in for a bit. I can go north of here into the Kumaon Himalaya with Peter S[metacek], youngest of the sons, or, I suppose I could go up to Nepal. But Peter has been ill with measles and the after-effects are slow. Manali, I gather, is out of the question. Chandigarh is cut off by the army: you can't get to Simla, and they anticipate that no one will go to Kashmir the whole year. The situation is apparently quite dreadful, much worse than anyone anticipated. I certainly intend to be back by May 1st or so . . .

Will you tell [John] Pawson I do want to be able to <u>use</u> the flat in May and June. None of that hanging round waiting for them to finish.

Nice birds here on my terrace. A Himalayan magpie, blue and white with a tail 2 feet long. The scarlet minivet, the Himalayan barbet and the funniest whistling thrushes that look like Barbara Cartland.[1] Then pheasants . . .

The V & A story[2] . . . just shows you. Things are both tough and vulnerable but no safer in a museum than in some old Rajasthan fort.

This letter is going to be posted in England by some friends of S[unil] who are flying to London tomorrow night. Apparently the cheapest ticket now is Air France, but with a 6-hour stopover in Paris. I shall try and

1. Barbara Cartland (1901–2000), prolific English author of 723 romances; her brother, the Conservative MP Ronald Cartland, had briefly employed Chatwin's mother.
2. On the night of 21 March a joint on a temporary water main at the Victoria and Albert Museum failed, causing serious flooding of the basement area.

get Vayadoot[1] down to Delhi because that Trunk Road is a nightmare to travel down, to say nothing of the cost . . .

My Dad has given us 6000 quid each from family capital: useful for paying off the mortgage: but I told them I'll only accept it providing they can call for it back if needed.

Must stop because they're going.

xxx with love B

PS I have an idea. I should like to go on holiday in Turkey in September with the car and windsurfer. So don't make too many plans.

'We've just had bad news from India.' Back at Homer End Elizabeth was telephoned in April by Dinah Swayne, who ran the office for Penelope Betjeman's trekking tours in the Western Himalayas.'I thought of Bruce immediately. Why do they know? But it was Penelope.' Penelope Betjeman had died on 11 April while leading a tour in the Kulu valley. Soon afterwards, Chatwin telephoned from India.'It was the only time I'd known him in tears,' says Elizabeth.'He was shattered.' In Wales, during his separation from Elizabeth, Penelope had become, he said,'a sort of mother to me'.

To Candida Lycett Greene[2]
Kulu | Himachal Pradesh | India | [April 1986]

PENELOPE DIED SITTING UPRIGHT LAUGHING AT HER PONY WHICH HAD STRAYED INTO A WHEATFIELD STOP IN ACCORDANCE WITH INDIAN CUSTOM HER ASHES WERE DIVIDED INTO TWO PARTS STOP ONE PART WAS SCATTERED AT KHANAG WHERE SHE DIED STOP THE SECOND PART INTO THE BEAS RIVER THIS MORNING TEN DAYS AFTER HER DEATH

---

1. Local independent airline.
2. Author (b.1942) and daughter of Penelope and John Betjeman.

To Patrick and Joan Leigh Fermor
Kulu | Himachal Pradesh | India | 24 April 1986

My dear Paddy and Joan,

I got your card at the same moment as news of Penelope's death – and decided to go up to Kulu at once. Yesterday morning, her friend Kranti Singh and I carried her ashes in a small brass pot to a rock in the middle of the R[iver] Beas which was carved all over, in Tibetan, with *Om mani padme hum*[1]. He tipped some into a whirlpool and I then threw the pot with the remainder into the white water. The flowers – wild tulips, clematis, and a sprig of English oakleaves (from the Botanical gardens in Manali) vanished at once into the foam.

The doctor, who was with her on the trek, gave 'heart-attack' as the cause of death: but the word 'attack' is far too strong for what happened. If ever there was a 'natural death', this was it. All morning she was in the best of spirits – although people in the party said she was already beginning to dread going back to England, to pack up her house etc. Around 10, she called in on her favourite Pahari temple. The priest, who knows her, welcomed her to join in the *puja*.[2] She received the blessing and then rode on towards a place called Khanag. There she dismounted to rest, laughed (and scolded) at her pony which had strayed into a wheat field, and was talking her head off to her Tibetan porter when her head tilted sideways and the talking stopped.

Although it's nowhere finished, I had – only two days before – been writing the final chapters of the book: of how Aborigines, when they feel death close, will make a kind of pilgrimage (sometimes a distance of thousands of miles) back to their 'conception site', their 'centre', the place where they belong. In the middle of nowhere in the desert I was taken to see three very old Aborigines, happily waiting to die on three metal bedsteads, side by side in the shade of an ironwood tree.

Penelope, as I'm sure you know, would cheerfully discuss the pros and cons of going back to India to die: she could never quite work out how to arrange it. Over the past year or so, she would discuss, quite

1. 'O the flower of the lotus,' Buddhist mantra.
2. Worship.

rationally, the building of her new 'Anglo-Indian' bungalow in Llandrindod Wells;[1] I don't think she ever believed in it. She had sworn never, ever to head another trek to Kulu, but when the offer came, her instinct must have told her to accept.

I'm writing this in a smoking tea-house waiting for the bus to take me and the Tibetan porters on a Penelope Memorial Walk.

Over the years I've heard so much about Kulu from her. On my first night, in the village behind Kranti's house, there was a dance of young boys in pleated white skirts (like evzones)[2] with cockades of monal pheasant feathers. The silver trumpets looked entirely Celtic, and the village houses with their dragon finials and mica-glinting roofs could easily be the Heorot[3] in *Beowulf*.

I said, months ago, that I'd go to Elizabeth's sister's wedding in Upstate New York on May 10. Since Delhi is about half way round the world, I'm going to slip off to Japan for a week (I have a Japanese publisher!). Then to England – at last! I do hope this catches you before you leave and that I'll find you both in London around 20 May.

Much love

Bruce

To John Pawson
Homer End | Ipsden | Oxford | 30 May 1986

1. Part of my anxiety about the shower stems from a previous experience. For my (or rather Christopher Gibbs') cubby-hole in Albany, John Prizeman[4] installed just such a shower with a zinc tray underneath. That, however, did not prevent it leaking and, over 10 years or so, causing dry rot damage to the tune of some thirty thousand quid – for

1. E.C.: 'She was going to get a Swedish ready-made house on a plot next to the Catholic Church so that she could pop in any time.'
2. Greek soldiers.
3. A great mead hall described in the Anglo-Saxon epic *Beowulf* as 'the foremost of halls under heaven'.
4. John Prizeman (1930–92), English architect.

which we were mercifully insured, but it did cause a very unpleasant scene.

2. [Can you ask] your people to rip out the existing shower as soon as possible or at least to make sure there are no drips. I also, as you may remember, have had an altercation with a dreadful woman downstairs over a leak when the plumbing was being put in.

3. We have used, very successfully, in the big room here an off-white which is Sanderson's 7-13 P, and I would like to repeat the same in the flat.

Otherwise all is well. I'm sorry I didn't come over: but with a lot of friends from abroad in London, I was on the run. Work on the book recommences this morning.

All my love to Caius,[1] Bruce Chatwin

To Sunil Sethi
Homer End | Ipsden | Oxford | 25 June 1986

Dear Sunilito,

I have you terribly on my conscience: the truth is, at the end of the day, when I've written myself into a standstill, I develop such a horror of words that to write a simple thank-you letter is worse than Tantalus rolling the stone. It absolutely goes without saying how incredibly grateful we are, to you and Shalini, for 'the winter', no less.

I have not been entirely idle on your behalf, however. I have talked to Shelley Wanger at *House and Garden* who is very interested in the Sarabhai house[2] – and positively wishes you'd write that famous letter. I have made tentative enquiries about the most discreet of 'house

1. Pawson's new baby son. Elizabeth and Bruce were joint godparents.
2. S.S.: 'The story was about an original house designed by Le Corbusier for Mani Sarabhai, a young widow with two sons. She belonged to a famous family of textile magnates in Ahmedabad, known for their patronage of the arts. She asked the boys what features they would like in the house; one wanted a slide and the other a swimming pool. So the architect designed a house incorporating a slide that dips from an upper storey into the swimming pool in the garden below.' The house featured in Sethi's book *Indian Interiors* (1990).

photographers' [Derry Moore] and believe he would love to do it, and work with you. So, the ball is in your court!

I have also been to Smythsons.[1] There seem to me to be two possibilities: one an elongated address book with a green leather binding and space for oodles of numbers; the other a slightly more portentous affair with marbled end papers, less space, and more gilding. The choice is yours. Either's fine by me. But how to get it out to you?

The book creaks on, at snail's pace: but it is some book. I'm not too discouraged because it really is <u>about something</u>. E. is well, and obviously cock-a-hoop to be back among the sheep: not without the usual attendant dramas!

Japan was the nastiest place I've ever been, except, of course, to where I then went, the USA. The most decadent corrupt country in the world, well on the way to ruin, if you ask me. Europe on the other hand strikes me as being rather less hopeless: certainly with the Libyan bombing,[2] the scales have fallen from people's eyes. Paris without Americans was unbelievably charming – and the French, to my surprise, were revelling in their absence.

No possibility, I suppose, of your visit here!

Much love, to you and Shalini

Bruce

To Ninette Dutton
Homer End | Ipsden | Oxford | 26 June 1986

Dearest Nin,

I'm sorry for the apparently endless delay in writing. The fact is that I've been straining to get the first draft finished: and by the end of the day, the nausea for words – even words to one's dearest! – becomes posi-

---

1. Bond Street stationers. S.S.: 'We chose the leather-bound address book, and still have it.'
2. On 15 April 1986 the United States had bombed Libya in operation 'El Dorado Canyon'.

tively stifling. Coupled with the hideous complications of our post – I may have told you, three or four months' worth, presumably scattered somewhere on the streets of Kathmandu. .

The news – no longer new – was that our best of all possible friends Penelope Betjeman, dismounted her horse while leading a trek in the Western Himalaya, sat down to rest on a mossy bank covered with violets and wild strawberries, hooted with laughter at her pony as the Tibetan boy tried to lead it up the path and, then, as he looked up, he was in the nick of time to see her curl up like a child going to sleep. Perhaps half a second and that was that. I was starting out on a trek of my own. We had saddled up, brought the provisions, when I bought *The Times of India* and found a perfectly beautiful third leader describing the death of the daughter of the Founder of the Modern Indian Army, Lord Chetwode. It was called 'Journey to the beginning'. She had been there with her mother in 1933 and couldn't really think of anywhere else as home. Her ashes, in accordance with Hindu custom, were half saved in a brass pot: so ten days later, I and her friend Kranti Singh stood on a rock in the river Beas, her favourite river in the world, and tipped her in. The ashes, I have to say, were not like the Western world's idea of ashes. They were bits of skull and bouquets of budding English oak from the ex-Resident's garden, the pheasant-eye narcissus and Tulipa cashmeriana. Anyway they all went into the rushing snow-water and we let out a loud Penelope-ish 'ha! ha!' – and that was that!

After leaving Kulu, I went down to Delhi by plane with a vague idea in my head that since, in a week's time, I had to be at my sister-in-law's wedding, it might be possible to make a stopover in Japan. Which it was, and which I'm afraid I hated. Such a treadmill, and so poisonously ingrown, that after the exhilarating breezes currently coming out of China, I profess myself a Sinophile and a Japanophobe (if that's a word!). Not that rather wonderful things didn't keep happening to me: but the $96 to the airport with no cheaper way, struck this mean old bastard with horror.

Then the USA where as you'll know the really pleasant surprise was seeing Tisi [Dutton] about the only one too! What a madhouse! I was completely put off kilter by a friend of mine[1] for whom I had said, three years ago and in a moment of extreme weakness, that I'd write an article on her Tuscan tower, where I sometimes write. She needless to say wanted it in *House and Garden* so she could rent it to the rich. I was left holding the can, with an ultimatum that it had to be done by the end of the week: so all my days and quite a lot of the nights was consumed writing this wretched piece, which because it was so wretched was inordinately difficult to do. Alas! our planned lunch with T[isi] fell through. I hope she <u>does</u> get going with Bob and Victoria Hughes.[2] They were here last weekend, reading the book too, with snorts and guffaws, so that was also quite encouraging. Robyn D[avidson] and Salman are in a split-up situation of high oriental drama. The passions of the Thousand and One nights have been generated and it'll take quite a long time for the episode to simmer down . . . must end.

Elizabeth sends fondest love and I, B. When's the American lap?

PS Invitation to the Perth Festival in Feb. Think I'll miss. We may have a bit of time then: and if so will come anyway.

---

1. Beatrice von Rezzori. 'A Tower in Tuscany,' *House & Garden*, January 1987.
2. Robert Hughes (*b*.1938), Australian-born art critic and friend of Ninette Dutton; m. 2nd 1981–96 Victoria Whistler.

CHAPTER ELEVEN

HOMER END: 1986–8

When in India in April Chatwin had visited Penelope Betjeman's pyre in a bushy glade below Khanag. As he sat, pausing for breath, at the top of the Jalori pass, an old sadhu sitting outside a shrine had asked to tell his fortune. 'The old man looked at his palm and blanched,' says Elizabeth. 'Bruce got a terrible intimation of mortality.'

Since his return to Homer End in May he had suffered from night sweats and asthma. Over the summer, he developed a hoarse voice and noticed 'some vague skin lumps'. Looking tired and drawn, he worked hard on his book, determined to finish it before finding out what his illness was.

One hot day early in August 1986 Elizabeth drove Chatwin to Reading. She wrote to her mother: 'On the way back B had a horrible attack when he started to go blue & was just gasping. He can only go for little slow walks & is always cold & sits wrapped up with a heater on all the time. He's very weak & looks awful & sleeps a lot. He's only got a tiny bit more of the book to do & most of it is at two typists, one seems to be fast and the other very slow. Maybe by the end of this week he'll be able to go away. We think Switzerland wd be the best place.'

He finished The Songlines *ten days later, 17 years and 3 months after signing the initial contract.*

To Jean-Claude Fasquelle[1]

Homer End | Ipsden | Oxford | 16 August 1986

Dear Jean-Claude, Many thanks for your letter. Yes. A new manuscript exists. There'll probably be some teething problems with it, but the moment a clear copy is available, you shall have it. French title, *Les Voies-Chansons*. This is an idea I've been mulling over for about 20 years and, now it's done, I feel completely done in. My next plan is to come and learn Russian at the Confrérie Jésuite Orthodoxe à Meudon! When and as I feel a bit stronger.

As always, Bruce

Too weak to work with Elisabeth Sifton on the manuscript in New York, Chatwin arranged to meet her in Zurich where he flew on 17 August. The next day he was admitted to a clinic in Muhlebachstrasse 'constantly coughing up and with acute diarrhoea', according to the report of Dr Keller, the Swiss doctor who treated him. By the time Sifton arrived, Chatwin was back in the Hotel Opera where he had booked her a room. They worked on The Songlines *every morning for five days, and then he said: 'Now I must get well. You can go now.' Sifton refused to leave until he had telephoned Elizabeth. When Elizabeth turned up on 1 September, he was unable to move, although he did manage, two days later, to write a note to Deborah Rogers: 'As for the cover there is a black and white engraving of an aboriginal family by – God bless and trust him to see – William Blake.'*

His parents were already on the Continent in a camper-van, motoring south to their holiday home in Provence, when, says Hugh, 'Margharita had another of her psychic "There's something the matter with . . ." moments – this time with Bruce. She stopped and telephoned Elizabeth. The outcome was, they changed their itinerary. "We cancelled our holiday and turned left for Zurich."'

On 12 September, hugely dehydrated and coughing up sputum,

---

1. Chatwin's editor at Grasset.

Chatwin was helped onto a plane by Elizabeth, Charles and Margharita. 'He came very near to dying on the flight,' says Elizabeth who accompanied him back to Heathrow. There, an ambulance waited to drive him to the Churchill Hospital in Oxford.

At 3.34 p.m. Chatwin was admitted to the John Warin emergency ward for infectious diseases. He was identified simply as 'an HIV positive 46-year-old travel writer'. Two days later, the ward registrar Dr Richard Bull wrote in his medical notes: 'Patient told he is seropositive, has pre-AIDS but true AIDS not yet certain.' Chatwin would cling to that uncertainty.

On 26 September, from a biopsy, the Radcliffe laboratory identified as Penicillium Marneffei *a mould fungus that is a natural pathogen of the bamboo rat in South Asia. It was then known only, as Dr Bull wrote in his report 'in Thai and Chinese farmers'. Not long from those parts, this discovery cheered Chatwin, who metabolised his illness into something rich and strange.*

His Evaluation Sheet reveals that while doctors did discuss with Chatwin 'that he <u>may</u> have AIDS' – and made Elizabeth aware 'he has not a good prognosis' – the exact nature of his illness was concealed from Charles, Margharita and Hugh: 'Family to be told he has pneumonia.'

'To me it was all very simple,' says Hugh Chatwin, who, in common with Charles and Margharita, would remain in ignorance of Chatwin's illness and sexuality until his last months. 'He would not let down his father.'

In Zurich, when he first received his diagnosis, Chatwin had asked Elizabeth to keep the news from his family. 'He minded terribly,' she says. 'He always thought he could tell his mother but not his father. "I don't want him to think badly of me." He hoped he could hold out until they had found a cure.'

At this stage, the doctors preferred not to make known the result of the brain scan. This revealed no deleterious effect upon the left side of his brain, the generative side; but some damage to the right side could be expected to impair his ability to reason.

To Gertrude Chanler

Homer End | Ipsden | Oxford | 'but still in hospital' | [13 October 1986]

My dear Gertrude,

So very many thanks for your sweet letter: this is the first one I have written since 'the collapse'.

Trust me to pick up a disease never recorded among Europeans. The fungus that has attacked my bone marrow has been recorded among 10 Chinese peasants (China is presumably where I got it), a few Thais and a killer-whale cast up on the shores of Arabia. The great test comes when we find out whether I can go on producing red blood cells on my own.

That is the worst of the news! Otherwise things are very cheery. Your eldest daughter has become a <u>real</u> nurse. I am very well looked after: really, our National Health Service for all its faults is a wonder. Where else can you get the benefit of the first rank research brains for free?

I cannot tell you how grateful I am for your support when I was in Zurich. It meant so much to me because I was beginning to panic. I went to Zurich thinking I'd picked up some Indian amoeba. Concentrating so hard on the book I had no idea how ill I was, but I never expected this! I bought a lot of watercolours and was intending to go up into the mountains to paint, but one day I could walk, the next not.

By the time this reaches you, you'll be out of the eye operation.[1] As you say, one does steadily fall to bits, but you are so wonderfully brave and seem to take everything in your stride as I must learn to do.

With all my love and a thousand thanks.

Bruce

1. For a cataract.

To Ninette Dutton

In an Oxford hospital but as from Homer End | Ipsden | Oxford |
17 October 1986

Dearest Nin,

Lovely to get your letter, Cheered me up a lot. Tisi told me, <u>very</u> discreetly that there was someone in your life – and so it should be. I'm delighted for you. This is a scribble written flat on my back – because O misery – I have caught in China an extremely rare (i.e no white man has had it) fungus of the bone marrow which as you know produces red corpuscles. I was in Switzerland trying to recuperate from having <u>finished</u> and delivered the book when the thing struck like a whirlwind. E. came out and we flew home just in time. The hospital staff thought it a wonder I lived through the night. But after 5 weeks of drugs, blood transfusion and expert care, there is talk of my going home. But alas, no wintering in Australia! because my blood has to be monitored constantly. So that is the news from this end. Something I never dreamed of, but will survive. E. is being marvellous. Much love, Bruce

To Charles Way

Homer End | Ipsden | Oxford | 25 October 1986

Dear Charlie,

Good for you! Of course in your hands I thoroughly approve of the BBC adaptation.[1] The one thing I slightly dread is that they choose readers who are unaware of what a Welsh – and more particularly what a Border accent is. They should be sat down for an hour or so in a pub in Hay-on-Wye and then they'd know for sure. The radio Book at Bedtime for *In Patagonia* was so horrible that I threw my portable radio away and refused to listen to any more instalments. All faked-up, English-joking South America. Really chilling!

1. The BBC radio play of *On the Black Hill*, directed by Adrian Mourby, went out on Radio 4, 2 March 1987.

I'm thrilled to think that I may, after all, see the play. Apparently, in Hereford at least it was sold out . . .[1]

As always B

To Murray Bail
Homer End | Ipsden | Oxford | 3 November 1986

Dear Murray,

Where am I? you ask. The fact is I very nearly croaked. In China I have to have caught a very rare fungus of the bone marrow: so rare that it is not described in medical literature and only known to 10 peasants in Western China (now dead) and a single killer-whale cast up on the shores of Arabia. I am, therefore, an <u>A1</u> medical curiosity. I'd been feeling rather low all summer, but not that low and thought, naively, that it was probably some Indian amoeba from the drinking water at Rohet. I finished the book – title *The Songlines* – which, to all the publishers distaste, I insist on calling a novel. I handed in the manuscript and left the very next day for Switzerland, thinking that a combination of mountain air and walks would revive me, and that first rate medicine was always at hand. Fat chance! The next thing I knew, on my first day in Zurich was that I could hardly walk along the street. I found by a miracle the great expert in tropical diseases[2] and the moment he looked at my blood, he exclaimed 'I cannot understand why you're alive.' Then the fun started. E. flew out and flew me home, to an Oxford hospital, where I was not expected to live through the night. It was not unpleasant. I was hallucinating like mad and was convinced that the view from my window – a car park, a wall and the tops of some trees – were an enormous painting by Paolo Veronese.[3]

1. Bruce would see the play the following year, in Brentford.
2. Dr Robert Keller at Allgemeine Medizin, 17 Muhlebachstrasse.
3. Venetian painter (1528–88) celebrated for large works like *The Feast at the House of Levi*. In *Looking Back*, Somerset Maugham describes sitting down to view this painting on one of his last visits to Venice; and how, as he gazed at it, he suddenly saw Jesus turn and look him full in the face.

Can we ever escape 'Art'? Then roughly six weeks of blood transfusions, and a drug that had to be administered intravenously and
made me feel terrible. I'm out now; spend most of the day in bed. But
the doctors are pleased with me – so far! – and although my legs are
still numb from the knees down I can totter about half a mile. But no
Australian visit. They want to monitor my blood count once a week
for at least a year (they may relent, depending on my 'progress'). The
real test comes when they take off the second anti-fungal drug (a pill,
Thank God!). Then we shall really see. Sorry to weary you with this
doleful and ego-centric tale, but the self is all I can think of. Reading
early tales of Gogol in new edition of the Garnett translation, Chicago
Univ press (2 vols). But this morning I've employed a researcher to
begin a new work.

Love to M[argaret]. E is wonderful at coping.

As ever B

To Nicholas Shakespeare
Homer End | Ipsden | Oxford | [November 1986]

My dear Nick,

Yes. Quite a drama! A fungus of the bone marrow that destroyed
all my red blood corpuscles. Known only among 10 Chinese peasants
and the corpse of a killer whale cast up on the shores of Arabia. Obviously, therefore, I caught it in China last winter. I'd no idea I was so
ill: because I was finishing the book (now in proof) I blocked it out
almost completely and went straight off to Switzerland. The 'thing'
struck 2 days later and, within five I couldn't walk. However, the right
drug was found. Be lovely to see you sometime. Do give a call one
evening.

Bruce

To Jonathan Miller[1]

Homer End | Ipsden | Oxford | [November 1986]

I am very serious about *Bajazet*.[2] I believe there's some way that Racine can be made to work for a non-French audience through being declaimed/intoned in the bravura passages with the help of music. Having just finished a new book, I'm relaxing. So you call me, Bruce

To Ninette Dutton

9am | Homer End | Ipsden | Oxford | 13 November 1986

Dearest Nin,

An hour ago E. and I were complaining that the Greek (Mount Hymettus, my eye!) honey we had bought at vast expense tasted of precisely nothing, when the postman arrived with your package.[3] We had a piece of toast each, in my bedroom, <u>at home</u> – and finished our breakfast with something quite delicious. Thank you and bless you. It hardly leaked at all: all we got were sticky fingers when opening it.

I'm at home feeling quite normal and, though I tire quite easily, I had yesterday an eight-hour working day with the copy editor from Cape's. We had a fearful struggle changing back to the original the changes made by the Americans to the copy. They refuse, for example, to admit use of the pronoun 'which', replacing it invariably by 'that' – which as we know makes prose so <u>flat</u>. Anyway despite my slightly numb and wobbly legs – apparently inevitable when one's legs were

---

1. British theatre and opera director, author, physician (*b*.1934).
2. E.C.: 'Bruce was crazy about this play, its claustrophobia and "prison atmosphere"; he and Jonathan Miller used to have long conversations. Bruce longed for someone to do it and then after he died Peter Eyre directed it at the Almeida Theatre.' Notebooks: 'Racine: note the astonishing swift reversals of fortune. The outcome of Andromache is fated from the start . . . There is no way out for the players. Yet in act II scene iii Orestes is buoyant with hope for the future: only to be dashed 2 stepped stanzas in the next scene.'
3. Dutton had sent some leatherwood honey from Tasmania.

reduced to spindles – we went for a short holiday in Cornwall[1] – a change for E. who, after bringing me an extra hot meal to the hospital every day for six weeks, was, to say the least, exhausted.

I have got to the stage when I'm fed up with reading and longing to start some new work. I've read Bob H[ughes]'s blockbuster *The Fatal Shore*: it has a kind of Tolstoyan sweep to it. What a tale! As fascinating about the mentality of the English in the 18/19th centuries as of the origins of Oz. Other news is that Werner Herzog intends to start filming the *Viceroy of Ouidah* (title change to *Cobra Verde*) in Feb. The script deviates wildly from the book: but so what! Precisely as it should be to make a good film.[2]

With much love from E. and I, Bruce

To Charles Way
Homer End | Ipsden | Oxford | 14 November 1986

The BBC would want L[ouis] and B[enjamin]'s intimate thoughts – and how corny they must want them to be. The point being that the writer, if he is not brought up in that milieu, cannot write about what he cannot know – or occasionally guess at. I don't envy you the task. Am out of hospital and proposing to work today for a couple of hours, as ever Bruce

To Derek Hill
Homer End | Ipsden | Oxford | 18 November 1986

My dearest Derek,

I'm terribly upset for you about your brother. One's hold on life is so extremely tenuous; but when the blow comes, nothing, it seems, can lessen its effect.

1. E.C.: 'We went to see Land's End and the wind nearly tore the door off the car. We stayed in The Abbey Hotel, Penzance, owned by Jean Shrimpton, "the Shrimp". When we lived in Mount Street, she was having an affair with Terence Stamp who lived on the same landing, and we used to see her running up and down.'
2. In August 1985 the singer David Bowie had also offered for the film rights.

I feel <u>fairly</u> normal: and was up to cooking blinis last night for a huge pot of caviare that someone brought to the hospital at a time when I was being fed intravenously. We decided to save it for Elizabeth's birthday. The only trouble is my legs which don't function as they should: not surprising in that they were spindles attached to knobbly knees for 2½ months.

To Cary and Edith Welch
Homer End | Ipsden | Oxford | 12 December 1986

My dear Dahlinks,

What a lovely surprise! Your letter which has come this morning is about half as long as the telex I got from Simon and Schuster four years back in which my present publisher, Elizabeth Sifton, was accused of <u>enticing</u> yours truly away from their incompetent clutches. I also have to report that when, in the summer, obviously a prey to my malady, I turned arsonist and destroyed heaps of old notebooks, card indexes, correspondence, I also found a whole boxful of <u>your</u> letters going back to the early 60's, and now doubtless a treasure to be hoarded.

Tell me, did J. J. Klejeman[1] really dump all those antiquities in the East River? I'd like to know if, and under what circumstances, he did so. I'm at present at work on a tale – a Hoffmann-like tale set in Prague – in which a collector of Meissen porcelain (a man I met there in 1967)[2] systematically destroys his collection on his deathbed, so that it will not pass into the hands of the National Museum.

My illness was a dramatic episode. I have always known – from a

---

1. John J. Klejman owned a gallery on Madison Avenue devoted to antiquities, or what Welch called 'tickwiddies'; upon his death, his gallery was rumoured to have been discovered empty.
2. Rudolph Just (1895–1972), Prague lawyer, cavalry officer and manager of the Bata shoe company, which financed his travels and art-collecting. Chatwin had met him for four hours in 1967. The maid was peeling potatoes on a plate made for Frederick the Great and after a walk through the town Just said to Chatwin: 'I'm going to a brothel.' On 11 December 2003, Sotheby's auctioned the remains of Just's collection for more than £1 million.

fortune-teller or from my own instinctive promptings? – that I would be terribly ill in middle-age, and would recover. All summer, while I was putting the final touches to the book, I was obviously sickening, but preferred to put it out of my mind – even though, on a sweltering summer day, I'd be wrapped in shawls beside the Aga scribbling onto a yellow pad. I imagined I'd recover if only I could reach some mountain pastures, and so gaily set off for Switzerland: only to find, next morning, that I couldn't drag myself a hundred yards down the sidewalk. Obviously, something was seriously wrong. Thinking I was prey to some Indian amoeba, I consulted a specialist in tropical medicine, who took one look at my blood count, and, next day, said amiably: 'I cannot understand why you're alive. You have no red blood corpuscles left.' He failed to make a diagnosis,[1] having run through a complete set of tests; and Elizabeth came to fetch me home in a definitely dying condition. I have a vague recollection of being wheeled to the plane; another, of the ambulance at London airport and then a blank. By the time I got to Oxford I was not expected to last the night. I did incidentally have the 'dark night experience', followed by the Pearly Gates. In my delirium I had visions of being in a colourful and vaguely medieval court where women offered me grapes on tazzas. At one point I called to Elizabeth, 'Where's King Arthur? He was here a minute ago.'

Anyway, although I was on life support, they still couldn't find the cause until, on the fourth day, the young immunologist rushed into my room and said 'Have you, in the past five years, been in a bats' cave? We think you've got a fungus of the bone marrow, which starts off growing on bat shit.' Yes. I had been in bat caves, in Java and in Australia. But when they grew the fungus, as one grows a culture for yoghurt, it was not mine after all. The most expert mycologists were consulted: samples were flown to the U.S., and the answer, which finally emerged, was that I had, indeed, a fungus of the marrow, but one which was known only from the corpse of a killer-whale cast up on the shores of Arabia and from ten healthy Chinese peasants, all of whom had died. Had I been

---

1. E.C.: 'Dr Keller tested him positive for HIV. That's when I rang our surgery in Nettlebed and they said "Where do you want to go?" and I said "Oxford."'

consorting with killer-whales? Or with Chinese peasants? 'Peasants,' I said decisively. Indeed, we had. Last December we were in Western Yunnan, following the traces of the Austro-American botanist, Joseph Rock, whose book *The Kingdom of the Na-Khi* was admired by Ezra Pound.[1] We went to peasant feasts, slept in peasant houses[2], inhaled the dust of peasant winnowing; and it must be in Yunnan that I inhaled the particles of fungal dust, which set the malady in motion. I lost half my weight; came out in lumps and scabs, and looked entirely like the miniature of Akbar's courtier in the Bodleian whose name I've forgotten.[3] I had a fearsome drug administered on the drip constantly for six weeks. I had blood transfusions, and in the end I made a rather startling recovery: at least, one which my doctors did not expect. It'll mean a change in one's life, though. Apparently, one can't ever quite get rid of a fungus like this, so I shall be on pills indefinitely; will have to report from time to time, and <u>not</u> alas go travelling into dangerously exotic places. The last stipulation I fully intend to ignore. In the meantime, rather than face the sodden gloom of an English winter, we are setting out for Grasse where we have borrowed a flat and where I hope to bash out my tale of the Czechoslovakian porcelain collector.

I must stop now. We have to go to London, and have a date with Leigh Bruce,[4] who is collecting the keys of my flat for Clem and Jessie [Wood] to stay in over Christmas. Talked to H[oward H[odgkin] for the first time in ages last night, and may see him this afternoon. Things turn full circle.

Will write again from Grasse with address.

much love Bruce

E. sends hers, too, to you and E[dith]

Nice to hear news of your Knellingtons, and also of the Tizzerets.

---

1. Ezra Pound (1885–1972), American poet, discovered Rock's *The Ancient Na-khi Kingdom of Southwest China* (1948) when he was locked up as a lunatic in St Elizabeth's hospital, in Washington, in 1956.
2. E.C.: 'We didn't sleep in peasant houses – we were in a hotel in Lijiang. You weren't allowed to stay anywhere else. It was still very strict.'
3. E.C.: 'A miniature of someone skeletal in bed, dead white and dying.'
4. Son of Jessie Wood.

I was intending to call on the Tizzer [George Ortiz] but for reasons described above failed to do so. Now I shall go down to the library where your scroll will join its brothers.

To Pam Bell
Homer End | Ipsden | Oxford | 15 December 1986

Dearest Pam,

This is an interim p/c to thank you for your letter and to <u>confirm</u> that I am much, much better. Quite a turn, though. I was flown from Switzerland in a state of collapse; was not expected to last the night – and got a definite glimpse of the Pearly Gates. My best to your Ma. Much love, Bruce XXX

The 'flat' near Grasse where Chatwin and Elizabeth now went to stay was in fact the Chateau de Seillans, an eleventh-century fort at the edge of a 60-foot cliff, belonging to Shirley Conran, the best-selling author and mother of Jasper. Chatwin had known Shirley since the late 1970s, first meeting her at a Hatchards Author-of-the-Year party. 'Suddenly this fair-headed chap was at my elbow and I said "What do you think is the best way to see a country?" "By boot." My first impression was that he was a Yorkshireman and he'd said "By boat." "Suppose it's a place like Switzerland . . . ?"' She described Chatwin, to whom she bore a resemblance, as 'the older brother I never dreamed of having', and invited him to convalesce at her house in the south of France. From December 1986 he based himself when abroad at the Chateau de Seillans.

To Ninette Dutton
Chateau Seillans | Seillans | France | 19 January 1987

Dearest Nin,

We're hiding out in the South of France to escape one of the really awful winters on record. We read of fearsome cold in England and

France. We see a bank of grey cloud over the sea. But here we bask –
so far! – in a snug little microclimate that gives us temperatures in the
80's on our terrace. I feel and look much better, but there are, it seems,
one or two complications, so we may have to pack up and return to
Oxford. I pray not! Last week, we went to Italy to see a succession of
old friends in Tuscany;[1] in Florence my legs, which are still liable to go
lilac and blue in the cold, completely froze up on me. All the same, we
had a lovely time.

I've been completely out of touch, having had no mail for a month.
The only excitement has been Werner Herzog's production of a film of
The Viceroy of Ouidah which he proposes to call *Cobra Verde*. We've
just signed the purchase, not the option, contract – and at the moment
some 600 Africans are recreating the King of Dahomey's palace in modern
Ghana. Anyway, it kept me <u>very</u> amused during these rather trying
months – and it would be nice to think that at the end of it I'd touch
some paper money: more at least than I'm ever likely to earn writing
books – and all without my having to lift a finger. Werner is doing a
production of *Lohengrin* at Bayreuth on July 28th – and that is our one
date for the summer.

The Australian book *The Songlines* is in proof though Cape's have
not seen fit, yet, to send me a copy. I only hope it's all right. There
are masses of details I'd like to have checked, but <u>physically</u> could
not.

In the meantime, I've begun something new: a very fanciful tale set
in the Prague of my distant memory, about a compulsive collector of
Meissen porcelain – with tangents into Jewish mysticism, the Golem, the
fantastical Emperor Rudolf, alchemy etc. This, again, is also keeping me
amused: I feel instantly better (though tired) when writing, and depressed
when not . . .

With lots of love from Elizabeth and myself Bruce

---

1. Teddy Millington-Drake, Gregor and Beatrice Von Rezzori, Matthew and Maro
Spender, Roberto Calasso.

To Derek Hill

Chateau de Seillans | Seillans | France | [January 1987]

We've had a succession of brilliant days over Christmas, but now it's balmy and grey. Whoever was 'the mastermind' at Le Thoronet[1] has, in my view, to have seen the Seljuk madrassas in Anatolia on the way to the 2nd Crusade. We take little trips about twice a week. Much love B

To Richard Bull[2]

Chateau de Seillans | Seillans | France | 8 February 1987

Dear Richard,

Enclosed are two sets of analysis from the laboratory in Grasse. When talking to the doctor[3] over the phone I got slightly the wrong end of the stick. What he meant to say was that, the second time round, the haemoglobin was the same but that the total picture was marginally improved.

We're going back to Italy, for a week, as from Friday. I'll call you from there.

Many thanks, all well here. As always, Bruce

To Roberto Calasso

Chatwin's entry to Robert Calasso's visitor's book | Milan | Italy | 20 February 1987

Une Histoire de la Bourgeoisie Française

In a restaurant[4] we sat next to two hatchet-faced women who argued

---

1. Unfinished Cistercian monastery near Draguignan. He urged Murray Bail to visit. For Bail, the austerity and elegance summed up Chatwin's aesthetic: 'Everything has been removed. It was plain, immaterial and resonant because of the emptiness.'
2. The registrar at the John Warin ward at the Churchill Hospital in Oxford.
3. E.C.: 'We picked a doctor with an Alsatian name out of the yellow pages.'
4. Restaurant la Chicane, near Lyons.

mercilessly as to whether an '<u>Alaska</u>' was the same as '*une île flotante*' or '*une omelette norvégienne*'. One of the husbands was fat, piglike, and wore six gold rings: the other was a reincarnation of Monsieur Homais.[1] He was, it turned out, also a pharmacist. He averred that there was one dish he could never tire of: '*un gigot d'agneau, pommes dauphinoises.*' Over coffee he said the following:

  '*Je vais vous raconter l'histoire d'un homme qui est parti pour son voyage de noces avec sa nouvelle femme, et, pendant le voyage, elle était tuée, meutriée par quelqu'un. Et lui, pour oublier ses tristes souvenirs est parti pour* . . .' and at this point one expected the words 'Tahiti' or '*la Nouvelle Calédonie*' . . . but no! . . .'*il est parti pour la Belgique où il est devenu président d'une société de fabrication du chocolat . . . de la laiterie . . . et même les produits chimiques*'

To Elisabeth Sifton
Homer End | Ipsden | Oxford | 15 March 1987

Dearest E,

  . . . Could you send copies of *The Songlines* to the following.
Bill Katz 2 copies: one marked for Jasper Johns[2]
Clarence Brown
Josef Brodsky[3]
Joseph Campbell[4]
James Ivory
Mrs Aristotle Onassis (I always do!)
Diane Johnson[5]

1. Chatwin had recently bought a first edition of *Madame Bovary*. Monsieur Homais, the apothecary in Flaubert's novel, is the embodiment of a pompous bourgeois.
2. American artist (*b.*1930) in whose house in the Caribbean Chatwin had stayed with Katz.
3. Russian poet (1940–96) and 1987 Nobel Laureate.
4. American mythologist (1904–87).
5. American satirical novelist (*b.*1934).

John Duff[1]
+ an Australian friend Pamela Bell

Much love, B

See you Labour Day.

To George Ortiz
Accra | Ghana | 23 March 1987

Have been swanning around in Ghana for 10 days where Werner Herzog is making my book *The Viceroy of Ouidah* into a movie. In the evenings we would go to the Ayatollah Drinks Bar – no credit given! See you soon, Bruce.

To Bill Buford
Homer End | Ipsden | Oxford | [April 1987]

My dear Bill,

Wow! I suspect – sadly for us but not for you – that we run the risk of losing the world's best magazine editor into the ranks of the world's best writers! Seriously, I found it first rate.[2] Soccer violence is something I've followed, from afar, with a certain grim fascination – but obviously I don't know anything about it at close quarters.

One thought strikes me. About 3 years ago I went to the Rugby final, Wales v France at Cardiff, on a filthy foggy day in winter. Then the mood of the crowd was almost liturgical; everyone singing the Welsh national Anthem etc. Why, therefore, should soccer violence

---

1. New York sculptor – 'he had once been a surfer and was a student of Zen' – off whom Chatwin had bought 'a fibreglass wallpiece the colour of watermelon'.
2. *Among the Thugs* (1990) documented football hooliganism in Britain. Bill Buford (*b*.1954) edited the then Cambridge-based magazine *Granta*, for which Chatwin had written.

be so different – unless, as you say, it is organised for the purpose of seeking out and damaging an enemy of the imagination? I couldn't agree with you more: that violence is not necessarily the product of adverse social conditions. It strikes me that the dominant mood of this country is a desperate need to find a substitute for the enemies it has lost cf The Falklands – and that this mood, in various manifestations, is to be found in all levels of society. There's a point at which your skinheads and members of White's Club see exactly eye to eye.

Can I take a strong personal interest in the manuscript? As I've said to you, now is not really the moment to offer advice. Just go straight ahead – it'll be fine. One minor point: there's something absolutely chilling about your first version: the Welsh station. I wonder if you shouldn't give a very detailed and graphic description – it can be half-fictionalised – where the station was, the kind of people on the platform, the look of the station-master – and then, suddenly, their announcement. I may be wrong, but I found that episode so compelling that I feel it should start the book. If you begin with a plane ride to Turin, you already know there's violence ahead. On an obscure Welsh railway station, you don't, and therefore set up a tension which'll carry you straight through the book. Another very minor comment: as it's so very tough as a concept, I think there are ways of slightly toughening up the syntax and vocabulary. I could show you what I mean when we meet: I'm going to ground in France for the next two weeks and will be back by May 1 at Homer: or if not Elizabeth will know how I'm to be reached.

With all my congratulations. Best, Bruce
PS In haste on the way to the airport.
At all costs stay dead pan.

In April 1987, during a miraculous period of remission, Chatwin stayed at the Paris Ritz as a judge for the International Ritz-Hemingway Award. Elizabeth says, 'Mohamed Al Fayed was running the prize. It was very strange. There were pornographic video-tapes to put in the TV and a mirror in the ceiling over our bed.'

To Derek Hill

Hotel Ritz | 15 Place Vendôme | Paris | France | [April 6 1987]

Dearest Derek,

Home again!

The comforts here are not exactly those of Athos, but . . .

Incidentally, are we going to Athos again? In the autumn?

Bruce

To Ninette Dutton

Homer End | Ipsden | Oxford | 9 April 1987

Dearest Nin,

A quick note before leaving for London airport – and Nice! Elizabeth's gone to India to do one of her Himalayan treks: perhaps the last, because the man who owns the company is seriously ill in London.[1] Anyhow, it'll be good for her to get a few whiffs of mountain air – after nursing me for 9 months! It's much, much better: the only after-effect is a permanent pins-and-needles in my feet, but since it was once above the knee, that, too, seems to be going.

How lovely to think you'll be here again soon. My plans are to go to France till around May 1st, come back for 10 days, or so, and then skip away again. I've been lent, for a year or more, that little chateau in the village once lived in by Max Ernst. It's super comfortable; and though over-built up for my taste the country to the back is magnificent and unspoiled. One thing is certain, I <u>must</u> be out of England when the book comes out in June. I hate all the publishing hoo-haa and, as I've discovered to my cost, you can't give one interview without opening the floodgates. I can't wait to get back to the south.

The book, for all the apparent obscurity of its subject, does seem to be making a bit of a stir. Bob H[ughes], to whom I talked last night, is very keen: but I suspect I'll have trodden on one or two corns.

1. Kranti Singh later died of kidney failure.

All of which adds up to the fact that we probably won't be in England from mid June to mid July: but will be at Seillans. So somehow we'll manage to meet. There are lots of rooms in the chateau and it's 40 minutes from Nice airport. Otherwise we could come to Italy where we have masses of friends.

In haste, much love Bruce

PS We've been having the most horrendous gale, trees knocked side ways. Really, this is a very uncomfortable country.

To Murray Bail
as from Homer End | Ipsden | Oxford | [May 1987]

Dear Murray,

In fact, I'm writing this from the South of France, where, when I was ill in the winter, I was lent, very chivalrously, a chateau: not a very large chateau, but a chateau nonetheless. The weather is hideously hot. We came here from Paris, utterly drained: not least by the Musée d'Orsay, which in its lapidary stupidity, must be one of the nastiest museums in the world. I suggest that the only time to go there is winter, in a wheel-chair, with a wide-brimmed panama to shield one's attention from the fantastical architectural hoo-haa up above. I also – for what reason I'm hard to explain – bought myself a first edition of *Madame Bovary*: a talisman? a livre de chevet? God knows! From here, we intend to go, of all things, to the Bayreuth Festival where my pal, Werner Herzog, is doing a production of Lohengrin: his work on cutting my film ie *The Viceroy of Ouidah* (retitled Cobra Verde) will begin in August. From Bayreuth we are going to Prague: I need to do a spot of research. Then, in September, I'm supposed to be going to America, but thinking hard how I can get out of it. Then . . . ? Madrid? Perhaps! Whenever I've been in Madrid I've been penniless and the series of doss-houses I've occupied, usually in the vicinity of the station, would not do for Maisie Drysdale. There is always the Ritz, right next to the Prado, which as value for money, is said to be the best hotel in Europe. But what kind of money? yes. Thank you for the tip that [Thomas] Bernhard's *Gath-*

ering Evidence is out at Knopf. You should just see the savaging he gets at the hand of English reviewers, blind and completely barmey. The review of *Concrete* by some arse was enough to bring one to the pass-port-burning stage. But then England, unlike Ireland, Scotland or Wales, is an utterly barbarian country. I thought that Bernhard's *Wittgenstein's Nephew* was marvellous, especially his account of getting the Grillparzer Prize and his insight – very close to home! – that one's dear, dear friends are appalled when, instead of dying, one re-emerges relatively fit.

Let me know about Kenya. I may be of help. Please stay in touch throughout the summer (ours if we have any!) and let's hope to meet in the fall.

Love to M[argaret] as always, and to you

Bruce

PS Papa Hemingway, I suggest, did stay at the Ritz: not in the early days perhaps, but certainly later. I wish you'd been a fly on the wall at the International Hemingway Award, at the Paris Ritz, of which I was one of the judges![1]

On 28 May 1987 Tom Maschler sent a finished copy of The Songlines *to Chatwin at Seillans. 'Dear Bruce, Here it is. This is a fabulous book. Your best to date and that is saying something.' It was published on 25 June 1987 and dedicated to Elizabeth.*

Foremost among those to whom he sent a copy was Robin Lane Fox. 'Bruce wrote to me: "This is a failed attempt to write the book that you above all people believed in. But time is short. Of course, it's fragmentary and probably baffling and you never expected it would have anything to do with Australia, but I send it to you in the hope there are snatches which will make you remember what you loved." I wrote back: "I think you are better in fragments than in a full-flown novel, but best of all I thought you were better in full-blown features."'

1. On 7 April 1987 Peter Taylor was awarded the $50,000 prize for his novel *A Summons to Memphis*, set in Tennessee. E.C.: 'The next year Bruce ganged up with the other judges and said none of the books were worth anything, and they agreed.'

To Michael Davie[1]
Homer End | Ipsden | Oxford | 24 June 1987

Dear Michael. Thank you. Thank you especially for rescuing me from the ever-increasing horde of travel-writers. We're here for most of July – after the 8th or so . . . so as we're in walking distance from Ewelme. Bruce

To Colin Thubron[2]
as from: Homer End | Ipsden | Oxford | 9 July 1987

My dear Colin,

Well. That was way in excess of any demands of friendship, etc! I am most touched and grateful to you on two main counts: a. that you took the point, and, out of that chaotic mass of material, managed to extract the sense of what I would liked to have said (rather than did say, which, of course, is quite another matter.) b. that you should have had to spend such amounts of time and energy. People seem to have no idea just how long it takes to put a piece like yours together.

Anyway, here's to you – and I'm sure that China will be as rewarding – and more – as the Russians. I can't wait!

We seem to be haring around the fringes of the Iron Curtain all summer: then back here – end of September when we must meet up.

Incidentally: one little thing I did not put in. When visiting the excavation at Swartkrans with Bob Brain, one of the questions uppermost in my mind was man's use of fire: the myth of Prometheus is absolutely crucial, to my mind, in understanding the condition of the First Man – since it is with fire that Man could adequately protect himself at night from the predators. When I was an archaeological student, it

1. Author, former editor of the Melbourne *Age* and journalist (1924–2005). His interview with Chatwin had appeared in the *Observer* on 21 June; he lived four miles from Homer End.
2. English travel writer and novelist (*b*.1939); Thubron's interview with Chatwin had appeared in the *Daily Telegraph*, 27 June 1987.

was accepted wisdom that fire – that is, domesticated fire – was <u>late</u> in Africa. 70,000 was the first recorded date as opposed to 500,000 from the Pekin[g] Cave. On the other hand, many excavators in Africa have hoped – and even thought they detected – traces of fire among the remains of Homo habilis, our first ancestor.

Bob and I discussed the pros and cons of the first hearth over lunch. Then, in the first few cubic centimetres which we – or rather the foreman George [Moenda] – excavated that afternoon, there were some fragments of bone which looked most definitely charred! Since the level in question would date somewhere close to 2 million, I got very excited – though he, sanguine as ever, was inclined to pooh-pooh the discovery. This morning, however, I had a letter in which he says the bones were definitely burned. In other words, I <u>may</u>, conceivably, have turned up at Swartkrans on the day the world's earliest hearth was found.[1]

Time – as you say in your piece – will tell![2]

As always

Bruce

To Charles and Brenda Tomlinson
Homer End | Ipsden | Oxford | 14 July 1987

Dear Charles and Brenda,

How kind of you to write! All in all *The Songlines* is a pretty odd production: the fact that I wrote the last chapter just before what was all but the last gasp gives it a very rough quality – to say the least! But I

1. Chatwin later telephoned Thubron: 'If the condition of man is to be walking through a howling wilderness . . . if, for example, the sources of aggression are directed against not other human beings but against the wild beast etc, then our condition is OK. This is the moment to talk. If hostility is against forces which are outside our control . . . if language is the medium of diplomacy (of uniting v. the beast etc) then we can see how it came into being. It was thus through language that the earliest hominids saved themselves. If man's underlying core of instinct is like theirs, then he's moral . . .'
2. Brain's article was the cover story of *Nature* magazine, December 1988.

have an idea that what's written is written with all the glaring defects: and if I'd tried to deliver everything I had in mind, the result might be even more incoherent than it is.

When in Yunnan, I bought a number of these little marble plaques: which were set into screens and have Taoist overtones. They're not very old: mid 19 century at best, but they do preserve the feeling of mountain poetry a little. The poem on this one roughly translated is

The clouded cliffs jut up

jaggedly in ragged points

Hope you like it. We're off to Czechoslovakia via the Bayreuth Festival – Lord preserve us!

much love B & E

To Murray Bail
Homer End | Ipsden | Oxford | 17 July 1987

Holden's Performance [Bail's new novel] has just reached me – and is going to Czechoslovakia on Mon. I am ⅔rds through a piece of wild 'Pragueois' writing which I hope to finish by the end of the year. Vague plans may mature for an Australian winter (ours) but I'm not sure. As always B

Lots of mistakes in *The Songlines* too but the Sydney office saved me from the worst Australian ones.

To Jean-Claude Fasquelle
Homer End | Ipsden | Oxford | 17 Juillet 1987

Dear Jean-Claude,

I know you'll be on holiday, but could your secretary send a copy of *Les Jumeaux de Black Hill* to:

M. E. Bavanoff-Rosimé, Chateau de Bellevue, Meaulne, St Bonnet-Tronçais.

This is the son of a most astonishing Russian constructivist sculptor of the early Soviet period whom I met by chance at Vichy. See you in the autumn,

Bruce

To Sunil Sethi
Homer End | Ipsden | Oxford | [July 1987]

Lovely to get your card. Yes. *The Songlines* – Lord knows how or why is No 1 on the best-seller list – for this week![1] Not next week! I seem to be the victim of hype – all a bit of bravura on my part to demonstrate that I was in the land of the living – but very bad for the head. We are off to Deutschland on Monday to the Bayreuth Festival and then to Czechoslovakia: the scene of my next novel! E is commissioned to write a guide to Rajasthan[2] so will soon be back – after New York and Madagascar! Much love as always B

To George Ortiz
Prague (now Vienna) | Czechoslovakia | 7 August 1987

I <u>am</u> sorry I never made it to Geneva: our arrangements in July got a bit out of hand. Now they are even worse: Prague, Budapest, Vienna, Rome, London, New York, Toronto – all in the space of a month. The Chatwin yo-yo is functioning again. But in the autumn, I promise, a special trip to see you – and catch up.
As always Bruce

1. On 20 July *The Songlines* reached Number 1 on the *Sunday Times* bestseller list. In October Tom Maschler wrote to Chatwin's new agent Gillon Aitken: 'You will not be surprised to hear that SL is, for me, one of the most wonderful books I have ever published and for it to have been at number one (ahead of the newly published Douglas Adams) is a high point in my publishing career.'
2. E.C.: 'No, a guide to Gujarat. I never did it because I didn't know how to work a computer.'

To Murray Bail
Austria | On the road | 7 August 1987

Holden's Performance saw us through some fairly dismal days in Czecho-slovakia. It's first rate, and you should be highly pleased with it. The sound you make on paper was like having you in the next room, mate! It was then grabbed from me by the leading young publisher of Prague, Jan Zelenka, and fell into good hands. Vague plans for Sydney in Jan. As always B

To Nicholas Shakespeare
Steiermark | Austria | 7 August 1987

Whew! The grimness of Czechoslovakia has to be seen. We spent the past week in flooded mosquito ridden campsites overrun with tourists from the D.D.R. Not a bed to be had! In the end we dived for the luxury of the Hotel Sacher in Vienna – never mind the price! Lovely dinner! Bruce

To Ninette Dutton
Steiermark | Austria | 7 August 1987

Probabilities[1] came with us to Prague. First rate! Exactly the right tone, speed of execution etc for the subject matter. And I now know far more about you! I particularly liked 'A Day To Remember'. Mucha[2] was away. His wife – ? or not wife – told me to call back the day we were leaving but wasn't there.

Much love B

On his way to the Harbourfront Festival in Toronto, Chatwin stayed in New York where he had a meeting with the London-based literary

1. Short stories by Ninette Dutton (1987).
2. Jiří Mucha, son of the artist Alfonse Mucha, was married to a Scot. His mistress lived in a house opposite.

agent Gillon Aitken and his New York partner, Andrew Wylie. In
September, in a much-publicised split, Chatwin and Salman
Rushdie decided to leave their London literary agent, Deborah
Rogers, and move to Wylie, Aitken and Stone.

To Deborah Rogers
Homer End | Ipsden | Oxford | 16 September 1987

My dear Deborah,

It is with deep sadness, not to say grief, that I sit down to write to you. You must believe me when I say that what follows is not a decision I have taken lightly, or without anguish. It is, however, irreversible. For some time now I have felt the need to have my affairs coordinated in the hands of a single person and have appointed Andrew Wylie, of Wylie, Aitken and Stone, as my sole agent for world rights.

He has also agreed to take charge of the back-list and all the negotiations pending. I will write to George and Anne[1] from Italy, but the post will take several days. And if this letter seems hopelessly inadequate, cruel and short, it is because I simply do not know how to go on . . .

with all my love to you
Bruce

To Greg Gatenby
Chateau de Seillans | Seillans | France | 20 September 1987

My dear Greg,

I hope I didn't seem too gaga or remote in Toronto.[2] There's something about a book tour – which pray God, I never do again! – that stews

1. Georges and Anne Borchardt, co-founders of the New York-based literary agency which had looked after Chatwin's American rights.
2. On 15 September, at the invitation of the organiser Greg Gatenby, Chatwin had appeared in Toronto at the Harbourfront Festival. Just before going on stage, he vomited in the dressing room and asked to be rushed back to his hotel. E.C.: 'He was suddenly awfully tired; I stamped my foot and said: "He's too tired. If you want to see him, come to the hotel."'

one up into a fever. My albeit fleeting impression of Canada was 100% in favour – I really had the best possible time – and, who knows, might easily want to immerse myself in the Yukon.[1]

As always, Bruce

– and I am also very sorry for the cock-up over the time etc.

I see you've got my old friend Charles T[omlinson] coming – who as my next door neighbour saw that work of mine in embryo.

To Gillon Aitken
Chateau de Seillans | Seillans | France | [September 1987]

Dear Gillon,

... I'll also be writing to Jean-Claude Fasquelle at Grasset – with whom I've always had a good time. The atmosphere at Grasset always amuses me intensely. I have informed [Roberto] Calasso who thought it, incidentally, a most sensible move,

As ever, Bruce

To Jean-Claude Fasquelle
Chateau de Seillans | Seillans | France | [September 1987]

Dear Jean-Claude,

You may have learned – or will do soon enough – that I decided to move my affairs from Deborah Rogers to Wylie, Aitken and Stone. You should perhaps know that I have a long-standing relationship with Gillon – although, until recently, there has never been any question of my joining him. I have, for some time, felt that he was the best person for the job, but this is between us ...

As always Bruce

1. Gatenby had discussed with Chatwin the possibility of him starting a Writer in Residence Programme on Baffin Island.

To Deborah Rogers

Chateau de Seillans | Seillans | France | 25 September 1987

My dear Deborah,

I realise this is all very terrible. I know from people in New York and London how upset you are. I know we should some day go over the ground. I know it was a snap decision, for better or worse. I know it's bound to affect our friendship, and that makes me miserable.

But on one point I must make myself clear. I gather that, on both sides of the Atlantic, there had been talk of Andrew Wylie propositioning me or 'luring' me away, either from you or [Georges] Borchardt. This, frankly, is nonsense. Others may have tried it: not him. As you know, in 1976 I deferred to you and to our old association rather than go to Gillon Aitken.[1] I have over the years kept in touch with him. One of his clients, whose way of life is rather similar to my own, is the only writer with whom I have an annual 'state of the game' conversation.[2] You were aware that, for a long time, I felt that communication between myself and Georges Borchardt was at a low ebb: probably my fault as much as his. You knew I felt the need for a

---

1. Gillon Aitken (*b.*1938) had met Chatwin in New York in 1974 when setting up a literary agency with Anthony Sheil and Lois Wallace. In a draft introduction for *What Am I Doing Here*, Chatwin wrote: 'Two days before I flew to Buenos Aires I met Gillon Aitken at a party. He asked me what I did. I said I was a journalist. He said he was a literary agent. I asked him whether, when I came back, he could place an article with an American magazine. The title would be "Letter from the End of the World."

'He invited me to his office. I told him what I knew of Patagonia – and what I hoped to find. He took notes and said:

'"This is a book and you must write it."'

G.A.: 'He regarded his connection to Deborah as evanescent and appointed me his agent in New York. He kept talking about Patagonia and he talked so much about it I said: "You must stop talking about it, you must go. Go, go, go." I got him to do an outline and on the basis of his letter sold the book to Harper and Row for $12,500. I rang Bruce to tell him and he'd gone. Two years later I was again in New York and looked across the room and there he was and he with his hands covered his face as a gesture of apology. I went up and said: "What happened?" He'd gone back to Deborah – or never left her.'

2. Probably Paul Theroux.

change, and you made various suggestions as to whom I should approach. However, in May of 1986, at Joe Fox's[1] on Long Island, I broached the question of U.S. representation with Gillon: at the time I have to tell you I was thinking of using a lawyer rather than an agent to vet the contracts. He told me he had just joined forces with Andrew Wylie, and arranged for me to meet him in New York. We had a preliminary discussion, without there being any question of my leaving you.

Since then, the situation has changed. In one year the status of Cape's has changed. Sonny[2] has gone off to America, Elisabeth [Sifton] has gone to Sonny, and there is the mess – and mess it is! – with Summit Books. I have also been unhappy about the way in which contracts were drafted.

Before leaving for America, I asked you to tell me whether or not I had an option clause on the *Songlines* contract, so that I would not be in an invidious position while talking to the new Viking team, who, it must be said, have done magnificent things for the book. I still do not know the answer. Instead of which Georges [Borchardt] rang up Peter Mayer[3] to arrange with him that I would be following Elisabeth to Knopf. So I may. But he did not have my permission to do this: nor was it an answer to my question. This, I'm afraid, rammed home to me the fact that I have been spending far too much time getting brewed up over niggling matters when I should be doing something else. The temptation to put one's affairs into a single, coordinated agency became irresistible.

I met Gillon and Wylie in New York, and the rest followed. The fact that Salman [Rushdie] had decided to do the same thing did not enter into these discussions: they did, however, suggest I call him when I got back to London.

I am, however, very sorry to have misled you on one point. I felt it

1. Editor at Random House.
2. Sonny Mehta had published Chatwin in paperback at Picador in London, before moving to New York as Editor-in-chief at Knopf.
3. CEO of Viking Penguin.

might be easier to break the news that I had gone to Wylie: this is somewhat inaccurate. I have gone, in fact, to the agency Wylie, Aitken and Stone and since I am based in Europe not the U.S. it will be Gillon who will handle the day to day business. As I explained to Anne [Borchardt] in a letter, my trouble is that, under a somewhat bland mask, I am from my Sotheby's days a rather hard-nosed business pro. Not for nothing did I once draw up a new form of draft contract, revolutionary in its day, which ultimately gave the art auction business a new flexibility. But that's all old stuff.

In the meantime, can I please ask you that this transition be conducted as smoothly and unobtrusively as possible.

with all my love to you, Bruce

To Ninette Dutton
Chateau de Seillans | Seillans | France | 26 September 1987

An interim p/c collapsing after a very strenuous tour of the US and Canada will be in Seillans chateau de S . . . the whole of Oct, Nov, Dec much love B

To Andrew Wylie[1]
Chateau de Seillans | Seillans | France | 29 September 1987

Dear Andrew,
    I'm a firm believer in the iron fist in the velvet glove. When in doubt, put on a second velvet glove, cheers, Bruce C.

1. Chatwin's new agent in New York; Wylie (b.1948), known as 'the Jackal' ever since this episode, was in negotiation with Georges Borchardt, Chatwin's previous American agent, in regard to his release from Summit Books and transfer to Penguin.

To Deborah Rogers
Chateau de Seillans | Seillans | France | 30 September 1987

My dear Deborah,

I have investigated the story you told me, and I have to tell you it has a perfectly innocent origin, resulting from a phone call I myself made early last summer. The fact that others spread it around was somewhat less innocent, but let that be . . .

I am sorry. I am sad – but the arrangement I have made with Wylie, Aitken and Stone must stand. I don't want to be put in the position of having to explain myself. Perhaps we should put it down to my 'incurable restlessness'?[1]

To Anne-Marie Mykyta
Homer End | Ipsden | Oxford | 21 October 1987

My dearest Anne-Marie,

A. Thank you for buying it, let alone finishing it. B. for your charming last line. I've been in the wars recently, with an impossible malady picked up in W China – but I'm quite well again

Forgive the haste. I have a mountain of mail to catch up. All my love to you, Bruce

---

1. His rift with Rogers continued to preoccupy Chatwin after he and Elizabeth returned to Homer End. On 24 October his sister-in-law Sheila Chanler arrived for a Sunday lunch at which were also present Michael Ignatieff, Salman Rushdie and Murray Bail. Chanler wrote in her diary: 'Murray an Australian, dry subtle man v likeable. Lunch noisy and confusing. Lots of cross-fire conversations on hot literary topics, one situation in particular concerning B's former agent now involved in some sinister plot and all v disturbing to B.' Bail wrote in his notebook: 'B. told with a certain relish of a Russian he'd met in Prague, a dark ex-monk who, after being harsh with women, would slash his face with a razor, his face criss-crossed multiplying the torment.'

To Harriet Harvey-Wood[1]
Homer End | Ipsden | Oxford | 22 October 1987

Dear Harriet Harvey-Wood,

Of course, I'd be <u>interested</u> in coming but I haven't a clue where I'll be next July. What's the latest I can let you know?

Yours ever, Bruce Chatwin

To Harriet Harvey-Wood
Homer End | Ipsden | Oxford | 22 November 1987

Dear Harriet Harvey-Wood,

Forgive me, I can't remember if I've replied to your letter of Oct 27 or not. Ach! The disorganisation! Yes: Do please be in touch around May: then I'll know better how the land lies.

As ever, Bruce Chatwin

To Murray Bail
Homer End | Ipsden | Oxford | 11 December 1987

My dear Murray,

Well, it was good to get a glimpse of you. I agree with you about the London literati: the only possible use I can think of for a spaceship would be to take them out of our orbit — but then more would grow!

Salman and I had a rather thick time of it recently vis-à-vis

---

1. Head of Literature at the British Council (*b.*1934). 'I'd asked him to come to our Contemporary Writers Seminar which we had every year in Cambridge. We got together a team of about 20 British writers, young and old, known and unknown, together with a group of about 50 people from overseas who had anything to do with contemporary writing, laid on industrial quantities of food and drink, especially drink, and hoped something would happen. Usually it did.'

changing our agent. Tremendous hullabaloo in the press! But it seems to have simmered down now. In the old days, writers – 'so-called' – were thought to be neurotic, self-obsessed, primadonna-ish people, forever suffering from 'blocks', emotional problems etc. and agents were calm hard-working people who would sort out their problems. Now the Tables are turned. The 'writers' simply sit down and write their books and, as an additional burden, have to cope with hopelessly neurotic publicity-seeking agents who think nothing of airing their neuroses, and their business! to the press. However, as I said, it's simmering down, and I, for what it's worth, yesterday, finished a novel. Quite a carry on! The title – *Utz* simple as that! The most that can be said for it is that it was designed as an entertainment to carry me through those rather beleaguered months. Admittedly, it does bear very little relation to anything I've ever done. A kind of Middle European fairy-story – with some savage digs at the art business! We shall see . . .

I had a very odd week in Paris, at a conference for Russian and other dissidents who, regrettably nowadays seem to perform the role of clown for people who wish their anti-Marxist views confirmed. If you think that Mr Gorbachev has things to contend with from the Old Bolshevik Guard, that is nothing to the New Guard. There is in Russia a political 'secret' society called Pamiat (which means 'remembrance'). It has a million signed up members in Moscow alone: and what it wants to remember are the virtues of Russian soil, the Russian Orthodox Church, Russian facial features etc as opposed to slit-eyes, hook noses and other aberrations of human nature. It wants to raise the Russian Church to Khomeini-ite levels of fanaticism, and is, among other things, anti-industrial, anti-nuclear, ecological etc.

Hans Magnus Enzensberger,[1] who went to Russia recently, says that, at a reception, he spoke to a full Russian general at the Kremlin who was wearing on his finger a cameo insignia of Nicholas II with the eagles. Such people think of Stalin as a Jewish-puppet, you must realise. Anyhow,

1. Hans Magnus Enzensberger (*b.*1929) German polymath, author and editor.

it all puts a new slant on things . . . I'm going to have a go at seeing what I can do to write a Russian novel . . .[1]

On the other hand, I'm dying to get away to a sunny place where I can swim. I almost went to Madagascar for a magazine. I've always thought I might like Madagascar – and could call in on Zanzibar. But I couldn't get away until the book was done, and now it's the rainy season and I didn't feel like slewing around in red mud.

My love to you and Margaret
And from Elizabeth.

To Colin Thubron
Homer End | Ipsden | Oxford | 7 January 1988

Forgive me for being a bit slow in the uptake about *Behind the Wall*.[2] I was up to my gills in a new book and – well, you know how it is – one reads <u>nothing</u> that isn't immediately useful for the work in hand! Absolutely first rate! I know it so much less well than you: but every word rang true. The claustrophobia of that society: also its reserves of wisdom. I have a mildly different 'take' on Russia, but in China I was with you every step of the way.

E. & I are going on our first proper holiday: to an island off Guadaloupe – for 15 days. As always, Bruce.

1. On 13 October 1986 Tom Maschler had written to Chatwin looking forward 'to more extraordinary things. No doubt totally different from what you would have written otherwise. Perhaps this will be in the direction of fiction, and perhaps will also be the "international" novel (Russian, France, etc) you have spoken of. If you recall, that is the book which I told you would be an enormous commercial break-through in addition to being great literature.' On 11 February 1988 Maschler would write again to Chatwin: 'I've said it before, and I'll say it again, there is simply no writer in England for whose work I have a greater passion than yours. This statement is made with all my heart.'
2. *Behind the Wall: A Journey Through China*, by Colin Thubron (1987).

To J. Howard Woolmer
Homer End | Ipsden | Oxford | 7 January 1988

Dear Howard,

How kind to send the Cormac McCarthys.[1] I've read *The Orchard Keeper* which is splendid, and am taking *Suttree* with me to the Caribbean next week. Hope we'll meet again soon.

I'm sorry for the scrappy note – I've got a month of correspondence to wade through before lunch. As ever, Bruce.

To Susannah Clapp
Homer End | Ipsden | Oxford | [January 1988]

My dearest Susannah,

I haven't been able to raise you on the phone today. Never mind. We're off to Guadaloupe, no less. For a couple of weeks swimming. It's one of the cheapest places to fly to, because it's part of metropolitan France and the fares are subsidised. We're booked to fly back on the 25th, but may, depending on various imponderables, go down to the South of France. I left the car in a garage for repairs on October 15, saying I'd be back the next day – and now look!

Gillon Aitken will have sent over a copy of the *Utz* annotated by Michael Ignatieff. I don't agree with everything he says but most of it I do. I jotted down my reactions in the margin and would love it if you'd take a squint.[2]

I want to show it, too, to my friend Diana Phipps[3] who is a Czech – and had first hand memories of Prague until 1949 when she and her

---

1. American novelist and playwright (*b.*1933). Woolmer, a dealer in rare books, had met Chatwin at a gallery opening in London. 'We discussed several writers, primarily Cormac McCarthy, Bruce hadn't read McCarthy at the time so I sent him copies of *The Orchard Keeper* and *Suttree*.'
2. Clapp had edited *In Patagonia* and *The Viceroy of Ouidah* for Cape.
3. Diana Sternberg (*b.*1936) to whom he dedicated *Utz*; m. 1957 Henry Ogden Phipps (1931–62).

family left – to Vichy! (except that they went to Paris instead). One of the few facts I have about my model for Utz is that he <u>did</u> go annually to Vichy – until 1968.

Much love, B

To Gillon Aitken
Homer End | Ipsden | Oxford | 8 January 1988

Dear Gillon,

. . . While I'm away can you think over the following.

For the benefit of all concerned, we should get onto paper a formal agreement between ourselves. We have not yet finally agreed on the rates of commission. I'm easy about this. I have always thought that the 20% European sales is a bit stiff, but I would have your guidance on this point. Seeing that Salman [Rusdhie] and I came, as it were, as a package, I wonder if I could have the same terms as him. Or whether we could agree on a flat rate of commission to cover the US, the UK and abroad. As things are going, there may, in the future, be separate agreements with the ex-Commonwealth etc. Anyway, it won't be a problem between us.

The second point is this. Deborah Rogers never made it clear to me the question of the 'agent of record': in fact, it was the first I'd ever heard of it. Surely we should agree that if, for any reason <u>either</u> of us wished to terminate the agreement, then the 'agency of record' should not continue beyond a fixed term, say, three years or five. To agree this between ourselves would, I feel, give a certain leverage with DR/GB. It is obviously very messy for me to be having to deal with two agencies.[1]

As always
Bruce

1. Deborah Rogers continues to be Chatwin's agent of record.

To Murray Bail

Homer End | Ipsden | Oxford | 8 February 1988

My dear Murray,

So we went to the West Indies for a holiday: I honestly can't spare the time to come your way this winter. Besides, I'm rapidly coming to the conclusion that, unless someone pays you to go club class, air travel (for more than 3 hours) has already become impossible. We went first to a pair of islands called Les Saintes, off Guadaloupe which are peopled by a very strange clan of mestizo Indian-negro-Breton fishermen. Most striking to look at. Proud, disdainful, not giving one inch to tourists like ourselves: the girls wearing a kind of tutu, the boys with blond hair in rasta-plaits. Nothing happened to interrupt our days of sleeping or taking a boat to the coral reefs except for the ludicrous incident when squatting in the bush I inadvertently let my balls brush against a plant which is the toxic plant of the West Indies.[1] And since we were on our way to Mass, the agony of standing in church was indescribable. I hope you'll forgive my invoking your name as a possible reviewer for the Botany Bay book to the *Los Angeles Times* review section. I didn't feel I could take it in, knowing so little of the history.

Has *The Day of Judgement* by Salvatore Satta come your way? A tremendous evocation of place – the place being the town of Nuoro in Eastern Sardinia. I read it ages ago in French because it's published by my Italian publisher. Also, at the age of 19 I went alone on a walking tour of Eastern Sardinia. It was terrifying to walk at dusk up the main street of Orgolos, the legendary 'home' of the Sardinian bandit, looking for a bed and having every door slammed in one's face. One pal G[eorge] S[teiner] reviewed it for the *New Yorker*, but I don't think he really got the measure of it. Yes. I've known the Musil[2] for some time.

---

1. EC: 'We were staying at a hotel at the end of Les Saintes and on a long walk through the forest passed a sign saying "Attention!" but we didn't think what it was for. Bruce went for a shit and squatted down and within minutes he was in agony. From church, he went straight to the doctor.'
2. Robert Musil (1880–1947), Austrian author of the unfinished modernist novel *A Man Without Qualities*.

Very marvellous! I may, at any minute, be off to the Sudan on some mildly nefarious business.[1] That is, if I recover from a bad bout of flu (I am recovering!).

I wish I could give up writing, don't you? More and more this book business tempts me into silence. There have been some frightfully funny incidents here: the best is that Virago Press were about to publish as an astonishing new 'find' a novel by a young Pakistani girl called Rahila Khan[2] or something like it, with some quite sexy scenes between Pakistani girls and white boys: all very suitable to bring 'literature' to Britain's Asiatic community, all set for a big promotion etc. – when it was discovered that Rahila Khan was an Anglican clergyman in Brighton called the Rev Toby Forward! Great?

Next, at the Whitbread Prize there were 3 categories, the best novel, the best first novel, the best biography. The best book of the 3 was, at the beery businessman's dinner, then judged to be the winner.

The three were:

1. My friend Francis Wyndham who treated the whole affair with wonderful panache.

2. A paraplegic (or something worse) who had overcome his disability to write a book[3] – and was of course declared the winner.

3. Ian McEwan[4], who, when given a hard-luck slap on the back by one of the organisers, said: 'Next year there'll be a man with an iron lung.'

Much love to you both, B & E

1. On 12 February 1988 Gillon Aitken had written to Georges Borchardt: 'Bruce wishes to make a charitable donation to the Commissioner for Refugees of the Democratic Republic of the Sudan and Ethiopian Aid of $3,000 from the first payment accruing to him following the sale of paperback rights in *In Patagonia* and *Viceroy of Ouidah* and a similar donation of $3,000 from the second payment.'
2. *Down the Road, Worlds Away*, by Rahila Khan. Virago published the book in June 1987, but pulped it when the author was discovered to be not a shy girl in her twenties, married with two children and living on a south London housing estate, but a white clergyman based in Brighton.
3. *Under the Eye of the Clock*, by Christopher Nolan.
4. Ian McEwan (*b*.1948), English novelist and screenwriter, shortlisted for *The Child in Time*.

The categorisation of his own book troubled Chatwin, who, feeling that he must defend and protect the status of The Songlines *as a novel, asked Tom Maschler to issue this statement.*

To Tom Maschler
Homer End | Ipsden | Oxford | 8 February 1988

I am most honoured to be nominated for the Thomas Cook Travel Award; but *The Songlines* has been published as fiction on both sides of the Atlantic . . . The journey it describes is an invented journey, it is not a travel book in the generally accepted sense. To avoid any possible confusion, I must ask to withdraw from the shortlist.

To Cary Welch
Homer End | Ipsden | Oxford | 22 February 1988

My dear Cary,

Either we'll have met in London by the time you get this – or else it'll have to be thought of as an interim letter. I have just sent off to agents, publishers etc a new work: the theme? Art-collecting – or rather the convolutions of a man who gets stuck behind the Iron Curtain and will do anything to save the collection until one day . . .

The book was my response to convalescence last year: I had thought I'd use that time to read and re-read all the great Russian novels. Instead, hardly able to hold a pen, I launched forth on my story: a tale of Marxist Czechoslovakia conceived in the spirit and style of the Rococo. God knows how people will receive it.

My book *The Songlines*, which as you may be aware was written, the last third of it, in semi-hallucination,[1] has brought me a host of new friends from 'every quarter'. But the latest is a simply astonishing

1. In Charles Chatwin's last words of admiration for his son's work, he pointed out to Hugh 'Bruce's stamina at having delivered three books to publishers – half of his output – during the last three years of his life, when ill.'

person. He is called Kevin Volans[1], an Anglo South-African composer
– and composer of genius – who has gone into the field in Africa rather
as Brahms or Dvorak went looking for folksongs. He has filled his
head with the sounds of the veldt, with Zulu chant, the shepherds
pipes echoing across the valleys of Lesotho – and without in any way
being 'ethnic' he has produced an entirely new modern music that also
makes me think of Schubert. He is the favourite composer of the
Kronos Quartet, who, it would appear are the best string quartet in
America for modern music. Unfortunately, their record of Kevin's work
entitled 'White Man Sleeps', which is a huge hit in the U.S. omits the
4th movement which is so utterly transporting that one gasps with
wonder.

Anyway this is to me one of the really nice things that's happened
to me. The longer I live the more anarchic my attitude to institutions.
In the end the people who run them are professional time-wasters. I
think you survived the Met[2] for quite long enough: for what should
and could be a rewarding task ends up a drudgery. One has to be free
to pursue one's loonier concerns. The New Hampshire retreat sounds
heavenly. I do have reason for visiting your neck of the woods sometime in the foreseeable future: but I'm completely befuddled by the
dates. My current interest is the astonishing revival of Orthodoxy in
Russia. I don't know if you know but I now think of myself as orthodox
and will be going back at some point to Athos to stay with my Serbian
friends at the monastery of Chilandari[3] . . . but this is beside the point.

1. Kevin Volans (*b.*1949) had studied under Stockhausen in Cologne and was composer-
in-residence at Queen's University, Belfast. His compositions blend the music of Europe
and his native South Africa. *Cover Him With Grass: In Memoriam Bruce Chatwin* was
recorded in 1989. His opera about Rimbaud, based on an idea by Chatwin, *The Man
Who Strides the Wind*, premiered in London at the Almeida in 1993, with a libretto by
Roger Clarke.
2. Welch was special consultant (1979–87) for the department of Islamic art at the
Metropolitan Museum of Art.
3. One of Chatwin's hallucinations, following his collapse in Zurich, was of the Christos
Pantokrator. According to Kallistos Ware, a titular Metropolitan Bishop of the Greek
Orthodox faith living in Oxford: 'He felt he was lying in the middle of the church in
the Serbian monastery of Chilandari during a vigil service.' Chatwin came to see Ware
several times over the summer, to discuss the possibility of becoming Orthodox. 'What

I find myself prey to indecision as to where to go next. Rephrasing Cyril Connolly, one could say 'Inside every traveller an anchorite is longing to stay put.'

Forgive this rather rambling scrawl. E. and I went to some islands off Guadaloupe for a swimming holiday but alas we both came back with a horrible stomach bug which has affected my liver in a pseudo-hepatitis.[1]

Feeling better today,
Much love B

To Murray Bail
Homer End | Ipsden | Oxford | [February 1988]

My dear Murray,

. . . Thanks for sending us the Australian short stories.[2] Why you've not put yourself in it is beyond my comprehension. I'll talk to you about them one day – I like Murnane: but so often, in the others, there is an evenness of texture which I find rather disturbing. I won't go on now.

We're off on a world tour – I hope! – and the air ticket may bring us to Sydney in March.

Love as always. B

---

he wanted was to be received by baptism on the Holy Mountain since the Holy Mountain had played such a decisive part in his conversion. I was quite convinced by the firmness of his purpose, although I realised his illness was beginning to affect him. I asked Elizabeth: "Does he understand?" There was no doubt, she said: he understood very clearly what it was he was doing.' But Chatwin's second trip to Athos, though arranged for September, during which he hoped also to attend the 900th anniversary celebrations for the founding of St John's monastery on Patmos, never took place. 'Unfortunately, his health deteriorated rapidly and he could not go,' says Ware. 'I offered to receive him myself, but we were overtaken by events.'

1. E.C.: 'It took weeks to diagnose what was wrong. It was a return of the fungus, in fact. It got so bad, he went back to the Churchill Hospital.'

2. Bail had edited *The Faber Book of Contemporary Australian Short Stories* (1988).

To Ninette Dutton

Homer End | Ipden | Oxford | 29 February 1988

Dearest Nin,

Sorry for the protracted silence. Time has flown with astonishing rapidity. The first news is that I finished and edited a new book: the title UTZ. Tout court! Anyhow it seems to have caught the imagination of the publisher because we're suddenly inundated with money which we don't really want. My temperament tells me to give it away: but that's not so easy. And it's certainly a change from being on the deadline. I've also started something new: which will probably fail, utterly, for being too ambitious. I have a scene in which an utterly beguiling American woman in her early 70's – courageous to the point of camping alone in Wyoming – takes her picnic lunch into Central Park and is mugged by a black kid. That's how it appears to be, except that she soon has her attacker sitting beside her, using _her_ knife not his to cut up the chicken, and there follows a long animated discussion in which he refuses $50 but accepts $10. This incident is based on the experience of one of my mother-in-law's friends in Rock Creek Park, Washington.[1] I hope you will like her as a character because I have called her Ninette and have hauled in a bit of you. The whole book is way into the future and may take years to write.

Otherwise . . . E. and I went away snorkelling in the West Indies. We only had 2½ weeks and really that is not enough for Australia. Even so, the flights from Paris to Martinique were gruelling – and we both came down with a mysterious virus that laid us out nearly cold for a couple of weeks. Banish the thought that holidays in the sun are therapeutic!

Cyril Connolly's most famous aphorism is: 'Inside every fat man a thin one is wildly signalling to be let out'. How about this one? 'Inside every traveller an anchorite is longing to stay put.'

Murray [Bail] has had a great success with his book of Australian Stories: though I can't see why yours should not have been included. Much less flat than the usual ones!

Lots of love to you, Bruce

1. E.C.: 'Where she was raped. She went immediately to the police.'

To Nicholas Shakespeare
Churchill Hospital | Oxford | [March 1988]

Dear Nick,

One quite useful technique – which I used for the fantastic compression necessary for *The Viceroy* – is to get a board with a huge sheet of graph paper divided into squares. You can write the 'synopsis' sections on little cards and pin them on with drawing pins. You then have a flexible way of setting out the story with the possibility of change.

Much love,

B

Better! Keep your fingers crossed.

On 8 March 1988 Tom Maschler passed on to Maggie Traugott at Cape this note from Chatwin. 'Bruce was, frankly, disappointed by your blurb for UTZ *since he felt you did not really get to the heart and content of the book.'*

To Tom Maschler

No idea of the illusionist city of Prague.

No idea of the 'private' world of Utz's little figures was a strategy for blocking out the horrors of the 20th century; that the porcelains were real, the horrors so much flim-flam.

No indication of the technique which allows the reader an insight into the fictional process (or how a storyteller sets about it).

One of the principle themes of the book is that Old Europe <u>survives</u>.

Marta epitomises the fact that the techniques of political indoctrination fail and are bound to fail.

No idea that Utz identifies himself as Harlequin, the Trickster, and runs his own private commedia – outwitting everyone until, finally, he finds his Columbine

No idea of the Jewish element. Utz is ¼ Jewish – or of the somewhat subversive notion that the collecting of images, ie art-collecting is inimical to Jahweh – which is why the Jews have always been so good at it.

Art collecting = idol-worship = blasphemy against the created world of God.

To Harriet Harvey-Wood
Homer End | Ipsden | Oxford | 5 May 1988

Dear Harriet Harvey-Wood,

It's no good. I've been in hospital on and off for 3 months a. with an ordinary stomach disorder of the tropics b. with undiagnosed malaria (temperature of 106°) caught on the famous trip to Ghana [in March 1987].

I simply can't face any engagements and have work to do.

Yours sincerely,

Bruce Chatwin

CHAPTER TWELVE

OXFORD AND FRANCE: 1988–9

Since his return from Guadaloupe, Chatwin had been spending more time in the Churchill Hospital. Dr Juel-Jensen, who had retired in November, wrote in his last report that Chatwin's P24 antigen was positive again. 'I fear that all is not well.' Chatwin's new doctor, David Warrell, recorded that Bruce had explosive diarrhoea, no appetite and complained of pains in his spleen. On 12 March 1988 Chatwin was taken off Ketoconzacole. Two weeks later, the fungus returned with new virulence, this time for good. Seventeen months after the possibility was first raised, a skin biopsy indicated that the spots on his face were 'highly suspicious' of Kaposi's sarcoma. On 29 April one of the specialists in the John Warin ward described Chatwin as a 'very nice 47-year-old travel writer with AIDS.' It had taken twenty months to establish once and for all what the clinic had initially suspected.

The fungus infected his brain. Chatwin was suffering from a toxic brain syndrome which began to manifest itself in hypomania. It impaired his ability to think and act rationally, while sparing his verbal fluency and his ability to beguile. His non-stop talk, his grandiose schemes, his unrestrained buying sprees (which would require him to be sectioned), his wish to convert to the Greek Orthodox faith, his charitable trusts, threw those around him into turmoil. At the same time, his hypomania made him a concentrate of himself: someone funny, private, romantic, persuasive who believed fiercely in his own stories.

To Gertrude Chanler
Homer End | Ipsden | Oxford | 6 May 1988

Dear Gertrude,

I need your help. I'd prefer to tell you the details in person but I have indeed been hammered over the past two years and I hope I have been hammered by God. The fact is that I made the leap into Faith. Elizabeth and I have not had an easy marriage, but it survives everything because neither of us have loved anyone else. If ever I had a regret, it is that I could not have become a monk – an idea which kept occurring to me in the cauchemar of Sotheby's. I'd explain to you one day why I could never join the Catholic Church,[1] since I believe that the churches of the Eastern Rite are the True Church. I have recently learned that there is no contradiction between the Anglican and Orthodox. God willing, it seems possible that I could become a lay brother.

This does not mean that I would cease to write. I have been gifted with the pen and will continue to the best of my ability. I have been doing very well. My income for this tax year from April the first is around $600,000.[2] But I want none of it for myself. If I were alone in the world I would hope to give it away to the sick.

I do have responsibilities: to Elizabeth, to my parents and to Hugh (whose instability since his motor accident has always worried me). I have devoted certain royalties to my charity, The Radcliffe Memorial Trust, which is run by the man who saved my life. But I must be prevented from giving too much away.

It does seem that my inexplicable fever was malaria: the temperature returned to normal nine hours after taking anti-malarial pills. You can imagine what 3½ months of raging fever has done to the system. But I don't regret a second of it.

1. E.C.: 'Bruce had been very well coached by the Jesuit Father Murray. Then, two days before our marriage, the parish priest in Geneseo, Father Carron, gave me a nasty little pamphlet spelling out 32 reasons why I should not marry a non-Catholic. Bruce felt it was a slap in the face. He was furious.'
2. E.C.: 'He was by this time putting noughts onto his sums.'

My grey matter functioned perfectly and I took a number of most rational decisions.

I am entirely concerned with the matter of healing. There is no point in setting out to write a book about healing. If a book has to be born, it will be born. Nor is there any point to the enterprise unless one knows what to heal and how, and actually does the healing oneself – even if this means changing the bedpans of the terminally ill.

I hope to divide my life into four parts: a. religious instruction b. learning about disease c. learning to heal d. the rest of the time free to give my undivided attention to Elizabeth and the house. A tall order, but with God's help not impossible. There's no point either in becoming a martyr. Because of my bronchial and circulation problems Elizabeth and I would have to spend most of the winter in a mild climate but I do not intend to buy a house.

I cannot do this work if I am fettered to possessions. I have envied and grasped at possessions but they are very bad for me. I want to be free of them. I don't want to land Elizabeth with extra burdens, but I do want to give her <u>all</u> I have in the form of a breakable trust with the proviso that it stay on this side of the Atlantic and the residue go to medicine. I shall make several presents to close friends and that will be that.

She is not fully aware of this yet, and she would, of course, have to hand me out lumps of pocket money, for books, air fares, etc. I have never known the extent of her capital, but I believe I would increase her existing assets by at least twice if all mine were totted up.

But you know how frugal she is. She said it is in her Iselin blood.[1] She is retentive of possessions whereas I have always thought that by giving or dispersing, you attract more. The real difficulty is to get her to spend money on herself.[2] <u>Everything</u> frivolous becomes an extravagance.

I have been very worried that she is over-exhausting herself and

1. E.C: 'True. The Iselins are dyed-in-the-wool Swiss bankers with a Puritan work ethic.'
2. E.C: 'He always said I didn't spend enough money. He was used to living on his wits and not having any. I couldn't live on my wits and I didn't have very much.'

might make herself ill: a. by the strain of looking after me (not easy!) b. by the house, the cooking and the garden. c. most exhausting of all by the sheep. She loves the sheep but, literally, they tear her apart. I think she needs a horse instead and stabling when she goes to India or with me to the sun. It's wonderful riding country all around and the field is big enough for a horse and a donkey. There would be nothing better to unwind her than to ride a few miles each day. This will all cost money. I will give her all I have, but she still might hesitate. Can you help?

Do show this to John [Chanler] or any priest. But I'd rather it doesn't go any further.

Bless you, Bruce

John Chanler replied to Gertrude:'Ma, I have very carefully read Bruce's letter twice . . . obviously some of it is a pure fantasy. His marriage to Lib is a fantasy. They don't communicate on even a basic level. He should discuss his finances and she should discuss her finances together and Bruce should not put Lib's financial situation in your head.

'If he had this much income in 1987 then he is a rich man and can afford to support Lib and not make her feel guilty about spending money. She is so careful with her money because she never can be sure of getting any money from him. If they had a true marriage it is not his money, or her money, but our money. It belongs to both of them.

'I would suggest that your reply to Bruce is that you are happy that he has come to some conclusions but that you don't feel comfortable in making any commitments or decisions without talking in person with both him and Lib in person together and now is not convenient.

'The horse routine is not a real good idea at all.'

To Gertrude Chanler

Homer End | Ipsden | Oxford | 17 May 1988

Dearest Gertrude,

The horse![1] Obviously she has to be an Arab mare, not perhaps up to competition standard, but breedable. What I suggest is this, you and I go dutch on the purchase, the fence needed to prevent her getting in the garden, a prefabricated wooden stable, saddle etc. We also go dutch on her upkeep – with the proviso, if money matters go wrong (and if they don't get rid of Mrs Thatcher we shall have a Labour government) there will be a 'safety-net' so that the horse doesn't have to be sold for 'economic reasons'.

I get better by the day – although the neuropathy in my legs makes me very tottery. Yesterday, I went to the neurologist who said he could treat it right away, but with steroids – which is obviously out! The nerves should heal entirely within five years.[2]

Fondest love, Bruce

That summer, to the alarm of passers-by, a man in a wheelchair hurtled up the Burlington Arcade towards Piccadilly. It had begun to rain and across his lap he wore a cheap plastic mackintosh. The traffic was dense in Piccadilly, but this did not perturb him. He raised his arm and declared:'Stop all cars!' Then he urged his companion, Kevin Volans, to push. 'His mind was soaring,' says Volans. 'He was really enjoying himself.'

Chatwin was on a shopping spree. Attached to his wheelchair clanked several plastic bags. These, hurriedly packed by astonished dealers in Cork Street and Bond Street, contained items of enormous value. A Bronze Age arm band for which he had written out a cheque for £65,000; an Etruscan head worth £150,000; a

1. E.C.: 'I didn't have any home for it. I'd given up horses when I moved to Homer End – a horse is much more work and money than sheep. Bruce was ringing up Arab breeders and finding out how much they cost.'
2. Chatwin's medical report of 13 June read: 'Still convinced that he is making a unique recovery.'

jade prehistoric English cutting knife; a flint Norwegian hand-axe and an Aleutian Islands hat.

On another outing, he crossed Duke Street and called at Artemis where Adrian Eales worked, a former Sotheby's colleague who had bought Holwell Farm from Elizabeth. Chatwin specifically asked for an engraving, The Melancholy of Michaelangelo, *by the sixteenth-century artist Giorgio Ghisi. By rare chance, Eales had the print in stock. The price: £20,000. Chatwin told him he was building a collection for Elizabeth. He was then wheeled to the Ritz where he had rented a room. During the afternoon more dealers were summoned to his bed. When he was finished, he turned to his friend Christopher Gibbs with an ebullient eye. 'Tomorrow, musical instruments, women's clothes and incunables!'*

To Gertrude Chanler
Homer End | Ipsden | Oxford | 26 June 1988

My dear Gertrude,

Everything seems to be going to plan. You mustn't worry about the horse because I am not going to consider the horse unless we have a full time groom. I am fairly certain we have the money for it.

I have been buying your daughter the beginnings of an art collection which I hope will be wonderful.

In New York we bought the wax model for Giovanni da Bologna's Neptune[1] which has to be one of the most beautiful small sculptures in existence. We are making arrangements to give it to the Bargello in Florence with the use of it in our life times. We also bought an incredible German drawing of the mid fifteenth century.[2]

With lots of love Bruce

1. E.C.: 'It was real: a little nude of wax, from the antique dealer Blumka on Madison Avenue. It was lost in storage. Bruce added umpteen noughts to the insurance statement and someone saw and it was stolen, along with an Indian bracelet.'
2. E.C.: 'A drawing for a carved box, of wild men and women in a tangle of leaves and owls.'

As fast as he bought works of art, Chatwin started to shed posses-sions. Robin Lane Fox says, 'I received through the post a hard brown A4 envelope with Bruce's handwriting on it and inside four black and white photographs of Nuristan boys in trailing vine leaves. "Dear Robin, you will understand that these are what I want you most to have and remember."'

Michael Ignatieff was sent a rare first edition of Isaac Babel's Red Cavalry *not long after making a visit to Homer End. Early in July 1988 Ignatieff wrote to thank Chatwin – 'few books are more precious to me than that, and few friends more beloved than you. So I will always keep it on the topmost shelf of the heart and think of your absurd and loveable generosity.' Ignatieff went on eloquently to express the concerns and fears which he shared with Chatwin's family and friends. 'I came away from my visit with you full of dark and strange thoughts. You seemed in a realm of exultation – extreme physical dilapidation seems to have sent you shooting up into the sky with the angels. And your talk – adorable as always – was as wild as I've ever heard it: vows of purity, ortho-doxy, crofts in the Shetlands, the art of the sublime, and the UR virus all contending, barging each other aside in your speech. Over it all hung an unmistakeable air of* Nunc Dimittis, *cheerful, joyous even, but hard to bear for those of us who would much rather prefer for you to remain with us a bit longer instead of ascending into the smoke or the monk's cell. Even harder to bear was some feeling – forgive me if I'm wrong – that you are in the grips of something, mastered by something, a fever, a conversion, an intoxication, I don't know what to call it, that is forcing its pace on you, forcing you to accelerate, to struggle breathlessly behind it, chucking away your life behind you as you pursue it. Over everything you said there was the image of Time running, running, and you at your wit's end to catch up.*

'It's quite possible that you experience this apparent frenzy from inside some deep calm, some serenity that I heard in your music from the savannas. But those who love you – and see only the outside – see someone haunted and in breathless pursuit.

'I'm not sure it is among the offices of friendship to convey my sense of foreboding & disquiet at how I saw you. I may just be expressing a friend's regret at losing you to a great wave of conviction, to some gust of certainty, that leaves me here, rooted to the spot, and you carried far away. In which case, I can only wave you onto your journey.'

To the Editor of the *London Review of Books*
Oxford Team for Research into Infectious Tropical Diseases,
Oxford University | 7 July 1988

Aids Panic

In a review of three American books, *And the band played on,* *Crisis: Heterosexual Behaviour in the Age of Aids* and *The Forbidden Zone*, Mr John Ryle (LRB, 19 May) begins: 'There is no good news about Aids. With a total of 85,000 cases reported at the beginning of this year the World Health Organisation estimate of the true figure is nearer 150,000. Their global estimate for HIV infection is between five and ten million. Most HIV-positive individuals have no symptoms and don't know they are infected: but the majority of them – possibly all of them – will eventually develop Aids and die; in the meantime, of course, they may infect anyone they have sex with and any children they bear.' This is hogwash. The word 'Aids' is one of the cruellest and silliest neologisms of our time. 'Aid' means help, succour, comfort – yet with a hissing sibilant tacked onto the end it becomes a nightmare. It should never be used in front of patients. HIV (Human Immuno-Deficiency Virus) is a perfectly easy name to live with. 'Aids' causes panic and despair and has probably done something to facilitate the spread of the disease. In France, not even M. Le Pen could do much with le Sida. He had a go, but was made to look completely ridiculous. HIV is not some gay Gotterdammerung: it is another African virus, a very dangerous one, presenting the greatest challenge to medicine since tuberculosis, but one for which a cure will be found. Any virus, be it chicken-pox, mumps or HIV, will create a kind of mirror image of itself known as an 'antibody' which in time will stabilise the infected person. That should be the pattern.

But HIV is a very slippery customer. There is no positive evidence of antibodies at work, only negative evidence that a great many infected people are alive. In one case in the US an infected person suddenly became HIV negative. We should, in fact, take Mr Ryle's own figures. There have been 800,000 infected persons in the United States, of whom 80,000 have died. That means nine survivors to one death. This can mean only one thing: that some mechanism, pharmaceutical or otherwise, is keeping them alive.

One point cannot be emphasised too strongly. An infected person must never use anyone else's toothbrush or an electric razor. We all have gingivitis from time to time.

What is most horrifying about Mr Ryle's article is the callous cruelty with which he condemns hundreds of thousands of people to death. If a young man who has just been told that he is HIV positive got hold of the article, the chances are he might commit suicide. There have been many such cases.

Bruce Chatwin

To Kath Strehlow

Dedication written in *The Songlines* on Strehlow's visit to Homer End,
9 July 1988

For Kath with love beyond the grave, Bruce.

To Harry Marshall[1]

Dictated by Bruce Chatwin | Homer End | Ipsden | Oxford | 25 July [1988]

Dear Harry,

Since we met my life's taken a number of zig-zag directions. I've had malaria anaemia semi paralysis of the hands and feet – all now better but I'm still a wheelchair case.

---

1. Chatwin had met Marshall, a young documentary-maker, on 17 July 1987. H.M.: 'We were going to make a film together and planned to go to Russia and look at the roots of modern Russian art in icons.' The following day Chatwin signed a copy of *The Songlines*. 'To Harry, a sequence of non-sequiturs'.

On the intellectual front I've been collecting Russian icons, trying to arrange to become an Orthodox Priest[1] & have evolved certain notions about virology which I'm told by the professors will transform their discipline. Anyway I'm an Oxford don & member of the team for research into tropical medicine.

This means that any TV appearances are out at present, but in the autumn we might reconsider outside the framework of Peter's series. I promise to give you an exclusive. Best, Bruce

To Cary Welch
The Radcliffe Medical Foundation | 'Expanding the Frontiers of Medicine' | Manor House | Headley Way | Headington | Oxford |
25 July 1988

Dear Cary,

We live in a time of new viruses: a time of Pandora's Box. Climatic change is the motor of evolution, and the sweeping changes in climate that have affected many parts of Africa offer ideal conditions for a virus that may have been stable over many thousands of years to burst its bounds, and set off to colonise the world.

The most pressing medical problem since tuberculosis is HIV (Human Immuno-deficiency Virus), vulgarly known as Aids. The word Aids should never be used by the medical profession, since it plays into the hands of the gutter press, and causes panic and despair: in France, not even M. le Pen could do much with 'le S.I.D.A.' There is, in fact, no cause for panic. H.I.V. is not a late twentieth century Gotterdammerung: it is another African virus.

My friend, David Warrell, is Professor of tropical medicine and infectious diseases at Oxford University. He is one of the finest clinical physicians in this country. He has spent many years in the Far East, working

1. In *The Songlines* Chatwin writes of his uncle Geoffrey Milward – a friend of Emir Feisal and who had fought with Lawrence – 'who died, chanting the suras of the Glorious Koran, in a hospital for holy men in Cairo'.

in the field to advance the study of cerebral malaria. He is a world authority on snake-bite; but he has recently returned to Oxford to lead a team of researchers into HIV.

As you probably know the virus constantly mutates and there seems little hope at present of preparing a vaccine. Excellent results have been achieved by the laboratories in describing the virus; but in the future we shall have to look elsewhere. The stable form of the primordial HIV must exist in Africa, and we intend to find it. The pessimists will say it is like looking for the proverbial needle in a haystack. The problem may be simpler: that of the archaeologist who knows where to dig.

Once the stable virus is found, it may be possible to produce a vaccine. In any case, the answer will probably not come out of the laboratory, but from the field.

The Oxford Team runs a two-fold operation. It has a programme of laboratory and clinical research based in Nairobi, the aim of which is:

a) to alleviate the sufferings of those stricken by the HIV disease in Kenya and Uganda;

b) to keep a watchful eye on any new mutation of the virus;

c) to find the 'primordial' virus.

Back in Oxford we have a most urgent need to build an isolation unit of twelve or fifteen beds, in which exceptional cases can be flown in, observed and nursed under optimal conditions. Of course, this would not be confined to 'foreigners': the exceptional case might come from Oxford nor would it be confined to HIV cases alone: any virus from anywhere in the world that showed peculiar characteristics would be included. The team intends to study dengue fever, lassa fever, rabies, cerebral malaria and fulminating chicken-pox. All this will cost money, but the sums needed immediately are not immense. The Oxford Team is expert in making money go a long way – although in this field of research there will never be enough.

Any contribution, however small, will be most welcome. In the UK there are a number of ways in which donations can receive tax relief. This will vary from case to case and the manner in which the donation is given. For any further information would you please contact Mr David Davies of the Radcliffe Medical Foundation, Manor House, Headley Way, Headington, Oxford OX3 9DZ to whom all contributions should be sent?

I would like to think of this letter as an endless chain. If you have friends or relations who you think would be interested, I would gladly send it to them.

love   Bruce

To Gertrude Chanler

[Elizabeth's handwriting] Homer End | Ipsden | Oxford | 16 August 1988

Dear Gertrude,

Elizabeth came back worried about our nephew, Kevin.[1] From the sound of it, I think he should take an art course, preferably the Sotheby Art Course in N[ew] Y[ork]. These tend to get overbooked, but I think I can fix it with David Nash. He can then decide if he wants to go on in the art business or take a higher degree. In any case he would be an invaluable ally in reforming the Laughlin Collection[2] – apart from the fun!

Love B

Dear Mummy,

As you can see this was dictated. Makes perfectly good sense except for the end. Still grandiose. The pills are working a bit but it's slow. Am now trying to prevent wild travel schemes. I will try and pay my air fare with the travellers checks I brought over if the agent will accept them. Will need money to send him to Athos but can probably get it from my mutual fund. If it takes too long can I borrow it from you?

1. John Chanler's son.
2. The collection of French eighteenth-century drawings made by Gertrude's father, Irwin Laughlin (half of which is now in the National Gallery in Washington), on which Chatwin drew the idea to form The Homer Collection. He planned to leave it to Elizabeth.

Haven't got a nurse yet, but hoping for something to turn up. Have a one day a week girl who lives less than 2 miles away. Have started taking lambs to kill and hope to get on with it in the next few weeks. Elizabeth.

To Murray Bail

[Elizabeth's handwriting] | Homer End | Ipsden | Oxford | 28 August 1988

Dear Murray,

You must forgive me if I don't quite subscribe to your view of yourself as an ungenerous, selfish intolerant old codger. The best bit of news in the entire letter was the fact that you say the divorce is very far off.[1] By the time you've lived through this for a year or 2, you'll be back again in each other's arms. On the other hand, I do see the need for a change of scene and that you must unclutter yourself from Australia by coming, not Lord knows to Tuscany, but by living somewhere which you can then write about, not as an Australian, but as a kind of world citizen. Being Australian, I do see, is very specific. My book *Utz* is nearly out and a copy follows under separate cover. All my love to you both,

Bruce

He's still incredibly weak and immobilised. I wrote to his dictation. I really hope we'll be able to make it in the winter but he certainly couldn't do anything at the moment. We may be starting a new form of therapy tomorrow and I hope they'll take him on and that there's a chance of success – love, Elizabeth

To Ninette Dutton

[Elizabeth's handwriting] Homer End | Ipsden | Oxford | 28 August 1988

Dearest Nin,

I haven't really been sick except that I had undiagnosed malaria for

1. Bail divorced in 1991; he m. 2nd Helen Garner.

13½ months and the fungus came back, necessitating a blood transfusion and the nurse put blood straight from the fridge into my system, thereby <u>completely</u> screwing up the nerves in my legs and hands. I am much better but it is incredibly slow to repair anything to do with the nervous system. I hope to be much better by the winter and we're both looking forward to coming to Australia. Any chance of being able to stay with you for an extended period? I hope to be writing again by then.

We see a lot of Rebecca Hossack[1] these days.

Much love, Bruce

Nin – I wrote this at his dictation. I just hope he will be able to travel. We are embarking on a new course of therapy/alternative medicine this week to see if they can do anything to strengthen him and get the nerves repaired. Pray for him – Elizabeth.

To Emma Bunker
[Elizabeth's handwriting] | Homer End | Ipsden | Oxford |
1 September 1988

Dear Emmy,

You can study nomads in the Inner Mongolian milieu. You can also catch outrageous diseases in the same area.

I caught a fungus of the bone marrow which is presumably in Yunnan Mongolia and Tibet. It was otherwise known from 10 Chinese corpses. I was the only European.

As to HIV, the situation is much less of a problem here than in America because people have learned not to be hysterical. Many people seem to move from HIV negative to positive without any medication.

In France they are even more advanced. A man called Jean Franchome has even developed a vaccine from the people who have

---

1. In March 1988 Rebecca Hossack opened a gallery in Windmill Street, the first in Europe to exhibit Australian Aboriginal painting.

recovered. I hope I have got his name right. But if you are interested I can find out much more about him.

I shall be in San Francisco shortly after Christmas on our way to Australia.

Much love,

Bruce [his handwriting]

To Paul Theroux

[Elizabeth's handwriting] | Homer End | Ipsden | Oxford |
[October 1988]

Dear Paul,

Many thanks for your card. I am more or less bed ridden and would love a visit if it was convenient.

Bruce

Utz, *which Chatwin had managed to write during his remission in 1987, was published on 22 September. Few readers appreciated it more than Charles Chatwin. 'He slipped into the mode of seriously pleased father,' says Hugh. 'He remarked: "A real gem of a book. The surprise is to find out that what has been holding you is a love story."' The novel was one of six shortlisted for the 1988 Booker Prize, along with Salman Rushdie's* The Satanic Verses. *Tom Maschler wrote to Gillon Aitken:'Bruce as you know is determined to be present at the Booker Prize dinner.' He wished to bring along Elizabeth, Diana Melly, Kevin Volans and Roger Clarke. On the afternoon of 25 October Chatwin was telephoned with advance information that he had not won and should spare himself the journey to that evening's televised dinner at the Guildhall (where the prize was awarded to Peter Carey for* Oscar and Lucinda). *On 27 October Maschler sent Chatwin a bound copy of* Utz *as a souvenir of the event.'You really didn't miss anything.'*

To Matthew Spender
[Elizabeth's handwriting] Homer End | Ipsden | Oxford |
3 November 1988

Dear Matthew, Thanks for your communications, always encouraging when one is a bit low. I'm afraid I can't get very worked up about the Booker & just try to go on producing my strange books. Obviously I'm taking a year's respite at present. Love to Maro.

Bruce [his handwriting]

To David Miller[1]
[Elizabeth's handwriting] Homer End | Ipsden | Oxford |
3 November 1988

It simply doesn't matter about the Booker because it's a complete lottery. I wish I remembered you in your cot, but I can't say that I do. Thank you for writing.

Yours sincerely, Bruce Chatwin.

To Charles Way
[Elizabeth's handwriting] Homer End | Ipsden | Oxford |
10 November 1988

Dear Charlie,

I am not that unwell but owing to a bad blood transfusion I am numb in my hands and quite unable to use my legs.

The most that can be said about the Booker prize nomination is that it passed off. I was advised at the last minute not to go and it was one of the best pieces of advice I have had recently.

1. David Miller (*b.*1966), an undergraduate at Cambridge reading theology. His mother June MacLellan had worked with Chatwin at Sotheby's. She moved after her marriage to Edinburgh, where Chatwin visited her and saw Miller in his cot.

I have always had an idea Alun Lewis[1] must be a very moving poet and have taken your tip and ordered his work from the bookshop.

I look forward to see you before too long.

Best regards, Bruce

To Sarah Bennett[2]

[Elizabeth's handwriting] Homer End | Ipsden | Oxford |

12 November 1988

Dear Sarah,

I am not as ill as all that, but I don't have the use of my legs having had a unit of blood at refrigerated temperature in the course of a transfusion

It is strange to think of you living on the doorstep of my childhood haunts. We lived at Tamworth-in-Arden. My old great uncle[3] was the architect in charge of the Beauchamp Chapel which is where I got my feeling for history.

It would be really nice to see you sometime.

with love Bruce

On 20 November Chatwin left England for the last time, returning to the Chateau de Seillans. He started making notes for his Russian novel, but he was becoming daily more resistant to remedies. On 19 December Elizabeth wrote to Kath Strehlow on his behalf to say that he was unable, after all, to write the foreword for her late husband's Songs of Central Australia. *'He is really too weak & ill*

1. C.W.: 'I had a thought that Bruce would like the poetry of Alun Lewis [1915 – 44] who died at the very early age of 28, in Burma, it is generally agreed by his own hand. The poem I could always quote was a romantic one which describes the last time Alun ever saw his newly-wedded wife Gweno in a boarding house in Liverpool the night before he left for India. It's called "Goodbye". Verse 5 reads: *Everything we renounce except ourselves;/Selfishness is the last of all to go;/Our sighs are exhalations of the earth,/Our footprints leave a track across the snow.'*
2. Chatwin's secretary at Sotheby's, Sarah Inglis-Jones (*b*.1943) m. 1971 John Bennett.
3. Philip Chatwin.

to do anything. We've come here as it's warmer & brighter than England in the winter & he loves being away from there. He dictates to me occasionally the beginning of a new book but hasn't the energy to do anything else. He is having some treatment from a doctor in Paris, which at first after an intensive 2 weeks of non-stop IVs had a very good effect. However, a lot of that has now worn off & he's very depressed . . . Keep up the prayers – all of them help.'

To Nicholas Shakespeare

[Elizabeth's handwriting] Chateau de Seillans | Seillans | France |
29 December 1988

Your pretty p/c from Morocco arrived 2 days ago. So what's so awful about writing another book. You can't escape your vocation. What is the publication date of *Maria* – ?[1] We are here till mid-March with a trip for medication in Paris at some stage. It's wonderfully warm and sunny & certainly improves one's mood. Love, Bruce and Elizabeth

Early in the New Year Chatwin was taken for another transfusion to the Sunny Bank Anglo-American Hospital in Cannes. The remainder of the time he stayed at the Chateau de Seillans in a former priest's room with a barrel-vaulted ceiling on the ground floor leading to the terrace. In the first week of January he invited Werner Herzog to Seillans. 'Bruce said; "Werner, I'm dying." And I said, "Yes, I'm aware of that." And then he said: "You must carry my rucksack, you are the one who must carry it."'

Another visitor was Kevin Volans who played him the Songlines *string quartet which had premiered at the Lincoln Centre in New York in November. The white fungus in Chatwin's mouth made speaking difficult. He was incontinent, thin, exhausted by coughing. All he could say was: 'Lovely.'*

1. Shakespeare's novel *The Vision of Elena Silves* was published in September 1989 and dedicated to Chatwin.

Shirley Conran arrived the same afternoon; Francis Wyndham and the Mellys the next day, Saturday 14 January. Also at Seillans was a homeopathic doctor from London, David Curtin. Elizabeth had contacted Curtin to oversee Chatwin's return to England. She hoped to fly back with Chatwin on Monday and put him in The Lighthouse, an Aids hospice off Ladbroke Grove, where Curtin could treat him. She says,'I later asked him:"What were you going to give Bruce?" "Gold."'

Gregor Von Rezzori wrote:'When he was on his deathbed and even phone conversations exhausted him he couldn't take my last call. His wife Elizabeth offered to pass on a message. I asked her to tell him from me: Schemnitz Chemnitz Nagybanya Ofenbanya Vöröspatàk.'

Chatwin deteriorated fast. He spent most of Sunday 15 January, his last day conscious, lying on the terrace. Teddy Millington-Drake telephoned from Italy to tell Shirley Conran that Alberto Moravia had loved Utz *and written a full-page'rave'review. 'I went straight and told Bruce and he gave a long slow smile and he just said:"Better than the Booker."' When the sun went in that afternoon, it grew cold very quickly. Elizabeth carried Chatwin inside and lay him on their bed.*

Elizabeth says,'In the middle of the night he started making this terrible noise. I said, "Bruce, Bruce, turn your head," but he was unconscious. He'd gone into a coma.'

He never regained consciousness. He was taken by ambulance to the state hospital in Nice, where he died at 1.30 p.m. on Wednesday 18 January, four months short of his forty-ninth birthday.

On 20 January 1989 Elizabeth arranged for Chatwin to be cremated in Nice.'I had a Greek service at the crematorium and a service at my church in Watlington and a memorial service at the Greek Orthodox Cathedral of Santa Sophia in Bayswater, which everybody came to.'

ACKNOWLEDGEMENTS

———◁○▷———

This book could not have been completed without the assistance of Hugh Chatwin. We are enormously grateful to him for his patience, explications and insights, particularly into his brother's early years.

We would like to express our immense gratitude to the following: Nigel Acheson, Peter Adam, Gillon Aitken, Stella Astor, Margaret Bail, Murray Bail, the late Monica Barnett, Magnus Bartlett, Andrew Batey, the late Pam Bell, Sarah Bennett, Ray Boulton, Bob Brain, Peter Bratt, the late Gerald Brenan, Clarence Brown, Bill Buford, Richard Bull, Emma Bunker, Roberto Calasso, Michael Cannon, the late Gertrude Chanler, the late Charles and Margharita Chatwin, Lisa Choeygal, Susannah Clapp, the late Michael Davie, the late Ninette Dutton, Tisi Dutton, Jean-Claude Fasquelle, the late John Fleming, Belinda Foster-Melliar, Ivry Freyberg, Valerian Freyberg, Sven Gahlin, Phillippe Garner, Greg Gatenby, Graham C. Greene, Curtis Harnack, Harriet Harvey-Wood, Shirley Hazzard, the late John Hewett, the late Derek Hill, Hugh Honour, James Ivory, Bill Katz, David King, Robin Lane Fox, the late Joan Leigh Fermor, Patrick Leigh Fermor, the late Peter Levi, Lydia Livingstone, Ted Lucie-Smith, Candida Lycett Greene, Christopher MacLehose, Harry Marshall, Tom Maschler, David Mason, Candida Melly, Diana Melly, David Miller, Jonathan Miller, Keith Milow, Beatrice Monti, Desmond Morris, Anne-Marie Mykyta, George Ortiz, John Pawson, the late Edward Peregrine, John Peregrine, Lynda Pranger, Robyn Ravlich, the late Gregor Von Rezzori, Tegai Roberts, Deborah Rogers, Alison and Brendan Rosse, Hannah Rothschild, Miranda Rothschild, Salman Rushdie, Millicent Jane Saunders, Toly Sawenko, Sunil Sethi, Elisabeth Sifton, Jim Silberman,

Peter Smetacek, the late Susan Sontag, Matthew Spender, Kath Strehlow, David Sulzberger, the late Stephen Tennant, Paul Theroux, David Thomas, Colin Thubron, Charles and Brenda Tomlinson, Penelope Tree, Petronella Vaarzon-Morel, Kallistos Ware, David Warrell, Charles Way, the late Cary Welch, Edith Welch, Martin Wilkinson, the late Peter Willey, J. Howard Woolmer, Andrew Wylie, Francis Wyndham, Jorge Torres Zavaleta.

We would like to thank the editors of *The London Review of Books* for permission to reproduce Chatwin's letter of 7 July 1988 (Vol.10, Issue 13).

For permission to use their own letters, diaries and unpublished manuscripts, we would like to thank Murray Bail; John Barnett and the estate of his late wife Monica; Clarence Brown; Sheila Chanler and the estate of her late husband John; Robert Erskine; Michael Ignatieff; James Ivory; John Kasmin; Candida Lycett-Greene and the estate of the late Penelope Betjeman; Desmond Morris; David Nash; the estate of the late Stuart Piggott; David Plante; David Rieff and the estate of the late Susan Sontag; Kenneth Rose; the estate of the late Stephen Tennant; the estate of the late Cary Welch.

For access to collections of Bruce Chatwin's papers and related material we would like to thank: Colin Harris and Judith Priestman at the Bodleian Library in Oxford; the Churchill Hospital in Oxford; Gemma McCallion at the Public Record Office of Northern Ireland; Kate Arnold-Forster and Nancy Fulford at Reading University; the Burns Library in Boston; Lalice Hatayama of the Charles E. Young Library in Los Angeles; Elaina Richardson at Yaddo.

We would also like to thank the estate and publisher of the late W. G. Sebald for permission to quote from 'The Mystery of the Red-Brown Skin,' in *Campo Santo*, trans. Anthea Bell (Hamish Hamilton, 2005); Nicholas Robinson, Michael Bloch and the estate and publisher of the late James Lees-Milne for permission to quote from *Diaries, 1971–83*, and *Diaries, 1984–97* (John Murray, 2008); Murray Bail for permission to quote from *Notebooks 1970–2003* (Harvill, 2006). Don Bachardy and Kate Bucknall for permission to quote from Christopher Isherwood's forthcoming diaries *Liberation: Diaries Volume 3, 1970–1983* (Faber, 2010); Kenneth Pearson & Patricia Connor for permission to quote from *The*

Dorak Affair (Michael Joseph, 1967); Patrick Leigh Fermor and Deborah Devonshire for permission to quote from *In Tearing Haste: Letters between Deborah Devonshire and Patrick Leigh Fermor*, ed. Charlotte Mosley (John Murray, 2008); Diana di Caraci and the estate of the late Teddy Millington-Drake for permission to quote from *Shapes on the Horizon* (London, 1996); the estate and publisher of the late Leo Lerman for permission to quote from *The Grand Surprise – The Journals of Leo Lerman*, ed. Stephen Pascal (Knopf, 2007); David Mason for permission to quote from 'On Bruce Chatwin's Ashes', *Mondo Greco*, premier issue (Spring 1999); Johnathan Gathorne-Hardy and the estate of the late Gerald Brenan for permission to quote from *The Interior Castle: A life of Gerald Brenan* (Sinclair-Stevenson, 1992); the estate and publisher of the late Frances Partridge for permission to quote from *Ups and Downs: Diaries 1972–5* (Weidenfeld & Nicolson, 2001).

The quotation of Cyril Connolly is taken from *The Unquiet Grave: A Word Cycle*, by Palinurus (1944). The quotation of Osip Mandelstam is taken from *The Noise of Time*, trans. Clarence Brown (Quartet Books, 1988).

We have made every effort to trace copyright holders. We greatly regret any omissions, but these will be rectified in future editions.

INDEX

31901050290925